SCHAUM'S OUTLINE OF

THEORY AND PROBLEMS

of

BUSINESS STATISTICS

•

by

LEONARD J. KAZMIER, Ph.D.
Arizona State University

SCHAUM'S OUTLINE SERIES
McGRAW-HILL BOOK COMPANY

New York   St. Louis   San Francisco   Auckland   Bogotá   Düsseldorf   Johannesburg
London   Madrid   Mexico   Montreal   New Delhi   Panama   Paris
São Paulo   Singapore   Sydney   Tokyo   Toronto

0-07-033460-9

6 7 8 9 10 11 12 13 14 15 16 17 18 19 20   **SH SH 8 7 6 5 4 3 2**

Library of Congress Cataloging in Publication Data

Kazmier, Leonard J.

   Theory and problems of business statistics.
   (Schaum's outline series)
   Includes index.

   1. Statistics. I. Title.

HA29.K36   519.5   76-41396

ISBN 0-07-033460-9

Preface

This Outline covers the basic methods of statistical description, statistical inference, and decision analysis under conditions of uncertainty which are typically included in elementary and intermediate-level courses in business and economic statistics.

The purpose of this book is to present the concepts and methods of statistical analysis clearly and concisely. Along these lines, verbal explanations have been minimized in favor of presenting specific examples of the use of the various concepts and methods of analysis. Because this Outline has been developed particularly for those who have an interest in the *application* of statistical techniques, mathematical derivations of the computational formulas are omitted.

Although the book has been developed as a supplement to existing textbooks, the presentation of the concepts and techniques is sufficiently complete to enable its use as a course text as well. In terms of content, both the classical and contemporary methods of statistical analysis are included, and the chapter contents have been grouped so as to be consistent with the organization of most textbooks concerned with the application of statistical methods in business and economics. Similarly, most of the examples and problems relate to applications in business and economics. The Solved Problems at the end of each chapter include complete solutions, while the Supplementary Problems includes only check answers. Instructors can obtain a *Solutions Manual* for all of the Supplementary Problems by writing directly to the author on stationery with the institutional letterhead.

I am indebted to the Literary Executor of the late Sir Ronald A. Fisher, F.R.S., to Dr. Frank Yates, F.R.S., and to the Longman Group Ltd., London, for permission to adapt and reprint Tables III and IV from their book, *Statistical Tables for Biological, Agricultural and Medical Research*.

I express my personal appreciation to Mrs. Harriet Malkin, editor with the Schaum's Outline Series, for her assistance and advice in all stages of this project. Thanks are also extended to Elizabeth Ruiz and Lorna Miller, who typed most of the preliminary test chapters as well as the final manuscript for this book. Finally, I wish to express gratitude to an anonymous reviewer who read the entire manuscript with an exceptionally penetrating eye, and to the students at Arizona State University who used and evaluated preliminary test versions of the chapters in this book.

LEONARD J. KAZMIER

CONTENTS

Page

Chapter **1** ANALYZING BUSINESS DATA 1
Definition of Business Statistics. Descriptive and Inferential Statistics. Classical Statistics and Bayesian Decision Analysis. Discrete and Continuous Variables. Significant Digits. Rounding of Data.

Chapter **2** STATISTICAL PRESENTATIONS 8
Frequency Distributions. Class Intervals. Histograms and Frequency Polygons. Frequency Curves. Cumulative Frequency Distributions. Relative Frequency Distributions. "And Under" Types of Frequency Distributions. Bar Charts and Line Graphs. Pie Charts.

Chapter **3** DESCRIBING BUSINESS DATA:
MEASURES OF LOCATION 28
Measures of Location in Data Sets. The Arithmetic Mean. The Arithmetic Mean for Grouped Data. The Weighted Mean. The Median. The Median for Grouped Data. The Mode. The Mode for Grouped Data. Relationship among the Mean, Median, and Mode. Quartiles, Deciles, and Percentiles. Quartiles, Deciles, and Percentiles for Grouped Data.

Chapter **4** DESCRIBING BUSINESS DATA:
MEASURES OF VARIABILITY 44
Measures of Variability in Data Sets. The Range. Modified Ranges. The Average Deviation. The Average Deviation for Grouped Data. The Variance and Standard Deviation. The Variance and Standard Deviation for Grouped Data. Shortcut Calculations of the Variance and Standard Deviation. Use of the Standard Deviation. The Coefficient of Variation. Pearson's Coefficient of Skewness.

Chapter **5** PROBABILITY 65
Basic Definitions of Probability. Expressing Probability. Mutually Exclusive and Nonexclusive Events. The Rules of Addition. Independent Events, Dependent Events, and Conditional Probability. The Rules of Multiplication. Joint Probability Tables. Permutations. Combinations.

Chapter **6** DISCRETE PROBABILITY DISTRIBUTIONS:
BINOMIAL, HYPERGEOMETRIC, AND POISSON 89
Probability Distributions. The Expected Value and Variance of Discrete Random Variables. The Binomial Distribution. The Binomial Distribution Expressed by Proportions. The Hypergeometric Distribution. The Poisson Distribution. Poisson Approximation of Binomial Probabilities.

CONTENTS

Page

Chapter 7 CONTINUOUS PROBABILITY DISTRIBUTIONS: NORMAL AND EXPONENTIAL 109

Continuous Random Variables. The Normal Probability Distribution. Normal Approximation of Binomial Probabilities. Normal Approximation of Poisson Probabilities. The Exponential Probability Distribution.

Chapter 8 SAMPLING DISTRIBUTIONS AND CONFIDENCE INTERVALS FOR THE POPULATION MEAN 125

Point Estimation and Sampling. Sampling Distribution of the Mean. Confidence Intervals for the Mean Using the Normal Distribution. Determining the Required Sample Size for Estimating the Mean. Student's t Distributions and Confidence Intervals for the Mean. Chebyshev's Inequality and Confidence Intervals for the Mean. Summary Table for Interval Estimation of the Population Mean.

Chapter 9 OTHER CONFIDENCE INTERVALS 142

Confidence Intervals for the Difference between Two Population Means Using the Normal Distribution. Student's t Distributions and Confidence Intervals for the Difference between Means. Confidence Intervals for the Proportion Using the Normal Distribution. Determining the Required Sample Size for Estimating the Proportion. Confidence Intervals for the Difference between Two Population Proportions. The χ^2 (Chi-Square) Distributions and Confidence Intervals for the Standard Deviation and Variance.

Chapter 10 TESTING HYPOTHESES CONCERNING THE VALUE OF THE POPULATION MEAN 155

Basic Steps in Hypothesis Testing. Testing a Hypothesized Value of the Mean Using the Normal Distribution. Type I and Type II Errors in Hypothesis Testing. Determining the Required Sample Size for Testing the Mean. Testing a Hypothesized Value of the Mean Using Student's t Distributions. Testing a Hypothesized Value of the Mean Using Chebyshev's Inequality. Summary Table for Testing a Hypothesized Value of the Mean.

Chapter 11 TESTING OTHER HYPOTHESES 175

Testing the Difference between Two Means Using the Normal Distribution. Testing the Difference between Two Means Using Student's t Distributions. Testing the Difference between Two Means Based on Paired Observations. Testing a Hypothesized Proportion Using the Binomial Distributions. Testing a Hypothesized Proportion Using the Normal Distribution. Determining Required Sample Size for Testing the Proportion. Testing the Difference between Two Population Proportions. Testing a Hypothesized Value of the Variance Using the Chi-Square Distributions. The F Distributions and Testing the Difference between Two Variances.

Chapter 12 THE CHI-SQUARE TEST 195

The Chi-Square Test as a Hypothesis-Testing Procedure. Goodness of Fit Tests. Minimum Expected Frequencies and the Correction for Continuity. Tests for Independence of Two Variables (Contingency Table Tests). Testing the Differences among k Proportions.

CONTENTS

Page

Chapter *13*   ANALYSIS OF VARIANCE 218
General Concepts Associated with Testing the Differences among k Means. One-Way Analysis of Variance. Two-Way Analysis of Variance. Two-Way Analysis without Interaction (Randomized Block Design). Two-Way Analysis with Interaction (n Observations per Cell). Additional Considerations.

Chapter *14*   BAYESIAN DECISION ANALYSIS:
DECISION TABLES AND DECISION TREES 236
The Structure of Decision Tables. Decision Making Based upon Probabilities Alone. Decision Making Based upon Economic Consequences Alone. Decision Making Based upon Both Probabilities and Economic Consequences: The Expected Value Criterion. Decision Tree Analysis. Expected Utility as the Decision Criterion.

Chapter *15*   BAYESIAN DECISION ANALYSIS:
THE USE OF SAMPLE INFORMATION 257
The Expected Value of Perfect Information (*EVPI*). Bayes' Theorem. Prior and Posterior Probability Distributions. Bayesian Posterior Analysis and the Value of Sample Information (after Sampling). Preposterior Analysis: The Expected Value of Sample Information (*EVSI*) prior to Sampling. Expected Net Gain from Sampling (*ENGS*) and Optimum Sample Size.

Chapter *16*   BAYESIAN DECISION ANALYSIS:
APPLICATION OF THE NORMAL DISTRIBUTION 277
Introduction. Determining the Parameters of the Normal Distribution. Defining the Linear Payoff Functions and Determining the Best Act. Linear Piecewise Loss Functions and the Expected Value of Perfect Information (*EVPI*). Bayesian Posterior Analysis. Preposterior Analysis and the Expected Value of Sample Information (*EVSI*). Expected Net Gain from Sampling (*ENGS*) and Optimum Sample Size. Bayesian Decision Analysis vs. Classical Decision Procedures.

Chapter *17*   LINEAR REGRESSION AND CORRELATION
ANALYSIS 297
Objectives and Assumptions of Regression Analysis. The Scatter Diagram. The Method of Least Squares for Fitting a Regression Line. The Standard Error of Estimate and Prediction Intervals. Inference Concerning the Parameters of the Regression Line. Objectives and Assumptions of Correlation Analysis. The Coefficient of Determination. The Coefficient of Correlation. Significance of the Correlation Coefficient. Pitfalls and Limitations Associated with Regression and Correlation Analysis.

Chapter *18*   MULTIPLE REGRESSION AND CORRELATION
ANALYSIS 313
Objectives and Assumptions of Linear Multiple Regression Analysis. Concepts in Multiple Regression Analysis. Analysis of Variance in Linear Regression Analysis. Objectives and Assumptions of Multiple Correlation Analysis. Concepts in Multiple Correlation Analysis. Pitfalls and Limitations Associated with Multiple Regression and Correlation Analysis.

CONTENTS

Page

Chapter *19* TIME SERIES ANALYSIS 326

The Classical Time Series Model. Trend Analysis. Measurement of Seasonal Variations. Applying Seasonal Adjustments. Forecasting Based on Trend and Seasonal Factors. Analysis of Cyclical and Irregular Variations. Cyclical Forecasting and Business Indicators.

Chapter *20* INDEX NUMBERS FOR BUSINESS AND
ECONOMIC DATA 344

Introduction. Construction of Simple Indexes. Construction of Aggregate Price Indexes. Link Relatives. Shifting the Base Period. Splicing Two Series of Index Numbers. The Consumer Price Index (CPI). Other Published Indexes.

APPENDIX 355

1. Binomial Probabilities
2. Values of $e^{-\lambda}$
3. Poisson Probabilities
4. Proportions of Area of the Standard Normal Distribution
5. Table of Random Numbers
6. Proportions of Area for the t Distributions
7. Proportions of Area for the χ^2 Distributions
8. Values of F Exceeded with Probabilities of 5 and 1 Percent
9. Unit Normal Loss Function

INDEX 371

Chapter 1

Analyzing Business Data

1.1 DEFINITION OF BUSINESS STATISTICS

Business statistics refers to the techniques by which quantitative data are collected, organized, presented, and analyzed. The focal point of modern statistical analysis is decision making under conditions of uncertainty.

1.2 DESCRIPTIVE AND INFERENTIAL STATISTICS

Descriptive statistics include the techniques which are concerned with summarizing and describing numerical data. These methods can either be graphical or involve computational analysis (see Chapters 2, 3, and 4).

EXAMPLE 1. The monthly sales volume for a product during the past year can be described and made meaningful by preparing a bar chart or a line graph (as described in Section 2.8). The relative sales by month can be highlighted by calculating an index number for each month such that the deviation from 100 for any given month indicates the percentage deviation of sales in that month as compared with average monthly sales during the entire year.

Inferential statistics are those techniques by which decisions about a statistical population are made based only on a sample having been observed or a judgment having been obtained. Because such decisions are made under conditions of uncertainty, the use of probability concepts is required. Whereas the measured characteristics of a sample are called *sample statistics*, measured characteristics of a statistical population, or universe, are called *population parameters*. The process of measuring the characteristics of all of the members of a defined population is called a *census*. Chapters 5 through 7 are concerned with probability concepts, and most of the chapters which follow Chapter 7 are concerned with the application of these concepts in statistical inference.

EXAMPLE 2. In order to estimate the voltage required to cause an electrical device to fail, a sample of such devices can be subjected to increasingly higher voltages until each device fails. Based on these sample results, the probability of failure at various voltage levels for the other devices in the sampled population can be estimated.

1.3 CLASSICAL STATISTICS AND BAYESIAN DECISION ANALYSIS

The methods of *classical statistics* are concerned with the analysis of sampled (objective) data for the purpose of inference, with the exclusions of any personal judgments or opinions (see Chapters 8–13, 17, and 18). *Bayesian decision analysis* incorporates the use of managerial judgments in the statistical analysis and also places special emphasis on the possible economic gains or the possible losses associated with alternative decision acts (see Chapters 14–16).

EXAMPLE 3. By the classical approach to statistical inference, the uncertain level of sales for a new product would be estimated solely on the basis of market studies carried out in a number of locations selected in accordance with the requirements of scientific sampling. By the Bayesian approach, the judgments of managers who have had experience with similar products would be obtained and used as the basis of arriving at an estimated sales volume. This subjective estimate could then be combined with objective sample data to arrive at a combined estimate of the sales volume.

1.4 DISCRETE AND CONTINUOUS VARIABLES

A *discrete variable* can only have observed values at isolated points along a scale of values. In business statistics, such data typically occur through the process of *counting* ; hence, the values generally are expressed as integers (whole numbers) only. A *continuous variable* can assume a value at any fractional point along a specified interval of values. Continuous data are generated by the process of *measuring*.

EXAMPLE 4. Examples of discrete data are the number of persons per household, the units of an item in inventory, and the number of assembled components which are found to be defective. Examples of continuous data are the weight of each shipment, the length of time before the first failure of a device, and the average number of persons per household in a large community. Note that an *average number* of persons can be a fractional value and is thus a continuous variable, even though the *number* per household is a discrete variable.

1.5 SIGNIFICANT DIGITS

The measurement of continuous data is never exact because the level of accuracy could always be improved by obtaining (or developing) a more sensitive measuring instrument. Although the process of counting does generally result in discrete data that are exact, even discrete data may be only approximately counted (e.g., today's U.S. Treasury balance). Therefore, in the numbers expressing data we distinguish *significant digits*, which represent accurate information, from digits which are not accurate and often only serve to locate the decimal point.

EXAMPLE 5. Suppose we asked a sample of students how much each one spent, to the nearest dollar, on recreational activities during the past month. Reporting the result as being "an average of $25.45 per student" would be misleading and statistically inappropriate, because this figure would imply accuracy to the nearest cent while the accuracy of the data collected was to the nearest dollar.

The result of a statistical computation can contain no more significant digits than the *least accurate* input data. Therefore, only the significant digits of the result should be reported, to avoid giving a false impression of accuracy.

EXAMPLE 6. Suppose an individual has accumulated several categories of assets and their respective values have been measured at the levels of accuracy indicated below. Because the least accurate measurement included in this sum was to the nearest $100, the total assets should also be reported only to the nearest $100:

Securities	$4900	(nearest $100)
Savings account	2625	(nearest $1)
Cash on hand	81.27	
Total assets	$7606.27 = $7600	

Since the accuracy is to the nearest $100, there are only two significant digits in the total asset amount, with two zeros included to locate the decimal point.

The number of significant digits included in a reported value indicates the maximum error associated with the reported value and the numeric limits within which the true value is located, as well as the level of accuracy associated with the value.

EXAMPLE 7.   The reported value "$3800" could contain two, three, or four significant digits, according to whether the zeros are included only to locate the position of the decimal or whether one or both zeros in fact represent measured values.

> If "$3800" has two significant digits, then the measurement was made to the nearest hundred dollars, the maximum error is $50, and the true value is located somewhere between $3750 and $3850.

> If "$3800" has three significant digits, then the measurement was made to the nearest ten dollars, the maximum error is $5, and the true value is located somewhere between $3795 and $3805.

> If "$3800" has four significant digits, then the measurement was made to the nearest dollar, the maximum error is 50¢, and the true value is located somewhere between $3799.50 and $3800.50.

As a general rule, *leading zeros*, such as in $00389, are never considered to be significant digits. *Embedded zeros* which are followed by at least one significant digit, such as in $3800.57, are all considered to be significant. *Trailing zeros* may or may not be significant, according to the level of accuracy in the original data (see Example 7).

1.6 ROUNDING OF DATA

Rounding a number to the nearest unit (tenth, or other decimal place) reduces it to the number of significant digits warranted in the particular computation. When the remainder to be rounded off is "exactly 5," the convention is to round to the nearest *even* number. By this practice the additions due to rounding will tend to counterbalance the subtractions due to rounding in the long run.

EXAMPLE 8.
> 18.758 (rounded to the nearest tenth) = 18.8
>
> 15.449 (rounded to the nearest hundredth) = 15.45
>
> 15.449 (rounded to the nearest tenth) = 15.4
>
> 18.05 (rounded to the nearest tenth) = 18.0
>
> 89.1750 (rounded to the nearest hundredth) = 89.18

Solved Problems

DESCRIPTIVE AND INFERENTIAL STATISTICS

1.1.   Indicate which of the following terms or operations are concerned with a sample or sampling (S), and those which are concerned with a population (P):   (a) Group measures called *parameters*,   (b) use of *inferential statistics*,   (c) taking a *census*,   (d) judging the quality of an incoming shipment of fruit by inspecting several crates of the large number included in the shipment.

(a) P,   (b) S,   (c) P,   (D) S

CLASSICAL STATISTICS AND
BAYESIAN DECISION ANALYSIS

1.2. Indicate which of the following types of information could be used only in Bayesian decision analysis (B), and those which could be used in either classical or Bayesian analysis (CB): (*a*) Managerial judgment about the likely level of sales for a new product, (*b*) survey results for a sample of previous customers, (*c*) combining managerial forecasts of sales with sample sales data.

(*a*) B, (*b*) CB, (*c*) B

DISCRETE AND CONTINUOUS VARIABLES

1.3. For the following types of values, designate discrete variables (D) and continuous variables (C): (*a*) Weight of the contents of a package of cereal, (*b*) diameter of a bearing, (*c*) number of defective items produced, (*d*) number of individuals in a geographic area who are collecting unemployment benefits, (*e*) the average number of prospective customers contacted per sales representative during the past month, (*f*) dollar amount of sales.

(*a*) C, (*b*) C, (*c*) D, (*d*) D, (*e*) C, (*f*) D (*Note:* Although monetary amounts are discrete, when the amounts are large they are often treated as continuous data.)

SIGNIFICANT DIGITS

1.4. Round the following sum appropriately, and indicate the number of significant digits in the answer.

$$
\begin{array}{ll}
\$\ 54.40 & \\
127 & \text{(nearest \$1)} \\
125.53 & \\
\underline{400} & \text{(nearest \$100)} \\
\$706.93 &
\end{array}
$$

$700 (with one significant digit; the two zeros are included only to locate the decimal point).

1.5. Round the following difference appropriately, and indicate the number of significant digits in the answer.

$$
\begin{array}{ll}
\$3500 & \text{(nearest \$100)} \\
\underline{-125.87} & \\
\$3374.13 &
\end{array}
$$

$3400 (with two significant digits)

1.6. Round the following difference appropriately, and indicate the number of significant digits in the answer.

$$
\begin{array}{ll}
\$5830 & \text{(nearest \$1)} \\
\underline{-27.55} & \\
\$5802.45 &
\end{array}
$$

$5802 (with four significant digits)

1.7. Round the following sum appropriately, assuming that all digits included in the entries are significant.

$$\begin{array}{r} 3.825 \text{ lb} \\ 21.5 \\ 80.00 \\ 19.0 \\ \underline{57.513} \\ 181.838 \end{array}$$

181.8 lb (with four significant digits)

1.8. Identify the number of significant digits in each of the following values, which are measured on a continuous scale: (*a*) 37.875, (*b*) 38,397, (*c*) 1593.4, (*d*) 0.812, (*e*) 0.0031, (*f*) 5007, (*g*) 3700, (*h*) 450.0, (*i*) 0.0500.

(*a*) 5, (*b*) 5, (*c*) 5, (*d*) 3, (*e*) 2, (*f*) 4, (*g*) 2, 3, or 4 depending on whether the measurement is to the nearest hundred, ten, or whole-number value, (*h*) 4, (*i*) 3 (only the leading zeros are not significant in this case)

1.9. For each of the following values, identify the interval within which the true value is located: (*a*) 16 oz, (*b*) 12.0 oz, (*c*) 8.45 cm, (*d*) $500 (to the nearest $100), (*e*) $495 (to the nearest $1), (*f*) 85.875 m.

(*a*) 15.5 to 16.5 oz, (*b*) 11.95 to 12.05 oz, (*c*) 8.445 to 8.455 cm, (*d*) $450 to $550, (*e*) $494.50 to $495.50, (*f*) 85.8745 to 85.8755 m

1.10. For the values in Problem 1.9, indicate the maximum amount of error associated with each value: (*a*) 16 oz, (*b*) 12.0 oz, (*c*) 8.45 cm, (*d*) $500 (to the nearest $100), (*e*) $495 (to the nearest $1), (*f*) 85.875 m.

(*a*) 0.5 oz, (*b*) 0.05 oz, (*c*) 0.005 cm, (*d*) $50, (*e*) $0.50, (*f*) 0.0005 m

ROUNDING OF DATA

1.11. Indicate how each of the following values would be rounded:

(*a*)   5789 (to the nearest hundred)   (*d*)   28.65 (to the nearest tenth)

(*b*)   6501 (to the nearest thousand)   (*e*)   19.95 (to the nearest tenth)

(*c*)   130.055 (to the nearest unit)   (*f*)   32.505 (to the nearest hundredth)

(*a*) 5800, (*b*) 7000, (*c*) 130, (*d*) 28.6, (*e*) 20.0, (*f*) 32.50

1.12. Indicate how each of the following values would be rounded:

(*a*)   57.8755 (to four significant digits)

(*b*)   24.54 (to three significant digits)

(*c*)   92.445 (to four significant digits)

(*d*)   8.875 (to three significant digits)

(*e*)   15.05 (to the first place beyond the decimal)

(*f*)   113.35 (to the first place beyond the decimal)

(*a*) 57.88, (*b*) 24.5, (*c*) 92.44, (*d*) 8.88, (*e*) 15.0, (*f*) 113.4

Supplementary Problems

DESCRIPTIVE AND INFERENTIAL STATISTICS

1.13. Indicate which of the following terms or operations are concerned with a sample or sampling (S), and those which are concerned with a population (P): (*a*) Universe, (*b*) group measures called *statistics*, (*c*) application of probability concepts, (*d*) inspection of every item which is manufactured.

Ans. (*a*) P, (*b*) S, (*c*) S, (*d*) P

CLASSICAL STATISTICS AND BAYESIAN DECISION ANALYSIS

1.14. Indicate which of the following types of information could be used only in Bayesian decision analysis (B) and those which could be used in either classical or Bayesian analysis (CB): (*a*) Objective data, (*b*) sample data, (*c*) subjective data, (*d*) combining objective data with subjective data.

Ans. (*a*) CB, (*b*) CB, (*c*) B, (*d*) B

DISCRETE AND CONTINUOUS VARIABLES

1.15. For the following types of values, designate discrete variables (D) and continuous variables (C): (*a*) Number of units of an item held in stock, (*b*) ratio of current assets to current liabilities, (*c*) total tonnage shipped, (*d*) total value of inventory, (*e*) quantity shipped, in units, (*f*) volume of traffic on a toll road, (*g*) attendance at the company's annual meeting.

Ans. (*a*) D, (*b*) C, (*c*) C, (*d*) D, (*e*) D, (*f*) D, (*g*) D

SIGNIFICANT DIGITS

1.16. Round the following sums and differences appropriately and indicate the number of significant digits in each answer.

(*a*)	67.90 tons	(*b*)	$3824.37	(*c*)	12,000 oz (nearest 1000 oz)
	150 (nearest ton)		−700 (nearest $100)		−121 oz
	37.8		$3124.37		11,879 oz
	255.70 tons				

Ans. (*a*) 256 tons, (*b*) $3100, (*c*) 12,000 oz

1.17. Assuming that the following measurements are appropriately recorded, indicate the number of significant digits included in each measurement: (*a*) 49 g, (*b*) 4009 g, (*c*) 0.075 g, (*d*) 27.00 m, (*e*) 2700 m, (*f*) 270 m, (*g*) 10.01 lb, (*h*) 1001 lb, (*i*) 0.010 lb.

Ans. (*a*) 2, (*b*) 4, (*c*) 2, (*d*) 4, (*e*) 2, 3, or 4, (*f*) 2 or 3, (*g*) 4, (*h*) 4, (*i*) 2

1.18. For each of the following values, identify the interval within which the true value is located: (*a*) $32, (*b*) $3200 (two significant digits), (*c*) $3200 (to the nearest $10), (*d*) 0.5 oz, (*e*) 0.50 oz, (*f*) 50.0 oz, (*g*) 155 lb, (*h*) 155.5 lb, (*i*) 150 lb (two significant digits).

Ans. (*a*) $31.50 to $32.50, (*b*) $3150 to $3250, (*c*) $3195 to $3205, (*d*) 0.45 to 0.55 oz, (*e*) 0.495 to 0.505 oz, (*f*) 49.95 to 50.05 oz, (*g*) 154.5 to 155.5 lb, (*h*) 155.45 to 155.55 lb, (*i*) 145 to 155 lb

1.19. For the values in Problem 1.18, indicate the maximum amount of possible error associated with each value.

>   *Ans.*   (*a*) $0.50,   (*b*) $50,   (*c*) $5,   (*d*) 0.05 oz,   (*e*) 0.005 oz,   (*f*) 0.05 oz,   (*g*) 0.5 lb,   (*h*) 0.05 lb,   (*i*) 5 lb

ROUNDING OF DATA

1.20. Indicate how each of the following values would be rounded.

(*a*) 27.27 (to the nearest tenth)	(*h*) $63.50 (to the nearest dollar)
(*b*) 27.27 (to the nearest unit)	(*i*) $64.50 (to the nearest dollar)
(*c*) 188.549 (to four significant digits)	(*j*) $64.51 (to the nearest dollar)
(*d*) 188.549 (to three significant digits)	(*k*) 0.05049 (to two significant digits)
(*e*) 325.455 (to the nearest hundredth)	(*l*) 0.05050 (to two significant digits)
(*f*) 325.455 (to the nearest tenth)	(*m*) 0.05050 (to one significant digit)
(*g*) 325.455 (to the nearest unit)	

>   *Ans.*   (*a*) 27.3,   (*b*) 27,   (*c*) 188.5,   (*d*) 189,   (*e*) 325.46,   (*f*) 325.5,   (*g*) 325,   (*h*) $64,   (*i*) $64,   (*j*) $65,   (*k*) 0.050,   (*l*) 0.050,   (*m*) 0.05

Chapter 2

Statistical Presentations

2.1 FREQUENCY DISTRIBUTIONS

A *frequency distribution* is a table in which possible values for a variable are grouped into classes, and the number of observed values which fall into each class is recorded. Data organized in a frequency distribution are called *grouped data*. In contrast, for *ungrouped data* every observed value of the random variable is listed.

EXAMPLE 1. A frequency distribution of weekly wages is shown in Table 2.1.

2.2 CLASS INTERVALS

For each class in a frequency distribution, the lower and upper *class limits* indicate the values included within the class. (See the first column of Table 2.1.) In contrast, the *class boundaries*, or *exact limits*, are the specific points along the measurement scale which serve to separate adjoining classes. Class boundaries can be determined by identifying the points which are halfway between the upper and lower limits, respectively, of adjoining classes. The *class interval* indicates the range of values included within a class, and can be determined by subtracting the lower class boundary from the upper class boundary for the class. Finally, for certain summary purposes the values in a class are often represented by the *class midpoint*, which can be determined by adding one half of the class interval to the lower boundary of the class.

EXAMPLE 2. Table 2.2 presents class boundaries and corresponding class midpoints.

Computationally, it is generally desirable that all class intervals in a given frequency distribution be equal. A formula which can be used to determine the approximate class interval is

$$\text{Approximate interval} = \frac{\begin{bmatrix} \text{Largest value in} \\ \text{ungrouped data} \end{bmatrix} - \begin{bmatrix} \text{Smallest value in} \\ \text{ungrouped data} \end{bmatrix}}{\text{Number of classes desired}} \tag{2.1}$$

EXAMPLE 3. For the ungrouped data which were grouped in Table 2.1, suppose the highest observed wage was \$258 and the lowest observed wage was \$142. Given the objective of having six classes with equal class intervals:

$$\text{Approximate interval} = \frac{258 - 142}{6} = \$19.33$$

The closest convenient class size is thus \$20.

For data that are distributed in a highly nonuniform way, such as annual salary data for a variety of occupations, *unequal class intervals* may be desirable. In such a case, the larger class intervals are used for the ranges of values where there are relatively few observations.

8

**Table 2.1 A Frequency Distribution of Weekly
Wages for 100 Unskilled Workers**

Weekly wage	Number of workers (f)
$140–159	7
160–179	20
180–199	33
200–219	25
220–239	11
240–259	4
	Total 100

Table 2.2 Weekly Wages for 100 Unskilled Workers

Weekly wage (class limits)	Class boundaries*	Class midpoint	Number of workers
$140–159	$139.50–159.50	$149.50	7
160–179	159.50–179.50	169.50	20
180–199	179.50–199.50	189.50	33
200–219	199.50–219.50	209.50	25
220–239	219.50–239.50	229.50	11
240–259	239.50–259.50	249.50	4
			Total 100

*In general, only one additional significant digit is expressed in class boundaries as compared with class limits. However, because with monetary units the next more precise unit of measurement after "nearest dollar" is usually defined as "nearest cent," in this case two additional digits are expressed.

2.3 HISTOGRAMS AND FREQUENCY POLYGONS

A *histogram* is a bar graph of a frequency distribution. As indicated in Fig. 2-1, typically the class boundaries are entered along the horizontal axis of the graph while the number of observations are listed along the vertical axis.

EXAMPLE 4.   A histogram for the frequency distribution of weekly wages in Table 2.2 is shown in Fig. 2-1.

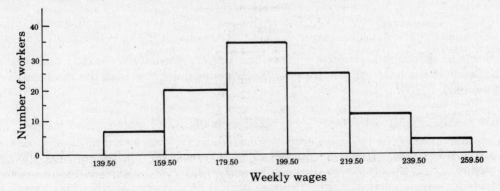

Fig. 2-1.

A *frequency polygon* is a line graph of a frequency distribution.   As indicated in Fig. 2-2, the two axes of this graph are similar to those of the histogram except that the midpoint of each class typically is identified along the horizontal axis.   The number of observations in each class is represented by a dot above the midpoint of the class, and these dots are joined by a series of line segments to form a "many-sided figure," or polygon.

EXAMPLE 5.   A frequency polygon for the distribution of weekly wages in Table 2.2 is shown in Fig. 2-2.

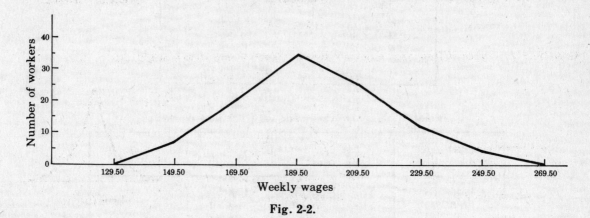

Fig. 2-2.

2.4   FREQUENCY CURVES

A frequency curve is a smoothed frequency polygon.

EXAMPLE 6.   Figure 2-3 is a frequency curve for the distribution of weekly wages in Table 2.2.

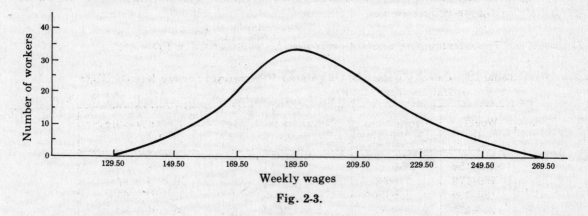

Fig. 2-3.

In terms of skewness a frequency curve can be   (1) *negatively skewed*: nonsymmetrical with the "tail" to the left,   (2) *positively skewed*: nonsymmetrical with the "tail" to the right, or   (3) *symmetrical*.

EXAMPLE 7.   The concept of frequency curve skewness is illustrated graphically in Fig. 2-4.

In terms of kurtosis, a frequency curve can be   (1) *platykurtic*: flat, with the observations distributed relatively evenly across the classes,   (2) *leptokurtic*: peaked, with the observations concentrated within a narrow range of values, or   (3) *mesokurtic*: neither flat nor peaked, in terms of the distribution of observed values.

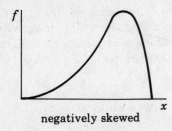
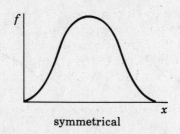
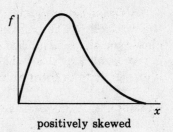

| negatively skewed | symmetrical | positively skewed |

Fig. 2-4.

EXAMPLE 8. Types of frequency curves in terms of kurtosis are shown in Fig. 2-5.

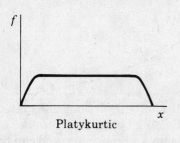
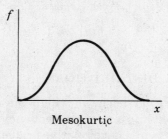
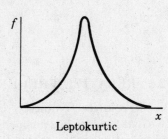

| Platykurtic | Mesokurtic | Leptokurtic |

Fig. 2-5.

2.5 CUMULATIVE FREQUENCY DISTRIBUTIONS

A *cumulative frequency distribution* identifies the cumulative number of observations included below the upper boundary of each class in the distribution.   The cumulative frequency for a class can be determined by adding the observed frequency for that class to the cumulative frequency for the preceding class.

EXAMPLE 9. The calculation of cumulative frequencies is illustrated in Table 2.3.

Table 2.3   Calculation of the Cumulative Frequencies for the Weekly Wage Data of Table 2.2

Weekly wage	Upper class boundary	Number of workers (f)	Cumulative frequency (cf)
$140–159	$159.50	7	7
160–179	179.50	20	20 + 7 = 27
180–199	199.50	33	33 + 27 = 60
200–219	219.50	25	25 + 60 = 85
220–239	239.50	11	11 + 85 = 96
240–259	259.50	4	4 + 96 = 100
		Total 100	

The graph of a cumulative frequency distribution is called an *ogive* (pronounced "ō-jive").   For the less-than type of cumulative distribution, this graph indicates the cumulative frequency below each class boundary of the frequency distribution.   When such a line graph is smoothed, it is called an *ogive curve*.

EXAMPLE 10. An ogive curve for the cumulative frequency distribution in Table 2.3 is given in Fig. 2-6.

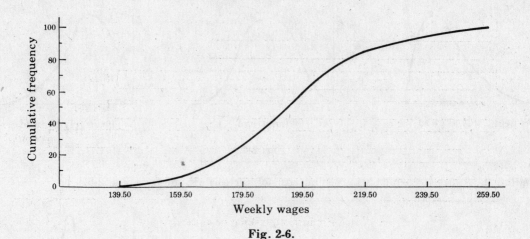

Fig. 2-6.

2.6 RELATIVE FREQUENCY DISTRIBUTIONS

A *relative frequency distribution* is one in which the number of observations associated with each class has been converted into a relative frequency by dividing by the total number of observations in the entire distribution.   Each relative frequency is thus a proportion, and can be converted into a percentage by multiplying by 100%.

One of the advantages associated with constructing a relative frequency distribution is that the cumulative distribution and the ogive for such a distribution indicate the cumulative proportion (or percentage) of observation up to the various possible values of the variable.   A *percentile* value is the cumulative percentage of observations up to a designated value of a variable.   (See Problems 2.16 to 2.20.)

2.7 "AND UNDER" TYPES OF FREQUENCY DISTRIBUTIONS

Consider the following class limits for two adjoining classes:

5 and under 8

8 and under 11

For such "and under" class limits, the class boundaries are identical in value to the stated class limits.   Thus, the upper and lower boundaries for the first class above are 5.0 and 8.0, respectively.   (See Problems 2.21 and 2.22.)

2.8 BAR CHARTS AND LINE GRAPHS

A *bar chart* depicts amounts or frequencies for different categories of data by a series of bars.   The difference between a bar chart and a histogram is that a histogram always relates to data in a frequency distribution, whereas a bar chart depicts amounts for any types of categories.

EXAMPLE 11. The bar chart in Fig. 2-7 depicts factory sales of passenger cars for plants in the United States.   The data are categorized by year.   (*Source*: *Survey of Current Business*, U.S. Department of Commerce.)

A *component bar chart* portrays subdivisions within the bars on the chart.   For example, each bar in Fig. 2-7 could be subdivided into separate parts (and perhaps color-coded) to indicate

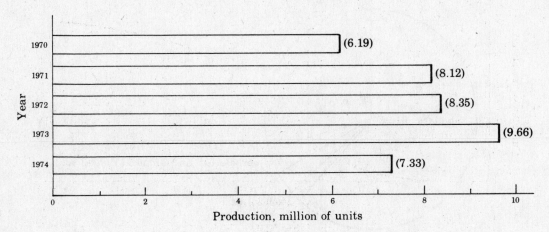

Fig. 2-7.

the relative contribution of each of the automobile manufacturers to the total factory sales (production) for the year.   (See Problem 2.24.)

Whenever the categories used represent a time segment, as is true for the data of Fig. 2-7, the data can also be described by means of a *line graph*.   A line graph portrays changes in amounts in respect to time by a series of line segments.

EXAMPLE 12.   The data of Fig. 2-7 are presented as a line graph in Fig. 2-8.

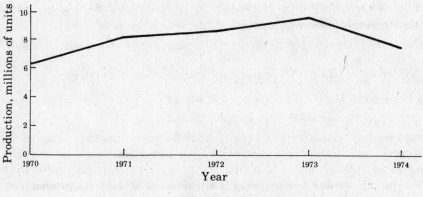

Fig. 2-8.

2.9   PIE CHARTS

The *pie chart* is a graphic device which is particularly appropriate for portraying the divisions of a total amount, such as the distribution of a company's sales dollar.

EXAMPLE 13.   Figure 2-9 is a pie chart depicting the distribution per dollar of sales in the Ford Motor Company in 1974 (data obtained from the *Annual Report*).

A *percentage pie chart* is one in which the values have been converted into percentages in order to make them easier to compare.   Since the values in Fig. 2-9 cumulate to exactly $1.00, such a conversion would not improve the readability of the chart in this case.   (See Problem 2.26.)

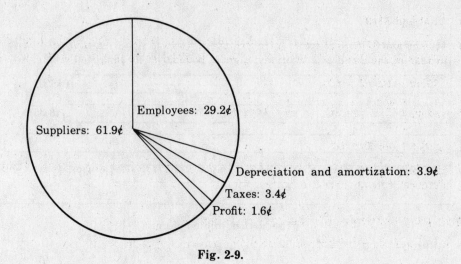

Fig. 2-9.

Solved Problems

FREQUENCY DISTRIBUTIONS, CLASS INTERVALS, AND RELATED GRAPHIC METHODS

2.1. With reference to Table 2.4,

    (*a*)   what are the lower and upper limits of the first class?

    (*b*)   what are the lower and upper boundaries of the first class?

    (*c*)   the class interval used is the same for all classes of the distribution. What is the interval size?

    (*d*)   what is the midpoint of the first class?

    (*e*)   what are the lower and upper boundaries of the class in which the largest number of apartment rental rates was tabulated?

    (*f*)   suppose a monthly rental rate of $239.50 was reported. Identify the lower and upper limits of the class in which this observation would be tallied.

Table 2.4   Frequency Distribution of Monthly Apartment Rental Rates for 200 Apartments

Rental rate	Number of apartments
$150–179	3
180–209	8
210–239	10
240–269	13
270–299	33
300–329	40
330–359	35
360–389	30
390–419	16
420–449	12
Total	200

(a) $150 and $179

(b) $149.50 and $179.50 (*Note*:   As in Example 2, two additional digits are expressed in this case instead of the usual one additional digit in boundaries as compared with class limits.)

(c)   179.50 − 149.50 = $30

(d) $149.50 + \dfrac{30}{2} = 149.50 + 15.00 = \$164.50$

(e) $299.50 and $329.50

(f) $240 and $269 (*Note*: $239.50 is first rounded to $240 as the nearest dollar using the "even number" rule described in Section 1.6.)

2.2.   Construct a histogram for the data of Table 2.4.

A histogram for the data of Table 2.4 appears in Fig. 2-10.

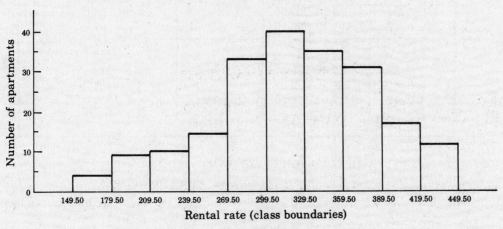

Fig. 2-10.

2.3   Construct a frequency polygon and a frequency curve for the data of Table 2.4.

Figure 2-11 is a graphic presentation of the frequency polygon and frequency curve for the data in Table 2.4.

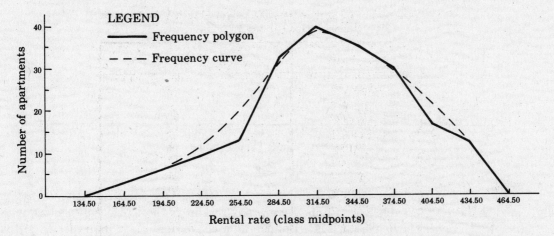

Fig. 2-11.

2.4. Describe the frequency curve in Fig. 2-11 from the standpoint of skewness.

The frequency curve appears to be somewhat negatively skewed.

2.5. Construct a cumulative frequency distribution for the data of Table 2.4.

See Table 2.5.

Table 2.5   Cumulative Frequency Distribution of Apartment Rental Rates

Rental rate	Class boundaries	Number of apartments	Cumulative frequency (*cf*)
$150–179	$149.50–179.50	3	3
180–209	179.50–209.50	8	11
210–239	209.50–239.50	10	21
240–269	239.50–269.50	13	34
270–299	269.50–299.50	33	67
300–329	299.50–329.50	40	107
330–359	329.50–359.50	35	142
360–389	359.50–389.50	30	172
390–419	389.50–419.50	16	188
420–449	419.50–449.50	12	200
		Total 200	

2.6. Present the cumulative frequency distribution in Table 2.5 graphically by means of an ogive curve.

The ogive curve for the data of Table 2.5 is shown in Fig. 2-12.

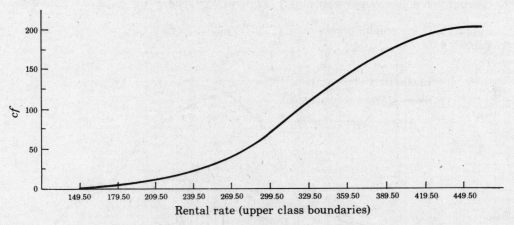

Fig. 2-12.

2.7. Refer to the data in Table 2.6. Suppose we wish to organize these prices into a frequency distribution with about five classes. Determine a convenient class interval, given that all class intervals are to be uniform in size.

Table 2.6   Average Price of Regular Grade Gasoline for Selected Areas in the U.S., March 1975

Area	Price per gallon, ¢	Area	Price per gallon, ¢
Atlanta	53.4	Los Angeles–Long Beach	53.5
Baltimore	55.1	Milwaukee	50.1
Boston	53.9	Minneapolis–St. Paul	50.3
Buffalo	53.4	New York–Northeastern N.J.	55.2
Chicago	54.8	Philadelphia	52.9
Cincinnati	53.3	Pittsburgh	53.4
Cleveland	53.9	St. Louis	52.3
Dallas	49.1	San Diego	55.3
Detroit	53.7	San Francisco–Oakland	56.8
Houston	47.9	Seattle	52.7
Kansas City	49.6	Washington D.C.	55.2

Source: *News*, U.S. Department of Labor, Bureau of Labor Statistics, April 22, 1975.

$$\text{Approximate interval} = \frac{\begin{bmatrix}\text{Largest value in} \\ \text{ungrouped data}\end{bmatrix} - \begin{bmatrix}\text{Smallest value in} \\ \text{ungrouped data}\end{bmatrix}}{\text{Number of classes desired}}$$

$$= \frac{56.8 - 47.9}{5} = 1.78$$

In this case, it is convenient to round the interval to 2.0.

2.8   Construct the frequency distribution for the data of Table 2.6 using a class interval of 2.0 and setting the lower limit of the first class at 47.0.

The required construction appears in Table 2.7.

Table 2.7   Frequency Distribution for Average Price of Gasoline in Selected Areas in the U.S., March 1975

Price per gallon, ¢	Number of areas
47.0–48.9	1
49.0–50.9	4
51.0–52.9	3
53.0–54.9	9
55.0–56.9	5
	Total 22

2.9.   For the frequency distribution in Table 2.7, determine   (*a*) the class limits of the class with the highest values, (*b*) the class boundaries of the class with the highest values, (*c*) the midpoint of the class with the highest values, (*d*) the midpoint of the class with the highest number of observations.

(*a*) 55.0–56.9,   (*b*) 54.95–56.95,   (*c*) 54.95 + 2.0/2 = 55.95,   (*d*) 52.95 + 1.0 = 53.95

2.10. Construct a histogram for the frequency distribution in Table 2.7.

The histogram is shown in Fig. 2-13.

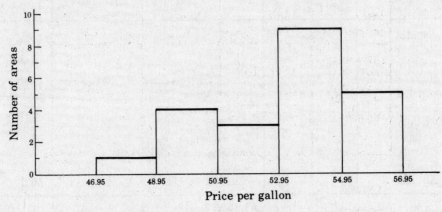

Fig. 2-13.

2.11. Construct a frequency polygon and frequency curve for the data in Table 2.7.

The frequency polygon and frequency curve appear in Fig. 2-14.

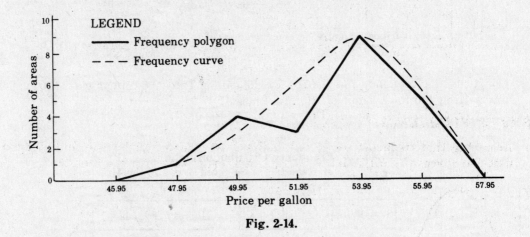

Fig. 2-14.

2.12. Describe the frequency curve in Fig. 2-14 in terms of skewness.

The frequency curve is negatively skewed.

2.13. Construct a cumulative frequency distribution for the frequency distribution in Table 2.7, including class boundaries as well as class limits in the table.

See Table 2.8 for the cumulative frequency distribution.

2.14. Present the cumulative frequency distribution of Table 2.8 graphically by means of an ogive and an ogive curve.

The ogive and ogive curve are shown in Fig. 2-15.

Table 2.8 Cumulative Frequency Distribution for Average Price of Gasoline in Selected Areas in the U.S., March 1975

Price per gallon, ¢	Class boundaries	Number of areas	Cumulative frequency (*cf*)
47.0–48.9	46.95–48.95	1	1
49.0–50.9	48.95–50.95	4	5
51.0–52.9	50.95–52.95	3	8
53.0–54.9	52.95–54.95	9	17
55.0–56.9	54.95–56.95	5	22
		Total 22	

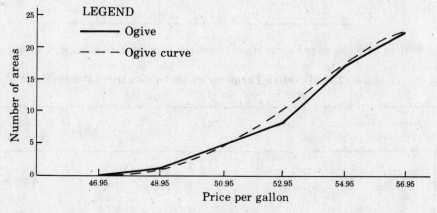

Fig. 2-15.

FORMS OF FREQUENCY CURVES

2.15. Assuming that frequency curve (*a*) in Fig. 2-16 is both symmetrical and mesokurtic, describe curves (*b*), (*c*), (*d*), (*e*), and (*f*) in terms of skewness and kurtosis.

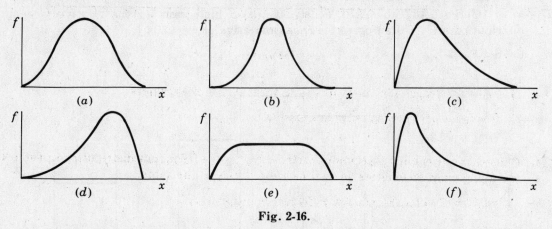

Fig. 2-16.

Curve (*b*) is symmetrical and leptokurtic; curve (*c*), positively skewed and mesokurtic; curve (*d*), negatively skewed and mesokurtic; curve (*e*), symmetrical and platykurtic; and curve (*f*), positively skewed and leptokurtic.

RELATIVE FREQUENCY DISTRIBUTIONS

2.16. Using the instructions in Section 2.6, determine   (a) the relative frequencies and   (b) the cumulative proportions for the data in Table 2.9.

Table 2.9   Average Number of Injuries per Thousand Man-Hours in a Particular Industry

Average number of injuries per thousand man-hours	Number of firms
1.5–1.7	3
1.8–2.0	12
2.1–2.3	14
2.4–2.6	9
2.7–2.9	7
3.0–3.2	5
	Total 50

The relative frequencies and cumulative proportions for the data in Table 2.9 are given in Table 2.10.

Table 2.10   Relative Frequencies and Cumulative Proportions for Average Number of Injuries

Average number of injuries per thousand man-hours	Number of firms	(a) Relative frequency	(b) Cumulative proportion
1.5–1.7	3	0.06	0.06
1.8–2.0	12	0.24	0.30
2.1–2.3	14	0.28	0.58
2.4–2.6	9	0.18	0.76
2.7–2.9	7	0.14	0.90
3.0–3.2	5	0.10	1.00
	Total 50	Total 1.00	

2.17. With reference to Table 2.10, construct   (a) a histogram for the relative frequency distribution and   (b) an ogive for the cumulative proportions.

(a) See Fig. 2-17.

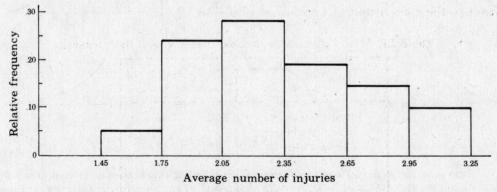

Fig. 2-17.

(b) See Fig. 2-18.

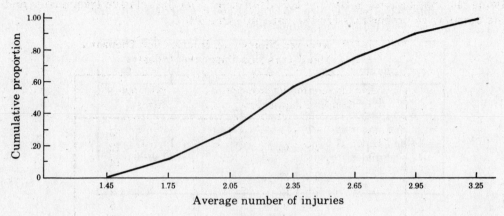

Fig. 2-18.

2.18. (a)   Referring to Table 2.10, what proportion of firms are in the category of having had an average of at least 3.0 injuries per thousand man-hours?   (b) What percentage of firms were at or below an average of 2.0 injuries per thousand man-hours?

(a) 0.10,   (b) 6% + 24% = 30%

2.19. (a)   Referring to Table 2.10, what is the percentile value associated with an average of 2.95 injuries per thousand man-hours?   (b) What is the average number of accidents at the 58th percentile?

(a) 90th percentile,   (b) 2.35

2.20. By graphic interpolation on an ogive curve, we can determine the approximate percentiles for various values of the variable, and vice versa.   Referring to Fig. 2-18,   (a) what is the approximate percentile associated with an average of 2.5 accidents?   (b) What is the approximate average number of accidents at the 50th percentile point?

(a) 65th percentile (This is the approximate height of the ogive corresponding to 2.50 along the horizontal axis.)
(b) 2.25 (This is the approximate point along the horizontal axis which corresponds to the 0.50 height of the ogive.)

"AND UNDER" TYPES OF FREQUENCY DISTRIBUTIONS

2.21. Identify the class boundaries for the data of Table 2.11.

Table 2.11   Time Required to Process and Prepare Mail Orders

Time, minutes	Number of orders
5 and under 8	10
8 and under 11	17
11 and under 14	12
14 and under 17	6
17 and under 20	2
	Total 47

From Table 2.11,

**Table 2.12   Time Required to Process and Prepare Mail Orders
(with Class Boundaries)**

Time, minutes	Number of orders	Class boundaries
5 and under 8	10	5.0– 8.0
8 and under 11	17	8.0–11.0
11 and under 14	12	11.0–14.0
14 and under 17	6	14.0–17.0
17 and under 20	2	17.0–20.0
	Total 47	

2.22.   Construct a frequency polygon for the frequency distribution in Table 2.12.

The frequency polygon appears in Fig. 2-19.

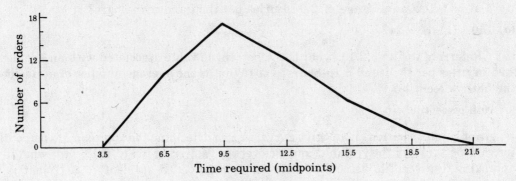

Fig. 2-19.

BAR CHARTS

2.23.   Table 2.13 reports certain financial results included in the 1974 *Annual Report* of the United States Steel Corporation.   Construct a vertical bar chart portraying the annual earnings of the company from 1969 to 1974.

**Table 2.13   Total Earnings, Dividends, and Retained
Earnings of the United States Steel
Corporation, 1969–74, Millions of Dollars**

Year	Earnings	Dividends	Retained earnings
1969	217	130	87
1970	148	130	18
1971	154	98	56
1972	157	87	70
1973	326	87	239
1974	635	119	516

The bar chart appears in Fig. 2-20.

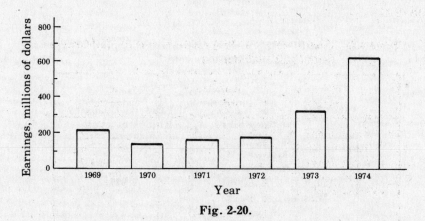

Fig. 2-20.

2.24. Construct a component bar chart for the data of Table 2.13 such that the division of total earnings between dividends (*D*) and retained earnings (*R*) is indicated for each year.

Figure 2-21 presents a component bar chart for the data in Table 2.13.

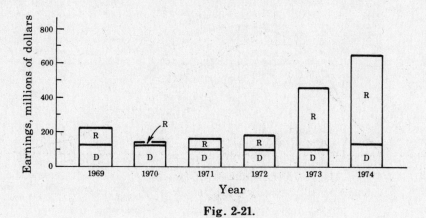

Fig. 2-21.

LINE GRAPHS

2.25. Construct a line graph for the retained earnings reported in Table 2.13.

The line graph is given in Fig. 2-22.

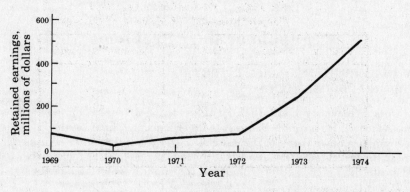

Fig. 2-22.

PIE CHARTS

2.26. Table 2.14 is based on values supplied in the *Annual Report* of the Boeing Company for 1974. Construct a percentage pie chart for the order backlog according to category of order.

Table 2.14 Order Backlog in the Boeing Company
at the End of 1974, Millions of Dollars

Category	Amount
Commercial aircraft	$2732
Missiles and space	408
Military aircraft	639
Other	45
Total	$3824

See Fig. 2-23.

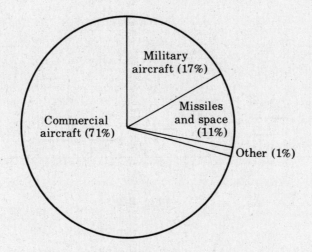

Fig. 2-23.

Supplementary Problems

FREQUENCY DISTRIBUTIONS, CLASS INTERVALS, AND RELATED GRAPHIC METHODS

2.27. Table 2.15 is a frequency distribution for the gasoline mileage obtained for 25 sampled trips for company-owned vehicles. (*a*) What are the lower and upper limits of the last class? (*b*) What are the lower and upper boundaries of the last class? (*c*) What class interval is used? (*d*) What is the midpoint of the last class? (*e*) Suppose the mileage per gallon was found to be 19.9 for a particular trip. Indicate the lower and upper limits of the class in which this result was included.

  Ans. (*a*) 24.0 and 25.9, (*b*) 23.95 and 25.95, (*c*) 2.0, (*d*) 24.95, (*e*) 18.0 and 19.9

**Table 2.15 Automobile Mileage for 25
Trips by Company Vehicles**

Miles per gallon	Number of trips
14.0–15.9	3
16.0–17.9	5
18.0–19.9	10
20.0–21.9	4
22.0–23.9	2
24.0–25.9	1
	Total 25

2.28. Construct a histogram for the data of Table 2.15.

2.29. Construct a frequency polygon and a frequency curve for the data of Table 2.15.

2.30. Describe the frequency curve constructed in Problem 2.29 from the standpoint of skewness.

Ans.   The frequency curve appears to be somewhat positively skewed.

2.31. Construct a cumulative frequency distribution for the data of Table 2.15 and construct an ogive to present this distribution graphically.

2.32. Table 2.16 presents the amounts of 40 personal loans in a consumer finance company. Suppose we wish to arrange the loan amounts in a frequency distribution with a total of seven classes. Assuming equal class intervals, what would be a convenient class interval for this frequency distribution?

Table 2.16   The Amounts of 40 Personal Loans

$900	$1000	$300	$2000
500	550	1100	1000
450	950	300	2000
1900	600	1600	450
1200	750	1500	750
1250	1300	1000	850
2500	850	1800	600
550	350	900	3000
1650	1400	500	350
1200	700	650	1500

Ans. $400

2.33. Construct the frequency distribution for the data of Table 2.16, beginning the first class at a lower class limit of $300 and using a class interval of $400.

2.34. Prepare a histogram for the frequency distribution constructed in Problem 2.33.

2.35. Construct a frequency polygon and frequency curve for the frequency distribution constructed in Problem 2.33.

2.36. Describe the frequency curve constructed in Problem 2.35 in terms of skewness.

Ans.   The frequency curve is clearly positively skewed.

2.37. Construct a cumulative frequency distribution for the frequency distribution constructed in Problem 2.33 and construct an ogive curve for these data.

FORMS OF FREQUENCY CURVES

2.38. Describe each of the following curves in terms of skewness or kurtosis, as appropriate: (a) A frequency curve with a "tail" to the right, (b) a frequency curve which is relatively peaked, (c) a frequency curve which is relatively flat, (d) a frequency curve with a "tail" to the left.

   Ans. (a) Positively skewed, (b) leptokurtic, (c) platykurtic, (d) negatively skewed

RELATIVE FREQUENCY DISTRIBUTIONS

2.39. Construct a relative frequency table for the frequency distribution presented in Table 2.17.

Table 2.17 Lifetime of Cutting Tools in an Industrial Process

Hours before replacement	Number of tools
0.0– 24.9	2
25.0– 49.9	4
50.0– 74.9	12
75.0– 99.9	30
100.0–124.9	18
125.0–149.9	4
	Total 70

2.40. Construct a histogram for the relative frequency distribution prepared in Problem 2.39.

2.41. Referring to Table 2.17, (a) what percentage of cutting tools lasted at least 125 hr? (b) What percentage of cutting tools had a lifetime of at least 100 hr?

   Ans. (a) 6%, (b) 31%

2.42. Prepare a table of cumulative proportions for the frequency distribution in Table 2.17.

2.43. Referring to the table constructed in Problem 2.42, (a) what is the tool lifetime associated at the 26th percentile of the distribution? (b) What is the percentile associated with a tool lifetime of 99.95 hr?

   Ans. (a) 74.95 hr, (b) 69th percentile

2.44. Construct the ogive for the cumulative proportions determined in Problem 2.42.

2.45. Refer to the ogive prepared in Problem 2.44 and determine the following values approximately by graphic interpolation: (a) The tool lifetime at the 50th percentile of the distribution, (b) the percentile associated with a tool lifetime of 60 hr.

   Ans. (a) Approx. 89 hr, (b) approx. 16th percentile

"AND UNDER" TYPES OF FREQUENCY DISTRIBUTIONS

2.46. By reference to the frequency distribution in Table 2.18, determine (a) the lower limit of the first class, (b) the upper limit of the first class, (c) the lower boundary of the first class, (d) the upper boundary of the first class, (e) the midpoint of the first class.

**Table 2.18 Ages of a Sample of Applicants
for a Training Program**

Age	Number of applicants
18 and under 20	5
20 and under 22	18
22 and under 24	10
24 and under 26	6
26 and under 28	5
28 and under 30	4
30 and under 32	2
	Total 50

Ans. (*a*) 18, (*b*) 20, (*c*) 18, (*d*) 20, (*e*) 19.0

2.47. Construct a frequency polygon for the frequency distribution in Table 2.18.

BAR CHARTS

2.48. The data in Table 2.19 are taken from the Survey of *Current Business* published by the U.S. Department of Commerce. Construct a vertical bar chart for these data.

**Table 2.19 Construction of New One-Family
Structures in the United States,
1970–74, Thousands of Units**

Year	Housing starts
1970	813
1971	1151
1972	1349
1973	1132
1974	888

LINE GRAPHS

2.49. Construct a line graph for the housing starts for single-family structures which are reported in Table 2.19.

PIE CHARTS

2.50. The values in Table 2.20 are taken from the *Annual Report* of the Valley National Bank (Arizona) for 1974. Construct a percentage pie chart for the sources of time deposits during that year.

**Table 2.20 Valley National Bank: Sources of the Average Balance of
Time Deposits during 1974, Thousands of Dollars**

Savings Accounts	$506,884
Premium Savings Plans	402,160
Certificates of Deposit—Regular	469,191
Certificates of Deposit—Public	101,538
	Total $1,479,773

Chapter 3

Describing Business Data:
Measures of Location

3.1 MEASURES OF LOCATION IN DATA SETS

A measure of location is a value which is calculated for a group of data and which is used to describe the data in some way. Typically, we wish the value to be representative of all of the values in the group, and thus some kind of *average* is desired. In the statistical sense an "average" is a *measure of central tendency* for a collection of values. This chapter covers the various statistical procedures concerned with measures of location.

3.2 THE ARITHMETIC MEAN

The *arithmetic mean*, or *arithmetic average*, is defined as the sum of the values in the data group divided by the number of values.

In statistics, a descriptive measure of a population, or a *population parameter*, is typically represented by a Greek letter, whereas a descriptive measure of a sample, or a *sample statistic*, is represented by a Roman letter. Thus, the arithmetic mean for a population of values is represented by the symbol μ (read "mū"), while the arithmetic mean for a sample of values is represented by the symbol $\bar{X}$ (read "X bar"). The formulas for the population mean and the sample mean are

$$\mu = \frac{\Sigma X}{N} \qquad\qquad (3.1)$$

$$\bar{X} = \frac{\Sigma X}{n} \qquad\qquad (3.2)$$

Operationally, the two formulas are identical; in both cases one sums all of the values (ΣX) and then divides by the number of values. However, the distinction in the denominators is that in statistical analysis the upper-case N typically indicates the number of items in the population, while the lower-case n indicates the number of items in the sample.

EXAMPLE 1. During a particular summer month, the eight salesmen in a heating and air-conditioning firm sold the following number of central air-conditioning units: 8, 11, 5, 14, 8, 11, 16, 11. Considering this month as the statistical population of interest, the mean number of units sold is

$$\mu = \frac{\Sigma X}{N} = \frac{84}{8} = 10.5 \text{ units}$$

Note: For purposes of comparison we generally report the measures of location to one additional significant digit beyond the original level of measurement throughout this chapter. In any final reports, these values should be rounded to the number of significant digits in the original data, as explained in Section 1.5.

3.3 THE ARITHMETIC MEAN FOR GROUPED DATA

When data have been grouped in a frequency distribution, the midpoint of each class is used as an approximation of all values contained in the class. The midpoint is represented by the symbol X_c, wherein the subscript c stands for "class," and the symbol f represents the observed frequency of values in each respective class. Thus, the formulas for the population mean and the sample mean computed for grouped data are

$$\mu = \frac{\Sigma(fX_c)}{\Sigma f} \quad \text{or, more simply,} \quad \mu = \frac{\Sigma(fX)}{N} \qquad (3.3)$$

$$\bar{X} = \frac{\Sigma(fX_c)}{\Sigma f} \quad \text{or, more simply,} \quad \bar{X} = \frac{\Sigma(fX)}{n} \qquad (3.4)$$

Operationally, both formulas indicate that each class midpoint (X_c) is multiplied by the associated class frequency (f), the products are summed (Σ), and then the sum is divided by the total number of observations (Σf) represented in the frequency distribution.

EXAMPLE 2. The grouped data in Table 3.1 are taken from the frequency distribution presented in Section 2.1. The mean is represented by the symbol $\bar{X}$ because the group of workers is assumed to be a sample from a larger population of workers.

Table 3.1 Weekly Wages of 100 Unskilled Workers (Rounded to the Nearest Dollar)

Weekly wage	Class midpoint (X)	Number of workers (f)	fX
$140–159	$149.50	7	$ 1,046.50
160–179	169.50	20	3,390.00
180–199	189.50	33	6,253.50
200–219	209.50	25	5,237.50
220–239	229.50	11	2,524.50
240–259	249.50	4	998.00
		Total 100	$\Sigma fX = \$19,450.00$

$$\bar{X} = \frac{\Sigma(fX)}{n} = \frac{19,450}{100} = \$194.50$$

3.4 THE WEIGHTED MEAN

The *weighted mean* or *weighted average* is an arithmetic mean in which each value is weighted according to its importance in the overall group. The formulas for the population and sample weighted means are identical:

$$\mu_w \text{ or } \bar{X}_w = \frac{\Sigma(wX)}{\Sigma w} \qquad (3.5)$$

Operationally, each value in the group (X) is multiplied by the appropriate weight factor (w), and the products are then summed and divided by the sum of the weights.

EXAMPLE 3. In a multiproduct company, the profit margins for the company's four product lines during the past fiscal year were: line A, 4.2%; line B, 5.5%; line C, 7.4%; and line D, 10.1%. The *unweighted* mean profit margin is

$$\mu = \frac{\Sigma X}{N} = \frac{27.2}{4} = 6.8\%$$

However, unless the four products are equal in sales, this unweighted average is incorrect. Assuming the sales totals in Table 3.2, the weighted mean correctly describes the overall average.

Table 3.2 Profit Margin and Sales Volume for Four Product Lines

Product line	Profit margin (X)	Sales (w)	wX
A	4.2%	$30,000,000	$1,260,000
B	5.5	20,000,000	1,100,000
C	7.4	5,000,000	370,000
D	10.1	3,000,000	303,000
		Σw = $58,000,000	ΣwX = $3,033,000

$$\mu_w = \frac{\Sigma(wX)}{\Sigma w} = \frac{\$3,033,000}{\$58,000,000} = 5.2\%$$

3.5 THE MEDIAN

The *median* of a group of items is the value of the middle item when all the items in the group are arranged in either ascending or descending order, in terms of value. For a group with an even number of items, the median is assumed to be midway between the two values adjacent to the middle. When a large number of values is contained in the group, the following formula to determine the position of the median in the ordered group is useful:

$$\text{Med} = X_{[(n/2)+(1/2)]} \qquad (3.6)$$

EXAMPLE 4. The eight salesmen described in Example 1 sold the following number of central air-conditioning units, in ascending order: 5, 8, 8, 11, 11, 11, 14, 16. The value of the median is

$$\text{Med} = X_{[(n/2)+(1/2)]} = X_{[(8/2)+(1/2)]} = X_{4.5} = 11.0$$

The value of the median is between the fourth and fifth value in the ordered group. Since both these values equal "11" in this case, the median equals 11.

3.6 THE MEDIAN FOR GROUPED DATA

For grouped data, the class which contains the median value has to be determined first, and then the position of the median within the class is determined by interpolation. The class which contains the median is the first class for which the cumulative frequency equals or exceeds one-half the total number of observations. Once this class is identified, the specific value of the median is determined by the formula

$$\text{Med} = B_L + \left(\frac{\frac{N}{2} - cf_B}{f_c}\right) i \qquad (3.7)$$

where B_L = lower boundary of the class containing the median
N = total number of observations in the frequency distribution (n for a sample)
cf_B = the cumulative frequency in the class preceding ("before") the class containing the median
f_c = the number of observations in the class containing the median
i = the size of the class interval

EXAMPLE 5. The grouped data in Table 3.3 are taken from the frequency distribution presented in Section 2.1. In this case, the class containing the median is the class with the $100/2 = 50$th value. The first class whose cumulative frequency equals or exceeds 50 is the class with the limits \$180–199; thus, interpolation to determine the specific value of the median is done within this class.

Table 3.3 Weekly Wages of 100 Unskilled Workers

Weekly wage	Number of workers (f)	Cumulative frequency (cf)
\$140–159	7	7
160–179	20	27
180–199	33	60
200–219	25	85
220–239	11	96
240–259	4	100
Total 100		

$$\text{Med} = B_L + \left(\frac{\frac{n}{2} - cf_B}{f_c}\right)i = 179.50 + \left(\frac{50 - 27}{33}\right)20 = \$193.44$$

3.7 THE MODE

The *mode* is the value which occurs most frequently in a set of values. Such a distribution is described as being *unimodal*. For a small data set in which no measured values are repeated, there is no mode. When two nonadjoining values are about equal in having maximum frequencies associated with them, the distribution is described as being *bimodal*. Distributions of measurements with several modes are referred to as being *multimodal*.

EXAMPLE 6. The eight salesmen described in Example 1 sold the following number of central air-conditioning units: 8, 11, 5, 14, 8, 11, 16, and 11. The mode for this group of values is the value with the greatest frequency, or Mode = 11.

3.8 THE MODE FOR GROUPED DATA

For data grouped in a frequency distribution with equal class intervals, first the class containing the mode is determined by identifying the class with the greatest number of observations. Some statisticians then designate the mode as being at the midpoint of the modal class. However, most statisticians interpolate within the modal class on the basis of the following formula:

$$\text{Mode} = B_L + \left(\frac{d_1}{d_1 + d_2}\right)i \qquad (3.8)$$

where B_L = lower boundary of the class containing the mode
d_1 = difference between the frequency in the modal class and the frequency in the preceding class
d_2 = difference between the frequency in the modal class and the frequency in the following class
i = the size of the class interval

EXAMPLE 7. Refer to the grouped data in Table 2.1 (page 9). The modal class is the class with the limits \$180–199. Thus,

$$\text{Mode} = B_L + \left(\frac{d_1}{d_1 + d_2}\right)i = 179.50 + \left(\frac{13}{13 + 8}\right)20 = \$191.88$$

3.9 RELATIONSHIP AMONG THE MEAN, MEDIAN, AND MODE

For grouped data represented by a frequency curve, the difference among the values of the mean, median, and mode are indicative of the form of the curve in terms of skewness. For a unimodal distribution which is symmetrical, the mean, median, and mode all coincide in value (see Fig. 3-1a). For a positively skewed distribution, the mean is largest in value and the median is larger than the mode but smaller than the mean (see Fig. 3-1b). For a negatively skewed distribution, the mean is smallest in value and the median is below the mode but above the mean (see Fig. 3-1c). One well-known measure of skewness which utilizes the observed difference between the mean and median of a group of values is Pearson's Coefficient of Skewness, described in Section 4.11.

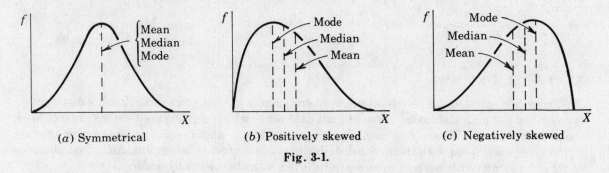

(a) Symmetrical   (b) Positively skewed   (c) Negatively skewed

Fig. 3-1.

EXAMPLE 8. For the frequency distribution of wages discussed in Examples 2, 5, and 7, we can observe that the mean is \$194.50, the median is \$193.44, and the mode is \$191.88, thus indicating that the distribution is somewhat positively skewed, or skewed to the right.

3.10 QUARTILES, DECILES, AND PERCENTILES

The quartiles, deciles, and percentiles are very similar to the median in that they also subdivide a distribution of measurements according to the proportion of frequencies observed. Whereas the median divides a distribution into two halves, the quartiles divide it into four quarters, the deciles divide it into 10 tenths, and the percentile points divide it into 100 parts. For ungrouped data, formula (3.6) for the median is modified according to the fractional point of interest. For example:

$$Q_1 \text{ (first quartile)} = X_{[(n/4)+(1/2)]} \qquad (3.9)$$

$$D_3 \text{ (third decile)} = X_{[(3n/10)+(1/2)]} \qquad (3.10)$$

$$P_{70} \text{ (seventieth percentile)} = X_{[(70n/100)+(1/2)]} \qquad (3.11)$$

EXAMPLE 9. The eight salesmen described in Example 1 sold the following number of central air-conditioning units, in ascending order: 5, 8, 8, 11, 11, 11, 14, 16. Find the position of the third quartile for this distribution.

$$Q_3 = X_{[(3n/4)+(1/2)]} = X_{[(24/4)+(1/2)]} = X_{6.5} = 12.5$$

In this case the value is between the sixth and seventh value in the ordered group.

3.11 QUARTILES, DECILES, AND PERCENTILES FOR GROUPED DATA

For grouped data, formula (3.7) for the median is modified according to the fractional point of interest. In using this modified formula, *first the appropriate class containing the point of interest is determined* by reference to cumulative frequencies, and then the interpolation is done as before. Example formulas in this case are

$$Q_1 \text{ (first quartile)} = B_L + \left(\frac{\frac{n}{4} - cf_B}{f_c}\right)i \qquad (3.12)$$

$$D_3 \text{ (third decile)} = B_L + \left(\frac{\frac{3n}{10} - cf_B}{f_c}\right)i \qquad (3.13)$$

$$P_{70} \text{ (seventieth percentile)} = B_L + \left(\frac{\frac{70n}{100} - cf_B}{f_c}\right)i \qquad (3.14)$$

EXAMPLE 10. The cumulative frequencies in Table 3.3 (page 33) can be used to determine the 90th percentile point for these wage rates. In this case, note that the class containing this value is the first class whose cumulative frequency exceeds $\frac{90n}{100}$, or 90. This is the class with the limits $220–239, and so the lower boundary used in the formula is $219.50.

$$P_{90} = B_L + \left(\frac{\frac{90n}{100} - cf_B}{f_c}\right)i = 219.50 + \left(\frac{90 - 85}{11}\right)20 = \$228.59$$

Solved Problems

THE MEAN, MEDIAN, AND MODE FOR UNGROUPED DATA

3.1. For a sample of 15 customers at a small convenience market, the following sales amounts arranged in ascending order of magnitude are observed: $0.10, 0.10, 0.25, 0.25, 0.25, 0.35, 0.40, 0.53, 0.90, 1.25, 1.35, 2.45, 2.71, 3.09, 4.10. Determine the (a) mean, (b) median, and (c) mode for these sales amounts.

(a) $\bar{X} = \dfrac{\Sigma X}{n} = \dfrac{18.08}{15} = \$1.21$

(b) $\text{Med} = X_{[(n/2)+(1/2)]} = X_{[(15/2)+(1/2)]} = X_8 = \$0.53$

(c)   Mode = most frequent value = $0.25

3.2. How would you describe the distribution in Problem 3.1 from the standpoint of skewness?

With the mean being substantially larger than the mode, and with the median also being larger than the mode but smaller than the mean, the distribution of values is positively skewed, or skewed to the right.

3.3. If you were asked for a description of the data in Problem 3.1 by reporting the "typical" amount of purchase per customer in the sample, which measure of central tendency, or average, would you report? Why?

For a highly skewed distribution such as this, the arithmetic mean is not descriptive of the typical value in the group. The choice between the median and mode as a better measure depends on the degree to which observations are concentrated at the modal point. In this case, the degree of concentration is not all that great, and so "$0.25" is not really descriptive of the typical purchase amount either. For these reasons, the best choice for these data appears to be the median, and "$0.53" can be considered typical in the sense that approximately half the sales amounts were lower and half were higher.

3.4. A sample of 20 production workers in a small company earned the following wages for a given week, rounded to the nearest dollar and arranged in ascending order: $140, 140, 140, 140, 140, 140, 140, 140, 155, 155, 165, 165, 180, 180, 190, 200, 205, 225, 230, 240. Calculate the (a) mean, (b) median, and (c) mode for this group of wages.

(a) $\bar{X} = \dfrac{\Sigma X}{n} = \dfrac{3410}{20} = \$170.50$

(b) Median $= X_{[(n/2)+(1/2)]} = X_{[(20/2)+(1/2)]} = X_{10.5} = \$160.00$

(c) Mode = most frequent value = $140.00

3.5. For the wage data in Problem 3.4, describe the distribution in terms of skewness.

With the mean being the largest value and with the median being between the mean and the mode, the distribution can be described as being positively skewed, or skewed to the right.

3.6. Given that you were placed in each of the following positions in turn, indicate which measure of "average" you might be inclined to report for the data in Problem 3.4, and in what sense each value can be considered "typical." (a) As vice-president responsible for collective bargaining. (b) As the president of the employee bargaining unit.

(a) You would be inclined to choose the arithmetic mean to best present the company's position and you could observe that this mean takes every individual's wage into consideration. You might also (incorrectly) be tempted to state that the arithmetic average is the only "real" average.

(b) You would be inclined to choose either the mode or the median, in this order, as your description of what is "typical" in this firm. The mode is "typical" in that clearly many more workers are at this wage level than at any other wage level. The median is "typical" in the sense that half of the workers earn less than this amount and half earn more than this amount.

3.7. A work-standards expert observes the amount of time required to type a sample of 10 business letters in an office with the following results listed in ascending order to the nearest minute: 5, 5, 5, 7, 9, 14, 15, 15, 16, 18. Determine the (a) mean, (b) median, and (c) mode for this group of values.

(a) $\bar{X} = \dfrac{\Sigma X}{n} = \dfrac{109}{10} = 10.9$ min

(b) Med $= X_{[(n/2)+(1/2)]} = X_{[(10/2)+(1/2)]} = X_{5.5} = 11.5$ min

(c) Mode = most frequent value = 5.0 (but see next problem)

3.8. Compare the values of the mean, median, and mode in Problem 3.7 and comment on the form of the distribution.

The results appear unusual in that the mean is not the extreme value (either highest or lowest). The reason for this is that for practical purposes there really is not just one mode. Rather, the values appear to be clustered at two different points in the distribution, forming a bimodal distribution.

THE MEAN, MEDIAN, AND MODE FOR GROUPED DATA

3.9. Reproduced in Table 3.4 is the frequency distribution given in Problem 2.1. Determine the average rental rate in terms of the (a) mean, (b) median, and (c) mode. Assume that these are all of the apartments in a given geographic area.

Table 3.4   Frequency Distribution for Monthly Apartment Rental Rates

(1) Rental rate	(2) Class midpoint (X)	(3) Number of apartments (f)	(4) fX	(5) Cumulative frequency (cf)
$150–179	$164.50	3	$ 493.50	3
180–209	194.50	8	1,556.00	11
210–239	224.50	10	2,245.00	21
240–269	254.50	13	3,308.50	34
270–299	284.50	33	9,388.50	67
300–329	314.50	40	12,580.00	107
330–359	344.50	35	12,057.50	142
360–389	374.50	30	11,235.00	172
390–419	404.50	16	6,472.00	188
420–449	434.50	12	5,214.00	200
		Total 200	$\Sigma(fX) = \$64,550.00$	

(a) $\mu = \dfrac{\Sigma(fX)}{N} = \dfrac{64,550}{200} = \$322.75$

(b) $\text{Med} = B_L + \left(\dfrac{\frac{N}{2} - cf_B}{f_c}\right)i = 299.50 + \left(\dfrac{100 - 67}{40}\right)30 = \$324.25$

(*Note:* $299.50 is the lower boundary of the class containing the $\frac{N}{2}$, or 100th, measurement.)

(c) $\text{Mode} = B_L + \left(\dfrac{d_1}{d_1 + d_2}\right)i = 299.50 + \left(\dfrac{7}{7 + 5}\right)30 = \$317.00$

(*Note:* $299.50 is the lower boundary of the class containing the highest frequency.)

3.10. Comment on the form of the distribution for the apartment rental rates in Problem 3.9.

Although the frequency polygon for these data as presented in Fig. 2-11 seems to be indicative of some degree of negative skewness, the comparison of the values of the mean, median, and mode does not clearly support such a conclusion. The mean is smaller than the median, but it is larger than the mode. The reason for this is that there is not a very great departure from symmetry. (See Problem 4.22, in which Pearson's coefficient of skewness is applied to these rental data.)

3.11. In conjunction with an annual audit, a public accounting firm makes note of the time required to audit 50 account balances, as indicated in Table 3.5. Compute the (a) mean, (b) median, and (c) mode for the audit time required for this sample of records.

Table 3.5 Time Required to Audit Account Balances

(1) Audit time (nearest minute)	(2) Class midpoint (X)	(3) Number of records (f)	(4) fX	(5) Cumulative frequency (cf)
10–19	14.5	3	43.5	3
20–29	24.5	5	122.5	8
30–39	34.5	10	345.0	18
40–49	44.5	12	534.0	30
50–59	54.5	20	1090.0	50
		Total 50	$\Sigma(fX) = 2135.0$	

(a) $\bar{X} = \dfrac{\Sigma(fX)}{n} = \dfrac{2135.0}{50} = 42.7$ min

(b) Med $= B_L + \left(\dfrac{\frac{n}{2} - cf_B}{f_c}\right)i = 39.5 + \left(\dfrac{25 - 18}{12}\right)10.00 = 45.3$ min

(*Note:* 39.5 is the lower boundary of the class containing the $\frac{n}{2}$, or 25th, measurement.)

(c) Mode $= B_L + \left(\dfrac{d_1}{d_1 + d_2}\right)i = 49.5 + \left(\dfrac{8}{8 + 20}\right)10.0 = 52.36$ min

(*Note:* 49.5 is the lower boundary of the class with the highest frequency. Also note that $d_2 = 20 - 0 = 20$ in this case.)

3.12. Comment on the form of the distribution for the audit times reported in Problem 3.11.

The mean is smaller in value than either the median or mode, and the median is smaller than the mode. Thus, the distribution is clearly negatively skewed, or skewed to the left.

3.13. Reproduced in Table 3.6 are the data reported in Problem 2.16. Determine the (a) mean, (b) median, and (c) mode for this sample of 50 firms.

Table 3.6 Average Number of Injuries per Thousand Man-Hours in a Particular Industry

Average number of injuries	Class midpoint (X)	Number of firms (f)	fX	Cumulative frequency (cf)
1.5–1.7	1.6	3	4.8	3
1.8–2.0	1.9	12	22.8	15
2.1–2.3	2.2	14	30.8	29
2.4–2.6	2.5	9	22.5	38
2.7–2.9	2.8	7	19.6	45
3.0–3.2	3.1	5	15.5	50
		Total 50	$\Sigma(fX) = 116.0$	

(a) $\bar{X} = \dfrac{\Sigma(fX)}{n} = \dfrac{116.0}{50} = 2.32$ injuries

(b) Med $= B_L + \left(\dfrac{\frac{n}{2} - cf_B}{f_c}\right)i = 2.05 + \left(\dfrac{25-15}{14}\right)0.3 = 2.26$ injuries

(*Note:* 2.05 is the lower boundary of the class containing the $\frac{n}{2}$, or 25th, measurement.)

(c) Mode $= B_L + \left(\dfrac{d_1}{d_1 + d_2}\right)i = 2.05 + \left(\dfrac{2}{2+5}\right)0.3 = 2.14$ injuries

(*Note:* 2.05 is the lower boundary of the class containing the $\frac{n}{2}$, or 25th, measurement.)

3.14. Comment on the form of the distribution for the data of Problem 3.13.

The sample mean is larger than either the median or the mode, and the median is also larger than the mode. This comparison indicates that the distribution is positively skewed, or skewed to the right.

3.15. The frequency distribution in Table 3.7 is reproduced from Problem 2.21. Determine the (a) mean, (b) median, and (c) mode for these data. Note the basis for determining class boundaries and class midpoints for such an "and under" frequency distribution.

Table 3.7 Time Required to Process and Prepare Mail Orders

Time (in minutes)	Class boundaries	Class midpoint (X)	Number of orders (f)	fX	Cumulative frequency (cf)
5 and under 8	5.0–8.0	6.5	10	65.0	10
8 and under 11	8.0–11.0	9.5	17	161.5	27
11 and under 14	11.0–14.0	12.5	12	150.0	39
14 and under 17	14.0–17.0	15.5	6	93.0	45
17 and under 20	17.0–20.0	18.5	2	37.0	47
			Total 47	$\Sigma(fX) = 506.5$	

(a) $\bar{X} = \dfrac{\Sigma(fX)}{n} = \dfrac{506.5}{47} = 10.8$ min

(b) Med $= B_L + \left(\dfrac{\frac{n}{2} - cf_B}{f_c}\right)i = 8.0 + \left(\dfrac{23.5-10}{17}\right)3.0 = 10.4$ min

(*Note:* 8.0 is the lower boundary of the class containing the $\frac{n}{2}$, or 23.5th, measurement.)

(c) Mode $= B_L + \left(\dfrac{d_1}{d_1 + d_2}\right)i = 8.0 + \left(\dfrac{7}{7+5}\right)3.0 = 9.75 \cong 9.8$ min

(*Note:* 8.0 is the lower boundary of the class containing the highest frequency.)

3.16. Comment on the form of the distribution for the order processing times analyzed in Problem 3.15.

Since the mean is the largest of the measures of central tendency and since the median is also larger than the mode, the distribution is positively skewed.

THE WEIGHTED MEAN

3.17. Table 2.6 presents the average price of regular grade gasoline for 22 selected metropolitan areas in March 1975. Suppose that the (a) median and (b) arithmetic mean were computed for these data. Describe the meaning each of these values would have.

(a) The median would indicate the average, or typical, price in the sense that half the metropolitan areas would have gasoline prices below this value and half would have prices above this value.

(b) The meaning of the arithmetic mean as an unweighted value is questionable at best. Clearly, it would *not* indicate the mean gasoline prices being paid by all of the gasoline purchasers living in the 22 metropolitan areas, because the small metropolitan areas would be represented equally with the large areas in such an average. In order to determine a suitable mean for all purchasers in these metropolitan areas, a weighted mean (using regular-grade gasoline sales as weights) would have to be computed.

3.18. Referring to Table 3.8, determine the overall percentage defective of all items assembled during the sampled week.

Table 3.8 Percentage of Defective Items in an Assembly Department in a Sampled Week

Shift	Percentage defective (X)	Number of items, in thousands (w)	wX
1	1.1	210	231.0
2	1.5	120	180.0
3	2.3	50	115.0
		$\Sigma w = 380$	$\Sigma(wX) = 526.0$

Using formula (*3.5*),

$$\bar{X}_\omega = \frac{\Sigma(wX)}{\Sigma w} = \frac{526.0}{380} = 1.4\% \text{ defective}$$

QUARTILES, DECILES, AND PERCENTILES

3.19. For the data in Problem 3.1, determine the values at the (a) second quartile, (b) second decile, and (c) 40th percentile point for these sales amounts.

(a) $Q_2 = X_{[(2n/4)+(1/2)]} = X_{(7.5+0.5)} = X_8 = \$0.53$

(*Note:* By definition, the second quartile is always at the same point as the median.)

(b) $D_2 = X_{[(2n/10)+(1/2)]} = X_{(3.0+0.5)} = X_{3.5} = \$0.25$

(*Note:* This is the value midway between the third and fourth sales amounts, arranged in ascending order.)

(c) $P_{40} = X_{[(40n/100)+(1/2)]} = X_{(6.0+0.5)} = X_{6.5} = 0.375 \cong \$0.38$

3.20. For the measurements in Problem 3.4, determine the values at the (a) third quartile, (b) ninth decile, (c) 50th percentile point, and (d) 84th percentile point for this group of wages.

(a) $Q_3 = X_{[(3n/4)+(1/2)]} = X_{15.5} = \$195.00$

(*Note:* This is the value midway between the 15th and 16th wage amounts, arranged in ascending order.)

(b) $D_9 = X_{[(9n/10)+(1/2)]} = X_{18.5} = \$227.50$

(c) $P_{50} = X_{[(50n/100)+(1/2)]} = X_{10.5} = \$160.00$

(*Note:* By definition the 50th percentile point is always at the same point as the median.)

(d) $P_{84} = X_{[(84n/100)+(1/2)]} = X_{(16.8+0.5)} = X_{17.3} = \$211.00$

(*Note:* This is the value which is *three-tenths* of the way between the 17th and 18th wage amounts, arranged in ascending order.)

3.21. Referring to Table 3.4 (page 37), determine the values at the (*a*) first quartile, (*b*) third decile, (*c*) 80th percentile point, and (*d*) 17th percentile point.

(a) $Q_1 = B_L + \left(\dfrac{\frac{N}{4} - cf_B}{f_c}\right)i = 269.50 + \left(\dfrac{50 - 34}{33}\right)30 = \$284.05$

(*Note:* \$269.50 is the lower boundary of the class containing the $\frac{n}{4}$, or 50th, measurement.)

(b) $D_3 = B_L + \left(\dfrac{\frac{3N}{10} - cf_B}{f_c}\right)i = 269.50 + \left(\dfrac{60 - 34}{33}\right)30 = \$293.14$

(*Note:* \$269.50 is the lower boundary of the class containing the $\frac{3N}{10}$, or 60th, measurement.)

(c) $P_{80} = B_L + \left(\dfrac{\frac{80N}{100} - cf_B}{f_c}\right)i = 359.50 + \left(\dfrac{160 - 142}{30}\right)30 = \$377.50$

(*Note:* \$359.50 is the lower boundary of the class containing the $\frac{80N}{100}$, or 160th, measurement.)

(d) $P_{17} = B_L + \left(\dfrac{\frac{17N}{100} - cf_B}{f_c}\right)i = 239.50 + \left(\dfrac{34 - 21}{13}\right)30 = \$269.50$

(*Note 1:* \$239.50 is the lower boundary of the class containing the $\frac{17N}{100}$, or 34th, measurement.)

(*Note 2:* The 17th percentile is at the upper boundary of the class. This is logical, since we need to go through the entire class to get to the 34th item in the distribution.)

3.22. Referring to Table 3.5 (page 38), determine the values at the (*a*) third quartile, (*b*) first decile, and (*c*) 90th percentile point.

(a) $Q_3 = B_L + \left(\dfrac{\frac{3n}{4} - cf_B}{f_c}\right)i = 49.5 + \left(\dfrac{37.5 - 30}{20}\right)10 = 53.25 \cong 53.2 \text{ min}$

(*Note:* 49.5 is the lower boundary of the class containing the $\frac{3n}{4}$, or 37.5th, measurement.)

(b) $D_1 = B_L + \left(\dfrac{\frac{n}{10} - cf_B}{f_c}\right)i = 19.5 + \left(\dfrac{5 - 3}{5}\right)10 = 23.5 \text{ min}$

(*Note:* 19.5 is the lower boundary of the class containing the $\frac{n}{10}$, or fifth, measurement.)

(c) $P_{90} = B_L + \left(\dfrac{\frac{90n}{100} - cf_B}{f_c}\right)i = 49.5 + \left(\dfrac{45 - 30}{20}\right)10 = 57.0 \text{ min}$

(*Note:* 49.5 is the lower boundary of the class containing the $\frac{90n}{100}$, or 45th, measurement.)

3.23. For the "and under" frequency distribution reported in Table 3.7 (page 39), determine the values of the　(a) second quartile,　(b) ninth decile, and　(c) 75th percentile point.

(a)　$Q_2 = B_L + \left(\dfrac{\frac{2n}{4} - cf_B}{f_c}\right)i = 8.0 + \left(\dfrac{23.5 - 10}{17}\right)3.0 = 10.4$ min

(b)　$D_9 = B_L + \left(\dfrac{\frac{9n}{10} - cf_B}{f_c}\right)i = 14.0 + \left(\dfrac{42.3 - 39}{6}\right)3.0 \cong 15.6$ min

(c)　$P_{75} = B_L + \left(\dfrac{\frac{75n}{100} - cf_B}{f_c}\right)i = 11.0 + \left(\dfrac{35.25 - 27}{12}\right)3.0 = 13.1$ min

Supplementary Problems

THE MEAN, MEDIAN, AND MODE FOR UNGROUPED DATA

3.24. The number of cars sold by each of the 10 salesmen in an automobile dealership during a particular month, arranged in ascending order, is: 2, 4, 7, 10, 10, 10, 12, 12, 14, 15.　Determine the　(a) mean,　(b) median, and　(c) mode for the number of cars sold.

Ans.　(a) 9.6,　(b) 10.0,　(c) 10.0

3.25. Which value in Problem 3.24 best describes the "typical" sales volume per salesman?

Ans.　10.0

3.26. The weights of a sample of outgoing packages in a mailroom, weighed to the nearest ounce, are found to be: 21, 18, 30, 12, 14, 17, 28, 10, 16, 25 oz.　Determine the　(a) mean,　(b) median, and　(c) mode for these weights.

Ans.　(a) 19.1,　(b) 17.5,　(c) there is no mode

3.27. How can a mode be obtained for the package weights described in Problem 3.26?

Ans.　A mode can be obtained by constructing a frequency distribution for the data.　In such a case, a larger sample size would be desirable.

3.28. The following examination scores, arranged in ascending order, were achieved by 20 students enrolled in a decision analysis course: 39, 46, 57, 65, 70, 72, 72, 75, 77, 79, 81, 81, 84, 84, 84, 87, 93, 94, 97, 97.　Determine the　(a) mean,　(b) median, and　(c) mode for these scores.

Ans.　(a) 76.7,　(b) 80.0,　(c) 84.0

3.29. Describe the distribution of test scores in Problem 3.28 in terms of skewness.

Ans.　Negatively skewed.

3.30. The number of accidents which occurred during a given month in the 13 manufacturing departments of an industrial plant was: 2, 0, 0, 3, 3, 12, 1, 0, 8, 1, 0, 5, 1.　Calculate the　(a) mean,　(b) median, and　(c) mode for the number of accidents per department.

Ans.　(a) 2.8,　(b) 1.0,　(c) 0

3.31. Describe the distribution of accident rates reported in Problem 3.30 in terms of skewness.

Ans.   Positively skewed.

THE MEAN, MEDIAN, AND MODE FOR GROUPED DATA

3.32. With reference to Table 2.15 (page 25), determine the typical mileage which was obtained in terms of the   (*a*) mean,   (*b*) median, and   (*c*) mode.

Ans.   (*a*) 18.95,   (*b*) 18.85,   (*c*) 18.86

3.33. Comment on the form of the distribution of the mileage figures in Problem 3.32 in terms of skewness.

Ans.   The distribution is relatively symmetrical.

3.34. The frequency distribution in Table 3.9 is based on data supplied in Problem 2.34. Compute the   (*a*) mean,   (*b*) median, and   (*c*) mode of the loan amounts.

Table 3.9   The Amounts of 40 Personal Loans

Loan amount	Number of loans
$ 300–699	13
700–1099	11
1100–1499	6
1500–1899	5
1900–2299	3
2300–2699	1
2700–3099	1
	Total 40

Ans.   (*a*) $1109.50,   (*b*) $954.05,   (*c*) $646.17

3.35. Describe the form of the frequency distribution of personal loan amounts in Problem 3.34.

Ans.   Positively skewed.

3.36. From Table 2.17 (page 26), determine the average lifetime of the cutting tools by computing the   (*a*) mean,   (*b*) median, and   (*c*) mode.

Ans.   (*a*) 87.45,   (*b*) 89.12,   (*c*) 89.95

3.37. Describe the frequency distribution of the tool lifetime in Problem 3.36 in terms of skewness.

Ans.   There is a slight negative skewness.

3.38. Referring to the "and under" frequency distribution in Table 2.18 (page 27), compute the (*a*) mean,   (*b*) median, and   (*c*) mode for the applicants' ages.

Ans.   (*a*) 23.3,   (*b*) 22.4,   (*c*) 21.2

3.39. Comment on the form of the distribution in Table 2.18.

Ans.   The distribution is positively skewed.

THE WEIGHTED MEAN

3.40. Suppose the retail prices of the selected items have changed as indicated in Table 3.10. Determine the mean percentage change in retail prices *without* reference to the average expenditures included in the table.

Table 3.10   Changes in the Retail Prices of Selected Items During a Particular Year

Item	Percent increase	Average expenditure per month (before increase)
Milk	10%	$10.00
Ground beef	−6	15.00
Apparel	−8	15.00
Gasoline	20	25.00

Ans.   4.0%

3.41. Referring to Table 3.10, determine the mean percentage change by weighting the percent increase for each item by the average amount per month spent on that item before the increase.

Ans.   6.0%

3.42. Is the mean percentage price change calculated in Problem 3.40 or 3.41 more appropriate as a measure of the impact of the price changes on this particular consumer?   Why?

Ans.   The weighted mean in Problem 3.41 is more appropriate.

QUARTILES, DECILES, AND PERCENTILES

3.43. Determine the values at the   (*a*) first quartile,   (*b*) second decile, and   (*c*) 30th percentile point for the sales amounts in Problem 3.24.

Ans.   (*a*) 7.0,   (*b*) 5.5,   (*c*) 8.5

3.44. From Problem 3.26, determine the weights at the   (*a*) third quartile,   (*b*) third decile, and   (*c*) 70th percentile point.

Ans.   (*a*) 25.0 oz,   (*b*) 15.0 oz,   (*c*) 23.0 oz

3.45. Determine the   (*a*) second quartile,   (*b*) ninth decile, and   (*c*) 50th percentile point for the examination scores in Problem 3.28.

Ans.   (*a*) 80.0,   (*b*) 95.5,   (*c*) 80.0

3.46. In general, which quartile, decile, and percentile point, respectively, are equivalent to the median?

Ans.   Second quartile, fifth decile, and 50th percentile point.

3.47. Determine the values at the   (*a*) first quartile,   (*b*) first decile, and   (*c*) 10th percentile point for the automobile mileage data in Table 2.15 (page 25).

Ans.   (*a*) 17.25,   (*b*) 15.62,   (*c*) 15.62

3.48. For the amounts of the personal loans reported in Problem 3.34, determine the values at the (a) second quartile, (b) second decile, and (c) 90th percentile point.

Ans.   (a) $954.05, (b) $545.65, (c) $2032.83

3.49. Determine the values at the (a) third quartile, (b) seventh decile, and (c) 75th percentile for the hours lifetime of cutting tools, as reported in Table 2.17 (page 26).

Ans.   (a) 106.20, (b) 101.34, (c) 106.20

3.50. Determine the values at the (a) first quartile, (b) seventh decile, and (c) 80th percentile point for the data in Table 2.18 (page 27).

Ans.   (a) 20.8, (b) 24.7, (c) 26.4

Chapter 4

Describing Business Data:
Measures of Variability

4.1 MEASURES OF VARIABILITY IN DATA SETS

The measures of central tendency described in Chapter 3 are useful for identifying the "typical" value in a group of values. In contrast, *measures of variability* are concerned with describing a group of values in terms of the variability among the items included within the group. Several techniques are available for measuring the extent of variability in data sets. The ones which are described in this chapter are the *range, modified ranges, average deviation, standard deviation,* and *coefficient of variation.*

EXAMPLE 1. Suppose that two different packaging machines result in a mean weight of 10 oz of cereal being packaged, but that in one case all packages are within 0.10 oz of this weight while in the other case the weights may vary by as much as one ounce in either direction. Measuring the variability, or dispersion, of the amounts being packaged would be every bit as important as measuring the average in this case.

The concept of skewness has been described in Sections 2.4 and 2.9. Pearson's *coefficient of skewness* is described in Section 4.11.

4.2 THE RANGE

The *range*, or R, is the difference between the highest and lowest values for items which have not been grouped in a frequency distribution. Thus, where H represents the highest value in the group and L represents the lowest value, the range for ungrouped data is

$$R = H - L \qquad (4.1)$$

EXAMPLE 2. During a particular summer month, the eight salesmen in a heating and air-conditioning firm sold the following numbers of central air-conditioning units: 8, 11, 5, 14, 8, 11, 16, 11. The range of the number of units sold is

$$R = H - L = 16 - 5 = 11.0 \text{ units}$$

Note: For purposes of comparison, we generally report the measures of variability to one additional significant digit beyond the original level of measurement throughout this chapter. In any final reports, these values should be rounded to the number of significant digits in the original data, as explained in Section 1.5.

For data grouped in a frequency distribution, the range is generally defined as the difference between the upper boundary of the highest class, $B_U(H)$, and the lower boundary of the lowest-valued class, $B_L(L)$. Thus, the range for grouped data is

$$R = B_U(H) - B_L(L) \qquad (4.2)$$

44

EXAMPLE 3. The grouped data in Table 4.1 are taken from the frequency distribution of weekly wages for 100 unskilled workers, as presented in Sections 2.1 and 3.3. The range is

$$R = B_U(H) - B_L(L) = 259.50 - 139.50 = \$120.00$$

Table 4.1   Weekly Wages of 100 Unskilled Workers

Weekly wage	Class boundaries	Number of workers (f)	Cumulative frequency (cf)
$140–159	$139.50–159.50	7	7
160–179	159.50–179.50	20	27
180–199	179.50–199.50	33	60
200–219	199.50–219.50	25	85
220–239	219.50–239.50	11	96
240–259	239.50–259.50	4	100
		Total 100	

4.3   MODIFIED RANGES

A *modified range* is a range for which a certain percent of the extreme values at each end of the distribution has been eliminated. Typical modified ranges are the *middle 50 percent*, *middle 80 percent*, and *middle 90 percent*.

The procedure by which a modified range is determined is to first locate the appropriate two percentile points (see Sections 3.10 and 3.11), and then take the difference between the values at these points. For instance, for the middle 80 percent range the appropriate percentile points are the 10th percentile point and the 90th percentile point, because between these two points the middle 80 percent of the values are located.

EXAMPLE 4. The ungrouped data for the central air-conditioning sales presented in Example 2, in ascending order, are: 5, 8, 8, 11, 11, 11, 14, 16. To compute the middle 50 percent range, we first determine the values at the appropriate percentile points and then subtract the lower from the higher value:

$$P_{75} = X_{[(75n/100)+(1/2)]} = X_{[6+(1/2)]} = X_{6.5} = 12.5$$
$$P_{25} = X_{[(25n/100)+(1/2)]} = X_{[2+(1/2)]} = X_{2.5} = 8.0$$

$$\text{Middle } 50\% \, R = P_{75} - P_{25} = 12.5 - 8.0 = 4.5 \text{ units}$$

EXAMPLE 5. The middle 90 percent range for the frequency distribution of wages given in Table 4.1 is

$$\text{Middle } 90\% \, R = P_{95} - P_{05} = 237.68 - 153.79 = \$83.89$$

where $P_{95} = B_L + \left(\dfrac{\frac{95n}{100} - cf_B}{f_c}\right) i = 219.50 + \left(\dfrac{95 - 85}{11}\right) 20 = \$237.68$

$P_{05} = B_L + \left(\dfrac{\frac{5n}{100} - cf_B}{f_c}\right) i = 139.50 + \left(\dfrac{5 - 0}{7}\right) 20 = \$153.79$

4.4   THE AVERAGE DEVIATION

The *average deviation*, or *AD*, is based on the difference between each value in the data set and the mean of the group. It is the mean of these deviations which is computed (some statisticians use the difference between each value and the median).   If the mean of the sum of the plus and minus differences between each value and the arithmetic mean were computed, the answer would in fact always be zero.   For this reason, it is the *absolute values* of the differences which are summed.

$$\text{Population } AD = \frac{\Sigma \, | \, X - \mu \, |}{N} \qquad (4.3)$$

$$\text{Sample } AD = \frac{\Sigma \, | \, X - \bar{X} \, |}{n} \qquad (4.4)$$

EXAMPLE 6.   For the air-conditioning sales data given in Example 2, the arithmetic mean is 10.5 units (see Section 3.2).   Using the calculations in Table 4.2, the average deviation is determined as follows:

$$AD = \frac{\Sigma \, | \, X - \mu \, |}{N} = \frac{21.0}{8} = 2.625 \cong 2.6 \text{ units}$$

Table 4.2   **Worksheet for Calculating the Average Deviation for Ungrouped Data**

X	$(X - \mu)$	$\mid X - \mu \mid$
5	−5.5	5.5
8	−2.5	2.5
8	−2.5	2.5
11	0.5	0.5
11	0.5	0.5
11	0.5	0.5
14	3.5	3.5
16	5.5	5.5
		Total 21.0

Thus, we can say that on the average, a salesman's unit sales of air-conditioners differs by 2.6 units from the group mean, in either direction.

4.5   THE AVERAGE DEVIATION FOR GROUPED DATA

For data grouped in a frequency distribution, the midpoint of each class is taken to represent all of the measurements included in that class.   This is the same approach which is used in determining the arithmetic mean for grouped data, as described in Section 3.3. Accordingly

$$\text{Population } AD = \frac{\Sigma(f \, | \, X - \mu \, |)}{N} \qquad (4.5)$$

$$\text{Sample } AD = \frac{\Sigma(f \, | \, X - \bar{X} \, |)}{n} \qquad (4.6)$$

EXAMPLE 7.   For the weekly wage data given in Table 4.1, the arithmetic mean is \$194.50 (see Section 3.3).   The average deviation is determined as follows, from the calculations in Table 4.3.

$$AD = \frac{\Sigma(f \, | \, X - \bar{X} \, |)}{n} = \frac{1960.00}{100} = \$19.60$$

Table 4.3 Worksheet for Calculating the Average Deviation for Grouped Data

Weekly wage	Class midpoint (X)	Number of workers (f)	$\mid X - \bar{X} \mid$	$(f \mid X - \bar{X} \mid)$
$140–159	$149.50	7	$45.00	$ 315.00
160–179	169.50	20	25.00	500.00
180–199	189.50	33	5.00	165.00
200–219	209.50	25	15.00	375.00
220–239	229.50	11	35.00	385.00
240–259	249.50	4	55.00	220.00
		Total 100		Total $1960.00

4.6 THE VARIANCE AND STANDARD DEVIATION

The *variance* is similar to the average deviation in that it is based on the difference between each value in the data set and the mean of the group. It differs in that these differences are squared before being summed. For a population, the variance is represented by the lower-case Greek σ^2 (read "sigma squared"); the formula is

$$\sigma^2 = \frac{\Sigma(X - \mu)^2}{N} \qquad (4.7)$$

Unlike the situation for other sample statistics we have discussed, the variance for a sample is not computationally exactly equivalent to the variance for a population. Rather, the denominator in the sample variance formula is slightly different. Essentially, a correction factor is included in this formula, so that the sample variance is an unbiased estimator of the population variance (see Section 8.1). The sample variance is represented by s^2; its formula is

$$s^2 = \frac{\Sigma(X - \bar{X})^2}{n - 1} \qquad (4.8)$$

Note: In some textbooks, the denominator in the above formula is "n" rather than "$n - 1$". This difference has implications for other formulas discussed in later chapters. Technically, because the correction factor for use as an estimator is included in the formula, it would be appropriate that it be designated by the parameter symbol with a "cap", that is, $\hat{\sigma}^2$. However, the majority of books in statistics define s^2 to be a corrected estimator, and not simply as the variance of a sample group.

In general, it is difficult to interpret the meaning of the value of a variance because the units in which it is expressed are not the same as the observations in the data set. For this reason, the square root of the variance, represented by Greek σ (or s for a sample) and called the *standard deviation* is more frequently used. The formulas are

Population standard deviation: $\qquad \sigma = \sqrt{\dfrac{\Sigma(X - \mu)^2}{N}} \qquad (4.9)$

Sample standard deviation: $\qquad s = \sqrt{\dfrac{\Sigma(X - \bar{X})^2}{n - 1}} \qquad (4.10)$

The standard deviation is particularly useful in conjunction with the so-called normal probability distribution (see Section 4.9).

EXAMPLE 8.   For the air-conditioning sales data given in Example 2 the arithmetic mean is 10.5 units (see Section 3.2).   Considering these monthly sales data to be the statistical population of interest, the standard deviation is determined from the calculations in Table 4.4 as follows:

$$\sigma = \sqrt{\frac{\Sigma(X - \mu)^2}{N}} = \sqrt{\frac{86}{8}} = \sqrt{10.75} = 3.3$$

Table 4.4   Worksheet for Calculating the Population Standard Deviation for Ungrouped Data

X	$X - \mu$	$(X - \mu)^2$
5	−5.5	30.25
8	−2.5	6.25
8	−2.5	6.25
11	0.5	0.25
11	0.5	0.25
11	0.5	0.25
14	3.5	12.25
16	5.5	30.25
		Total 86.00

4.7   THE VARIANCE AND STANDARD DEVIATION FOR GROUPED DATA

For data grouped in a frequency distribution, the midpoint of each class is taken to represent all of the measurements included in that class.   This is the same approach as used for computing the average deviation in Section 4.5.   Accordingly, the formulas for grouped population and sample data are

Population variance: $\qquad \sigma^2 = \dfrac{\Sigma f(X - \mu)^2}{N}$ $\qquad\qquad\qquad\qquad$ (4.11)

Sample variance: $\qquad s^2 = \dfrac{\Sigma f(X - \bar{X})^2}{n - 1}$ $\qquad\qquad\qquad\qquad$ (4.12)

The formulas for the standard deviation for grouped population and sample data are

Population standard deviation: $\sigma = \sqrt{\dfrac{\Sigma f(X - \mu)^2}{N}}$ $\qquad\qquad$ (4.13)

Sample standard deviation: $s = \sqrt{\dfrac{\Sigma f(X - \bar{X})^2}{n - 1}}$ $\qquad\qquad$ (4.14)

EXAMPLE 9.   For the weekly wage data presented in Example 3, the sample mean is $194.50, as determined in Section 3.3.   From Table 4.5, the sample standard deviation for these grouped values is determined as follows:

$$s = \sqrt{\frac{\Sigma f(X - \bar{X})^2}{n - 1}} = \sqrt{\frac{58{,}700}{99}} = \sqrt{592.9292} = \$24.35$$

Table 4.5   Worksheet for Calculating the Sample Standard Deviation for Grouped Data

Weekly wage	Class midpoint (X)	Number of workers (f)	$X - \bar{X}$	$(X - \bar{X})^2$	$f(X - \bar{X})^2$
$140–159	$149.50	7	$-45.00	$2,025	$14,175
160–179	169.50	20	-25.00	625	12,500
180–199	189.50	33	-5.00	25	825
200–219	209.50	25	15.00	225	5,625
220–239	229.50	11	35.00	1,225	13,475
240–259	249.50	4	55.00	3,025	12,100
		Total 100			Total $58,700

4.8   SHORTCUT CALCULATIONS OF THE VARIANCE AND STANDARD DEVIATION

The formulas in Sections 4.6 and 4.7 are frequently called *deviations formulas*, because in each case the specific deviations of individual values from the group mean must be determined. Alternative formulas which are mathematically equivalent but which do not require the determination of each deviation have been developed. Because these formulas are generally easier to use for computations, they are frequently called *computational formulas*.

For ungrouped data, the computational formulas are

Population variance: $$\sigma^2 = \frac{\Sigma X^2 - N\mu^2}{N} \qquad (4.15)$$

Population standard deviation: $$\sigma = \sqrt{\frac{\Sigma X^2 - N\mu^2}{N}} \qquad (4.16)$$

Sample variance: $$s^2 = \frac{\Sigma X^2 - n\bar{X}^2}{n - 1} \qquad (4.17)$$

Sample standard deviation: $$s = \sqrt{\frac{\Sigma X^2 - n\bar{X}^2}{n - 1}} \qquad (4.18)$$

EXAMPLE 10. For the air-conditioning sales data presented in Example 2, we calculate the population standard deviation below by the use of the alternative computational formula and Table 4.6 to demonstrate that the answer is the same as the answer obtained with the deviation formula in Example 8. The mean for these data is 10.5 units.

$$\sigma = \sqrt{\frac{\Sigma X^2 - N\mu^2}{N}} = \sqrt{\frac{968 - 8(10.5)^2}{8}} = \sqrt{10.75} = 3.3 \text{ units}$$

Table 4.6 Worksheet for Calculating
the Population Standard
Deviation for Ungrouped
Data

X	X^2
5	25
8	64
8	64
11	121
11	121
11	121
14	196
16	256
	Total 968

For grouped data, the computational formulas are

Population variance:
$$\sigma^2 = \frac{\Sigma f X^2 - N\mu^2}{N} \qquad (4.19)$$

Population standard deviation:
$$\sigma = \sqrt{\frac{\Sigma f X^2 - N\mu^2}{N}} \qquad (4.20)$$

Sample variance:
$$s^2 = \frac{\Sigma f X^2 - n\bar{X}^2}{n-1} \qquad (4.21)$$

Sample standard deviation:
$$s = \sqrt{\frac{\Sigma f X^2 - n\bar{X}^2}{n-1}} \qquad (4.22)$$

EXAMPLE 11. For the weekly wage data presented in Example 3, we calculate the sample standard deviation below by the use of the alternative computational formula and Table 4.7 to demonstrate that the answer is the same as the answer obtained with the deviation formula in Example 9. The sample mean for these data is $194.50.

$$s = \sqrt{\frac{\Sigma f X^2 - n\bar{X}^2}{n-1}} = \sqrt{\frac{3,841,725 - 100(194.50)^2}{100-1}} = \sqrt{592.9292} = \$24.35$$

Table 4.7 Worksheet for Calculating the Sample Standard Deviation for Grouped Data

Weekly wage	Class midpoint (X)	Number of workers (f)	X^2	fX^2
$140–159	$149.50	7	$22,350.25	$ 156,451.75
160–179	169.50	20	28,730.25	574,605.00
180–199	189.50	33	35,910.25	1,185,038.25
200–219	209.50	25	43,890.25	1,097,256.25
220–239	229.50	11	52,670.25	579,372.75
240–259	249.50	4	62,250.25	249,001.00
		Total 100		Total $3,841,725.00

4.9 USE OF THE STANDARD DEVIATION

The standard deviation is the most important measure of dispersion, in that it is used in conjunction with a number of methods of statistical inference discussed in later chapters of this book. A description of these uses is beyond the scope of the present chapter. However, as one example of the use of the standard deviation, consider a frequency distribution that is both symmetrical and mesokurtic. In statistical analysis, such a frequency curve is called a *normal curve*. For a distribution which is *normally distributed*, it is known that approximately 68 percent of the measurements are located within one standard deviation of the mean and approximately 95 percent of the measurements are located within two standard deviation units of the mean. These observations are presented diagramatically in Figs. 4-1(*a*) and (*b*), respectively.

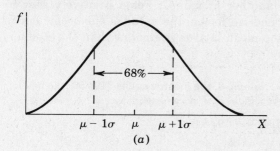
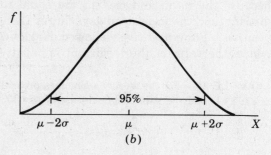

(*a*)   (*b*)

Fig. 4-1.

EXAMPLE 12. The electrical billings in a municipal area for the month of June are observed to be normally distributed. If the mean of the billings is calculated to be $42.00 with a standard deviation of $12.00, then it follows that approximately 68 percent of the billed amounts are within $12.00 of the mean, or between $30.00 and $54.00. It also follows that approximately 95 percent of the billed amounts are within $24.00 of the mean, or between $18.00 and $66.00.

4.10 THE COEFFICIENT OF VARIATION

The *coefficient of variation*, V, indicates the relative magnitude of the standard deviation as compared with the mean of the distribution of measurements. Thus, the formulas are

Population:
$$V = \frac{\sigma}{\mu} \qquad\qquad (4.23)$$

Sample:
$$V = \frac{s}{\bar{X}} \qquad\qquad (4.24)$$

The coefficient of variation is useful when we wish to compare the variability of two data sets relative to the general level of values (and thus relative to the mean) in each set.

EXAMPLE 13. For two common stock issues in the electronics industry, the daily mean closing market price during a one-month period for stock A was $150 with a standard deviation of $5. For stock B, the mean price was $50 with a standard deviation of $3. On an absolute comparison basis, the variability in the price of stock A was greater, because of the larger standard deviation. But relative to the price level, the respective coefficients of variation should be compared:

$$V(A) = \frac{\sigma}{\mu} = \frac{5}{150} = 0.033 \quad \text{and} \quad V(B) = \frac{\sigma}{\mu} = \frac{3}{50} = 0.060$$

Therefore, relative to the average price level for each stock issue, we can conclude that stock B has been almost twice as variable in price as stock A.

4.11 PEARSON'S COEFFICIENT OF SKEWNESS

Pearson's *coefficient of skewness* measures the departure from symmetry by expressing the difference between the mean and the median relative to the standard deviation of the group of measurements. The formulas are

$$\text{Population skewness} = \frac{3(\mu - \text{Med})}{\sigma} \qquad (4.25)$$

$$\text{Sample skewness} = \frac{3(\bar{X} - \text{Med})}{s} \qquad (4.26)$$

For a symmetrical distribution the value of the coefficient of skewness will always be zero, because the mean and median are equal to one another in value. For a positively skewed distribution, the mean is always larger than the median; hence, the value of the coefficient is positive. For a negatively skewed distribution, the mean is always smaller than the median; hence, the value of the coefficient is negative.

EXAMPLE 14. For the weekly wage data presented in Example 3, the mean wage is $194.50, the median is $193.44, and the standard deviation is $24.35. The coefficient of skewness is

$$\text{Skewness} = \frac{3(\bar{X} - \text{Med})}{s} = \frac{3(194.50 - 193.44)}{24.35} = +0.13$$

Solved Problems

THE RANGES, AVERAGE DEVIATION, AND STANDARD DEVIATION FOR UNGROUPED DATA

4.1. For a sample of 15 customers at a small convenience market, the following sales amounts arranged in ascending order of magnitude are observed: $0.10, 0.10, 0.25, 0.25, 0.25, 0.35, 0.40, 0.53, 0.90, 1.25, 1.35, 2.45, 2.71, 3.09, 4.10. Determine the (a) range and (b) middle 50 percent range for these sample data.

(a) $R = H - L = \$4.10 - 0.10 = \$4.00$

(b) Middle 50% $R = P_{75} - P_{25} = 2.175 - 0.25 = 1.925 \cong \$1.92$

where $P_{75} = X_{[(75n/100)+(1/2)]} = X_{(11.25+0.50)} = X_{11.75} = 1.35 + 0.825 = \$2.175$

(*Note:* This is the interpolated value *three-fourths* of the distance between the 11th and 12th ordered sales amounts.)

$P_{25} = X_{[(25n/100)+(1/2)]} = X_{(3.75+0.50)} = X_{4.25} = \$0.25$

4.2. Compute the average deviation for the data in Problem 4.1. The sample mean for this group of values was determined to be $1.21 in Problem 3.1.

The average deviation is calculated as follows, using Table 4.8.

$$AD = \frac{\sum |X - \bar{X}|}{n} = \frac{\$15.45}{15} = \$1.03$$

Table 4.8   Worksheet for Calculating the Average Deviation for Ungrouped Data

X	$X - \bar{X}$	$\lvert X - \bar{X} \rvert$
$0.10	-1.11	$ 1.11
0.10	-1.11	1.11
0.25	-0.96	0.96
0.25	-0.96	0.96
0.25	-0.96	0.96
0.35	-0.86	0.86
0.40	-0.81	0.81
0.53	-0.68	0.68
0.90	-0.31	0.31
1.25	0.04	0.04
1.35	0.14	0.14
2.45	1.24	1.24
2.71	1.50	1.50
3.09	1.88	1.88
4.10	2.89	2.89
		Total $15.45

Table 4.9   Worksheet for Calculating the Sample Standard Deviation for Ungrouped Data

X	$X - \bar{X}$	$(X - \bar{X})^2$	X^2
$0.10	-1.11	1.2321	0.0100
0.10	-1.11	1.2321	0.0100
0.25	-0.96	0.9216	0.0625
0.25	-0.96	0.9216	0.0625
0.25	-0.96	0.9216	0.0625
0.35	-0.86	0.7396	0.1225
0.40	-0.81	0.6561	0.1600
0.53	-0.68	0.4624	0.2809
0.90	-0.31	0.0961	0.8100
1.25	0.04	0.0016	1.5625
1.35	0.14	0.0196	1.8225
2.45	1.24	1.5376	6.0025
2.71	1.50	2.2500	7.3441
3.09	1.88	3.5344	9.5481
4.10	2.89	8.3521	16.8100
		Total 22.8785	Total 44.6706

4.3. Determine the sample standard deviation for the data in Problems 4.1 and 4.2 by using (*a*) the deviations formula and (*b*) the alternative computational formula, and demonstrate that the answers are equivalent.

From Table 4.9,

$$(a) \quad s = \sqrt{\frac{\Sigma(X - \bar{X})^2}{n - 1}} = \sqrt{\frac{22.8785}{15 - 1}} = \sqrt{1.6342} \cong \$1.28$$

$$(b) \quad s = \sqrt{\frac{\Sigma X^2 - n\bar{X}^2}{n - 1}} = \sqrt{\frac{44.6706 - 15(1.21)^2}{15 - 1}} = \sqrt{1.6221} \cong \$1.27$$

The answers are slightly different only because of rounding error, associated with the fact that the sample mean was rounded to two places in respect to the decimal point.

4.4. A sample of 20 production workers in a small company earned the following wages for a given week, rounded to the nearest dollar and arranged in ascending order: $140, 140, 140, 140, 140, 140, 140, 140, 155, 155, 165, 165, 180, 180, 190, 200, 205, 225, 230, 240.   Determine the (*a*) range and (*b*) middle 80 percent range for this sample.

(*a*) $R = H - L = 240 - 140 = \$100$

(*b*) Middle 80% $R = P_{90} - P_{10} = 227.50 - 140.00 = \$87.50$

where $P_{90} = X_{[(90n/100)+(1/2)]} = X_{[18+(1/2)]} = X_{18.5} = \$225 + 2.50 = \$227.50$
$P_{10} = X_{[(10n/100)+(1/2)]} = X_{[2+(1/2)]} = X_{2.5} = \$140.00$

4.5. Compute the average deviation for the wages in Problem 4.4. The sample mean for these wages was determined to be $170.50 in Problem 3.4.

From Table 4.10, the average deviation is

$$AD = \frac{\Sigma \, |X - \bar{X}|}{n} = \frac{\$572.00}{20} = \$28.60$$

Table 4.10 Worksheet for Calculating the Average Deviation for Ungrouped Data

X	$X - \bar{X}$	$|X - \bar{X}|$
$140	$-30.50	$ 30.50
140	−30.50	30.50
140	−30.50	30.50
140	−30.50	30.50
140	−30.50	30.50
140	−30.50	30.50
140	−30.50	30.50
140	−30.50	30.50
155	−15.50	15.50
155	−15.50	15.50
165	− 5.50	5.50
165	− 5.50	5.50
180	9.50	9.50
180	9.50	9.50
190	19.50	19.50
200	29.50	29.50
205	34.50	34.50
225	54.50	54.50
230	59.50	59.50
240	69.50	69.50
		Total $572.00

Table 4.11 Worksheet for Calculating the Sample Variance and Standard Deviation for Ungrouped Data

X	$X - \bar{X}$	$(X - \bar{X})^2$
$140	$-30.50	$ 930.25
140	−30.50	930.25
140	−30.50	930.25
140	−30.50	930.25
140	−30.50	930.25
140	−30.50	930.25
140	−30.50	930.25
140	−30.50	930.25
155	−15.50	240.25
155	−15.50	240.25
165	− 5.50	30.25
165	− 5.50	30.25
180	9.50	90.25
180	9.50	90.25
190	19.50	380.25
200	29.50	870.25
205	34.50	1,190.25
225	54.50	2,970.25
230	59.50	3,540.25
240	69.50	4,830.25
		Total $21,945.00

4.6. Determine the (a) sample variance and (b) sample standard deviation for the data in Problems 4.4 and 4.5, using the deviations formulas.

With reference to Table 4.11,

(a) $s^2 = \dfrac{\Sigma(X - \bar{X})^2}{n - 1} = \dfrac{21,945.00}{20 - 1} = \$1155.00$

(b) $s = \sqrt{\dfrac{\Sigma(X - \bar{X})^2}{n - 1}} = \sqrt{1155.00} \cong 33.99$

4.7. A work-standards expert observes the amount of time required to type a sample of 10 business letters in an office with the following results listed in ascending order to the nearest minute: 5, 5, 5, 7, 9, 14, 15, 15, 16, 18. Determine the (a) range and (b) middle 70 percent range for the sample.

(a) $R = H - L = 18 - 5 = 13$ min

(b) Middle 70% $R = P_{85} - P_{15} = 16.0 - 5.0 = 11.0$ min

where $P_{85} = X_{[(85n/100)+(1/2)]} = X_{(8.5+0.5)} = X_9 = 16.0$ min

$P_{15} = X_{[(15n/100)+(1/2)]} = X_{(1.5+0.5)} = X_2 = 5.0$ min

4.8. Compute the average deviation for the typing time in Problem 4.7. The sample mean was determined to be 10.9 min in Problem 3.7.

From Table 4.12,

$$AD = \frac{\Sigma\,|\,X - \bar{X}\,|}{n} = \frac{47.0}{10} = 4.7 \text{ min}$$

Table 4.12 Worksheet for Calculating the Average Deviation for Ungrouped Data

X	$X - \bar{X}$	$|\,X - \bar{X}\,|$
5	−5.9	5.9
5	−5.9	5.9
5	−5.9	5.9
7	−3.9	3.9
9	−1.9	1.9
14	3.1	3.1
15	4.1	4.1
15	4.1	4.1
16	5.1	5.1
18	7.1	7.1
		Total 47.0

Table 4.13 Worksheet for Calculating the Sample Variance and Standard Deviation for Ungrouped Data

X	X^2
5	25
5	25
5	25
7	49
9	81
14	196
15	225
15	225
16	256
18	324
	Total 1431

4.9. Determine the (a) sample variance and (b) sample standard deviation for the data in Problems 4.7 and 4.8, using the alternative computational formulas.

With reference to Table 4.13,

(a) $s^2 = \dfrac{\Sigma X^2 - n\bar{X}^2}{n - 1} = \dfrac{1431 - 10(10.9)^2}{10 - 1} = 26.99 \cong 27 \text{ min}$

(b) $s = \sqrt{\dfrac{\Sigma X^2 - n\bar{X}^2}{n - 1}} = \sqrt{26.99} \cong 5.2 \text{ min}$

THE RANGES, AVERAGE DEVIATION, AND STANDARD DEVIATION FOR GROUPED DATA

4.10. Determine the (a) range and (b) middle 50 percent range for the rental rates in Table 2.5 (page 16). Assume that these are all of the apartments in a given geographic area.

(a) $R = B_U(H) - B_L(L) = 449.50 - 149.50 = \$300.00$

(b) Middle 50% $R = P_{75} - P_{25} = 367.50 - 284.05 = \$83.45$

where $P_{75} = B_L + \left(\dfrac{\frac{75N}{100} - cf_B}{f_c}\right) i = 359.50 + \left(\dfrac{150 - 142}{30}\right) 30 = \$367.50$

$P_{25} = B_L + \left(\dfrac{\frac{25N}{100} - cf_B}{f_c}\right) i = 269.50 + \left(\dfrac{50 - 34}{33}\right) 30 = \$284.05$

4.11. Compute the average deviation for the rental rate data in Table 2.5. The population mean was determined to be $322.75 in Problem 3.9.

Using Table 4.14,

$$AD = \frac{\Sigma(f \mid X - \mu \mid)}{N} = \frac{\$9925.50}{200} = \$49.63$$

Table 4.14   Worksheet for Calculating the Average Deviation for Grouped Data

Rental rate	Class midpoint (X)	Number of apartments (f)	$\mid X - \mu \mid$	$f \mid X - \mu \mid$
$150–179	$164.50	3	$158.25	$ 474.75
180–209	194.50	8	128.25	1026.00
210–239	224.50	10	98.25	982.50
240–269	254.50	13	68.25	887.25
270–299	284.50	33	38.25	1262.25
300–329	314.50	40	8.25	330.00
330–359	344.50	35	21.75	761.25
360–389	374.50	30	51.75	1552.50
390–419	404.50	16	81.75	1308.00
420–449	434.50	12	111.75	1341.00
		Total 200		Total $9925.50

4.12. From Problem 4.11, determine the population standard deviation by using (a) the deviations formula and (b) the alternative computational formula, and demonstrate that the answers are equivalent.

(a) From Table 4.15,

$$\sigma = \sqrt{\frac{\Sigma f(X - \mu)^2}{N}} = \sqrt{\frac{768,487.50}{200}} = \sqrt{3842.4375} \cong \$61.99$$

Table 4.15   Worksheet for Calculating the Standard Deviation by the Deviation Formula

Rental rate	Class midpoint (X)	Number of apartments (f)	$X - \mu$	$(X - \mu)^2$	$f(X - \mu)^2$
$150–179	$164.50	3	$158.25	$25,043.0625	$ 75,129.1875
180–209	194.50	8	128.25	16,448.0625	131,584.5000
210–239	224.50	10	98.25	9,653.0625	96,530.6250
240–269	254.50	13	68.25	4,658.0625	60,554.8125
270–299	284.50	33	38.25	1,463.0625	48,281.0625
300–329	314.50	40	8.25	68.0625	2,722.5000
330–359	344.50	35	21.75	473.0625	16,557.1875
360–389	374.50	30	51.75	2,678.0625	80,341.8750
390–419	404.50	16	81.75	6,683.0625	106,929.0000
420–449	434.50	12	111.75	12,488.0625	149,856.7500
		Total 200			Total $768,487.5000

(b) From Table 4.16,

$$\sigma = \sqrt{\frac{\Sigma fX^2 - N\mu^2}{N}} = \sqrt{\frac{21,602,000.00 - 200(322.75)^2}{200}} = \sqrt{3842.4375} \cong \$61.99$$

Table 4.16   Worksheet for Calculating the Standard Deviation by the Alternative Computational Formula

Rental rate	Class midpoint (X)	Number of apartments (f)	X^2	fX^2
$150–179	$164.50	3	$ 27,060.25	$ 81,180.75
180–209	194.50	8	37,830.25	302,642.00
210–239	224.50	10	50,400.25	504,002.50
240–269	254.50	13	64,770.25	842,013.25
270–299	284.50	33	80,940.25	2,671,028.25
300–329	314.50	40	98,910.25	3,956,410.00
330–359	344.50	35	118,680.25	4,153,808.75
360–389	374.50	30	140,250.25	4,207,507.50
390–419	404.50	16	163,620.25	2,617,924.00
420–449	434.50	12	188,790.25	2,265,483.00
		Total 200		Total $21,602,000.00

4.13. In conjunction with an annual audit, a public accounting firm collects the data reported in Table 4.17. Determine the (a) range and (b) middle 80 percent range for this sample of records.

Table 4.17   Time Required to Audit Account Balances

Audit time (in minutes)	Class boundaries	Number of records (f)	Cumulative frequency (cf)
10–19	9.5–19.5	3	3
20–29	19.5–29.5	5	8
30–39	29.5–39.5	10	18
40–49	39.5–49.5	12	30
50–59	49.5–59.5	20	50
		Total 50	

(a) $R = B_U(H) - B_L(L) = 59.5 - 9.5 = 50.0$ min

(b) Middle 80% $R = P_{90} - P_{10} = 57.0 - 23.5 = 33.5$ min

where $P_{90} = B_L + \left(\dfrac{\frac{90n}{100} - cf_B}{f_c}\right) i = 49.5 + \left(\dfrac{45 - 30}{20}\right) 10 = 57.0$ min

$P_{10} = B_L + \left(\dfrac{\frac{10n}{100} - cf_B}{f_c}\right) i = 19.5 + \left(\dfrac{5 - 3}{5}\right) 10 = 23.5$ min

4.14. Compute the average deviation for the audit time data in Table 4.17. The sample mean was determined to be 42.7 min in Problem 3.11.

With reference to Table 4.18,

$$AD = \frac{\Sigma(f\,|X - \bar{X}|)}{n} = \frac{515.2}{50} \cong 10.3$$

Table 4.18 Worksheet for Calculating the Average Deviation

Audit time (in minutes)	Class midpoint (X)	Number of records (f)	$|X - \bar{X}|$	$(f\,|X - \bar{X}|)$
10–19	14.5	3	28.2	84.6
20–29	24.5	5	18.2	91.0
30–39	34.5	10	8.2	82.0
40–49	44.5	12	1.8	21.6
50–59	54.5	20	11.8	236.0
		Total 50		Total 515.2

4.15. Determine the (a) sample variance and (b) sample standard deviation for the data in Table 4.17 by using the deviations formulas.

From Table 4.19,

(a) $s^2 = \dfrac{\Sigma f(X - \bar{X})^2}{n - 1} = \dfrac{7538}{49} = 153.84$

(b) $s = \sqrt{\dfrac{\Sigma f(X - \bar{X})^2}{n - 1}} = \sqrt{153.84} \cong 12.4$

Table 4.19 Worksheet for Computing the Variance and Standard Deviation

Audit time (in minutes)	Class midpoint (X)	Number of records (f)	$X - \bar{X}$	$(X - \bar{X})^2$	$f(X - \bar{X})^2$
10–19	14.5	3	−28.2	795.24	2385.72
20–29	24.5	5	−18.2	331.24	1656.20
30–39	34.5	10	− 8.2	67.24	672.40
40–49	44.5	12	1.8	3.24	38.88
50–59	54.5	20	11.8	139.24	2784.80
		Total 50			Total 7538.00

4.16. Reproduced in Table 4.20 are the average number of injuries per thousand man-hours, as reported in Problem 2.16. Determine the (a) range and (b) middle 90 percent range for this sample of 50 firms.

Table 4.20 Average Number of Injuries per Thousand Man-Hours in a Particular Industry

Average number of injuries	Class boundaries	Number of firms (f)	Cumulative frequency (cf)
1.5–1.7	1.45–1.75	3	3
1.8–2.0	1.75–2.05	12	15
2.1–2.3	2.05–2.35	14	29
2.4–2.6	2.35–2.65	9	38
2.7–2.9	2.65–2.95	7	45
3.0–3.2	2.95–3.25	5	50
		Total 50	

(a) $R = B_U(H) - B_L(L) = 3.25 - 1.45 = 1.80$ injuries

(b) Middle 90% $R = P_{95} - P_{05} = 3.10 - 1.70 = 1.40$ injuries

where $P_{95} = B_L + \left(\dfrac{\frac{95n}{100} - cf_B}{f_c}\right) i = 2.95 + \left(\dfrac{47.5 - 45}{5}\right) 0.30 = 3.10$ injuries

$P_{05} = B_L + \left(\dfrac{\frac{5n}{100} - cf_B}{f_c}\right) 0.30 = 1.45 + \left(\dfrac{2.5 - 0}{3}\right) 0.30 = 1.70$ injuries

4.17. Compute the average deviation for the number of injuries in Table 4.20. The sample mean was determined to be 2.32 injuries per thousand man-hours in Problem 3.13.

With reference to Table 4.21,

$$AD = \frac{\Sigma(f \mid X - \bar{X} \mid)}{n} = \frac{17.76}{50} \cong 0.36 \text{ injury}$$

Table 4.21 Worksheet for Calculating the Average Deviation

Average number of injuries	Class midpoint (X)	Number of firms (f)	$\mid X - \bar{X} \mid$	$(f \mid X - \bar{X} \mid)$
1.5–1.7	1.6	3	0.72	2.16
1.8–2.0	1.9	12	0.42	5.04
2.1–2.3	2.2	14	0.12	1.68
2.4–2.6	2.5	9	0.18	1.62
2.7–2.9	2.8	7	0.48	3.36
3.0–3.2	3.1	5	0.78	3.90
		Total 50		Total 17.76

4.18. Determine the (a) sample variance and (b) sample standard deviation for the injuries data in Table 4.20, using the alternative computational formulas.

From Table 4.22,

(a) $s^2 = \dfrac{\Sigma fX^2 - n\bar{X}^2}{n - 1} = \dfrac{277.94 - 50(2.32)^2}{50 - 1} = \dfrac{8.82}{49} = 0.18$

(b) $s = \sqrt{\dfrac{\Sigma fX^2 - n\bar{X}^2}{n - 1}} = \sqrt{0.1800} \cong 0.42$

Table 4.22   Worksheet for Calculating the Variance and Standard Deviation

Average number of injuries	Class midpoint (X)	Number of firms (f)	X^2	fX^2
1.5–1.7	1.6	3	2.56	7.68
1.8–2.0	1.9	12	3.61	43.32
2.1–2.3	2.2	14	4.84	67.76
2.4–2.6	2.5	9	6.25	56.25
2.7–2.9	2.8	7	7.84	54.88
3.0–3.2	3.1	5	9.61	48.05
		Total 50		Total 277.94

4.19. The frequency distribution in Table 4.23 is reproduced from Problem 2.21. Determine the (a) range and (b) standard deviation, by the use of the alternative computational formula. Note the basis for determining class boundaries and class midpoints for such an "and under" frequency distribution. The sample mean was determined to be 10.8 min in Problem 3.15.

Table 4.23   Time Required to Process and Prepare Mail Orders

Time (in minutes)	Class boundaries	Class midpoint (X)	Number of orders (f)	X^2	fX^2
5 and under 8	5.0–8.0	6.5	10	42.25	422.50
8 and under 11	8.0–11.0	9.5	17	90.25	1534.25
11 and under 14	11.0–14.0	12.5	12	156.25	1875.00
14 and under 17	14.0–17.0	15.5	6	240.25	1441.50
17 and under 20	17.0–20.0	18.5	2	342.25	684.50
			Total 47		Total 5957.75

(a) $R = B_U(H) - B_L(L) = 20.0 - 5.0 = 15.0$ min

(b) $s = \sqrt{\dfrac{\Sigma fX^2 - n\bar{X}^2}{n-1}} = \sqrt{\dfrac{5957.75 - 47(10.8)^2}{47-1}} = \sqrt{10.34} \cong 3.2$ min

THE COEFFICIENT OF VARIATION

4.20. Determine the coefficient of variation for the apartment rental rate data analyzed in Problems 4.10 to 4.12.

Since $\mu = \$322.75$ and $\sigma = \$61.99$,

$$V = \frac{\sigma}{\mu} = \frac{61.99}{322.75} = 0.19$$

4.21. The mean number of injuries per thousand man-hours for the 50 sample firms analyzed in Problems 4.16 to 4.18 was 2.32 with a standard deviation of 0.42. A sample of 50 firms in a second industry has a mean of 3.50 injuries with a standard deviation of 0.70. Compare the variability of the firms in the two industries (a) on an absolute basis and (b) on the basis of the variability being relative to the mean injury rate in each industry.

(a) On an absolute basis, the firms in the first industry are less variable in injury rate than the firms in the second industry, because the standard deviation $s_1 = 0.42$ is less than the standard deviation $s_2 = 0.70$.

(b) In order to compare the variability relative to the respective means, the coefficients of variation are computed and compared:

$$V_1 = \frac{s_1}{\bar{X}_1} = \frac{0.42}{2.32} = 0.18$$

$$V_2 = \frac{s_2}{\bar{X}_2} = \frac{0.70}{3.50} = 0.20$$

Therefore, on a relative basis the variability of the injury rates among firms in the first industry is still somewhat less than the variability in the second industry.

PEARSON'S COEFFICIENT OF SKEWNESS

4.22. Compute the coefficient of skewness for the apartment rental rates, for which the mean and median were determined in Problem 3.9, and for which the standard deviation was determined in Problem 4.12.

Since $\mu = \$322.75$, Med $= \$324.25$, and $\sigma = \$61.99$,

$$\text{Skewness} = \frac{3(\mu - \text{Med})}{\sigma} = \frac{3(322.75 - 324.25)}{61.99} = -0.07$$

Therefore, the distribution is slightly negatively skewed, or skewed to the left.

4.23. Compute the coefficient of skewness for the audit time data, for which the mean and median were determined in Problem 3.11, and for which the standard deviation was determined in Problem 4.15. Compare this value with the coefficient computed in Problem 4.22.

Since $\bar{X} = 42.7$ min, Med $= 45.3$ min, and $s = 12.4$,

$$\text{Skewness} = \frac{3(\bar{X} - \text{Med})}{s} = \frac{3(42.7 - 45.3)}{12.4} = -0.63$$

As for the rental rate data in Problem 4.22, this coefficient also indicates a negatively skewed distribution. However, with a coefficient of -0.63 as compared with -0.07, there is clearly a greater degree of negative skewness for the audit-time data.

Supplementary Problems

THE RANGES, AVERAGE DEVIATION, AND STANDARD DEVIATION FOR UNGROUPED DATA

4.24. The number of cars sold by each of the 10 salesmen in an automobile dealership during a particular month, arranged in ascending order, is: 2, 4, 7, 10, 10, 10, 12, 12, 14, 15. Determine the (a) range and (b) middle 80 percent range for these data.

Ans. (a) 13,   (b) 11.5

4.25. Compute the average deviation for the sales data in Problem 4.24.   The mean for these values was determined to be 9.6 in Problem 3.24.

   Ans. $3.16 \cong 3.2$

4.26. From Problem 4.24, determine the standard deviation by using the deviations formula and considering the group of values as constituting a statistical population.

   Ans. $3.955 \cong 4.0$

4.27. The weights of a sample of outgoing packages in a mailroom, weighed to the nearest ounce, are found to be: 21, 18, 30, 12, 14, 17, 28, 10, 16, 25 oz.   Determine the   (*a*) range and   (*b*) middle 50 percent range for these weights.

   Ans.   (*a*) 20.0,   (*b*) 11.0

4.28. Compute the average deviation for the sampled packages in Problem 4.27.   The sample mean was determined to be 19.1 oz in Problem 3.26.

   Ans. $5.52 \cong 5.5$

4.29. Determine the   (*a*) sample variance and   (*b*) sample standard deviation for the data in Problem 4.27, by use of the computational versions of the respective formulas.

   Ans.   (*a*) 45.7,   (*b*) 6.8

4.30. The following examination scores, arranged in ascending order, were achieved by 20 students enrolled in a decision analysis course: 39, 46, 57, 65, 70, 72, 72, 75, 77, 79, 81, 81, 84, 84, 84, 87, 93, 94, 97, 97.   Determine the   (*a*) range and   (*b*) the middle 90 percent range for these ungrouped data.

   Ans.   (*a*) 58.0,   (*b*) 54.5

4.31. Compute the average deviation for the examination scores in Problem 4.30.   The mean examination score was determined to be 76.7 in Problem 3.28.

   Ans. $11.76 \cong 11.8$

4.32. Considering the examination scores in Problem 4.30 to be a statistical population, determine the standard deviation by use of   (*a*) the deviations formula and   (*b*) the alternative computational formula.

   Ans.   (*a*) $15.294 \cong 15.3$,   (*b*) $15.294 \cong 15.3$

4.33. The number of accidents which occurred during a given month in the 13 manufacturing departments of an industrial plant was: 2, 0, 0, 3, 3, 12, 1, 0, 8, 1, 0, 5, 1.   Determine the   (*a*) range and   (*b*) middle 50 percent range for the number of accidents.

   Ans.   (*a*) 12.0,   (*b*) 3.5

4.34. Compute the average deviation for the data in Problem 4.33.   The mean number of accidents was determined to be 2.8 in Problem 3.30.

   Ans. $2.646 \cong 2.6$

4.35. Considering the accident data in Problem 4.33 to be a statistical population, compute the standard deviation by using the alternative computational formula.

   Ans. $3.465 \cong 3.5$

THE RANGES, AVERAGE DEVIATION, AND STANDARD DEVIATION FOR GROUPED DATA

4.36. Determine the (a) range and (b) middle 80 percent range for the mileage data in Table 2.15 (page 25).

Ans.   (a) 12.00, (b) 6.83

4.37. Compute the average deviation for the mileage data in Table 2.15. The mean mileage was determined to be 18.95 in Problem 3.32.

Ans.   1.76

4.38. Considering the mileage data in Table 2.15 to be for a sample of trips, compute the standard deviation for these data by use of the (a) deviations formula and (b) alternative computational formula. The mean mileage was determined to be 18.95 in Problem 3.32.

Ans.   (a) 2.517 ≅ 2.52, (b) 2.517 ≅ 2.52

4.39. From Table 3.9 (page 41), determine the (a) range and (b) middle 50 percent range for the amounts of personal loans.

Ans.   (a) $2800.00, (b) $892.31

4.40. Compute the average deviation for the personal loan data in Table 3.9. The mean for this sample was determined to be $1109.50 in Problem 3.34.

Ans. $512.00

4.41. Determine the sample standard deviation for the data in Table 3.9 by using the alternative computational formula.

Ans. $627.49

4.42. Determine the (a) range and (b) middle 90 percent range for the lifetime of the cutting tools in Table 2.17 (page 26).

Ans.   (a) 149.95 hr, (b) 93.75 hr

4.43. Compute the average deviation for the lifetime of cutting tools reported in Table 2.17. The mean lifetime was determined to be 87.45 hr in Problem 3.36.

Ans.   18.57 hr

4.44. Considering the data in Table 2.17 to be a statistical population, compute the (a) population variance and (b) population standard deviation by using the deviations formulas. The mean lifetime was determined to be 87.45 hr in Problem 3.36.

Ans.   (a) 714.29, (b) 26.73 hr

4.45. From Table 2.18 (page 27), determine the (a) range and (b) average deviation for the age of the applicants. The mean age was determined to be 23.3 in Problem 3.38.

Ans.   (a) 14.0, (b) 2.656 ≅ 2.7 yr

4.46. Compute the sample standard deviation for the data in Table 2.18 by using the alternative computational formula. The mean age was determined to be 23.3 in Problem 3.38.

Ans.   3.4 yr

THE COEFFICIENT OF VARIATION

4.47. Determine the coefficient of variation for the loan amounts analyzed in Problems 4.39 to 4.41.

Ans. $V = 0.57$

4.48. In comparison with the tool-life data analyzed in Problems 4.42 to 4.44, the mean and standard deviation of lifetime for a second brand of tools was determined to be $\mu_2 = 61.50$ hr and $\sigma_2 = 22.30$ hr. Compute the coefficient of variation for (a) the first brand of tools and (b) the second brand of tools. (c) Indicate for which brand the variability of tool life is *relatively* greater.

Ans. (a) $V_1 = 0.31$, (b) $V_2 = 0.36$. (c) Relative variability of the second brand is greater.

PEARSON'S COEFFICIENT OF SKEWNESS

4.49. Compute the coefficient of skewness for the loan amounts, for which the mean and median were determined in Problem 3.34 and for which the standard deviation was computed in Problem 4.41. Interpret this coefficient.

Ans. +0.74, indicating a positively skewed distribution.

4.50. Determine the coefficient of skewness for the lifetime of cutting tools, for which the mean and median were determined in Problem 3.36, and for which the standard deviation was determined in Problem 4.44. Interpret the coefficient.

Ans. −0.19, indicating a negatively skewed distribution.

Chapter 5

Probability

5.1 BASIC DEFINITIONS OF PROBABILITY

Historically, three different conceptual approaches have been developed for defining probability and for determining probability values: the classical, relative frequency, and subjective approaches.

By the *classical approach* to probability, if there are a possible outcomes favorable to the occurrence of an event A and b possible outcomes unfavorable to the occurrence of A, and all outcomes are equally likely and mutually exclusive, then the probability that A will occur is

$$P(A) = \frac{a}{a + b} \tag{5.1}$$

The classical approach to probability is based on the assumption that each outcome is equally likely. Because this approach (when it is applicable) permits determination of probability values before any sample events are observed, it has also been called the *a priori approach*.

EXAMPLE 1. In a well-shuffled deck of cards which contains four aces and 48 other cards, the probability of an ace (A) being obtained on a single draw is

$$P(A) = \frac{4}{4 + 48} = \frac{4}{52} = \frac{1}{13}$$

By the *relative frequency approach*, the probability is determined on the basis of the proportion of times that a favorable outcome occurs in a number of observations or experiments. No prior assumption of equal likelihood is involved. Because determination of the probability values is based on observation and collection of data, this approach has also been called the *empirical approach*.

EXAMPLE 2. Before including coverage for certain types of dental problems in health insurance policies for employed adults, an insurance company wishes to determine the probability of occurrence of such problems, so that the insurance rate can be set accordingly. Therefore, the statistician collects data for 10,000 adults in the appropriate age categories and finds that 100 people have experienced the particular dental problem during the past year. The probability of occurrence is thus

$$P(A) = \frac{100}{10,000} = 0.01, \text{ or } 1\%$$

Both the classical and relative frequency approaches yield *objective* probability values, in the sense that the probability values indicate the relative rate of occurrence of the event in the long run. In contrast, the *subjective approach* to probability is particularly appropriate when there is only one opportunity for the event to occur, and it will either occur or not occur that one time. By the subjective approach, the probability of an event is the *degree of belief* by an individual that the event will occur, based on all evidence available to him. Because the probability value is a personal judgment, the subjective approach has also been called the *personalistic approach*.   This approach to probability has been developed relatively recently, and is related to Bayesian decision analysis (see Section 1.3 and Chapters 14 through 16).

EXAMPLE 3.   Because of taxes and alternative uses for his funds, an investor has determined that the purchase of land parcels is worthwhile only if there is at least a probability of 0.90 that the land will appreciate in value by 50 percent or more during the next 4 years.   In evaluating a certain parcel of land he studies price changes in the area during recent years, considers present price levels, studies the current and likely future status of land development projects, and reviews the statistics concerned with the economic development of the overall geographic area.   On the basis of this review he concludes that there is a probability of about 0.75 that the required appreciation in value will in fact occur, and so he decides not to invest in the parcel of land.

5.2   EXPRESSING PROBABILITY

The symbol P is used to designate the probability of an event.   Thus $P(A)$ denotes the probability that event A will occur in a single observation or experiment.

The smallest value that a probability statement can have is 0 (indicating the event is impossible) and the largest value it can have is 1 (indicating the event is certain to occur).   Thus, in general:

$$0 \le P(A) \le 1 \tag{5.2}$$

In a given observation or experiment, an event must either occur or not occur.   Therefore, the sum of the probability of occurrence plus the probability of nonoccurrence always equals 1.   Thus, where A' indicates the nonoccurrence of event A, we have:

$$P(A) + P(A') = 1 \tag{5.3}$$

A *Venn diagram* is a diagram related to set theory in mathematics by which the events which can occur in a particular observation or experiment can be portrayed.   An enclosed figure represents a sample space, and portions of the area within the space are designated to represent particular events, or classes of events, within the sample space.

EXAMPLE 4.   Figure 5.1 represents the probabilities of the two events, A and A' (read "not-A").   Because $P(A) + P(A') = 1$, all of the area within the diagram is accounted for.

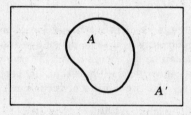

Fig. 5-1

As an alternative to probability values, probabilities can also be expressed in terms of *odds*.   The odds for the occurrence of an event are

$$\text{Odds} = \text{No. of favorable outcomes} : \text{No. of unfavorable outcomes} \tag{5.4}$$

Odds of $5:2$ (read "five to two") indicate that for every five elementary events constituting success there are two elementary events constituting failure.   Note that by the classical approach to probability discussed in Section 5.1 the probability value equivalent to an odds ratio of $5:2$ is $P = a/(a + b) = 5/(5 + 2) = 5/7$.

CHAP. 5] PROBABILITY 67

EXAMPLE 5. Suppose success is defined as drawing any face card *or* an ace from a well-shuffled deck of 52 cards. The odds associated with success are 16 : 36, or 4 : 9. The probability of success is $16/(16 + 36) = 16/52 = 4/13$.

5.3 MUTUALLY EXCLUSIVE AND NONEXCLUSIVE EVENTS

Two or more events are *mutually exclusive*, or *disjoint*, if they cannot occur together. That is, the occurrence of one event automatically precludes the occurrence of the other event (or events). For instance, suppose we consider the two possible events "ace" and "king" in respect to a card being drawn from a deck of playing cards. These two events are mutually exclusive, because any given card cannot be both an ace and a king.

Two or more events are *nonexclusive*, or *joint*, when it is possible for them to occur together. Note that this definition does *not* indicate that such events must necessarily always occur together. For instance, suppose we consider the two possible events "ace" and "spade." These events are not mutually exclusive, because a given card can be both an ace and a spade; however, it does not follow that every ace is a spade or every spade is an ace.

EXAMPLE 6. In a study of consumer behavior, an analyst classifies the people who enter a stereo shop according to sex ("male" or "female") and according to age ("under 30" or "30 and over"). The two events, or classifications, "male" and "female" are mutually exclusive, since any given person would be classified in one category or the other. Similarly, the events "under 30" and "30 and over" are also mutually exclusive. However, the events "male" and "under 30" are not mutually exclusive, because a randomly chosen person could have both characteristics.

5.4 THE RULES OF ADDITION

The rules of addition are used when we wish to determine the probability of one event *or* another (or both) occurring in a single observation. Symbolically, we can represent the probability of event A or event B occurring by $P(A \text{ or } B)$. In the language of set theory this is called the *union* of A and B and the probability is designated by $P(A \cup B)$.

There are two variations of the rule of addition, depending on whether the two events are mutually exclusive. The rule of addition for mutually exclusive events is

$$P(A \text{ or } B) = P(A \cup B) = P(A) + P(B) \tag{5.5}$$

EXAMPLE 7. When drawing a card from a deck of playing cards, the events "ace" (A) and "king" (K) are mutually exclusive. The probability of drawing either an ace or a king in a single draw is

$$P(A \text{ or } K) = P(A) + P(K) = \frac{4}{52} + \frac{4}{52} = \frac{8}{52} = \frac{2}{13}$$

(*Note:* Problem 5.4 extends the application of this rule to three events.)

For events that are *not* mutually exclusive, the probability of the joint occurrence of the two events is subtracted from the sum. We can represent the probability of joint occurrence by $P(A$ and $B)$. In the language of set theory this is called the *intersection* of A and B and the probability is designated by $P(A \cap B)$. Thus, the rule of addition for events that are not mutually exclusive is

$$P(A \text{ or } B) = P(A) + P(B) - P(A \text{ and } B) \tag{5.6}$$

Formula (*5.6*) is also often called the *general rule of addition*, because for events that are mutually exclusive the last term would always be equal to zero. Thus, the formula is then algebraically the same as formula (*5.5*) for mutually exclusive events.

EXAMPLE 8.   When drawing a card from a deck of playing cards, the events "ace" and "spade" are not mutually exclusive.   The probability of drawing an ace (A) or spade (S) (or both) in a single draw is

$$P(A \text{ or } S) = P(A) + P(S) - P(A \text{ and } S) = \frac{4}{52} + \frac{13}{52} - \frac{1}{52} = \frac{16}{52} = \frac{4}{13}$$

Venn diagrams can be used to portray the rationale underlying the two rules of addition.   In Fig. 5-2(a), note that the probability of A or B occurring is conceptually equivalent to adding the proportion of area included in A and B.   In Fig. 5-2(b), for events that are not mutually exclusive, some elements are included in *both* A and B; thus, there is overlap between these event sets.   When the areas included in A and B are added together for such events that are not mutually exclusive, the area of overlap is essentially added in twice.   Thus, the rationale of subtracting $P(A \text{ and } B)$ in the rule of addition for nonexclusive events is to correct the sum for the overlap represented in the Venn diagram.

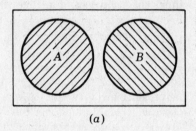 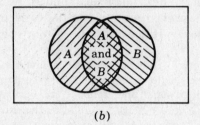

(a)   (b)

Fig. 5-2

5.5   INDEPENDENT EVENTS, DEPENDENT EVENTS, AND CONDITIONAL PROBABILITY

Two events are *independent* when the occurrence or nonoccurrence of one event has no effect on the probability of occurrence of the other event.   Two events are *dependent* when the occurrence or nonoccurrence of one event *does* affect the probability of occurrence of the other event.

EXAMPLE 9.   The outcomes associated with tossing a fair coin twice in succession are considered to be independent events, because the outcome of the first toss has no effect on the respective probabilities of a head or tail occurring on the second toss.   The drawing of two cards *without replacement* from a deck of playing cards are dependent events, because the probabilities associated with the second draw are dependent on the outcome of the first draw.   Specifically, if an "ace" occurred on the first draw, then the probability of an "ace" occurring on the second draw is the ratio of the number of aces still remaining in the deck to the total number of cards remaining in the deck, or 3/51.

When two events are dependent, the concept of *conditional probability* is employed to designate the probability of occurrence of the related event.   The expression $P(B \mid A)$ indicates the probability of event B occurring *given* that event A has occurred.   Note that "$B \mid A$" is *not* a fraction.

Conditional probability expressions are not required for independent events because by definition there is no relationship between the occurrence of such events.   Therefore, if events A and B are independent, $P(B)$ would always be equal to $P(B \mid A)$.   In fact, one approach by which the independence of two events A and B can be tested is by comparing

$$P(B) \overset{?}{=} P(B \mid A) \tag{5.7}$$

or

$$P(A) \overset{?}{=} P(A \mid B) \tag{5.8}$$

By reference to the Venn diagram in Fig. 5-3, the rationale underlying the algebraic formula for a conditional probability value can be illustrated. If we wish to determine the probability of B given A, then note that once A is given as having occurred, the original Venn diagram (sample space) is reduced to the smaller diagram in the right portion of Fig. 5-3. That is, the entire remaining diagram includes the occurrence A and part of the remaining diagram includes A *and* B. Now, since it follows from the classical approach that the probability of B (after A has occurred) is the proportion of the total remaining elementary events which include B, the algebraic formula for determining the probability of B given A is

$$P(B \mid A) = \frac{P(A \text{ and } B)}{P(A)} \tag{5.9}$$

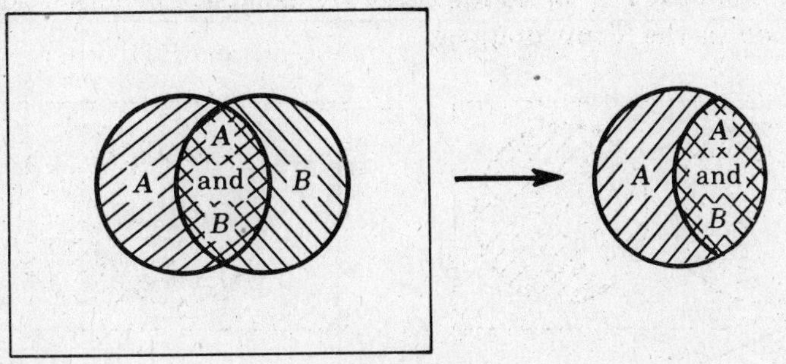

Fig. 5-3

There is often some confusion regarding the distinction between mutually exclusive and nonexclusive events on the one hand, and the concepts of independence and dependence on the other hand. Particularly, note the difference between events that are mutually exclusive and events that are independent. Mutual exclusiveness indicates that two events cannot both occur, whereas independence indicates that the probability of occurrence of one event is not affected by the occurrence of the other event. Therefore it follows that if two events are mutually exclusive, this is a particular example of highly *dependent* events, because the probability of one event given that the other has occurred would always be equal to zero. See Problem 5.10. In respect to formula (5.9) and Fig. 5-3, $P(A \text{ and } B)$ is always zero for mutually exclusive events and there is no area of intersection on the Venn diagram, resulting in $P(B \mid A) = 0$.

5.6 THE RULES OF MULTIPLICATION

The rules of multiplication are concerned with determining the probability of the joint occurrence of A and B. As mentioned earlier, this is the intersection of A and B; the probability is designated by $P(A \cap B)$. There are two variations of the rule of multiplication, according to whether the two events are independent or dependent. The rule of multiplication for independent events is

$$P(A \text{ and } B) = P(A \cap B) = P(A)P(B) \tag{5.10}$$

EXAMPLE 10. By formula (5.10), if a fair coin is tossed twice the probability that both outcomes will be "heads" is $(\frac{1}{2}) \times (\frac{1}{2}) = (\frac{1}{4})$.

(*Note:* Problem 5.11 extends the application of this rule to three events.)

The tree diagram is particularly useful as a method of portraying the possible events associated with sequential observations, or sequential trials. Figure 5-4 is an example of such a diagram for the events associated with tossing a coin twice, and identifies the outcomes that are possible and the probability at each point in the sequence.

EXAMPLE 11. By reference to Fig. 5-4, we see that there are four types of sequences, or joint events, that are possible: H and H, H and T, T and H, and T and T. By the rule of multiplication for independent events, the probability of joint occurrences for any one of these sequences in this case is 1/4, or 0.25. Since these are the only sequences which are possible, and since they are mutually exclusive sequences, by the rule of addition the sum of the four probabilities should be 1, which it is.

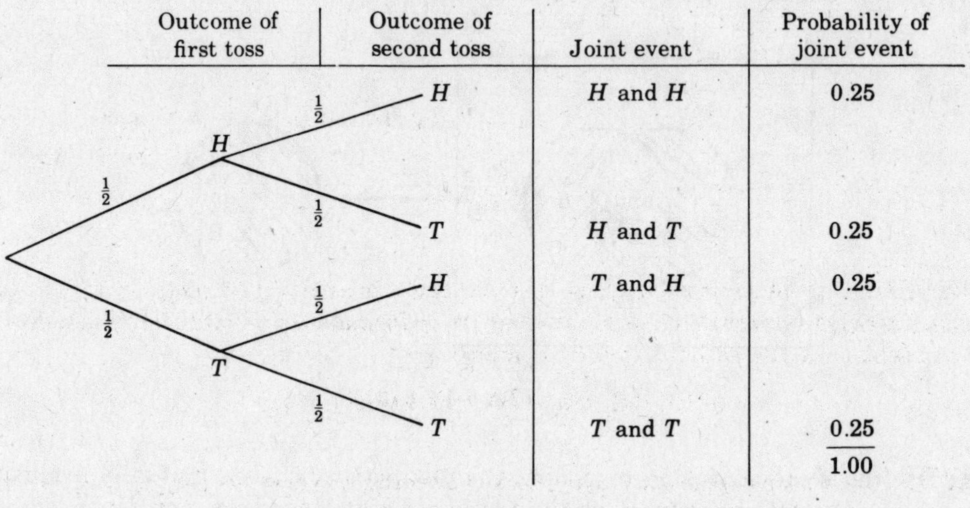

Outcome of first toss	Outcome of second toss	Joint event	Probability of joint event
	H	H and H	0.25
	T	H and T	0.25
	H	T and H	0.25
	T	T and T	0.25
			1.00

Fig. 5-4

For dependent events the probability of the joint occurrence of A and B is the probability of A multiplied by the *conditional* probability of B given A. An equivalent value is obtained if the two events are reversed in position. Thus the rule of multiplication for dependent events is

$$P(A \text{ and } B) = P(A)P(B \mid A) \qquad (5.11)$$

or

$$P(A \text{ and } B) = P(B)P(A \mid B) \qquad (5.12)$$

Formula (5.11) [or (5.12)] is often called the *general rule of multiplication*, because for events that are independent the conditional probability value, $P(B \mid A)$, would be the same as the respective unconditional probability value, $P(B)$, which then corresponds to (5.10) for independent events.

EXAMPLE 12. Suppose that a set of 10 spare parts is known to contain eight good parts (G) and two defective parts (D). Given that two parts are selected randomly without replacement, the sequence of possible outcomes and the probabilities are portrayed by the tree diagram in Fig. 5-5 (subscripts indicate sequential position of outcomes). Based on the multiplication rule for dependent events, the probability that the two parts selected are both good is

$$P(G_1 \text{ and } G_2) = P(G_1)P(G_2 \mid G_1) = \left(\frac{8}{10}\right) \times \left(\frac{7}{9}\right) = \frac{56}{90} = \frac{28}{45}$$

(*Note:* Problems 5.12(*b*) and 5.13 extend the application of this rule to three events.)

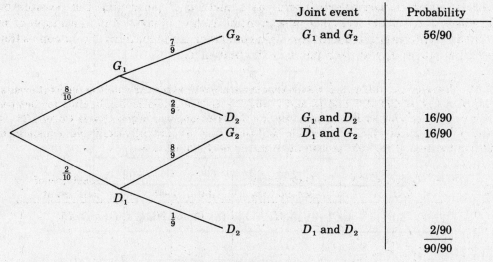

Joint event	Probability
G_1 and G_2	56/90
G_1 and D_2	16/90
D_1 and G_2	16/90
D_1 and D_2	2/90
	90/90

Fig. 5-5

If the probability of joint occurrence of two events is available directly without use of the multiplication rules as such, then as an alternative to formulas (5.7) and (5.8) the independence of two events A and B can be tested by comparing

$$P(A \text{ and } B) \overset{?}{=} P(A)P(B) \qquad\qquad (5.13)$$

EXAMPLE 13. By our knowledge of a playing deck of 52 cards, we know that only one card is both an ace (A) and a spade (S), and thus that $P(A \text{ and } S) = 1/52$. We also know that the probability of drawing any ace is 4/52 and the probability of drawing any spade is 13/52. We thus can verify that the events "ace" and "spade" are independent events, as follows:

$$P(A \text{ and } S) \overset{?}{=} P(A)P(S)$$

$$\frac{1}{52} \overset{?}{=} \frac{4}{52} \times \frac{13}{52}$$

$$\frac{1}{52} = \frac{1}{52} \text{ (therefore the events } are \text{ independent)}$$

5.7 JOINT PROBABILITY TABLES

A *joint probability table* is a table in which all possible events for one variable (or observation) are listed as column headings, all possible events for a second variable are listed as row headings, and the value entered in each resulting cell is the probability of each joint occurrence. Often, the probabilities in such a table are based on observed frequencies of occurrence for the various joint events, rather than being *a priori* in nature. The table of joint-occurrence frequencies which can serve as the basis for constructing a joint probability table is called a *contingency table*.

EXAMPLE 14. Table 5.1(a) is a contingency table which describes 200 people who entered a stereo shop according to sex and age, while Table 5.2(b) is the associated joint probability table. The frequency reported in each cell of the contingency table is converted into a probability value by dividing by the total number of observations, in this case, 200.

Table 5.1(*a*)　Contingency Table for Stereo Shop Customers

Age	Sex		Total
	Male	Female	
Under 30	60	50	110
30 and over	80	10	90
Total	140	60	200

Table 5.1(*b*)　Joint Probability Table for Stereo Shop Customers

Age	Sex		Marginal probability
	Male (*M*)	Female (*F*)	
Under 30 (*U*)	0.30	0.25	0.55
30 and over (*O*)	0.40	0.05	0.45
Marginal probability	0.70	0.30	1.00

In the context of joint probability tables, a *marginal probability* is so named because it is a marginal total of a column or a row. Whereas the probability values in the cells are probabilities of joint occurrence, the marginal probabilities are the unconditional probabilities of particular events.

EXAMPLE 15.　The probability of 0.30 in row 1 and column 1 of Table 5.1(*b*) indicates that there is a probability of 0.30 that a randomly chosen person from this group of 200 people will be a male and under 30. The marginal probability of 0.70 for column 1 indicates that there is a probability of 0.70 that a randomly chosen person will be a male.

Recognizing that a joint probability table also includes all of the unconditional probability values as marginal totals, we can use formula (*5.9*) for determining any particular conditional probability value.

EXAMPLE 16.　Suppose we are interested in the probability that a randomly chosen person in Table 5.1(*b*) is "under 30" (*U*) given that he is a "male" (*M*). The probability is, using formula (*5.9*),

$$P(U \mid M) = \frac{P(M \text{ and } U)}{P(M)} = \frac{0.30}{0.70} = \frac{3}{7} \cong 0.43$$

5.8　PERMUTATIONS

By the classical approach to determining probabilities presented in Section 5.1, the probability value is based on the ratio of the number of equally likely outcomes that are favorable to the total number of outcomes that are possible. When the problems are simple, the number of outcomes can be counted directly. However, for more complex problems the methods of permutations and combinations are required to determine the number of possible outcomes.

The number of *permutations* of *n* objects is the number of ways in which the objects can be arranged in terms of order:

$$\text{Permutations of } n \text{ objects} = n! = (n) \times (n-1) \times \cdots \times (2) \times (1) \qquad (5.14)$$

The symbol $n!$ is read "n factorial." In permutations and combinations problems, n is always positive. Also, note that by definition $0! = 1$ in mathematics.

EXAMPLE 17. Three members of a social organization have volunteered to serve as officers for the following year, to take positions as President, Treasurer, and Secretary. The number of ways (permutations) in which the three can assume the positions is

$$n! = 3! = (3)(2)(1) = 6 \text{ ways}$$

This result can be portrayed by a sequential diagram. Suppose that the three people are designated as A, B, and C. The number of possible arrangements, or permutations, is presented in Fig. 5-6.

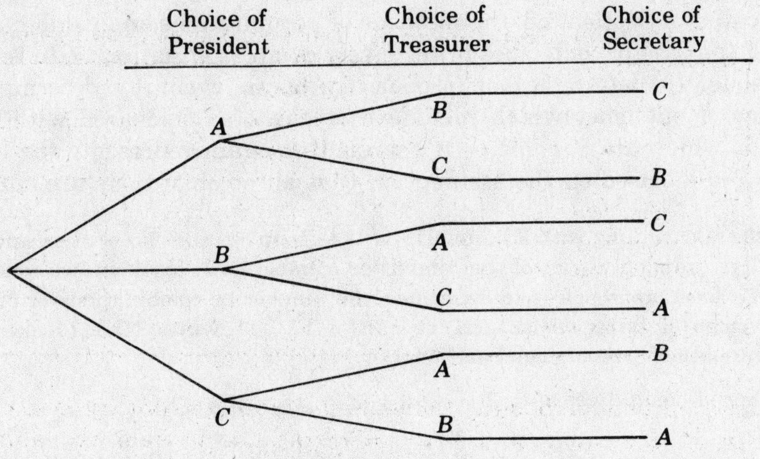

Fig. 5-6

Typically, we are concerned about the number of permutations of some *subgroup* of the n objects, rather than all n objects as such. That is, we are interested in the number of permutations of n objects taken r at a time, where r is less than n:

$$_nP_r = \frac{n!}{(n-r)!} \qquad (5.15)$$

EXAMPLE 18. In Example 17, suppose there are 10 members in the social organization and no nominations have yet been presented for the offices of President, Treasurer, and Secretary. The number of different arrangements of three officers elected from the 10 club members is

$$_nP_r = {_{10}P_3} = \frac{10!}{(10-3)!} = \frac{10!}{7!} = \frac{(10)(9)(8)(7!)}{7!} = (10)(9)(8) = 720$$

5.9 COMBINATIONS

In the case of permutations, the order in which the objects are arranged is important. In the case of *combinations*, we are concerned with the number of different groupings of objects that can occur *without* regard to their order. Therefore, an interest in combinations always concerns the number of different subgroups that can be taken from n objects. The number of combinations of n objects taken r at a time is

$$_nC_r = \frac{n!}{r!(n-r)!} \qquad (5.16)$$

In many textbooks, the combination of n objects taken r at a time is represented by $\binom{n}{r}$. Note that this is *not* a fraction.

EXAMPLE 19. Suppose that three members from a small social organization containing a total of 10 members are to be chosen to form a committee. The number of different groups of three people which can be chosen, *without regard to the different orders in which each group might be chosen*, is

$$_nC_r = {}_{10}C_3 = \frac{10!}{3!(10-3)!} = \frac{(10)(9)(8)(7!)}{3!(7!)} = \frac{(10)(9)(8)}{(3)(2)} = \frac{720}{6} = 120$$

As indicated in Section 5.8, the methods of permutations and combinations provide a basis for counting the possible outcomes in relatively complex situations. In terms of combinations, we can frequently determine the probability of an event by determining the number of combinations of outcomes which include that event as compared with the total number of combinations which are possible. Of course, this again represents the classical approach to probability and is based on the assumption that all combinations are equally likely.

EXAMPLE 20. Continuing with Example 19, if the group contains six women and four men, what is the probability that a random choice of the committee members will result in two women and one man being selected? The basic approach is to determine the number of combinations of outcomes which contain exactly two women (of the six women) and one man (of the four men) and then to take the ratio of this number to the total number of possible combinations:

Number of committees with 2 W and 1 $M = {}_6C_2 \times {}_4C_1$

$$= \frac{6!}{2!4!} \times \frac{4!}{1!3!} = 15 \times 4 = 60$$

Total number of possible combinations $= {}_{10}C_3$

$$= \frac{10!}{3!7!} = \frac{(10)(9)(8)}{(3)(2)(1)} = \frac{720}{6} = 120$$

$$P(2W \text{ and } 1M) = \frac{{}_6C_2 \times {}_4C_1}{{}_{10}C_3} = \frac{60}{120} = 0.50$$

In Example 20, the so-called *multiplication principle for sequential outcomes* is used. In general, if one event can occur in n_1 ways and a second event can occur in n_2 ways, then

Total No. of ways two events can occur in combination $= (n_1) \times (n_2) \qquad (5.17)$

Solved Problems

DETERMINING PROBABILITY VALUES

5.1. For each of the following situations, indicate whether the classical, relative frequency, or subjective approach would be most useful for determining the required probability value.

(a) Probability that there will be a recession next year.

(b) Probability that a six-sided die will show either a "one" or "six" on a single toss.

(c) Probability that from a shipment of 20 parts known to contain one defective part, one randomly chosen part will turn out to be defective.

(d) Probability that a randomly chosen part taken from a large shipment of parts will turn out to be defective.

(e) Probability that a randomly chosen person who enters a large department store will make a purchase in that store.

(f) Probability that the Dow-Jones Industrials Average will increase by at least 50 points during the next six months.

(a) Subjective, (b) classical, (c) classical, (d) relative frequency (Since there is no information about the overall proportion of the defective parts, the proportion of defective parts in a sample would be used as the basis for estimating the probability value.), (e) relative frequency, (f) subjective

5.2. Determine the probability value applicable in each of the following situations.

(a) Probability of industrial injury in a particular industry on an annual basis. A random sample of 10 firms, employing a total of 8000 people, reported that 400 industrial injuries occurred during a recent 12-month period.

(b) Probability of betting on a winning number in the game of roulette. The numbers on the wheel include a "0," "00," and "1" through "36."

(c) Probability that a fast-foods franchise outlet will be financially successful. The prospective investor obtains data for other units in the franchise system, studies the development of the residential area in which the outlet is to be located, and considers the sales volume required for financial success based on the required capital investment and operational costs. Overall, it is the investor's judgment that there is an 80% chance that the outlet will be financially successful and a 20% chance that it will not.

(a) By the relative frequency approach, $P = 400/8000 = 0.05$. Because this probability value is based on a sample, it is an estimate of the unknown true value. Also, the implicit assumption is made that safety standards have not changed since the 12-month sampled period.

(b) By the classical approach, $P = 1/38$. This value is based on the assumption that all numbers are equally likely, and therefore a well-balanced wheel is assumed.

(c) Based on the subjective approach, the value arrived at through the prospective investor's judgment is $P = 0.80$. Note that such a judgment should be based on knowledge of all available information within the scope of the time which is available to collect such information.

5.3. For each of the following reported odds ratios determine the equivalent probability value, and for each of the reported probability values determine the equivalent odds ratio.

(a) A purchasing agent estimates that the odds are 2:1 that a shipment will arrive on schedule.

(b) The probability that a new component will not function properly when assembled is assessed as being $P = 1/5$.

(c) The odds that a new product will succeed are estimated as being 3:1.

(d) The probability that the home team will win the opening game of the season is assessed as being 1/3.

(a) The probability that the shipment will arrive on schedule is $P = 2/(2 + 1) = 2/3 \cong 0.67$.

(b) The odds that it will not function properly are 1:4.

(c) The probability that the product will succeed is $P = 3/(3 + 1) = 3/4 = 0.75$.

(d) The odds that the team will win are 1:2.

APPLYING THE RULES OF ADDITION

5.4.   Determine the probability of obtaining an ace (A), king (K), or a deuce (D) when one card is drawn from a well-shuffled deck of 52 playing cards.

From formula *(5.5)*,

$$P(A \text{ or } K \text{ or } D) = P(A) + P(K) + P(D) = \frac{4}{52} + \frac{4}{52} + \frac{4}{52} = \frac{12}{52} = \frac{3}{13}$$

(*Note:*   The events are mutually exclusive.)

5.5.   With reference to Table 5.2, what is the probability that a randomly chosen family will have household income (a) between \$8000 and \$12,999, (b) less than \$13,000, (c) at one of the two extremes of being either less than \$8000 or at least \$30,000?

Table 5.2   Annual Household Income for 500 Families

Category	Income range	Number of families
1	Less than \$8000	60
2	8000–12,999	100
3	13,000–19,999	160
4	20,000–29,999	140
5	30,000 and above	40
		Total 500

(a) $P(2) = \dfrac{100}{500} = \dfrac{1}{5} = 0.20$

(b) $P(1 \text{ or } 2) = \dfrac{60}{500} + \dfrac{100}{500} = \dfrac{160}{500} = \dfrac{8}{25} = 0.32$

(c) $P(1 \text{ or } 5) = \dfrac{60}{500} + \dfrac{40}{500} = \dfrac{100}{500} = \dfrac{1}{5} = 0.20$

(*Note:*   The events are mutually exclusive.)

5.6.   Of 300 business students, 100 are currently enrolled in accounting and 80 are currently enrolled in business statistics.   These enrollment figures include 30 students who are in fact enrolled in both courses.   What is the probability that a randomly chosen student will be enrolled in either accounting (A) or business statistics (B)?

From formula *(5.6)*,

$$P(A \text{ or } B) = P(A) + P(B) - P(A \text{ and } B) = \frac{100}{300} + \frac{80}{300} - \frac{30}{300} = \frac{150}{300} = \frac{1}{2} = 0.50$$

(*Note:*   The events are not mutually exclusive.)

5.7. Of 100 individuals who applied for computer programming positions with a large firm during the past year, 40 had some prior work experience (W), and 30 had a professional certificate (C). However, 20 of the applicants had both work experience and a certificate, and thus are included in both of the counts.

  (*a*) Construct a Venn diagram to portray these events.

  (*b*) What is the probability that a randomly chosen applicant had either work experience or a certificate (or both)?

  (*c*) What is the probability that a randomly chosen applicant had either work experience or a certificate *but not both* ?

  (*a*) See Fig. 5-7.

  (*b*) $P(W$ or $C) = P(W) + P(C) - P(W$ and $C)$
$$= 0.40 + 0.30 - 0.20 = 0.50$$

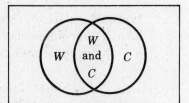

  (*Note:* The events are not mutually exclusive.)

  (*c*) $P(W$ or C, but not both) $= P(W$ or $C) - P(W$ and $C)$
$$= 0.50 - 0.20 = 0.30$$

Fig. 5-7

INDEPENDENT EVENTS, DEPENDENT EVENTS, AND CONDITIONAL PROBABILITY

5.8. For Problem 5.7, (*a*) determine the conditional probability that a randomly chosen applicant has a certificate given that he has some previous work experience. (*b*) Apply an appropriate test to determine if work experience and certification are independent events.

  (*a*) $P(C \mid W) = \dfrac{P(C \text{ and } W)}{P(W)} = \dfrac{0.20}{0.40} = 0.50$

  (*b*) $P(C) \overset{?}{=} P(C|W)$. Since $0.30 \neq 0.50$, events W and C are dependent. Independence could also be tested by applying the multiplication rule for independent events—see Problem 5.14(*a*).)

5.9. Two separate product divisions included in a large firm are Marine Products (M) and Office Equipment (O). The probability that the Marine Products division will have a profit margin of at least 10 percent this fiscal year is estimated to be 0.30, the probability that the Office Equipment division will have a profit margin of at least 10 percent is 0.20, and the probability that both divisions will have a profit margin of at least 10 percent is 0.06.

  (*a*) Determine the probability that the Office Equipment division will have at least a 10 percent profit margin given that the Marine Products division achieved this profit criterion.

  (*b*) Apply an appropriate test to determine if achievement of the profit goal in the two divisions is statistically independent.

  (*a*) $P(O \mid M) = \dfrac{P(O \text{ and } M)}{P(M)} = \dfrac{0.06}{0.30} = 0.20$

  (*b*) $P(O) \overset{?}{=} P(O \mid M)$. Since $0.20 = 0.20$, the two events are independent. (Independence could also be tested by applying the multiplication rule for independent events—see Problem 5.14(*b*).)

5.10. Suppose an optimist estimates that the probability of his earning a final grade of "A" in the business statistics course is 0.60 and the probability of a "B" is 0.40. Of course, he cannot earn both grades as final grades, since they are mutually exclusive.

(*a*) Determine the conditional probability of his earning a "B" given that he has in fact received the final grade of "A," by use of the appropriate computational formula.

(*b*) Apply an appropriate test to demonstrate that such mutually exclusive events are dependent events.

(*a*) $P(\text{B} \mid \text{A}) = \dfrac{P(\text{B and A})}{P(\text{A})} = \dfrac{0}{0.60} = 0$

(*b*) $P(\text{B}) \underset{?}{=} P(\text{B} \mid \text{A})$.   Since $0.40 \neq 0$, the events are dependent.   See Section 5.5.

APPLYING THE RULES OF MULTIPLICATION

5.11. In general, the probability that a prospect will make a purchase when he is contacted by a salesman is $P = 0.40$. If a salesman selects three prospects randomly from a file and makes contact with them, what is the probability that all three prospects will make a purchase?

Since the actions of the prospects are assumed to be independent of one another, the rule of multiplication for independent events is applied.

$$P(\text{all 3 are purchasers}) = P(\text{first is a purchaser}) \times P(\text{second is a purchaser})$$
$$\times\ P(\text{third is a purchaser})$$
$$= (0.40) \times (0.40) \times (0.40) = 0.064$$

5.12. Of 12 accounts held in a file, four contain a procedural error in posting account balances.

(*a*) If an auditor randomly selects two of these accounts (without replacement), what is the probability that neither account will contain a procedural error? Construct a tree diagram to represent this sequential sampling process.

(*b*) If the auditor samples three accounts, what is the probability that none of the accounts includes the procedural error?

(*a*) In this case the events are dependent, because the outcome on the first sampled account affects the probabilities which apply to the second sampled account. Where E_1' means no error in the first sampled account and E_2' means no error in the second sampled account

$$P(E_1' \text{ and } E_2') = P(E_1')P(E_2' \mid E_1') = \frac{8}{12} \times \frac{7}{11} = \frac{56}{132} = \frac{14}{33} \cong 0.42$$

In Fig. 5-8, E stands for an account with the procedural error, E' stands for an account with no procedural error, and the subscript indicates the sequential position of the sampled account.

(*b*) $P(E_1' \text{ and } E_2' \text{ and } E_3') = P(E_1')\,P(E_2' \mid E_1')\,P(E_3' \mid E_1' \text{ and } E_2')$

$$= \frac{8}{12} \times \frac{7}{11} \times \frac{6}{10} = \frac{336}{1320} = \frac{42}{165} \cong 0.25$$

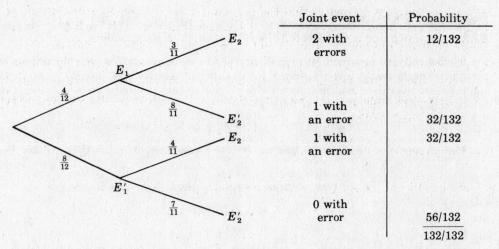

Joint event	Probability
2 with errors	12/132
1 with an error	32/132
1 with an error	32/132
0 with error	56/132
	132/132

Fig. 5-8

5.13. When sampling *without* replacement from a finite population, the probability values associated with various events are dependent on what events (sampled items) have already occurred. On the other hand, when sampling *with* replacement the events are always independent.

(a) Suppose that three cards are chosen randomly and without replacement from a playing deck of 52 cards. What is the probability that all three cards are aces?

(b) Suppose that three cards are chosen randomly from a playing deck of 52 cards, but that after each selection the card is replaced and the deck is shuffled before the next selection of a card. What is the probability that all three cards are aces?

(a) The rule of multiplication for dependent events applies in this case:

$$P(A_1 \text{ and } A_2 \text{ and } A_3) = P(A_1)\,P(A_2 \mid A_1)\,P(A_3 \mid A_1 \text{ and } A_2)$$

$$= \frac{4}{52} \times \frac{3}{51} \times \frac{2}{50} = \frac{24}{132,600} = \frac{1}{5525} \cong 0.0002$$

(b) The rule of multiplication for independent events applies in this case:

$$P(A_1 \text{ and } A_2 \text{ and } A_3) = P(A)\,P(A)\,P(A)$$

$$= \frac{4}{52} \times \frac{4}{52} \times \frac{4}{52} = \frac{64}{140,608} = \frac{1}{2197} \cong 0.0005$$

5.14. Test the independence   (a) of the two events described in Problems 5.7 and 5.8, and   (b) for the two events described in Problem 5.9, using the rule of multiplication for independent events.

(a) $P(W \text{ and } C) \stackrel{?}{=} P(W)P(C)$
       $0.20 \stackrel{?}{=} (0.40) \times (0.30)$
       $0.20 \neq 0.12$

   Therefore, events W and C are dependent.   This corresponds with the answer to Problem 5.8(b).

(b) $P(M \text{ and } O) \stackrel{?}{=} P(M)P(O)$
       $0.06 \stackrel{?}{=} (0.30) \times (0.20)$
       $0.06 = 0.06$

   Therefore, events M and O are independent.   This corresponds with the answer to Problem 5.9(b).

5.15. From Problem 5.7, what is the probability that a randomly chosen applicant has neither work experience nor a certificate? Are these events independent?

Symbolically, what is required is $P(W'$ and $C')$ for these events that are not mutually exclusive but possibly dependent events. However, in this case neither $P(W' \mid C')$ nor $P(C' \mid W')$ is available, and therefore the rule of multiplication for dependent events cannot be used. Instead, the answer can be obtained by subtraction, as follows:

$$P(W' \text{ and } C') = 1 - P(W \text{ or } C) = 1 - 0.50 = 0.50$$

We can now also demonstrate that the events are dependent rather than independent:

$$P(W' \text{ and } C') \stackrel{?}{=} P(W')P(C')$$
$$0.50 \stackrel{?}{=} [1 - P(W)][1 - P(C)]$$
$$0.50 \stackrel{?}{=} (0.60)(0.70)$$
$$0.50 \neq 0.42$$

The conclusion that the events are dependent coincides with the answer to Problem 5.14(a), which is directed to the complement of each of these two events.

5.16. Refer to Problem 5.11. (a) Construct a tree diagram to portray the sequence of three contacts, using S for sale and S' for no sale. (b) What is the probability that the salesman will make *at least* two sales? (c) What is the probability that the salesman will make *at least* one sale?

(a) See Fig. 5-9.

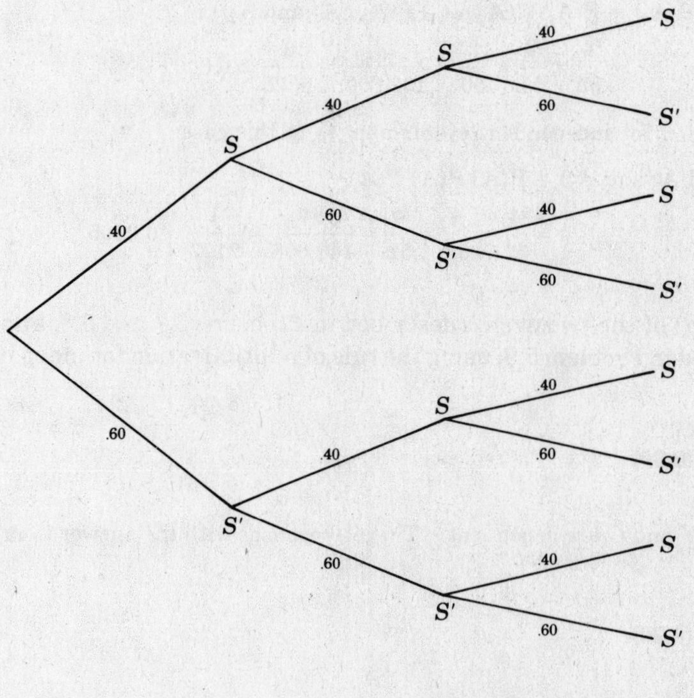

	Joint event	Probability
S	3 sales	0.064
S'	2 sales	0.096
S	2 sales	0.096
S'	1 sale	0.144
S	2 sales	0.096
S'	1 sale	0.144
S	1 sale	0.144
S'	0 sales	0.216
		1.000

Fig. 5-9.

(b) "At least" two sales includes either two *or* three sales. Further, by reference to Fig. 5-9 we note that the two sales can occur by any of three different sequences. Therefore, we use the rule of multiplication for independent events to determine the probability of each sequence and the rule of addition to indicate that any of these sequences constitutes "success":

$$P(\text{at least 2 sales}) = P(S \text{ and } S \text{ and } S) + P(S \text{ and } S \text{ and } S')$$
$$+ P(S \text{ and } S' \text{ and } S) + P(S' \text{ and } S \text{ and } S)$$
$$= (0.064) + (0.096) + (0.096) + (0.096) = 0.352$$

(c) Instead of following the approach in part (b), it is easier to obtain the answer to this question by subtraction:

$$P(\text{at least 1 sale}) = 1 - P(\text{no } S)$$
$$= 1 - P(S' \text{ and } S' \text{ and } S')$$
$$= 1 - 0.216 = 0.784$$

5.17. In Problem 5.12 it was established that four of 12 accounts contain a procedural error.

(a) If an auditor samples one account randomly, what is the probability that it will contain the error?

(b) If an auditor samples two accounts randomly, what is the probability that at least one will contain the error?

(c) If an auditor samples three accounts randomly, what is the probability that at least one will contain the error?

(a) $P(E) = \dfrac{\text{No. of accts. with error}}{\text{Total No. of accts.}} = \dfrac{4}{12} = \dfrac{1}{3} \cong 0.33$

(b) $P(\text{at least one } E) = P(E_1 \text{ and } E_2) + P(E_1 \text{ and } E_2') + P(E_1' \text{ and } E_2)$

$$= P(E_1) P(E_2 \mid E_1) + P(E_1) P(E_2' \mid E_1) + P(E_1') P(E_2 \mid E_1')$$

$$= \left(\frac{4}{12}\right)\left(\frac{3}{11}\right) + \left(\frac{4}{12}\right)\left(\frac{8}{11}\right) + \left(\frac{8}{12}\right)\left(\frac{4}{11}\right)$$

$$= \frac{12}{132} + \frac{32}{132} + \frac{32}{132} = \frac{76}{132} = \frac{19}{33} \cong 0.58$$

or

$P(\text{at least one } E) = 1 - P(\text{no } E)$

$$= 1 - P(E_1' \text{ and } E_2')$$

$$= 1 - P(E_1') P(E_2' \mid E_1')$$

$$= 1 - \left(\frac{8}{12}\right)\left(\frac{7}{11}\right)$$

$$= 1 - \frac{56}{132} = \frac{76}{132} = \frac{19}{33} \cong 0.58$$

(c) $P(\text{at least one } E) = 1 - P(\text{no } E)$

$$= 1 - P(E_1' \text{ and } E_2' \text{ and } E_3')$$

$$= 1 - P(E_1') P(E_2' \mid E_1') P(E_3' \mid E_1' \text{ and } E_2')$$

$$= 1 - \left(\frac{8}{12}\right)\left(\frac{7}{11}\right)\left(\frac{6}{10}\right)$$

$$= 1 - \frac{336}{1320} = \frac{984}{1320} = \frac{123}{165} \cong 0.75$$

JOINT PROBABILITY TABLES

5.18. Table 5.3 is a contingency table which presents voter reactions to a new property tax plan according to party affiliation. (*a*) Prepare the joint probability table for these data. (*b*) Determine the marginal probabilities and indicate what they mean.

Table 5.3 Contingency Table for Voter Reactions to a New Property Tax Plan

Party affiliation	Reaction			Total
	In favor	Neutral	Opposed	
Democratic	120	20	20	160
Republican	50	30	60	140
Independent	50	10	40	100
Total	220	60	120	400

(*a*) See Table 5.4.

Table 5.4 Joint Probability Table for Voter Reactions to a New Property Tax Plan

Party affiliation	Reaction			Marginal probability
	In favor (F)	Neutral (N)	Opposed (O)	
Democratic (D)	0.30	0.05	0.05	0.40
Republican (R)	0.125	0.075	0.15	0.35
Independent (I)	0.125	0.025	0.10	0.25
Marginal probability	0.55	0.15	0.30	1.00

(*b*) Each marginal probability value indicates the unconditional probability of the event identified as the column or row heading. For example, if a person is chosen randomly from this group of 400 voters, the probability that he will be in favor of the tax plan is $P(F) = 0.55$. If a voter is chosen randomly, the probability that he is a Republican is $P(R) = 0.35$.

5.19. Referring to Table 5.4, determine the following probabilities: (*a*) $P(O)$, (*b*) $P(R$ and $O)$, (*c*) $P(I)$, (*d*) $P(I$ and $F)$, (*e*) $P(O \mid R)$, (*f*) $P(R \mid O)$, (*g*) $P(R$ or $D)$, (*h*) $P(D$ or $F)$.

(*a*) $P(O) = 0.30$ (the marginal probability)

(*b*) $P(R$ and $O) = 0.15$ (the joint probability in the table)

(*c*) $P(I) = 0.25$ (the marginal probability)

(*d*) $P(I$ and $F) = 0.125$ (the joint probability in the table) (e)　$P(O \mid R) = \dfrac{P(O \text{ and } R)}{P(R)} = \dfrac{0.15}{0.35} = \dfrac{3}{7} \cong 0.43$ (the probability that the voter is opposed to the plan given that he is a Republican)

(f)　$P(R \mid O) = \dfrac{P(R \text{ and } O)}{P(O)} = \dfrac{0.15}{0.30} = 0.50$ (the probability that the voter is a Republican given that he is opposed to the plan)

(g)　$P(R \text{ or } D) = P(R) + P(D) = 0.35 + 0.40 = 0.75$ (the probability that the voter is either a Democrat or a Republican, which are mutually exclusive events)

(h)　$P(D \text{ or } F) = P(D) + P(F) - P(D \text{ and } F) = 0.40 + 0.55 - 0.30 = 0.65$ (the probability that the voter is either a Democrat or in favor of the proposal, which are not mutually exclusive events)

PERMUTATIONS AND COMBINATIONS

5.20. The five individuals constituting the top management of a small manufacturing firm are to be seated together at a banquet table. (a) Determine the number of different seating arrangements that are possible for the five individuals. (b) Suppose that only three of the five officers will be asked to represent the company at the banquet. How many different arrangements at the banquet table are possible, considering that any three of the five individuals may be chosen?

(a)　$_nP_n = n! = (5)(4)(3)(2)(1) = 120$

(b)　$_nP_r = \dfrac{n!}{(n-r)!} = \dfrac{5!}{(5-3)!} = \dfrac{(5)(4)(3)(2)(1)}{(2)(1)} = 60$

5.21. For Problem 5.20(b) suppose we are not concerned about the number of different possible seating arrangements, but rather, about the number of different groupings of three officers (out of the five) which might attend the banquet. How many different groupings are there?

Using formula (5.16),

$$_nC_r = \binom{n}{r} = \frac{n!}{r!(n-r)!} = \frac{5!}{3!(5-3)!} = \frac{(5)(4)(3)(2)(1)}{(3)(2)(1)(2)(1)} = 10$$

5.22. A sales representative must visit six cities during a trip.

(a) If there are 10 cities in the geographic area he is to visit, how many different groupings of six cities are there that he might visit?

(b) Suppose that there are 10 cities in the geographic area he is to visit, and further, that the sequence in which he schedules his visits at the six selected cities is also of concern. How many different sequences are there of six cities chosen from the total of 10 cities?

(c) Suppose that the six cities to be visited have been designated, but that the sequence of visiting the six cities has not been designated. How many sequences are possible for the six designated cities?

(a)　$_nC_r = \binom{n}{r} = \frac{n!}{r!(n-r)!} = \frac{10!}{6!(10-6)!} = \frac{(10)(9)(8)(7)(6)(5)(4)(3)(2)(1)}{(6)(5)(4)(3)(2)(1)(4)(3)(2)(1)} = 210$

(b) $\ _nP_r = \dfrac{n!}{(n-r)!} = \dfrac{10!}{(10-6)!} = \dfrac{(10)(9)(8)(7)(6)(5)(4)(3)(2)(1)}{(4)(3)(2)(1)} = 151{,}200$

(c) $\ _nP_n = n! = 6! = (6)(5)(4)(3)(2)(1) = 720$

5.23. Of the ten cities described in Problem 5.22, suppose that six are in fact "primary" markets for the product in question while the other four are "secondary" markets. If the salesman chooses the six cities to be visited on a random basis, what is the probability that (a) four of them will be primary market cities and two will be secondary market cities, (b) all six will turn out to be primary market cities?

(a) $\ P = \dfrac{\text{No. of combinations which include four and two cities, respectively}}{\text{Total number of different combinations of six cities}}$

$$P = \frac{_6C_4 \times _4C_2}{_{10}C_6} = \frac{\dfrac{6!}{4!\,2!}\,\dfrac{4!}{2!\,2!}}{\dfrac{10!}{6!\,4!}} = \frac{(15)(6)}{210} = \frac{90}{210} = \frac{3}{7} \cong 0.43$$

(b) $\ P = \dfrac{_6C_6 \times _4C_0}{_{10}C_6} = \dfrac{\dfrac{6!}{6!\,0!}\,\dfrac{4!}{0!\,4!}}{\dfrac{10!}{6!\,4!}} = \dfrac{(1)(1)}{210} = \dfrac{1}{210} \cong 0.005$

For this problem, the answer can also be obtained by applying the multiplication rule for dependent events. The probability of selecting a primary market city on the first choice is 6/10. Following this result, the probability on the next choice is 5/9. On this basis, the probability that all six will be primary market cities is

$$P = \left(\frac{6}{10}\right)\left(\frac{5}{9}\right)\left(\frac{4}{8}\right)\left(\frac{3}{7}\right)\left(\frac{2}{6}\right)\left(\frac{1}{5}\right) = \left(\frac{1}{210}\right) \cong 0.0005$$

5.24. In respect to the banquet described in Problem 5.20, determine the probability that the group of three officers chosen from the five will include (a) one particular officer, (b) two particular officers, (c) three particular officers.

(a) $\ P = \dfrac{\text{No. of combinations which include the particular officer}}{\text{Total number of different combinations of three officers}}$

$$P = \frac{_1C_1 \times _4C_2}{_5C_3} = \frac{\dfrac{1!}{1!\,0!}\,\dfrac{4!}{2!\,2!}}{\dfrac{5!}{3!\,2!}} = \frac{(1)(6)}{10} = \frac{6}{10} = 0.60$$

In this case, this probability value is equivalent simply to observing that 3/5 of the officers will be chosen, and thus that the probability that any given individual will be chosen is 3/5, or 0.60.

(b) $\ P = \dfrac{_2C_2 \times _3C_1}{_5C_3} = \dfrac{\dfrac{2!}{2!\,0!}\,\dfrac{3!}{1!\,2!}}{\dfrac{5!}{3!\,2!}} = \dfrac{(1)(3)}{10} = \dfrac{3}{10} = 0.30$

(c) $\quad P = \dfrac{{}_3C_3 \times {}_2C_0}{{}_5C_3} = \dfrac{\dfrac{3!}{3!\,0!}\,\dfrac{2!}{0!\,2!}}{\dfrac{5!}{3!\,2!}} = \dfrac{(1)(1)}{10} = \dfrac{1}{10} = 0.10$

Supplementary Problems

DETERMINING PROBABILITY VALUES

5.25. Determine the probability value for each of the following events.

(a) Probability of randomly selecting one account receivable which is delinquent, given that 5 percent of the accounts are delinquent.

(b) Probability that a land investment will be successful. In the given area, only half of such investments are generally successful, but the particular investor's decision methods have resulted in his having a 30 percent better record than the average investor in the area.

(c) Probability that the sum of the dots showing on the face of two dice which are tossed is seven.

Ans.   (a) 0.05,   (b) 0.65,   (c) 1/6

5.26. For each of the following reported odds ratios determine the equivalent probability value, and for each of the reported probability values determine the equivalent odds ratio.

(a) Probability of $P = 2/3$ that a target delivery date will be met.

(b) Probability of $P = 9/10$ that a new product will exceed the breakeven sales level.

(c) Odds of $1:2$ that a competitor will achieve a technological breakthrough.

(d) Odds of $5:1$ that a new product will be profitable.

Ans.   (a) $2:1$,   (b) $9:1$,   (c) $P = 1/3$,   (d) $P = 5/6$

APPLYING THE RULES OF ADDITION

5.27. During a given week the probability that a particular common stock issue will increase (I) in price, remain unchanged (U), or decline (D) in price is estimated to be $0.30, 0.20$, and 0.50, respectively.

(a) What is the probability that the stock issue will increase in price or remain unchanged?

(b) What is the probability that the price of the issue will change during the week?

Ans.   (a) 0.50,   (b) 0.80

5.28. Of 500 employees, 200 participate in a company's profit-sharing plan (P), 400 have major-medical insurance coverage (M), and 200 employees participate in both programs. Construct a Venn diagram to portray the events designated P and M.

5.29. Refer to the Venn diagram prepared in Problem 5.28. What is the probability that a randomly-selected employee   (a) will be a participant in at least one of the two programs,   (b) will not be a participant in either program?

Ans.   (a) 0.80,   (b) 0.20

5.30. The probability that a new marketing approach will be successful (S) is assessed as being 0.60. The probability that the expenditure for developing the approach can be kept within the original budget (B) is 0.50. The probability that both of these objectives will be achieved is estimated at 0.30. What is the probability that at least one of these objectives will be achieved?

Ans.   0.80

INDEPENDENT EVENTS, DEPENDENT EVENTS, AND CONDITIONAL PROBABILITY

5.31. For the situation described in Problem 5.28,   (a) determine the probability that an employee will be a participant in the profit-sharing plan (P) given that he has major-medical insurance coverage (M), and   (b) determine if the two events are independent or dependent by reference to the conditional probability value.

Ans.   (a) 0.50,   (b) dependent

5.32. For Problem 5.30, determine   (a) the probability that the new marketing approach will be successful (S) given that the development cost was kept within the original budget (B), and   (b) if the two events are independent or dependent by reference to the conditional probability value.

Ans.   (a) 0.60,   (b) independent

5.33. The probability that automobile sales will increase next month (A) is estimated to be 0.40.   The probability that the sale of replacement parts will increase (R) is estimated to be 0.50.   The probability that both industries will experience an increase in sales is estimated to be 0.10.   What is the probability that   (a) automobile sales have increased during the month given that there is information that replacement parts sales have increased,   (b) replacement parts sales have increased given information that automobile sales have increased during the month?

Ans.   (a) 0.20,   (b) 0.25

5.34. For Problem 5.33, determine if the two events are independent or dependent by reference to one of the conditional probability values.

Ans.   Dependent

APPLYING THE RULES OF MULTIPLICATION

5.35. During a particular period, 80 percent of the common stock issues in an industry which includes just 10 companies have increased in market value.   If an investor chose two of these issues randomly, what is the probability that both issues increased in market value during this period?

Ans.   56/90 ≅ 0.62

5.36. The overall proportion of defective items in a continuous production process is 0.10.   What is the probability that   (a) two randomly chosen items will both be nondefective (D'),   (b) two randomly chosen items will both be defective (D),   (c) at least one of two randomly chosen items will be nondefective (D')?

Ans.   (a) 0.81,   (b) 0.01,   (c) 0.99

5.37. Test the independence of the two events described in Problem 5.28 by using the rule of multiplication for independent events.   Compare your answer with the result of the test in Problem 5.31(b).

Ans.   Dependent

5.38. Test the independence of the two events described in Problem 5.30 by using the rule of multiplication for independent events.   Compare your answer with the result of the test in Problem 5.32(b).

Ans.   Independent

5.39. From Problem 5.35, suppose an investor chose three of these stock issues randomly.   Construct a tree diagram to portray the various possible results for the sequence of three stock issues.

5.40. Referring to the tree diagram prepared in Problem 5.39, determine the probability that   (a) only one of the three issues increased in market value,   (b) two issues increased in market value,   (c) at least two issues increased in market value.

   Ans.   (a) $48/720 \cong 0.07$,   (b) $336/720 \cong 0.47$,   (c) $672/720 \cong 0.93$

5.41. Referring to Problem 5.36, suppose a sample of four items is chosen randomly.   Construct a tree diagram to portray the various possible results in terms of individual items being defective (D) or nondefective (D').

5.42. Referring to the tree diagram prepared in Problem 5.41, determine the probability that   (a) none of the four items is defective,   (b) exactly one item is defective,   (c) one or fewer items are defective.

   Ans.   (a) $0.6561 \cong 0.66$,   (b) $0.2916 \cong 0.29$,   (c) $0.9477 \cong 0.95$

JOINT PROBABILITY TABLES

5.43. Table 5.5 is a contingency table which presents a classification of 150 sampled companies according to four industry groups and according to whether return on equity is above or below the average return in this sample of 150 firms.   Prepare the joint probability table based on these sample data.

Table 5.5   Contingency Table for Return on Equity According to Industry Group

Industry category	Return on equity		Total
	Above average (A)	Below average (B)	
I	20	40	60
II	10	10	20
III	20	10	30
IV	25	15	40
Total	75	75	150

5.44. Referring to the joint probability table prepared in Problem 5.43, indicate the following probabilities: (a) $P(\text{I})$,   (b) $P(\text{II})$,   (c) $P(\text{III})$,   (d) $P(\text{IV})$.

   Ans.   (a) 0.40,   (b) 0.13,   (c) 0.20,   (d) 0.27

5.45. Referring to the joint probability table prepared in Problem 5.43, determine the following probabilities: (a) $P(\text{I and } A)$,   (b) $P(\text{II or } B)$,   (c) $P(A)$,   (d) $P(\text{I or II})$,   (e) $P(\text{I and II})$, (f) $P(A \text{ or } B)$,   (g) $P(A \,|\, \text{I})$,   (h) $P(\text{III} \,|\, A)$.

   Ans.   (a) 0.13,   (b) 0.57,   (c) 0.50,   (d) 0.53,   (e) 0,   (f) 1.0,   (g) 0.33,   (h) 0.27

PERMUTATIONS AND COMBINATIONS

5.46. Suppose there are eight different management trainee positions to be assigned to eight employees in a company's junior management training program.   In how many different ways can the eight individuals be assigned to the eight different positions?

   Ans.   40,320

5.47. Referring to the situation described in Problem 5.46, suppose only six different positions are available for the eight qualified individuals.   In how many different ways can six individuals from the eight be assigned to the six different positions?

   Ans.   20,160

5.48. Referring to the situation described in Problem 5.47, suppose that the six available positions can all be considered comparable, and not really different for practical purposes.   In how many ways can the six individuals be chosen from the eight qualified people to fill the six positions?

   Ans.   28

5.49. A project group of two engineers and three technicians is to be assigned from a departmental group which includes five engineers and nine technicians.   How many different project groups can be assigned from the fourteen available personnel?

   Ans.   840

5.50. For the personnel assignment situation described in Problem 5.49, suppose the five individuals are assigned randomly from the fourteen personnel in the department, without reference to whether each person is an engineer or a technician.   What is the probability that the project group will include   (*a*) exactly two engineers,   (*b*) no engineers,   (*c*) no technicians?

   Ans.   (*a*) $P \cong 0.42$,   (*b*) $P \cong 0.06$,   (*c*) $P \cong 0.0005$

Chapter 6

Discrete Probability Distributions: Binomial, Hypergeometric, and Poisson

6.1 PROBABILITY DISTRIBUTIONS

When probability values are assigned to all possible values of a random variable X, either by a listing or by a mathematical function, the result is a *probability distribution*. A *random variable* is one whose value is determined by chance processes that are not under the control of the observer. The sum of the probabilities of all possible outcomes must equal 1. In the context of probability distributions, individual probability values may be denoted by the symbol $f(x)$, which recognizes that a mathematical function is involved, by $P(x = X)$, which recognizes that the random variable can have various values, or simply by $P(X)$.

For a *discrete random variable* all possible values of the random variable can be listed in a table with accompanying probabilities. The specific discrete probability models described in this chapter are the binomial, hypergeometric, and Poisson probability distributions. For a *continuous random variable* all possible fractional values of the variable cannot be listed, and so the probabilities which are determined by a mathematical function are typically portrayed by a density function, or probability curve. Several specific continuous probability distributions are described in Chapter 7. See Section 1.4 for a discussion of the difference between discrete and continuous variables.

EXAMPLE 1. The number of station wagons that have been requested for rental at a car rental agency during a 50-day period is identified in Table 6.1. The observed frequencies have been converted into probabilities for this 50-day period in the last column of the table. Thus, we can observe that the probability of exactly seven station wagons being requested on a randomly chosen day in this period is 0.20, and the probability of six or more being requested is 0.56.

Table 6.1 Daily Demand for Rental of Station Wagons during a 50-Day Period

Possible demand X	Number of days	Probability $P(X)$
3	3	0.06
4	7	0.14
5	12	0.24
6	14	0.28
7	10	0.20
8	4	0.08
	50	1.00

6.2 THE EXPECTED VALUE AND VARIANCE OF DISCRETE RANDOM VARIABLES

Just as for collections of sample and population data, it is often useful to describe a probability distribution in terms of its *mean* (see Section 3.2) and *variance* (see Section 4.6). The mean is called the *expected value* of the probability distribution. The expected value of a discrete random variable X is denoted by $E(X)$; it is the weighted average of all possible values of the variable with the respective probabilities used as weights. Because the sum of the weights (probabilities) is always equal to 1, formula (*3.5*) for the weighted mean can be simplified. The expected value of a discrete probability distribution is

$$E(X) = \sum X P(X) \tag{6.1}$$

EXAMPLE 2. Based on the data in Table 6.1, the calculation of the expected value for the probability distribution is presented in Table 6.2. The expected value is 5.66 station wagons. Note that the expected value for discrete data can be a fractional value, because it represents the long-run average value, not the specific value for any given observation.

Table 6.2   Expected Value Calculation for Station Wagon Demand

Possible demand X	Probability $P(X)$	Weighted value $XP(X)$
3	0.06	0.18
4	0.14	0.56
5	0.24	1.20
6	0.28	1.68
7	0.20	1.40
8	0.08	0.64
	1.00	$E(X) = 5.66$

The variance of a random variable X is denoted by $\text{Var}(X)$; it is computed in respect to $E(X)$ as the mean of the probability distribution. The general deviations form of the formula for the variance of a discrete probability distribution is

$$\text{Var}(X) = \sum [X - E(X)]^2 P(X) \tag{6.2}$$

The computational form of the formula for the variance of a discrete probability distribution, which does not require the determination of deviations from the mean, is

$$\text{Var}(X) = \sum X^2 P(X) - \left[\sum XP(X) \right]^2$$

$$= E(X^2) - [E(X)]^2 \tag{6.3}$$

EXAMPLE 3. The worksheet for the calculation of the variance for the probability distribution of demand for station wagon rentals is presented in Table 6.3, using the computational version of the formula. As indicated below, the variance has a value of 1.74.

$$\text{Var}(X) = E(X^2) - [E(X)]^2 = 33.78 - (5.66)^2 = 33.78 - 32.04 = 1.74$$

Table 6.3 Worksheet for the Calculation of the Variance for Station Wagon Demand

Possible demand X	Probability P(X)	Weighted value XP(X)	Squared demand X^2	Weighted square $X^2P(X)$
3	0.06	0.18	9	0.54
4	0.14	0.56	16	2.24
5	0.24	1.20	25	6.00
6	0.28	1.68	36	10.08
7	0.20	1.40	49	9.80
8	0.08	0.64	64	5.12
		$E(X) = 5.66$		$E(X^2) = 33.78$

6.3 THE BINOMIAL DISTRIBUTION

The binomial distribution is a discrete probability distribution which is applicable whenever a sampling process can be assumed to conform to a Bernoulli process. A *Bernoulli process* is a sampling process in which:

(1) There are two mutually exclusive possible outcomes on each trial, or observation. For convenience these are called *success* and *failure*.

(2) The series of trials, or observations, constitute independent events.

(3) The probability of success, denoted by p, remains constant from trial to trial. That is, the process is stationary.

The binomial distribution can be used to determine the probability of obtaining a designated number of successes in a Bernoulli process. Three values are required: the designated number of successes (X); the number of trials, or observations, (n); and the probability of success in each trial (p). The formula for determining the probability of a designated number of successes X in a binomial distribution is

$$P(X) = {}_nC_X p^X(1-p)^{n-X} = \binom{n}{X}p^X(1-p)^{n-X}$$

$$= \frac{n!}{X!(n-X)!}p^X(1-p)^{n-X} \qquad (6.4)$$

EXAMPLE 4. The probability that a randomly chosen sales prospect will make a purchase is 0.20. If a salesman calls on six prospects, the probability that he will make exactly four sales is determined as follows:

$$P(X = 4) = {}_6C_4(0.20)^4(0.80)^2 = \frac{6!}{4!\,2!}(0.20)^4(0.80)^2$$

$$= \frac{6 \times 5 \times 4 \times 3 \times 2}{(4 \times 3 \times 2)(2)}(0.0016)(0.64) = 0.01536 \cong 0.015$$

Generally, there is an interest in the cumulative probability of "X or more" successes or "X or fewer" successes occurring in n trials. In such a case, the probability of each outcome included within the designated interval must be determined, and then these probabilities are summed.

EXAMPLE 5. For Example 4, the probability that the salesman will make four or more sales is determined as follows:

$$P(X \geq 4) = P(X = 4) + P(X = 5) + P(X = 6)$$
$$= 0.01536 + 0.001536 + 0.000064 = 0.016960 \cong 0.017$$

where $P(X = 4) = 0.01536$ (from Example 4)

$$P(X = 5) = {}_6C_5(0.20)^5(0.80)^1 = \frac{6!}{5!\,1!}(0.20)^5(0.80) = 6(0.00032)(0.80) = 0.001536$$

$$P(X = 6) = {}_6C_6(0.20)^6(0.80)^0 = \frac{6!}{6!\,0!}(0.000064)(1) = (1)(0.000064) = 0.000064$$

(*Note:* Recall that any value raised to the zero power is equal to 1.)

Because use of the binomial formula involves considerable arithmetic when the sample is relatively large, and particularly when we wish to determine the probability that the outcome will occur within a range of values, tables of binomial probabilities are often used. See Appendix 1, which identifies the probability of each designated number of successes.

EXAMPLE 6. If the probability that a randomly chosen sales prospect will make a purchase is 0.20, the probability that a salesman who calls on 15 prospects will make fewer than three sales is

$$P(X < 3) = P(X \leq 2) = P(X = 0) + P(X = 1) + P(X = 2)$$
$$= 0.0352 + 0.1319 + 0.2309 \text{ (from Appendix 1)}$$
$$= 0.3980 \cong 0.40$$

The values of p referenced in Appendix 1 do not exceed $p = 0.50$. If the value of p in a particular application exceeds 0.50, the problem has to be transformed so that the event is defined in terms of the number of "failures" rather than the number of successes (see Problem 6.9).

The expected value (mean) and variance for a given binomial distribution could be determined by listing the probability distribution in a table and applying the formulas presented in Section 6.2. However, the expected number of successes can be computed directly:

$$E(X) = np \tag{6.5}$$

The variance of the number of successes can also be computed directly:

$$\text{Var}(X) = np(1 - p) \tag{6.6}$$

EXAMPLE 7. For Example 6, the expected number of sales (as a long-run average) and the variance associated with making calls on 15 prospects are

$$E(X) = np = 15(0.20) = 3.0 \text{ sales}$$
$$\text{Var}(X) = np(1 - p) = 15(0.20)(0.80) = 2.4$$

6.4 THE BINOMIAL DISTRIBUTION EXPRESSED BY PROPORTIONS

Instead of expressing the random binomial variable as the number of successes X, we can designate it in terms of the *proportion* of successes, $\bar{p}$, which is the ratio of the number of successes to the number of trials:

$$\bar{p} = \frac{X}{n} \tag{6.7}$$

In such cases, formula (6.4) is modified only in respect to defining the proportion. Thus, the probability of observing exactly $\bar{p}$ proportion of successes in n Bernoulli trials is

$$P\left(\bar{p} = \frac{X}{n}\right) = {}_nC_X p^X (1 - p)^{n-X} \tag{6.8}$$

or

$$P\left(\bar{p} = \frac{X}{n}\right) = {}_nC_X \pi^X (1 - \pi)^{n-X} \tag{6.9}$$

In formula (6.9), π (Greek "pī") is the equivalent of p except that it specifically indicates that the probability of success in an individual trial is a population parameter.

EXAMPLE 8. The probability that a randomly selected salaried employee is a participant in a company-sponsored stock investment program is 0.40. If five salaried employees are chosen randomly, the probability that the proportion of participants is exactly 0.60 is

$$P\left(\bar{p} = 0.60 = \frac{3}{5}\right) = {}_5C_3 (0.40)^3 (0.60)^2 = \frac{5!}{3!\,2!}(0.064)(0.36) = 0.2304 \cong 0.23$$

When the binomial variable is expressed as a proportion, the distribution is still discrete and not continuous. Only the proportions for which the number of successes X is a whole number can occur. For instance, in Example 8 it is not possible for there to be a proportion of 0.50 participants out of a sample of five. The use of the binomial table in respect to proportions simply requires converting the designated proportion $\bar{p}$ to number of successes X.

EXAMPLE 9. The probability that a randomly selected employee is a participant in a company-sponsored stock investment program is 0.40. If 10 employees are chosen randomly, the probability that the proportion of participants is at least 0.70 is

$$P(\bar{p} \geq 0.70) = P(X \geq 7) = P(X = 7) + P(X = 8) + P(X = 9) + P(X = 10)$$
$$= 0.0425 + 0.0106 + 0.0016 + 0.0001 = 0.0548$$

The expected value for a binomial probability distribution expressed by proportions is equal to the population proportion, which may be designated by either p or π:

$$E(\bar{p}) = p \tag{6.10}$$

or

$$E(\bar{p}) = \pi \tag{6.11}$$

The variance of the proportion of successes for a binomial probability distribution is

$$\text{Var}(\bar{p}) = \frac{p(1 - p)}{n} \tag{6.12}$$

or

$$\text{Var}(\bar{p}) = \frac{\pi(1 - \pi)}{n} \tag{6.13}$$

6.5 THE HYPERGEOMETRIC DISTRIBUTION

When sampling is done *without replacement* of each sampled item taken from a finite population of items, the Bernoulli process does not apply because there is a systematic change in the probability of success as items are removed from the population. When sampling without replacement is used in a situation which would otherwise qualify as a Bernoulli process, the hypergeometric distribution is the appropriate discrete probability distribution.

Given that X is the designated number of successes, N is the total number of items in the population, X_T is the total number of "successes" included in the population, and n is the number of items in the sample, the formula for determining hypergeometric probabilities is

$$P(X \mid N, X_T, n) = \frac{\binom{N - X_T}{n - X}\binom{X_T}{X}}{\binom{N}{n}} \qquad (6.14)$$

EXAMPLE 10. Of six employees, three have been with the company five or more years. If four employees are chosen randomly from the group of six, the probability that exactly two will have five or more years seniority is

$$P(X = 2 \mid N = 6, X_T = 3, n = 4) = \frac{\binom{6 - 3}{4 - 2}\binom{3}{2}}{\binom{6}{4}} = \frac{\binom{3}{2}\binom{3}{2}}{\binom{6}{4}} = \frac{\frac{3!}{2!\,1!}\frac{3!}{2!\,1!}}{\frac{6!}{4!\,2!}} = \frac{(3)(3)}{15} = 0.60$$

Note that in Example 10, the required probability value is computed by determining the number of different combinations which would include two high-seniority and two low-seniority employees as a ratio of the total number of combinations of four employees taken from the six. Thus, the hypergeometric formula is a direct application of the rules of combinatorial analysis described in Section 5.9.

When the population is large and the sample is relatively small, the fact that sampling is done without replacement has little effect on the probability of success in each trial. A convenient rule of thumb is that a binomial distribution can be used as an approximation of a hypergeometric probability value when $n < 0.05N$. That is, the sample size should be less than 5 percent of the population size. Different texts use somewhat different rules for determining when such approximation is appropriate.

6.6 THE POISSON DISTRIBUTION

The *Poisson distribution* can be used to determine the probability of a designated number of successes when the events occur in a continuum of time or space. Such a process is called a *Poisson process*; it is similar to the Bernoulli process (see Section 6.3) except that the events occur over a continuum rather than occurring on fixed trials or observations. An example of such a process is the arrival of incoming calls at a telephone switchboard. As was the case for the Bernoulli process, it is assumed that the events are independent and that the process is stationary.

Only one value is required to determine the probability of a designated number of successes in a Poisson process: the average number of successes for the specific time or space dimension of interest. This average number is generally represented by λ (Greek "lambda") or μ. The formula for determining the probability of a designated number of successes X in a Poisson distribution is

$$P(X \mid \lambda) = \frac{\lambda^X e^{-\lambda}}{X!} \qquad (6.15)$$

Here e is the constant 2.7183 used in connection with natural logarithms, and the values of $e^{-\lambda}$ may be obtained from Appendix 2.

EXAMPLE 11. An average of five calls for service per hour are received by a machine repair department. The probability that exactly three calls for service will be received in a randomly selected hour is

$$P(X = 3 \mid \lambda = 5.0) = \frac{(5)^3 e^{-5}}{3!} = \frac{(125)(0.00674)}{6} = 0.1404$$

Alternatively, a table of Poisson probabilities may be used. Appendix 3 identifies the probability of each designated number of successes for various values of λ.

EXAMPLE 12. We can determine the answer to Example 11 by use of Appendix 3 for Poisson probabilities as follows:

$$P(X = 3 \mid \lambda = 5.0) = 0.1404$$

When there is an interest in the probability of "X or more" or "X or fewer" successes, the rule of addition for mutually exclusive events is applied.

EXAMPLE 13. If an average of five service calls per hour is received at a machine repair department, the probability that *fewer than* three calls will be received during a randomly chosen hour is determined as follows:

$$P(X < 3 \mid \lambda = 5.0) = P(X \le 2) = P(X = 0) + P(X = 1) + P(X = 2)$$
$$= 0.0067 + 0.0337 + 0.0842 = 0.1246$$

where $P(X = 0 \mid \lambda = 5.0) = 0.0067$ (from Appendix 3)

$P(X = 1 \mid \lambda = 5.0) = 0.0337$

$P(X = 2 \mid \lambda = 5.0) = 0.0842$

Because a Poisson process is assumed to be stationary, it follows that the mean of the process is always proportional to the length of the time or space continuum. Therefore, if the mean is available for one interval size, the mean for any other required interval size can be determined. *This is important, because the value of λ which is used must apply to the interval of interest.*

EXAMPLE 14. On the average, 12 people per hour ask questions of a decorating consultant in a fabric store. The probability that three or more people will approach the consultant with questions during a 10-min period is determined as follows:

$$\text{Average per hour} = 12$$

$$\lambda = \text{average per 10 min} = \frac{12}{6} = 2.0$$

$$P(X \ge 3 \mid \lambda = 2.0) = P(X = 3 \mid \lambda = 2.0) + P(X = 4 \mid \lambda = 2.0) + P(X = 5 \mid \lambda = 2.0) + \cdots$$
$$= 0.1804 + 0.0902 + 0.0361 + 0.0120 + 0.0034 + 0.0009 + 0.0002 = 0.3232$$

where $P(X = 3 \mid \lambda = 2.0) = 0.1804$ (from Appendix 3) $P(X = 7 \mid \lambda = 2.0) = 0.0034$

$P(X = 4 \mid \lambda = 2.0) = 0.0902$ $P(X = 8 \mid \lambda = 2.0) = 0.0009$

$P(X = 5 \mid \lambda = 2.0) = 0.0361$ $P(X = 9 \mid \lambda = 2.0) = 0.0002$

$P(X = 6 \mid \lambda = 2.0) = 0.0120$

The expected value for a Poisson probability distribution is equal to the mean of the distribution:

$$E(X) = \lambda \qquad\qquad (6.16)$$

The variance of the number of events for a Poisson probability distribution is also equal to the mean of the distribution:

$$\text{Var}(X) = \lambda \qquad\qquad (6.17)$$

6.7 POISSON APPROXIMATION OF BINOMIAL PROBABILITIES

When the number of observations or trials n in a Bernoulli process is large, computations are quite tedious. Further, tabled probabilities for very small values of p are not generally available. Fortunately, the Poisson distribution is suitable as an approximation of binomial probabilities when n is large and p or $(1 - p)$ is small. A convenient rule of thumb is that such approximation can be made when $n \geq 30$, and $np < 5$ or $n(1 - p) < 5$. Different texts use somewhat different rules for determining when such approximation is appropriate.

The mean of the Poisson probability distribution which is used to approximate binomial probabilities is

$$\lambda = np \qquad (6.18)$$

EXAMPLE 15. For a large shipment of transistors from a supplier, 1 percent of the items is known to be defective. If a sample of 30 transistors is randomly selected, the probability that two or more transistors will be defective can be determined by use of the binomial probabilities in Appendix 1:

$$P(X \geq 2 \mid n = 30, p = 0.01) = P(X = 2) + P(X = 3) + \cdots = (0.0328) + (0.0031) + (0.0002) = 0.0361$$

The Poisson approximation of the above probability value is

$$P(X \geq 2 \mid \lambda = 0.3) = P(X = 2) + P(X = 3) + \cdots = (0.0333) + (0.0033) + (0.0002) = 0.0368$$

Thus, the difference between the Poisson approximation and the actual binomial probability value is 0.0007.

When n is large but neither np nor $n(1 - p)$ is less than 5.0, binomial probabilities can be approximated by use of the normal probability distribution (see Section 7.3).

Solved Problems

DISCRETE RANDOM VARIABLES

6.1. The number of trucks arriving hourly at a warehouse facility has been found to follow the probability distribution in Table 6.4. Calculate (a) the expected number of arrivals X per hour and (b) the variance of this probability distribution.

Table 6.4   Hourly Arrival of Trucks at a Warehouse

Number of trucks X	0	1	2	3	4	5	6
Probability $P(X)$	0.05	0.10	0.15	0.25	0.30	0.10	0.05

From Table 6.5,

(a) $E(X) = 3.15$

(b) $\text{Var}(X) = E(X^2) - [E(X)]^2 = 12.05 - (3.15)^2 = 12.05 - 9.9225 = 2.1275 \cong 2.13$

Table 6.5 Worksheet for the Calculation of the Expected Value and the Variance for Truck Arrivals

Number of trucks X	Probability $P(X)$	Weighted value $XP(X)$	Squared number X^2	Weighted square $X^2P(X)$
0	0.05	0	0	0
1	0.10	0.10	1	0.10
2	0.15	0.30	4	0.60
3	0.25	0.75	9	2.25
4	0.30	1.20	16	4.80
5	0.10	0.50	25	2.50
6	0.05	0.30	36	1.80
		$E(X) = 3.15$		$E(X^2) = 12.05$

6.2. Table 6.6 identifies the probability that a computer system will be "down" the indicated number of periods per day during the initial installation phase for the system. Calculate (a) the expected number of times per day that the computer is inoperative and (b) the variance of this probability distribution.

Table 6.6 Number of Inoperative Periods per Day for a New Computer System

Number of periods X	4	5	6	7	8	9
Probability $P(X)$	0.01	0.08	0.29	0.42	0.14	0.06

Using Table 6.7,

(a) $E(X) = 6.78$

(b) $\text{Var}(X) = E(X^2) - [E(X)]^2 = 47.00 - (6.78)^2 = 47.00 - 45.9684 \cong 1.03$

Table 6.7 Worksheet for the Calculation of the Expected Value and the Variance of Computer Malfunction

Number of periods X	Probability $P(X)$	Weighted value $XP(X)$	Squared number X^2	Weighted square $X^2P(X)$
4	0.01	0.04	16	0.16
5	0.08	0.40	25	2.00
6	0.29	1.74	36	10.44
7	0.42	2.94	49	20.58
8	0.14	1.12	64	8.96
9	0.06	0.54	81	4.86
	1.00	$E(X) = 6.78$		$E(X^2) = 47.00$

6.3. Table 6.8 lists the possible outcomes associated with the toss of two six-sided dice and the probability associated with each outcome. These probabilities were determined by use of the rules of addition and multiplication discussed in Sections 5.4 and 5.6. For example, a "3" can be obtained by a combination of a "1" and "2", or a combination of a "2" and "1". Each sequence has a probability of occurrence of $(1/6) \times (1/6) = 1/36$, and since the two sequences are mutually exclusive, $P(X = 3) = 1/36 + 1/36 = 2/36$. Determine (a) the expected number on the throw of two dice and (b) the standard deviation of this distribution.

Table 6.8 Possible Outcomes on the Toss of Two Dice

Number on two dice X	2	3	4	5	6	7	8	9	10	11	12
Probability $P(X)$	$\frac{1}{36}$	$\frac{2}{36}$	$\frac{3}{36}$	$\frac{4}{36}$	$\frac{5}{36}$	$\frac{6}{36}$	$\frac{5}{36}$	$\frac{4}{36}$	$\frac{3}{36}$	$\frac{2}{36}$	$\frac{1}{36}$

From Table 6.9,

(a) $E(X) = 7$

(b) $\text{Var}(X) = E(X^2) - [E(X)]^2 = 54.83 - (7)^2 = 54.83 - 49 = 5.83$

$\sigma = \sqrt{\text{Var}(X)} = \sqrt{5.83} \cong 2.41$

Table 6.9 Worksheet for the Calculation of the Expected Value and the Variance Associated with the Toss of Two Dice

Number X	Probability $P(X)$	Weighted value $XP(X)$	Squared number X^2	Weighted square $X^2P(X)$
2	1/36	2/36	4	4/36
3	2/36	6/36	9	18/36
4	3/36	12/36	16	48/36
5	4/36	20/36	25	100/36
6	5/36	30/36	36	180/36
7	6/36	42/36	49	294/36
8	5/36	40/36	64	320/36
9	4/36	36/36	81	324/36
10	3/36	30/36	100	300/36
11	2/36	22/36	121	242/36
12	1/36	12/36	144	144/36
	36/36	$E(X) = 252/36 = 7.0$		$E(X^2) = 1974/36 \cong 54.83$

THE BINOMIAL DISTRIBUTION

6.4. Because of high interest rates, a firm reports that 30 percent of its accounts receivable from other business firms are overdue. If an accountant takes a random sample of five such accounts, determine the probability of each of the following events by use of the formula for binomial probabilities: (a) none of the accounts is overdue, (b) exactly two accounts are overdue, (c) most of the accounts are overdue, (d) exactly 20 percent of the accounts are overdue.

(a) $P(X = 0) = {}_5C_0(0.30)^0(0.70)^5 = \dfrac{5!}{0!\,5!}(0.30)^0(0.70)^5 = (1)(1)(0.16807) = 0.16807$

(b) $P(X = 2) = {}_5C_2(0.30)^2(0.70)^3 = \dfrac{5!}{2!\,3!}(0.30)^2(0.70)^3 = (10)(0.09)(0.343) = 0.3087$

(c) $P(X \geq 3) = P(X = 3) + P(X = 4) + P(X = 5) = 0.1323 + 0.02835 + 0.00243 = 0.16308$

where $P(X = 3) = \dfrac{5!}{3!\,2!}(0.30)^3(0.70)^2 = (10)(0.027)(0.49) = 0.1323$

$P(X = 4) = \dfrac{5!}{4!\,1!}(0.30)^4(0.70)^1 = (5)(0.0081)(0.70) = 0.02835$

$P(X = 5) = \dfrac{5!}{5!\,0!}(0.30)^5(0.70)^0 = (1)(0.00243)(1) = 0.00243$

(d) $P\!\left(\dfrac{X}{n} = 0.20\right) = P(X = 1) = {}_5C_1(0.30)^1(0.70)^4 = \dfrac{5!}{1!\,4!}(0.30)^1(0.70)^4$

$= (5)(0.30)(0.2401) = 0.36015$

6.5.   A mail-order firm has a circular which elicits a 10 percent response rate. Suppose 20 of the circulars are mailed as a market test in a new geographic area. Assuming that the 10 percent response rate is applicable in the new area, determine the probabilities of the following events by use of Appendix 1: (a) no one responds, (b) exactly two people respond, (c) a majority of the people respond, (d) less than 20 percent of the people respond.

(a) $P(X = 0 \mid n = 20, p = 0.10) = 0.1216$

(b) $P(X = 2 \mid n = 20, p = 0.10) = 0.2852$

(c) $P(X \geq 11 \mid n = 20, p = 0.10) = P(X = 11) + P(X = 12) + \cdots = 0.0000 \cong 0$

(d) $P\!\left(\dfrac{X}{n} < 0.20 \mid n = 20, p = 0.10\right) = P(X \leq 3 \mid n = 20, p = 0.10)$

$= P(X = 0) + P(X = 1) + P(X = 2) + P(X = 3)$

$= 0.1216 + 0.2702 + 0.2852 + 0.1901 = 0.8671$

6.6.   The binomial formula can be viewed as being comprised of two parts: a combinations formula to determine the number of different ways in which the designated event can occur and the rule of multiplication to determine the probability of each sequence. Suppose that three items are selected randomly from a process known to produce 10 percent defectives. Construct a three-step tree diagram portraying the selection of the three items and using D for a defective item being selected and D' for a nondefective item being selected. Also, enter the appropriate probability values in the diagram and use the multiplication rule for independent events to determine the probability of each possible sequence of three events occurring.

See Fig. 6-1.

First item	Second item	Third item	Probability of each sequence

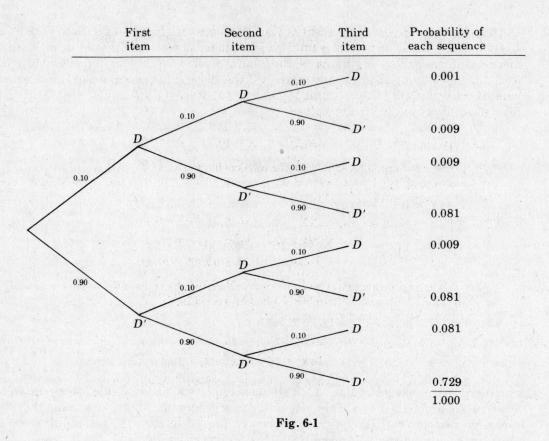

Fig. 6-1

6.7. From Problem 6.6, determine the probability that exactly one of the three sampled items is defective, referring to Fig. 6-1 and using the addition rule for mutually exclusive events.

Beginning from the top of the tree diagram, the fourth, sixth, and seventh sequences include exactly one defective item. Thus,

$$P(X = 1) = (D \text{ and } D' \text{ and } D') + (D' \text{ and } D \text{ and } D') + (D' \text{ and } D' \text{ and } D)$$
$$= 0.081 + 0.081 + 0.081 = 0.243$$

6.8. From Problems 6.6 and 6.7, determine the probability of obtaining exactly one defective item by use of the binomial formula, and note the correspondence between the values in the formula and the values obtained from the tree diagram.

Using formula (6.4),

$$P(X = 1) = {}_3C_1(0.10)^1(0.90)^2 = \frac{3!}{1!\,2!}(0.10)(0.81)$$

$$= 3(0.081) = 0.243$$

Thus, the first part of the binomial formula indicates the number of different groups of positions which can include the designated number of successes (in this case there are three ways in which one defective item can be included in the group of three items). The second part of the formula represents the rule of multiplication for the specified independent events.

6.9. During a particular year, 70 percent of the common stocks listed on the New York Stock Exchange increased in market value while 30 percent were unchanged or declined in market value. At the beginning of the year a stock advisory service chose 10 stock issues as being "specially recommended." If the 10 issues represent a random selection, what is the probability that (a) all 10 issues, (b) at least eight issues, (c) fewer than four issues increase in market value?

(a) $P(X = 10 \mid n = 10, p = 0.70) = P(X' = 0 \mid n = 10, (1 - p) = 0.30) = 0.0282$

    (*Note:* When p is greater than 0.50, the problem has to be transformed and stated in terms of X' (read "not X") and it follows that $X' = n - X$. Thus, "all 10 increase" is the same event as "none decrease.")

(b) $P(X \geq 8 \mid n = 10, p = 0.70) = P(X' \leq 2 \mid n = 10, (1 - p) = 0.30)$

$$= P(X' = 0) + P(X' = 1) + P(X' = 2)$$

$$= 0.0282 + 0.1211 + 0.2335 = 0.3828$$

    (*Note:* When an inequality is involved in transforming the probability statement into terms of X' from X, the inequality symbol is simply reversed in the process of transformation, and $X' = n - X$, as for the equality situation.)

(c) $P(X < 4 \mid n = 10, p = 0.70) = P(X' > 6 \mid n = 10, (1 - p) = 0.30)$

$$= P(X' = 7) + P(X' = 8) + P(X' = 9) + P(X' = 10)$$

$$= 0.0090 + 0.0014 + 0.0001 + 0.0000 = 0.0105$$

6.10. Using Appendix 1, determine:

(a) $P(X = 5 \mid n = 9, p = 0.50)$

(b) $P(X = 7 \mid n = 15, p = 0.60)$

(c) $P(X \leq 3 \mid n = 20, p = 0.05)$

(d) $P(X \geq 18 \mid n = 20, p = 0.90)$

(e) $P(X > 8 \mid n = 10, p = 0.70)$

(a) $P(X = 5 \mid n = 9, p = 0.50) = 0.2461$

(b) $P(X = 7 \mid n = 15, p = 0.60) = P(X' = 8 \mid n = 15, (1 - p) = 0.40) = 0.1181$

(c) $P(X \leq 3 \mid n = 20, p = 0.05) = P(X = 0) + P(X = 1) + P(X = 2) + P(X = 3)$

$$= 0.3585 + 0.3774 + 0.1887 + 0.0596 = 0.9842$$

(d) $P(X \geq 18 \mid n = 20, p = 0.90) = P(X' \leq 2 \mid n = 20, (1 - p) = 0.10)$

$$= P(X' = 0) + P(X' = 1) + P(X' = 2)$$

$$= 0.1216 + 0.2702 + 0.2852 = 0.6770$$

(e) $P(X > 8 \mid n = 10, p = 0.70) = P(X' < 2 \mid n = 10, (1 - p) = 0.30)$

$$= P(X' = 0) + P(X' = 1) = 0.0282 + 0.1211 = 0.1493$$

6.11. If a fair coin is tossed five times, the probability distribution in respect to the number of heads observed is based on the binomial distribution with $n = 5$ and $p = 0.50$ (see Table

6.10). Determine (a) the expected number of heads and (b) the variance of the probability distribution by use of the general formulas for discrete random variables.

Table 6.10 Binomial Probability Distribution of the Number of Heads Occurring in Five Tosses of a Fair Coin

Number of heads X	0	1	2	3	4	5
Probability $P(X)$	0.031	0.156	0.313	0.313	0.156	0.031

(a) $E(X) = 2.5$

(b) $\text{Var}(X) = E(X^2) - [E(X)]^2 = 7.496 - (2.5)^2 = 7.496 - 6.25 = 1.246 \cong 1.25$

Table 6.11 Worksheet for the Calculation of the Expected Value and the Variance for Problem 6.11

Number of heads X	Probability $P(X)$	Weighted value $XP(X)$	Squared number X^2	Weighted square $X^2P(X)$
0	0.031	0	0	0
1	0.156	0.156	1	0.156
2	0.313	0.626	4	1.252
3	0.313	0.939	9	2.817
4	0.156	0.624	16	2.496
5	0.031	0.155	25	0.775
		$E(X) = 2.500$		$E(X^2) = 7.496$

6.12. Referring to Problem 6.11, determine (a) the expected number of heads and (b) the variance of the probability distribution by use of the special formulas applicable for binomial probability distributions. (c) Compare your answers.

(a) $E(X) = np = 5(0.50) = 2.5$

(b) $\text{Var}(X) = np(1-p) = (5)(0.50)(0.50) = 1.25$

(c) The answers obtained with the special formulas which are applicable for binomial distributions correspond with the answers obtained by the lengthier general procedure applicable for discrete random variables.

THE HYPERGEOMETRIC DISTRIBUTION

6.13. A manager randomly selects $n = 3$ individuals from a group of 10 employees in his department for assignment to a wage classification study. Assuming that four of the employees were assigned to a similar project previously, construct a three-step tree diagram portraying the selection of the three individuals in terms of whether each individual chosen has had experience E or has no previous experience E' in such a study. Further, enter the appropriate probability values in the diagram and use the multiplication rule for dependent events to determine the probability of each possible sequence of three events occurring.

See Fig. 6-2.

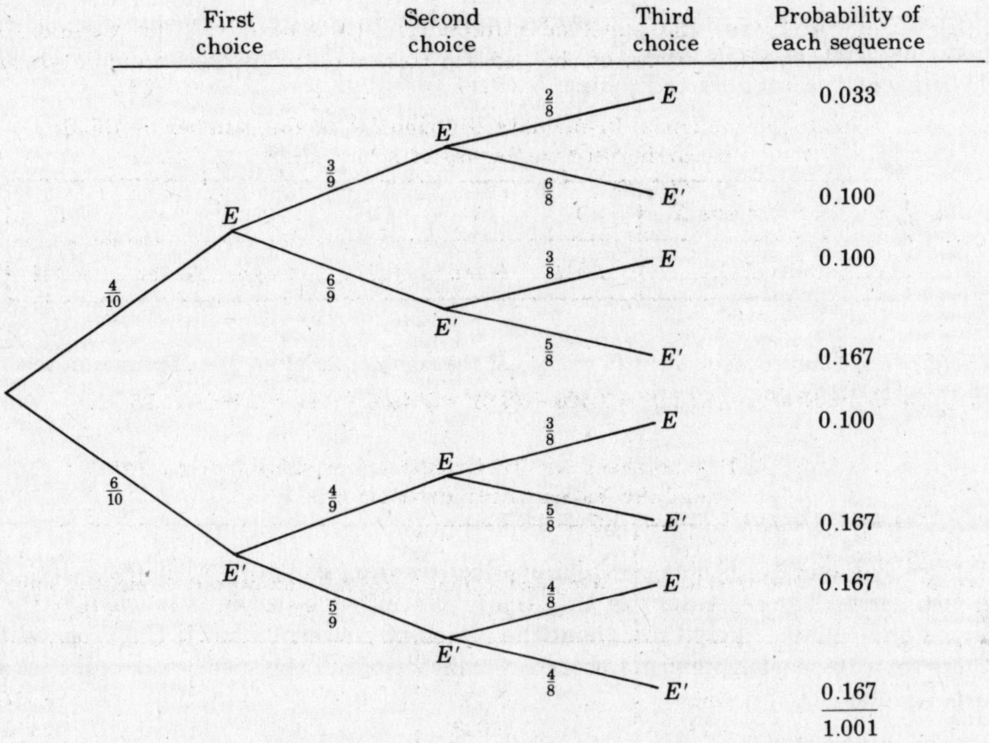

First choice	Second choice	Third choice	Probability of each sequence

Fig. 6-2

6.14. Referring to Problem 6.13, determine the probability that exactly two of the three employees selected have had previous experience in a wage classification study by reference to Fig. 6-2 and use of the addition rule for mutually exclusive events.

Beginning from the top of the tree diagram, the second, third, and fifth sequences include exactly two employees with experience. Thus, by the rule of addition for these mutually exclusive sequences:

$$P(X = 2) = (E \text{ and } E \text{ and } E') + (E \text{ and } E' \text{ and } E) + (E' \text{ and } E \text{ and } E)$$
$$= 0.100 + 0.100 + 0.100 = 0.30$$

6.15. Referring to Problem 6.13, determine the probability that exactly two of the three employees have had the previous experience, using the formula for determining hypergeometric probabilities.

From formula (6.14),

$$P(X \mid N, X_T, n) = \frac{\binom{N - X_T}{n - X}\binom{X_T}{X}}{\binom{N}{n}}$$

$$P(X = 2 \mid N = 10, X_T = 4, n = 3) = \frac{\binom{10 - 4}{3 - 2}\binom{4}{2}}{\binom{10}{3}} = \frac{\binom{6}{1}\binom{4}{2}}{\binom{10}{3}} = \frac{\left(\frac{6!}{1!\,5!}\right)\left(\frac{4!}{2!\,2!}\right)}{\left(\frac{10!}{3!\,7!}\right)} = \frac{(6)(6)}{120} = 0.30$$

6.16. Section 6.5 states that the hypergeometric formula is a direct application of the rules of combinatorial analysis described in Section 5.9. To demonstrate this, apply the hypergeometric formula to Problem 5.23(a).

$$P(X = 4 \mid N = 10, X_T = 6, n = 6) = \frac{\binom{10-6}{6-4}\binom{6}{4}}{\binom{10}{6}} = \frac{\frac{4!}{2!2!}\frac{6!}{4!2!}}{\frac{10!}{6!4!}}$$

$$= \frac{(6)(15)}{210} = \frac{90}{210} = \frac{3}{7} \cong 0.43$$

(*Note:* This result is equivalent to the use of the combinatorial analysis formula in the solution to Problem 5.23(a).)

THE POISSON PROBABILITY DISTRIBUTION

6.17. On the average, five people per hour conduct transactions at a "special service" desk in a commercial bank. Assuming that the arrival of such people is independently distributed and equally likely throughout the period of concern, what is the probability that more than 10 people will wish to conduct transactions at the special services desk during a particular hour?

Using Appendix 3,

$$P(X > 10 \mid \lambda = 5.0) = P(X \geq 11 \mid \lambda = 5.0) = P(X = 11) + P(X = 12) + \cdots$$
$$= 0.0082 + 0.0034 + 0.0013 + 0.0005 + 0.0002 = 0.0136$$

6.18. On the average, a ship arrives at a certain dock every second day. What is the probability that two or more ships will arrive on a randomly selected day?

Since the average per two days = 1.0, then λ = average per day = 1.0/2 = 0.5. Substituting from Appendix 3,

$$P(X \geq 2 \mid \lambda = 0.5) = P(X = 2) + P(X = 3) + \cdots$$
$$= 0.0758 + 0.0126 + 0.0016 + 0.0002 = 0.0902$$

6.19. Each 500-ft roll of sheet steel includes two flaws, on the average. A flaw is a scratch or mar which would affect the use of that segment of sheet steel in the finished product. What is the probability that a particular 100-ft segment will include no flaws?

If the average per 500-ft roll = 2.0, then λ = average per 100-ft roll = 2.0/5 = 0.40. Thus, from Appendix 3,

$$P(X = 0 \mid \lambda = 0.40) = 0.6703$$

6.20. An insurance company is considering the addition of coverage for a relatively rare ailment in the major-medical insurance field. The probability that a randomly selected individual will have the ailment is 0.001, and 3000 individuals are included in the group which is insured.

(a) What is the expected number of people who will have the ailment in the group?

(b) What is the probability that no one in this group of 3000 people will have this ailment?

(a) The distribution of the number of people who will have the ailment would follow the binomial probability distribution with $n = 3000$ and $p = 0.001$.

$$E(X) = np = (3000)(0.001) = 3.0 \text{ people}$$

(b) Tabled binomial probabilities are not available for $n = 3000$ and $p = 0.001$. Also, algebraic solution of the binomial formula is not appealing, because of the large numbers which are involved. However, we can use the Poisson distribution to approximate the binomial probability, because $n \geq 30$ and $np < 5$. Therefore:

$$\lambda = np = (3000)(0.001) = 3.0$$

$$P_{\text{Binomial}}(X = 0 \mid n = 3000, p = 0.001) \cong P_{\text{Poisson}}(X = 0 \mid \lambda = 3.0) = 0.0498$$

(from Appendix 3).

Supplementary Problems

DISCRETE RANDOM VARIABLES

6.21. The arrival of customers during randomly chosen 10-min intervals at a drive-in facility specializing in photo development and film sales has been found to follow the probability distribution in Table 6.12. Calculate the expected number of arrivals for 10-min intervals and the variance of the arrivals.

Table 6.12   Arrivals of Customers at a Photo-processing Facility during 10-min Intervals

Number of arrivals X	0	1	2	3	4	5
Probability $P(X)$	0.15	0.25	0.25	0.20	0.10	0.05

Ans. $E(X) = 2.0$, $\text{Var}(X) = 1.9$

6.22. The newsstand sales of a monthly magazine have been found to follow the probability distribution in Table 6.13. Calculate the expected value and the variance.

Table 6.13   Newsstand Sales of a Monthly Magazine

Number of magazines, thousands, X	15	16	17	18	19	20
Probability $P(X)$	0.05	0.10	0.25	0.30	0.20	0.10

Ans. $E(X) = 17.80$, $\text{Var}(X) = 1.66$

6.23. A salesman has found that the probability of his making various numbers of sales per day, given that he calls on 10 sales prospects, is presented in Table 6.14. Calculate the expected number of sales per day and the variance of the number of sales.

Table 6.14 Sales per Day when 10 Prospects Are Contacted

Number of sales X	1	2	3	4	5	6	7	8
Probability $P(X)$	0.04	0.15	0.20	0.25	0.19	0.10	0.05	0.02

Ans. $E(X) = 4.00$, $\text{Var}(X) = 2.52$

6.24. Referring to Problem 6.23, suppose the salesman earns a commission of $15 per sale. Determine his expected daily commission earnings by (*a*) substituting the commission amount for each of the sales numbers in Table 6.14 and calculating the expected commission amount, and (*b*) multiplying the expected sales number calculated in Problem 6.23 by the commission rate.

Ans. (*a*) $60.00, (*b*) $60.00

THE BINOMIAL DISTRIBUTION

6.25. There is a 90 percent chance that a particular type of component will perform adequately under high temperature conditions. If the device involved has four such components, determine the probability of each of the following events by use of the formula for binomial probabilities.

(*a*) All of the components perform adequately and therefore the device is operative.

(*b*) The device is inoperative because one of the four components fails.

(*c*) The device is inoperative because one or more of the components fail.

Ans. (*a*) 0.6561, (*b*) 0.2916, (*c*) 0.3439

6.26. Verify the answers to Problem 6.25 by constructing a tree diagram and determining the probabilities by the use of the appropriate rules of multiplication and of addition.

6.27. Verify the answers to Problem 6.25 by use of Appendix 1.

6.28. Using the table of binomial probabilities, determine:

(*a*) $P(X = 8 \mid n = 20, p = 0.30)$ (*d*) $P(X = 5 \mid n = 10, p = 0.40)$

(*b*) $P(X \geq 10 \mid n = 20, p = 0.30)$ (*e*) $P(X > 5 \mid n = 10, p = 0.40)$

(*c*) $P(X \leq 5 \mid n = 20, \ p = 0.30)$ (*f*) $P(X < 5 \mid n = 10, p = 0.40)$

Ans. (*a*) 0.1144, (*b*) 0.0479, (*c*) 0.4165, (*d*) 0.2007, (*e*) 0.1663, (*f*) 0.6330

6.29. Using the table of binomial probabilities, determine:

(*a*) $P(X = 4 \mid n = 12, \ p = 0.70)$ (*d*) $P(X < 3 \mid n = 8, \ p = 0.60)$

(*b*) $P(X \geq 9 \mid n = 12, \ p = 0.70)$ (*e*) $P(X = 5 \mid n = 10, \ p = 0.90)$

(*c*) $P(X \leq 3 \mid n = 8, \ \ p = 0.60)$ (*f*) $P(X > 7 \mid n = 10, \ p = 0.90)$

Ans. (*a*) 0.0078, (*b*) 0.4925, (*c*) 0.1738, (*d*) 0.0499, (*e*) 0.0015, (*f*) 0.9298

6.30. Suppose that 40 percent of the hourly employees in a large firm are in favor of union representation, and a random sample of 10 employees is contacted and asked for an anonymous response. What is the probability that (*a*) a majority of the respondents, (*b*) fewer than half of the respondents will be in favor of union representation?

Ans. (*a*) 0.1663, (*b*) 0.6330

6.31. Determine the probabilities in Problem 6.30, if 60 percent in the firm are in favor of union representation.

Ans.   (*a*) 0.6330,   (*b*) 0.1663

6.32. Refer to the probability distribution in Problem 6.23. Does this probability distribution appear to follow a binomial probability distribution? (*Hint*:   Convert the $E(X)$ found in Problem 6.23 into a proportion and use this value as the p for the comparison binomial distribution with $n = 10$.)

Ans.   The two probability distributions correspond quite closely.

THE HYPERGEOMETRIC DISTRIBUTION

6.33. In a class containing 20 students, 15 are dissatisfied with the text used. If a random sample of four students is asked about the text, determine the probability that   (*a*) exactly three, and   (*b*) at least three are dissatisfied with the text.

Ans.   (*a*) $P \cong 0.47$,   (*b*) $P \cong 0.75$

6.34. Verify the answers to Problem 6.33 by constructing a tree diagram and determining the probabilities by use of the appropriate rules of multiplication and of addition.

6.35. In Section 6.5 it is suggested that the binomial distribution can generally be used to approximate hypergeometric probabilities when $n < 0.05N$. Demonstrate that the binomial approximation of the probability values requested in Problem 6.33 is quite poor. (*Hint*:   Use X_T/N as the p value for the binomial table with $n = 4$.)

6.36. A departmental group includes five engineers and nine technicians. If five individuals are randomly chosen and assigned to a project, what is the probability that the project group will include exactly two engineers? (*Note*:   This is a restatement of Problem 5.50(*a*), for which the answer was determined by combinatorial analysis.)

Ans. $P \cong 0.42$

THE POISSON PROBABILITY DISTRIBUTION

6.37. On the average, six people per hour use a self-service banking facility during the prime shopping hours in a department store. What is the probability that

(*a*) exactly six people will use the facility during a randomly selected hour?

(*b*) fewer than five people will use the facility during a randomly selected hour?

(*c*) no one will use the facility during a 10-min interval?

(*d*) no one will use the facility during a 5-min interval?

Ans.   (*a*) 0.1606,   (*b*) 0.2851,   (*c*) 0.3679,   (*d*) 0.6065

6.38. Suppose that the manuscript for a textbook has a total of 50 errors or typos included in the 500 pages of material, and the errors are distributed randomly throughout the text. What is the probability that

(*a*) a chapter covering 30 pages has two or more errors?

(*b*) a chapter covering 50 pages has two or more errors?

(*c*) a randomly selected page has no error?

Ans. (*a*) 0.8008,   (*b*) 0.9596,   (*c*) 0.9048

6.39. Only one generator per thousand is found to be defective after assembly in a manufacturing plant, and the defective generators are distributed randomly throughout the production run.

(*a*) What is the probability that a shipment of 500 generators includes no defective generator?

(b) What is the probability that a shipment of 100 generators includes at least one defective generator?

Ans. By the Poisson approximation of binomial probabilities, (a) 0.6065, (b) 0.0952

6.40. Refer to the probability distribution in Problem 6.21. Does this probability distribution of arrivals appear to follow a Poisson probability distribution? (*Hint:* Use the $E(X)$ calculated in Problem 6.21 as the mean (λ) for determining the comparison Poisson distribution.)

Ans. The two probability distributions correspond quite closely.

(*Note:* Problems 7.16–7.22 involve the use of all of the probability distributions covered in Chapters 6 and 7.)

Chapter 7

Continuous Probability Distributions: Normal and Exponential

7.1 CONTINUOUS RANDOM VARIABLES

As contrasted to a discrete random variable, a *continuous random variable* is one which can have any fractional value within a defined range of values. (See Section 1.4.) Thus, for probability distributions, it is not possible to list every possible value for a continuous random variable along with a corresponding probability value. Rather, the most convenient approach is to construct a probability density function, or probability curve, based on the mathematical function involved. The proportion of area included between any two points under the probability curve identifies the probability that a randomly selected continuous variable has a value between those points.

EXAMPLE 1. For the continuous probability distribution in Fig. 7-1, the probability that a randomly selected shipment will have a net weight between 6000 and 8000 lb is equal to the proportion of the total area under the curve which is included within the shaded area. That is, the total area under the probability density function is defined as being equal to 1, and the proportion of this area which is included between the two designated points can be determined by applying the method of integration (from calculus) in conjunction with the mathematical function for this probability curve.

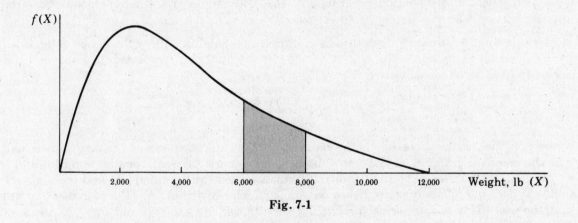

Fig. 7-1

Several specific continuous probability distributions are applicable to a wide variety of continuous variables under designated circumstances. Therefore, probability tables have been prepared for these continuous distributions, making it unnecessary for the applied statistician to be involved in integration of areas under probability curves. The specific continuous probability distributions described in this chapter are the normal and exponential probability distributions.

7.2 THE NORMAL PROBABILITY DISTRIBUTION

The *normal probability distribution* is a continuous probability distribution which is *both symmetrical* and *mesokurtic* (defined in Section 2.4).   The curve representing the normal probability distribution is often described as being bell-shaped, as exemplified by the probability density function in Fig. 7-2.

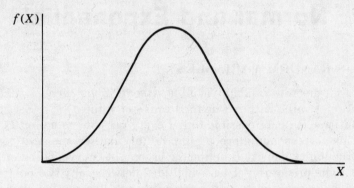

Fig. 7-2

The normal probability distribution is important in statistical inference for three distinct reasons:

(1) The measurements produced in many random processes are known to follow this distribution.

(2) Normal probabilities can often be used to approximate other probability distributions, such as the binomial and Poisson distributions.

(3) Distribution of such statistics as the sample mean and sample proportion often follow the normal distribution regardless of the distribution of the parent population (see Section 8.2).

As with any continuous probability distribution, a probability value can only be determined for an interval of values. The height of the density function, or probability curve, for a normally distributed variable is given by

$$f(X) = \frac{1}{\sqrt{2\pi\sigma^2}} e^{-[(X-\mu)^2/2\sigma^2]} \tag{7.1}$$

where π is the constant 3.1416, e is the constant 2.7183, μ is the mean of the distribution, and σ is the standard deviation of the distribution.   Since every different combination of μ and σ would generate a different normal probability distribution (all symmetrical and mesokurtic), tables of normal probabilities are based on one particular distribution: the *standard normal distribution*.   This is the normal probability distribution with $\mu = 0$ and $\sigma = 1$. Any normally distributed set of values X can be converted into standard normal values z by use of the formula

$$z = \frac{X - \mu}{\sigma} \tag{7.2}$$

Appendix 4 indicates proportions of area for various intervals of values for the standard normal probability distribution, with the lower boundary of the interval always beginning at the mean. Converting designated values of the variable X into standard normal values makes use of this table possible, and makes use of the equation for the density function of any given normal distribution unnecessary.

EXAMPLE 2. The lifetime of an electrical component is known to follow a normal distribution with a mean $\mu = 2000$ hr and a standard deviation $\sigma = 200$ hr. The probability that a randomly selected component will last between 2000 and 2400 hr is determined as follows.

Figure 7-3 portrays the probability curve (density function) for this problem and also indicates the relationship between the hours X scale and the standard normal z scale. Further, the area under the curve corresponding to the interval "2000 to 2400" has been shaded.

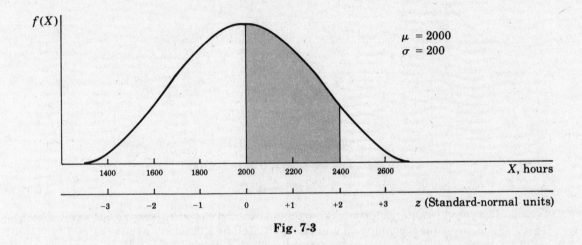

Fig. 7-3

The lower boundary of the interval is at the mean of the distribution, and therefore is at the value $z = 0$. The upper boundary of the designated interval in terms of a z value is

$$z = \frac{X - \mu}{\sigma} = \frac{2400 - 2000}{200} = \frac{400}{200} = +2.0$$

By reference to Appendix 4, we find that

$$P(0 \leq z \leq +2.0) = 0.4772$$

Therefore,
$$P(2000 \leq X \leq 2400) = 0.4772$$

Of course, not all problems involve an interval with the mean as the lower boundary. However, Appendix 4 can be used to determine the probability value associated with any designated interval, either by appropriate addition or subtraction of areas or by recognizing that the curve is symmetrical. Example 3 and Problems 7.1–7.8 include several varieties of such applications.

EXAMPLE 3. In respect to the electrical components described in Example 2, suppose we are interested in the probability that a randomly selected component will last *more* than 2200 hours.

Note that the total proportion of area to the right of the mean of 2000 in Fig. 7-4 is 0.5000. Therefore, if we determine the proportion between the mean and 2200, we can subtract this value from 0.5000 to obtain the probability of the hours X being greater than 2200, which is shaded in Fig. 7-4.

$$z = \frac{2200 - 2000}{200} = +1.0$$

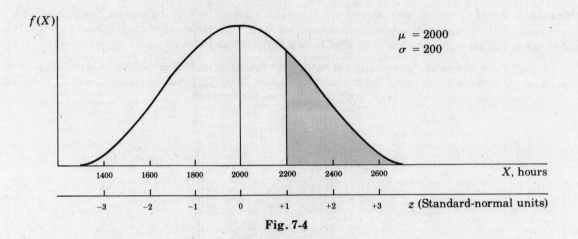

Fig. 7-4

$$P(0 \leq z \leq +1.0) = 0.3413 \qquad \text{(from Appendix 4)}$$

$$P(z > +1.0) = 0.5000 - 0.3413 = 0.1587$$

Therefore, $$P(X > 2200) = 0.1587$$

Where the mean μ for a population can be calculated by the formulas presented in Sections 3.2 and 3.3, the expected value of a normally distributed random variable is

$$E(X) = \mu \qquad (7.3)$$

Where the variance σ^2 for a population can be calculated by the formulas presented in Sections 4.6 to 4.8, the variance of a normally distributed random variable is

$$\text{Var}(X) = \sigma^2 \qquad (7.4)$$

7.3 NORMAL APPROXIMATION OF BINOMIAL PROBABILITIES

When the number of observations or trials n is relatively large, the normal probability distribution can be used to approximate binomial probabilities. A convenient rule of thumb is that such approximation is acceptable when $n \geq 30$, and both $np \geq 5$ and $n(1 - p) \geq 5$. This rule, combined with the one given in Section 6.7 for the Poisson approximation of binomial probabilities, means that whenever $n \geq 30$, binomial probabilities can be approximated by either the normal or the Poisson distribution, depending on the values of np and $n(1 - p)$. Different texts use somewhat different rules for determining when such approximations are appropriate.

When the normal probability distribution is used as an approximation of a binomial probability distribution, the mean and standard deviation are based on the expected value and variance of the number of successes for a binomial distribution, as given in Section 6.3. The mean number of "successes" is

$$\mu = np \qquad (7.5)$$

The standard deviation of the number of "successes" is

$$\sigma = \sqrt{np(1 - p)} \qquad (7.6)$$

EXAMPLE 4. For a large group of sales prospects, it is known that 20 percent of those contacted personally by a sales representative will make a purchase. If a sales representative contacts 30 prospects, we can determine the probability that 10 or more will make a purchase by reference to the binomial probabilities in Appendix 1:

$$P(X \geq 10 | n = 30, p = 0.20) = P(X = 10) + P(X = 11) + \cdots$$
$$= 0.0355 + 0.0161 + 0.0064 + 0.0022 + 0.0007 + 0.0002$$
$$= 0.0611 \text{ (the binomial probability value)}$$

The normal approximation of the binomial probability value is

$$\mu = np = (30)(0.20) = 6.0$$

$$\sigma = \sqrt{np(1 - p)} = \sqrt{(30)(0.20)(0.80)} = \sqrt{4.8} \cong 2.19$$

$$P_{\text{Binomial}}(X \geq 10 | n = 30, p = 0.20) \cong P_{\text{Normal}}(X \geq 9.5 | \mu = 6.0, \sigma = 2.19)$$

(*Note:* This includes the correction for continuity discussed below.)

$$z = \frac{X - \mu}{\sigma} = \frac{9.5 - 6.0}{2.19} = \frac{3.5}{2.19} \cong +1.60$$

$$P(X \geq 9.5 | \mu = 6.0, \sigma = 2.19) = P(z \geq +1.60)$$
$$= 0.5000 - P(0 \leq z \leq +1.60) = 0.5000 - 0.4452$$
$$= 0.0548 \quad \text{(the normal approximation)}$$

In Example 4, the class of events "10 or more" is assumed to begin at 9.5 when the normal approximation is used. This subtraction of one-half unit is called the *correction for continuity*, and is required because even though there are no events that are possible in the interval between 9 successes and 10 successes, the area under the normal curve has to be allocated between the two adjoining classes. If Example 4 had asked for the probability of "more than 10" successes, the appropriate correction for continuity would involve adding 0.5 to 10, and determining the area for the interval beginning at 10.5. In general, when use of the correction for continuity is appropriate, 0.5 is either added or subtracted according to the form of the probability value which is required:

(1)　Subtract 0.5 from X when $P(X \geq X_i)$ is required.

(2)　Subtract 0.5 from X when $P(X < X_i)$ is required.

(3)　Add 0.5 to X when $P(X \leq X_i)$ is required.

(4)　Add 0.5 to X when $P(X > X_i)$ is required.

The correction for continuity has little effect and therefore may be omitted when there is a large number of values of the random variable X included in the probability distribution. No general rule of thumb exists for such omission. However, it is always warranted if the resulting z value is not affected in the second decimal place.

7.4　NORMAL APPROXIMATION OF POISSON PROBABILITIES

When the mean λ of a Poisson distribution is relatively large, the normal probability distribution can be used to approximate Poisson probabilities. A convenient rule of thumb is that such approximation is acceptable when $\lambda \geq 10.0$.

The mean and standard deviation of the normal probability distribution are based on the expected value and the variance of the number of successes in a Poisson process, as identified in Section 6.6. This mean is

$$\mu = \lambda \tag{7.7}$$

The standard deviation is

$$\sigma = \sqrt{\lambda} \tag{7.8}$$

EXAMPLE 5. The average number of calls for service received by a machine repair department per 8-hr shift is 10.0. We can determine the probability that more than 15 calls will be received during a randomly selected 8-hr shift using Appendix 3:

$$P(X>15|\lambda=10.0) = P(X=16) + P(X=17) + \cdots$$

$$= 0.0217 + 0.0128 + 0.0071 + 0.0037 + 0.0019 + 0.0009 + 0.0004 + 0.0002 + 0.0001$$

$$= 0.0488 \quad \text{(the Poisson probability)}$$

The normal approximation of the Poisson probability value is

$$\mu = \lambda = 10.0$$

$$\sigma = \sqrt{\lambda} = \sqrt{10.0} \cong 3.16$$

$$P_{\text{Poisson}}(X > 15|\lambda = 10.0) \cong P_{\text{Normal}}(X \geq 15.5|\mu = 10.0, \sigma = 3.16)$$

(*Note:* This includes the correction for continuity, discussed below.)

$$z = \frac{X - \mu}{\sigma} = \frac{15.5 - 10.0}{3.16} = \frac{5.5}{3.16} \cong +1.74$$

$$P(z \geq +1.74) = 0.5000 - P(0 \leq z \leq +1.74) = 0.5000 - 0.4591 = 0.0409$$

(the normal approximation)

The correction for continuity applied in Example 5 is the same type of correction described for the normal approximation of binomial probabilities. The rules provided in Section 7.3 as to when 0.5 is added to and subtracted from X apply equally to the situation in which the normal probability distribution is used to approximate Poisson probabilities.

7.5 THE EXPONENTIAL PROBABILITY DISTRIBUTION

If events, or successes, occur in the context of a Poisson process, as described in Section 6.6, then the length of time or space between successive events follows an *exponential probability distribution*. Because the time or space is a continuum, this is a continuous distribution. As for the case of any continuous distribution, it is not meaningful to ask, "What is the probability that the first request for service will arrive in *exactly* one minute?" Rather, we must designate an *interval* within which the event is to occur, such as by asking, "What is the probability that the first request for service will arrive *within* a minute?"

Since the Poisson process is stationary, the exponential distribution applies whether we are concerned with the time (or space) *until* the very first event, the time *between* two successive events, or the time until the first event occurs after any randomly selected point.

Where λ is the mean number of occurrences for the *interval of interest* (see Section 6.6), the exponential probability that the first event will occur *within* the designated interval of time or space is

$$P(T \leq t) = 1 - e^{-\lambda} \tag{7.9}$$

Similarly, the exponential probability that the first event *will not* occur within the designated interval of time or space is

$$P(T > t) = e^{-\lambda} \tag{7.10}$$

For both of the above formulas the value of $e^{-\lambda}$ may be obtained from Appendix 2.

EXAMPLE 6. An average of five calls per hour is received by a machine repair department. Beginning at a random point in time, the probability that the first call for service will arrive within a half hour is

Average per hour $= 5.0$

λ = Average per half hour $= 2.5$

$P = 1 - e^{-\lambda} = 1 - e^{-2.5} = 1 - 0.08208 = 0.91792$ (from Appendix 2)

The expected value and the variance of an exponential probability distribution, where the variable is designated as time T, are

$$E(T) = \frac{1}{\lambda} \tag{7.11}$$

$$\mathrm{Var}(T) = \frac{1}{\lambda^2} \tag{7.12}$$

Solved Problems

THE NORMAL PROBABILITY DISTRIBUTION

7.1. The packaging process in a breakfast cereal company has been adjusted so that an average of $\mu = 13.0$ oz of cereal is placed in each box. Of course, not all packages have precisely 13.0 oz because of random sources of variability. The standard deviation of the actual net weight is $\sigma = 0.1$ oz, and the distribution of weights is known to follow the normal probability distribution. Determine the probability that a randomly chosen box will contain between 13.0 and 13.2 oz of cereal and illustrate the proportion of area under the normal curve which is associated with this probability value.

From Fig. 7-5,

$$z = \frac{X - \mu}{\sigma} = \frac{13.2 - 13.0}{0.1} = +2.0$$

$$P(13.0 \leq X \leq 13.2) = P(0 \leq z \leq +2.0) = 0.4772 \qquad \text{(from Appendix 4)}$$

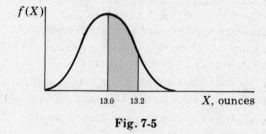
Fig. 7-5

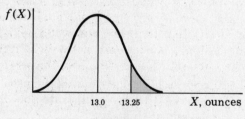
Fig. 7-6

7.2. For the situation described in Problem 7.1, what is the probability that the weight of the cereal will exceed 13.25 oz? Illustrate the proportion of area under the normal curve which is relevant in this case.

With reference to Fig. 7-6,

$$z = \frac{X - \mu}{\sigma} = \frac{13.25 - 13.0}{0.1} = +2.5$$

$$P(X > 13.25) = P(z > +2.5) = 0.5000 - 0.4938 = 0.0062$$

7.3. From Problem 7.1, what is the probability that the weight of the cereal will be between 12.9 and 13.1 oz? Illustrate the proportion of area under the normal curve which is relevant in this case.

Referring to Fig. 7-7,

$$z_1 = \frac{X_1 - \mu}{\sigma} = \frac{12.9 - 13.0}{0.1} = -1.0$$

$$z_2 = \frac{X_2 - \mu}{\sigma} = \frac{13.1 - 13.0}{0.1} = +1.0$$

$$P(12.9 \le X \le 13.1) = P(-1.0 \le z \le +1.0) = 0.3413 + 0.3413 = 0.6826$$

(*Note:* This is the proportion of area from $-1.0z$ to μ plus the proportion from μ to $+1.0z$. Note that because the normal probability distribution is symmetrical, areas to the left of the mean for negative z values are equivalent to areas to the right of the mean.)

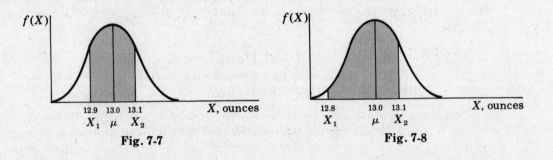

Fig. 7-7   Fig. 7-8

7.4. What is the probability that the weight of the cereal in Problem 7.1, will be between 12.8 and 13.1 oz? Illustrate the proportion of area under the normal curve which is relevant in this case.

With reference to Fig. 7-8,

$$z_1 = \frac{X_1 - \mu}{\sigma} = \frac{12.8 - 13.0}{0.1} = \frac{-0.2}{0.1} = -2.0$$

$$z_2 = \frac{X_2 - \mu}{\sigma} = \frac{13.1 - 13.0}{0.1} = \frac{0.1}{0.1} = +1.0$$

$$P(12.8 \le X \le 13.1) = P(-2.0 \le z \le 1.0) = 0.4772 + 0.3413 = 0.8185$$

7.5. From Problem 7.1, what is the probability that the weight of the cereal will be between 13.1 and 13.2 oz? Illustrate the proportion of area under the normal curve which is relevant in this case.

Referring to Fig. 7-9,

$$z_1 = \frac{X_1 - \mu}{\sigma} = \frac{13.1 - 13.0}{0.1} = +1.0$$

$$z_2 = \frac{X_2 - \mu}{\sigma} = \frac{13.2 - 13.0}{0.1} = +2.0$$

$$P(13.1 \le X \le 13.2) = P(+1.0 \le z \le +2.0) = 0.4772 - 0.3413 = 0.1359$$

(*Note:* The probability is equal to the proportion of area from 13.0 to 13.2 minus the proportion of area from 13.0 to 13.1.)

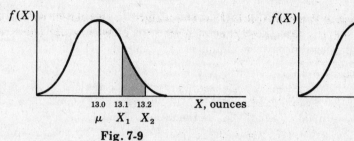

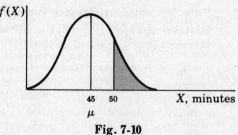

Fig. 7-9   Fig. 7-10

7.6. The amount of time required for a certain type of automobile transmission repair at a service garage is normally distributed with the mean $\mu = 45$ min and the standard deviation $\sigma = 8.0$ min. The service manager plans to have work begin on the transmission of a customer's car 10 min after the car is dropped off, and he tells the customer that the car will be ready within 1 hr total time. What is the probability that he will be wrong? Illustrate the proportion of area under the normal curve which is relevant in this case.

From Fig. 7-10,

$$P(\text{Error}) = P(X > 50 \text{ min}), \text{ since actual work is to begin in 10 min}$$

$$z = \frac{X - \mu}{\sigma} = \frac{50 - 45}{8.0} = \frac{5.0}{8.0} = +0.62$$

$$P(X > 50) = P(z > +0.62) = 0.5000 - 0.2324 = 0.2676$$

7.7. Referring to Problem 7.6, what is the required working time allotment such that there is a 90 percent chance that the transmission repair will be completed within that time? Illustrate the proportion of area which is relevant.

Essentially, the solution is based on obtaining the value of z from Appendix 4 by using that table in the reverse of the usual direction and then converting the z value to a value of X.

Specifically, if the proportion of area shaded in Fig. 7-11 is 0.90, then because a proportion of 0.50 is to the left of the mean it follows that a proportion of 0.40 is between the mean and the unknown value of X. By looking in the *body* of Appendix 4, the closest we can come to a proportion of 0.40 is 0.3997, and the z value associated with this proportion is $z = +1.28$. We now convert this z value to a value of X by substituting in the following formula:

$$X = \mu + z\sigma \tag{7.13}$$

$$X = 45 + (+1.28)(8.0) = 45 + 10.24 = 55.24 \text{ min}$$

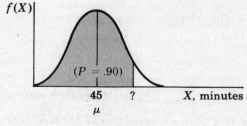

Fig. 7-11

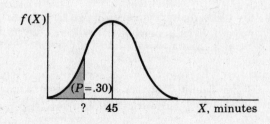

Fig. 7-12

7.8. With reference to Problem 7.6, what is the working time allotment such that there is a probability of just 30 percent that the transmission repair can be completed within that time? Illustrate the proportion of area which is relevant.

Since a proportion of area of 0.30 is to the left of the unknown value of X in Fig. 7-12, it follows that a proportion of 0.20 is between the unknown value and the mean. By reference to Appendix 4, the proportion of area closest to this is 0.1985, for $z = -0.52$. The z value is negative because the unknown value is to the left of the mean. Finally, the z value is converted to the required value of X:

$$X = \mu + z\sigma$$
$$X = 45 + (-0.52)(8.0) = 45 - 4.16 = 40.84 \text{ min}$$

NORMAL APPROXIMATION OF BINOMIAL AND POISSON PROBABILITIES

7.9. Of the people who enter a large shopping mall, it has been found that 70 percent will make at least one purchase. For a sample of $n = 50$ individuals, what is the probability that at least 40 people make one or more purchases each?

The normal approximation of the required binomial probability value can be used, because $n \geq 30$, $np \geq 5$ and $n(1-p) \geq 5$.

$$\mu = np = (50)(0.70) = 35.0$$
$$\sigma = \sqrt{np(1-p)} = \sqrt{(50)(0.70)(0.30)} = \sqrt{10.5} = 3.24$$
$$P_{\text{Binomial}}(X \geq 40 | n = 50, p = 0.70) \cong P_{\text{Normal}}(X \geq 39.5 | \mu = 35.0, \sigma = 3.24)$$

(*Note:* The correction for continuity is included, as described in Section 7.3.)

$$z = \frac{X - \mu}{\sigma} = \frac{39.5 - 35.0}{3.24} = \frac{4.5}{3.24} = +1.39$$
$$P(X \geq 39.5) = P(z \geq +1.39) = 0.5000 - 0.4177 = 0.0823$$

7.10. For the situation described in Problem 7.9, what is the probability that fewer than 30 of the 50 sampled individuals make at least one purchase?

Since, from Problem 7.9, $\mu = 35.0$ and $\sigma = 3.24$,

$$P_{\text{Binomial}}(X < 30 | n = 50, p = 0.70) \cong P_{\text{Normal}}(X \leq 29.5 | \mu = 35.0, \sigma = 3.24)$$

(*Note:* The correction for continuity is included).

$$z = \frac{X - \mu}{\sigma} = \frac{29.5 - 35.0}{3.24} = \frac{-5.5}{3.24} = -1.70$$
$$P(X \leq 29.5) = P(z \leq -1.70) = 0.5000 - 0.4554 = 0.0446$$

7.11. Calls for service are known to arrive randomly and as a stationary process at an average of five calls per hour. What is the probability that more than 50 calls for service will be received during an 8-hr shift?

Because the mean for the 8-hr period for this Poisson process exceeds $\lambda = 10$, the normal probability distribution can be used to approximate the Poisson probability value. Since $\mu = \lambda = 40.0$ and $\sigma = \sqrt{\lambda} = \sqrt{40.0} = 6.32$,

$$P_{\text{Poisson}}(X > 50 | \lambda = 40.0) \cong P_{\text{Normal}}(X \geq 50.5 | \mu = 40.0, \sigma = 6.32)$$

(*Note:* The correction for continuity is included.)

$$z = \frac{X - \mu}{\sigma} = \frac{50.5 - 40.0}{6.32} = \frac{10.5}{6.32} = +1.66$$

$$P(X \geq 50.5) = P(z \geq +1.66) = 0.5000 - 0.4515 = 0.0485$$

7.12. Referring to Problem 7.11, what is the probability that 35 or fewer calls for service will be received during an 8-hr shift?

Since $\mu = 40.0$ and $\sigma = 6.32$,

$$P_{\text{Poisson}}(X \leq 35 \mid \lambda = 40.0) \cong P_{\text{Normal}}(X \leq 35.5 \mid \mu = 40.0, \sigma = 6.32)$$

(*Note:* The correction for continuity is included.)

$$z = \frac{X - \mu}{\sigma} = \frac{35.5 - 40.0}{6.32} = \frac{-4.5}{6.32} = -0.71$$

$$P(X \leq 35.5) = P(z \leq -0.71) = 0.5000 - 0.2612 = 0.2388$$

THE EXPONENTIAL PROBABILITY DISTRIBUTION

7.13. On the average, a ship arrives at a certain dock every second day. What is the probability that after the departure of a ship 4 days will pass before the arrival of the next ship?

Average per 2 days = 1.0

λ = average per 4-day period = $1.0 \times 2 = 2.0$

$P(T > 4) = e^{-\lambda} = e^{-2.0} = 0.13534$ (from Appendix 2)

7.14. Each 500-ft roll of sheet steel includes two flaws, on the average. What is the probability that as the sheet steel is unrolled the first flaw occurs within the first 50-ft segment?

Average per 500-ft roll = 2.0

λ = average per 50-ft segment = $2.0/10 = 0.20$

$P(T \leq 50) = 1 - e^{-\lambda} = 1 - e^{-0.20} = 1 - 0.81873 = 0.18127$ (from Appendix 2)

7.15. An application that is concerned with use of the exponential distribution can be transformed into Poisson distribution form, and vice versa. To illustrate such transformation, suppose that an average of four aircraft per 8-hr day arrive for repairs at a repair facility. (*a*) What is the probability that the first arrival does *not* occur during the first hour of work? (*b*) Demonstrate that the equivalent Poisson-oriented problem is the probability that there will be *no* arrivals in the 1-hr period. (*c*) What is the probability that the first arrival occurs within the first hour? (*d*) Demonstrate that the equivalent Poisson-oriented problem is the probability that there will be one or more arrivals during the 1-hr period.

(*a*) $\lambda = 0.5$ (per hr)

$P(T > 1) = e^{-\lambda} = e^{-0.5} = 0.60653$ (from Appendix 2)

(*b*) $P(X = 0 \mid \lambda = 0.5) = 0.6065$ (from Appendix 3)

(c) $\lambda = 0.5$ (per hr)

$P(T \le 1) = 1 - e^{-\lambda} = 1 - e^{-0.5} = 1 - 0.60653 = 0.39347$ (from Appendix 2)

(d) $P(X \ge 1 \mid \lambda = 0.5) = 1 - P(X = 0) = 1.0000 - 0.6065 = 0.3935$ (from Appendix 3)

Thus, in the case of both transformations the answers are identical, except for the number of digits which happen to be carried in the two tables.

MISCELLANEOUS PROBLEMS ON PROBABILITY DISTRIBUTIONS

(*Note:*   Problems 7.16–7.22 involve the use of all of the probability distributions covered in Chapters 6 and 7.)

7.16.   A shipment of ten engines includes one that is defective.   If seven engines are chosen randomly from this shipment, what is the probability that none of the seven is defective?

Using the hypergeometric distribution (see Section 6.5),

$$P(X|N,X_T,n) = \frac{\binom{N - X_T}{n - X}\binom{X_T}{X}}{\binom{N}{n}}$$

$$P(X = 0|N = 10, X_T = 1, n = 7) = \frac{\binom{10 - 1}{7 - 0}\binom{1}{0}}{\binom{10}{7}} = \frac{\left(\frac{9!}{7!\,2!}\right)\left(\frac{1!}{0!\,1!}\right)}{\left(\frac{10!}{7!\,3!}\right)} = \frac{(36)(1)}{120} = 0.30$$

7.17.   Suppose that in Problem 7.16 the overall proportion of engines with some defect is 0.10, but that a very large number are being assembled in an engine-assembly plant.   What is the probability that a random sample of seven engines will include no defective engines?

Using the binomial distribution (see Section 6.3),

$$P(X = 0|n = 7, p = 0.10) = 0.4783 \qquad \text{(from Appendix 1)}$$

7.18.   Suppose that the proportion of engines which contain a defect in an assembly operation is 0.10, and a sample of 200 engines is included in a particular shipment.   What is the probability that at least 30 of the 200 engines contain a defect?

Use of the normal approximation of the binomial probability distribution described in Section 7.3 is acceptable, because $n \ge 30$, $np \ge 5$ and $n(1-p) \ge 5$.

$$\mu = np = (200)(0.10) = 20.0$$

$$\sigma = \sqrt{np(1-p)} = \sqrt{(200)(0.10)(0.90)} = \sqrt{18.00} \cong 4.24$$

$$P_{\text{Binomial}}(X \ge 30 \mid n = 200, p = 0.10) \cong P_{\text{Normal}}(X \ge 29.5 \mid \mu = 20.0, \sigma = 4.24)$$

(*Note:*   The correction for continuity is included.)

$$z = \frac{X - \mu}{\sigma} = \frac{29.5 - 20.0}{4.24} = \frac{9.5}{4.24} = +2.24$$

$$P(X \ge 29.5) = P(Z \ge +2.24) = 0.5000 - 0.4875 = 0.0125 \quad \text{(from Appendix 4)}$$

7.19. Suppose that the proportion of engines which contain a defect in an assembly operation is 0.01, and a sample of 200 engines is included in a particular shipment. What is the probability that three or fewer engines contain a defect?

Use of the Poisson approximation of the binomial probability distribution (see Section 6.7) is acceptable in this case because $n \geq 30$ and $np < 5$.

$$\lambda = np = (200)(0.01) = 2.0$$

$$P_{\text{Binomial}}(X \leq 3|n = 200, \ p = 0.01) \cong P_{\text{Poisson}}(X \leq 3|\lambda = 2.0)$$
$$= 0.1353 + 0.2707 + 0.2707 + 0.1804 = 0.8571$$

(from Appendix 3)

7.20. An average of 0.5 customer per minute arrives at a checkout stand. After an attendant opens the stand, what is the probability that he will have to wait at least 3 min before the first customer arrives?

Using the exponential probability distribution described in Section 7.5,

$$\text{Average per minute} = 0.5$$
$$\lambda = \text{average for 3 min} = 0.5 \times 3 = 1.5$$
$$P(T > 3) = e^{-\lambda} = e^{-1.5} = 0.22313 \qquad \text{(from Appendix 2)}$$

7.21. An average of 0.5 customer per minute arrives at a checkout stand. What is the probability that five or more customers will arrive in a given 5-min interval?

From Section 6.6 on the Poisson probability distribution,

$$\text{Average per minute} = 0.5$$
$$\lambda = \text{average for 5 min} = 0.5 \times 5 = 2.5$$
$$P(X \geq 5|\lambda = 2.5) = 0.0668 + 0.0278 + 0.0099 + 0.0031 + 0.0009 + 0.0002 = 0.1087$$

(from Appendix 3)

7.22. An average of 0.5 customer per minute arrives at a checkout stand. What is the probability that more than 20 customers arrive at the stand during a particular interval of 0.5 hr?

Use of the normal approximation of the Poisson probability distribution described in Section 7.4 is acceptable because $\lambda \geq 10.0$.

$$\text{Average per minute} = 0.5$$
$$\lambda = \text{average for 30 min} = 0.5 \times 30 = 15.0$$
$$\mu = \lambda = 15.0$$
$$\sigma = \sqrt{\lambda} = \sqrt{15.0} \cong 3.87$$

$$P_{\text{Poisson}}(X > 20 \mid \lambda = 15.0) \cong P_{\text{Normal}}(X \geq 20.5 \mid \mu = 15.0, \ \sigma = 3.87)$$

(*Note:* The correction for continuity is included.)

$$z = \frac{X - \mu}{\sigma} = \frac{20.5 - 15.0}{3.87} = \frac{5.50}{3.87} = +1.42$$

$$P(X \geq 20.5) = P(z \geq +1.42) = 0.5000 - 0.4222 = 0.0778 \qquad \text{(from Appendix 4)}$$

Supplementary Problems

THE NORMAL PROBABILITY DISTRIBUTION

7.23. The reported scores on a nationally standardized achievement test for high school graduates has a mean of $\mu = 500$ with the standard deviation $\sigma = 100$. The scores are approximately normally distributed. What is the probability that the score of a randomly chosen individual will be (a) between 500 and 650? (b) Between 450 and 600?

   Ans.   (a) 0.4332,   (b) 0.5328

7.24. For a nationally standardized achievement test the mean is $\mu = 500$ with $\sigma = 100$. The scores are normally distributed. What is the probability that a randomly chosen individual will have a score (a) below 300? (b) Above 650?

   Ans.   (a) 0.0228,   (b) 0.0668

7.25. For a nationally standardized achievement test the mean is $\mu = 500$ with $\sigma = 100$. The scores are normally distributed. What score is at the (a) 50th percentile point, (b) 30th percentile point, and (c) 90th percentile point?

   Ans.   (a) 500,   (b) 448,   (c) 628

7.26. The useful life of a certain brand of steel-belted radial tires has been found to follow a normal distribution with $\mu = 38,000$ miles and $\sigma = 3000$ miles. (a) What is the probability that a randomly selected tire will have a useful life of at least 35,000 miles? (b) What is the probability that it will last more than 45,000 miles?

   Ans.   (a) 0.8413,   (b) 0.0099

7.27. A dealer orders 500 of the tires specified in Problem 7.26 for resale. Approximately what number of tires will last (a) between 40,000 and 45,000 miles? (b) 40,000 miles or more?

   Ans.   (a) 121,   (b) 126

7.28. An individual buys four of the tires described in Problem 7.26. What is the probability that all four tires will last (a) at least 38,000 miles? (b) At least 35,000 miles?

   Ans.   (a) 0.0625,   (b) 0.5010

7.29. The amount of time required per individual at a bank teller's window has been found to be approximately normally distributed with $\mu = 130$ sec and $\sigma = 45$ sec. What is the probability that a randomly selected individual will (a) require less than 100 sec to complete his transactions? (b) Spend between 2.0 and 3.0 min at the teller's window?

   Ans.   (a) 0.2514,   (b) 0.4536

7.30. Under the conditions specified in Problem 7.29, (a) within what length of time do the 20 percent of individuals with the simplest transactions complete their business at the window? (b) At least what length of time is required for the individuals in the top 5 percent of required time?

   Ans.   (a) 92 sec,   (b) 204 sec

NORMAL APPROXIMATION OF BINOMIAL AND POISSON PROBABILITIES

7.31. For the several thousand items stocked by a mail order firm, there is an overall probability of 0.08 that a particular item (including specific size and color, etc.) is out of stock. If a shipment covers orders for 120 different items, what is the probability that 15 or more items are out of stock?

   Ans.   0.0495

7.32. For the shipment described in Problem 7.31, what is the probability that there are between 10 and 15 items out of stock?

   Ans.   0.4887

7.33. During the 4 P.M. to 6 P.M. peak period in an automobile service station, one car enters the station every 3 min, on the average.   What is the probability that at least 25 cars enter the station for service between 4 P.M. and 5 P.M.?

   Ans.   0.1562

7.34. For the service-station arrivals in Problem 7.33, what is the probability that fewer than 30 cars enter the station between 4 P.M. and 6 P.M. of a randomly selected day?

   Ans.   0.0485

THE EXPONENTIAL PROBABILITY DISTRIBUTION

7.35. On the average, six people per hour use a self-service banking facility during the prime shopping hours in a department store.

   (*a*)   What is the probability that at least 10 min will pass between the arrival of two customers?

   (*b*)   What is the probability that after a customer leaves, another customer does not arrive for at least 20 min?

   (*c*)   What is the probability that a second customer arrives within 1 min after a first customer begins his banking transaction?

   Ans.   (*a*) 0.36788.   (*b*) 0.13534,   (*c*) 0.09516

7.36. Suppose that the manuscript for a textbook has a total of 50 errors or typos included in the 500 pages of material, and the errors are distributed randomly throughout the text.   As the technical proofreader begins reading a particular chapter, what is the probability that the first error in that chapter   (*a*) is included within the first five pages?   (*b*) Occurs beyond the first 15 pages?

   Ans.   (*a*) 0.39347,   (*b*) 0.22313

MISCELLANEOUS PROBLEMS

   (*Note:*   Problems 7.37–7.44 involve the use of all of the probability distributions covered in Chapters 6 and 7.)

7.37. The frequency distribution of the length of stay in a community hospital has been found to be approximately symmetrical and mesokurtic, with $\mu = 8.4$ days, and $\sigma = 2.6$ days (with fractions of days measured).   What is the probability that a randomly chosen individual will be in the hospital for   (*a*) less than 5.0 days?   (*b*) More than 8.0 days?

   Ans.   (*a*) 0.0951,   (*b*) 0.5596

7.38. A firm which manufactures and markets a wide variety of low-priced innovative toys (such as a ball which will bounce in unexpected directions) has found that in the long run 40 percent of the toys which it develops have at least moderate market success.   If six new toys have been developed for market introduction next summer, what is the probability that at least three of them will have moderate market success?

   Ans.   0.4557

7.39. The firm in Problem 7.38 has 60 toy ideas in the process of development for introduction during the next few years. If all 60 of these are eventually marketed, what is the probability that at least 30 of them will have moderate market success?

Ans.   0.0735

7.40. From Problems 7.38 and 7.39, above, suppose 5 percent of the toys which are marketed turn out to be outstanding sales successes. If 60 new toys are introduced during the next few years, what is the probability that none of them will turn out to be an outstanding sales success?

Ans.   0.0498

7.41. Customers arrive at a refreshment stand located in a sports arena at an average rate of two per minute. What is the probability that five or more people will approach the stand for refreshments during a randomly chosen minute?

Ans.   0.0526

7.42. From Problem 7.41, what is the probability that after the refreshment stand opens two full minutes pass before the first customer arrives?

Ans.   0.01832

7.43. For the situation described in Problem 7.41, what is the probability that more than 50 people will come to the stand during a half hour period?

Ans.   0.8907

7.44. Of the eight hotels located in a resort area, three can be described as being mediocre in terms of customer services. A travel agent chooses two of the hotels randomly for two clients planning vacations in the resort area. What is the probability that at least one of the clients will end up in one of the mediocre hotels?

Ans.   0.6429

Chapter 8

Sampling Distributions and Confidence Intervals for the Population Mean

8.1 POINT ESTIMATION AND SAMPLING

Because of such factors as time and cost, the parameters of a population are frequently estimated on the basis of sample statistics. As defined in Section 1.2, a *population parameter* is a summary measure of a population, whereas a summary measure of a sample is called a *sample statistic.*

EXAMPLE 1. The mean μ and standard deviation σ of a population of measurements are population parameters.   The mean $\bar{X}$ and standard deviation s of a sample of measurements are sample statistics.

A number of criteria are used by mathematical statisticians to choose appropriate estimators of population parameters based on sample data.   One of the most important characteristics of an estimator is that it be unbiased.   An *unbiased estimator* is a sample statistic having an expected value which is equal to the parameter being estimated.   As explained in Section 6.2, an expected value is the long-run average of the sample statistic.

Table 8.1 presents some frequently used point estimators of population parameters.   In every case, the appropriate estimator of a population parameter simply is the corresponding sample statistic.   However, note that in Section 4.6, formula *(4.8)* for the sample variance includes a "correction factor."   Without this, the sample variance would be a biased estimator of the population variance.

Table 8.1   Frequently Used Point Estimators

Population parameter	Estimator
Mean, μ	$\bar{X}$
Difference between the means of two populations, $\mu_1 - \mu_2$	$\bar{X}_1 - \bar{X}_2$
Proportion, π	$\bar{p}$
Difference between the proportions in two populations, $\pi_1 - \pi_2$	$\bar{p}_1 - \bar{p}_2$
Standard deviation, σ	$s *$

*This estimator is based on the assumption that the correction for biasedness was included in the formula for s. If this correction were not included, the appropriate estimator would be $s \sqrt{n/(n - 1)}$.

If a sample statistic is to be used to estimate the specific value of a parameter (i.e., as a point estimator), it must be based on a random sample taken from the target population of interest. A *random sample* is collected by such a procedure that every element in the population has a known probability of being chosen, and with no known sources of systematic bias being included in the procedure.   Random samples are also called *probability samples* or *scientific samples*; they can be collected using a number of specific sampling techniques. A common technique is the *simple random sample*, where every population element has an equal chance of being included in the sample. In this case elements are chosen on a chance basis, such as by "picking names out of a hat" or by the use of a table of random numbers.

EXAMPLE 2. Appendix 5 is a short form of a table of random numbers. Suppose an auditor wishes to choose 10 accounts randomly from a set of 89 numbered accounts. In using this table, we do not generally begin at line 1 and column 1. Instead, we begin at an arbitrary point. Suppose we begin reading numbers (as pairs) on line 20, column 6 and read the numbers horizontally, by line. The 10 account numbers selected are 28, 33, 72, 09, 23, 87, 92, 96, 10, and 20. However, since there are only 89 accounts, the two numbers 92 and 96 do not identify actual accounts. Therefore, the next two account numbers (62, 84) are included in the sample instead. If a repetition of numbers is obtained, such repeated numbers are also ignored.

8.2 SAMPLING DISTRIBUTION OF THE MEAN

A population distribution represents the distribution of a population of values, and a sample distribution represents the distribution of a sample of values collected from a population. In contrast to such distributions of individual measurements, a *sampling distribution* is a probability distribution which applies to the possible values of a sample statistic. Thus, the *sampling distribution of the mean* is the probability distribution for the possible values of the sample mean $\bar{X}$ based on a particular sample size.

For any given sample size n taken from a population with mean μ, the value of the sample mean $\bar{X}$ will vary somewhat from sample to sample. This variability serves as the basis for the sampling distribution. The sampling distribution of the mean is described by determining the expected value $E(\bar{X})$, or mean, of the distribution and the standard deviation of the distribution of means $\sigma_{\bar{x}}$. Because this standard deviation indicates the accuracy of the sample mean as a point estimator, $\sigma_{\bar{x}}$ is usually called the *standard error of the mean*. In general, the expected value of the mean and the standard error of the mean are defined as

$$E(\bar{X}) = \mu \tag{8.1}$$

$$\sigma_{\bar{x}} = \frac{\sigma}{\sqrt{n}} \tag{8.2}$$

EXAMPLE 3. Suppose the mean of a very large population is $\mu = 50.0$ and the standard deviation of the measurements is $\sigma = 12.0$. We determine the sampling distribution of the sample means for a sample size of $n = 36$, in terms of the expected value and the standard error of the distribution, as follows:

$$E(\bar{X}) = \mu = 50.0$$

$$\sigma_{\bar{x}} = \frac{\sigma}{\sqrt{n}} = \frac{12.0}{\sqrt{36}} = \frac{12.0}{6} = 2.0$$

When sampling from a population which is finite, you should include a *finite correction factor* in the formula for the standard error of the mean. As a rule of thumb, the correction is negligible and may be omitted when $n < 0.05N$; that is, when the sample size is less than 5 percent of the population size. The formula for the standard error of the mean with the finite correction factor included is

$$\sigma_{\bar{x}} = \frac{\sigma}{\sqrt{n}} \sqrt{\frac{N-n}{N-1}} \tag{8.3}$$

If the standard deviation of the population is not known, the standard error of the mean can be estimated by using the sample standard deviation as an estimator of the population standard deviation. To differentiate this standard error from one based on a known σ, it is designated by the symbol $s_{\bar{x}}$ (or by $\hat{\sigma}_{\bar{x}}$ in some texts). The formula for the estimated standard error of the mean is

$$s_{\bar{x}} = \frac{s}{\sqrt{n}}$$ (8.4)

The formula for the estimated standard error of the mean with the finite correction factor included is

$$s_{\bar{x}} = \frac{s}{\sqrt{n}} \sqrt{\frac{N - n}{N - 1}}$$ (8.5)

(*Note:* Formulas (8.4) and (8.5) are based on the assumption that the correction for biasedness was included in the formula for s, as explained in Section 4.6. If this correction were not included, the divisor for s in the formulas would be $\sqrt{n - 1}$ instead of $\sqrt{n}$.)

EXAMPLE 4. An auditor takes a random sample of size $n = 16$ from a set of $N = 100$ accounts receivable. The standard deviation of the amounts of the receivables for the entire group of 100 accounts is not known. However, the sample standard deviation is $s = \$57.00$. We determine the value of the standard error for the sampling distribution of the mean as follows:

$$s_{\bar{x}} = \frac{s}{\sqrt{n}} \sqrt{\frac{N - n}{N - 1}} = \frac{57.00}{\sqrt{16}} \sqrt{\frac{100 - 16}{100 - 1}} = \frac{57}{4} \sqrt{\frac{84}{99}}$$

$$= 14.25 \sqrt{0.8484} = 14.25(0.9211) = 13.126 \cong \$13.13$$

The standard error of the mean is estimated on the basis of the sample standard deviation in this example, and use of the finite correction factor is required because $16 > 0.05(100)$.

The standard error of the mean provides the principal basis for statistical inference concerning an unknown population mean, as presented in this and the next two chapters. A theorem in statistics that leads to the usefulness of the standard error of the mean is

Central limit theorem: As the sample size is increased, the sampling distribution of the mean approaches the normal distribution in form *regardless of the form of the population distribution.* For practical purposes, the sampling distribution of the mean can be assumed to be approximately normal whenever the sample size is $n \geq 30$.

Thus, given a "large" sample of $n \geq 30$, we can always use the normal probability distribution in conjunction with the standard error of the mean. Further, if the population is normally distributed and σ is known, the normal distribution can be used in statistical inference with small samples as well. The requirement that σ be known is explained in Section 8.5.

EXAMPLE 5. An auditor takes a sample of size $n = 36$ from a population of 1000 accounts receivable. The standard deviation of the population is unknown, but the standard deviation of the sample is $s = \$43.00$. If the true mean value of the accounts receivable for the population is $\mu = \$260.00$, what is the probability that the sample mean will be less than or equal to $\$250.00$?

The sampling distribution is described by the mean and standard error:

$$E(\bar{X}) = \mu = 260.00 \text{ (as given)}$$

$$s_{\bar{x}} = \frac{s}{\sqrt{n}} = \frac{43.00}{\sqrt{36}} = \frac{43.00}{6} \cong 7.17$$

(*Note:* s is used as an estimator of σ, and the finite correction factor is not required because $36 < 0.05(1000)$.)

$$z = \frac{\bar{X} - \mu}{s_{\bar{x}}} = \frac{250.00 - 260.00}{7.17} = \frac{-10.00}{7.17} = -1.39$$

Therefore,

$$P(\bar{X} \leq 250.00 \mid \mu = 260.00, s_{\bar{x}} = 7.17) = P(z \leq -1.39)$$

$$P(z \leq -1.39) = 0.5000 - P(-1.39 \leq z \leq 0)$$
$$= 0.5000 - 0.4177 = 0.0823$$

8.3 CONFIDENCE INTERVALS FOR THE MEAN USING THE NORMAL DISTRIBUTION

The methods of interval estimation in this section are based on the assumption that the normal probability distribution can be used. As discussed in Sections 8.2 and 8.5, this assumption is warranted (1) whenever $n \geq 30$, because of the central limit theorem, or (2) when $n < 30$ but the population is normally distributed and σ is known.

Although the sample mean is useful as an unbiased estimator of the population mean, there is no way of expressing the degree of accuracy of a point estimator. In fact, mathematically speaking, the probability that the sample mean is *exactly* correct as an estimator is $P = 0$.   A *confidence interval* for the mean is an estimate interval constructed in respect to the sample mean by which the probability that the interval includes the value of the population mean can be specified. The *degree of confidence* associated with a confidence interval indicates the percentage of such intervals which would include the parameter being estimated.

Confidence intervals for the mean typically are constructed with the unbiased estimator $\bar{X}$ at the center of the interval. However, Problems 8.14 and 8.15 demonstrate the construction of a so-called "one-sided" confidence interval, for which the sample mean is not at the center of the interval. When use of the normal probability distribution is warranted, the confidence interval for the mean is determined by

$$\bar{X} \pm z\sigma_{\bar{x}} \tag{8.6}$$

or

$$\bar{X} \pm zs_{\bar{x}} \tag{8.7}$$

The most frequently used confidence intervals are the 90 percent, 95 percent, and 99 percent intervals. The values of z required in conjunction with such intervals are given in Table 8.2.

Table 8.2   Selected Proportions of Area under the Normal Curve

z (the number of standard deviation units from the mean)	Proportion of area in the interval $\mu \pm z\sigma$
1.65	0.90
1.96	0.95
2.58	0.99

EXAMPLE 6. For a given week, a random sample of 30 hourly employees selected from a very large number of employees in a manufacturing firm has a sample mean wage of $\bar{X} = \$180.00$ with a sample standard deviation of $s = \$14.00$. We estimate the mean wage for all hourly employees in the firm with an interval estimate such that we can be 95 percent confident that the interval includes the value of the population mean, as follows:

$$\bar{X} \pm 1.96 s_{\bar{x}} = 180.000 \pm 1.96(2.56) = \$174.98 \text{ to } \$185.02$$

where $\bar{X} = \$180.00$ (as given)

$$s_{\bar{x}} = s/\sqrt{n} = 14.00/\sqrt{30} = 2.56$$

(*Note:* s is used as an estimator of σ and the finite correction factor is not required because presumably $n < 0.05N$.)

Thus, we can state that the mean wage level for all employees is between \$174.98 and \$185.02, with a 95 percent degree of confidence in this estimate.

In addition to estimating the value of the population mean as such, there is sometimes an interest in estimating the total quantity or amount in the population. See Problem 8.11(*b*).

8.4 DETERMINING THE REQUIRED SAMPLE SIZE FOR ESTIMATING THE MEAN

Suppose the desired size of a confidence interval and the degree of confidence to be associated with it are known. If σ is known or can be estimated in any way, such as from the results of similar studies, the required sample size based on use of the normal distribution is

$$n = \left(\frac{z\sigma}{E}\right)^2 \tag{8.8}$$

In formula (*8.8*), z is the value used for the specified degree of confidence, σ is the standard deviation of the population (or estimate thereof), and E is the "plus and minus" error factor allowed in the interval (always one-half the total confidence interval). (*Note:* When solving for sample size, any fractional result is always rounded up. Further, unless σ is known *and* the population is normally distributed, any computed sample size below 30 should be increased to 30 because formula (*8.8*) is based on use of the normal distribution.)

EXAMPLE 7. A personnel department analyst wishes to estimate the mean number of training hours annually for foremen in a division of the company within 3.0 hr (plus-or-minus) and with 90 percent confidence. Based on data from other divisions, he estimates the standard deviation of training hours to be $\sigma = 20.0$ hr. The minimum required sample size is

$$n = \left(\frac{z\sigma}{E}\right)^2 = \left(\frac{(1.65)(20.0)}{3}\right)^2 = \left(\frac{33.0}{3}\right)^2 = 11^2 = 121$$

8.5 STUDENT'S *t* DISTRIBUTIONS AND CONFIDENCE INTERVALS FOR THE MEAN

In Section 8.3 we indicated that use of the normal distribution in estimating a population mean is warranted for any large sample ($n \geq 30$), and for a small sample ($n < 30$) only if the population is normally distributed *and* σ is known. In this section we handle the situation in which the sample is small and the population is normally distributed, but σ is not known.

If a population is normally distributed, the sampling distribution of the mean for any sample size will also be normally distributed; this is true whether σ is known or not. However, in the process of inference each value of the mean is converted to a standard normal value, *and herein lies the problem.*   If σ is unknown, the conversion formula $(\bar{X} - \mu)/s_{\bar{x}}$ includes a variable in the denominator which is somewhat different for each sample mean.   The result is that including the variable $s_{\bar{x}}$ rather than the constant $\sigma_{\bar{x}}$ in the denominator results in converted values that are *not* distributed as z values.   Instead, the values are distributed according to Student's t distributions, which are platykurtic (flat) as compared with the normal distribution.   Appendix 6 indicates proportions of area under the t distributions, with the specific distribution being based on the degrees of freedom (df) involved.   For the case of a single sample, $df = n - 1$.

A t distribution is appropriate for inferences concerning the mean whenever σ is not known and the population is normally distributed, regardless of sample size.   However, as the sample size (and df) is increased, the t distribution approaches the normal distribution in form.   A rule of thumb is that a t distribution can be approximated by the normal distribution when $n \geq 30$ (or $df \geq 29$) for a single sample.   This substitution is a different matter from that covered by the central limit theorem, and the fact that a sample of $n \geq 30$ is required in both cases is coincidental.

Note that the values of t reported in Appendix 6 indicate the proportion in the upper "tail" of the distribution, rather than the proportion between the mean and a given point, as in Appendix 4 for the normal distribution.   Where $df = n - 1$, the confidence interval for estimating the population mean when σ is not known, $n < 30$, and the population is normally distributed is

$$\bar{X} \pm t_{df} s_{\bar{x}} \tag{8.9}$$

EXAMPLE 8.   The mean operating life for a random sample of $n = 10$ light bulbs is $\bar{X} = 4000$ hr with the sample standard deviation $s = 200$ hr.   The operating life of bulbs in general is assumed to be approximately normally distributed.   We estimate the mean operating life for the population of bulbs from which this sample was taken, using a 95 percent confidence interval, as follows:

$$95\% \text{ Int.} = \bar{X} \pm t_{df} s_{\bar{x}}$$
$$= 4000 \pm (2.262)(63.3)$$
$$= 3856.8 \text{ to } 4143.2 \cong 3857 \text{ to } 4143 \text{ hr}$$

where $\bar{X} = 4000$ (as given)

$t_{df} = t_{n-1} = t_9 = 2.262$

$s_{\bar{x}} = \dfrac{s}{\sqrt{n}} = \dfrac{200}{\sqrt{10}} = \dfrac{200}{3.16} = 63.3$

8.6 CHEBYSHEV'S INEQUALITY AND CONFIDENCE INTERVALS FOR THE MEAN

When the sample is small ($n < 30$) and the population is assumed *not* to be normally distributed, neither the normal probability distribution nor a t distribution can be used for constructing a confidence interval.   However, a general theorem developed by the Russian mathematician Chebyshev is useful:

Chebyshev's theorem: The proportion of measurements in a set of data that lies within k standard deviations of the mean is not less than $1 - 1/k^2$, where $k \geq 1$.

As applied to the sampling distribution of a mean, the probability that a sample mean will lie within k standard error units from the population mean is

$$P(\,|\,\bar{X} - \mu\,| \leq k\sigma_{\bar{x}}) \geq 1 - \frac{1}{k^2} \tag{8.10}$$

Formula (*8.10*) is generally referred to as *Chebyshev's inequality*. Note that it is based on the assumption that $\sigma_{\bar{x}}$ is known. If σ is not known then $s_{\bar{x}}$ can be used in its place, but with some risk because of the fluctuation of this value for small samples. Chebyshev's inequality is in fact rarely used for constructing confidence intervals for the mean, but it is the only appropriate method given a population that is decidedly non-normal and a sample that is small ($n < 30$).

In using Chebyshev's inequality in conjunction with interval estimation, the procedure is to set $1 - 1/k^2$ equal to the desired degree of confidence, solve for k, and then construct the interval using one of the following formulas, according to whether or not σ is known:

$$\bar{X} \pm k\sigma_{\bar{x}} \tag{8.11}$$

or

$$\bar{X} \pm ks_{\bar{x}} \tag{8.12}$$

EXAMPLE 9. For a given week, a random sample of 10 employees selected from a large group of hourly employees has a mean wage of $\bar{X}$ = \$180.00 with a sample standard deviation of s = \$14.00. What is the interval of wages such that there is at least 95 percent confidence that the true mean is included within the interval? Using Chebyshev's inequality formula (*8.10*), since $1 - 1/k^2 = 0.95$, we first solve for k:

$$\frac{1}{k^2} = 1.00 - 0.95 = 0.05$$
$$0.05k^2 = 1$$
$$k^2 = 20$$
$$k = \sqrt{20} = 4.47 \text{ standard error units}$$

Then, from formula (*8.12*),

$$\bar{X} \pm k\frac{s}{\sqrt{n}} = 180.00 \pm 4.47\left(\frac{14.00}{\sqrt{10}}\right)$$
$$= 180.00 \pm 4.47(4.43) = \$160.20 \text{ to } \$199.80$$

8.7 SUMMARY TABLE FOR INTERVAL ESTIMATION OF THE POPULATION MEAN

Table 8.3 Interval Estimation of the Population Mean

Population	Sample size	σ known	σ unknown
Normally distributed	Large ($n \geq 30$)	$\bar{X} \pm z\sigma_{\bar{x}}$	$\bar{X} \pm zs_{\bar{x}}$**
	Small ($n < 30$)	$\bar{X} \pm z\sigma_{\bar{x}}$	$\bar{X} \pm ts_{\bar{x}}$
Not normally distributed	Large ($n \geq 30$)	$\bar{X} \pm z\sigma_{\bar{x}}$*	$\bar{X} \pm zs_{\bar{x}}$†
	Small ($n < 30$)	$\bar{X} \pm k\sigma_{\bar{x}}$ where $1 - 1/k^2$ is defined using Chebyshev's inequality	$\bar{X} \pm ks_{\bar{x}}$†† where $1 - 1/k^2$ is defined using Chebyshev's inequality

*Central limit theorem is invoked.
**z is used as an approximation of t.
†Central limit theorem is invoked, and z is used as an approximation of t.
††Some statisticians consider this interval unreliable because of the fluctuation in the value of $s_{\bar{x}}$ for small samples.

Solved Problems

SAMPLING DISTRIBUTION OF THE MEAN

8.1. For a particular brand of TV picture tube, it is known that the mean operating life of the tubes is $\mu = 9000$ hr with a standard deviation of $\sigma = 500$ hr. Determine the expected value and standard error of the sampling distribution of the mean given a sample size of $n = 25$. Interpret the meaning of the computed values.

$$E(\bar{X}) = \mu = 9000$$

$$\sigma_{\bar{x}} = \frac{\sigma}{\sqrt{n}} = \frac{500}{\sqrt{25}} = \frac{500}{5} = 100$$

These calculations indicate that in the long run the mean of a large group of sample means, each based on a sample size of $n = 25$, will be equal to 9000 hr. Further, the variability of these sample means in respect to the expected value of 9000 hr is expressed by a standard deviation of 100 hr.

8.2. A financial analyst takes a 10 percent random sample of 300 accounts and finds that the mean account balance is $\bar{X} = \$148.50$ with a standard deviation of $s = \$35.75$. On the basis of this information, what is the estimated value of the standard error of the mean?

$$s_{\bar{x}} = \frac{s}{\sqrt{n}} \sqrt{\frac{N-n}{N-1}} = \frac{35.75}{\sqrt{30}} \sqrt{\frac{300-30}{300-1}}$$

$$= \frac{35.75}{5.4772} \sqrt{0.9030} = (6.5271)(0.9503) = \$6.20$$

8.3. For Problem 8.2, suppose that the actual mean for the population of 300 accounts is $\mu = \$138.00$. What is the probability of obtaining a sample mean balance of $148.50 or larger?

Since $E(\bar{X}) = \mu = \$138.00$ and $s_{\bar{x}} = \$6.20$ (from Problem 8.2),

$$z = \frac{\bar{X} - \mu}{s_{\bar{x}}} = \frac{148.50 - 138.00}{6.20} = \frac{10.50}{6.20} = +1.69$$

Therefore,

$$P(\bar{X} \geq 148.50) = P(z \geq +1.69)$$
$$P(z \geq +1.69) = 0.5000 - 0.4545 = 0.0455$$

(*Note:* Whether or not the population of account balances is normally distributed, the normal distribution can be used because the sample size is at least $n = 30$ (central limit theorem).)

8.4. This problem and the following two problems serve to illustrate the meaning of the sampling distribution of the mean by reference to a highly simplified population. Suppose a population consists of just the four values 3, 5, 7, and 8. Compute (*a*) the population mean, μ, and (*b*) the population standard deviation, σ.

With reference to Table 8.4,

(*a*) $\mu = \frac{\Sigma X}{N} = \frac{23}{4} = 5.75$

(b) $\sigma = \sqrt{\dfrac{\Sigma X^2}{N} - \left(\dfrac{\Sigma X}{N}\right)^2} = \sqrt{\dfrac{147}{4} - \left(\dfrac{23}{4}\right)^2}$

$= \sqrt{36.75 - (5.75)^2} = \sqrt{36.75 - 33.0625} = 1.92$

Table 8.4   Worksheet for Problem 8.4

X	X^2
3	9
5	25
7	49
8	64
$\Sigma X = 23$	$\Sigma X^2 = 147$

8.5. For the population described in Problem 8.4, suppose that simple random samples of size $n = 2$ each are taken from this population. For each sample the first sampled item is *not* replaced in the population before the second item is sampled.

(a)   List all possible pairs of values which can constitute a sample.

(b)   For each of the pairs identified in (a), compute the sample mean, $\bar{X}$, and demonstrate that the mean of all possible sample means, $\mu_{\bar{x}}$, is equal to the mean of the population from which the samples were selected.

(a) and (b)   From Table 8.5,

$$\mu_{\bar{x}} = \frac{\Sigma \bar{X}}{N_{\text{samples}}} = \frac{34.5}{6} = 5.75$$

[which equals μ as computed in Problem 8.4(a)].

Table 8.5   Possible Samples and Sample Means for Problem 8.5

Possible samples	$\bar{X}$
3, 5	4.0
3, 7	5.0
3, 8	5.5
5, 7	6.0
5, 8	6.5
7, 8	7.5
	$\Sigma \bar{X} = 34.5$

8.6. For the sampling situation described in Problems 8.4 and 8.5, compute the standard error of the mean by determining the standard deviation of the six possible sample means identified in Problem 8.5 in respect to the population mean, μ. Then compute the standard error of the mean based on σ being known and sampling from a finite population, using the appropriate formula from this chapter. Verify that the two standard error values are the same.

With reference to Table 8.5,

Table 8.6   Worksheet for Problem 8.6

$\bar{X}$	$\bar{X}^2$
4.0	16.00
5.0	25.00
5.5	30.25
6.0	36.00
6.5	42.25
7.5	56.25
$\Sigma \bar{X} = 34.5$	$\Sigma \bar{X}^2 = 205.75$

First method:

$$\sigma_{\bar{x}} = \sqrt{\frac{\Sigma \bar{X}^2}{N_S} - \left(\frac{\Sigma \bar{X}}{N_S}\right)^2} = \sqrt{\frac{205.75}{6} - \left(\frac{34.5}{6}\right)^2}$$

$$= \sqrt{34.2917 - (5.75)^2} = \sqrt{34.2917 - 33.0625} = 1.11$$

Second method:

$$\sigma_{\bar{x}} = \frac{\sigma}{\sqrt{n}} \sqrt{\frac{N - n}{N - 1}} = \frac{1.92}{\sqrt{2}} \sqrt{\frac{4 - 2}{4 - 1}}$$

$$= \frac{1.92}{1.414} \sqrt{0.6666} = 1.358(0.816) = 1.11$$

Of course, the second method is the one always used for determining the standard error of the mean in actual data situations. But conceptually, the first method illustrates more directly the meaning of the standard error of the mean.

CONFIDENCE INTERVALS FOR THE MEAN USING THE NORMAL DISTRIBUTION

8.7.   Suppose that the standard deviation of the tube life for a particular brand of TV picture tube is known to be $\sigma = 500$, but that the mean operating life is not known. Overall, the operating life of the tubes is assumed to be approximately normally distributed. For a sample of $n = 15$, the mean operating life is $\bar{X} = 8900$ hr. Construct (a) the 95 percent and   (b) the 90 percent confidence intervals for estimating the population mean.

The normal probability distribution can be used in this case because the population is normally distributed and σ is known.

(a) $\bar{X} \pm z\sigma_{\bar{x}} = 8900 \pm 1.96 \dfrac{\sigma}{\sqrt{n}}$

$$= 8900 \pm 1.96 \frac{500}{\sqrt{15}} = 8900 \pm 1.96 \left(\frac{500}{3.87}\right)$$

$$= 8900 \pm 1.96(129.20) = 8647 \text{ to } 9153$$

(b) $\bar{X} \pm z\sigma_{\bar{x}} = 8900 \pm 1.65(129.20) = 8687 \text{ to } 9113 \text{ hr}$

8.8. In respect to Problem 8.7, suppose that the population of tube life cannot be assumed to be normally distributed. However, the sample mean of $\bar{X} = 8900$ is based on a sample of $n = 35$. Construct the 95 percent confidence interval for estimating the population mean.

The normal probability distribution can be used in this case by invoking the central limit theorem, which indicates that for $n \geq 30$ the sampling distribution can be assumed to be normally distributed even though the population is not normally distributed. Thus,

$$\bar{X} \pm z\sigma_{\bar{x}} = 8900 \pm 1.96 \frac{\sigma}{\sqrt{n}} = 8900 \pm 1.96 \frac{500}{\sqrt{35}}$$

$$= 8900 \pm 1.96\left(\frac{500}{5.92}\right) = 8900 \pm 1.96(84.46) = 8734 \text{ to } 9066 \text{ hr}$$

8.9. In respect to Problem 8.8, suppose that the population can be assumed to be normally distributed, but that the population standard deviation is not known. Rather, the sample standard deviation $s = 500$ and $\bar{X} = 8900$. Estimate the population mean using a 90 percent confidence interval.

Because $n \geq 30$ the normal distribution can be used as an approximation of the t distribution. However, because the population is normally distributed, the central limit theorem need not be invoked. Therefore,

$$\bar{X} \pm zs_{\bar{x}} = 8900 \pm 1.65\left(\frac{500}{\sqrt{35}}\right) = 8900 \pm 1.65(84.46) = 8761 \text{ to } 9039 \text{ hr}$$

8.10. In respect to Problems 8.8 and 8.9, suppose that the population *cannot* be assumed to be normally distributed and, further, that the population σ is not known. As before, $n = 35$, $s = 500$, and $\bar{X} = 8900$. Estimate the population mean using a 99 percent confidence interval.

In this case the central limit theorem is invoked, as in Problem 8.8, and z is used as an approximation of t, as in Problem 8.9.

$$\bar{X} \pm zs_{\bar{x}} = 8900 \pm 2.58\left(\frac{500}{\sqrt{35}}\right) = 8900 \pm 2.58(84.46) = 8682 \text{ to } 9118 \text{ hr}$$

8.11. A marketing research analyst collects data for a random sample of 100 customers out of the 400 who purchased a particular "coupon special." The 100 people spent an average of $\bar{X} = \$24.57$ in the store with a standard deviation of $s = \$6.60$. Using a 95 percent confidence interval, estimate (a) the mean purchase amount for all 400 customers, and (b) the total dollar amount of purchases by the 400 customers.

(a) $s_{\bar{x}} = \dfrac{s}{\sqrt{n}} \sqrt{\dfrac{N-n}{N-1}} = \dfrac{6.60}{\sqrt{100}} \sqrt{\dfrac{400-100}{400-1}}$

$\quad = \dfrac{6.60}{10} \sqrt{0.7519} = 0.660(0.867) = 0.57$

$\bar{X} \pm zs_{\bar{x}} = 24.57 \pm 1.96(0.57) = \$23.45 \text{ to } \$25.69$

(b) $N(\bar{X} \pm zs_{\bar{x}}) = 400(\$23.45 \text{ to } \$25.69) = \$9380 \text{ to } \$10,276$

or

$$N\bar{X} \pm N(zs_{\bar{x}}) = 400(24.57) \pm 400(1.12)$$
$$= 9828 \pm 448 = \$9380 \text{ to } \$10,276$$

(*Note:* The confidence interval for the dollar amount of purchases is simply the total number of customers *in the population* multiplied by the confidence limits for the mean purchase amount per customer. Such a population value is referred to as the *total quantity* in some textbooks.)

DETERMINING THE REQUIRED SAMPLE SIZE FOR ESTIMATING THE MEAN

8.12. A prospective purchaser wishes to estimate the mean dollar amount of sales per customer at a toy store located at an airlines terminal. Based on data from other similar airports, the standard deviation of such sales amounts is estimated to be about $\sigma = \$0.80$. What size of random sample should he collect, as a minimum, if he wants to estimate the mean sales amount within 25¢ and with 99 percent confidence?

$$n = \left(\frac{z\sigma}{E}\right)^2 = \left[\frac{(2.58)(0.80)}{0.25}\right]^2 = (8.256)^2 = 68.16 \cong 69$$

8.13. Referring to Problem 8.12, what is the minimum required sample size if the distribution of sales amounts is not assumed to be normal and the purchaser wishes to estimate the mean sales amount within 50¢ with 99 percent confidence?

$$n = \left(\frac{z\sigma}{E}\right)^2 = \left[\frac{(2.58)(0.80)}{0.50}\right]^2 = (4.128)^2 = 17.04 \cong 18$$

However, because the population is not assumed to be normally distributed, the minimum sample size is $n = 30$, so that the central limit theorem can be invoked as the basis for using the normal probability distribution for constructing the confidence interval.

ONE-SIDED CONFIDENCE INTERVALS FOR THE POPULATION MEAN

8.14. Occasionally, a *one-sided confidence interval* may be of greater interest than the usual two-sided interval. Such would be the case if we are interested only in the highest (or only in the lowest) value of the mean at the indicated degree of confidence. An "upper 95 percent interval" extends from a computed lower limit to positive infinity, with a proportion of 0.05 of the area under the normal curve being to the left of the lower limit. Similarly, a "lower 95 percent confidence interval" extends from negative infinity to a computed upper limit, with a proportion of 0.05 of the area under the normal curve being to the right of the upper limit.

Suppose a prospective purchaser in a toy store at an airlines terminal observes a random sample of $n = 64$ sales and finds that the sample mean is $\bar{X} = \$4.63$ with the sample standard deviation $s = \$1.20$. Determine the upper 95 percent confidence interval so that the *minimum* value of the population mean is identified with a 95 percent degree of confidence.

$$s_{\bar{x}} = \frac{s}{\sqrt{n}} = \frac{1.20}{\sqrt{64}} = \frac{1.20}{8} = 0.15$$

Upper 95% Int. $= \bar{X} - zs_{\bar{x}} = 4.63 - 1.65(0.15) = \$4.38$ or higher

Thus, with a 95 percent degree of confidence we can state that the mean sales amount for the population of all customers is equal to or greater than $4.38.

8.15. With 99 percent confidence, what is the estimate of the maximum value of the mean sales amount in Problem 8.14?

Since $\bar{X} = \$4.63$ and $s_{\bar{x}} = 0.15$,

Lower 99% Int. $= \bar{X} + z s_{\bar{x}} = 4.63 + 2.33(0.15) = \$4.98$ or less

Thus, with a 99 percent degree of confidence we can state that the mean sales amount is no larger than $4.98.

CONFIDENCE INTERVALS FOR THE MEAN BASED ON USING THE t DISTRIBUTIONS

8.16. In Problem 8.7 we constructed confidence intervals for estimating the mean operating life of a particular brand of TV picture tube based on the assumption that the operating life of all tubes is approximately normally distributed and $\sigma = 500$, and given a sample of $n = 15$ with $\bar{X} = 8900$ hr. Suppose that σ is not known, but rather, that the sample standard deviation is $s = 500$.

(a) Construct the 95 percent confidence interval for estimating the population mean and compare this interval with the answer to Problem 8.7(a).

(b) Construct the 90 percent confidence interval for estimating the population mean and compare this interval with the answer to Problem 8.7(b).

(*Note:* Use of a t distribution is appropriate in this case because the population is assumed to be normally distributed, σ is not known, and the sample is small ($n < 30$).)

(a) $\bar{X} \pm t_{df} s_{\bar{x}} = 8900 \pm 2.145 \dfrac{s}{\sqrt{n}} = 8900 \pm 2.145 \dfrac{500}{\sqrt{15}}$

$= 8900 \pm 2.145 \left(\dfrac{500}{3.87} \right) = 8900 \pm 2.145(129.199) = 8623$ to 9177 hr

The confidence interval is wider than the one in Problem 8.7(a), reflecting the difference between the t distribution and the normal probability distribution.

(b) $\bar{X} \pm t_{df} s_{\bar{x}} = 8900 \pm 1.761(129.199) = 8672$ to 9128 hr

Again, the confidence interval is wider than the one in Problem 8.7(b).

8.17. As a commercial buyer for a private supermarket brand, suppose you take a random sample of 12 No. 303 cans of string beans at a canning plant. The net weight of the drained beans in each can is reported in Table 8.7. Determine (a) the mean net weight of string beans being packed in each can for this sample, and (b) the sample standard deviation. (c) Assuming that the net weights per can are normally distributed, estimate the mean weight per can of beans being packed using a 95 percent confidence interval.

Table 8.7 Net Weight of Beans Packed in 12 No. 303 Cans

Ounces per can	15.7	15.8	15.9	16.0	16.1	16.2
No. of cans	1	2	2	3	3	1

Table 8.8   Worksheet for Problem 8.17

X per can	No. of cans	Total X	X^2 per can	Total X^2
15.7	1	15.7	246.49	246.49
15.8	2	31.6	249.64	499.28
15.9	2	31.8	252.81	505.62
16.0	3	48.0	256.00	768.00
16.1	3	48.3	259.21	777.63
16.2	1	16.2	262.44	262.44
	$n = 12$	$\Sigma X = 191.6$		$\Sigma X^2 = 3059.46$

Referring to Table 8.8,

(a) $\bar{X} = \dfrac{\Sigma X}{n} = \dfrac{191.6}{12} = 15.97$ oz

(b) $s = \sqrt{\dfrac{n \Sigma X^2 - (\Sigma X)^2}{n(n-1)}} = \sqrt{\dfrac{12(3059.46) - (191.6)^2}{12(11)}} = \sqrt{0.0224} = 0.15$

(c) $\bar{X} \pm t_{df}s_{\bar{x}} = 15.97 \pm t_{11}\dfrac{s}{\sqrt{n}} = 15.97 \pm 2.201\left(\dfrac{0.15}{\sqrt{12}}\right)$

$\qquad = 15.97 \pm 2.201\left(\dfrac{0.15}{3.46}\right) = 15.97 \pm 2.201(0.043) = 15.88$ to 16.06 oz

CONFIDENCE INTERVALS FOR THE MEAN USING CHEBYSHEV'S INEQUALITY

8.18.   For a sample of size $n = 15$ TV picture tubes, the mean operating life is $\bar{X} = 8900$ hr with a standard deviation of $s = 500$ hr.   Construct a 90 percent confidence interval for the population mean if the operating life of all tubes cannot be assumed to be normally distributed.   Compare this interval with the one constructed in Problem 8.7(b) using the normal distribution, and the one constructed in Problem 8.16(b) using a t distribution.

Since

$$1 - \frac{1}{k^2} = 0.90 \quad \text{(by definition)}$$

$$\frac{1}{k^2} = 1.00 - 0.90 = 0.10$$

$$0.10k^2 = 1$$

$$k^2 = 10$$

$$k = \sqrt{10} = 3.162$$

Then

$$\bar{X} \pm k\frac{s}{\sqrt{n}} = 8900 \pm 3.162\frac{500}{\sqrt{15}} = 8900 \pm 3.16\left(\frac{500}{3.87}\right)$$

$$= 8900 \pm 3.16(129.199) = 8492 \text{ to } 9308 \text{ hr}$$

Thus, the interval is wider than the intervals based on the normal distribution and the t distribution, as would be expected.   (See Section 8.6.)

Supplementary Problems

SAMPLING DISTRIBUTION OF THE MEAN

8.19. The mean dollar value of the sales amounts for a particular consumer product last year is known to be $\mu = \$3400$ per retail outlet handling the item, with a standard deviation of $\sigma = \$200$. If a large number of outlets handle the product, determine the standard error of the mean for a sample of size $n = 25$.

Ans. $40.00

8.20. Referring to Problem 8.19, suppose only 100 retail outlets handle the product. Determine the standard error of the mean for the sample of $n = 25$ in this case, and compare your answer with the answer to Problem 8.19.

Ans. $34.80

8.21. Refer to Problem 8.19. What is the probability that the mean for a random sample of size $n = 25$ will be (a) greater than $3500; (b) between $3350 and $3450?

Ans. (a) 0.0062, (b) 0.7888

8.22. Refer to Problem 8.20. What is the probability that the mean for a random sample of size $n = 25$ will be (a) greater than $3500, (b) between $3350 and $3450? Compare your answers with the answers to Problem 8.21.

Ans. (a) 0.0021, (b) 0.8502

CONFIDENCE INTERVALS FOR THE MEAN

8.23. Suppose that you wish to estimate the mean sales amount per retail outlet for a particular consumer product during the past year. The number of retail outlets is large. Determine the 95 percent confidence interval given that the sales amounts are assumed to be normally distributed, $\bar{X} = \$3425$, $\sigma = \$200$, and $n = 25$.

Ans. $3346.60 to $3503.40

8.24. Referring to Problem 8.23, determine the 95 percent confidence interval given that the population is assumed to be normally distributed, $\bar{X} = \$3425$, $s = \$200$, and $n = 25$.

Ans. $3342.44 to $3507.56

8.25. For Problem 8.23, determine the 95 percent confidence interval given that the population is *not* assumed to be normally distributed, $\bar{X} = \$3425$, $s = \$200$, and $n = 50$.

Ans. $3369.55 to $3480.45

8.26. For a sample of 50 firms taken from a particular industry the mean number of employees per firm is 420.4 with a sample standard deviation of 55.7. There is a total of 380 firms in this industry. Determine the standard error of the mean to be used in conjunction with estimating the population mean by a confidence interval.

Ans. 7.33

8.27. For Problem 8.26, determine the 90 percent confidence interval for estimating the average number of workers per firm in the industry.

Ans. 408.3 to 432.5

8.28. For the situations described in Problems 8.26 and 8.27, determine the 90 percent confidence interval for estimating the total number of workers employed in the industry.

Ans. 155,154 to 164,350

8.29. An analyst in a personnel department randomly selects the records of 16 hourly employees and finds that the mean wage rate per hour is $7.50. The wage rates in the firm are assumed to be normally distributed. If the standard deviation of the wage rates is known to be $1.00, estimate the mean wage rate in the firm using an 80 percent confidence interval.

Ans. $7.18 to $7.82

8.30. Referring to Problem 8.29, suppose that the standard deviation of the population is not known, but that the standard deviation of the sample is $1.00. Estimate the mean wage rate in the firm using an 80 percent confidence interval.

Ans. $7.16 to $7.84

8.31. Suppose that the wage rates of the firm in Problem 8.29 cannot be assumed to be normally distributed. Estimate the mean wage rate in the firm using an 80 percent confidence interval.

Ans. $6.94 to $8.06

8.32. The mean diameter of a sample of $n = 12$ cylindrical rods included in a shipment is 2.350 mm with a standard deviation of 0.050 mm. The distribution of the diameters of all of the rods included in the shipment is assumed to be approximately normal. Determine the 99 percent confidence interval for estimating the mean diameter of all of the rods included in the shipment.

Ans. 2.307 to 2.393 mm

8.33. The mean diameter of a sample of $n = 100$ rods included in a shipment is 2.350 mm with a standard deviation of 0.050 mm. Estimate the mean diameter of all rods included in the shipment if the shipment contains 500 rods, using a 99 percent confidence interval.

Ans. 2.338 to 2.362 mm

8.34. The mean weight per rod for the sample of 100 rods in Problem 8.33 is 8.45 g with a standard deviation of 0.25 g. Estimate the total weight of the entire shipment (exclusive of packing materials), using a 99 percent confidence interval.

Ans. 4195 to 4255 g

8.35. A shipment of 100 defective machines has been received in a machine-repair department. For a random sample of 10 of the machines, the average time required to repair them is $\bar{X} = 85.0$ min with $s = 15.0$ min. Estimate the average amount of time per machine required to repair the machines in the shipment, using a 90 percent confidence interval.

Ans. 70.7 to 99.3 min

8.36. Estimate the total amount of working time required to repair all 100 machines in Problem 8.35, using a 90 percent confidence interval.

Ans. 7070 to 9930 min, or approx. 118 to 166 hr

DETERMINING THE REQUIRED SAMPLE SIZE FOR ESTIMATING THE MEAN

8.37. From historical records, the standard deviation of the sales level per retail outlet for a consumer product is known to be $\sigma = \$200$, and the population of sales amounts per outlet is assumed to be normally distributed.   What is the minimum sample size required to estimate the mean sales per outlet within $100 and with 95 percent confidence?

Ans. $15.37 \cong 16$

8.38. An analyst wishes to estimate the mean hourly wage of workers in a particular company within 25¢ and 90 percent confidence.   The standard deviation of the wage rates is estimated as being no larger than $1.00.   What is the number of personnel records that should be sampled, as a minimum, to satisfy this research objective?

Ans. $43.56 \cong 44$

ONE-SIDED CONFIDENCE INTERVALS FOR THE POPULATION MEAN

8.39. Instead of the two-sided confidence interval constructed in Problem 8.23, suppose we wish to estimate the minimum value of the mean level of sales per retail outlet for a particular consumer product during the past year.   As before, the distribution of sales amounts per store is assumed to be approximately normal.   Determine the minimum value of the mean using a 95 percent confidence interval given that $\bar{X} = \$3425$, $\sigma = \$200$, and $n = 25$.   Compare your confidence interval with the one constructed in Problem 8.23.

Ans.   Est. $\mu \geq \$3359$

8.40. Using the data in Problem 8.32, determine the 99 percent lower confidence interval for estimating the mean diameter of all the rods included in the shipment.   Compare the interval with the one constructed in Problem 8.32.

Ans.   Est. $\mu \leq 2.388$ mm

Chapter 9

Other Confidence Intervals

9.1 CONFIDENCE INTERVALS FOR THE DIFFERENCE BETWEEN TWO POPULATION MEANS USING THE NORMAL DISTRIBUTION

There is often a need to estimate the difference between two population means, such as the difference between the wage levels in two firms. As indicated in Section 8.1, the unbiased point estimate of $(\mu_1 - \mu_2)$ is $(\bar{X}_1 - \bar{X}_2)$. The confidence interval is constructed in a manner similar to that used for estimating the mean, except that the relevant standard error for the sampling distribution is the standard error of the *difference* between means. Use of the normal distribution is based on the same conditions as for the sampling distribution of the mean (see Section 8.2), except that two samples are involved. The formula used for estimating the difference between two population means is

$$(\bar{X}_1 - \bar{X}_2) \pm z\sigma_{\bar{x}_1 - \bar{x}_2} \qquad (9.1)$$

or

$$(\bar{X}_1 - \bar{X}_2) \pm zs_{\bar{x}_1 - \bar{x}_2} \qquad (9.2)$$

When the standard deviations of the two populations are known, the standard error of the difference between means is

$$\sigma_{\bar{x}_1 - \bar{x}_2} = \sqrt{\sigma_{\bar{x}_1}^2 + \sigma_{\bar{x}_2}^2} \qquad (9.3)$$

When the standard deviations of the populations are not known, the estimated standard error of the difference between means is

$$s_{\bar{x}_1 - \bar{x}_2} = \sqrt{s_{\bar{x}_1}^2 + s_{\bar{x}_2}^2} \qquad (9.4)$$

The values of the standard errors of the respective means included in these formulas are calculated by the formulas given in Section 8.2, including the possibility of using finite correction factors when appropriate.

EXAMPLE 1. The mean weekly wage for a sample of $n = 30$ employees in a large manufacturing firm is $\bar{X} = \$180.00$ with a sample standard deviation of $s = \$14.00$. In another large firm a random sample of $n = 40$ hourly employees has a mean weekly wage of $170.00 with a sample standard deviation of $s = \$10.00$. The 99 percent confidence interval for estimating the difference between the mean weekly wage levels in the two firms is

$$99\% \text{ Int.} = (\bar{X}_1 - \bar{X}_2) \pm zs_{\bar{x}_1 - \bar{x}_2}$$
$$= \$10.00 \pm 2.58(3.01)$$
$$= \$2.23 \text{ to } \$17.77$$

142

where $\bar{X}_1 - \bar{X}_2 = \$180.00 - 170.00 = \$10.00$

$z = 2.58$

$$s_{\bar{x}_1} = \frac{s_1}{\sqrt{n_1}} = \frac{14.00}{\sqrt{30}} = \frac{14.00}{5.477} = 2.56$$

$$s_{\bar{x}_2} = \frac{s_2}{\sqrt{n_2}} = \frac{10.00}{\sqrt{40}} = \frac{10.00}{6.325} = 1.58$$

$$s_{\bar{x}_1 - \bar{x}_2} = \sqrt{s_{\bar{x}_1}^2 + s_{\bar{x}_2}^2} = \sqrt{(2.56)^2 + (1.58)^2} = \sqrt{6.5536 + 2.4964} \cong 3.01$$

Thus, we can state the average weekly wage in the first firm is greater than the average in the second firm by an amount somewhere between \$2.23 and \$17.77, with 99 percent confidence in this interval estimate.

In addition to the two-sided confidence interval, a one-sided confidence interval for the difference between means can also be constructed. (See Problem 9.4.)

9.2 STUDENT'S t DISTRIBUTIONS AND CONFIDENCE INTERVALS FOR THE DIFFERENCE BETWEEN MEANS

The general formula for estimating the difference between means when using the t distribution is similar to that used with the normal distribution in Section 9.1. Use of a t distribution is appropriate when a sample is small ($n < 30$), the population is normally distributed, and σ is not known (see Section 8.5). Where $df = n_1 + n_2 - 2$, the confidence interval is

$$(\bar{X}_1 - \bar{X}_2) \pm t_{df}s_{\bar{x}_1 - \bar{x}_2} \tag{9.5}$$

EXAMPLE 2. For a random sample of $n = 10$ bulbs, the mean bulb life is $\bar{X} = 4000$ hr with $s = 200$. The bulb life is assumed to be normally distributed. For another brand of bulb whose useful life is also assumed to be normally distributed, a random sample of $n = 8$ has a sample mean $\bar{X} = 4600$ and a sample standard deviation $s = 250$. The 90 percent confidence interval for estimating the difference between the mean operating life of the two brands of bulbs is

90% Int. $= \bar{X}_1 - \bar{X}_2 \pm t_{df}s_{\bar{x}_1 - \bar{x}_2} = -600 \pm 1.746(108.65) = -789.7 \text{ to } -410.3 \cong -790 \text{ to } -410$

where $\bar{X}_1 - \bar{X}_2 = 4000 - 4600 = -600$ (as given)

$t_{df} = t_{(n_1 + n_2 - 2)} = t_{16} = 1.746$

$$s_{\bar{x}_1} = \frac{s_1}{\sqrt{n_1}} = \frac{200}{\sqrt{10}} = \frac{200}{3.16} = 63.3$$

$$s_{\bar{x}_2} = \frac{s_2}{\sqrt{n_2}} = \frac{250}{\sqrt{8}} = \frac{250}{2.83} = 88.3$$

$$s_{\bar{x}_1 - \bar{x}_2} = \sqrt{s_{\bar{x}_1}^2 + s_{\bar{x}_2}^2} = \sqrt{(63.3)^2 + (88.3)^2} = \sqrt{4006.89 + 7796.89} = 108.65 \text{ hr}$$

In other words, the estimated difference, with a 90 percent degree of confidence, is that the *second* brand has a longer operating life of somewhere between 410 hr and 790 hr, as compared with the first brand.

As explained in Section 8.5, a rule of thumb is that a t distribution can be approximated by the normal distribution when $n \geq 30$ (or $df \geq 29$) for a single sample. For estimating the difference between two sample means, the rule followed in this book is that such approximation is acceptable when $df \geq 29$. Thus, each of the two samples can be small ($n < 30$) and yet the normal distribution might be used because $df \geq 29$ for the difference between means. However, in such small sample cases note that because the central limit theorem cannot be invoked, the two populations must be assumed to be normally distributed.

9.3 CONFIDENCE INTERVALS FOR THE PROPORTION USING THE NORMAL DISTRIBUTION

As explained in Section 6.4, the probability distribution which is applicable to proportions is the binomial probability distribution.   However, the mathematics associated with constructing a confidence interval for an unknown population proportion on the basis of the binomial distribution are rather involved.   Therefore, most textbooks utilize the normal distribution as an approximation of the binomial for constructing confidence intervals for proportions.   As explained in Section 7.3, such approximation is appropriate when $n \geq 30$ and both $np \geq 5$ and $n(1 - p) \geq 5$.   However, when the population proportion p (or π) is not known, many statisticians suggest that a sample $n \geq 100$ should be taken.

The variance of the distribution of proportions (see Section 6.4) serves as the basis for the standard error.   Given an observed sample proportion, $\bar{p}$, the estimated standard error of the proportion is

$$s_{\bar{p}} = \sqrt{\frac{\bar{p}(1 - \bar{p})}{n}} \qquad (9.6)$$

In the context of statistical estimation, the population proportion p (or π) would not be known because that is the value being estimated.   If the population is finite then use of the finite correction factor is appropriate (see Section 8.2).   As was the case for the standard error of the mean, use of this correction is generally not considered necessary if $n < 0.05N$.   The formula for the standard error of the proportion which includes the finite correction factor is

$$s_{\bar{p}} = \sqrt{\frac{\bar{p}(1 - \bar{p})}{n}} \sqrt{\frac{N - n}{N - 1}} \qquad (9.7)$$

Finally, the confidence interval for a population proportion is

$$\bar{p} \pm z s_{\bar{p}} \qquad (9.8)$$

In addition to the two-sided confidence interval, a one-sided confidence interval for the population proportion can also be constructed.   (See Problem 9.12.)

EXAMPLE 3. A marketing research firm contacts a random sample of 100 men in a large community and finds that a sample proportion of 0.40 prefer the razor blades manufactured by the client firm to all other brands.   The 95 percent confidence interval for the proportion of all men in the community who prefer the client firm's razor blades is determined as follows:

$$s_{\bar{p}} = \sqrt{\frac{\bar{p}(1 - \bar{p})}{n}} = \sqrt{\frac{(0.40)(0.60)}{100}} = \sqrt{\frac{0.24}{100}} = \sqrt{0.0024} \cong 0.05$$

$$\bar{p} \pm z s_{\bar{p}} = 0.40 \pm 1.96(0.05)$$

$$= 0.40 \pm 0.098 \cong 0.40 \pm 0.10 = 0.30 \text{ to } 0.50$$

Therefore, with 95 percent confidence we estimate the proportion of all men in the community who prefer the client firm's blades to be somewhere between 0.30 and 0.50.

9.4 DETERMINING THE REQUIRED SAMPLE SIZE FOR ESTIMATING THE PROPORTION

Before a sample is actually collected, the minimum required sample size can be determined by specifying the degree of confidence required, the error which is acceptable, and by making an initial estimate of π, the unknown population proportion:

$$n = \frac{z^2 \pi (1 - \pi)}{E^2} \qquad (9.9)$$

In (9.9), z is the value used for the specified confidence interval, π is the initial estimate of the population proportion, and E is the "plus and minus" error factor allowed in the interval (always one half the total confidence interval).

If an initial estimate of π is not possible, then it should be estimated as being 0.50.   Such an estimate is "conservative" in that it is the value for which the largest sample size would be required.   Under such an assumption, the general formula for sample size is simplified as follows:

$$n = \left(\frac{z}{2E}\right)^2 \qquad (9.10)$$

(*Note:*   When solving for sample size, any fractional result is always rounded up.   Further, any computed sample size below 30 should be increased to 30 because formulas (9.9) and (9.10) are based on use of the normal distribution.   Some statisticians suggest that the minimum sample size should be 100.)

EXAMPLE 4.   For the study in Example 3, suppose that before data were collected it was specified that the 95 percent interval estimate should be within ± 0.05 and no prior judgment was made about the likely value of π.   The minimum sample size which should be collected is

$$n = \left(\frac{z}{2E}\right)^2 = \left(\frac{1.96}{2(0.05)}\right)^2 = \left(\frac{1.96}{0.10}\right)^2 = (19.6)^2 = 384.16 = 385$$

In addition to estimating the population proportion, the *total number* in a category of the population can also be estimated.   (See Problem 9.7(b).)

9.5 CONFIDENCE INTERVALS FOR THE DIFFERENCE BETWEEN TWO POPULATION PROPORTIONS

In order to estimate the difference between the proportions in two populations, the unbiased point estimate of $(\pi_1 - \pi_2)$ is $(\bar{p}_1 - \bar{p}_2)$.   See Section 8.1.   The confidence interval involves use of the standard error of the *difference* between proportions.   Use of the normal distribution is based on the same conditions as for the sampling distribution of the proportion, except that two samples are involved.   The confidence interval for estimating the difference between two population proportions is

$$(\bar{p}_1 - \bar{p}_2) \pm z s_{\bar{p}_1 - \bar{p}_2} \qquad (9.11)$$

The standard error of the difference between proportions is determined by (9.12), wherein the value of each respective standard error of the proportion is calculated as described in Section 9.3:

$$s_{\bar{p}_1 - \bar{p}_2} = \sqrt{s_{\bar{p}_1}^2 + s_{\bar{p}_2}^2} \qquad (9.12)$$

EXAMPLE 5.   In Example 3 it was reported that a proportion of 0.40 men out of a random sample of 100 in a large community preferred the client firm's razor blades to all others.   In another large community, 60 men out of a random sample of 200 men prefer the client firm's blades.   The 90 percent confidence interval for the difference in the proportion of men in the two communities preferring the client firm's blades is

$$90\% \text{ Int.} = (\bar{p}_1 - \bar{p}_2) \pm z s_{\bar{p}_1 - \bar{p}_2}$$
$$= (0.10) \pm 1.65(0.059)$$
$$= 0.003 \text{ to } 0.197$$

where $\bar{p}_1 - \bar{p}_2 = 0.40 - 0.30 = 0.10$

$z = 1.65$

$$s_{\bar{p}_1}^2 = \frac{\bar{p}_1(1 - \bar{p}_1)}{n_1} = \frac{(0.40)(0.60)}{100} = 0.0024$$

$$s_{\bar{p}_2}^2 = \frac{\bar{p}_2(1 - \bar{p}_2)}{n_2} = \frac{(0.30)(0.70)}{200} = 0.00105$$

$$s_{\bar{p}_1 - \bar{p}_2} = \sqrt{s_{\bar{p}_1}^2 + s_{\bar{p}_2}^2} = \sqrt{0.0024 + 0.00105} = \sqrt{0.00345} \cong 0.059$$

9.6 THE χ^2 (CHI-SQUARE) DISTRIBUTIONS AND CONFIDENCE INTERVALS FOR THE STANDARD DEVIATION AND VARIANCE

Given a normally distributed population of values, the χ^2 (chi-square) distributions can be shown to be the appropriate probability distributions for the ratio $(n - 1)s^2/\sigma^2$. There is a different chi-square distribution according to the value of $n - 1$, which represents the degrees of freedom (df). Thus,

$$\chi_{df}^2 = \frac{(n - 1)s^2}{\sigma^2} \qquad (9.13)$$

Because the sample variance is the unbiased estimator of the population variance, the long-run expected value of the above ratio is equal to the degrees of freedom, or $(n - 1)$. However, in any given sample the sample variance is not generally identical in value to the population variance. Since the ratio above is known to follow a chi-square distribution, this probability distribution can be used for statistical inference concerning an unknown variance or standard deviation.

Chi-square distributions are not symmetrical. Therefore, a two-sided confidence interval for a standard deviation involves the use of two different χ^2 values, rather than the "plus-and-minus" approach used with the confidence intervals based on the normal distribution. Given that s^2 has been corrected for biasedness (see Section 4.6), the formula for constructing a confidence interval for the population standard deviation is

$$\sqrt{\frac{(n - 1)s^2}{\chi_{df,\text{upper}}^2}} \leq \sigma \leq \sqrt{\frac{(n - 1)s^2}{\chi_{df,\text{lower}}^2}} \qquad (9.14)$$

The confidence interval for the population variance is

$$\frac{(n - 1)s^2}{\chi_{df,\text{upper}}^2} \leq \sigma^2 \leq \frac{(n - 1)s^2}{\chi_{df,\text{lower}}^2} \qquad (9.15)$$

Appendix 7 indicates the proportions of area under the chi-square distributions according to various degrees of freedom, df. In the general formula above, the subscripts "upper" and "lower" identify the percentile points on the particular χ^2 distribution to be used for constructing the confidence interval. For example, for a 90 percent confidence interval the "upper" is $\chi_{0.95}^2$ and the "lower" is $\chi_{0.05}^2$. By excluding the lowest 5 percent and highest 5 percent of the chi-square distribution, what remains is the "middle" 90 percent.

As the degrees of freedom are increased, the chi-square distribution approaches the normal distribution with $\mu = df$ and $\sigma = \sqrt{2df}$. As a rule of thumb, we shall consider such approximation acceptable when $df \geq 30$ (in the present type of application, when $n \geq 31$). Note, however, that use of the chi-square distribution or the normal approximation of it for estimating a variance is based on the necessary assumption that the population being sampled is normally distributed.

EXAMPLE 6.   The mean weekly wage for a sample of 30 hourly employees in a large firm is $\bar{X}$ = \$180.00 with a sample standard deviation of s = \$14.00.   The weekly wage amounts in the firm are known to be approximately normally distributed.   The 95 percent confidence interval for estimating the standard deviation of weekly wages is

$$\sqrt{\frac{(n-1)s^2}{\chi^2_{df,\text{upper}}}} \leq \sigma \leq \sqrt{\frac{(n-1)s^2}{\chi^2_{df,\text{lower}}}}$$

$$\sqrt{\frac{(29)(196.00)}{\chi^2_{29,0.975}}} \leq \sigma \leq \sqrt{\frac{(29)(196.00)}{\chi^2_{29,0.025}}}$$

$$\sqrt{\frac{5684.00}{45.72}} \leq \sigma \leq \sqrt{\frac{5684.00}{16.05}}$$

$$\sqrt{124.3220} \leq \sigma \leq \sqrt{354.1433}$$

$$11.15 \leq \sigma \leq 18.82$$

In the above example, note that because the column headings in Appendix 7 are right-tail probabilities, rather than percentile values, the column headings which are used are the complementary values of the required "upper" and "lower" percentile values.

As an alternative to a two-sided confidence interval, a one-sided confidence interval for the variance or standard deviation can also be constructed.   (See Problem 9.14.)

Solved Problems

CONFIDENCE INTERVALS FOR THE DIFFERENCE BETWEEN TWO POPULATION MEANS USING THE NORMAL DISTRIBUTION

9.1.   For the study reported in Problem 8.11, suppose that there were 900 customers who did not purchase the "coupon special" but who did make other purchases in the store during the period of the study.   For a sample of 200 of these customers, the mean purchase amount was $\bar{X}$ = \$19.60 with a sample standard deviation of s = \$8.40.

(a)   Estimate the mean purchase amount for the noncoupon customers, using a 95 percent confidence interval.

(b)   Estimate the difference between the mean purchase amount of coupon and noncoupon customers, using a 90 percent confidence interval.

(a) $s_{\bar{x}} = \dfrac{s}{\sqrt{n}} \sqrt{\dfrac{N-n}{N-1}} = \dfrac{8.40}{\sqrt{200}} \sqrt{\dfrac{900-200}{900-1}} = \dfrac{8.40}{14.142} \sqrt{0.7786} = (0.594)(0.882) = 0.52$

$\bar{X} \pm z s_{\bar{x}} = 19.60 \pm 1.96(0.52) = \$18.58$ to $\$20.62$

(b) $s_{\bar{x}_1 - \bar{x}_2} = \sqrt{s^2_{\bar{x}_1} + s^2_{\bar{x}_2}} = \sqrt{(0.57)^2 + (0.52)^2} = \sqrt{0.3249 + 0.2704} = \sqrt{0.5953} = 0.772$

$(\bar{X}_1 - \bar{X}_2) \pm z s_{\bar{x}_1 - \bar{x}_2} = (24.57 - 19.60) \pm 1.65(0.772) = \$3.70$ to $\$6.24$

Thus, we can state with 90 percent confidence that the mean level of sales for coupon customers exceeds that for noncoupon customers by an amount somewhere between \$3.70 and \$6.24.

9.2. A random sample of 50 households in community A has a mean household income of $\bar{X} = \$13,800$ with a standard deviation $s = \$2200$. A random sample of 50 households in community B has a mean of $\bar{X} = \$14,600$ with a standard deviation of $s = \$2800$. Estimate the difference in the average household income in the two communities using a 95 percent confidence interval.

$$s_{\bar{x}_1} = \frac{s_1}{\sqrt{n_1}} = \frac{2200}{\sqrt{50}} = \frac{2200}{7.07} = \$311.17$$

$$s_{\bar{x}_2} = \frac{s_2}{\sqrt{n_2}} = \frac{2800}{\sqrt{50}} = \frac{2800}{7.07} = \$396.04$$

$$s_{\bar{x}_1 - \bar{x}_2} = \sqrt{s_{\bar{x}_1}^2 + s_{\bar{x}_2}^2} = \sqrt{(311.17)^2 + (396.04)^2} = \sqrt{96,826.77 + 156,847.68} = \$503.66$$

$$(\bar{X}_1 - \bar{X}_2) \pm z s_{\bar{x}_1 - \bar{x}_2} = (13,800 - 14,600) \pm 1.96(503.66)$$
$$= -800 \pm 987.17 = \$187.17 \text{ to } -\$1,787.17$$

With a 95 percent degree of confidence, the limits of the confidence interval indicate that the mean in the *first* community might actually exceed the mean in the second community by $\$187.17$, while at the other limit the mean of the *second* community might exceed that in the first by as much as $\$1787.17$. In other words, the possibility that there is no actual difference between the two population means is included within this 95 percent confidence interval.

CONFIDENCE INTERVALS FOR THE DIFFERENCE BETWEEN TWO MEANS USING t DISTRIBUTIONS

9.3. In one canning plant the average net weight of string beans being packed in No. 303 cans for a sample of $n = 12$ cans is $\bar{X}_1 = 15.97$ oz, with $s_1 = 0.15$ oz. At another canning plant the average net weight of string beans being packed in No. 303 cans for a sample of $n_2 = 15$ cans is $\bar{X}_2 = 16.14$ oz with a standard deviation of $s_2 = 0.09$ oz. The distributions of the amounts packed are assumed to be approximately normal. Estimate the difference between the average net weight of beans being packed in No. 303 cans at the two plants, using a 90 percent confidence interval.

$$s_{\bar{x}_1} = \frac{s_1}{\sqrt{n_1}} = \frac{0.15}{\sqrt{12}} = \frac{0.15}{3.46} = 0.043$$

$$s_{\bar{x}_2} = \frac{s_2}{\sqrt{n_2}} = \frac{0.09}{\sqrt{15}} = \frac{0.09}{3.87} = 0.023$$

$$s_{\bar{x}_1 - \bar{x}_2} = \sqrt{s_{\bar{x}_1}^2 + s_{\bar{x}_2}^2} = \sqrt{(0.043)^2 + (0.023)^2} = \sqrt{0.001849 + 0.000529} = 0.049$$

$$(\bar{X}_1 - \bar{X}_2) \pm t_{df} s_{\bar{x}_1 - \bar{x}_2} = (15.97 - 16.14) \pm t_{25}(0.049)$$
$$= (-0.17) \pm 1.708(0.049) = -0.25 \text{ to } -0.09 \text{ oz}$$

In other words, with 90 percent confidence we can state the average net weight being packed at the *second* plant is somewhere between 0.09 and 0.25 oz more than at the first plant.

ONE-SIDED CONFIDENCE INTERVALS FOR THE DIFFERENCE BETWEEN TWO MEANS

9.4. Just as for the mean, as explained in Problem 8.14, a difference between means can be estimated by the use of a one-sided confidence interval. Referring to the data in Problem

9.1(b), estimate the minimum difference between the mean purchase amounts of "coupon" and "noncoupon" customers by constructing a 90 percent upper confidence interval.

Since, from Problem 9.1(b), $\bar{X}_1 - \bar{X}_2 = \$4.97$ and $s_{\bar{x}_1 - \bar{x}_2} = 0.772$,

$$\text{Est. } (\mu_1 - \mu_2) \geq (\bar{X}_1 - \bar{X}_2) - zs_{\bar{x}_1 - \bar{x}_2}$$
$$\geq \$4.97 - (1.28)(0.772)$$
$$\geq \$3.98$$

9.5. For the income data reported in Problem 9.2, estimate the maximum difference between the mean income levels in the first and second community (in this order) by constructing a 95 percent lower confidence interval.

Since, from Problem 9.2, $\bar{X}_1 - \bar{X}_2 = -\$800$ and $s_{\bar{x}_1 - \bar{x}_2} = \$503.66$,

$$\text{Est. } (\mu_1 - \mu_2) \leq (\bar{X}_1 - \bar{X}_2) + zs_{\bar{x}_1 - \bar{x}_2}$$
$$\leq -\$800 + 1.65(503.66)$$
$$\leq \$31.04$$

CONFIDENCE INTERVALS FOR ESTIMATING THE POPULATION PROPORTION

9.6. A college administrator collects data on a nationwide random sample of 230 students enrolled in graduate programs in business administration, and finds that 54 of these students have undergraduate degrees in business. Estimate the proportion of such students nationwide who have undergraduate degrees in business administration, using a 90 percent confidence interval.

$$\bar{p} = \frac{54}{230} = 0.235$$

$$s_{\bar{p}} = \sqrt{\frac{\bar{p}(1 - \bar{p})}{n}} = \sqrt{\frac{(0.235)(0.765)}{230}} = \sqrt{\frac{0.179775}{230}} = \sqrt{0.0007816} = 0.028$$

$$\bar{p} \pm zs_{\bar{p}} = 0.235 \pm 1.65(0.028)$$
$$= 0.235 \pm 0.046 \cong 0.19 \text{ to } 0.28$$

It is assumed here that the number of such students nationwide is large enough that the finite correction factor is not required.

9.7. In a large metropolitan area in which a total of 800 gasoline service stations are located, for a random sample of $n = 36$, 20 of the stations carry a particular nationally advertised brand of oil. Using a 95 percent confidence interval estimate (a) the proportion of all stations in the area which carry the oil, and (b) the total number of service stations in the area which carry the oil.

(a) $\bar{p} = \dfrac{20}{36} = 0.5555 \cong 0.56$

$$s_{\bar{p}} = \sqrt{\frac{\bar{p}(1 - \bar{p})}{n}} = \sqrt{\frac{(0.56)(0.44)}{36}} = \sqrt{\frac{0.2464}{36}} = \sqrt{0.006844} = 0.083$$

$$\bar{p} \pm zs_{\bar{p}} = 0.56 \pm 1.96(0.083) = 0.40 \text{ to } 0.72$$

(b) (*Note:* As in the solution to Problem 8.11(b) for the mean and the total quantity, the *total number* in a category of the population is determined by multiplying the confidence limits for the proportion by the total number of all elements in the population.)

$$N(\bar{p} \pm zs_{\bar{p}}) = 800(0.40 \text{ to } 0.72) = 320 \text{ to } 576 \text{ stations}$$

or

$$N(\bar{p}) \pm N(zs_{\bar{p}}) = 800(0.56) \pm 800(0.16) = 320 \text{ to } 576 \text{ stations}$$

DETERMINING THE REQUIRED SAMPLE SIZE FOR ESTIMATING THE PROPORTION

9.8. A university administrator wishes to estimate the proportion of students enrolled in graduate programs in business administration who also have undergraduate degrees in business administration within ±0.05 and with 90 percent confidence. What sample size should he collect, as a minimum, if there is no basis for estimating the approximate value of the proportion before the sample is taken?

Using formula (*9.10*),

$$n = \left(\frac{z}{2E}\right)^2 = \left(\frac{1.65}{2(0.05)}\right)^2 = (16.5)^2 = 272.25 = 273$$

9.9. In respect to Problem 9.8, what is the minimum sample size required if prior data and information indicate that the proportion will be no larger than 0.30?

From formula (*9.9*),

$$n = \frac{z^2 \pi(1 - \pi)}{E^2} = \frac{(1.65)^2(0.30)(0.70)}{(0.05)^2} = \frac{(2.7225)(0.21)}{0.0025} = 228.69 = 229$$

CONFIDENCE INTERVALS FOR THE DIFFERENCE BETWEEN TWO POPULATION PROPORTIONS

9.10. In attempting to gauge voter sentiment regarding a school bonding proposal, a superintendent of schools collects random samples of $n = 100$ in each of the two major residential areas included within the school district. In the first area 70 of the 100 sampled voters indicate that they intend to vote for the proposal, while in the second area 50 of 100 sampled voters indicate this intention. Estimate the difference between the actual proportions of voters in the two areas who intend to vote for the proposal, using 95 percent confidence limits.

$$s_{\bar{p}_1}^2 = \frac{\bar{p}_1(1 - \bar{p}_1)}{n_1} = \frac{(0.70)(0.30)}{100} = \frac{0.21}{100} = 0.0021$$

$$s_{\bar{p}_2}^2 = \frac{\bar{p}_2(1 - \bar{p}_2)}{n_2} = \frac{(0.50)(0.50)}{100} = \frac{0.25}{100} = 0.0025$$

Therefore,

$$s_{\bar{p}_1 - \bar{p}_2} = \sqrt{s_{\bar{p}_1}^2 + s_{\bar{p}_2}^2} = \sqrt{0.0021 + 0.0025} = \sqrt{0.0046} = 0.068$$

$$(\bar{p}_1 - \bar{p}_2) \pm zs_{\bar{p}_1 - \bar{p}_2} = (0.70 - 0.50) \pm 1.96(0.068) = 0.07 \text{ to } 0.33$$

Thus, the difference in the population proportions is somewhere between 0.07 and 0.33 (or 7 to 33 percent). In this solution it is assumed that the number of voters in each area is large enough that the finite correction factor is not required.

ONE-SIDED CONFIDENCE INTERVALS FOR PROPORTIONS

9.11. Just as for the mean and difference between means (see Problems 8.14, 9.4, and 9.5), a proportion or difference between proportions can be estimated by the use of a one-sided confidence interval. For the data of Problem 9.6, find the minimum proportion of the graduate students who have an undergraduate degree in business administration, using a 90 percent confidence interval.

Since, from Problem 9.6, $\bar{p} = 0.235$ and $s_{\bar{p}} = 0.028$,

$$\bar{p} - zs_{\bar{p}} = 0.235 - 1.28(0.028) = 0.199 \text{ or higher}$$

9.12. For the data of Problem 9.10, what is the upper 95 percent confidence interval for the difference in the proportions of people in the first and second neighborhoods who intend to vote for the bonding proposal?

$$(\bar{p}_1 - \bar{p}_2) - zs_{\bar{p}_1 - \bar{p}_2} = (0.70 - 0.50) - 1.65(0.068) = 0.09 \text{ or higher}$$

Thus, with a 95 percent degree of confidence we can state that the *minimum* difference between the proportions of voters in the two neighborhoods who intend to vote in favor of the school bonding proposal is 0.09.

CONFIDENCE INTERVALS FOR THE STANDARD DEVIATION AND VARIANCE

9.13. For the random sample of $n = 12$ cans of string beans in Problem 8.17, the mean was $\bar{X} = 15.97$ oz, the variance was $s^2 = 0.0224$, and the standard deviation was $s = 0.15$. Estimate the (a) variance and (b) standard deviation for all No. 303 cans of beans being packed in the plant, using 90 percent confidence intervals.

(a) $$\frac{(n-1)s^2}{\chi^2_{df,\text{upper}}} \leq \sigma^2 \leq \frac{(n-1)s^2}{\chi^2_{df,\text{lower}}}$$

$$\frac{(11)(0.0224)}{\chi^2_{11,0.95}} \leq \sigma^2 \leq \frac{(11)(0.0224)}{\chi^2_{11,0.05}}$$

$$\frac{0.2464}{19.68} \leq \sigma^2 \leq \frac{0.2464}{4.57}$$

$$0.0125 \leq \sigma^2 \leq 0.0539$$

(b) $$\sqrt{0.0125} \leq \sigma \leq \sqrt{0.0539}$$

$$0.11 \leq \sigma \leq 0.23$$

9.14. Just as for other confidence intervals (see Problems 8.14, 9.4, and 9.11), a population standard deviation or variance can be estimated by the use of a one-sided confidence interval. The usual concern is in respect to the upper limit of the standard deviation or variance, and thus, the lower confidence interval is the most frequent type of one-sided interval. For the data of Problem 9.3, what is the lower 90 percent confidence interval for estimating the population standard deviation?

$$\text{Est. } \sigma \le \sqrt{\frac{(n-1)s^2}{\chi^2_{df,\text{lower}}}} \le \sqrt{\frac{(11)(0.0224)}{\chi^2_{11,0.90}}}$$

$$\le \sqrt{\frac{0.2464}{5.58}} \le \sqrt{0.04416} \le 0.21$$

Thus, with a 90 percent degree of confidence we can state that the standard deviation of the population is no larger than 0.21.

Supplementary Problems

CONFIDENCE INTERVALS FOR THE DIFFERENCE BETWEEN TWO POPULATION MEANS

9.15. For a particular consumer product, the mean dollar sales per retail outlet last year in a sample of $n_1 = 10$ stores was $\bar{X}_1 = \$3425$ with $s_1 = \$200$. For a second product the mean dollar sales per outlet in a sample of $n_2 = 12$ stores was $\bar{X}_2 = \$3250$ with $s_2 = \$175$. The sales amounts per outlet are assumed to be normally distributed for both products. Estimate the difference between the mean level of sales per outlet last year using a 95 percent confidence interval.

Ans. $6.14 to $343.86

9.16. From the data in Problem 9.15, suppose the two sample sizes were $n_1 = 20$ and $n_2 = 24$. Determine the 95 percent confidence interval for the difference between the two means.

Ans. $62.83 to $287.17

9.17. Using the data in Problem 9.15, suppose that we are only interested in the minimum difference between the sales levels of the first and second product. Determine the lower limit of such an estimation interval at the 95 percent degree of confidence.

Ans. $35.36 or more

9.18. For a sample of 50 firms taken from a particular industry, the mean number of employees per firm is $\bar{X}_1 = 420.4$ with $s_1 = 55.7$. There is a total of 380 firms in this industry. In a second industry which includes 200 firms, the mean number of employees in a sample of 50 firms is $\bar{X}_2 = 392.5$ employees with $s_2 = 87.9$. Estimate the difference in the mean number of employees per firm in the two industries, using a 95 percent confidence interval.

Ans. 2.3 to 53.5

9.19. Construct the 99 percent confidence interval for the difference between means for Problem 9.18.

Ans. −5.8 to 61.6

9.20. For a sample of 30 employees in one large firm, the mean hourly wage is $\bar{X}_1 = \$7.50$ with $s_1 = \$1.00$. In a second large firm, the mean hourly wage for a sample of 40 employees is $\bar{X}_2 = \$7.05$ with $s_2 = \$1.20$. Estimate the difference between the mean hourly wage at the two firms, using a 90 percent confidence interval.

Ans. $0.02 to $0.88 per hour

9.21. For the data in Problem 9.20, suppose we are concerned with determining the maximum difference between the mean wage rates, using a 90 percent confidence interval. Construct such a lower confidence interval.

Ans.   Est. $(\mu_1 - \mu_2) \leq \$0.78$ per hour

CONFIDENCE INTERVALS FOR ESTIMATING THE POPULATION PROPORTION

9.22. For a random sample of 100 households in a large metropolitan area, the number of households in which at least one adult is currently unemployed and seeking a full-time job is 12. Estimate the percentage of households in the area in which at least one adult is unemployed, using a 95 percent confidence interval. (*Note:* Percentage limits can be obtained by first determining the confidence interval for the proportion, and then multiplying these limits by 100.)

Ans.   5.7% to 18.3%

9.23. Suppose the confidence interval obtained in Problem 9.22 is considered to be too wide for practical purposes (i.e. it is lacking in precision). Instead, we desire that the 95 percent confidence interval be within two percentage points of the true percentage unemployed. What is the minimum sample size required to satisfy this specification, (*a*) if we make no assumption about the true percentage unemployed before collecting a larger sample, and (*b*) if, on the basis of the sample collected in Problem 9.22, we assume that the true percentage unemployed is no larger than 18 percent?

Ans.   (*a*) 2401,   (*b*) 1418

9.24. A small manufacturer has purchased a batch of 200 small electronic parts from the "excess inventory" of a larger firm. For a random sample of 50 of the parts, five are found to be defective. Estimate the proportion of all of the parts in the shipment which are defective, using a 95 percent confidence interval.

Ans.   0.03 to 0.17

9.25. For Problem 9.24, estimate the total number of parts in the shipment which are defective, using a 90 percent confidence interval.

Ans.   8 to 32

9.26. For the situation in Problem 9.24, suppose the price of the electronics parts was such that the small manufacturer would be satisfied with his purchase as long as the true proportion defective does not exceed 0.20. Construct a one-sided 95 percent confidence interval and observe whether the upper limit of this interval exceeds the proportion 0.20.

Ans.   Est. $\pi \leq 0.16$

CONFIDENCE INTERVALS FOR THE DIFFERENCE BETWEEN TWO POPULATION PROPORTIONS

9.27. In contrast to the data in Problem 9.22, in a second metropolitan area a random sample of 100 households yields only six households in which at least one adult is unemployed and seeking a full-time job. Estimate the difference in the percentage of households in the two areas which include an unemployed adult, using a 90 percent confidence interval.

Ans.   −0.6% to +12.6%

9.28. Referring to Problem 9.27, what is the maximum percentage by which the unemployment in the first metropolitan area exceeds the percentage unemployment in the second area, using a 90 percent one-sided confidence interval?

Ans.   Est. Dif. $\leq 11.1\%$

CONFIDENCE INTERVALS FOR THE STANDARD DEVIATION AND VARIANCE

9.29. For a particular consumer product, the mean dollar sales per retail outlet last year in a sample of $n = 10$ stores was $\bar{X} = \$3425$ with $s = \$200$. The sales amounts per outlet are assumed to be normally distributed. Estimate the *(a)* variance and *(b)* standard deviation of dollar sales of this product in all stores last year, using a 90 percent confidence interval.

  Ans.   *(a)* $21{,}278 \leq \sigma^2 \leq 108{,}271$,   *(b)* $145.9 \leq \sigma \leq 329.0$

9.30. With reference to Problem 9.29, there is particular concern about how *large* the standard deviation of dollar sales might be. Construct the 90 percent one-sided confidence interval which identifies this value.

  Ans. $\sigma \leq 293.9$

Chapter 10

Testing Hypotheses Concerning the Value of the Population Mean

10.1 BASIC STEPS IN HYPOTHESIS TESTING

In hypothesis testing we begin with an assumed (hypothesized) value of a population parameter. After a random sample is collected, we compare the sample statistic, such as the sample mean ($\bar{X}$), with the hypothesized parameter, such as the hypothesized population mean (μ). Then, we either *accept* or *reject* the hypothesized value as being correct. The hypothesized value is rejected only if the sample result clearly is unlikely to occur when the hypothesis is true.

Step 1:   Formulate the null hypothesis and the alternative hypothesis. The *null hypothesis* (H_0) is the hypothesized parameter value which is compared with the sample result. It is rejected *only if* the sample result is unlikely to have occurred given the correctness of the hypothesis. The *alternative hypothesis* (H_1) is accepted only if the null hypothesis is rejected.

EXAMPLE 1. An auditor wishes to test the assumption that the mean value of all accounts receivable in a given firm is \$260.00 by taking a sample of $n = 36$ and computing the sample mean. He wishes to reject the assumed value of \$260.00 only if it is clearly contradicted by the sample mean, and thus the hypothesized value should be given the "benefit of the doubt" in the testing procedure. The null and alternative hypotheses for this test are H_0: $\mu = \$260.00$ and H_1: $\mu \neq \$260.00$.

Step 2:   Specify the level of significance to be used. The level of significance is the statistical standard which is specified for rejecting the null hypothesis. If a 5 percent level of significance is specified, then the null hypothesis is rejected only if the sample result is so different from the hypothesized value that a difference of that amount or larger would occur by chance with a probability of 0.05 or less.

Note that if the 5 percent level of significance is used, there is a probability of 0.05 of rejecting the null hypothesis when it is true. This is called *Type I error*. The probability of Type I error is always equal to the level of significance that is used as the standard for rejecting the null hypothesis; it is designated by the lowercase Greek α ("alpha"), and thus, α also designates the level of significance. The most frequently used levels of significance in hypothesis testing are the 5 percent and 1 percent levels.

A *Type II error* occurs if the null hypothesis is accepted when it is false. Determining the probability of Type II error is explained in Section 10.3. Table 10.1 summarizes the types of decisions and the possible consequences of the decisions which are made in hypothesis testing.

Step 3:   Select the test statistic. The test statistic will either be the sample statistic (the unbiased estimator of the parameter being tested), or a transformed version of the sample statistic. For example, in order to test a hypothesized value of the population mean, the mean of a random sample taken from that population could serve as the test statistic. However, if the sampling distribution of the mean is normally distributed, then the value of the sample mean typically is transformed into a z value.

Table 10.1 Consequences of Decisions in Hypothesis Testing

Possible decisions	Possible states	
	Null hypothesis true	Null hypothesis false
Accept null hypothesis	Correctly accepted	Type II error
Reject null hypothesis	Type I error	Correctly rejected

Step 4: Establish the critical value or values of the test statistic.   Having specified the null hypothesis, the level of significance, and the test statistic to be used, we now establish the critical value(s) of the test statistic.   There may be one or two such values, depending on whether a so-called one-tail or two-tail test is involved (see Section 10.2).   In either case, a *critical value* identifies the value of the test statistic required to reject the null hypothesis.

Step 5: Determine the actual value of the test statistic.   For example, in testing a hypothesized value of the population mean a random sample is collected and the value of the sample mean is determined.   If the critical value was established as a z value, then the sample mean is converted into a z value.

Step 6: Make the decision.   The observed value of the sample statistic is compared with the critical value (or values) of the test statistic.   The null hypothesis is then either accepted or rejected.   If the null hypothesis is rejected, the alternative hypothesis is accepted.   In turn, this decision will have relevance to other decisions to be made by operating managers, such as whether a standard of performance is being maintained or which of two marketing strategies should be used.

10.2 TESTING A HYPOTHESIZED VALUE OF THE MEAN USING THE NORMAL DISTRIBUTION

The normal probability distribution can be used for testing a hypothesized value of the population mean   (1) whenever $n \geq 30$, because of the central limit theorem, or   (2) when $n < 30$ but the population is normally distributed and σ is known.   (See Section 8.2.)

A *two-tail test* is used when we are concerned about a possible deviation in *either* direction from the hypothesized value of the mean.   The formula used to establish the critical values of the sample mean is similar to the formula for determining confidence limits for estimating the population mean (see Section 8.3), except that the hypothesized value of the population mean, μ_0, is the reference point rather than the sample mean.   The critical values of the sample mean for a two-tailed test, according to whether σ is known, are

$$\mu_0 \pm z\sigma_{\bar{x}} \qquad (10.1)$$

or

$$\mu_0 \pm zs_{\bar{x}} \qquad (10.2)$$

EXAMPLE 2.   For the null hypothesis formulated in Example 1, determine the critical values of the sample mean for testing the hypothesis at the 5 percent level of significance.   Given that the standard deviation of the accounts receivable amounts is known to be $\sigma = \$43.00$, the critical values are

Hypotheses: H_0: μ = \$260.00; H_1: $\mu \neq$ \$260.00

Level of significance: $\alpha = 0.05$

Testing statistic: $\bar{X}$ based on a sample of $n = 36$ and with $\sigma = 43.00$

$\bar{X}_{CR}$ = critical values of the sample mean

$\bar{X}_{CR} = \mu_0 \pm z\sigma_{\bar{x}} = 260.00 \pm 1.96 \dfrac{\sigma}{\sqrt{n}}$

$\qquad = 260.00 \pm 1.96 \dfrac{43.00}{\sqrt{36}} = \$245.95 \text{ and } \$274.05$

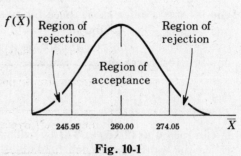

Fig. 10-1

Therefore, in order to reject the null hypothesis the sample mean must have a value which is less than \$245.95 *or* greater than \$274.05. Thus, there are two regions of rejection in the case of a two-tail test (see Fig. 10-1). The z values of ± 1.96 are used to establish the critical limits because for the standard normal distribution a proportion of 0.05 of the area remains in the two tails, which corresponds to the specified $\alpha = 0.05$.

Instead of establishing critical values in terms of the sample mean as such, the critical values in hypothesis testing typically are specified in terms of z values. For the 5 percent level of significance the critical values z for a two-tail test are -1.96 and $+1.96$, for example. When the value of the sample mean is determined, it is transformed to a z value so that it can be compared with the critical values of z. The transformation formula, according to whether σ is known, is

$$z = \frac{\bar{X} - \mu_0}{\sigma_{\bar{x}}} \qquad (10.3)$$

or

$$z = \frac{\bar{X} - \mu_0}{s_{\bar{x}}} \qquad (10.4)$$

EXAMPLE 3. For the hypothesis-testing problem in Examples 1 and 2, suppose the sample mean is $\bar{X} = \$240.00$. We determine whether the null hypothesis should be accepted or rejected by transforming this mean to a z value and comparing it to the critical values of ± 1.96 as follows:

$$\sigma_{\bar{x}} = 7.17 \qquad \text{(from Example 2)}$$

$$z = \frac{\bar{X} - \mu_0}{\sigma_{\bar{x}}} = \frac{240.00 - 260.00}{7.17} = \frac{-20.00}{7.17} = -2.79$$

This value of z is in the left-tail region of rejection of the hypothesis-testing model portrayed in Fig. 10-2. Thus, the null hypothesis is rejected and the alternative, that $\mu \neq \$260.00$, is accepted. Note that the same conclusion is reached by comparing the sample mean of $\bar{X} = \$240.00$ with the critical limits for the mean identified in Fig. 10-1.

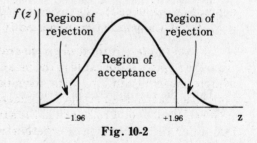

Fig. 10-2

A *one-tail test* is appropriate when we are concerned about possible deviations in only one direction from the hypothesized value of the mean. The auditor in Example 1 may not be concerned that the true average of all accounts receivable exceeds \$260.00, but only that it might be less than \$260.00. Thus, if he gives the benefit of the doubt to the stated claim that the true mean is *at least* \$260.00, the null and alternative hypotheses are

$$H_0: \quad \mu \geq \$260.00 \quad \text{and} \quad H_1: \quad \mu < \$260.00$$

There is only one region of rejection for a one-tail test, and for the above example the test is a lower-tail test. The region of rejection for a one-tail test is always in the tail which represents support of the *alternative* hypothesis. As for a two-tail test, the critical value can be determined for the mean as such or in terms of a z value. However, critical values for one-tail tests differ from those for two-tail tests because the given proportion of area is all in one tail of the distribution. Table 10.2 presents the values of z needed for one-tail and two-tail tests. The general formula to establish the critical value of the sample mean for a one-tail test, according to whether σ is known, is

$$\mu_0 + z\sigma_{\bar{x}} \qquad (10.5)$$

or

$$\mu_0 + zs_{\bar{x}} \qquad (10.6)$$

In formulas (10.5) and (10.6), above, note that z can be negative, resulting in a subtraction of the second term in each formula.

Table 10.2   Critical Values of z in Hypothesis Testing

Level of significance	Type of test	
	One-tail	Two-tail
5%	+1.65 (or −1.65)	±1.96
1%	+2.33 (or −2.33)	±2.58

EXAMPLE 4. Assume that the auditor in Examples 1 through 3 began with the null hypothesis that the mean value of all accounts receivable is at least $260.00. Given that the sample mean is $240.00, we test this hypothesis at the 5 percent level of significance by the following two separate procedures.

(1) Determining the critical value of the sample mean, where H_0: $\mu \geq \$260.00$ and H_1: $\mu < \$260.00$.

$$\bar{X}_{CR} = \mu_0 + z\sigma_{\bar{x}} = 260 + (-1.65)(7.17) = \$248.17$$

Since $\bar{X} = \$240.00$, it is in the region of rejection. The null hypothesis is therefore rejected and the alternative hypothesis, that $\mu < \$260.00$, is accepted.

(2) Specifying the critical value in terms of z, where critical z ($\alpha = 0.05$) $= -1.65$:

$$z = \frac{\bar{X} - \mu_0}{\sigma_{\bar{x}}} = \frac{240.00 - 260.00}{7.17} = -2.79$$

Thus, the null hypothesis is rejected. Figure 10-3 portrays the critical value for this one-tail test in terms of $\bar{X}$ and z.

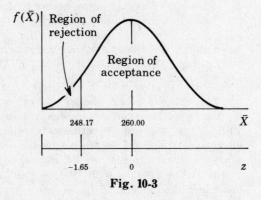

Fig. 10-3

10.3   TYPE I AND TYPE II ERRORS IN HYPOTHESIS TESTING

In this section Type I and Type II errors (defined in Section 10.1) are discussed entirely in respect to one-tail tests of a hypothesized mean. However, the basic concepts illustrated here apply to other hypothesis-testing models as well.

The probability of Type I error is always equal to the level of significance used in testing the null hypothesis. This is so because by definition the proportion of area in the region of rejection is equal to the proportion of sample results that would occur in that region given that the null hypothesis is true.

The probability of Type II error is generally designated by the Greek β ("beta"). The only way it can be determined is in respect to a *specific* value included within the range of the alternative hypothesis.

EXAMPLE 5. As in Example 4, the null hypothesis to be tested is that the mean of all accounts receivable is at least $260.00, and this test is to be carried out at the 5 percent level of significance. Further, the auditor indicates that he would consider an actual mean of $240.00 (or less) to be an important and material difference from the hypothesized value of the mean. As before, $\sigma = \$43.00$ and the sample size is $n = 36$ accounts. The determination of the probability of Type II error requires that we

(1) formulate the null and alternative hypotheses for this testing situation,

(2) determine the critical value of the sample mean to be used in testing the null hypothesis at the 5 percent level of significance,

(3) identify the probability of Type I error associated with using the critical value computed above as the basis for the decision rule,

(4) identify the probability of Type II error associated with the decision rule given the specific alternative mean value of $240.00.

The complete solution is

(1) H_0: $\mu \geq 260.00$; H_1: $\mu < 260.00$
(2) $\bar{X}_{CR} = \mu_0 + z\sigma_{\bar{x}} = 260.00 + (-1.65)(7.17) = \$248.17$

where $\sigma_{\bar{x}} = \dfrac{\sigma}{\sqrt{n}} = \dfrac{43.00}{\sqrt{36}} = \dfrac{43.00}{6} = 7.17$

(3) The probability of Type I error equals 0.05 (the level of significance used in testing the null hypothesis).

(4) The probability of Type II error is the probability that the mean of the random sample will equal or exceed $248.17 given that the mean of all accounts is actually at $240.00.

$$z = \frac{X_{CR} - \mu_1}{\sigma_{\bar{x}}} = \frac{248.17 - 240.00}{7.17} = \frac{8.17}{7.17} = +1.14$$

$$P(\text{Type II error}) = P(z \geq +1.14) = 0.5000 - 0.3729 = 0.1271 \cong 0.13$$

Figure 10-4 illustrates the approach followed in Example 5. In general, the critical value of the mean determined in respect to the null hypothesis is "brought down" and used as the

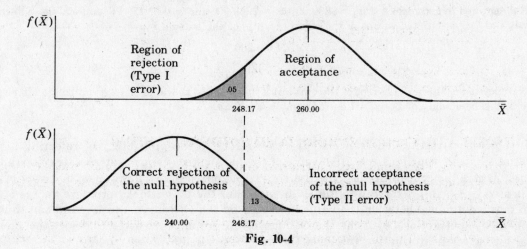

Fig. 10-4

critical value in respect to the specific alternative hypothesis. Problem 10.13 illustrates the determination of the probability of Type II error for a two-tail test.

With the level of significance and sample size held constant, the probability of Type II error decreases as the specific alternative value of the mean is set farther from the value in the null hypothesis. It increases as the alternative value is set closer to the value in the null hypothesis. *An operating characteristic (OC) curve* portrays the probability of accepting the null hypothesis given various alternative values of the true mean. Figure 10–5 is the *OC* curve applicable to any lower-tail test of a hypothesized mean carried out at the 5 percent level of significance and based on the use of the normal probability distribution. Note that it is applicable to any such test because the values on the horizontal axis are stated in units of the standard error of the mean. For any values to the left of μ_0, the probability of acceptance indicates the probability of Type II error. To the right of μ_0, the probabilities indicate correct acceptance of the null hypothesis.

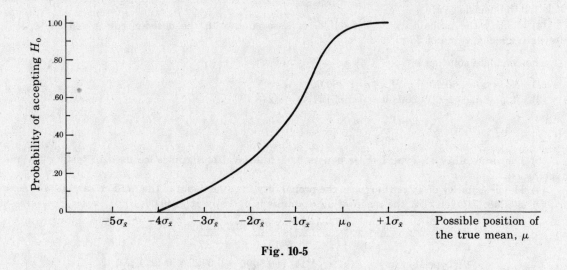

Fig. 10-5

EXAMPLE 6. We can verify the probability of Type II error determined in Example 5 by reference to Fig. 10-5, as follows:

As identified in Example 5, $\mu_0 = \$260.00$, $\mu_1 = \$240.00$, and $\sigma_{\bar{x}} = 7.17$. Therefore, the difference between the two designated values of the mean in units of the standard error is

$$\frac{\mu_1 - \mu_0}{\sigma_{\bar{x}}} = \frac{240 - 260}{7.17} = -2.8.$$

By reference to Fig. 10-5, the height of the curve at a horizontal-axis value of -2.8 can be seen to be just above 0.10. The actual computed value in Example 5 is 0.13.

In hypothesis testing, the concept of *power* refers to the probability of rejecting a null hypothesis given a specific alternative value of the parameter (in our examples, the population mean). Where the probability of Type II error is designated β, it follows that the power of the test is always $1 - \beta$. Referring to Fig. 10-5, note that the power for alternative values of the mean is the difference between the value indicated by the *OC* curve and 1.0, and can thus be obtained "by subtraction" by using the *OC* curve. A graph constructed to depict the various power levels, given alternative values of the mean, is called a *power curve*.

EXAMPLE 7. Referring to Example 5, we can determine the power of the test given a specific alternative value of the mean of $240.00 as follows:

Since $\beta = P(\text{Type II error}) = 0.13$ (from Example 5),

$$\text{Power} = 1 - \beta = 1.00 - 0.13 = 0.87$$

(*Note:* This is the probability of correctly rejecting the null hypothesis when $\mu = \$240.00$.)

10.4 DETERMINING THE REQUIRED SAMPLE SIZE FOR TESTING THE MEAN

Before a sample is actually collected, the required sample size can be determined by specifying   (1) the hypothesized value of the mean,   (2) a specific alternative value of the mean such that the difference from the null-hypothesized value is considered important,   (3) the level of significance to be used in the test,   (4) the probability of Type II error which is to be permitted, and   (5) the value of the population standard deviation, σ.   The formula for determining the minimum sample size required in conjunction with testing a hypothesized value of the mean, based on use of the normal distribution, is

$$n = \frac{(z_0 - z_1)^2 \sigma^2}{(\mu_1 - \mu_0)^2} \tag{10.7}$$

In (*10.7*), z_0 is the critical value of z used in conjunction with the specified level of significance (α-level) while z_1 is the value of z in respect to the designated probability of Type II error (β-level).   The value of σ must either be known or be estimated on some general or historical basis.   Formula (*10.7*) can be used for either one-tail or two-tail tests.   The only value that differs is the value of z_0 which is used for the two types of tests (see Examples 8 and 9).

(*Note:* When solving for minimum sample size, any fractional result is always rounded up.   Further, unless σ is known *and* the population is normally distributed, any computed sample size below 30 should be increased to 30 because (*10.7*) is based on the use of the normal distribution.)

EXAMPLE 8. An auditor wishes to test the assumption that the mean value of all accounts receivable is at least $260.00.   He considers that the difference would be material and important if the true mean is at the specific alternative of $240.00.   The acceptable levels of Type I error (α) and Type II error (β) are 0.05 and 0.10 respectively.   The standard deviation of the accounts receivable amounts is known to be $\sigma = \$43.00$.   The size of the sample which should be collected, as a minimum, to carry out this test is

$$n = \frac{(z_0 - z_1)^2 \sigma^2}{(\mu_1 - \mu_0)^2} = \frac{(-1.65 - 1.28)^2 (43.00)^2}{(240.00 - 260.00)^2} = \frac{(8.5849)(1849)}{400} = 39.68 \cong 40$$

(*Note:* Because z_0 and z_1 would always have opposite algebraic signs, the result is that the two z values are always accumulated in the numerator above.   If the accumulated value is a negative value, the process of squaring results in a positive value.)

EXAMPLE 9. Suppose the auditor in Example 8 is concerned about a discrepancy in either direction from the null-hypothesized value of $260.00, and that a discrepancy of $20 in either direction would be considered important.   Given the other information and specifications in Example 8, the minimum size of the sample which should be collected is

$$n = \frac{(z_0 - z_1)^2 \sigma^2}{(\mu_1 - \mu_0)^2} = \frac{(-1.96 - 1.28)^2 \sigma^2}{(240.00 - 260.00)^2} \quad \text{or} \quad \frac{[1.96 - (-1.28)]^2 \sigma^2}{(280.00 - 260.00)^2}$$

$$= \frac{(-3.24)^2 (43.00)^2}{(-20)^2} \quad \text{or} \quad \frac{(3.24)^2 (43.00)^2}{(20)^2} = \frac{(10.4976)(1849)}{400} = 48.53 \cong 49$$

(*Note:* Because any deviation can only be in a given direction, we use either the $+1.96$ or the -1.96 as the value of z_0 in conjunction with the then relevant value of z_1. As in Example 8, the two z values will in effect always be accumulated before being squared.)

10.5 TESTING A HYPOTHESIZED VALUE OF THE MEAN USING STUDENT'S *t* DISTRIBUTIONS

The t distributions (see Section 8.5) are appropriate for use as the test statistic when the sample is small ($n < 30$), the population is normally distributed, and σ is not known. The procedure used for testing an assumed value of a population mean is identical to that described in Section 10.2, except for the use of t as the test statistic. The test statistic used is

$$t = \frac{\bar{X} - \mu_0}{s_{\bar{x}}} \qquad (10.8)$$

EXAMPLE 10. The null hypothesis has been formulated that the mean operating life of light bulbs of a particular brand is at least 4200 hr. The mean operating life for a random sample of $n = 10$ light bulbs is $\bar{X} = 4000$ hr with a sample standard deviation of $s = 200$ hr. The operating life of bulbs in general is assumed to be normally distributed. We test the null hypothesis at the 5 percent level of significance as follows:

$$H_0: \quad \mu \geq 4200 \qquad H_1: \quad \mu < 4200$$

$$\text{Critical } t \ (df = 9, \alpha = 0.05) = -1.833$$

$$s_{\bar{x}} = \frac{s}{\sqrt{n}} = \frac{200}{\sqrt{10}} = \frac{200}{3.16} = 63.3 \text{ hr}$$

$$t = \frac{\bar{X} - \mu_0}{s_{\bar{x}}} = \frac{4000 - 4200}{63.3} = \frac{-200}{63.3} = -3.16$$

Therefore, the null hypothesis is rejected and the alternative hypothesis, that the true mean operating life is less than 4000 hours, is accepted.

10.6 TESTING A HYPOTHESIZED VALUE OF THE MEAN USING CHEBYSHEV'S INEQUALITY

The use of Chebyshev's inequality for the purpose of testing an assumed value of the mean is appropriate when the sample is small ($n < 30$) and the population is assumed *not* to be normally distributed. See Section 8.6. The form of Chebyshev's inequality which is appropriate in the context of hypothesis testing, and which indicates the maximum probability that the sample mean is located more than k standard error units from the population mean, is

$$p(\mid \bar{X} - \mu \mid > k\sigma_{\bar{x}}) < \frac{1}{k^2} \qquad (10.9)$$

To use this inequality, we simply determine the difference between the sample mean and hypothesized mean in units of the standard error of the mean, (k), and then compare the value $1/k^2$ to the designated level of significance. For example, for significance at the 5 percent level the minimum value of k required to reject the null hypothesis is 4.47, because $1/(4.47)^2 = 0.05$.

(*Note*: Any test using Chebyshev's inequality must be a two-tail test, since the population distribution is not assumed to be symmetrical.)

EXAMPLE 11. It is hypothesized that the mean weekly wage in a particular firm is $200.00, and there is good reason to believe that the distribution of weekly wage amounts does not follow the normal distribution. For a random sample of $n = 10$ employees, selected from a large group of hourly employees the mean wage is $\bar{X} = \$180.00$ with a sample standard deviation of $s = \$14.00$. Should the null hypothesis be accepted or rejected using the 5 percent level of significance? Using Chebyshev's inequality, since H_0: $\mu = \$200.00$ and H_1: $\mu \neq \$200.00$,

$$s_{\bar{x}} = \frac{s}{\sqrt{n}} = \frac{14.00}{\sqrt{10}} = \frac{14.00}{3.1623} = \$4.43$$

$$k = \frac{\bar{X} - \mu_0}{s_{\bar{x}}} = \frac{180.00 - 200.00}{4.43} = \frac{-20.00}{4.43} = -4.51$$

$$P = \frac{1}{k^2} = \frac{1}{-4.51^2} = \frac{1}{20.34} = 0.049$$

Since the probability of the observed difference occurring by chance is less than 0.05, the null hypothesis is rejected, and the alternative hypothesis that the population mean is different from $200.00 is accepted.

10.7 SUMMARY TABLE FOR TESTING A HYPOTHESIZED VALUE OF THE MEAN

Table 10.3   Testing a Hypothesized Value of the Mean

Population	Sample size	σ known	σ unknown
Normally distributed	Large ($n \geq 30$)	$z = \dfrac{\bar{X} - \mu_0}{\sigma_{\bar{x}}}$	$z = \dfrac{\bar{X} - \mu_0}{s_{\bar{x}}}$**
	Small ($n < 30$)	$z = \dfrac{\bar{X} - \mu_0}{\sigma_{\bar{x}}}$	$t = \dfrac{\bar{X} - \mu_0}{s_{\bar{x}}}$
Not normally distributed	Large ($n \geq 30$)	$z = \dfrac{\bar{X} - \mu_0}{\sigma_{\bar{x}}}$*	$z = \dfrac{\bar{X} - \mu_0}{s_{\bar{x}}}$†
	Small ($n < 30$)	$k = \dfrac{\bar{X} - \mu_0}{\sigma_{\bar{x}}}$ where $1/k^2$ is determined based on Chebyshev's inequality	$k = \dfrac{\bar{X} - \mu_0}{s_{\bar{x}}}$†† where $1/k^2$ is determined based on Chebyshev's inequality

*Central limit theorem is invoked.
**z is used as an approximation of t.

†Central limit theorem is invoked and z is used as an approximation of t.

††Some statisticians consider this test unreliable, because of the fluctuation in the value of $s_{\bar{x}}$ for small samples.

Solved Problems

TESTING A HYPOTHESIZED VALUE OF THE MEAN USING THE NORMAL DISTRIBUTION

10.1. A representative of a community group informs the prospective developer of a shopping center that the average income per household in the area is $15,000. Suppose that for the type of area involved household income can be assumed to be approximately normally distributed, and that the standard deviation can be accepted as being equal to $\sigma = \$2000$, based on an earlier study. For a random sample of $n = 15$ households, the mean household income is found to be $\bar{X} = \$14,000$. Test the null hypothesis that $\mu = \$15,000$ by establishing critical limits of the sample mean in terms of dollars, using the 5 percent level of significance.

(*Note:* The normal probability distribution can be used even though the sample is small, because the population is assumed to be normally distributed *and* σ is known.)

Since H_0: $\mu = \$15,000$ and H_1: $\mu \neq \$15,000$, the critical limits of $\bar{X}$ ($\alpha = 0.05$) are

$$\bar{X}_{CR} = \mu_0 \pm z\sigma_{\bar{x}} = \mu_0 \pm z\left(\frac{\sigma}{\sqrt{n}}\right) = 15,000 \pm 1.96\left(\frac{2000}{\sqrt{15}}\right)$$

$$= 15,000 \pm 1.96\left(\frac{2000}{3.87}\right) = 15,000 \pm 1.96(516.80) = \$13,987 \text{ and } \$16,013$$

Since the sample mean of $\bar{X} = \$14,000$ is in the region of acceptance of the null hypothesis, the community representative's claim cannot be rejected at the 5 percent level of significance.

10.2. Test the hypothesis in Problem 10.1, by using the standard normal variable z as the test statistic.

$$H_0: \quad \mu = \$15,000 \qquad H_1: \quad \mu \neq \$15,000$$

Critical z ($\alpha = 0.05$) = ± 1.96, thus

$$\sigma_{\bar{x}} = \frac{\sigma}{\sqrt{n}} = \frac{2000}{\sqrt{15}} = \frac{2000}{3.87} = \$516.80$$

$$z = \frac{\bar{X} - \mu_0}{\sigma_{\bar{x}}} = \frac{14,000 - 15,000}{516.80} = \frac{-1000}{516.80} = -1.93$$

Since the computed z of -1.93 is in the region of acceptance of the null hypothesis, the community representative's claim cannot be rejected at the 5 percent level of significance.

10.3. With reference to Problems 10.1 and 10.2, the prospective developer is not really concerned about the possibility that the average household income is higher than the claimed $15,000, but only that it might be lower. Accordingly, reformulate the null and alternate hypotheses and carry out the appropriate statistical test, still giving the benefit of the doubt to the community representative's claim.

$$H_0: \quad \mu \geq \$15,000 \qquad H_1: \quad \mu < \$15,000$$
$$\text{Critical } z \ (\alpha = 0.05) = -1.65$$
$$z = -1.93 \quad \text{(from Problem 10.2)}$$

Therefore, on the basis of this one-tail test the null hypothesis is rejected at the 5 percent level of significance, and the alternative hypothesis, that the true household income is less than $15,000, is accepted. The reason for the change in the decision from Problem 10.2 is that the 5 percent region of rejection is located entirely in one tail of the distribution.

10.4. For Problem 10.3, suppose that the population standard deviation is not known, which typically would be the case, and the population of income figures is not assumed to be normally distributed. For a sample of $n = 30$ households, the sample standard deviation is $s = \$2000$ and the sample mean remains $\bar{X} = \$14,000$. Test the null hypothesis that the mean household income in the population is at least $\$15,000$, using the 5 percent level of significance.

   (*Note:* The normal probability distribution can be used both because of the central limit theorem and because z can be used as an approximation of t when $n \geq 30$.)

$$H_0: \quad \mu \geq \$15,000 \qquad H_1: \quad \mu < 15,000$$
$$\text{Critical } z \ (\alpha = 0.05) = -1.65$$

$$s_{\bar{x}} = \frac{s}{\sqrt{n}} = \frac{2000}{\sqrt{30}} = \frac{2000}{5.48} = \$364.96$$

$$z = \frac{\bar{X} - \mu_0}{s_{\bar{x}}} = \frac{14,000 - 15,000}{364.96} = \frac{-1000}{364.96} = -2.74$$

Thus, the null hypothesis is rejected at the 5 percent level of significance. Notice that the computed value of z in this case is arithmetically smaller in value and more clearly in the region of rejection as compared with Problem 10.3. This is due entirely to the increase in sample size from $n = 15$ to $n = 30$, which results in a smaller value for the standard error of the mean.

10.5. A manufacturer contemplating the purchase of new tool-making equipment has specified that on the average the equipment should not require more than 10 min of set-up time per hour of operation. The purchasing agent visits a company where the equipment being considered is installed; from records there he notes that 40 randomly selected hours of operation included a total of 7 hr and 30 min of set-up time, and the standard deviation of set-up time per hour was 3.0 min. Based on this sample result, can the assumption that the equipment meets set-up time specifications be rejected at the 1 percent level of significance?

$$H_0: \quad \mu \leq 10 \text{ min (per hour)} \qquad H_1: \quad \mu > 10 \text{ min (per hour)}$$
$$\text{Critical } z \ (\alpha = 0.01) = +2.33$$

$$\bar{X} = \frac{\Sigma X}{n} = \frac{450 \text{ min}}{40} = 11.25 \text{ min}$$

$$s_{\bar{x}} = \frac{s}{\sqrt{n}} = \frac{3.0}{\sqrt{40}} = \frac{3.0}{6.32} = 0.47 \text{ min}$$

$$z = \frac{\bar{X} - \mu_0}{s_{\bar{x}}} = \frac{11.25 - 10}{0.47} = \frac{1.25}{0.47} = +2.66$$

Therefore, the null hypothesis is rejected at the 1 percent level of significance, and the alternative hypothesis, that the average set-up time for this equipment is greater than 10 min per hour of operation, is accepted.

10.6. The standard deviation of the tube life for a particular brand of TV picture tube is known to be $\sigma = 500$ hr, and the operating life of the tubes is normally distributed. The manufacturer claims that average tube life is at least 9000 hr. Test this claim at the 5 percent level of significance by designating it as the null hypothesis and given that for a sample of $n = 15$ tubes the mean operating life was $\bar{X} = 8800$ hr.

$$H_0: \quad \mu \geq 9000 \qquad H_1: \quad \mu < 9000$$

$$\text{Critical } z \ (\alpha = 0.05) = -1.65$$

$$\sigma_{\bar{x}} = \frac{\sigma}{\sqrt{n}} = \frac{500}{\sqrt{15}} = \frac{500}{3.87} = 129.20$$

$$z = \frac{\bar{X} - \mu_0}{\sigma_{\bar{x}}} = \frac{8800 - 9000}{129.20} = \frac{-200}{129.20} = -1.55$$

Therefore, the null hypothesis cannot be rejected at the 5 percent level of significance.

10.7. In respect to Problem 10.6, suppose the sample data were obtained for a sample of $n = 35$ sets. Test the claim at the 5 percent level of significance.

$$H_0: \quad \mu \geq 9000 \qquad H_1: \quad \mu < 9000$$

$$\text{Critical } z \ (\alpha = 0.05) = -1.65$$

$$\sigma_{\bar{x}} = \frac{\sigma}{\sqrt{n}} = \frac{500}{\sqrt{35}} = \frac{500}{5.92} = 84.46$$

$$z = \frac{\bar{X} - \mu_0}{\sigma_{\bar{x}}} = \frac{8800 - 9000}{84.46} = \frac{-200}{84.46} = -2.37$$

Therefore, the null hypothesis is rejected at the 5 percent level of significance.

10.8. A marketing research analyst collects data for a random sample of 100 customers out of the 400 who purchased a particular "coupon special." The 100 people spent an average of $\bar{X} = \$24.57$ in the store with a standard deviation of $s = \$6.60$. Before seeing these sample results, the marketing manager had claimed that the average purchase by those responding to the coupon offer would be at least \$25.00. Can his claim be rejected, using the 5 percent level of significance?

$$H_0: \quad \mu \geq \$25.00 \qquad H_1: \quad \mu < \$25.00$$

$$\text{Critical } z \ (\alpha = 0.05) = -1.65$$

$$s_{\bar{x}} = \frac{s}{\sqrt{n}} \sqrt{\frac{N-n}{N-1}} = \frac{6.60}{\sqrt{100}} \sqrt{\frac{400-100}{400-1}} = \frac{6.60}{10} \sqrt{0.7519} = 0.660(0.867) = 0.57$$

(The finite correction factor is required because $n > 0.05\,N$.)

$$z = \frac{\bar{X} - \mu_0}{s_{\bar{x}}} = \frac{24.57 - 25.00}{0.57} = \frac{-0.43}{0.57} = -0.75$$

Therefore, the claim cannot be rejected at the 5 percent level of significance.

TYPE I AND TYPE II ERRORS IN HYPOTHESIS TESTING

10.9. For Problem 10.3, suppose the prospective developer would consider it an important discrepancy if the average household income is at or below \$13,500, as contrasted to the \$15,000 claimed income level. Identify the probability of Type I error and the probability of Type II error associated with this one-tail testing procedure.

$$P(\text{Type I error}) = 0.05 \ (\text{the } \alpha\text{-level, or level of significance})$$

$$P(\text{Type II error}) = P(\text{critical limit of } \bar{X} \text{ will be exceeded given } \mu = \$13,500)$$

$$\text{Lower Critical Limit of } \bar{X} = \mu_0 + z\sigma_{\bar{x}} = 15,000 + (-1.65)(516.80) = \$14,147.28$$

·where $\mu_0 = \$15,000$

$z = -1.65$

$$\sigma_{\bar{x}} = \frac{\sigma}{\sqrt{n}} = \frac{2000}{\sqrt{15}} = \frac{2000}{3.87} = \$516.80$$

$$P(\text{Type II error}) = P(\bar{X} \geq 14,147.28 \mid \mu_1 = 13,500, \sigma_{\bar{x}} = 516.80)$$

$$z_1 = \frac{\bar{X} - \mu_1}{\sigma_{\bar{x}}} = \frac{14,147.28 - 13,500}{516.80} = \frac{647.28}{516.80} = +1.25$$

$$P(\text{Type II error}) = P(z_1 \geq +1.25) = 0.5000 - 0.3944 = 0.1056 \cong 0.11$$

10.10. In respect to Problems 10.3 and 10.9, the specific null-hypothesized value of the mean is $\mu_0 = \$15,000$ and the specific alternative value is $\mu_1 = \$13,500$. Based on the sample of $n = 15$, $\sigma_{\bar{x}} = 516.80$ and the critical value of the sample mean is $\bar{X}_{CR} = \$14,147.28$. (a) Explain what is meant by calling the last value above a "critical" value. (b) If the true value of the population mean is $\mu = \$13,000$, what is the power of the statistical test?

(a)   The $14,147.28 value is the "critical" value of the sample mean in that if the sample mean equals or exceeds this value the null hypothesis (H_0: $\mu \geq \$15,000$) will be accepted, whereas if the sample mean is less than this value the null hypothesis will be rejected and the alternative hypothesis (H_1: $\mu < \$15,000$) will be accepted.

(b)   Power $= P$(Rejecting the null hypothesis given a specific value of μ). In this case, Power $= P(\bar{X} < 14,147.28 \mid \mu = 13,000, \sigma_{\bar{x}} = 516.80)$

$$z = \frac{\bar{X} - \mu}{\sigma_{\bar{x}}} = \frac{14,147.28 - 13,000}{516.80} = \frac{1147.28}{516.80} = +2.22$$

$$\text{Power} = P(z < +2.22) = 0.5000 + 0.4868 = 0.9868 \cong 0.99$$

In other words, given a true mean of $\mu = \$13,000$ there is about a 99 percent chance that the null hypothesis will be (correctly) rejected, and about a 1 percent chance that it will be (incorrectly) accepted (Type II error).

10.11. Referring to Problem 10.10,

(a)   What is the power of the statistical test if the true mean is $\mu = \$14,000$? Compare this answer with the value obtained for $\mu = \$13,000$ in the answer to Problem 10.10(b).

(b)   What is the power of the statistical test if the true mean is $\mu = \$14,500$? Compare this answer with the values obtained for $\mu = \$13,000$ in Problem 10.10(b) and for $\mu = \$14,000$ in (a) above.

(a)   Power $= P(\bar{X} < 14,147.28 \mid \mu = 14,000, \sigma_{\bar{x}} = 516.80) = P(z < 0.28)$

$$= 0.5000 + 0.1103 = 0.6103 \cong 0.61$$

where $z = \frac{\bar{X} - \mu_1}{\sigma_{\bar{x}}} = \frac{14,147.28 - 14,000}{516.80} = \frac{147.28}{516.80} = +0.28$

The power of the test in this case is substantially lower than the power of 0.99 in Problem 10.10(b). This would be expected, since the present mean of $\mu = \$14,000$ is closer in value to the null-hypothesized $\mu \geq \$15,000$.

(b)   Power $= P(\bar{X} < 14{,}147.28 \mid \mu = 14{,}500,\ \sigma_{\bar{x}} = 516.80) = P(z < -0.68)$

$\qquad\qquad = 0.5000 - 0.2518 = 0.2482 \cong 0.25$

where $\quad z = \dfrac{\bar{X} - \mu_1}{\sigma_{\bar{x}}} = \dfrac{14{,}147.28 - 14{,}500}{516.80} = \dfrac{-352.72}{516.80} = -0.68$

The power of the test is substantially lower than the previous values of 0.99 and 0.61.

10.12. In Problems 10.9, 10.10, and 10.11, the power of the one-tail statistical test associated with alternative values of the population mean of \$14,500, \$14,000, \$13,500, and \$13,000 was determined to be 0.25, 0.61, 0.89, and 0.99, respectively. Determine the *OC* values associated with these alternative values of the population mean, and also for the case where $\mu = \$15{,}000$ (with H_0: $\mu \geq \$15{,}000$).

Since *OC* value $= P$(accepting the null hypothesis given a specific value of μ), *OC* value $= 1 - \text{Power}$ (for each specific value of μ), as reported in Table 10.4.

Table 10.4   Power and *OC* Values

Value of μ	Power	*OC* Value
\$15,000	0.05	0.95
14,500	0.25	0.75
14,000	0.61	0.39
13,500	0.89	0.11
13,000	0.99	0.01

In Table 10.4, since \$15,000 is the point at which the range of the null-hypothesized values begin, the "power" is in fact the probability of incorrect rejection of the null hypothesis, and is also therefore equal to the level of significance and the probability of Type I error. Similarly, when μ is less than \$15,000 in the table, the *OC* value is the probability of incorrectly accepting the null hypothesis, and is thus the probability of Type II error.

10.13. For Problems 10.1 and 10.2, suppose that the prospective developer would consider it important if the average household income per year differs from the claimed \$15,000 by \$1500 or more in either direction. Given that the null hypothesis is being tested at the 5 percent level of significance, identify the probability of Type I and Type II error.

(*Note:* This solution is an extension of the explanation given in Section 10.3 in that a two-tail test rather than a one-tail test is involved.)

P(Type I error) $= 0.05$ (the α-level, or level of significance)

P(Type II error) $= P$(lower critical limit of $\bar{X}$ will be exceeded given $\mu = \$13{,}500$)   or

$\qquad\qquad\qquad = P(\bar{X}$ will be below the upper critical limit given $\mu = \$16{,}500)$

(*Note:* Either calculation will yield the solution for the probability of Type II error. These two values are *not* accumulated because the specific alternative value can be only at one point in a given situation.)

Since, from Problem 10.1, lower critical limit of $\bar{X} = \$13{,}987$ and $\sigma_{\bar{x}} = \$516.80$,

P(Type II error) $= P(\bar{X} \geq 13{,}987 \mid \mu_1 = 13{,}500,\ \sigma_{\bar{x}} = 516.80) = P(z_1 \geq +0.94)$

$\qquad\qquad\qquad\qquad = 0.5000 - 0.3264 = 0.1736 \cong 0.17$

where $\quad z_1 = \dfrac{\bar{X} - \mu_1}{\sigma_{\bar{x}}} = \dfrac{13{,}987 - 13{,}500}{516.80} = \dfrac{487}{516.80} = +0.94$

DETERMINING THE REQUIRED SAMPLE SIZE
FOR TESTING THE MEAN

10.14. Suppose the prospective developer of the shopping center in Problem 10.3 wishes to test the null hypothesis H_0: $\mu \geq \$15,000$ at the 5 percent level of significance and he considers it an important difference if the average household income level is at (or below) $13,500. Because he is particularly concerned about the error of developing a shopping center in an area where it cannot be supported, he sets the desired level of Type II error at $\beta = 0.01$. If the standard deviation for such income data is assumed to be $\sigma = \$2000$, determine the size of the sample required to achieve the developer's objectives in regard to Type I and Type II error if no assumption is made about the normality of the population.

$$ n = \frac{(z_0 - z_1)^2 \sigma^2}{(\mu_1 - \mu_0)^2} = \frac{[-1.65 - (+2.33)]^2 (2000)^2}{(15,000 - 13,500)^2} = \frac{(-3.98)^2 (4,000,000)}{(1,500)^2} $$

$$ = \frac{63,361,600}{2,250,000} = 28.1607 = 29 \text{ households} $$

However, because the population is not assumed to be normally distributed, the required sample size is increased to $n = 30$, so that the central limit theorem can be invoked as the basis for using the normal probability distribution.

10.15. The manufacturer contemplating the purchase of tool-making equipment in Problem 10.5 has specified in the null hypothesis that the average set-up time for new equipment being considered is equal to or less than 10 min per hour (H_0: $\mu \leq 10$). Suppose he would be particularly concerned if the average set-up time per hour is 12 min or more. He estimates that the standard deviation is about $\sigma = 3.0$ min, and assumes that a variable such as set-up time is likely to be normally distributed. Because of the long-run cost implications of this decision, he designates that the probability of both Type I error and Type II error should be held to 0.01. How many randomly selected hours of equipment operation should be sampled, as a minimum, to satisfy his testing objectives?

$$ n = \frac{(z_0 - z_1)^2 \sigma^2}{(\mu_1 - \mu_0)^2} = \frac{[2.33 - (-2.33)]^2 (3.0)^2}{(12 - 10)^2} $$

$$ = \frac{(4.66)^2 (9)}{(2)^2} = \frac{21.7156(9)}{4} = \frac{195.4404}{4} = 48.86 = 49 \text{ hr} $$

TESTING A HYPOTHESIZED VALUE OF THE MEAN USING
STUDENT'S t DISTRIBUTIONS

10.16. As a modification of Problem 10.3, a representative of a community group informs the prospective developer of a shopping center that the average household income in the community is *at least* $\mu = \$15,000$. As before, the population of income figures in the community is assumed to be normally distributed. For a random sample of $n = 15$ households taken in the community the sample mean is $\bar{X} = \$14,000$ and the sample standard deviation is $s = \$2000$. Test the null hypothesis at the 5 percent level of significance.

(*Note:* The t distribution is appropriate because the sample is small ($n < 30$), σ is not known, and the population is assumed to be normally distributed.)

$$H_0: \quad \mu \geq \$15{,}000 \qquad H_1: \quad \mu < \$15{,}000$$

$$\text{Critical } t \ (df = 14, \ \alpha = 0.05) = -1.761$$

$$s_{\bar{x}} = \frac{s}{\sqrt{n}} = \frac{2000}{\sqrt{15}} = \frac{2000}{3.87} = 516.80$$

$$t = \frac{\bar{X} - \mu_0}{s_{\bar{x}}} = \frac{14{,}000 - 15{,}000}{516.80} = \frac{-1000}{516.80} = -1.93$$

Thus, the null hypothesis is rejected at the 5 percent level of significance. The decision is the same as in Problem 10.3 in which σ was known, except that in the former case z was the test statistic, and the critical value was $z = -1.65$.

10.17. Of 100 juniors and seniors majoring in accounting in a college of business administration, a random sample of $n = 12$ students has a mean grade-point average of 2.7 (where A = 4.0) with a sample standard deviation of $s = 0.4$. Grade-point averages for juniors and seniors are assumed to be normally distributed. Test the hypothesis that the overall grade-point average for all students majoring in accounting is at least 3.0, using the 1 percent level of significance.

$$H_0: \quad \mu \geq 3.0 \qquad H_1: \quad \mu < 3.0$$

$$\text{Critical } t \ (df = 11, \ \alpha = 0.01) = -2.718$$

$$s_{\bar{x}} = \frac{s}{\sqrt{n}} \sqrt{\frac{N-n}{N-1}} = \frac{0.4}{\sqrt{12}} \sqrt{\frac{100-12}{100-1}}$$

$$= \frac{0.4}{3.46} \sqrt{\frac{88}{99}} = 0.116(0.943) = 0.109$$

(The finite correction factor is required because $n > 0.05N$.)

$$t = \frac{\bar{X} - \mu_0}{s_{\bar{x}}} = \frac{2.7 - 3.0}{0.109} = \frac{-0.30}{0.109} = -2.752$$

Therefore, the null hypothesis is rejected at the 1 percent level of significance. If we had neglected to use the finite correction factor the computed t-value would have been -2.59, and we would have inappropriately accepted the null hypothesis.

10.18. As a commercial buyer for a private supermarket brand, suppose you take a random sample of 12 No. 303 cans of string beans at a canning plant. The average weight of the drained beans in each can is found to be $\bar{X} = 15.97$ oz, with $s = 0.15$. The claimed average net weight of the drained beans per can is 16.0 oz. Can this claim be rejected at the 10 percent level of significance?

$$H_0: \quad \mu \geq 16.0 \qquad H_1: \quad \mu < 16.0$$

$$\text{Critical } t \ (df = 11, \ \alpha = 0.10) = -1.363$$

$$s_{\bar{x}} = \frac{s}{\sqrt{n}} = \frac{0.15}{\sqrt{12}} = \frac{0.15}{3.46} = 0.043 \text{ oz}$$

$$t = \frac{\bar{X} - \mu_0}{s_{\bar{x}}} = \frac{15.97 - 16.00}{0.043} = \frac{-0.03}{0.043} = -0.70$$

Therefore, the claim cannot be rejected at the 10 percent level of significance.

TESTING A HYPOTHESIZED VALUE OF THE MEAN
USING CHEBYSHEV'S INEQUALITY

10.19. For the situation in Problems 10.1 and 10.2, suppose that the population standard deviation σ is not known and that the population is *not* assumed to be normally distributed. As before, the community representative claims that average household income per year is $\mu = \$15{,}000$. For a random sample of 15 households in the area, the mean is $\bar{X} = \$14{,}000$ with a sample standard deviation of $s = \$2000$. Test the hypothesized value of the mean at the 5 percent level of significance.

$$H_0: \quad \mu = \$15{,}000 \qquad H_1: \quad \mu \neq \$15{,}000$$

$$s_{\bar{x}} = \frac{s}{\sqrt{n}} = \frac{2000}{\sqrt{15}} = \frac{2000}{3.87} = \$516.80$$

$$k = \frac{\bar{X} - \mu_0}{s_{\bar{x}}} = \frac{14{,}000 - 15{,}000}{516.80} = \frac{-1000}{516.80} = -1.93$$

$$P = \frac{1}{k^2} = \frac{1}{(-1.93)^2} = \frac{1}{3.7249} = 0.268 \cong 0.27$$

Therefore, based on Chebyshev's inequality the probability of a difference of \$1000 or larger occurring by chance given a true null hypothesis is 0.27. Since this value is larger than 0.05, the null hypothesis cannot be rejected.

10.20. For Problem 10.19, suppose that the null hypothesis is changed to $H_0: \quad \mu \geq \$15{,}000$ so that a one-tail test is appropriate. Can this hypothesis be tested by use of Chebyshev's inequality?

No, it cannot. Because Chebyshev's inequality is not based on the assumption of a normal population, or even of a symmetrically distributed population, the probability value obtained always relates to the two "tails" of the distribution and cannot be adjusted to apply to a one-tail test.

Supplementary Problems

TESTING A HYPOTHESIZED VALUE OF THE MEAN

10.21. A fast-foods chain will build a new outlet in a proposed location if at least 200 cars per hour pass the location during certain prime hours. For 20 randomly sampled hours during the prime periods, the average number of cars passing the location is $\bar{X} = 208.5$ with $s = 30.0$. The statistical population is assumed to be approximately normal. The management of the chain conservatively adopted the null hypothesis that the traffic volume does *not* satisfy their requirement, i.e. $H_0: \quad \mu \leq 200.0$. Can this hypothesis be rejected at the 5 percent level of significance?

Ans. No.

10.22. Suppose the sample results in Problem 10.21 are based on a sample of $n = 50$ hr. Can the null hypothesis be rejected at the 5 percent level of significance?

Ans. Yes.

10.23. The mean sales amount per retail outlet for a particular consumer product during the past year is found to be $\bar{X} = \$3425$ in a sample of $n = 25$ outlets. Based on sales data for other similar products, the distribution of sales is assumed to be normal and the standard deviation of the population is assumed to be $\sigma = \$200$. Suppose it was claimed that the true sales amount per outlet is at least $3500. Test this claim at the (a) 5 percent and (b) 1 percent level of significance.

    Ans.   (a) Reject H_0,   (b) accept H_0.

10.24. In Problem 10.23, suppose that no assumption was made about the population standard deviation, but that $s = \$200$. Test the claim at the (a) 5 percent and (b) 1 percent level of significance.

    Ans.   (a) Reject H_0,   (b) accept H_0.

10.25. For a sample of 50 firms taken from a particular industry the mean number of employees per firm is 420.4 with a sample standard deviation of 55.7. There is a total of 380 firms in this industry. Before the data were collected, it was hypothesized that the mean number of employees per firm in this industry does not exceed 408 employees. Test this hypothesis at the 5 percent level of significance.

    Ans.   Reject H_0.

10.26. Suppose the analyst in Problem 10.25 neglected to use the finite correction factor in determining the value of the standard error of the mean. What would be the result of the test, still using the 5 percent level of significance?

    Ans.   Accept H_0.

10.27. The manufacturer of a new compact car claims that the car will average at least 35 miles per gallon in general highway driving. For 40 test runs, the car averaged 34.5 miles per gallon with a standard deviation of 2.3 miles per gallon. Can the manufacturer's claim be rejected at the 5 percent level of significance?

    Ans.   No.

10.28. Referring to Problem 10.27, before the highway tests were carried out, a consumer advocate claimed that the compact car would *not* exceed 35 miles per gallon in general highway driving. Can this claim be rejected at the 5 percent level of significance? Consider the implications of your answer to this question and in Problem 10.27 regarding which hypothesis is designated as the null hypothesis.

    Ans.   No.

10.29. An analyst in a personnel department randomly selects the records of 16 hourly employees and finds that the mean wage rate is $\bar{X} = \$7.50$ with a standard deviation of $s = \$1.00$. The wage rates in the firm are assumed to be normally distributed. Test the null hypothesis H_0: $\mu = \$8.00$, using the 10 percent level of significance.

    Ans.   Reject H_0.

10.30. Referring to Problem 10.29, test the null hypothesis given no information as to whether the population of wage rates is normally distributed.

    Ans.   Accept H_0.

10.31. A random sample of 30 employees at the Secretary II level in a large organization take a standardized typing test. The sample results are $\bar{X} = 63.0$ wpm (words per minute) with $s = 5.0$ wpm. Test the null hypothesis that the secretaries in general do *not* exceed a typing speed of 60 wpm, using the 1 percent level of significance.

    Ans.   Reject H_0.

10.32. An automatic soft ice cream dispenser has been set to dispense 4.00 oz per serving. For a sample of $n = 10$ servings, the average amount of ice cream is $\bar{X} = 4.05$ oz with $s = 0.10$ oz. The amounts being dispensed are assumed to be normally distributed. Basing the null hypothesis on the assumption that the process is "in control," should the dispenser be reset as a result of a test at the 5 percent level of significance?

Ans.   No.

10.33. A shipment of 100 defective machines has been received in a machine-repair department. For a random sample of 10 machines, the average repair time required is $\bar{X} = 85.0$ min with $s = 15.0$ min. Test the null hypothesis H_0: $\mu = 100.0$ min, using the 10 percent level of significance and based on the assumption that the distribution of repair time is approximately normal.

Ans.   Reject H_0.

10.34. Suppose that the distribution of repair time in Problem 10.33 cannot be assumed to be approximately normal. Test the null hypothesis H_0: $\mu = 100.0$ at the 10 percent level of significance.

Ans.   Reject H_0.

TYPE I AND TYPE II ERRORS IN HYPOTHESIS TESTING

10.35. With reference to Problem 10.31, suppose it is considered an important difference from the hypothesized value of the mean if the average typing speed is at least at 64.0 wpm. Determine the probability of   (a) Type I error and   (b) Type II error.

Ans.   (a) $\alpha = 0.01$,   (b) $\beta = 0.0192 \cong 0.02$.

10.36. For Problem 10.35, determine the probability of Type II error   (a) if the level of significance is changed to the 5 percent level, and   (b) if the level of significance is kept at the 1 percent level, but the sample size was $n = 60$ instead of $n = 30$.

Ans.   (a) $\beta = 0.0030 = 0.003$,   (b) $\beta < 0.001$.

10.37. For the testing procedure described in Problem 10.27, suppose it is considered an important discrepancy from the claim if the average mileage is 34.0 miles per gallon or less. Given this additional information, determine   (a) the minimum OC value if the null hypothesis is true, and   (b) the minimum power associated with the statistical test if the discrepancy from the claim is an important one.

Ans.   (a) $OC = 0.95$,   (b) power $= 0.8729 \cong 0.87$.

10.38. Determine the minimum power of the test in Problem 10.37, given that it is considered an important discrepancy if the true mileage is   (a) 0.5 mile per gallon, and   (b) 0.1 mile per gallon less than the claim. Comparing the several power values, consider the implication of the standard used to define an "important discrepancy."

Ans.   (a) Power $= 0.4013 \cong 0.40$,   (b) power $= 0.0869 \cong 0.09$.

DETERMINING THE REQUIRED SAMPLE SIZE FOR TESTING THE MEAN

10.39. Before collecting any sample data, the prospective investor in Problem 10.21 stipulates that the level of Type I error should be no larger than $\alpha = 0.01$, and that if the number of cars passing the site is at or above $\mu = 210$ per hour then the level of Type II error should also not exceed $\beta = 0.01$. He estimates that the population standard deviation is no larger than $\sigma = 40$. What sample size is required to achieve his objectives?

Ans. $n = 347.45 = 348$.

10.40. For the testing situation described in Problem 10.23, it is considered an important discrepancy if the mean sales amount per outlet is $100 less than the claimed amount. What sample size is required if the test is to be carried out at the 1 percent level of significance, allowing a maximum probability of Type II error of $\beta = 0.05$?

    Ans. $n = 63.36 = 64$.

Chapter 11

Testing Other Hypotheses

11.1 TESTING THE DIFFERENCE BETWEEN TWO MEANS USING THE NORMAL DISTRIBUTION

The procedure associated with testing the difference between two means is similar to that for testing a hypothesized value of the mean (see Sections 10.1 and 10.2), except that the standard error of the difference between means is used as the basis for determining the z value associated with the sample result. Use of the normal distribution is based on the same conditions as in the one-sample case, except that two independent samples are involved. The general formula for determining the z value for testing the difference between two means, according to whether the σ values for the two populations are known, is

$$z = \frac{(\bar{X}_1 - \bar{X}_2) - (\mu_1 - \mu_2)_0}{\sigma_{\bar{x}_1 - \bar{x}_2}} \qquad (11.1)$$

or

$$z = \frac{(\bar{X}_1 - \bar{X}_2) - (\mu_1 - \mu_2)_0}{s_{\bar{x}_1 - \bar{x}_2}} \qquad (11.2)$$

As implied by (11.1) and (11.2), we may begin with any assumed difference, $(\mu_1 - \mu_2)_0$, which is to be tested. However, the usual null hypothesis tested is that the two samples have been obtained from populations with means that are equal. In this case $(\mu_1 - \mu_0)_0 = 0$, and the above formulas are simplified as follows:

$$z = \frac{\bar{X}_1 - \bar{X}_2}{\sigma_{\bar{x}_1 - \bar{x}_2}} \qquad (11.3)$$

or

$$z = \frac{\bar{X}_1 - \bar{X}_2}{s_{\bar{x}_1 - \bar{x}_2}} \qquad (11.4)$$

In general, the standard error of the difference between means is computed as described in Section 9.1 [see formulas (9.3) and (9.4)]. However, in testing the difference between two means, the null hypothesis of interest is generally not only that the sample means were obtained from populations with equal means, but that the two samples were in fact obtained from the *same* population of values. This means that $\sigma_1 = \sigma_2$, which we can simply designate σ. Thus, the assumed common variance is often estimated by pooling the two sample variances, and the estimated value of σ^2 is then used as the basis for the standard error of the difference. The pooled estimate of the population variance is

$$\hat{\sigma}^2 = \frac{(n_1 - 1)s_1^2 + (n_2 - 1)s_2^2}{n_1 + n_2 - 2} \qquad (11.5)$$

The estimated standard error of the difference based on the assumption that the population standard deviations are equal is

$$\hat{\sigma}_{\bar{x}_1 - \bar{x}_2} = \sqrt{\frac{\hat{\sigma}^2}{n_1} + \frac{\hat{\sigma}^2}{n_2}} \qquad (11.6)$$

The assumption that the two sample variances were obtained from the same population can itself be tested as the null hypothesis (see Section 11.9).

Tests concerned with the difference between means can be either two-tail or one-tail, as illustrated in the following examples.

EXAMPLE 1. The mean weekly wage for a sample of $n_1 = 30$ employees in a large manufacturing firm is $\bar{X}_1 = \$180.00$ with a sample standard deviation of $s_1 = \$14.00$. In another large firm a random sample of $n_2 = 40$ employees has a mean wage of $\bar{X}_2 = \$170.00$ with a sample standard deviation of $s_2 = \$10.00$. The standard deviations of the two populations of wage amounts are not assumed to be equal. We test the hypothesis that there is no difference between the mean weekly wage amounts in the two firms, using the 5 percent level of significance, as follows:

$$H_0: \quad \mu_1 = \mu_2 \qquad \bar{X}_1 = \$180.00 \qquad \bar{X}_2 = \$170.00$$

$$H_1: \quad \mu_1 \neq \mu_2 \qquad s_1 = \$14.00 \qquad s_2 = \$10.00$$

$$n_1 = 30 \qquad n_2 = 40$$

Critical z ($\alpha = 0.05$) $= \pm 1.96$

$$z = \frac{\bar{X}_1 - \bar{X}_2}{s_{\bar{x}_1 - \bar{x}_2}}$$

$$= \frac{180 - 170}{3.01} = \frac{10.0}{3.01} = +3.32$$

where $s_{\bar{x}_1} = \dfrac{s_1}{\sqrt{n_1}} = \dfrac{14.00}{\sqrt{30}} = \dfrac{14.00}{5.477} = 2.56$

$s_{\bar{x}_2} = \dfrac{s_2}{\sqrt{n_2}} = \dfrac{10.00}{\sqrt{40}} = \dfrac{10.00}{6.325} = 1.58$

$s_{\bar{x}_1 - \bar{x}_2} = \sqrt{s_{\bar{x}_1}^2 + s_{\bar{x}_2}^2} = \sqrt{(2.56)^2 + (1.58)^2} = \sqrt{6.5536 + 2.4964} = 3.01$

Thus, the null hypothesis is rejected, and the alternative hypothesis, that the average weekly wage in the two firms is different, is accepted.

EXAMPLE 2. Before seeing the sample results in Example 1, a wage analyst believed that the average wage in the first firm was greater than the average wage in the second firm. In order to subject his belief to a critical test, he gives the benefit of the doubt to the opposite possibility, and formulates the null hypothesis that the average wage in the first firm is equal to or less than the average in the second firm. We test this hypothesis at the 1 percent level of significance, again without assuming that the standard deviations of the two populations are equal, as follows:

$$H_0: \quad \mu_1 \leq \mu_2 \qquad H_1: \quad \mu_1 > \mu_2$$

Critical z ($\alpha = 0.01$) $= +2.33$

Computed $z = +3.32$ (from Example 1)

Thus, the null hypothesis is rejected and the alternative hypothesis, that the average wage in the first firm is *greater than* the average wage in the second firm, is accepted.

11.2 TESTING THE DIFFERENCE BETWEEN TWO MEANS USING STUDENT'S t DISTRIBUTIONS

When the difference between two means is tested by the use of the t distributions, a necessary assumption is that the variances of the two populations are equal. Therefore, in such a test, the estimated standard error of the mean is calculated from (11.5) and (11.6). The several requirements associated with the appropriate use of the t distributions are described in Sections 8.5 and 10.5.

EXAMPLE 3. For a random sample of $n_1 = 10$ bulbs, the mean bulb life was $\bar{X}_1 = 4000$ hr with $s_1 = 200$. For another brand of bulbs whose useful life is also assumed to be normally distributed, a random sample of $n_2 = 8$ has a sample mean of $\bar{X}_2 = 4300$ hr and a sample standard deviation of $s = 250$. We test the hypothesis that there is no difference between the mean operating life of the two brands of bulbs, using the 1 percent level of significance, as follows:

$$H_0: \quad \mu_1 = \mu_2 \qquad \bar{X}_1 = 4000 \text{ hr} \qquad \bar{X}_2 = 4300 \text{ hr}$$

$$H_1: \quad \mu_1 \neq \mu_2 \qquad s_1 = 200 \text{ hr} \qquad s_2 = 250 \text{ hr}$$

$$n_1 = 10 \qquad n_2 = 8$$

$$df = n_1 + n_2 - 2 = 10 + 8 - 2 = 16$$

$$\text{Critical } t(df = 16, \alpha = 0.01) = \pm 2.921$$

$$\hat{\sigma}^2 = \frac{(n_1 - 1)s_1^2 + (n_2 - 1)s_2^2}{n_1 + n_2 - 2} = \frac{(9)(200)^2 + (7)(250)^2}{10 + 8 - 2} = \frac{360{,}000 + 437{,}500}{16} = 49{,}843.75$$

$$\hat{\sigma}_{\bar{x}_1 - \bar{x}_2} = \sqrt{\frac{\hat{\sigma}^2}{n_1} + \frac{\hat{\sigma}^2}{n_2}} = \sqrt{\frac{49{,}843.75}{10} + \frac{49{,}843.75}{8}} = \sqrt{11{,}214.843} = 105.9$$

$$t = \frac{\bar{X}_1 - \bar{X}_2}{\hat{\sigma}_{\bar{x}_1 - \bar{x}_2}} = \frac{4000 - 4300}{105.9} = \frac{-300}{105.9} = -2.83$$

Therefore, the computed t is in the region of acceptance of the null hypothesis, and the null hypothesis cannot be rejected at the 1 percent level of significance.

11.3 TESTING THE DIFFERENCE BETWEEN TWO MEANS BASED ON PAIRED OBSERVATIONS

The procedures in Sections 11.1 and 11.2 are based on the assumption that the two samples were collected independently of one another. However, in many situations the samples are collected as pairs of values, such as when determining the productivity level of each worker before and after a training program. These are referred to as *paired observations*, or *matched pairs*. Also, as contrasted to independent samples, two samples that contain paired observations are called *dependent samples*.

For paired observations, the appropriate test for the difference between the means of the two samples is to first determine the difference d between each pair of values, and then test the null hypotheses that the average difference in the population is zero. Thus, from the computational standpoint the test is applied to the one sample of d values.

The mean and standard deviation of the sample d values are obtained by use of the basic formulas in Chapters 3 and 4, except that d is substituted for X. The mean difference for a set of paired observations is

$$\bar{d} = \frac{\Sigma d}{n} \tag{11.7}$$

The deviations formula and the computational formula for the standard deviation of the differences between paired observations are, respectively

$$s_d = \sqrt{\frac{\Sigma(d - \bar{d})^2}{n - 1}} \qquad (11.8)$$

$$s_d = \sqrt{\frac{\Sigma\, d^2 - n\bar{d}^2}{n - 1}} \qquad (11.9)$$

The standard error of the mean difference between paired observations is obtained by formula (8.4) for the standard error of the mean, except that d is again substituted for X:

$$s_{\bar{d}} = \frac{s_d}{\sqrt{n}} \qquad (11.10)$$

Because the standard error of the mean difference is computed on the basis of the differences observed in the paired samples (that is, σ_d is unknown) and because values of d generally can be assumed to be normally distributed, the t distributions are appropriate for testing the null hypothesis that $\bar{d} = 0$.

The degrees of freedom is the number of *pairs* of observed values minus one, or $n - 1$. As discussed in Section 8.5, the standard normal z distribution can be used in place of the t distributions when $n \geq 30$. Example 4, illustrates a two-tail test, whereas Problem 11.5 exemplifies a one-tail test. Thus, the test statistic used to test the hypothesis that there is no difference between the means of a set of paired observations is

$$t = \frac{\bar{d}}{s_{\bar{d}}} \qquad (11.11)$$

EXAMPLE 4. An automobile manufacturer collects mileage data for a sample of $n = 10$ cars in various weight categories by use of a standard grade of gasoline with and without a particular additive. Of course, the engines were tuned to the same specifications before each run, and the same drivers were used for the two gasoline conditions (with the driver in fact being unaware of which gasoline was being used on a particular run). Given the mileage data in Table 11.1, we test the hypothesis that there is no difference between the mean mileage obtained with and without the additive, using the 5 percent level of significance, as follows:

Table 11.1   Automobile Mileage Data and Worksheet for Computing the Mean Difference and the Standard Deviation of the Difference

Automobile	Mileage with additive	Mileage without additive	d	d^2
1	26.7	26.2	0.5	0.25
2	25.8	25.7	0.1	0.01
3	21.9	22.3	−0.4	0.16
4	19.3	19.6	−0.3	0.09
5	18.4	18.1	0.3	0.09
6	15.7	15.8	−0.1	0.01
7	14.2	13.9	0.3	0.09
8	12.6	12.0	0.6	0.36
9	11.9	11.5	0.4	0.16
10	10.3	10.0	0.3	0.09
Total	176.8	175.1	+1.7	1.31

Average with additive $= \dfrac{176.8}{10} = 17.68$ mpg;

Average without additive $= \dfrac{175.1}{10} = 17.51$ mpg

$$H_0: \quad \mu_1 = \mu_2 \quad \text{(or, for paired observations, that } \mu_d = 0\text{)}$$

$$H_1: \quad \mu_1 \neq \mu_2 \quad \text{(or, for paired observations, that } \mu_d \neq 0\text{)}$$

$$\text{Critical } t(df = 9, \alpha = 0.05) = \pm 2.262$$

$$\bar{d} = \frac{\Sigma d}{n} = \frac{1.7}{10} = 0.17$$

$$s_d = \sqrt{\frac{\Sigma d^2 - n\bar{d}^2}{n-1}} = \sqrt{\frac{1.31 - 10(0.17)^2}{10-1}} = \sqrt{\frac{1.31 - 10(0.0289)}{9}} = \sqrt{0.1134} = 0.337$$

$$s_{\bar{d}} = \frac{s_d}{\sqrt{n}} = \frac{0.337}{\sqrt{10}} = \frac{0.337}{3.16} = 0.107$$

$$t = \frac{\bar{d}}{s_{\bar{d}}} = \frac{0.17}{0.107} = +1.59$$

Therefore, the computed t is in the region of acceptance of the null hypothesis that there is no difference in the miles per gallon obtained with as compared to without the additive.

11.4 TESTING A HYPOTHESIZED PROPORTION USING THE BINOMIAL DISTRIBUTIONS

When a sampling process can be assumed to conform to a Bernoulli process (see Section 6.3), the binomial distributions can be used in conjunction with testing hypotheses regarding the population proportion.

Typically, tests of proportions based on using the binomial distributions are one-tail tests. Given the hypothesized value of the population proportion, the "region" of rejection is the set of sample observations which deviates from the hypothesized value and for which the probability of occurrence by chance does not exceed the specified level of significance. The test procedure for a one-tail test is illustrated by Example 5. See Problem 11.8 for a two-tail test using a binomial distribution.

EXAMPLE 5. The director of a college placement office claims that by March 1 at least 50 percent of the graduating seniors will have obtained full-time jobs. A random sample of 10 graduating seniors are polled on March 1, and only two indicate that they have concluded their job arrangements. Can the director's claim be rejected, using the 5 percent level of significance? By reference to the appropriate binomial distribution, $H_0: \pi \geq 0.50$ and $H_1: \pi < 0.50$.

Based on the binomial distribution, the probability values associated with fewer than five students having obtained jobs, given a population proportion of 0.50, are given in Table 11.2 (from Appendix 1, with $n = 10$ and $p = 0.50$).

Table 11.2   Probability Values Associated with
Fewer than Five out of Ten
Students Having Obtained Jobs

Number of students	Probability
0	0.0010
1	0.0098
2	0.0439
3	0.1172
4	0.2051

Critical values of test statistic: The test statistic is the number of students in the sample of $n = 10$ who have already obtained employment.   In order to reject the null hypothesis at the 5 percent level of significance, only "0" or "1" student would have to be observed to have jobs.   This is because the probabilities are accumulated in the "lower tail" of this binomial distribution to determine the region of rejection.   To attempt to include "2" students in the region of rejection results in a cumulative probability (for "0, 1, or 2") of 0.0547, which just exceeds the designated 0.05 test level.

Result of test: Based on the critical values identified above, observing that only two students out of a sample of 10 have obtained jobs is not low enough to reject the director's claim at the 5 percent level of significance.

(*Note*:   With a larger sample, the same relative difference from the hypothesized value might indeed lead to the rejection of the null hypothesis.   See Problem 11.7.)

11.5 TESTING A HYPOTHESIZED PROPORTION USING THE NORMAL DISTRIBUTION

As explained in Section 7.3, the normal distribution can be used as an approximation of a binomial distribution when $n \geq 30$ and both $np \geq 5$ and $n(1 - p) \geq 5$.   This is the basis upon which confidence intervals for the proportion are constructed in Section 9.3, where the standard error of the proportion is also discussed.

In hypothesis testing, the value of the standard error of the proportion used in conjunction with hypothesis testing is

$$\sigma_{\bar{p}} = \sqrt{\frac{\pi_0(1 - \pi_0)}{n}} \qquad (11.12)$$

The formula for the standard error of the proportion which includes the finite correction factor is

$$\sigma_{\bar{p}} = \sqrt{\frac{\pi_0(1 - \pi_0)}{n}} \sqrt{\frac{N - n}{N - 1}} \qquad (11.13)$$

The procedure associated with testing a hypothesized value of the population proportion is identical to that described in Section 10.2, except that the proportion rather than the mean is being tested.   Thus, the formula for the z statistic for testing a hypothesized value of the proportion is

$$z = \frac{\bar{p} - \pi_0}{\sigma_{\bar{p}}} \qquad (11.14)$$

EXAMPLE 6. In Example 5, the placement director claimed that at least 50 percent of the graduating seniors had finalized job arrangements by March 1. Suppose a random sample of $n = 30$ seniors are polled, rather than the 10 in Example 5, and only 10 of the students indicate that they have concluded their job arrangements by March 1. Can the placement director's claim be rejected at the 5 percent level of significance? We utilize z as the test statistic, as follows:

$$H_0: \quad \pi \geq 0.50 \qquad H_1: \quad \pi < 0.50$$

$$\text{Critical } z \, (\alpha = 0.05) = -1.65$$

(Use of the normal distribution is warranted because $n \geq 30$, $n\pi_0 \geq 5$, and $n(1 - \pi_0) \geq 5$.)

$$\sigma_{\bar{p}} = \sqrt{\frac{\pi_0(1 - \pi_0)}{n}} = \sqrt{\frac{(0.50)(0.50)}{30}} = \sqrt{\frac{0.25}{30}} = \sqrt{0.0083} = 0.09$$

(It is assumed that the sample is less than 5 percent of the population size, and so the finite correction factor is not used.)

$$z = \frac{\bar{p} - \pi_0}{\sigma_{\bar{p}}} = \frac{0.33 - 0.50}{0.09} = \frac{-0.17}{0.09} = -1.88$$

The z value obtained is in the region of rejection; thus, the director's claim can be rejected at the 5 percent level of significance.

11.6 DETERMINING REQUIRED SAMPLE SIZE FOR TESTING THE PROPORTION

Before a sample is actually collected, the required sample size for testing a hypothesized value of the proportion can be determined by specifying (1) the hypothesized value of the proportion, (2) a specific alternative value of the proportion such that the difference from the null-hypothesized value is considered important, (3) the level of significance to be used in the test, and (4) the probability of Type II error which is to be permitted. The formula for determining the minimum sample size required for testing a hypothesized value of the proportion is

$$n = \left[\frac{z_0\sqrt{\pi_0(1 - \pi_0)} - z_1\sqrt{\pi_1(1 - \pi_1)}}{\pi_1 - \pi_0} \right]^2 \qquad (11.15)$$

In (11.15), z_0 is the critical value of z used in conjunction with the specified level of significance (α-level) while z_1 is the value of z in respect to the designated probability of Type II error (β-level). As was true in Section 10.4, z_0 and z_1 always have opposite algebraic signs. The result is that the two products in the numerator will always be accumulated. Also formula (11.15) can be used in conjunction with either one-tail or two-tail tests and any fractional sample size is rounded up. In addition, the sample size should be large enough to warrant use of the normal probability distribution in conjunction with π_0 and π_1, as reviewed in Section 11.5.

EXAMPLE 7. A Congressman wishes to test the hypothesis that at least 60 percent of his constituents are in favor of labor legislation being introduced in Congress, using the 5 percent level of significance. He considers the discrepancy from this hypothesis to be important if only 50 percent (or fewer) favor the legislation, and is willing to accept a risk of Type II error of $\beta = 0.05$. The sample size which he should arrange to collect, as a minimum, to satisfy these decision-making specifications is

$$n = \left[\frac{z_0\sqrt{\pi_0(1-\pi_0)} - z_1\sqrt{\pi_1(1-\pi_1)}}{\pi_1 - \pi_0} \right]^2 = \left[\frac{-1.65\sqrt{(0.60)(0.40)} - (+1.65)\sqrt{(0.50)(0.50)}}{0.60 - 0.50} \right]^2$$

$$= \left[\frac{-1.65(0.49) - 1.65(0.50)}{0.10} \right]^2 = \left(\frac{-0.808 - 0.825}{0.10} \right)^2 = (-16.33)^2 = 266.67 = 267$$

11.7 TESTING THE DIFFERENCE BETWEEN TWO POPULATION PROPORTIONS

When we wish to test the hypothesis that the proportions in two populations are not different, the two sample proportions are pooled as a basis for determining the standard error of the difference between proportions. Note that this differs from the procedure used in Section 9.5 on statistical estimation, in which the assumption of no difference was *not* made. Further, the present procedure is conceptually similar to that presented in Section 11.1, in which the two sample variances are pooled as the basis for computing the standard error of the difference between means. The pooled estimate of the population proportion, based on the proportions obtained in two independent samples, is

$$\hat{\pi} = \frac{n_1\bar{p}_1 + n_2\bar{p}_2}{n_1 - n_2} \qquad (11.16)$$

The standard error of the difference between proportions used in conjunction with testing the assumption of no difference is

$$\hat{\sigma}_{\bar{p}_1 - \bar{p}_2} = \sqrt{\frac{\hat{\pi}(1-\hat{\pi})}{n_1} + \frac{\hat{\pi}(1-\hat{\pi})}{n_2}} \qquad (11.17)$$

The formula for the z statistic for testing the difference between two proportions is

$$z = \frac{\bar{p}_1 - \bar{p}_2}{\hat{\sigma}_{\bar{p}_1 - \bar{p}_2}} \qquad (11.18)$$

A test of the difference between proportions can be carried out as either a one-tail (see Problem 11.11) or a two-tail (see Example 8) test.

EXAMPLE 8. A sample of 50 households in one community shows that 10 of them are watching a TV special on the national economy. In a second community, 15 of a random sample of 50 households are watching the TV special. We test the hypothesis that the overall proportion of viewers in the two communities does not differ, using the 1 percent level of significance, as follows:

$$H_0: \quad \pi_1 = \pi_2 \qquad H_1: \quad \pi_1 \neq \pi_2$$

Critical z ($\alpha = 0.01$) $= \pm 2.58$

$$\hat{\pi} = \frac{n_1\bar{p}_1 + n_2\bar{p}_2}{n_1 + n_2} = \frac{50(0.20) + 50(0.30)}{50 + 50} = \frac{10 + 15}{100} = 0.25$$

$$\hat{\sigma}_{\bar{p}_1 - \bar{p}_2} = \sqrt{\frac{\hat{\pi}(1-\hat{\pi})}{n_1} + \frac{\hat{\pi}(1-\hat{\pi})}{n_2}} = \sqrt{\frac{(0.25)(0.75)}{50} + \frac{(0.25)(0.75)}{50}} = \sqrt{0.00375 + 0.00375} = 0.087$$

$$z = \frac{\bar{p}_1 - \bar{p}_2}{\hat{\sigma}_{\bar{p}_1 - \bar{p}_2}} = \frac{0.20 - 0.30}{0.087} = \frac{-0.10}{0.087} = -1.15$$

Thus, this z value is in the region of acceptance of the null hypothesis, and the hypothesis that there is no difference in the proportion of viewers in the two areas cannot be rejected.

11.8 TESTING A HYPOTHESIZED VALUE OF THE VARIANCE USING THE CHI-SQUARE DISTRIBUTIONS

As explained in Section 9.6, for a normally distributed population the ratio $(n - 1)s^2/\sigma^2$ follows a χ^2 probability distribution, with there being a different chi-square distribution according to degrees of freedom $(n - 1)$. Therefore, the statistic which is used to test a hypothesized value of the population variance is

$$\chi^2 = \frac{(n - 1)s^2}{\sigma_0^2} \qquad\qquad (11.19)$$

The test based on (11.19) can be either a one-tail test or a two-tail test, although most often hypotheses about a population variance relate to one-tail tests. Appendix 7 can be used to determine the critical value(s) of the chi-square statistic for various levels of significance.

EXAMPLE 9. The mean operating life for a random sample of $n = 10$ light bulbs is $\bar{X} = 4000$ hr with a standard deviation of $s = 200$ hr. The operating life of bulbs in general is assumed to be normally distributed. Suppose that before the sample was collected it was hypothesized that the population standard deviation is no larger than $\sigma = 150$. Based on the sample results, this hypothesis is tested at the 1 percent level of significance as follows:

$$H_0: \quad \sigma^2 \leq 22{,}500 \quad (\text{because } \sigma_0^2 = (150)^2 = 22{,}500) \qquad H_1: \quad \sigma^2 > 22{,}500$$

$$\text{Critical } \chi^2(df = 9, \alpha = 0.01) = 21.67$$

$$\chi^2 = \frac{(n - 1)s^2}{\sigma_0^2} = \frac{(9)(40{,}000)}{22{,}500} = \frac{360{,}000}{22{,}500} = 16.0$$

Therefore, the hypothesis that $\sigma \leq 150$ cannot be rejected at the 1 percent level of significance.

11.9 THE F DISTRIBUTIONS AND TESTING THE DIFFERENCE BETWEEN TWO VARIANCES

The F distributions can be shown to be the appropriate probability distributions for the ratio of the variances of two samples taken independently from the same normally distributed population, with there being a different F distribution for every combination of the degrees of freedom df associated with each sample. For each sample, $df = n - 1$. Thus, the statistic which is used to test the null hypothesis that there is no difference between two variances is

$$F_{df_1, df_2} = \frac{s_1^2}{s_2^2} \qquad\qquad (11.20)$$

Since each sample variance is an unbiased estimator of the population variance, the long-run expected value of the above ratio is about 1.0. (*Note*: The expected value is not exactly 1.0, but rather is $df_2/(df_2 - 2)$, for mathematical reasons that are beyond the scope of this outline.) However, for any given pair of samples the sample variances are not likely to be identical in value, even though the null hypothesis is true. Since this ratio is known to follow an F distribution, this probability distribution can be used in conjunction with testing the difference between two variances. Although a necessary mathematical assumption is that the two populations are normally distributed, the F test has been demonstrated to be relatively insensitive to departures from normality when each population is at least unimodal and the sample sizes are about equal.

Appendix 8 indicates the values of F exceeded by proportions of 0.05 and 0.01 of the distribution of F values. The degrees of freedom df associated with the numerator of the calculated F ratio are the column headings of this table and the degrees of freedom for the denominator are the row headings. The table does not identify any critical values of F for the lower tail of the distribution, partly because the F distribution is typically used in conjunction with one-tail tests. This is particularly true for the use of the F distributions in the analysis of variance (see Chapter 13). Another reason for providing only upper-tail F-values is that lower-tail values of F can be calculated by the so-called *reciprocal property* of the F distribution, as follows:

$$F_{df_1, df_2 \text{lower}} = \frac{1}{F_{df_2, df_1, \text{upper}}} \tag{11.21}$$

In applying formula (11.21), an F value at the lower 5 percent point is determined by entering an upper-tail value at the 5 percent point in the denominator. Note, however, that the two df values in the denominator are the reverse of the order in the required F value.

EXAMPLE 10. For the data in Example 3, bulb life is assumed to be normally distributed. We test the null hypothesis that the samples were obtained from populations with equal variances, using the 10 percent level of significance for the test, by use of the F distribution:

$$H_0: \quad \sigma_1^2 = \sigma_2^2 \qquad s_1 = 200 \text{ hr} \qquad s_2 = 250 \text{ hr}$$
$$H_1: \quad \sigma_1^2 \neq \sigma_2^2 \qquad s_1^2 = 40{,}000 \qquad s_2^2 = 62{,}500$$
$$n_1 = 10 \qquad n_2 = 8$$

For the test at the 10 percent level of significance, the upper 5 percent point for F and the lower 5 percent point for F are the critical values.

Critical $F_{9,7}$ (upper 5%) = 3.68

Critical $F_{9,7}$ (lower 5%) $= \dfrac{1}{F_{7,9} \text{(upper 5\%)}} = \dfrac{1}{3.29} = 0.304$

$$F_{df_1, df_2} = \frac{s_1^2}{s_2^2}$$

$$F_{9,7} = \frac{40{,}000}{62{,}500} = 0.64$$

Since the computed F ratio is neither smaller than 0.304 nor larger than 3.68, it is in the region of acceptance of the null hypothesis. Thus, the assumption that the variances of the two populations are equal cannot be rejected at the 10 percent level of significance.

Solved Problems

TESTING THE DIFFERENCE BETWEEN TWO MEANS USING THE NORMAL DISTRIBUTION

11.1. A developer is considering two alternative sites for a regional shopping center. Since household income in the community is one important consideration in such site selection, he wishes to test the null hypothesis that there is no difference between the mean household income amounts in the two communities. Consistent with this hypothesis, he assumes that the standard deviation of household income is also the same in the two communities. For a sample of $n_1 = 30$ households in the first community, the average annual income is $\bar{X}_1 = \$15{,}500$ with the sample standard deviation $s_1 = \$1800$. For a sample of $n_2 = 40$ households in the second community, $\bar{X}_2 = \$14{,}600$ and $s_2 = \$2400$. Test the null hypothesis at the 5 percent level of significance.

$$H_0: \quad \mu_1 = \mu_2 \text{ (or } \mu_1 - \mu_2 = 0) \qquad H_1: \quad \mu_1 \ne \mu_2 \text{ (or } \mu_1 - \mu_2 \ne 0)$$

$$\bar{X}_1 = \$15{,}500 \qquad \bar{X}_2 = \$14{,}600$$

$$s_1 = \$1800 \qquad s_2 = \$2400$$

$$n_1 = 30 \qquad n_2 = 40$$

Critical $z \ (\alpha = 0.05) = \pm 1.96$

$$\hat{\sigma}^2 = \frac{(n_1 - 1)s_1^2 + (n_2 - 1)s_2^2}{n_1 + n_2 - 2} = \frac{29(1800)^2 + 39(2400)^2}{30 + 40 - 2} = \frac{318{,}600{,}000}{68} = \$4{,}685{,}294$$

(The variances are pooled because of the assumption that the standard deviation values in the two populations are equal.)

$$\hat{\sigma}_{\bar{x}_1 - \bar{x}_2} = \sqrt{\frac{\hat{\sigma}^2}{n_1} + \frac{\hat{\sigma}^2}{n_2}} = \sqrt{\frac{4{,}685{,}294}{30} + \frac{4{,}685{,}294}{40}} = \sqrt{156{,}176.46 + 117{,}132.35} = \$522.79$$

$$z = \frac{\bar{X}_1 - \bar{X}_2}{\hat{\sigma}_{\bar{x}_1 - \bar{x}_2}} = \frac{15{,}500 - 14{,}600}{522.79} = \frac{900}{522.79} = +1.72$$

Therefore, the null hypothesis cannot be rejected at the 5 percent level of significance, and the hypothesis that the average income per household in the two communities does not differ is accepted.

11.2. With reference to Problem 11.1, before any data were collected it was the developer's judgment that income in the first community might be higher. In order to subject this judgment to a critical test, he gave the benefit of doubt to the other possibility and formulated the null hypothesis $H_0: \quad \mu_1 \le \mu_2$. Test this hypothesis at the 5 percent level of significance with the further assumption that the standard deviation values for the two populations are *not* necessarily equal.

$$H_0: \quad \mu_1 \le \mu_2 \text{ (or } \mu_1 - \mu_2 \le 0) \qquad H_1: \quad \mu_1 > \mu_2 \text{ (or } \mu_1 - \mu_2 > 0)$$

Critical $z \ (\alpha = 0.05) = +1.65$

$$s_{\bar{x}_1} = \frac{s_1}{\sqrt{n_1}} = \frac{1800}{\sqrt{30}} = \frac{1800}{5.48} = \$328.47$$

$$s_{\bar{x}_2} = \frac{s_2}{\sqrt{n_2}} = \frac{2400}{\sqrt{40}} = \frac{2400}{6.32} = \$379.75$$

$$s_{\bar{x}_1 - \bar{x}_2} = \sqrt{s_{\bar{x}_1}^2 + s_{\bar{x}_2}^2} = \sqrt{(328.47)^2 + (379.75)^2} = \sqrt{252{,}102.60} = \$502.10$$

$$z = \frac{\bar{X}_1 - \bar{X}_2}{s_{\bar{x}_1 - \bar{x}_2}} = \frac{15{,}500 - 14{,}600}{502.10} = \frac{900}{502.10} = +1.79$$

Therefore, the null hypothesis is rejected at the 5 percent level of significance, and the alternative hypothesis, that average household income is larger in the first community as compared with the second, is accepted.

11.3. In respect to Problems 11.1 and 11.2, before any data were collected it was the developer's judgment that the average income in the first community exceeds the average in the second community by at least $1500 per year. In this case, give this judgment the benefit of the doubt and test the assumption as the null hypothesis using the 5 percent level of significance. The population standard deviations are not assumed to be equal.

$$H_0: \quad \mu_1 - \mu_2 \geq 1500 \qquad H_1: \quad \mu_1 - \mu_2 < 1500$$

$$\text{Critical } z \ (\alpha = 0.05) = -1.65$$

$$s_{\bar{x}_1 - \bar{x}_2} = \$502.10 \quad \text{(from Problem 11.2)}$$

$$z = \frac{(\bar{X}_1 - \bar{X}_2) - (\mu_1 - \mu_2)_0}{s_{\bar{x}_1 - \bar{x}_2}} = \frac{(15{,}500 - 14{,}600) - 1500}{502.10} = \frac{-600}{502.10} = -1.19$$

Therefore, the null hypothesis cannot be rejected at the 5 percent level of significance. Although the sample difference of $900 does not meet the $1500 difference hypothesized by the developer, it is not different enough from his assumption when the assumption is given the benefit of the doubt by being designated as the null hypothesis.

TESTING THE DIFFERENCE BETWEEN TWO MEANS USING t DISTRIBUTIONS

11.4. Of 100 juniors and seniors majoring in accounting in a college of business administration, a random sample of $n_1 = 12$ students has a mean grade-point average of 2.7 (where A = 4.0) with a sample standard deviation of 0.4. For the 50 juniors and seniors majoring in computer information systems, a random sample of $n_2 = 10$ students has a mean grade-point average of $\bar{X}_2 = 2.9$ with a standard deviation of 0.3. The grade-point values are assumed to be normally distributed. Test the null hypothesis that the mean grade-point average for the two categories of students is not different, using the 5 percent level of significance.

$$H_0: \quad \mu_1 = \mu_2 \ (\text{or } \mu_1 - \mu_2 = 0) \qquad H_1: \quad \mu_1 \neq \mu_2 \ (\text{or } \mu_1 - \mu_2 \neq 0)$$

$$\bar{X}_1 = 2.7 \qquad \qquad \bar{X}_2 = 2.9$$

$$s_1 = 0.4 \qquad \qquad s_2 = 0.3$$

$$n_1 = 12 \qquad \qquad n_2 = 10$$

$$N_1 = 100 \qquad \qquad N_2 = 50$$

$$\text{Critical } t \ (df = 20, \alpha = 0.05) = \pm 2.086$$

(*Note*: Section 11.2 specifies that a necessary assumption when using a t distribution for testing a difference between means is that the variances are equal.) Therefore the two sample variances are pooled:

$$\hat{\sigma}^2 = \frac{(n_1 - 1)s_1^2 + (n_2 - 1)s_2^2}{n_1 + n_2 - 2} = \frac{(11)(0.4)^2 + (9)(0.3)^2}{12 + 10 - 2} = \frac{1.76 + 0.81}{20} = \frac{2.57}{20} = 0.128$$

$$\hat{\sigma}_{\bar{x}_1 - \bar{x}_2} = \sqrt{\frac{\hat{\sigma}^2}{n_1}\left(\frac{N_1 - n_1}{N_1 - 1}\right) + \frac{\hat{\sigma}^2}{n_2}\left(\frac{N_2 - n_2}{N_2 - 1}\right)} = \sqrt{\frac{0.128}{12}\left(\frac{100 - 12}{100 - 1}\right) + \frac{0.128}{10}\left(\frac{50 - 10}{50 - 1}\right)}$$

$$= \sqrt{0.011\left(\frac{88}{99}\right) + 0.013\left(\frac{40}{49}\right)} = \sqrt{0.011(0.889) + 0.013(0.816)} = \sqrt{0.020387} = 0.143$$

(For each sample, $n < 0.05N$, and thus use of the finite correction factor is required.)

$$t = \frac{\bar{X}_1 - \bar{X}_2}{\hat{\sigma}_{\bar{x}_1 - \bar{x}_2}} = \frac{2.7 - 2.9}{0.143} = \frac{-0.2}{0.143} = -1.40$$

Therefore, the null hypothesis that there is no difference between the grade-point averages for the two populations of students cannot be rejected at the 5 percent level of significance.

TESTING THE DIFFERENCE BETWEEN MEANS
BASED ON PAIRED OBSERVATIONS

11.5. A company training director wishes to compare a new approach to technical training, involving a combination of programmed instruction and laboratory problem-solving, with the traditional lecture-discussion approach. He matches twelve pairs of trainees according to prior background and academic performance, and assigns one member of each pair to the traditional class and the other to the new approach. At the end of the course, the level of learning is determined by an examination covering basic information as well as the ability to apply the information. Because the training director wishes to give the benefit of the doubt to the established instructional system, he formulates the null hypothesis that the mean performance for the established system is equal to or greater than the mean level of performance for the new system. Test this hypothesis at the 5 percent level of significance. The sample performance data are presented in the first three columns of Table 11.3.

Table 11.3   Training Program Data and Worksheet for Computing the Mean Difference and the Standard Deviation of the Difference

Trainee pair	Traditional method, X_1	New approach, X_2	d $(X_1 - X_2)$	d^2
1	89	94	−5	25
2	87	91	−4	16
3	70	68	2	4
4	83	88	−5	25
5	67	75	−8	64
6	71	66	5	25
7	92	94	−2	4
8	81	88	−7	49
9	97	96	1	1
10	78	88	−10	100
11	94	95	−1	1
12	79	87	−8	64
Total	988	1030	−42	378

$$\text{Mean performance (traditional method)} = \frac{988}{12} = 82.33$$

$$\text{Mean performance (new approach)} \quad = \frac{1030}{12} = 85.83$$

$$H_0: \quad \mu_1 \geq \mu_2 \,(\text{or } \mu_d \geq 0) \qquad H_1: \quad \mu_1 < \mu_2 \,(\text{or } \mu_d < 0)$$

$$\text{Critical } t \,(df = 11, \alpha = 0.05) = -1.796$$

$$\bar{d} = \frac{\Sigma d}{n} = \frac{-42}{12} = -3.5$$

$$s_d = \sqrt{\frac{\Sigma d^2 - n\bar{d}^2}{n-1}} = \sqrt{\frac{378 - 12(-3.5)^2}{11}} = \sqrt{\frac{378 - 147}{11}} = \sqrt{\frac{231}{11}} = \sqrt{21} = 4.58$$

$$s_{\bar{d}} = \frac{s_d}{\sqrt{n}} = \frac{4.58}{\sqrt{12}} = \frac{4.58}{3.46} = 1.32$$

$$t = \frac{\bar{d}}{s_{\bar{d}}} = \frac{-3.5}{1.32} = -2.65$$

Thus, the null hypothesis is rejected at the 5 percent level of significance, and we conclude that the mean level of performance for those trained by the new approach is superior to those trained by the traditional method.

TESTING A HYPOTHESIZED PROPORTION USING THE BINOMIAL DISTRIBUTIONS

11.6   When a production process is in control, no more than 1 percent of the components are defective and have to be removed in the inspection process.   For a random sample of $n = 10$ components, one is found to be defective.   On the basis of this sample result, can the null hypothesis that the process is in control be rejected at the 5 percent level of significance?

For the hypotheses H_0: $\pi \leq 0.01$ and H_1: $\pi > 0.01$, based on the binomial distribution, the probability of obtaining one or more defectives by chance given that $\pi = 0.01$ is 1.0 minus the probability of obtaining zero defectives (from Appendix 1, with $n = 10$, $p = 0.01$):

$$P(X \geq 1 \mid n = 10, p = 0.01) = 1.000 - 0.9044 = 0.0956$$

Since this probability is greater than 0.05, the null hypothesis cannot be rejected.   For this problem, two or more items would have to be found defective to reject the null hypothesis, because the probability associated with this "tail" of the distribution is less than 0.05.   Further, the probability of two or more items being defective is also less than 0.01:

$$P(X \geq 2 \mid n = 10, p = 0.01) = 0.0042 + 0.0001 + 0.0000 + \cdots = 0.0043$$

11.7.   With reference to Example 5 (page 179), suppose that a sample of $n = 20$ students are polled and only four indicate having jobs by March 1 (the same sample proportion as in Example 5).   Can the director's claim be rejected in this case, using the 5 percent level of significance?

For the hypotheses, H_0: $\pi \geq 0.05$ and H_1: $\pi < 0.50$, based on the binomial distribution, the probabilities of sample results divergent from the claim, and not exceeding a cumulative probability of 0.05 are as follows (from Appendix 1, with $n = 20$ and $p = 0.50$):

Number obtaining jobs	Probability	Cumulative probability
0	0.0000	
1	0.0000	
2	0.0002	
3	0.0011	0.0207
4	0.0046	
5	0.0148	
6	0.0370	

Therefore, for a one-tail test at the 5 percent level of significance (in fact, the 2.07 percent level) the critical number for rejection is five or fewer.   To include the category "6" would result in a probability greater than 0.05.

Given the sample result that only *four* students reported having jobs, the null hypothesis is rejected. Note that even though the sample proportion is the same as in Example 5, the larger sample size is associated with a lower sampling error and leads to a test that is more sensitive to detecting a difference.

11.8. It is hypothesized that 40 percent of the voters in a primary election will vote for the incumbent, and that the other 60 percent of the votes will be distributed among three other candidates. Of a random sample of 20 registered voters who plan to vote in the primary election, 12 indicate that they will vote for the incumbent. Test the hypothesis that the overall proportion of voters who will cast their ballots for the incumbent is $\pi = 0.40$, using the 5 percent level of significance.

Where H_0: $\pi = 0.40$ and H_1: $\pi \neq 0.40$, based on the binomial distribution, the probabilities of extreme observations in either "tail" of the distribution, and not exceeding a cumulative probability of 0.025 in each tail, are as follows (from Appendix 1, with $n = 20$, $p = 0.40$):

Number for the candidate	Probability	Cumulative probability
0	0.0000	
1	0.0005	
2	0.0031	0.0159
3	0.0123	
4	0.0350	
⋮	⋮	
12	0.0355	
13	0.0146	
14	0.0049	
15	0.0013	
16	0.0003	0.0211
17	0.0000	
18	0.0000	
19	0.0000	
20	0.0000	

Therefore, for the two-tail test the overall level of significance without exceeding 0.025 in each tail is in fact at $\alpha = 0.037$. The critical number in the sample for rejection is "three or fewer" or "13 or more". Because 12 voters indicated they intend to vote for the incumbent, the null hypothesis cannot be rejected.

TESTING PROPORTIONS USING THE NORMAL DISTRIBUTION

11.9. It is hypothesized that no more than 5 percent of the parts being produced in a manufacturing process are defective. For a random sample of $n = 100$ parts, 10 are found to be defective. Test the null hypothesis at the 5 percent level of significance.

$$H_0: \pi \leq 0.05 \quad H_1: \pi > 0.05$$

$$\text{Critical } z \ (\alpha = 0.05) = +1.65$$

(Use of the normal distribution is warranted because $n \geq 30$, $n\pi_0 \geq 5$ and $n(1 - \pi_0) \geq 5$.)

$$\sigma_{\bar{p}} = \sqrt{\frac{\pi_0(1 - \pi_0)}{n}} = \sqrt{\frac{(0.05)(0.95)}{100}} = \sqrt{\frac{0.0475}{100}} = \sqrt{0.000475} = 0.022$$

$$z = \frac{\bar{p} - \pi_0}{\sigma_{\bar{p}}} = \frac{0.10 - 0.05}{0.022} = \frac{0.05}{0.022} = +2.27$$

Therefore, with 10 parts out of 100 found to be defective, the hypothesis that the proportion defective in the population is at or below 0.05 is rejected, using the 5 percent level of significance in the test.

11.10. For Problem 11.9, the manager stipulates that the probability of stopping the process for adjustment when it is in fact not necessary should be at only a 1 percent level, while the probability of *not* stopping the process when the true proportion defective is at $\pi = 0.10$ can be set at 5 percent. What sample size should be obtained, as a minimum, to satisfy these test objectives?

$$n = \left[\frac{z_0\sqrt{\pi_0(1 - \pi_0)} - z_1\sqrt{\pi_1(1 - \pi_1)}}{\pi_1 - \pi_0} \right]^2 = \left[\frac{2.33\sqrt{(0.05)(0.95)} - (-1.65)\sqrt{(0.10)(0.90)}}{0.10 - 0.05} \right]^2$$

$$= \left(\frac{2.33(0.218) + 1.65(0.300)}{0.05} \right)^2 = \left(\frac{1.003}{0.05} \right)^2 = (20.06)^2 = 402.4 = 403 \text{ parts}$$

For industrial sampling purposes this is a rather large sample, so the manager might well want to reconsider the test objectives in regard to the designated P (Type I error) of 0.01 and P (Type II error) of 0.05.

11.11. A manufacturer is evaluating two types of equipment for the fabrication of a component. A random sample of $n_1 = 50$ is collected for the first brand of equipment, and five items are found to be defective. A random sample of $n_2 = 80$ is collected for the second brand and six items are found to be defective. The fabrication rate is the same for the two brands. However, because the first brand costs substantially less, the manufacturer gives this brand the benefit of the doubt and formulates the hypothesis H_0: $\pi_1 \leq \pi_2$. Test this hypothesis at the 5 percent level of significance.

$$H_0: \quad \pi_1 \leq \pi_2 \qquad H_1: \quad \pi_1 \geq \pi_2$$

$$\text{Critical } z \ (\alpha = 0.05) = +1.65$$

$$\hat{\pi} = \frac{n_1\bar{p}_1 + n_2\bar{p}_2}{n_1 + n_2} = \frac{50(0.10) + 80(0.075)}{50 + 80} = \frac{5 + 6}{130} = 0.085$$

$$\hat{\sigma}_{\bar{p}_1 - \bar{p}_2} = \sqrt{\frac{\hat{\pi}(1 - \hat{\pi})}{n_1} + \frac{\hat{\pi}(1 - \hat{\pi})}{n_2}} = \sqrt{\frac{(0.085)(0.915)}{50} + \frac{(0.085)(0.915)}{80}}$$

$$= \sqrt{\frac{0.0778}{50} + \frac{0.0778}{80}} = \sqrt{0.0016 + 0.0010}, = 0.051$$

$$z = \frac{\bar{p}_1 - \bar{p}_2}{\hat{\sigma}_{\bar{p}_1 - \bar{p}_2}} = \frac{0.10 - 0.075}{0.051} = \frac{0.025}{0.051} = +0.49$$

Thus, the null hypothesis cannot be rejected at the 5 percent level of significance.

TESTING A HYPOTHESIZED VALUE OF THE VARIANCE
USING THE CHI-SQUARE DISTRIBUTIONS

11.12. Suppose it is hypothesized that the standard deviation of household income per year in a particular community is \$3000. For a sample of $n = 15$ randomly selected households, the standard deviation is $s = \$2000$. The household income figures for the population are assumed to be normally distributed. On the basis of this sample result, can the null hypothesis be rejected using the 5 percent level of significance?

$$H_0: \quad \sigma^2 = (\$3000)^2 = \$9,000,000 \qquad H_1: \quad \sigma^2 \neq \$9,000,000$$

Critical $\chi^2(df = 14, \alpha = 0.05) = 5.63$ and 26.12 (respectively, for the two-tail test)

$$\chi^2 = \frac{(n-1)s^2}{\sigma_0^2} = \frac{(14)(2000)^2}{(3000)^2} = \frac{14(4,000,000)}{9,000,000} = \frac{56,000,000}{9,000,000} = 6.22$$

The computed value is in the region of acceptance of the null hypothesis, and thus the null hypothesis cannot be rejected.

11.13. For Problem 11.12, suppose the null hypothesis was that the population standard deviation is *at least* \$3000. Test this hypothesis at the 5 percent level of significance.

$$H_0: \quad \sigma^2 \geq \$9,000,000 \qquad H_1: \quad \sigma^2 < \$9,000,000$$

Critical $\chi^2(df = 14, \alpha = 0.05) = 6.57$ (lower-tail critical value)

$$\chi^2 = 6.22 \text{ (from Problem 11.12)}$$

Therefore, in the case of this one-tail test the null hypothesis is rejected at the 5 percent level of significance, and the alternative hypothesis, that $\sigma^2 < \$9,000,000$ (that $\sigma < \$3000$), is accepted.

TESTING THE DIFFERENCE BETWEEN TWO VARIANCES

11.14. In Problem 11.4, concerned with testing the difference between two sample means by using a t distribution, a necessary assumption was that the two population variances are equal. The two sample variances were $s_1^2 = 0.16$ and $s_2^2 = 0.09$, with $n_1 = 12$ and $n_2 = 10$, respectively. Test the null hypothesis that the two population variances are equal, using a 10 percent level of significance.

$$H_0: \quad \sigma_1^2 = \sigma_2^2 \qquad s_1^2 = 0.16 \qquad s_2^2 = 0.09$$

$$H_1: \quad \sigma_1^2 \neq \sigma_2^2 \qquad n_1 = 12 \qquad n_2 = 10$$

Critical $F_{11,9}$ (upper 5%) = 3.10 (from Appendix 8)

$$\text{Critical } F_{11,9} \text{ (lower 5\%)} = \frac{1}{F_{9,11} \text{ (upper 5\%)}} = \frac{1}{2.90} = 0.345$$

$$F_{df_1,df_2} = \frac{s_1^2}{s_2^2} = \frac{0.16}{0.09} = 1.78$$

Therefore, the hypothesis of no difference between the variances cannot be rejected.

11.15. In Problem 11.1, the assumption was made that the variance of household income was not different in the two communities. Test the null hypothesis that the two variances are equal, using the 10 percent level of significance.

$$H_0: \quad \sigma_1^2 = \sigma_2^2 \qquad s_1^2 = (1800)^2 = 3,240,000 \qquad s_2^2 = (2400)^2 = 5,760,000$$

$$H_1: \quad \sigma_1^2 \neq \sigma_2^2 \qquad n_1 = 30 \qquad n_2 = 40$$

(*Note*: Because of limitations in Appendix 8, the specific F values for 29 and 39 degrees of freedom cannot be determined. Therefore, the approximate F values are determined by using the nearest degrees of freedom of 30 and 40, respectively.)

$$\text{Critical } F_{30,40} \text{ (upper 5\%)} = 1.74$$

$$\text{Critical } F_{30,40} \text{ (lower 5\%)} = \frac{1}{F_{40,30} \text{ (upper 5\%)}} = \frac{1}{1.79} = 0.559$$

$$F_{df_1, df_2} = \frac{s_1^2}{s_2^2} = \frac{3,240,000}{5,760,000} = 0.562$$

At the 10 percent level of significance the F statistic is just within the region of acceptance of the null hypothesis. Further, the critical F value for the lower tail was slightly overstated because of the approximation noted above. Therefore, the null hypothesis cannot be rejected on the basis of these sample data.

Supplementary Problems

TESTING THE DIFFERENCE BETWEEN TWO MEANS

11.16. As reported in Problem 9.15, for one consumer product the mean dollar sales per retail outlet last year in a sample of $n_1 = 10$ stores was $\bar{X}_1 = \$3425$ with $s_1 = \$200$. For a second product the mean dollar sales per outlet in a sample of $n_2 = 12$ stores was $\bar{X}_2 = \$3250$ with $s_2 = \$175$. The sales amounts per outlet are assumed to be normally distributed for both products. Test the null hypothesis that there is no difference between the mean dollar sales for the two products using the 1 percent level of significance.

   Ans.   Accept H_0.

11.17. For the data in Problem 11.16, suppose the two sample sizes were $n_1 = 20$ and $n_2 = 24$. Test the difference between the two means at the 1 percent level of significance.

   Ans.   Reject H_0.

11.18. For a sample of 30 employees in one large firm, the mean hourly wage is $\bar{X}_1 = \$7.50$ with $s_1 = \$1.00$. In a second large firm, the mean hourly wage for a sample of 40 employees is $\bar{X}_2 = \$7.05$ with $s_2 = \$1.20$. Test the hypothesis that there is no difference between the average wage rate being earned in the two firms, using the 5 percent level of significance and assuming that the variances of the two populations are not necessarily equal.

   Ans.   Accept H_0.

11.19. In Problem 11.18, suppose the null hypothesis being tested was that the average wage in the second firm was equal to or greater than the average wage rate in the first firm. Can this hypothesis be rejected at the 5 percent level of significance?

   Ans.   Yes.

11.20. A random sample of $n_1 = 10$ salesmen are placed on one incentive system while a random sample $n_2 = 10$ other salesman are placed under a second incentive system. During the comparison period, the salesmen under the first system have average weekly sales of $\bar{X}_1 = \$5000$ with a standard deviation of $s_1 = \$1200$ while the salesmen under the second system have sales of $\bar{X}_2 = \$4600$ with a standard deviation of $\$1000$. Test the null hypothesis that there is no difference between the mean sales per week for the two incentive systems, using the 5 percent level of significance.

   Ans.   Accept H_0.

11.21. In order to compare two electronic calculators in respect to a planned purchase of several such units, a manager obtains a "loaner" from each company and has 10 operators use each machine to perform a standard set of computations typical of those encountered in the office. Of course, in carrying out the comparison the manager was careful to use operators who did not have an established preference or skill with either type of machine, and he randomly assigned five of the operators to use Calculator A first, while the other five used Calculator B first. The time required to perform the standard set of computations, to the nearest minute, is reported in Table 11.4. Test the null hypothesis that there is no difference between the average time required to perform the calculations on the two machines, using the 5 percent level of significance.

Ans. Reject H_0.

Table 11.4   **Time Required to Perform a Standard Set of Computations on Two Electronic Calculators (Nearest Minute)**

Operator	1	2	3	4	5	6	7	8	9	10
Calculator A	12	16	15	13	16	10	15	17	14	12
Calculator B	10	17	18	16	19	12	17	15	17	14

TESTING A HYPOTHESIZED PROPORTION USING THE BINOMIAL DISTRIBUTION

11.22. Suppose we hypothesize that a coin is fair in the absence of having the opportunity to examine it directly. The coin is tossed, and the result is that it comes up "heads" all five times. Test the null hypothesis at the (a) 5 percent and (b) 10 percent level of significance.

Ans. (a) Accept H_0, (b) reject H_0.

11.23. A salesman claims that on the average he obtains orders from at least 30 percent of his prospects. For a random sample of 10 prospects he is able to obtain just one order. Can his claim be rejected on the basis of the sample result, at the 5 percent level of significance?

Ans. No.

11.24. The sponsor of a television "special" expected that at least 40 percent of the viewing audience would watch the show in a particular metropolitan area. For a random sample of 20 households with television sets turned on, only four households are watching the program. Based on this limited sample size, test the null hypothesis that at least 40 percent of the viewing audience are watching the program, using the 10 percent level of significance.

Ans. Reject H_0.

TESTING PROPORTIONS USING THE NORMAL DISTRIBUTION

11.25. With reference to Problem 11.23, suppose the salesman is able to obtain orders from 20 out of 100 randomly selected prospects. Can his claim be rejected at the (a) 5 percent and (b) 1 percent level of significance?

Ans. (a) Yes, (b) no.

11.26. With reference to Problem 11.24, the sample is expanded so that 100 households with sets turned on are contacted. Of the 100 households, 30 households are viewing the special. Can the sponsor's assumption that at least 40 percent of the households would watch the program be rejected at the (a) 10 percent and (b) 5 percent level of significance?

Ans. (a) Yes, (b) yes.

11.27. For Problems 11.24 and 11.26, suppose the sponsor specifies that as the result of the study the probability of rejecting a true claim should be no larger than $P = 0.02$, and the probability of accepting the claim given that the percentage viewing the program is actually 30 percent or less should be no larger than $P = 0.05$. What sample size is required in the study, as a minimum, to satisfy this requirement?

Ans. 312 households

11.28. For Problems 11.24 and 11.26, it was suggested that the program might appeal differently to urban versus suburban residents, but there was a difference of opinion among the production staff regarding the direction of the difference. For a random sample of 50 urban households, 20 reported watching the program. For a random sample of 50 suburban households, 30 reported watching the program. Can the difference be considered significant at the (*a*) 10 percent and (*b*) 5 percent level?

Ans. (*a*) Yes, (*b*) yes.

TESTING A HYPOTHESIZED VALUE OF THE VARIANCE AND THE DIFFERENCE BETWEEN TWO VARIANCES

11.29. Based on the operating characteristics provided by the process designer, the standard deviation of casting diameters is hypothesized to be no larger than 3.0 mm. For a sample of $n = 12$ castings, the sample standard deviation is $s = 4.2$ mm. The distribution of the diameters is assumed to be approximately normal. Can the null hypothesis that the true standard deviation is no larger than 3.0 mm be rejected at the (*a*) 5 percent and (*b*) 1 percent level of significance?

Ans. (*a*) Yes, (*b*) no.

11.30. In Problem 11.16, under the assumption that the variances of the two populations were equal, the null hypothesis that the means are equal could not be rejected using the t test at the 1 percent level of significance. At the 10 percent level of significance, was the assumption that the two variances are not different warranted?

Ans. Yes.

11.31. A new molding process is designed to reduce the variability of casting diameters. To test the new process, we conservatively formulate the hypothesis that the variance of casting diameters under the new process is equal to or greater than the variance for the old process. Rejection of this null hypothesis would then permit us to accept the alternative hypothesis that the variance associated with the new process is smaller than that associated with the old process. For a sample of $n_1 = 8$ castings produced by the new process $s_1 = 4.2$ mm. For a sample of $n_2 = 10$ castings produced by the old process $s_2 = 5.8$ mm. Can the null hypothesis be rejected at the 5 percent level of significance?

Ans. No.

THE MEANING OF SIGNIFICANCE

11.32. In the general press, it is often implied that results that are "statistically significant" are thereby also important. Consider the appropriateness of such a conclusion by considering the meaning of "significant" in the context of hypothesis testing.

Chapter 12

The Chi-Square Test

12.1 THE CHI-SQUARE TEST
AS A HYPOTHESIS-TESTING PROCEDURE

The procedures presented in this chapter are all concerned with comparing obtained sample frequencies that have been entered into certain categories with the expected frequencies based on a particular hypothesis in each case. Thus, the procedures presented are all hypothesis-testing procedures, and all of them therefore are concerned with the analysis of sample results.

The χ^2 (chi-square) distributions have been described in Sections 9.6 and 11.8. The test statistic described in Section 12.2 also follows the chi-square distributions, and since the use of this test statistic is associated with hypothesis testing, the basic steps in hypothesis testing described in Section 10.1 apply in this chapter as well.

This chapter covers use of the chi-square test for hypotheses concerned with *goodness of fit*, the *independence of two variables*, and the *differences among k sample proportions*. The latter procedure can be considered as an extension of testing the difference between two proportions, as described in Section 11.7.

12.2 GOODNESS OF FIT TESTS

The null hypothesis in a goodness of fit test is a stipulation concerning the expected pattern of frequencies in a series of categories. The expected pattern may conform to the assumption of equal likelihood and be uniform, or it may conform to such probability distributions as the binomial, Poisson, or normal.

EXAMPLE 1. A regional distributor of air-conditioning systems has subdivided his region into four territories. A prospective purchaser of the distributorship is told that installations of the equipment are about equally distributed among the four territories. The prospective purchaser takes a random sample of 40 installations performed during the past year from the company's files, and finds that the number installed in each of the four territories is as listed in the first row of Table 12.1 (where f_o means "observed

Table 12.1   Number of Installations of Air-Conditioning
Systems According to Territory

| | Territory | | | | |
	A	B	C	D	Total
Number installed in sample, f_o	6	12	14	8	40
Expected number of installations, f_e	10	10	10	10	40

frequency"). On the basis of the hypothesis that installations are equally distributed, the expected uniform distribution of the installations is given in the second row of Table 12.1 (where f_e means "expected frequency").

For the null hypothesis to be accepted, the differences between observed and expected frequencies must be attributable to sampling variability at the designated level of significance. Thus, the chi-square test statistic is based on the magnitude of this difference for each category in the frequency distribution. The chi-square value for testing the difference between an obtained and expected pattern of frequencies is

$$\chi^2 = \sum \frac{(f_o - f_e)^2}{f_e} \tag{12.1}$$

EXAMPLE 2. The calculation of the chi-square test statistic for the pattern of observed and expected frequencies in Table 12.1 is as follows

$$\chi^2 = \sum \frac{(f_o - f_e)^2}{f_e} = \frac{(6 - 10)^2}{10} + \frac{(12 - 10)^2}{10} + \frac{(14 - 10)^2}{10} + \frac{(8 - 10)^2}{10} = \frac{40}{10} = 4.0$$

The required value of the chi-square test statistic to reject the null hypothesis depends on the level of significance which is specified and the degrees of freedom. In goodness of fit tests, the degrees of freedom df are equal to the number of categories minus the number of parameter estimators based on the sample and minus 1. Where k = number of categories of data and m = number of parameter values estimated on the basis of the sample, the degrees of freedom in a chi-square goodness of fit test are

$$df = k - m - 1 \tag{12.2}$$

When the null hypothesis is that the frequencies are equally distributed, no parameter estimation is ever involved and $m = 0$. (Examples in which m is greater than zero are provided in Problems 12.6 and 12.8.) The subtraction of "1" is always included, because given a total number of observations, once observed frequencies have been entered in $k - 1$ categories of a table of frequencies, the last cell is in fact not "free" to vary. For instance, given that the first three categories in Table 12.1 have observed frequencies of 6, 12, and 14, respectively, it follows that the fourth category must have a frequency of 8 in order to cumulate to the designated sample size of $n = 40$.

EXAMPLE 3. Following is a complete presentation of the hypothesis-testing procedure associated with the data in Table 12.1, with the null hypothesis being tested at the 5 percent level of significance.

H_0: The number of installations are equally distributed among the four territories.

H_1: The number of installations are not equally distributed among the four territories.

$$df = k - m - 1 = 4 - 0 - 1 = 3$$

Critical χ^2 $(df = 3, \alpha = 0.05) = 7.81$ (from Appendix 7)

Computed $\chi^2 = 4.0$ (from Example 2)

Therefore, the null hypothesis that the installations are equally distributed among the four territories cannot be rejected at the 5 percent level of significance.

The expected frequencies may be based on any assumption regarding the form of the population frequency distribution. If the assumption is simply based on the historical pattern of frequencies, then, as in the case of the equally likely hypothesis, no parameter estimation is involved, and $df = k - m - 1 = k - 0 - 1 = k - 1$.

EXAMPLE 4. Historically, a manufacturer of TV sets has had 40 percent of his sales in small-screen sets (under 14 in.), 40 percent in the mid-range sizes (14 in. to 19 in.), and 20 percent in the large-screen category (21 in. and above). In order to ascertain appropriate prduction schedules for the next month, he takes a random sample of 100 purchases during the current period and finds that 55 of the sets purchased were small, 35 were middle-sized, and 10 were large. Below we test the null hypothesis that the historical pattern of sales still prevails, using the 1 percent level of significance.

H_0: The percentages of all purchases in the small-, medium-, and large-screen categories of TV sets are 40 percent, 40 percent, and 20 percent, respectively.

H_1: The present pattern of TV set purchases is different from the historical pattern in H_0.

$$df = k - m - 1 = 3 - 0 - 1 = 2$$

Critical χ^2 $(df = 2, \alpha = 0.01) = 9.21$

Computed χ^2 (See Table 12.2 for observed and expected frequencies.):

$$\chi^2 = \sum \frac{(f_o - f_e)^2}{f_e} = \frac{(55 - 40)^2}{40} + \frac{(35 - 40)^2}{40} + \frac{(10 - 20)^2}{20} = 11.25$$

Therefore, the null hypothesis is rejected at the 1 percent level of significance. Comparing the obtained and expected frequencies in Table 12.2, we find that the principal change involves more small sets and fewer large sets being sold, with some reduction in middle-sized sets also possibly occurring.

Table 12.2 **Observed and Expected Purchases of TV Sets by Screen Size**

	Screen size			
	Small	Medium	Large	Total
Observed frequency, f_o	55	35	10	100
Historical pattern, f_e	40	40	20	100

12.3 MINIMUM EXPECTED FREQUENCIES AND THE CORRECTION FOR CONTINUITY

Computed values of the chi-square test statistic are based on discrete counts, whereas the chi-square distribution is a continuous distribution. When the expected frequencies f_e for the cells are not small, this factor is not important in terms of the extent to which the distribution of the test statistic is approximated by the chi-square distribution. *A frequently used rule is that the expected frequency f_e for each cell, or category, should be at least 5.* Cells that do not meet this criterion should be combined with adjacent categories, when possible, so that this requirement is satisfied. The reduced number of categories then becomes the basis for determining the degrees of freedom df applicable in the test situation. See Problems 12.6 and 12.7.

It has been shown that when there is only one degree of freedom associated with the chi-square test, unless the sample is quite large, the computed χ^2 is systematically overstated because of the discrete nature of the data. The statistician Yates demonstrated that the following formula for chi-square which includes a *correction for continuity*, is appropriate when $df = 1$. As a rule of thumb, the correction factor has little effect and can be omitted when $n \geq 50$. Further, it should not be applied to any cell for which the difference between f_o and f_e is less than 0.5. The χ^2 statistic which includes the correction for continuity, and which is applicable when $df = 1$, is

$$\chi^2 = \sum \frac{(|f_o - f_e| - 0.5)^2}{f_e} \qquad (12.3)$$

EXAMPLE 5. In general, 20 percent of the prospects contacted by a firm's salesmen make a purchase. During a trial period, a new salesman makes 30 calls on prospects and completes three sales. The test of the null hypothesis that his pattern of sales does not differ from the historical pattern, using the 5 percent level of significance, is

H_0:   The new salesman's record conforms to the historical pattern of a 20 percent sales rate.

H_1:   The new salesman's record is different from the historical pattern.

$$df = k - m - 1 = 2 - 0 - 1 = 1$$

(Table 12.3 identifies the categories of data.)

Critical χ^2 ($df = 1$, $\alpha = 0.05$) = 3.84

Computed χ^2 (See Table 12.3 for observed and expected frequencies.):

$$\chi^2 = \sum \frac{(|f_o - f_e| - 0.5)^2}{f_e} = \frac{(|-3| - 0.5)^2}{6} + \frac{(|3| - 0.5)^2}{24} = \frac{(2.5)^2}{6} + \frac{(2.5)^2}{24} = 1.30$$

Therefore, the null hypothesis that his sales record conforms to the historical pattern cannot be rejected at the 5 percent level of significance.

Table 12.3   Observed and Expected Frequencies for Example 5

	Result of call		
	Sale	No sale	Total
f_o	3	27	30
f_e	6	24	30

12.4   TESTS FOR INDEPENDENCE OF TWO VARIABLES (CONTINGENCY TABLE TESTS)

In the case of goodness of fit tests there is only one variable, such as the screen size of TV sets which have been sold, and what is tested is the hypothesized pattern of frequencies, or the distribution, of the variable. The observed frequencies can be listed as a single row, or as a single column, of values. *Tests for independence* involve two variables, and what is tested is the assumption that the two variables are statistically independent. Independence implies that knowledge of the category in which an observation is classified in respect to one variable has no affect on the probability of being in one of the several categories of the other variables. Since two variables are involved, the observed frequencies are entered in a two-way classification table, or *contingency table* (see Section 5.7). The dimensions of such tables are defined by the expression $r \times k$, in which r indicates the number of rows and k indicates the number of columns.

EXAMPLE 6.   Table 12.4 is repeated from Section 5.7 and is an example of the simplest possible format for a contingency table, in that each of the two variables (sex and age) has only two classification levels, or categories. Thus, this is a 2×2 contingency table.

Table 12.4 Contingency Table for Stereo Shop
Customers

Age	Sex		Total
	Male	Female	
Under 30	60	50	110
30 and over	80	10	90
Total	140	60	200

If the null hypothesis of independence is rejected for classified data such as in Table 12.4, this indicates that the two variables are *dependent* and that there is a *relationship* between them. For Table 12.4, for instance, this would indicate that there is a relationship between age and the sex of stereo shop customers.

Given the hypothesis of independence of the two variables, the expected frequency associated with each cell of a contingency table should be proportionate to the total observed frequencies included in the column and in the row in which the cell is located as related to the total sample size. A convenient formula for determining the expected frequency for each cell of a contingency table is

$$f_e = \frac{\Sigma r \, \Sigma k}{n} \qquad\qquad (12.4)$$

The general formula for the degrees of freedom associated with a test for independence is

$$df = (r - 1)(k - 1) \qquad\qquad (12.5)$$

EXAMPLE 7. The expected frequencies for the data of Table 12.4 are reported in Table 12.5. For row 1, column 1, for instance, the calculation of the expected frequency is

$$f_e = \frac{\Sigma r \, \Sigma k}{n} = \frac{(110)(140)}{200} = \frac{15,400}{200} = 77$$

Note that in this case the three remaining expected frequencies can be obtained by subtraction from row and column totals, as an alternative to using (12.4). This is a direct indication that there is one degree of freedom for a 2×2 contingency table, and that only one cell frequency is "free" to vary.

Table 12.5 Table of Expected Frequencies for the
Observed Frequencies Reported in Table
12.4

Age	Sex		Total
	Male	Female	
Under 30	77	33	110
30 and over	63	27	90
Total	140	60	200

The chi-square test statistic for contingency tables is computed exactly as for the goodness of fit tests (see Sections 12.2 and 12.3).

EXAMPLE 8. Following is the test of the null hypothesis of independence for the data of Table 12.4, using the 1 percent level of significance.

H_0:   Sex and age of stereo shop customers are independent.

H_1:   Sex and age are dependent variables (there is a relationship between the variables sex and age).

$$df = (r - 1)(k - 1) = (2 - 1)(2 - 1) = 1$$

Critical $\chi^2 (df = 1, \alpha = 0.01) = 6.63$

$$\chi^2 = \sum \frac{(f_o - f_e)^2}{f_e} = \frac{(60 - 77)^2}{77} + \frac{(50 - 33)^2}{33} + \frac{(80 - 63)^2}{63} + \frac{(10 - 27)^2}{27} = 27.8$$

(*Note*: The correction for continuity was omitted, even though $df = 1$, because $n > 50$. The computed value with the continuity factor included is 26.19.)

Therefore, the null hypothesis of independence is rejected at the 1 percent level of significance. Referring to Table 12.4, we see that male customers are more likely to be over 30 years of age while female customers are more likely to be under 30. The result of the chi-square test is that this sample relationship cannot be ascribed to chance at the 1 percent level of significance.

12.5   TESTING THE DIFFERENCES AMONG k PROPORTIONS

Before demonstrating how the chi-square test can be used as an extension of the test for the difference between two proportions to the case of k proportions, we first indicate the formats of the chi-square test which are comparable to (1) testing a hypothesized proportion and (2) testing the difference between two proportions.

Testing a Hypothesized Proportion.   Given a hypothesized population proportion and an observed proportion for a random sample taken from the population, in Section 11.5 we used the normal probability distribution as an approximation for the binomial process in order to test the hypothesized value. Mathematically it can be shown that such a two-tail test is equivalent to a chi-square goodness of fit test involving the one row of frequencies and two categories (a 1×2 table). Since the chi-square test involves an analysis of differences between obtained and expected frequencies regardless of the direction of the differences, there is no chi-square test procedure which is the equivalent of a one-tail test concerning a population proportion.

EXAMPLE 9. A personnel department manager estimates that a proportion of $\pi = 0.40$ of the employees in a large firm will participate in a new stock investment program. A random sample of $n = 50$ employees are contacted and 10 indicate their intention to participate. The hypothesized value of the population proportion could be tested using the normal probability distribution, as described in Section 11.5. Following is the use of the chi-square test to accomplish the same objective, using the 5 percent level of significance.

$$H_0: \quad \pi = 0.40 \qquad H_1: \quad \pi \neq 0.40$$

$$df = k - m - 1 = 2 - 0 - 1 = 1$$

(There are two categories of observed frequencies, as indicated in Table 12.6.)

Critical $\chi^2 (df = 1, \alpha = 0.05) = 3.84$

Computed χ^2 (Table 12.6 indicates the observed and expected frequencies. Since $n = 50$, the correction for continuity is omitted.):

$$\chi^2 = \sum \frac{(f_o - f_e)^2}{f_e} = \frac{(10 - 20)^2}{20} + \frac{(40 - 30)^2}{30} = 8.33$$

Therefore, the null hypothesis is rejected at the 5 percent level of significance, and we conclude that the proportion of program participants in the entire firm is not 0.40.

Table 12.6   Observed and Expected Frequencies for Example 9

	Participation in program		
	Yes	No	Total
Number observed in sample, f_o	10	40	50
Number expected in sample, f_e	20	30	50

Testing the Difference Between Two Proportions.   A procedure for testing the difference between two proportions based on use of the normal probability distribution is presented in Section 11.7.   Mathematically, it can be shown that such a two-tail test is equivalent to a chi-square contingency-table test in which the observed frequencies are entered in a 2×2 table.   Again, there is no chi-square test equivalent to a one-tail test.

EXAMPLE 10.   Example 8 in Section 11.7 specifies that 10 out of 50 households in one community watched a TV special on the national economy and 15 out of 50 households in a second community watched the TV special.   In that example the null hypothesis H_0: $\pi_1 = \pi_2$ is tested at the 1 percent level of significance.   Below is the equivalent test using the chi-square test statistic.

$$H_0: \quad \pi_1 = \pi_2 \qquad H_1: \quad \pi_1 \neq \pi_2$$

$$df = (r - 1)(k - 1) = (2 - 1)(2 - 1) = 1$$

(The observed frequencies are entered in a 2×2 table, as indicated in Table 12.7.)

Table 12.7   Extent of TV Program Viewing in Two Communities

	Communities		
	Community 1	Community 2	Total
Number watching	10	15	25
Number not watching	40	35	75
Total	50	50	100

Critical χ^2 $(df = 1, \alpha = 0.01) = 6.63$

Computed χ^2 (The observed frequencies are presented in Table 12.7 while the expected frequencies—calculated by the method in Example 7—are presented in Table 12.8.   The correction for continuity is omitted because $n > 50$.):

$$\chi^2 = \sum \frac{(f_o - f_e)^2}{f_e} = \frac{(10 - 12.5)^2}{12.5} + \frac{(15 - 12.5)^2}{12.5} + \frac{(40 - 37.5)^2}{37.5} + \frac{(35 - 37.5)^2}{37.5} = 1.34$$

Therefore, the null hypothesis cannot be rejected at the 1 percent level of significance, and we conclude that the proportion of viewers in the two communities does not differ.

Table 12.8   Expected Frequencies for the Data of Table 12.7

	Communities		
	Community 1	Community 2	Total
Number watching	12.5	12.5	25
Number not watching	37.5	37.5	75
Total	50	50	100

Testing the Differences Among k Proportions.   Given the basic approach in Example 10, the chi-square test can be used to test the difference among k sample proportions by using a $2 \times k$ tabular design for the analysis of the frequencies.   In this case, there is no mathematically equivalent procedure based on the normal probability distribution.   The null hypothesis in this case is that there is no difference among the several population proportions (or, that the several different sample proportions could have been obtained by chance from the same population).

EXAMPLE 11.   From Example 10, suppose households in four communities are sampled in regard to the number viewing a TV special on the national economy.   Table 12.9 presents the observed sample data while Table 12.10 presents the expected frequencies, based on the method presented in Section 12.4.   The test of the null hypothesis that there are no differences among the population proportions, using the 1 percent level of significance, follows.

$$H_0: \quad \pi_1 = \pi_2 = \pi_3 = \pi_4 \qquad H_1: \quad \text{The null hypothesis is not true.}$$

(*Note*:   Rejection of the null hypothesis does not indicate that all of the equalities are untrue, but only that at least one equality is untrue.)

$$df = (r - 1)(k - 1) = (2 - 1)(4 - 1) = 3$$

Critical $\chi^2 (df = 3, \alpha = 0.01) = 11.35$

$$\chi^2 = \sum \frac{(f_o - f_e)^2}{f_e} = \frac{(10 - 12)^2}{12} + \frac{(15 - 12)^2}{12} + \frac{(5 - 12)^2}{12} + \frac{(18 - 12)^2}{12}$$

$$+ \frac{(40 - 38)^2}{38} + \frac{(35 - 38)^2}{38} + \frac{(45 - 38)^2}{38} + \frac{(32 - 38)^2}{38}$$

$$= 0.33 + 0.75 + 4.08 + 3.0 + 0.11 + 0.24 + 1.29 + 0.95 = 10.75$$

Therefore, the differences in the proportion of viewers among the four sampled communities are not large enough to reject the null hypothesis at the 1 percent level of significance.

Table 12.9   Extent of TV Program Viewing in Four Communities

| | Communities | | | | |
	1	2	3	4	Total
Number watching	10	15	5	18	48
Number not watching	40	35	45	32	152
Total	50	50	50	50	200

Table 12.10   Expected Frequencies for the Data of Table 12.9

| | Communities | | | | |
	1	2	3	4	Total
Number watching	12.0	12.0	12.0	12.0	48
Number not watching	38.0	38.0	38.0	38.0	152
Total	50	50	50	50	200

Solved Problems

GOODNESS OF FIT TESTS

12.1. It is claimed that an equal number of men and women patronize a retail outlet specializing in the sale of slacks and jeans. A random sample of 40 customers are observed, and of these 25 are men and 15 are women. Test the null hypothesis that the overall number of men and women customers is equal by applying the chi-square test and using the 5 percent level of significance.

Table 12.11   Obtained and Expected Frequencies for Problem 12.1

| | Customers | | |
	Men	Women	Total
Number in sample, f_o	25	15	40
Number expected, f_e	20	20	40

From Table 12.11,

H_0:   The number of men and women customers is equal.

H_1:   The number of men and women customers is not equal.

$$df = k - m - 1 = 2 - 0 - 1 = 1$$

Critical $\chi^2 (df = 1, \alpha = 0.05) = 3.84$

$$\chi^2 = \sum \frac{(|f_o - f_e| - 0.5)^2}{f_e} = \frac{(|25 - 20| - 0.5)^2}{20} + \frac{(|15 - 20| - 0.5)^2}{20}$$

$$= \frac{(4.5)^2}{20} + \frac{(4.5)^2}{20} = 2.02$$

(Note: The correction for continuity, as described in Section 12.3, is required.)

Therefore, the null hypothesis cannot be rejected at the 5 percent level of significance.

12.2.   With reference to Problem 12.1, suppose it had instead been claimed that twice as many men as compared with women are store customers.   Using the observed data in Table 12.11, test this hypothesis using the 5 percent level of significance.

From Table 12.12,

H_0:   There are twice as many men as there are women customers.

H_1:   There are not twice as many men as women customers.

$$df = k - m - 1 = 2 - 0 - 1 = 1$$

Critical $\chi^2 (df = 1, \alpha = 0.05) = 3.84$

$$\chi^2 = \sum \frac{(|f_o - f_e| - 0.5)^2}{f_e} = \frac{(|25 - 26.67| - 0.5)^2}{26.67} + \frac{(|15 - 13.33| - 0.5)^2}{13.33}$$

$$= \frac{(1.17)^2}{26.67} + \frac{(1.17)^2}{13.33} = 0.05 + 0.10 = 0.15$$

Therefore, the null hypothesis cannot be rejected at the 5 percent level of significance.   The fact that neither of the null hypotheses in Problems 12.1 and 12.2 could be rejected demonstrates the "benefit of the doubt" given to the null hypothesis in each case.   However, the size of the sample also affects the probability of sample results (see Problem 12.3).

**Table 12.12   Obtained and Expected
Frequencies for Problem 12.2**

	Customers		
	Men	Women	Total
Number in sample, f_o	25	15	40
Number expected, f_e	26.67	13.33	40

12.3.   For the situation described in Problem 12.1, suppose the same null hypothesis is tested, but that the sample frequencies in each category are exactly doubled.   That is, of 80 randomly selected customers 50 are men and 30 are women.   Test the null hypothesis at the 5 percent level of significance and compare your decision with the one in Problem 12.1.

From Table 12.13,

H_0: The number of men and women customers is equal.

H_1: The number of men and women customers is not equal.

$$df = k - m - 1 = 2 - 0 - 1 = 1$$

Critical χ^2 ($df = 1$, $\alpha = 0.05$) = 3.84

$$\chi^2 = \sum \frac{(f_o - f_e)^2}{f_e} = \frac{(50 - 40)^2}{40} + \frac{(30 - 40)^2}{40} = 5.0$$

(Because $n > 50$, the correction for continuity is omitted even though $df = 1$.)

Therefore, the null hypothesis is rejected at the 5 percent level of significance. Even though the sample data are proportionally the same as in Problem 12.1, the decision now is "reject H_0" instead of "accept H_0". This demonstrates the greater sensitivity of a statistical test associated with a larger sample size.

Table 12.13 Obtained and Expected Frequencies for Problem 12.3

	Customers		
	Men	Women	Total
Number in sample, f_o	50	30	80
Number expected, f_e	40	40	80

12.4. A manufacturer of refrigerators offers three basic product lines, which can be described as being "low," "intermediate," and "high" in terms of comparative price. Before a sales promotion aimed at highlighting the virtues of the high-priced refrigerators, the percentage sales in the three categories was 45, 30, and 25, respectively. Of a random sample of 50 refrigerators sold after the promotion, the number sold in the low, intermediate, and high-priced categories is 15, 15, and 20, respectively. Test the null hypothesis that the current pattern of sales does not differ from the historical pattern, using the 5 percent level of significance.

With reference to Table 12.14,

H_0: The present pattern of sales frequencies follows the historical pattern.

H_1: The present pattern of sales frequencies is different from the historical pattern.

$$df = k - m - 1 = 3 - 0 - 1 = 2$$

Critical χ^2 ($df = 2$, $\alpha = 0.05$) = 5.99

$$\chi^2 = \sum \frac{(f_o - f_e)^2}{f_e} = \frac{(15 - 22.5)^2}{22.5} + \frac{(15 - 15)^2}{15} + \frac{(20 - 12.5)^2}{12.5}$$

$$= \frac{(-7.5)^2}{22.5} + \frac{(0)^2}{15} + \frac{(7.5)^2}{12.5} = 7.0$$

Therefore, the null hypothesis is rejected at the 5 percent level of significance. Although such rejection does not itself indicate in what respect the present pattern of sales differs from the historical pattern, a review of Table 12.14 indicates that more high-priced and fewer low-priced refrigerators were sold than would be expected in terms of the historical pattern of sales.

Table 12.14   Obtained and Expected Frequencies for Problem 12.4

	Price category of refrigerator			
	Low	Intermediate	High	Total
Number sold, f_o	15	15	20	50
Number expected to be sold, f_e	22.5	15	12.5	50

12.5. Any probability distribution can serve as the basis for determining the expected frequencies associated with a goodness of fit test (see Section 12.2). Suppose it is hypothesized that the distribution of machine breakdowns per hour in any assembly plant conforms to a Poisson probability distribution, as described in Section 6.6. However, the particular Poisson distribution as determined by the mean of the distribution, λ, is not specified. Table 12.15 presents the observed number of breakdowns during 40 sampled hours.

(a) Determine the value of λ to be used to test the hypothesis that the number of machine breakdowns conforms to a Poisson probability distribution.

(b) Construct the table of expected frequencies based on use of the Poisson distribution identified in (a) for a sample of $n = 40$ hours.

Table 12.15   Observed Number of Machine Breakdowns During 40 Sampled Hours and Worksheet for the Calculation of the Average Number of Breakdowns per Hour

Number of breakdowns, X	Observed frequency, f_o	$f_o(X)$
0	0	0
1	6	6
2	8	16
3	11	33
4	7	28
5	4	20
6	3	18
7	1	7
	$\Sigma f_o = 40$	$\Sigma (f_o)(X) = 128$

(a) $\bar{X} = \dfrac{\Sigma (f_o)(X)}{\Sigma f_o} = \dfrac{128}{40} = 3.2$ breakdowns per hour

Therefore, we set the mean of the Poisson distribution at $\lambda = 3.2$.

(b)   The expected frequencies are determined by reference to Appendix 3 for the Poisson probability distribution. See Table 12.16.

Table 12.16 Determination of Expected Frequencies for the
Machine-Breakdown Problem According to the Poisson
Distribution with $\lambda = 3.2$ and $n = 40$

Number of breakdowns, X	Probability, P	Expected frequency, $f_e (= nP)$
0	0.0408	1.6
1	0.1304	5.2
2	0.2087	8.3
3	0.2226	8.9
4	0.1781	7.1
5	0.1140	4.6
6	0.0608	2.4
7	0.0278	1.1
8	0.0111	0.4
9	0.0040	0.2
10	0.0013	0.1
11	0.0004	0.0
12	0.0001	0.0
13	0.0000	0.0
Total	1.0001	39.9

12.6. Given the information in Tables 12.15 and 12.16, test the null hypothesis that the distribution of machine breakdowns per hour conforms to a Poisson probability distribution at the 5 percent level of significance.

H_0: The observed distribution of machine breakdowns per hour conforms to a Poisson-distributed variable.

H_1: The distribution of machine breakdowns does not conform to a Poisson-distributed variable.

Table 12.17 Observed and Expected Frequencies for the
Machine-Breakdown Problem and the Calculation
of the Chi-Square Value

Number of breakdowns	Observed frequency, f_o	Expected frequency, f_e	$\dfrac{(f_o - f_e)^2}{f_e}$
0	0 } 6	1.6 } 6.8	0.094
1	6	5.2	
2	8	8.3	0.011
3	11	8.9	0.496
4	7	7.1	0.001
5	4	4.6	
6	3	2.4	
7	1 } 8	1.1 } 8.8	0.073
8	0	0.4	
9	0	0.2	
10	0	0.1	
			$\chi^2 = \overline{0.675}$

Critical χ^2: Table 12.17 indicates the observed and expected frequencies to be compared. Note that in order to satisfy the requirement that each f_e be at least 5, a number of categories at each end of the frequency distribution had to be combined. Further, one parameter, λ, was estimated on the basis of the sample. Therefore, $df = k - m - 1 = 5 - 1 - 1 = 3$, and the critical χ^2 $(df = 3, \alpha = 0.05) = 7.81$.

Computed χ^2: As indicated in Table 12.17, the computed $\chi^2 = 0.675$.

Therefore, the null hypothesis that the number of machine breakdowns per hour is a Poisson-distributed variable cannot be rejected at the 5 percent level of significance.

12.7. In respect to the sample data presented in Problem 12.5, suppose that in an established similar assembly plant machine breakdowns per hour follow a Poisson distribution with $\lambda = 2.5$. Determine if the breakdowns in the present plant differ significantly from such a pattern, using the 5 percent level of significance.

In this case, no parameter is estimated on the basis of the sample, and the expected frequencies are determined on the basis of the Poisson distribution with the mean $\lambda = 2.5$.

H_0: The observed distribution of machine breakdowns per hour conforms to a Poisson-distributed variable with $\lambda = 2.5$.

H_1: The observed distribution of machine breakdowns does not conform to a Poisson-distributed variable with $\lambda = 2.5$.

Table 12.18 illustrates the determination of the expected frequencies.

Table 12.18 Determination of Expected Frequencies for the Machine-Breakdown Problem According to the Poisson Distribution with $\lambda = 2.5$ and with $n = 40$

Number of breakdowns, X	Probability, P	Expected frequency, f_e $(=nP)$
0	0.0821	3.3
1	0.2052	8.2
2	0.2565	10.3
3	0.2138	8.6
4	0.1336	5.3
5	0.0668	2.7
6	0.0278	1.1
7	0.0099	0.4
8	0.0031	0.1
9	0.0009	0.0
10	0.0002	0.0
Total	0.9999	40.0

Critical χ^2: Table 12.19 indicates the observed and expected frequencies to be compared. With the reduced number of categories being $k = 4$, and with no parameter estimated on the basis of the sample, $df = k - m - 1 = 4 - 0 - 1 = 3$, and critical χ^2 $(df = 3, \alpha = 0.05) = 7.81$.

Computed χ^2: As indicated in Table 12.19, the computed $\chi^2 = 6.85$.

Therefore, the null hypothesis that the number of machine breakdowns per hour is distributed as a Poisson variable with $\lambda = 2.5$ cannot be rejected at the 5 percent level of significance. As would be expected, the χ^2 test statistic is larger in this problem than in Problem 12.6, where λ was based on the sample mean itself. However, the test statistic is still in the region of acceptance of the null hypothesis.

Table 12.19   Observed and Expected Frequencies for the Machine-Breakdown Problem and the Calculation of the Chi-Square Value

Number of breakdowns, X	Observed frequency, f_o	Expected frequency, f_e	$\dfrac{(f_o - f_e)^2}{f_e}$
0	$\left.\begin{array}{c}0\\6\end{array}\right\}6$	$\left.\begin{array}{c}3.3\\8.2\end{array}\right\}11.5$	2.63
1			
2	8	10.3	0.51
3	11	8.6	0.67
4	$\left.\begin{array}{c}7\\4\\3\\1\\0\end{array}\right\}15$	$\left.\begin{array}{c}5.3\\2.7\\1.1\\0.4\\0.1\end{array}\right\}9.6$	3.04
5			
6			
7			
8			
			$\chi^2 = \overline{6.85}$

12.8. Table 12.20, taken from Problem 2.16, indicates the average number of injuries per thousand man-hours in a sample of 50 firms taken from a particular industry. The mean for this distribution was $\bar{X} = 2.32$ in Problem 3.13; the sample standard deviation was $s = 0.42$ in Problem 4.18. Test the null hypothesis that the observed frequencies in this sample follow a normal distribution, using the 5 percent level of significance.

H_0:　The frequency distribution follows a normal distribution.

H_1:　The frequency distribution does not follow a normal distribution.

The expected frequencies are determined in Table 12.21, based on use of Appendix 4 for the standard normal distribution and with use of the sample mean and sample standard deviation as estimators for the respective population parameters. Table 12.22 indicates the observed and expected frequencies to be compared.

Table 12.20   Industrial Injuries in 50 Firms

Average number of injuries per thousand man-hours	Number of firms
1.5–1.7	3
1.8–2.0	12
2.1–2.3	14
2.4–2.6	9
2.7–2.9	7
3.0–3.2	5
	$\overline{}$
	50

$$df = k - m - 1 = 4 - 2 - 1 = 1$$

Critical χ^2 ($df = 1$, $\alpha = 0.05$) = 3.84

Computed $\chi^2 = 1.65$ (as indicated in Table 12.22)

Therefore, the null hypothesis that the frequency distribution of accident rates follows the normal distribution cannot be rejected at the 5 percent level of significance, and the hypothesis is therefore accepted.

Table 12.21 Determination of Expected Frequencies for the Industrial Injuries in 50 Firms

Average number of injuries per thousand man-hours (class boundaries)	Class boundaries in standard-normal units, z*	Probability of being in each category, P†	Expected frequency ($=50 \times P$)
1.45–1.75	−2.07 to −1.36	0.09	4.5
1.75–2.05	−1.36 to −0.64	0.17	8.5
2.05–2.35	−0.64 to 0.07	0.27	13.5
2.35–2.65	0.07 to 0.79	0.26	13.0
2.65–2.95	0.79 to 1.50	0.15	7.5
2.95–3.25	1.50 to 2.21	0.07	3.5
		1.01	50.5

*Based on $\bar{X} = 2.32$ and $s = 0.42$; for example, for $X = 1.45$, $z = (X - \bar{X})/s = (1.45 - 2.32)/0.42 = -2.07$.

†The first probability value of 0.09 is the proportion of area in the entire "tail" to the left of $z = -1.36$ and the last probability value of 0.07 is the proportion of area in the entire "tail" to the right of $z = 1.50$. This procedure is necessary for the end classes so that the entire area under the normal curve is allocated in the frequency distribution.

Table 12.22 Observed and Expected Frequencies for the Industrial Injuries Data and the Determination of the χ^2 Value

Average number of injuries per thousand man-hours	Observed frequency, f_o	Expected frequency, f_e	$\dfrac{(f_o - f_e)^2}{f_e}$
1.5–1.7	3 } 15	4.5 } 13.0	0.31
1.8–2.0	12	8.5	
2.1–2.3	14	13.5	0.02
2.4–2.6	9	13.0	1.23
2.7–2.9	7 } 12	7.5 } 11.0	0.09
3.0–3.2	5	3.5	
			$\chi^2 = 1.65$

TESTS FOR INDEPENDENCE OF TWO VARIABLES (CONTINGENCY TABLE TESTS)

12.9. Table 12.23 (a contingency table taken from Problem 5.18) presents voter reactions to a new property tax plan according to party affiliation. From these data, construct a table of the expected frequencies based on the assumption that there is no relationship between party affiliation and reaction to the tax plan.

Table 12.23   Contingency Table for Voter Reactions to a
New Property Tax Plan

Party affiliation	Reaction			Total
	In favor	Neutral	Opposed	
Democratic	120	20	20	160
Republican	50	30	60	140
Independent	50	10	40	100
Total	220	60	120	400

The expected cell frequencies presented in Table 12.24 are determined by the formula $f_e = (\Sigma r \, \Sigma k)/n$ (see Section 12.4).

Table 12.24   Table of Expected Frequencies for the
Observed Frequencies Reported in Table 12.23

Party affiliation	Reaction			Total
	In favor	Neutral	Opposed	
Democratic	88	24	48	160
Republican	77	21	42	140
Independent	55	15	30	100
Total	220	60	120	400

12.10. Referring to Tables 12.23 and 12.24, test the null hypothesis that there is no relationship between party affiliation and voter reaction, using the 1 percent level of significance.

H_0:   Party affiliation and voter reaction are independent (there is no relationship).

H_1:   Party affiliation and voter reaction are not independent.

$$df = (r - 1)(k - 1) = (3 - 1)(3 - 1) = 4$$

Critical χ^2 ($df = 4$, $\alpha = 0.01$) = 13.28

$$\chi^2 = \sum \frac{(f_o - f_e)^2}{f_e} = \frac{(120 - 88)^2}{88} + \frac{(20 - 24)^2}{24} + \frac{(20 - 48)^2}{48} + \frac{(50 - 77)^2}{77}$$

$$+ \frac{(30 - 21)^2}{21} + \frac{(60 - 42)^2}{42} + \frac{(50 - 55)^2}{55} + \frac{(10 - 15)^2}{15} + \frac{(40 - 30)^2}{30}$$

$$= 11.64 + 0.67 + 16.33 + 9.47 + 3.86 + 7.71 + 0.45 + 1.67 + 3.33 = 55.13$$

Therefore, the null hypothesis is rejected at the 1 percent level of significance, and we conclude that there is a relationship between party affiliation and reaction to the new tax plan.

12.11. Table 12.25 indicates student reaction to expanding a college athletic program according to class standing, where "lower division" indicates freshman or sophomore class standing and "upper division" indicates junior or senior class standing. Test the null hypothesis that class standing and reaction to expanding the athletic program are independent variables, using the 5 percent level of significance.

H_0: Class standing and reaction to expanding the athletic program are independent.

H_1: Class standing and reaction to expanding the athletic program are not independent.

$$df = (r - 1)(k - 1) = (2 - 1)(2 - 1) = 1$$

Critical χ^2 ($df = 1$, $\alpha = 0.05$) = 3.84

Computed χ^2 (The expected cell frequencies are presented in Table 12.26.):

$$\chi^2 = \sum \frac{(f_o - f_e)^2}{f_e} = \frac{(20 - 18)^2}{18} + \frac{(19 - 21)^2}{21} + \frac{(10 - 12)^2}{12} + \frac{(16 - 14)^2}{14} = 1.03$$

(*Note:* The correction for continuity is omitted even though $df = 1$ because $n > 50$.)

Therefore, the null hypothesis cannot be rejected at the 5 percent level of significance, and the hypothesis that the two variables are independent is accepted.

Table 12.25   Student Reaction to Expanding the Athletic Program According to Class Standing

Reaction	Class standing		Total
	Lower division	Upper division	
In favor	20	19	39
Against	10	16	26
Total	30	35	65

Table 12.26   Table of Expected Frequencies for the Observed Frequencies Reported in Table 12.25

Reaction	Class standing		Total
	Lower division	Upper division	
In favor	18	21	39
Against	12	14	26
Total	30	35	65

TESTING THE DIFFERENCES AMONG k SAMPLE PROPORTIONS

12.12. Since Problem 12.1 involves a 1×2 table of observed frequencies, the procedure is equivalent to testing a hypothesized population proportion, as explained in Section 12.5.

(a) Formulate the null hypothesis as a hypothesized proportion and interpret the result of the test carried out in Problem 12.1 from this standpoint.

(b) Test the hypothesized proportion by using the normal probability distribution as the basis of the test and demonstrate that the result is equivalent to using the chi-square test.

(a) H_0: The proportion of men customers $\pi = 0.50$; H_1: $\pi \neq 0.50$

$$\text{Critical } \chi^2(df = 1, \alpha = 0.05) = 3.84$$

$$\chi^2 = 2.02 \quad \text{(from Problem 12.1)}$$

Therefore, we cannot reject the hypothesis that $\pi = 0.50$ at the 5 percent level of significance.

(b) H_0: $\pi = 0.50$ H_1: $\pi \neq 0.50$

$$\text{Critical } z \ (\alpha = 0.05) = \pm 1.96$$

Using formula (11.12),

$$\sigma_{\bar{p}} = \sqrt{\frac{\pi_0(1 - \pi_0)}{n}} = \sqrt{\frac{(0.50)(0.50)}{40}} = \sqrt{\frac{0.25}{40}} = \sqrt{0.00625} = 0.079$$

From formula (11.14),

$$z = \frac{\bar{p} - \pi_0}{\sigma_{\bar{p}}} = \frac{0.375 - 0.50}{0.079} = \frac{-0.125}{0.079} = -1.58$$

Therefore, the null hypothesis cannot be rejected at the 5 percent level of significance.

12.13. Because Problem 12.11 involves a 2×2 table of observed frequencies, the procedure is equivalent to testing the difference between two sample proportions. State the null and alternative hypothesis from this point of view and interpret the test carried out in Problem 12.11.

$$H_0: \quad \pi_1 = \pi_2 \qquad H_1: \quad \pi_1 \neq \pi_2$$

where π_1 = proportion of lower-division students in favor of expanding the athletic program
π_2 = proportion of upper-division students in favor of expanding the athletic program

$$\text{Critical } \chi^2(df = 1, \alpha = 0.05) = 3.84$$

$$\chi^2 = 1.03 \quad \text{(from Problem 12.11)}$$

Therefore, the null hypothesis cannot be rejected at the 5 percent level of significance, and the hypothesis that the proportion of lower-division students in favor of expanding the athletic program is equal to the proportion of upper-division students with this view is accepted.

12.14. Table 12.27 represents an extension of the study discussed in Problems 12.11 and 12.13. Formulate the null hypothesis from the viewpoint that a $2 \times k$ table of frequencies can be used to test the difference among k proportions, and carry out the test using the 5 percent level of significance.

$$H_0: \quad \pi_1 = \pi_2 = \pi_3 \qquad H_1: \quad \text{The null hypothesis is not true}$$

where π_1 = proportion of lower-division students in favor of expanding the athletic program
π_2 = proportion of upper-division students in favor of expanding the athletic program
π_3 = proportion of graduate students in favor of expanding the athletic program

$$df = (r - 1)(k - 1) = (2 - 1)(3 - 1) = 2$$

Table 12.27 Student Reaction to Expanding the Athletic Program According to Class Standing

Reaction	Class standing			Total
	Lower division	Upper division	Graduate	
In favor	20	19	15	54
Against	10	16	35	61
Total	30	35	50	115

Critical $\chi^2 (df = 2, \alpha = 0.05) = 5.99$

Computed χ^2 (The expected cell frequencies are presented in Table 12.28.):

$$\chi^2 = \frac{(f_o - f_e)^2}{f_e} = \frac{(20 - 14.1)^2}{14.1} + \frac{(19 - 16.4)^2}{16.4} + \frac{(15 - 23.5)^2}{23.5} + \frac{(10 - 15.9)^2}{15.9}$$

$$+ \frac{(16 - 18.6)^2}{18.6} + \frac{(35 - 26.5)^2}{26.5} = 11.23$$

Therefore, the null hypothesis is rejected at the 5 percent level of significance and we conclude that not all three population proportions are equal.

Table 12.28 Table of Expected Frequencies for the Observed Frequencies in Table 12.27

Reaction	Class standing			Total
	Lower division	Upper division	Graduate	
In favor	14.1	16.4	23.5	54
Against	15.9	18.6	26.5	61
Total	30	35	50	115

Supplementary Problems

GOODNESS OF FIT TESTS

12.15. Refer to Table 12.29 and test the null hypothesis that the consumer preferences are equal, using the 1 percent level of significance.

Ans. Reject H_0.

12.16. Using Table 12.29, test the hypothesis that Brand C is preferred by as many people as the other three brands combined at the 1 percent level of significance.

Ans. Accept H_0.

**Table 12.29   Consumer Panel Preferences for
Four Brands of Rhine Wine**

Brand				
A	B	C	D	Total
30	20	40	10	100

12.17. Table 12.30 reports the single most important safety feature desired by a random sample of car purchasers. Test the null hypothesis that the general population of car buyers is equally distributed in terms of primary preference for these safety features, using the (a) 5 percent and (b) 1 percent level of significance.

Table 12.30   Identification of Most Important Safety Feature Desired by Car Buyers

Safety feature					
Disk brakes	Collapsible steering wheel	Steel-belted radial tires	Automatic door locks	Speed warning indicator	Total
20	10	30	25	15	100

Ans.   (a) Reject H_0,   (b) accept H_0.

12.18. In a college course in business statistics, the historical distribution of the A, B, C, D, and E grades has been 10, 30, 40, 10, and 10 percent, respectively. A particular class taught by a new instructor completes the semester with 8 students earning a grade of A, 17 with B, 20 with C, 3 with D, and 2 with E. Test the null hypothesis that this sample does not differ significantly from the historical pattern, using the 5 percent level of significance.

Ans.   Accept H_0.

12.19. In general, 20 percent of the people stop to watch a cookingware demonstration in a department store. For a new demonstration format, only 3 of 40 people stop to watch the demonstration.   Test the hypothesis that this result is not significantly different from the expected number based on the general experience, using the 5 percent level of significance.

Ans.   Accept H_0.

12.20. Table 12.31 reports the number of transistors that do not meet a stringent quality requirement in 20 samples of $n = 10$ each. Test the null hypothesis that this distribution is not significantly different from the binomial distribution with $n = 10$ and $p = 0.30$, using the 5 percent level of significance.

Ans.   Reject H_0.

**Table 12.31   Number of Defective Transistors in 20 Samples of Size $n = 10$
Each**

Number defective	0	1	2	3	4	5	6	7	8	9	10
Number of samples	0	1	2	4	5	5	2	1	0	0	0

12.21. Refer to Table 2.15 (page 25). For these grouped data, $\bar{X} = 18.95$ and $s = 2.52$ (see Problems 3.32 and 4.38). Test the null hypothesis that this distribution of frequencies conforms to a normal probability distribution at the 5 percent level of significance.

Ans. Cannot be tested, because $df = 0$.

12.22. Refer to Table 2.18 (page 27). For this sample of grouped data, $\bar{X} = 23.3$ years and $s = 3.4$ years (see Problems 3.38 and 4.46). Test the null hypothesis that this distribution of frequencies follows a normal probability distribution, using the 1 percent level of significance.

Ans. Reject H_0.

TESTS FOR INDEPENDENCE OF TWO VARIABLES (CONTINGENCY TABLE TESTS)

12.23. As an extension of Problem 12.17, the opinions of men and women were tallied separately (see Table 12.32). Test the hypothesis that there is no relationship between sex and which safety feature is preferred, using the 1 percent level of significance.

Table 12.32 Identification of Most Important Safety Feature Desired by Car Buyers, According to Sex

Respondents	Disk brakes	Collapsible steering wheel	Steel-belted radial tires	Automatic door locks	Speed warning indicator	Total
Men	15	5	20	5	5	50
Women	5	5	10	20	10	50
Total	20	10	30	25	15	100

Ans. Reject H_0.

12.24. In order to investigate the relationship between employment status at the time a loan was arranged and whether or not the loan is now in default, a loan company manager chooses 100 accounts randomly, with the results indicated in Table 12.33. Test the null hypothesis that employment status and status of the loan are independent variables, using the 5 percent level of significance for the test.

Table 12.33 Employment Status and Loan Status for a Sample of 100 Accounts

Present status of loan	Employment status at time of loan		Total
	Employed	Unemployed	
In default	10	8	18
Not in default	60	22	82
Total	70	30	100

Ans. Accept H_0.

12.25. An elementary school principal categorizes parents into three income categories according to residential area, and into three levels of participation in school programs. From Table 12.34, test the hypothesis that there is no relationship between income and school program participation, using the 5 percent level of significance. Consider the meaning of the test results.

Table 12.34 Income Level and Participation in School
Programs by Parents of Elementary School
Students

Program participation	Income level			Total
	Low	Middle	High	
Never	28	48	16	92
Occasional	22	65	14	101
Regular	17	74	3	94
Total	67	187	33	287

Ans. Reject H_0.

TESTING THE DIFFERENCES AMONG k SAMPLE PROPORTIONS

12.26. Refer to Problems 12.15 to 12.25 and identify those applications of the chi-square test which are equivalent to testing a hypothesized population proportion. For each problem you identify, formulate such a null hypothesis.

Ans. Problems 12.16 and 12.19.

12.27. Refer to Problems 12.15 to 12.25 and identify those applications which are equivalent to testing the difference between two sample proportions. For each problem you identify, formulate such a null hypothesis.

Ans. Problem 12.24.

12.28. Refer to Problems 12.15 to 12.25 and identify those applications which are equivalent to testing the difference among k proportions, and formulate the null hypothesis in each case.

Ans. Problem 12.23.

Chapter 13

Analysis of Variance

13.1 GENERAL CONCEPTS ASSOCIATED WITH
TESTING THE DIFFERENCES AMONG k MEANS

Whereas the chi-square test is used to test the differences among k proportions (see Section 12.5), the analysis of variance is used to test the differences among k means. A basic assumption underlying the analysis of variance is that the several sample means were obtained from normally distributed populations having the same variance σ^2. However, the test procedure has been found to be relatively unaffected by violations of the normality assumption when the populations are unimodal and the sample sizes are approximately equal. Because the null hypothesis is that the population means are equal, the assumption of equal variance (*homogeneity of variance*) also implies that for practical purposes the test is concerned with the hypothesis that the means came from the same population. This is so because any normally distributed population is defined by the mean and variance (or standard deviation) as the two parameters. (See Section 7.2 for a general description of the normal probability distribution.) All of the computational procedures presented in this chapter are for fixed-effects models as contrasted with random-effects models. This distinction is explained in Section 13.6.

The basic concept underlying the analysis of variance was first developed by R. A. Fisher, and the F distribution was named in his honor. The conceptual rationale is as follows:

(1) Compute the mean for each sample group and then determine the standard error of the mean $s_{\bar{x}}$ *based only on the several sample means*. Computationally, this is the standard deviation of these several mean values.

(2) Now, given the formula $s_{\bar{x}} = s/\sqrt{n}$, it follows that $s = \sqrt{n}s_{\bar{x}}$ and that $s^2 = ns_{\bar{x}}^2$. Therefore, the standard error of the mean computed in (1) can be used to estimate the variance of the (common) population from which the several samples were obtained. This estimate of the population variance is called the *mean square between groups* (*MSB*).

(3) Compute the variance separately within each sample group and in respect to each group mean. Then pool these variance values by weighting them according to $n - 1$ for each sample. This weighting procedure for the variance is an extension of the procedure for combining and weighting two sample variances (see Section 11.1). The resulting estimate of the population variance is called the *mean square within groups* (*MSW*).

(4) If the null hypothesis that $\mu_1 = \mu_2 = \mu_3 = \cdots = \mu_k$ is true, then it follows that the two mean squares obtained in (2) and (3) are unbiased and independent estimators of the same population variance σ^2. However, if the null hypothesis is false, then the expected value of the *MSB* is larger than the *MSW*. Essentially, any differences among the population means will inflate *MSB* while having no affect on *MSW*.

(5) Based on the observation in (4), the F distribution can be used to test the difference between the two variances, as described in Section 11.9. A one-tail test is involved, and the general form of the F test in analysis of variance is

$$F_{df_1, df_2} = \frac{MSB}{MSW}$$ (13.1)

If the F ratio is in the region of rejection for the specified level of significance, then the hypothesis that the several sample means came from the same population is rejected.

Problem 13.1 illustrates the application of these five steps to a hypothesis-testing problem involving the difference among three means.

Although the above steps are useful for describing the conceptual approach underlying the analysis of variance, extension of this procedure for designs that are more complex than the simple comparison of k sample means is cumbersome. For this reason, in the sections which follow each design is described in terms of the linear model which identifies the components influencing the random variable. Also, a standard analysis-of-variance table which shows the calculation of the required mean square values is presented for each type of experimental design.

13.2 ONE-WAY ANALYSIS OF VARIANCE

The one-way analysis of variance model is concerned with testing the difference among k sample means when the subjects are assigned randomly to each of the several treatment groups. Therefore, the general explanation in Section 13.1 concerns the one-way classification model.

The linear equation which represents the one-way analysis of variance model is

$$X_{ik} = \mu + \alpha_k + e_{ik}$$ (13.2)

where μ = the overall mean of all k treatment populations
  α_k = effect of the treatment in the particular group k from which the value was sampled
  e_{ik} = the random error associated with the process of sampling

Table 13.1 is the summary table for the one-way analysis of variance, including all computational formulas. The application of these formulas to sample data is illustrated in Problems 13.2 to 13.4. The symbol system used in this table is somewhat different from that used in Section 13.1 because of the need to use a system which can be extended logically to two-way analysis of variance. Thus, MSB becomes the *mean square between the A treatment groups* (MSA). Further, MSW is now called the *mean square error* (MSE), indicating that

Table 13.1 Summary Table for One-Way Analysis of Variance
(Treatment Groups Need Not Be Equal)

Source of variation	Sum of squares, SS	Degrees of freedom, df	Mean square, MS	F ratio
Between treatment groups, A	$SSA = \sum_{k=1}^{K} \frac{T_k^2}{n_k} - \frac{T^2}{N}$	$K - 1$	$MSA = \dfrac{SSA}{K - 1}$	$F = \dfrac{MSA}{MSE}$
Sampling error, E	$SSE = SST - SSA$	$N - K$	$MSE = \dfrac{SSE}{N - K}$	
Total, T	$SST = \sum_{i=1}^{n} \sum_{k=1}^{K} X^2 - \frac{T^2}{N}$	$N - 1$		

this is the source of variability associated only with sampling error and not including any influences associated with treatments. Finally, note that the definition of symbols in the context of analysis of variance is not necessarily consistent with the use of these symbols in general statistical analysis. For example, α_k in (13.2) is concerned with the effect on a randomly sampled value originating from the treatment group in which the value is located; it has nothing to do with the concept of α in general hypothesis-testing procedures as defined in Section 10.1. Similarly, N in Table 13.1 designates the total size of the sample for all treatment groups combined, rather than a population size. New symbols included in Table 13.1 are T_k, which represents the sum (total) of the values in a particular treatment group, and T, which represents the sum of the sampled values in all groups combined.

Instead of the form of the null hypothesis described in Section 13.1, the general form of the null hypothesis in the analysis of variance makes reference to the relevant component of the linear model. Thus, for the one-way analysis of variance the null and alternative hypotheses are

$$H_0: \quad \alpha_k = 0 \text{ for all treatment levels} \qquad H_1: \quad \alpha_k \neq 0 \text{ for all treatment levels}$$

If the null hypothesis above is true, then it follows that $\mu_1 = \mu_2 = \mu_3 = \cdots = \mu_k$, as stated in Section 13.1.

13.3 TWO-WAY ANALYSIS OF VARIANCE

Two-way analysis of variance is based on two sets of classifications or treatments. For example, in analyzing the level of achievement in a training program we could consider both the effect of the method of instruction and the effect of prior school achievement. Similarly, we could investigate gasoline mileage according to the weight category of the car and according to the grade of gasoline. In data tables, the treatments identified in the column headings are typically called the A treatments; those in the row headings are called the B treatments.

Interaction in a two-factor experiment means that the two treatments are not independent, and that the particular effect of the treatment levels in one factor differs according to levels of the other factor. For example, in studying automobile mileage a higher-octane gasoline may improve mileage for certain types of cars but not for others. Similarly, the effectiveness of various methods of instruction may differ according to the ability levels of the students. In order to test for interaction, more than one observation or sampled measurement (i.e. *replication*) has to be included in each cell of the two-way data table. Section 13.4 presents the analytical procedure which is appropriate when there is only one observation per cell, and in which interaction between the two factors cannot be tested. The analytical procedure is extended to include replication and the analysis of interaction effects in Section 13.5.

13.4 TWO-WAY ANALYSIS WITHOUT INTERACTION
(RANDOMIZED BLOCK DESIGN)

The two-way analysis of variance model in which there is only one observation per cell is also often referred to as the *randomized block design*, because of one particular type of use for this model. What if we extend the idea of pairing (see Section 11.3) to the basic one-way analysis of variance model, and have groups of k *matched* individuals assigned randomly to each treatment level? In analysis of variance, such matched groups are called *blocks*, and because the individuals (or items) are randomly assigned based on the identification of block membership, the design is referred to as a randomized block design. In such a design the "blocks" dimension is not a treatment dimension as such. The objective of using this design is not for the specific purpose of testing for a "blocks" effect. Rather, by being able to assign some of the variability among subjects to prior achievement, for example, the MSE can be reduced and the resulting test of the A treatments effect is more sensitive.

The linear equation for the two-way analysis of variance model with no replication (i.e. with one observation per cell) is

$$X_{jk} = \mu + \beta_j + \alpha_k + e_{jk} \qquad (13.3)$$

where μ = the overall mean regardless of any treatment
$\quad\ \beta_j$ = effect of the treatment j or block j in the B dimension of classification
$\quad\ \alpha_k$ = effect of the treatment k in the A dimension of classification
$\quad\ e_{jk}$ = the random error associated with the process of sampling

Table 13.2 is the summary table for the two-way analysis of variance without replication. As compared with Table 13.1 for the one-way analysis of variance, the only new symbol in this table is T_j^2, which indicates that the total of each j group (for the B treatments, or blocks) is squared. See Problems 13.5 and 13.6 for application of these formulas.

Table 13.2 Summary Table for Two-Way Analysis of Variance with One Observation per Cell (Randomized Block Design)

Source of variation	Sum of squares, SS	Degrees of freedom, df	Mean square, MS	F ratio
Between treatment groups, A	$SSA = \sum_{k=1}^{K} \dfrac{T_k^2}{n_k} - \dfrac{T^2}{N}$	$K - 1$	$MSA = \dfrac{SSA}{K - 1}$	$F = \dfrac{MSA}{MSE}$
Between treatment groups, or blocks, B	$SSB = \dfrac{1}{K} \sum_{j=1}^{J} T_j^2 - \dfrac{T^2}{N}$	$J - 1$	$MSB = \dfrac{SSB}{J - 1}$	$F = \dfrac{MSB}{MSE}$
Sampling error, E	$SSE = SST - SSA - SSB$	$(J - 1)(K - 1)$	$MSE = \dfrac{SSE}{(J - 1)(K - 1)}$	
Total, T	$SST = \sum_{j=1}^{J} \sum_{k=1}^{K} X^2 - \dfrac{T^2}{N}$	$N - 1$		

13.5 TWO-WAY ANALYSIS WITH INTERACTION (n OBSERVATIONS PER CELL)

As explained in Section 13.3, when replication is included within a two-way design, the interaction between the two factors can be tested. Thus, when such a design is used, three different null hypotheses can be tested by the analysis of variance: that there are no column effects (the column means are not significantly different), that there are no row effects (the row means are not significantly different), and that there is no interaction between the two factors (the two factors are independent). A significant interaction effect indicates that the effect of treatments for one factor varies according to levels of the other factor. In such a case, the existence of column and/or row effects may not be meaningful from the standpoint of the application of research results.

The linear equation for the two-way analysis of variance model when replication is included is

$$X_{ijk} = \mu + \beta_j + \alpha_k + \iota_{jk} + e_{ijk} \qquad (13.4)$$

where μ = the overall mean regardless of any treatment

β_j = effect of the treatment j in the B (row) dimension

α_k = effect of the treatment k in the A (column) dimension

ι_{jk} = effect of interaction between treatment j (of factor B) and treatment k (of factor A) (where ι is the Greek "iota")

e_{ijk} = the random error associated with the process of sampling

Table 13.3 is the summary table for the two-way analysis of variance with replication. The formulas included in this table are based on the assumption that there are an equal number of observations in all of the cells. See Problem 13.7 for application of these formulas.

**Table 13.3 Summary Table for Two-Way Analysis of Variance
with More than One Observation per Cell**

Source of variation	Sum of Squares, SS	Degrees of freedom, df	Mean square, MS	F ratio
Between treatment groups, A	$SSA = \sum\limits_{k=1}^{K} \dfrac{T_k^2}{nJ} - \dfrac{T^2}{N}$	$K - 1$	$MSA = \dfrac{SSA}{K - 1}$	$F = \dfrac{MSA}{MSE}$
Between treatment groups, B	$SSB = \sum\limits_{j=1}^{J} \dfrac{T_j^2}{nK} - \dfrac{T^2}{N}$	$J - 1$	$MSB = \dfrac{SSB}{J - 1}$	$F = \dfrac{MSB}{MSE}$
Interaction (between factors A and B), I	$SSI = \dfrac{1}{n} \sum\limits_{j=1}^{J} \sum\limits_{k=1}^{K} \left(\sum\limits_{i=1}^{n} X \right)^2$ $- SSA - SSB - \dfrac{T^2}{N}$	$(J - 1)(K - 1)$	$MSI = \dfrac{SSI}{(J - 1)(K - 1)}$	$F = \dfrac{MSI}{MSE}$
Sampling error, E	$SSE = SST - SSA$ $- SSB - SSI$	$JK(n - 1)$	$MSE = \dfrac{SSE}{JK(n - 1)}$	
Total, T	$SST = \sum\limits_{i=1}^{n} \sum\limits_{j=1}^{J} \sum\limits_{k=1}^{K} X^2 - \dfrac{T^2}{N}$	$N - 1$		

13.6 ADDITIONAL CONSIDERATIONS

All of the computational procedures presented in this chapter are for fixed-effects models of the analysis of variance. In a *fixed-effects model*, all of the treatment levels of concern for a given factor are included in the experiment. For instance, in Problem 13.1 it is assumed that the only instructional methods of concern are the three methods included in the design. A *random-effects model*, however, includes only a random sample from all the possible treatment levels for the given factor in the experiment. For instance, out of ten different instructional methods, three might have been randomly chosen. A different computational method is required in the latter case because the null hypothesis is that there are no differences among the various instructional methods in general, and not just among the particular instructional methods which were included in the experiment. In most experiments the fixed-effects model is appropriate, and therefore the presentation in this chapter has been limited to such models.

The concepts presented in this chapter can be extended to more than two treatments, or factors. Designs involving three or more factors are called *factorial designs*, and in fact many statisticians include the two-way analysis of variance with replication in this category. Although a number of different null hypotheses can be tested with the same body of data by the use of factorial designs, the extension of such designs can lead to an extremely large number of categories (cells) in the data table, with related sampling problems. Because of such difficulties, designs have been developed which do not require that every possible combination of the treatment levels of every factor be included in the analysis. Such designs as the *Latin Square design* and *incomplete block designs* are examples of such developments and are described in specialized textbooks in the analysis of variance.

Whatever experimental design is used, rejection of a null hypothesis in the analysis of variance typically does not present the analyst with the basis for final decisions, because such rejection does not serve to pinpoint the exact differences among the treatment levels. For example, given that there is a significant difference in student achievement among three instructional methods, we would next want to determine which of the pairs of methods are different from one another. Various procedures have been developed for such pairwise comparisons carried out in conjunction with the analysis of variance.

Solved Problems

ONE-WAY ANALYSIS OF VARIANCE

13.1. Fifteen trainees in a technical program are randomly assigned to three different types of instructional approaches, all of which are concerned with developing a specified level of skill in blueprint reading. The achievement test scores at the conclusion of the instructional unit are reported in Table 13.4, along with the mean performance score associated with each instructional approach.   Use the analysis-of-variance procedure in Section 13.1 to test the null hypothesis that the three sample means were obtained from the same population at the 5 percent level of significance.

Table 13.4   Achievement Test Scores of Trainees under Three Methods of Instruction

Instructional method	Test scores					Total test scores	Mean test scores
A_1	86	79	81	70	84	400	80
A_2	90	76	88	82	89	425	85
A_3	82	68	73	71	81	375	75

From the hypotheses H_0: $\mu_1 = \mu_2 = \mu_3$ and H_1:   The means are not all mutually equal,

(1)   The overall mean of all 15 test scores is

$$\bar{X}_T = \frac{\Sigma X}{n} = \frac{1200}{15} = 80$$

The standard error of the mean, based on the three sample means reported, is

$$s_{\bar{x}} = \sqrt{\frac{\Sigma (\bar{X} - \bar{X}_T)^2}{\text{No. means} - 1}} = \sqrt{\frac{(80 - 80)^2 + (85 - 80)^2 + (75 - 80)^2}{3 - 1}} = \sqrt{\frac{50}{2}} = 5.0$$

(2) $MSB = ns_{\bar{x}}^2 = 5(5.0)^2 = 5(25) = 125$

(3) From the general formula:

$$s^2 = \frac{\Sigma(X - \bar{X})^2}{n - 1}$$

the variance for each of the three samples is

$$s_1^2 = \frac{(86 - 80)^2 + (79 - 80)^2 + (81 - 80)^2 + (70 - 80)^2 + (84 - 80)^2}{5 - 1} = \frac{154}{4} = 38.5$$

$$s_2^2 = \frac{(90 - 85)^2 + (76 - 85)^2 + (88 - 85)^2 + (82 - 85)^2 + (89 - 85)^2}{5 - 1} = \frac{140}{4} = 35.0$$

$$s_3^2 = \frac{(82 - 75)^2 + (68 - 75)^2 + (73 - 75)^2 + (71 - 75)^2 + (81 - 75)^2}{5 - 1} = \frac{154}{4} = 38.5$$

Then,

$$\hat{\sigma}^2\text{(pooled)} = \frac{(n_1 - 1)s_1^2 + (n_2 - 1)s_2^2 + (n_3 - 1)s_3^2}{n_1 + n_2 + n_3 - 3} = \frac{(4)(38.5) + 4(35.0) + 4(38.5)}{5 + 5 + 5 - 3} = \frac{448}{12} = 37.3$$

Therefore, $MSW = 37.3$.

(4) Since MSB is larger than MSW, a test of the null hypothesis is appropriate.

Critical F $(df = k - 1, kn - k; \alpha = 0.05) = F(2, 12; \alpha = 0.05) = 3.88$

(5) $F = MSB/MSW = 125/37.3 = 3.35$

Since this F ratio is not in the region of rejection of the null hypothesis at the designated 5 percent level of significance, the hypothesis of no difference among the population means cannot be rejected.

13.2. Repeat the analysis of variance for the data in Table 13.4 by using the general procedure described in Section 13.2 with the accompanying formulas in Table 13.1.

The various quantities required for substitution in the formulas in Table 13.1 are

$n_1 = 5$	$n_2 = 5$	$n_3 = 5$	$N = 15$
$T_1 = 400$	$T_2 = 425$	$T_3 = 375$	$T = 1200$
$T_1^2 = 160,000$	$T_2^2 = 180,625$	$T_3^2 = 140,625$	$T^2 = 1,440,000$

$$T^2/N = 1,440,000/15 = 96,000$$

$$\sum_{i=1}^{n} \sum_{k=1}^{K} X^2 = 86^2 + 79^2 + \cdots + 81^2 = 96,698$$

$$SST = \sum_{i=1}^{n} \sum_{k=1}^{K} X^2 - \frac{T^2}{N} = 96,698 - 96,000 = 698$$

$$SSA = \sum_{k=1}^{K} \frac{T_k^2}{n_k} - \frac{T^2}{N} = \frac{160,000}{5} + \frac{180,625}{5} + \frac{140,625}{5} - 96,000 = 250$$

$$SSE = SST - SSA = 698 - 250 = 448$$

Table 13.5 presents the analysis of variance (ANOVA) for the data in Table 13.4. As expected, the F ratio is identical to the one computed in Problem 13.1, and based on the 2 and 12 degrees of freedom, it is less than the critical F of 3.88 required for significance at the 5 percent level. Thus, we conclude that there is no effect associated with the treatment levels (methods of instruction) and thereby also conclude that the differences among the means are not significant at the 5 percent level.

Table 13.5 ANOVA Table for Analysis of Three Methods of Instruction (Data in Table 13.4)

Source of variation	Sum of squares, SS	Degrees of freedom, df	Mean square, MS	F ratio
Between treatment groups, A	250	$3 - 1 = 2$	$\dfrac{250}{2} = 125$	$\dfrac{125}{37.33} = 3.35$
Sampling error, E	448	$15 - 3 = 12$	$\dfrac{448}{12} = 37.33$	
Total, T	698	$15 - 1 = 14$		

ONE-WAY ANALYSIS OF VARIANCE WITH UNEQUAL GROUPS

13.3. Sometimes the data used as the basis for a one-way analysis of variance do not include equal group sizes for the several treatment levels. Table 13.6 reports the average words per minute typed on different brands of electric typewriters by randomly assigned individuals with no prior experience on these machines, after the same amount of instruction. Test the null hypothesis that the mean words per minute achieved for the three machines is not different, using the 5 percent level of significance.

Table 13.6 Average Words per Minute for Three Brands of Typewriters Based on a 15-min Test Period

Typewriter brand	Average words per minute					Total WPM	Mean WPM
A_1	79	83	62	51	77	352	70.4
A_2	74	85	72	—	—	231	77.0
A_3	81	65	79	55	—	280	70.0

For the hypothesis, H_0: $\alpha_k = 0$ for all treatment levels (typewriter brands) and H_1: $\alpha_k \neq 0$ for all treatment levels, the various quantities required for substitution in the standard formulas for the one-way analysis of variance are

$$n_1 = 5 \qquad n_2 = 3 \qquad n_3 = 4 \qquad N = 12$$

$$T_1 = 352 \qquad T_2 = 231 \qquad T_3 = 280 \qquad T = 863$$

$$T_1^2 = 123{,}904 \qquad T_2^2 = 53{,}361 \qquad T_3^2 = 78{,}400 \qquad T^2 = 744{,}769$$

$$T^2/N = 744{,}769/12 = 62{,}064.1$$

$$\sum_{i=1}^{n} \sum_{k=1}^{K} X^2 = 79^2 + 83^2 + \cdots + 55^2 = 63{,}441$$

$$SST = \sum_{i=1}^{n} \sum_{k=1}^{K} X^2 - \frac{T^2}{N} = 63{,}441 - 62{,}064.1 = 1{,}376.9$$

$$SSA = \sum_{k=1}^{K} \frac{T_k^2}{n_k} - \frac{T^2}{N} = \frac{123{,}904}{5} + \frac{53{,}361}{3} + \frac{78{,}400}{4} - 62{,}064.1 = 103.7$$

$$SSE = SST - SSA = 1{,}376.9 - 103.7 = 1{,}273.2$$

Table 13.7 presents the analysis of variance for this test. At the 5 percent level of significance, the critical value of F ($df = 2, 9$) is 4.26. The computed F ratio is thus in the region of acceptance of the null hypothesis, and we conclude that based on these sample results there are no differences among the three brands of typewriters in terms of typing speed. In fact, because MSA is smaller than MSE we can observe that the variability among the three typewriters is less than the expected variability given that there are no differences among the typewriter brands.

Table 13.7 ANOVA Table for the Analysis of Typing Speed on Three Brands of Typewriters

Source of variation	Sum of squares, SS	Degrees of freedom, df	Mean square, MS	F ratio
Between treatment groups, A (brand of typewriter)	103.7	$3 - 1 = 2$	$\dfrac{103.7}{2} = 51.8$	$\dfrac{51.8}{141.5} = 0.37$
Sampling error, E	1273.2	$12 - 3 = 9$	$\dfrac{1273.2}{9} = 141.5$	
Total, T	1376.9	$12 - 1 = 11$		

RELATIONSHIP OF ONE-WAY ANALYSIS OF VARIANCE TO THE t TEST FOR TESTING THE DIFFERENCE BETWEEN THE MEANS OF TWO INDEPENDENT SAMPLES

13.4. One-way analysis of variance can be considered an extension to k groups of testing the difference between the means of two independent samples by use of Student's t distribution. In both types of applications a necessary assumption is that the samples have been obtained from the same normally distributed population for which the population variance σ^2 is unknown (see Section 11.2). Therefore, it follows that when one-way analysis of variance is applied to a design in which $k = 2$, the result is directly equivalent to using the t distribution to test the difference. In fact, for the analysis in which $k = 2$, $F = t^2$ both in terms of the respective critical values required for significance and the respective computed values for the sample data. To demonstrate these observations, carry out (a) a t test and (b) the one-way analysis of variance for the difference between the means of the first two brands of typewriters reported in Table 13.6. Use the 5 percent level of significance to test the null hypothesis that there is no difference between the two means.

(a) Using the t test for independent groups:

$$H_0: \quad \mu_1 = \mu_2 \quad (\text{or } \mu_1 - \mu_2 = 0) \qquad \bar{X}_1 = 70.4 \qquad \bar{X}_2 = 77.0$$

$$H_1: \quad \mu_1 \neq \mu_2 \quad (\text{or } \mu_1 - \mu_2 \neq 0) \qquad n_1 = 5 \qquad n_2 = 3$$

$$\text{Critical } t \ (df = 6, \alpha = 0.05) = \pm 2.447$$

$$s_1^2 = \frac{\Sigma (X_1 - \bar{X}_1)^2}{n_1 - 1} = \frac{(79 - 70.4)^2 + (83 - 70.4)^2 + (62 - 70.4)^2 + (51 - 70.4)^2 + (77 - 70.4)^2}{5 - 1}$$

$$= \frac{723.20}{4} = 180.8$$

$$s_2^2 = \frac{\Sigma (X_2 - \bar{X}_2)^2}{n_2 - 1} = \frac{(74 - 77.0)^2 + (85 - 77.0)^2 + (72 - 77.0)^2}{3 - 1} = \frac{98.0}{2} = 49.0$$

$$\hat{\sigma}^2 = \frac{(n_1 - 1)s_1^2 + (n_2 - 1)s_2^2}{n_1 + n_2 - 2} = \frac{(4)180.8 + (2)49.0}{5 + 3 - 2} = \frac{821.2}{6} = 136.8667$$

$$\hat{\sigma}_{\bar{x}_1 - \bar{x}_2} = \sqrt{\frac{\hat{\sigma}^2}{n_1} + \frac{\hat{\sigma}^2}{n_2}} = \sqrt{\frac{136.8667}{5} + \frac{136.8667}{3}} = \sqrt{72.9955} = 8.54$$

$$t = \frac{\bar{X}_1 - \bar{X}_2}{\hat{\sigma}_{\bar{x}_1 - \bar{x}_2}} = \frac{70.4 - 77.0}{8.54} = \frac{-6.6}{8.54} = -0.77$$

Therefore, the computed t is in the region of acceptance of the null hypothesis, and the null hypothesis cannot be rejected at the 5 percent level of significance.

(*b*)   For the two treatment levels (typewriter brands), based on the one-way analysis of variance:

$$H_0: \quad \alpha_k = 0 \qquad n_1 = 5 \qquad n_2 = 3 \qquad N = 8$$

$$H_1: \quad \alpha \neq 0 \qquad T_1 = 352 \qquad T_2 = 231 \qquad T = 583$$

$$T_1^2 = 123{,}904 \qquad T_2^2 = 53{,}361 \qquad T^2 = 339{,}889$$

$$T^2/N = 339{,}889/8 = 42{,}486.1$$

$$\sum_{i=1}^{n} \sum_{k=1}^{K} X^2 = 79^2 + 83^2 + \cdots + 72^2 = 43{,}389$$

$$SST = \sum_{i=1}^{n} \sum_{k=1}^{K} X^2 - \frac{T^2}{N} = 43{,}389 - 42{,}486.1 = 902.9$$

$$SSA = \sum_{k=1}^{K} \frac{T_k^2}{n_k} - \frac{T^2}{N} = \frac{123{,}904}{5} + \frac{53{,}361}{3} - 42{,}486.1 = 81.7$$

$$SSE = SST - SSA = 902.9 - 81.7 = 821.2$$

Table 13.8 presents the analysis of variance for this test. At the 5 percent level of significance, the critical value of F ($df = 1, 6$) is 5.99. Since the computed F is in the region of acceptance of the null hypothesis, the assumption that there is no treatment effect cannot be rejected.

Table 13.8   ANOVA Table for the Analysis of Typing Speed on Two Brands of Typewriters

Source of variation	Sum of squares, SS	Degrees of freedom, df	Mean square, MS	F ratio
Between treatment groups, A (brand of typewriter)	81.7	$2 - 1 = 1$	$\dfrac{81.7}{1} = 81.7$	$\dfrac{81.7}{136.9} = 0.60$
Sampling error, E	821.2	$8 - 2 = 6$	$\dfrac{821.2}{6} = 136.9$	
Total, T	902.9	$8 - 1 = 7$		

Thus, the observation about the comparability of the two testing procedures is supported. In terms of the critical values, critical $F = 5.99$ and critical $t = \pm 2.447$. Thus, $(\pm 2.447)^2 = 5.99$. As for the computed values of F and t, $F = 0.60$ and $t = -0.77$; $(-0.77)^2 = 0.59 \cong 0.60$, with the slight difference being due solely to rounding error.

TWO-WAY ANALYSIS WITHOUT INTERACTION
(RANDOMIZED BLOCK DESIGN)

13.5. For the data in Table 13.4, suppose a randomized block design was in fact used and trainees were matched before the experiment, with a trainee from each ability group (based on prior course achievement) assigned to each method of instruction. Table 13.9 is a revision of Table 13.4 in that the values reported are reorganized to reflect the randomized block design. Note, however, that the same values are included in each A treatment group, except that they are reported according to the B ability groups and therefore are arranged in a different order. Test the null hypothesis that there is no difference in the mean performance among the three methods of instruction, using the 5 percent level of significance.

Table 13.9   Achievement Test Scores of Trainees under Three Methods of Instruction, According to Ability Level

Level of ability	Method of Instruction			Total, T_j	Mean, $\bar{X}_j$
	A_1	A_2	A_3		
B_1	86	90	82	258	86.0
B_2	84	89	81	254	84.7
B_3	81	88	73	242	80.7
B_4	79	76	68	223	74.3
B_5	70	82	71	223	74.3
Total, T_k	400	425	375	Grand total $T = 1200$	
Mean, $\bar{X}_k$	80	85	75		Grand mean $\bar{X} = 80.0$

The various quantities required for the analysis of variance table are

For j: $T_1 = 258$ $T_2 = 254$ $T_3 = 242$ $T_4 = 223$ $T_5 = 223$

$T_1^2 = 66{,}564$ $T_2^2 = 64{,}516$ $T_3^2 = 58{,}564$ $T_4^2 = 49{,}729$ $T_5^2 = 49{,}729$

For k: $T_1 = 400$ $T_2 = 425$ $T_3 = 375$

$T_1^2 = 160{,}000$ $T_2^2 = 180{,}625$ $T_3^2 = 140{,}625$

$n_1 = 5$ $n_2 = 5$ $n_3 = 5$

Overall: $T = 1200$, $T^2 = 1{,}440{,}000$, $N = 15$

$$\frac{T^2}{N} = \frac{1{,}440{,}000}{15} = 96{,}000$$

$$\sum_{j=1}^{J} \sum_{k=1}^{K} X^2 = 86^2 + 84^2 + \cdots + 71^2 = 96{,}698$$

$$SST = \sum_{j=1}^{J} \sum_{k=1}^{K} X^2 - \frac{T^2}{N} = 96{,}698 - 96{,}000 = 698$$

$$SSA = \sum_{k=1}^{K} \frac{T_k^2}{n_k} - \frac{T^2}{N} = \frac{160{,}000}{5} + \frac{180{,}625}{5} + \frac{140{,}625}{5} - 96{,}000 = 250$$

$$SSB = \frac{1}{K} \sum_{j=1}^{J} T_j^2 - \frac{T^2}{N} = \frac{1}{3}(66{,}564 + 64{,}516 + 58{,}564 + 49{,}729 + 49{,}729) - 96{,}000 = 367.3$$

$$SSE = SST - SSA - SSB = 698 - 250 - 367.3 = 80.7$$

Table 13.10 presents the analysis of variance (ANOVA) for this data. In respect to the linear equation representing this model, the two F ratios in Table 13.10 are concerned with the tests of the following null and alternative hypotheses:

$$H_0: \quad \alpha_k = 0 \quad \text{for all columns} \qquad H_0: \quad \beta_j = 0 \quad \text{for all rows}$$

$$H_1: \quad \alpha_k \neq 0 \quad \text{for all columns} \qquad H_1: \quad \beta_j \neq 0 \quad \text{for all rows}$$

In terms of practical implications, the first null hypothesis is concerned with testing the difference among the column means, which is the basic purpose of the analysis. The second null hypothesis is concerned with testing the difference among the row means. This is done to identify and control this source of variability due to individual differences and thereby reduce the variability ascribed to sampling error (see Section 13.4).

Using the 5 percent level of significance, the required F ratio for the rejection of the first null hypothesis ($df = 2, 8$) $= 4.46$ while the required F for the second null hypothesis ($df = 4, 8$) $= 3.84$. Thus, both of the calculated F ratios in Table 13.10 are in the region of rejection of the null hypothesis. We conclude that there is a significant difference in achievement test scores for the different methods of instruction, and also that there is a significant difference in achievement test scores for the different levels of ability. Note that this is in contrast to the result in Problem 13.2, where the data were treated as three independent samples. The MSE in the present analysis is substantially lower than that determined in Problem 13.2 because much of that variability could be identified as being due to differences in ability level.

Table 13.10 ANOVA Table for Analysis of Three Methods of Instruction According to Ability Level

Source of variation	Sum of squares, SS	Degrees of freedom, df	Mean square, MS	F ratio
Between treatment groups, A (method)	250.0	$3 - 1 = 2$	$\dfrac{250.0}{2} = 125.0$	$\dfrac{125}{10.1} = 12.4$
Between blocks, B (ability level)	367.3	$5 - 1 = 4$	$\dfrac{367.3}{4} = 91.8$	$\dfrac{91.8}{10.1} = 9.1$
Sampling error, E	80.7	$(5 - 1)(3 - 1) = 8$	$\dfrac{80.7}{8} = 10.1$	
Total, T	698.0	$15 - 1 = 14$		

RELATIONSHIP OF THE RANDOMIZED BLOCK DESIGN TO THE t TEST FOR TESTING THE DIFFERENCE BETWEEN TWO MEANS USING PAIRED OBSERVATIONS

13.6. When $k = 2$, the randomized block design is equivalent to the t test for the difference between the means of paired observations and $F = t^2$. This is similar to the case in Problem 13.4. To demonstrate these points, apply the analysis of variance to the data in Table 13.11, which is taken from Example 4 in Chapter 11. In Example 4 the critical t ($df = 9$, $\alpha = 0.05$) was ± 2.262, the computed t was $+1.59$ and thus the null hypothesis of no difference could not be rejected. Carry out the test at the 5 percent level of significance.

Table 13.11   **Automobile Mileage Obtained with and without a Gasoline Additive for Ten Sampled Cars**

Automobile	Mileage with additive (per gal.)	Mileage without additive (per gal.)	Total, T_j	Mean, $\bar{X}_j$
1	26.7	26.2	52.9	26.45
2	25.8	25.7	51.5	25.75
3	21.9	22.3	44.2	22.10
4	19.3	19.6	38.9	19.45
5	18.4	18.1	36.5	18.25
6	15.7	15.8	31.5	15.75
7	14.2	13.9	28.1	14.05
8	12.6	12.0	24.6	12.30
9	11.9	11.5	23.4	11.70
10	10.3	10.0	20.3	10.15
Total, T_k	176.8	175.1	Grand total $T = 351.9$	
Mean, $\bar{X}_k$	17.68	17.51		Grand mean $\bar{X} = 17.60$

The various quantities required for the analysis of variance table are

For j: $T_1=52.9$ $T_2=51.5$ $T_3=44.2$ $T_4=38.9$ $T_5=36.5$

        $T_1^2=2798.41$ $T_2^2=2652.25$ $T_3^2=1953.64$ $T_4^2=1513.21$ $T_5^2=1332.25$

        $T_6=31.5$ $T_7=28.1$ $T_8=24.6$ $T_9=23.4$ $T_{10}=20.3$

        $T_6^2=992.25$ $T_7^2=789.61$ $T_8^2=605.16$ $T_9^2=547.56$ $T_{10}^2=412.09$

For k: $T_1=176.8$ $T_2=175.1$

        $T_1^2=31{,}258.24$ $T_2^2=30{,}660.01$

        $n_1=10$ $n_2=10$

Overall: $T = 351.9$, $T^2 = 123{,}833.61$, $N = 20$

$$T^2/N = 123{,}833.61/20 = 6{,}191.68$$

$$\sum_{j=1}^{J}\sum_{k=1}^{K} X^2 = 26.7^2 + 25.8^2 + \cdots + 10.0^2 = 6{,}798.87$$

$$SST = \sum_{j=1}^{J}\sum_{k=1}^{K} X^2 - \frac{T^2}{N} = 6{,}798.87 - 6191.68 = 607.19$$

$$SSA = \sum_{k=1}^{K} \frac{T_k^2}{n_k} - \frac{T^2}{N} = \frac{31{,}258.24}{10} + \frac{30{,}660.01}{10} - 6{,}191.68 = 0.145$$

$$SSB = \frac{1}{K}\sum_{j=1}^{J} T_j^2 - \frac{T^2}{N} = \frac{1}{2}(2798.41 + \cdots + 412.09) - 6191.68 = 606.535$$

$$SSE = SST - SSA - SSB = 607.19 - 0.145 - 606.535 = 0.510$$

Table 13.12 presents the analysis of variance for the data of Table 13.11. The null hypothesis of interest, which is conceptually the same one tested in Example 4 of Chapter 11, is, for the treatment groups, H_0: $\alpha_k = 0$ and H_1: $\alpha_k \neq 0$. Critical F ($df = 1, 9$; $\alpha = 0.05$) $= 5.12$.

Since the computed value of F is less than the critical value of F, the hypothesis of no treatment effect (of no difference between the means) cannot be rejected at the 5 percent level of significance.

Note the very large value of the computed F for the blocks dimension. Referring to the data in Table 13.11 this result is not surprising, since the 10 automobiles were apparently in different weight categories and differed substantially in mileage achieved according to category.

Table 13.12 ANOVA Table for Analysis of Automobile Mileage with and without a Gasoline Additive

Source of variation	Sum of squares, SS	Degrees of freedom, df	Mean square, MS	F ratio
Between treatment groups, A	0.145	$2 - 1 = 1$	$\dfrac{0.145}{1} = 0.145$	$\dfrac{0.145}{0.057} = 2.54$
Between blocks, B (different automobiles)	606.535	$10 - 1 = 9$	$\dfrac{606.535}{9} = 67.39$	$\dfrac{67.39}{0.057} = 1182.28$
Sampling error, E	0.510	$(2-1)(10-1) = 9$	$\dfrac{0.510}{9} = 0.057$	
Total, T	607.190	$20 - 1 = 19$		

As expected, the critical value of F in this problem is equal to the square of the critical value used in the t test: $5.12 = (\pm 2.262)^2$. Also, except for the rounding error, the computed t^2 value in Example 4 of Chapter 11 is equal to the computed F of 2.54 here, with $t^2 = (1.59)^2 = 2.53$.

TWO-WAY ANALYSIS OF VARIANCE WITH INTERACTION (n OBSERVATIONS PER CELL)

13.7. Nine trainees in each of four different subject areas were randomly assigned to three different methods of instruction. Three students were assigned to each instructional method. With reference to Table 13.13, test the various null hypotheses which are of interest in respect to such a design at the 5 percent level of significance.

The various quantities required for the analysis of variance table are

For j: $T_1 = 717$ $T_2 = 709$ $T_3 = 722$ $T_4 = 732$

$T_1^2 = 514{,}089$ $T_2^2 = 502{,}681$ $T_3^2 = 521{,}284$ $T_4^2 = 535{,}824$

For k: $T_1 = 960$ $T_2 = 1020$ $T_3 = 900$

$T_1^2 = 921{,}600$ $T_2^2 = 1{,}040{,}400$ $T_3^2 = 810{,}000$

Overall: $T = 2880$, $T^2 = 8{,}294{,}400$, $N = 36$

$$T^2/N = 8{,}294{,}400/36 = 230{,}400$$

$$\sum_{j=1}^{J} \sum_{k=1}^{K} \left(\sum_{i=1}^{n} X \right)^2 = (70 + 79 + 72)^2 + (77 + 81 + 79)^2 + \cdots + (68 + 71 + 69)^2 = 694{,}694$$

Table 13.13   Achievement Test Scores of Trainees under Three Methods of Instruction and for Four Subject Areas

Subject area	Method of instruction			Total, T_j	Mean, $\bar{X}_j$
	A_1	A_2	A_3		
B_1	70 79 72	83 89 78	81 86 79	717	79.7
B_2	77 81 79	77 87 88	74 69 77	709	78.8
B_3	82 78 80	94 83 79	72 79 75	722	80.2
B_4	85 90 87	84 90 88	68 71 69	732	81.3
Total, T_k	960	1020	900	Grand total $T = 2880$	
Mean, $\bar{X}_k$	80	85	75		Grand mean $\bar{X} = 80$

$$\sum_{i=1}^{n}\sum_{j=1}^{J}\sum_{k=1}^{K} X^2 = 70^2 + 79^2 + 72^2 + 77^2 + \cdots + 69^2 = 232{,}000$$

$$SST = \sum_{i=1}^{n}\sum_{j=1}^{J}\sum_{k=1}^{K} X^2 - \frac{T^2}{N} = 232{,}000 - 230{,}400 = 1{,}600$$

$$SSA = \sum_{k=1}^{K}\frac{T_k^2}{nJ} - \frac{T^2}{N} = \frac{921{,}600}{(3)(4)} + \frac{1{,}040{,}400}{(3)(4)} + \frac{810{,}000}{(3)(4)} - 230{,}400 = 600$$

$$SSB = \sum_{j=1}^{J}\frac{T_j^2}{nK} - \frac{T^2}{N} = \frac{514{,}089}{(3)(3)} + \frac{502{,}681}{(3)(3)} + \frac{521{,}284}{(3)(3)} + \frac{535{,}824}{(3)(3)} - 230{,}400 = 30.8$$

$$SSI = \frac{1}{n}\sum_{j=1}^{J}\sum_{k=1}^{K}\left(\sum_{i=1}^{n} X\right)^2 - SSA - SSB - \frac{T^2}{N} = \frac{1}{3}(694{,}694) - 600 - 30.8 - 230{,}400 = 533.9$$

$$SSE = SST - SSA - SSB - SSI = 1{,}600.0 - 600.0 - 30.8 - 533.9 = 435.3$$

Table 13.14 presents the analysis of variance (ANOVA) for the data of Table 13.13. In respect to the linear equation for two-way analysis of variance with replication, the three F ratios reported in Table 13.14 are concerned with the following null and alternative hypotheses:

H_0: $\alpha_k = 0$ for all columns H_1: $\alpha_k \neq 0$ for all columns

H_0: $\beta_j = 0$ for all rows H_1: $\beta_j \neq 0$ for all rows

H_0: $\iota_{jk} = 0$ for all cells H_1: $\iota_{jk} \neq 0$ for all cells

Using the 5 percent level of significance, the required F ratio for the rejection of the first null hypothesis ($df = 2, 24$) is 3.40, for the second the required F ($df = 3, 24$) is 3.01, and for the third the required F ($df = 6, 24$) is 2.51. Thus, we conclude that there is a significant difference in test scores for the different methods of instruction, that there is no significant difference among the different subject areas, and that there is significant interaction between the two factors. The last conclusion indicates that the effectiveness of the three methods of instruction varies for the different subject areas. For example, in Table 13.13 notice that for subject area B_1 method A_1 was the least effective method while for subject area B_4, method A_3 was the least effective method. In reviewing this table, however, method A_2 is observed to be at least equal to the other methods for every subject area. Thus, the possibility of using different methods of instruction as being best for different subject areas does not appear to be the appropriate decision in this case, even though there was a significant interaction effect.

Table 13.14   ANOVA Table for Analysis of Three Methods of Instruction Applied in Four Subject Areas

Source of variation	Sum of squares, SS	Degrees of freedom, df	Mean square, MS	F ratio
Between treatment groups, A (method)	600.0	$3 - 1 = 2$	$\dfrac{600.0}{2} = 300.0$	$\dfrac{300.0}{18.1} = 16.57$
Between treatment groups, B (subject)	30.8	$4 - 1 = 3$	$\dfrac{30.8}{3} = 10.3$	$\dfrac{10.3}{18.1} = 0.57$
Interaction between method and subject, I	533.9	$(4-1)(3-1)=6$	$\dfrac{533.9}{6} = 89.0$	$\dfrac{89.0}{18.1} = 4.92$
Sampling error, E	435.3	$(4)(3)(3-1)=24$	$\dfrac{435.3}{24} = 18.1$	
Total, T	1600.0	$36 - 1 = 35$		

Supplementary Problems

ONE-WAY ANALYSIS OF VARIANCE

13.8. Four types of advertising displays were set up in 12 retail outlets, with three outlets randomly assigned to each of the displays, for the purpose of studying the point-of-sale impact of the displays. With reference to Table 13.15, test the null hypothesis that there are no differences among the mean sales values for the four types of displays, using the 5 percent level of significance.

Ans.   Critical F ($df = 3, 8$) = 4.07.   Computed $F = 4.53$.   Therefore, reject the null hypothesis that $\alpha_k = 0$ for all treatment levels.

TWO-WAY ANALYSIS WITHOUT INTERACTION (RANDOMIZED BLOCK DESIGN)

13.9. The designs produced by four automobile designers are evaluated by three different raters, as reported in Table 13.16. Test the null hypothesis that the average ratings of the designs do not differ, using the 1 percent level of significance.

Ans.   Critical F ($df = 3, 6$) = 9.78.   Computed $F = 12.29$.   Therefore, reject the null hypothesis that $\alpha_k = 0$ for all treatment (column) effects.

Table 13.15 Product Sales According to
Advertising Display Used

Type of display	Sales			Total sales	Mean sales
A_1	40	44	43	127	42.3
A_2	53	54	59	166	55.3
A_3	48	38	46	132	44.0
A_4	48	61	47	156	52.0

Table 13.16 Ratings of Automobile Designs

Rater	Designer				Total, T_j	Mean, $\bar{X}_j$
	1	2	3	4		
A	87	79	83	92	341	85.25
B	83	73	85	89	330	82.50
C	91	85	90	92	358	89.50
Total, T_k	261	237	258	273	Grand total $T = 1029$	
Mean rating, $\bar{X}_k$	87.0	79.0	86.0	91.0		Grand mean 85.75

Table 13.17 Weekly Sales in Thousands of Dollars with and without
Advertising, and with and without Discount Pricing

Discount pricing	With advertising	Without advertising	Total, T_j	Mean, $\bar{X}_j$
With discounting	9.8 10.6	6.0 5.3	31.7	7.925
Without discounting	6.2 7.1	4.3 3.9	21.5	5.375
Total, T_k	33.7	19.5	Grand total $T = 53.2$	
Mean, $\bar{X}_k$	8.425	4.875		Grand mean $\bar{X} = 6.650$

TWO-WAY ANALYSIS OF VARIANCE WITH INTERACTION (n OBSERVATIONS PER CELL)

13.10. The smallest data table for which two-way analysis of variance with interaction can be carried out is a 2×2 table with two observations per cell. Table 13.17, which presents sales data for a consumer product in eight randomly assigned regions, is one such table. Test the effect of the two factors and of the interaction between the two factors on the weekly sales levels, using the 1 percent level of significance. Consider the meaning of your test results.

Ans. At the 1 percent level of significance the critical values of F associated with the column, row, and interaction effects are, respectively, $F\ (df = 1,\ 4) = 21.20$; $F\ (df = 1,\ 4) = 21.20$; and $F\ (df = 1,\ 4) = 21.20$. The computed F ratios are, respectively, $F = 96.00$, $F = 49.52$, and $F = 7.66$. Therefore, there are significant column and row effects, but no significant interaction effects.

Chapter 14

Bayesian Decision Analysis:
Decision Tables and Decision Trees

14.1 THE STRUCTURE OF DECISION TABLES

From the standpoint of statistical decision theory, a decision situation under conditions of uncertainty can be represented by certain common ingredients which are included in the structure of the *decision table*, or payoff table, for the situation. Essentially, a decision table identifies the conditional gain (or loss) associated with every possible combination of decision acts and events; it also typically indicates the probability of occurrence for each of the mutually exclusive events.

Table 14.1 General Structure of a Decision Table

Events	Probability	Acts				
		A_1	A_2	A_3	$\cdots$	A_n
E_1	P_1	X_{11}	X_{12}	X_{13}	$\cdots$	X_{1n}
E_2	P_2	X_{21}	X_{22}	X_{23}	$\cdots$	X_{2n}
E_3	P_3	X_{31}	X_{32}	X_{33}	$\cdots$	X_{3n}
$\cdots$	$\cdots$	$\cdots$	$\cdots$	$\cdots$	$\cdots$	$\cdots$
E_m	P_m	X_{m1}	X_{m2}	X_{m3}	$\cdots$	X_{mn}

In Table 14.1, the *acts* are the alternative courses of action, or strategies, that are available to the decision maker. As the result of the analysis, one of these acts is chosen as being the best act. The basis for this choice is the subject matter of this chapter. As a minimum, there must be at least two possible acts available, so that the opportunity for choice in fact exists. An example of an act is the number of units of a particular item to be ordered for stock.

The *events* identify the occurrences which are outside of the decision maker's control and which determine the level of success for a given act. These events are often called "states of nature", "states", or "outcomes". The events are mutually exclusive and the listing should include all possible events. An example of an event is the level of market demand for a particular item during a stipulated time period.

The *probability* of each event is included as part of the general format of a decision table when such probability values are in fact available. However, one characteristic of Bayesian decision analysis is that such probabilities should always be available since they can be based on either objective data or be determined subjectively on the basis of judgment. Because the events in the decision table are mutually exclusive and exhaustive, the sum of the probability values should be 1.0.

Finally, the cell entries are the conditional values, or conditional economic consequences. These values are often called *payoffs* in the literature, and they are conditional in the sense that the economic result which is experienced depends on the decision act which is chosen and the event which occurs.

EXAMPLE 1. A heating and air-conditioning contractor must commit himself to the purchase of central air-conditioning units as of April 1 for resale and installation during the following summer season. Based on demand during the previous summer, current economic conditions, and competitive factors in the market, he estimates that there is a 0.10 probability of selling only 5 units, a 0.30 probability of selling 10 units, a 0.40 probability of selling 15 units, and a 0.20 probability of selling 20 units. The air-conditioning units can be ordered only in groups of five, with the cost per unit being $1000 and the retail price being $1300 (plus installation charges). Any unsold units at the end of the season are returned to the manufacturer for a net credit of $800, after deduction of shipping charges.

Table 14.2 is the decision table for this situation. Note that because we estimate that there will be a market demand for at least 5 units but not more than 20 units, these are logically also the limits for our possible acts (units ordered). Our stipulation that units can only be ordered in groups of five serves to simplify the problem and reduce the size of the decision table. The conditional values (payoffs) in Table 14.2 are based on a markup of $300 per unit sold and a loss of $200 for each unsold unit. Thus, for example, if 15 units are ordered for stock and only 10 are demanded, the economic result is a gain of $3000 on the 10 units sold less a loss of $1000 on the 5 units returned to the manufacturer, for a resulting payoff of $2000 at A_3, E_2 in the table.

Table 14.2   Decision Table for the Number of Air-Conditioning Units to Be Ordered

Market demand	Probability	Order quantity			
		A_1: 5	A_2: 10	A_3: 15	A_4: 20
E_1: 5	0.10	$1500	$ 500	$−500	$−1500
E_2: 10	0.30	1500	3000	2000	1000
E_3: 15	0.40	1500	3000	4500	3500
E_4: 20	0.20	1500	3000	4500	6000
	1.00				

In the following sections we refer to Example 1 in order to demonstrate the application of different decision criteria, or standards, that can be used to identify the decision act which is considered to be the best act. The methods in this chapter which involve the use of the probability values associated with each event are concerned only with the probabilities formulated during the initial structuring of the decision table. Because these values are formulated before the collection of any additional information, they are called *prior probabilities* in Bayesian decision analysis. See Chapters 15 and 16 for other areas of Bayesian decision analysis.

14.2 DECISION MAKING BASED UPON PROBABILITIES ALONE

A complete application of Bayesian decision analysis involves use of all of the information included in a decision table. However, in this section we briefly consider the criteria that would be used if the economic consequences were ignored (or not determined) and if the decision was based entirely on the probabilities associated with the possible events.

In such cases, one decision criterion which might be used is to identify the event with the *maximum probability* of occurrence, and to choose the decision act corresponding with that event.   Another basis for choosing the best act would be to calculate the *expectation* of the event, and to choose the act accordingly.   However, because neither of these criteria make reference to the economic consequences associated with the various decision acts and events, they represent an incomplete basis for choosing the best decision.

EXAMPLE 2. Table 14.3 presents the probability distribution for the market demand of central air-conditioning units in Example 1.   The event with the maximum probability is $E_3 = 15$, for which $P = 0.40$.   On the basis of the criterion of highest probability, the number of units ordered would be 15.

The calculation of the expected demand, $E(D)$, is also presented in Table 14.3 (see Section 6.2).   Since the air-conditioning units can only be ordered as whole units, and further, only in groups of five, the expected demand level of 13.5 units cannot be ordered.   Either 10 units would be ordered with the expectation of being 3.5 units short (as a long-run average), or 15 units would be ordered with the expectation of having an excess of 1.5 units, on the average.

Table 14.3   Probability Distribution of Market Demand
for Air-Conditioning Units and the Calculation
of the Expected Demand

Market demand, D	Probability, $P(D)$	$(D)P(D)$
E_1: 5	0.10	0.5
E_2: 10	0.30	3.0
E_3: 15	0.40	6.0
E_4: 20	0.20	4.0
	1.00	$E(D) = 13.5$

One difficulty associated with the two criteria described in Example 2 is that their long-run success cannot really be evaluated without some reference to economic consequences.   For example, suppose the contractor can order air conditioners for stock without any payment and with the opportunity to return unsold units at the manufacturer's expense.   In such a circumstance there would be no risk associated with overstocking, and the best decision would be to order 20 units so that the inventory would be adequate for the highest possible demand level.

14.3   DECISION MAKING BASED UPON ECONOMIC CONSEQUENCES ALONE

The decision matrix which is used in conjunction with decision making based only upon economic consequences is similar to Table 14.1, except for the absence of the probability distribution associated with the possible events.   Three criteria which have been described and used in conjunction with such a decision matrix are the maximin, maximax, and minimax regret criteria.

The *maximin criterion* is the standard by which the best act is the one for which the minimum value is larger than the minimum for any other decision act.   Use of this criterion leads to a highly conservative decision strategy, in that the decision maker is particularly concerned about the "worst that can happen" in respect to each act.   Computationally, the minimum value in each column of the decision table is determined, and the best act is the one for which the resulting value is largest.

EXAMPLE 3. Table 14.4 presents the economic consequences associated with the various acts and events for the problem described in Example 1. The minimum value associated with each decision act is listed along the bottom of this table. Of these values, the largest economic result (the maximum of the minima) is $1500. Since the act "$A_1$: Order 5 air-conditioning units" is associated with this outcome, this is the best decision act from the standpoint of the maximin criterion.

Table 14.4   Number of Air-Conditioning Units to Be Ordered
According to the Maximin Criterion

Market demand	A_1: 5	A_2: 10	A_3: 15	A_4: 20
E_1: 5	$1500	$ 500	$-500	$-1500
E_2: 10	1500	3000	2000	1000
E_3: 15	1500	3000	4500	3500
E_4: 20	1500	3000	4500	6000
Minimum	$1500	$500	$-500	$-1500

The *maximax criterion* is the standard by which the best act is the one for which the maximum value is larger than the maximum of any other decision act. This criterion is philosophically the opposite of the maximin criterion, since the decision maker is particularly oriented toward the "best that can happen" in respect to each act. Computationally, the maximum value in each column of the decision table is determined, and the best act is the one for which the resulting value is largest.

EXAMPLE 4. In Table 14.5 the *maximum* value associated with each decision act is listed along the bottom. The largest of these maximum values (the maximum of the maxima) is $6000, and thus the associated act "A_4: Order 20 air-conditioning units" would be chosen as the best act from the standpoint of the maximax criterion. Rather than going through the two-step procedure of identifying column maxima and then determining the maximum of these several values, a shortcut which can be used is simply to locate the largest value in the table.

Table 14.5   Number of Air-Conditioning Units to Be
Ordered According to the Maximax Criterion

Market demand	A_1: 5	A_2: 10	A_3: 15	A_4: 20
E_1: 5	$1500	$ 500	$-500	$-1500
E_2: 10	1500	3000	2000	1000
E_3: 15	1500	3000	4500	3500
E_4: 20	1500	3000	4500	6000
Maximum	$1500	$3000	$4500	$6000

Analysis by the *minimax regret* criterion is based on so-called regrets rather than on conditional values as such. A *regret*, or conditional *opportunity loss*, for each act is the difference between the economic outcome for the act and the economic outcome of the best act *given that a particular event has occurred*. Thus, the "best" or most desirable regret value is "0", which indicates that the act is perfectly matched with the given event. Also, note that even when there is an economic gain associated with a particular act and a given event, there may also be an opportunity loss because some other act would result in a higher gain with the given event.

The construction of a table of opportunity losses, or regrets, is illustrated in Example 5. The best act is identified as being the one for which the maximum possible regret is smallest. Philosophically, the minimax regret criterion is similar to the maximin criterion in terms of "assuming the worst". However, use of the concept of opportunity loss results in a broader criterion, in that the failure to improve an economic result is considered to be a type of loss.

EXAMPLE 5. Table 14.6 is the table of opportunity losses associated with the conditional values in Table 14.5. Computationally, the regret values are determined given each event in turn, that is, according to rows. For example, given that E_1 occurs, the best act (by reference to the payoff matrix in Table 14.5) is A_1, with a value of \$1500. If A_2 is chosen, the result is \$500, which differs from the best act by \$1000, and which is then the regret value for A_2. If A_3 is chosen, regret = \$1500 − (−\$500) = \$2000. If A_4 is chosen, regret = \$1500 − (−\$1500) = \$3000. The remaining opportunity loss values are similarly determined, with the best conditional value in each row serving as the basis for determining regret values in that row. For instance, in row 2, for E_2: 10, the best act is A_2: 10 with a conditional value of \$3000 in Table 14.5.

Table 14.6   Opportunity Loss Table for the Number of Air-Conditioning Units to Be Ordered and Application of the Minimax Regret Criterion

Market demand	A_1: 5	A_2: 10	A_3: 15	A_4: 20
E_1: 5	\$ 0	\$1000 (=\$1500 − 500)	\$2000 [=\$1500 − (−500)]	\$3000 [=\$1500 − (−1500)]
E_2: 10	1500 (=3000 − 1500)	0	1000 (=3000 − 2000)	2000 (=3000 − 1000)
E_3: 15	3000 (=4500 − 1500)	1500 (=4500 − 3000)	0	1000 (=4500 − 3500)
E_4: 20	4500 (=6000 − 1500)	3000 (=6000 − 3000)	1500 (=6000 − 4500)	0
Maximum regret	\$4500	\$3000	\$2000	\$3000

The maximum regret which can occur in conjunction with each decision act is listed along the bottom of Table 14.6. The smallest of these maxima (the minimum of the maximum regrets) is \$2000; "A_3: Order 15 units" would thus be chosen as the best act from the standpoint of the minimax regret criterion.

14.4   DECISION MAKING BASED UPON BOTH PROBABILITIES AND ECONOMIC CONSEQUENCES: THE EXPECTED VALUE CRITERION

The methods presented in this section utilize all of the information contained in the basic decision table (see Section 14.1). Thus, we consider both the probabilities associated with the possible events and the economic consequences for all combinations of the several acts and several events.

The *expected value* (EV) criterion is the standard by which the best act is the one for which the expected economic outcome is the highest, as a long-run average (see Section 6.2). Note that in the present case we are concerned about the long-run average economic result, and not simply the long-run average event value (demand level) discussed in Section 14.2. Computationally, the expected value for each act is determined by multiplying the conditional value for each event/act combination by the probability of the event, and summing these products for each act.

EXAMPLE 6. Table 14.7 repeats the information from Table 14.2, except that the expected values have been identified along the bottom. Table 14.8 illustrates the procedure by which such expected values are calculated. In Table 14.7, the largest expected value is $3250, and thus the associated act "A_3: Order 15 units" is the best act from the standpoint of the expected value criterion.

Table 14.7 Decision Table for the Number of Air-Conditioning Units to Be Ordered and Determination of the Best Act According to the Expected Value Criterion

Market demand	Probability	Order quantity			
		A_1: 5	A_2: 10	A_3: 15	A_4: 20
E_1: 5	0.10	$1500	$ 500	$-500	$-1500
E_2: 10	0.30	1500	3000	2000	1000
E_3: 15	0.40	1500	3000	4500	3500
E_4: 20	0.20	1500	3000	4500	6000
Expected value, EV		$1500	$2750	$3250	$2750

Table 14.8 Determination of the Expected Value for Decision A_4 in Table 14.7

Market demand	Conditional value for A_4: X	$P(X)$	$X P(X)$
E_1: 5	$-1500	0.10	$-150
E_2: 10	1000	0.30	300
E_3: 15	3500	0.40	1400
E_4: 20	6000	0.20	1200
			$\Sigma X P(X) = \$2750$

The expected value criterion often is referred to as the *Bayesian criterion*. Use of the adjective "Bayesian" here is distinct from the use of Bayes' theorem for revising a prior probability value (see Section 15.2). Thus, a reference to "Bayesian procedures" in decision analysis can involve use of the expected value criterion, revision of prior probability values, or both.

The best act identified by the expected value criterion can also be determined by identifying the act with the minimum expected opportunity loss (*EOL*) or expected regret. This is so because the act with the largest expected gain logically would have the smallest expected regret. In textbooks which refer to opportunity losses simply as *losses, expected losses* are understood to mean expected opportunity losses.

EXAMPLE 7. Table 14.9 repeats the opportunity loss values from Table 14.6. It also shows the probability of each event and the expected opportunity loss associated with each decision act. Table 14.10 illustrates the procedure by which each expected opportunity loss was calculated. As indicated in Table 14.9, the minimum expected opportunity loss is $800, and thus the associated act "Order 15 units" is the best act from the standpoint of minimizing the expected opportunity loss. Note that this is the same act as identified by use of the expected value criterion in Example 6.

Table 14.9   Opportunity Loss Table for the Number of Air-Conditioning
             Units to Be Ordered, and Computation of Expected
             Opportunity Losses

Market demand	Probability	Order quantity			
		A_1: 5	A_2: 10	A_3: 15	A_4: 20
E_1: 5	0.10	$ 0	$1000	$2000	$3000
E_2: 10	0.30	1500	0	1000	2000
E_3: 15	0.40	3000	1500	0	1000
E_4: 20	0.20	4500	3000	1500	0
Expected opportunity loss, EOL:		$2550	$1300	$800	$1300

Table 14.10   Determination of the Expected Opportunity Loss for
              Decision A_4 in Table 14.9

Market demand	Conditional opportunity loss for A_4: OL	$P(OL)$	$(OL)\,P(OL)$
E_1: 5	$3000	0.10	$300
E_2: 10	2000	0.30	600
E_3: 15	1000	0.40	400
E_4: 20	0	0.20	0
			EOL = $1300

14.5   DECISION TREE ANALYSIS

Frequently a decision problem is complicated by the fact that the economic consequences are not directly related to an initial decision, but rather, that subsequent events lead to
the need for additional decisions at each step of a sequential process.   The evaluation of the
alternative decision acts in the first step of such a sequential process must of necessity be
based on an evaluation of the events and decisions in the overall process.   *Decision tree
analysis* is the method which can be used to identify the best initial act, as well as the best
subsequent acts.   The decision criterion satisfied is the Bayesian expected value criterion (see
Section 14.4).

The first step in decision tree analysis is to construct the decision tree that corresponds to a
sequential decision situation.   The tree is constructed from left to right with appropriate
identification of *decision points* (sequential points at which a choice has to be made) and *chance
events* (sequential points at which a probabilistic event will occur).   The construction of a
valid decision tree for a sequential decision situation is particularly dependent on appropriate
analysis of the overall decision situation.   See Problem 14.12.

After a decision tree is constructed, the probability values associated with the chance
events and the economic consequences that can occur are entered in the diagram.   Many of
the economic consequences are several steps removed from the initial decision point.   In order
to determine the expected values of the alternative acts at the initial decision point, expected
values are systematically calculated from right to left in the decision tree.   This process is
sometimes called "folding back" (see Problem 14.13).   As the result of applying this analytical
process, the best act at the initial decision point can be identified.

14.6 EXPECTED UTILITY AS THE DECISION CRITERION

The expected value criterion is typically used in conjunction with both decision table analysis and decision tree analysis (see Section 14.4). However, when the decision maker perceives one or more of the economic consequences as being unusually large or small, the expected value criterion does not necessarily provide the basis for identifying the "best" decision. This is particularly likely for unique, rather than repetitive, situations.

EXAMPLE 8. Consider the decision acts in Table 14.11 and assume that the choice in respect to each pair will be made only once. Although it can easily be demonstrated that the expected value of A_2 is greater than that for A_1 in every case, most people would choose A_1 in preference to A_2 for each of these pairs. In the context of each choice being a one-time act, the choice of A_1 is rational even though the expected value is not maximized. The implication of such a conclusion is that monetary values may not adequately represent true values to the decision maker in one-time decision situations which include the possibility of exceptional losses and/or exceptional gains.

Table 14.11   Three Pairs of Alternative Decision Acts with Associated Consequences

A_1: Receive \$1,000,000 for certain.	A_2: Receive \$2,000,000 with a probability of 0.50 or receive \$100 with a probability of 0.50
A_1: Pay \$10.	A_2: Experience a loss of \$8000 with a probability of 0.001 or experience no loss with a probability of 0.999.
A_1: Receive \$15,000 with a probability of 0.50 or receive \$5000 with a probability of 0.50.	A_2: Receive \$50,000 with a probability of 0.50 or experience a loss of \$25,000 with a probability of 0.50.

Utility is a measure of value which expresses the true relative value of various outcomes, including economic consequences, for a decision maker. This book deals only with the utility of economic consequences. Any given utility scale can begin at an arbitrary minimum value and have an arbitrarily assigned maximum value. However, it is convenient to have utility values begin at a minimum of 0 and extend to a maximum of 1.00, and this is the scale most frequently used. With such a scale, an outcome with a utility of 0.60 is understood to be twice as desirable as one with a utility of 0.30. On the other hand, note that an economic outcome of \$60,000 is not necessarily twice as desirable as an outcome of \$30,000 for a decision maker with limited resources and in a one-time decision situation.

Using a *reference contract*, you can determine an individual's utility values for different monetary values. By this approach, the individual is asked to designate an *amount certain* that he would accept, or pay, as being equivalent to each of a series of uncertain situations involving risk. The first risk situation portrayed always includes the two extreme limits of the range of monetary values of interest, i.e. lower and upper limits having utilities of 0 and 1.0, respectively. See Problem 14.14.

Once a reference-contract procedure has been established, it can be continued by changing either the designated probabilities or one or more of the economic consequences in the risk situation. In this way, the set of utility values corresponding to a range of monetary values can be determined. See Problem 14.15.

After the utility values have been determined, the paired values may be plotted on a graph. A best-fitting smooth line can be drawn through the plotted points as an approximation of the decision maker's *utility function* for various monetary consequences. The standard convention is to plot the monetary values in respect to the horizontal axis and the utility values in respect to the vertical axis. This graph can be used as the basis for estimating the utility value of any monetary outcome between the designated monetary limits of the function. In turn, this makes it possible to substitute utility values for monetary values in a decision table, and to determine the best act by identifying that act for which the *expected utility* (*EU*) is maximized. See Problems 14.16 and 14.7.

The form of the utility function indicates whether a decision maker is a risk averter or a risk seeker (see Fig. 14-1). For the risk averter, each additional dollar along the horizontal axis is associated with a declining slope of the utility function. That is, one might say that each additional increment has positive value to the decision maker, but not as much as the preceding increments (the curve is concave). Conversely, Fig. 14-1(*c*) indicates that for the risk seeker each additional monetary increment has increasing value to the decision maker (the curve is convex). It can also be shown that the risk averter designates an amount certain that is consistently less than the *expected monetary value* of the risk situation, while the risk seeker designates an amount certain that is consistently greater than the expected monetary value of the risk situation. See Problem 14.16.

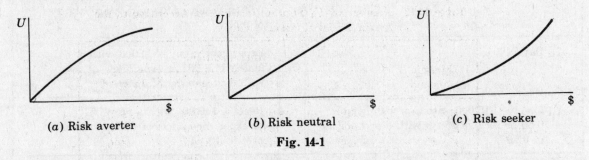

(a) Risk averter   (b) Risk neutral   (c) Risk seeker

Fig. 14-1

Overall, the form of the utility curve reflects a decision maker's attitude toward risk, and therefore is an important factor in determining which act is best *for him* at a particular moment. For a firm in financial jeopardy, a particular contract opportunity that includes the possibility of a high loss and subsequent business failure may not represent a good opportunity even though the expected monetary value associated with the contract is positive and represents a substantial return. The concept of utility provides the basis for demonstrating why both parties to a contract (such as insurer and insured) can experience a positive utility and why a risk situation which is "right" for one firm may not be right for another. However, if the utility function is linear or approximately so, as in Fig. 14-1(*b*), then the expected value criterion is equivalent to the expected utility criterion for that decision maker.

Solved Problems

DECISION TABLES

14.1. Based on a new technological approach, a manufacturer has developed a color TV set with a 36-in. picture tube. The owner of a small retail store estimates that at the selling price of $1800 the probability values associated with his selling 2, 3, 4 or 5 sets during the 3 months of concern are 0.30, 0.40, 0.20 and 0.10, respectively. Based only on these probability values, what number of sets should the retailer order for stock, assuming no reorders are possible during the period?

Based on the criterion of maximum probability, three sets would be ordered, since the probability of 0.40 associated with three sets being sold is higher than the probability of any other event.

On the other hand, the expectation of the demand level is

$$2(0.30) + 3(0.40) + 4(0.20) + 5(0.10) = 3.1$$

Based on this expectation of the event, the act which comes closest to corresponding with it is also that of ordering three sets.

14.2. For the inventory decision situation in Problem 14.1, the profit margin for each set sold is $200. If any sets are not sold during the three months, the total loss per set to the retailer will be $300. Based on these economic consequences alone, and ignoring the probability values identified in Problem 14.1, determine the best decision acts from the standpoint of the maximin and maximax criteria.

With reference to Table 14.12, for the maximin criterion the best act is A_1: Order two sets. For the maximax criterion, the best act is A_4: Order five sets.

Table 14.12   Number of TV Sets to Be Ordered According to the Maximin and Maximax Criteria

Market demand	Order quantity			
	A_1: 2	A_2: 3	A_3: 4	A_4: 5
E_1: 2	$400	$100	$-200	$-500
E_2: 3	400	600	300	0
E_3: 4	400	600	800	500
E_4: 5	400	600	800	1000
Minimum	$400	$100	$-200	$-500
Maximum	$400	$600	$800	$1000

14.3. Determine the best decision act from the standpoint of the minimax regret criterion for the decision situation described in Problems 14.1 and 14.2.

Table 14.13   Opportunity Loss Table for the Number of TV Sets to Be Ordered and Application of the Minimax Regret Criterion

Market demand	Order quantity			
	A_1: 2	A_2: 3	A_3: 4	A_4: 5
E_1: 2	$ 0	$300	$600	$900
E_2: 3	200	0	300	600
E_3: 4	400	200	0	300
E_4: 5	600	400	200	0
Maximum regret	$600	$400	$600	$900

Table 14.13 indicates the opportunity losses (regrets) for this decision situation. From the standpoint of the minimax regret criterion, the best act is A_2: Order three sets.

14.4. With reference to Problems 14.1 and 14.2, determine the best act from the standpoint of the expected value criterion.

Table 14.14 is the complete decision table for this problem and reports the expected monetary values associated with the possible decision acts. As indicated in the table, the best act from the standpoint of the expected value criterion is A_2: Order three sets.

14.5. Using Table 14.14, determine the best act for the Bayesian criterion by identifying the act with the lowest expected opportunity loss.

Table 14.15 repeats the opportunity loss values from Table 14.13 and identifies the expected opportunity loss associated with each act. As indicated in the table, the best act from the standpoint of minimizing the expected opportunity loss is A_2: Order three sets. This result was expected, since the act which satisfies the Bayesian criterion of maximizing the expected value will also be the act which has the minimum expected opportunity loss.

Table 14.14 Decision Table for the Number of TV Sets to Be Ordered and Application of the Expected Value Criterion

Market demand	Probability	Order quantity			
		A_1: 2	A_2: 3	A_3: 4	A_4: 5
E_1: 2	0.30	$400	$100	$-200	$-500
E_2: 3	0.40	400	600	300	0
E_3: 4	0.20	400	600	800	500
E_4: 5	0.10	400	600	800	1000
Expected value, EV		$400	$450	$300	$50

Table 14.15 Opportunity Loss Table for the Number of TV Sets to Be Ordered and Computation of Expected Opportunity Losses

Market demand	Probability	Order quantity			
		A_1: 2	A_2: 3	A_3: 4	A_4: 5
E_1: 2	0.30	$ 0	$300	$600	$900
E_2: 3	0.40	200	0	300	600
E_3: 4	0.20	400	200	0	300
E_4: 5	0.10	600	400	200	0
Expected opportunity loss, EOL		$220	$170	$320	$570

14.6. Table 14.16 presents the conditional values (returns) associated with five alternative types of investment decisions for a 1-yr period. Given that the probabilities associated with the possible states are not available, determine the best acts from the standpoint of the maximin and maximax criteria.

Table 14.16 Monetary Returns Associated with Several Investment Alternatives for a $10,000 Fund

State of economy	Investment decision				
	A_1 Savings account	A_2 Corporate bonds	A_3 Blue chip stocks	A_4 Speculative stocks	A_5 Stock options
E_1: Recession	$600	$500	$-2,500	$-5,000	$-10,000
E_2: Stable	600	900	800	400	-5,000
E_3: Expansion	600	900	4,000	10,000	20,000

Table 14.17 identifies the minimum and maximum values for each act in Table 14.16. As would be expected, the maximin criterion leads to the selection of the very conservative decision A_1: Invest in a savings account. The maximax criterion, on the other hand, leads to the selection of the decision act at the other extreme, A_5: Invest in stock options.

Table 14.17 Investment Decision To Be Made According to the Maximin and Maximax Criteria

Economic Consequence	Investment decision				
	A_1 Savings account	A_2 Corporate bonds	A_3 Blue chip stocks	A_4 Speculative stocks	A_5 Stock options
Minimum	$600	$500	$-2,500	$-5,000	$-10,000
Maximum	$600	$900	$4,000	$10,000	$20,000

14.7. Determine the best decision act from the standpoint of the minimax regret criterion for the situation described in Problem 14.6.

Table 14.18 indicates that the best act in this case is A_4: Invest in speculative stocks. Note the extent to which the maximum regret values for the first four acts are influenced by the

Table 14.18 Opportunity Loss Table for the Investment Decision Problem and Application of the Minimax Regret Criterion

State of economy	Investment decision				
	A_1 Savings account	A_2 Corporate bonds	A_3 Blue chip stocks	A_4 Speculative stocks	A_5 Stock options
E_1: Recession	$ 0	$ 100	$ 3,100	$ 5,600	$10,600
E_2: Stable	300	0	100	500	5,900
E_3: Expansion	19,400	19,100	16,000	10,000	0
Maximum regret	$19,400	$19,100	$16,000	$10,000	$10,600

possibility of the large gain with A_5, and that there is no consideration of probability values using the minimax regret criterion.

14.8. For Problem 14.6, suppose the probabilities associated with a recession, economic stability, and with an expansion are 0.30, 0.50, and 0.20 respectively. Determine the best act from the standpoint of the Bayesian criterion of maximizing the expected value.

Table 14.19 is the complete decision table for this problem and also indicates the expected monetary value associated with each decision act. The best act from the standpoint of the expected value criterion is A_2: Invest in corporate bonds.

Table 14.19   Decision Table for the Investment Decision Problem and the Determination of the Best Act According to Expected Value Criterion

State of economy	Probability	Investment decision				
		A_1 Savings account	A_2 Corporate bonds	A_3 Blue Chip stocks	A_4 Speculative stocks	A_5 Stock options
E_1: Recession	0.30	$600	$500	$-2,500	$-5,000	$-10,000
E_2: Stable	0.50	600	900	800	400	-5,000
E_3: Expansion	0.20	600	900	4,000	10,000	20,000
Expected value, EV		$600	$780	$450	$700	$-1,500

14.9. Thus far, we have been concerned with situations in which positive as well as negative economic consequences can occur. When the consequences are all *cost* values the same techniques can be applied *provided that all cost figures are identified as being negative values* (payouts). However, cost figures are frequently identified as "costs" but are reported as absolute values without the negative signs. In such a case, keep in mind that the minimum cost, rather than the maximum, is the "best" cost, and adjust the application of the various decision criteria accordingly. Using Table 14.20, determine the best acts from the standpoint of the maximin and maximax criteria by modifying the application of these criteria appropriately.

Table 14.20   Cost Table Associated with Three Product Inspection Plans

Proportion defective in shipment	Inspection plan		
	A_1 100% inspection	A_2 5% inspection	A_3 No inspection
E_1: 0.01	$100	$ 20	$ 0
E_2: 0.05	100	150	400

Since the lowest cost is the best cost and the highest cost is the worst cost, when the maximin criterion is applied the objective is to choose that act whose maximum cost is the smallest. In this context, the maximin criterion could be called the "minimax" criterion. As indicated in Table 14.21, the decision act which satisfies this criterion is A_1: 100% inspection. By using this criterion, the maximum cost which can occur is minimized.

In the context of a table of costs, using the maximax criterion involves choosing that act whose minimum value is the smallest. Thus, the criterion could be called the "minimin" criterion in this case. As indicated in Table 14.21, the criterion which satisfies the optimistic orientation represented by the maximax criterion (i.e. which minimizes the minimum cost) is A_3: No inspection.

Table 14.21 Quality Inspection Plan to Be Chosen by the Maximin and Maximax Criteria

Proportion defective in shipment	Inspection plan		
	A_1 100% inspection	A_2 5% inspection	A_3 No inspection
E_1: 0.01 E_2: 0.05	$100 100	$ 20 150	$ 0 400
Maximum cost	$100	$150	$400
Minimum cost	$100	$20	$ 0

14.10. Determine the best decision act from the standpoint of the minimax regret criterion for the situation in Problem 14.9.

Refer to Table 14.22. Because the best act for a given state is the one which results in the *lowest* cost, that is the act which is assigned an opportunity loss of zero. Thus, given E_1, A_3 is the best act in terms of having the lowest cost and thus has $0 regret. The act which minimizes the maximum regret which can occur is A_2: 5% inspection.

Table 14.22 Opportunity Loss Table for the Quality Inspection Plan Problem and Application of the Minimax Regret Criterion

Proportion defective in shipment	Inspection plan		
	A_1 100% inspection	A_2 5% inspection	A_3 No inspection
E_1: 0.01 E_2: 0.05	$100 0	$20 50	$ 0 300
Maximum regret	$100	$50	$300

14.11. From Problem 14.9, determine the best act from the standpoint of the general Bayesian criterion of maximizing the expected value, given that the probability is 0.80 that a shipment will contain a proportion of 0.01 defectives and the probability is 0.20 that a shipment will contain a proportion of 0.05 defectives.

When dealing with cost figures, the Bayesian criterion is satisfied by choosing that act for which the expected cost is minimized. Table 14.23 is a complete decision table for this problem and indicates that the best act from this standpoint is A_2: 5% inspection. Note that in terms of expected (long-run) cost, the "conservative" strategy of 100% inspection is the least preferred act.

Table 14.23 Decision Table for the Quality Inspection Plan Problem and Application of the Bayesian Criterion

Proportion defective in shipment	Probability	Inspection plan		
		A_1 100% inspection	A_2 5% inspection	A_3 No inspection
E_1: 0.01	0.80	$100	$ 20	$ 0
E_2: 0.05	0.20	100	150	400
Expected cost		$100	$46	$80

DECISION TREE ANALYSIS

14.12. A manufacturer has been presented with a proposal for a new product, and must decide whether or not to develop it. The cost of the development project is $200,000; the probability of success is 0.70. If development is unsuccessful, the project will be terminated. If it is successful, the manufacturer must then decide whether to begin manufacturing the product at a high level or at a low level. If demand is high, the incremental profit given a high level of manufacturing is $700,000; given a low level it is $150,000. If demand is low, the incremental profit given a high level of manufacturing is $100,000; given a low level it is $150,000. All of these incremental profit values are gross figures (i.e. *before* subtraction of the $200,000 development cost). The probability of high demand is estimated as $P = 0.40$, and of low demand as $P = 0.60$. Construct the decision tree for this situation.

Figure 14-2 is the decision tree for this problem. As is typical for such diagrams, each decision point is identified by a square and each chance event is identified by a circle.

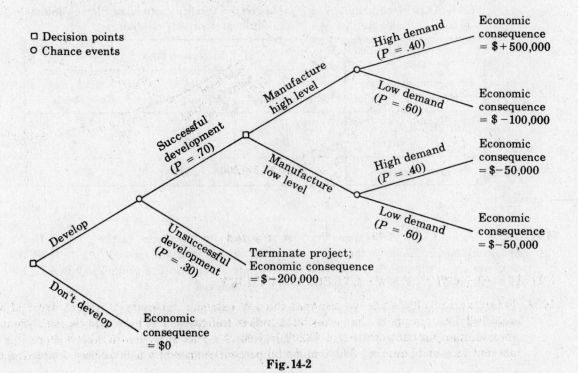

Fig. 14-2

14.13. Referring to Fig. 14-2, determine whether or not the manufacturer should proceed with the attempt to develop this product by determining the expected value associated with the alternative acts "Develop" and "Don't develop".

Figure 14-3 repeats the decision tree presented in Fig. 14-2, except that the expected values associated with each possible decision in the sequential process have been entered, and the nonpreferred act at each decision point has been eliminated from further consideration in each case by superimposing a double bar ($\parallel$) at that branch. Working from right to left, the expected value of the act "High-level manufacturing" is $140,000, which is determined as follows:

$$EV\,(\text{High-level manufacturing}) = (0.40)(500{,}000) + (0.60)(-100{,}000) = \$140{,}000$$

Similarly,

$$EV\,(\text{Low-level manufacturing}) = (0.40)(-50{,}000) + (0.60)(-50{,}000) = \${-}50{,}000$$

Comparing the two expected values, the best act is "High-level manufacturing"; the other act possibility is eliminated. Moving leftward to the next decision point (which is also the initial decision point in this case), the expected values for the two possible decision acts are

$$EV\,(\text{Develop}) = (0.70)(140{,}000) + (0.30)(-200{,}000) = \$38{,}000$$

$$EV\,(\text{Don't develop}) = \$0$$

Comparing the two expected values, the best act at the initial decision point is "Develop." In the calculation of the expected value for "Develop," note that the probability of 0.70 (for "Successful development") is multiplied by $140,000, with the $-50,000 in the adjoining branch being ignored because it is associated with a decision act eliminated in the previous step of analysis.

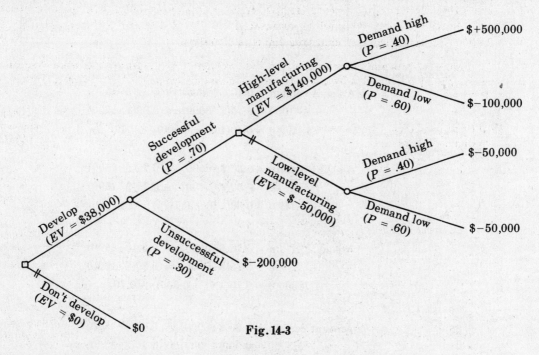

Fig. 14-3

UTILITY FUNCTIONS AND EXPECTED UTILITY

14.14. Referring to Table 14.2, we see that the two extreme monetary outcomes are $-1,500 and $+6,000. Suppose that a decision maker indicates that he would be indifferent to receiving an amount certain of $1200 in lieu of a risk situation in which there is a 50 percent chance of gaining $6000 and a 50 percent chance of a $1500 loss. Following the convention of assigning the extreme lower and upper monetary values with utility values of "0" and "1.0", respectively, determine the utility values associated with $-1500, $1200, and $6000.

We begin by assigning utility values to the two extreme monetary consequences:

$$U(\$-1500) = 0 \qquad U(\$6000) = 1.0$$

The utility associated with the amount certain of $1200 is determined as follows:

$$U(\text{amount certain}) = P(U \text{ of high outcome}) + (1-P)(U \text{ of low outcome})$$
$$U(\$1200) \qquad = 0.50(1.0) + 0.50(0)$$
$$U(\$1200) \qquad = 0.50$$

14.15. Continuing with Problem 14.14, suppose that four additional reference contracts are presented to the decision maker (see Table 14.24). Determine the utility values associated with each amount certain.

Table 14.24   Four Reference Contracts with Associated Amounts Certain

Contract number	Probability of $6000 gain	Probability of $1500 loss	Equivalent amount certain
1	0.10	0.90	$- 1000
2	0.30	0.70	0
3	0.70	0.30	3000
4	0.90	0.10	5000

Contract No. 1:

$$\text{Amount certain} = 0.10(\$+6000) \text{ vs. } 0.90(\$-1500)$$
$$\$-1000 = 0.10(\$+6000) \text{ vs. } 0.90(\$-1500)$$
$$U(\$-1000) = 0.10(1.0) + 0.90(0) = 0.10$$

Contract No. 2:

$$\text{Amount certain} = 0.30(\$+6000) \text{ vs. } 0.70(\$-1500)$$
$$\$0 = 0.30(\$+6000) \text{ vs. } 0.70(\$-1500)$$
$$U(\$0) = 0.30(1.0) + 0.70(0) = 0.30$$

Contract No. 3:

$$\text{Amount certain} = 0.70(\$+6000) \text{ vs. } 0.30(\$-1500)$$
$$\$3000 = 0.70(\$+6000) \text{ vs. } 0.30(\$-1500)$$
$$U(\$3000) = 0.70(1.0) + 0.30(0) = 0.70$$

Contract No. 4:

$$\text{Amount certain} = 0.90(\$+6000) \text{ vs. } 0.10(\$-1500)$$
$$\$5000 = 0.90(\$+6000) \text{ vs. } 0.10(\$-1500)$$
$$U(\$5000) = 0.90(1.0) + 0.10(0) = 0.90$$

Table 14.25 summarizes the utility values which are equivalent to several monetary values determined above and in Problem 14.14. Note that when the risk situation in the reference contract involves the two extreme outcomes with the associated utility values of "1.0" and "0", the utility value of the amount certain which is designated by the decision maker is always equal to the probability of the outcome which has the assigned utility of 1.0.

Table 14.25 Utility Values and Equivalent Monetary Values

Monetary value, $	−1500	−1000	0	1200	3000	5000	6000
Utility value	0	0.10	0.30	0.50	0.70	0.90	1.00

14.16. Referring to Table 14.25, construct a graph to portray the utility function for this decision maker. Describe his attitude toward the risks inherent in the reference contracts which were presented to him.

Figure 14-4 shows that this decision maker is a risk averter in the range of monetary consequences included in this problem. See Fig. 14-1. Basically, this indicates that the amount certain which he designates as being equivalent to the designated risk situation in the reference contract is always less than the associated expected monetary value, except for the two extreme end points of the utility curve. For instance, in Problem 14.14 the decision maker stated that for him a certain $1200 was equivalent to a probability of 0.50 of gaining $6000 and a probability of 0.50 of losing $1500. However, the expected value of this risk situation is 0.50($6000) + 0.50($−1500) = $3000 + ($−750) = $2250.

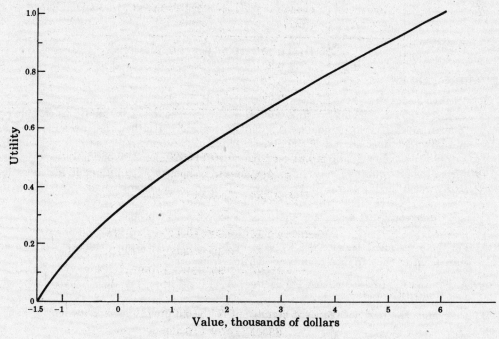

Fig. 14-4

14.17. Referring to the utility function in Fig. 14-4, determine the approximate utility values corresponding to each monetary value in Table 14.2, and determine the best act from the standpoint of maximizing the expected utility.

Table 14.26 identifies the utility values which are equivalent to the monetary consequences in Table 14.2. Using the criterion of maximizing the expected utility, the best act is A_3, as it was for the expected value criterion (see Example 6). However, note that whereas the expected monetary values for acts A_2 and A_4 were equal in Table 14.7, the expected utility values of these two acts are not.

Table 14.26 Decision Table for the Number of Air-Conditioning Units to Be Ordered and Determination of the Best Act According to the Expected Utility Criterion

Market demand	Probability	Order quantity			
		A_1: 5	A_2: 10	A_3: 15	A_4: 20
E_1: 5	0.10	0.55	0.38	0.21	0
E_2: 10	0.30	0.55	0.70	0.61	0.47
E_3: 15	0.40	0.55	0.70	0.86	0.78
E_4: 20	0.20	0.55	0.70	0.86	1.00
Expected utility, EU		0.550	0.668	0.720	0.653

Supplementary Problems

DECISION TABLES

14.18. An investment analyst estimates that there is about a 50 percent chance of an "upturn" in the chemical industry during the first quarter of the year, with the probabilities of "no change" and a "downturn" being about equal. A client is considering either the investment of $10,000 in a mutual fund specializing in chemical industry common stocks or investing in corporate AAA-rated bonds yielding 8.0 percent per year. If the chemical industry experiences an upturn during the first quarter, the value of the mutual fund shares (including dividends) will increase by 15.0 percent during the next 12 months. If there is no change, the value will increase by 3.0 percent. If there is a downturn, the value will *decrease* by 10.0 percent. Ignoring any commission costs, construct a decision table for this investment problem.

14.19. For the investment decision described in Problem 14.18, determine the best decision acts from the standpoint of the (a) maximin and (b) maximax criteria.

Ans. (a) A_2: Invest in AAA bonds, (b) A_1: Invest in mutual fund

14.20. Determine the best act from the standpoint of the minimax regret criterion for Problem 14.18.

Ans. A_2: Invest in AAA bonds

14.21. For Problem 14.18, determine the best act from the standpoint of the expected value criterion.

Ans. A_2: Invest in AAA bonds

14.22. A retailer buys a certain product for $3 per case and sells it for $5 per case. The high markup is reflective of the perishability of the product, since it has no value after 5 days. Based on experience with similar products, the retailer is confident that the demand for the item will be somewhere between 9 and 12 cases, inclusive.

Construct an appropriate decision table. Determine the best act from the standpoint of (a) the maximin criterion and (b) the maximax criterion.

Ans. (a) A_1: Order 9 cases, (b) A_4: Order 12 cases

14.23. Construct the table of opportunity losses (regrets) for Problem 14.22, and determine the best act from the standpoint of the minimax regret criterion.

Ans. A_2: Order 10 cases

14.24. Continuing with Problem 14.22, the retailer further estimates that the probability values associated with selling 9 to 12 cases of the item are 0.30, 0.40, 0.20, and 0.10, respectively. Determine the best decision acts from the standpoint of the (*a*) maximum probability criterion and (*b*) expectation of the event.

Ans.   (*a*) A_2: Order 10 cases, (*b*) A_2: Order 10 cases

14.25. Referring to Problems 14.22 and 14.23, determine the best order quantity from the standpoint of the (*a*) expected value criterion and (*b*) the criterion of minimizing the expected opportunity loss. Demonstrate that these are equivalent criteria by also identifying the "second best" and "worst" acts in respect to each criterion.

Ans.   (*a*) A_2: Order 10 cases, (*b*) A_2: Order 10 cases

14.26. In conjunction with the installation of a new marine engine, a charter vessel owner has the opportunity to buy spare propellers at $200 each for use during the coming cruise season. The propellers are custom fit for the vessel, and because the owner has already contracted to sell the boat after the cruise season, there is no value associated with having spare propellers left over after the season. If a spare propeller is not immediately available when needed, the cost of buying a needed spare propeller, including lost cruise time, is $400. Based on previous experience, the vessel owner estimates that the probability values associated with needing 0 to 3 propellers during the coming cruise season are 0.30, 0.30, 0.30, and 0.10, respectively. Construct a decision table for this problem, and determine the number of propellers that should be ordered from the standpoint of (*a*) the maximin criterion, (*b*) the maximax criterion.

Ans.   (*a*) A_4: Order three spare propellers, (*b*) A_1: Order no spare propellers

14.27. For the situation in Problem 14.26, determine the best act from the standpoint of the (*a*) maximum probability criterion and (*b*) the expectation of the event.

Ans.   (*a*) Indifferent between 0, 1 and 2 propellers; (*b*) A_2: Order 1 propeller

14.28. For Problem 14.26, determine the best act from the standpoint of the expected value criterion (in this case, expected cost).

Ans. A_2: Order 1 propeller

14.29. Several weeks before an annual "Water Carnival," a college social group must decide to order either blankets, beach umbrellas or neither for resale at the event. The monetary success of the decision to sell one of the two items is dependent on the weather conditions, as indicated in Table 14.27. Determine the best acts from the standpoint of the (*a*) maximin and (*b*) maximax criteria.

Ans.   (*a*) A_3: Neither, (*b*) A_2: Beach umbrellas

14.30. Determine the best act from the standpoint of the minimax regret criterion for Problem 14.29.

Ans. A_3: Neither

Table 14.27   Payoffs for the "Water Carnival" Decision Problem

Weather	A_1: Blankets	A_2: Beach umbrellas	A_3: Neither
Cool	$100	$-80	$0
Hot	-50	150	0

14.31. Continuing with Problem 14.29, one of the club members calls the weather bureau and learns that during the past 10 years the weather has been "hot" on 6 of the 10 days on the date when the Water Carnival is to be held.   Use this information to estimate the probabilities associated with the two weather conditions.   Then determine the best acts from the standpoint of the (a) maximum probability and (b) expected value criteria.

Ans.   (a) A_2: Beach umbrellas, (b) A_2: Beach umbrellas

DECISION TREE ANALYSIS

14.32. An investor is considering placing a $10,000 deposit to reserve a franchise opportunity in a new residential area for 1 year.   There are two areas of uncertainty associated with this sequential decision situation: whether or not a prime franchise competitor will decide to locate an outlet in the same area and whether or not the residential area will develop to be a moderate or large market.   The investor estimates that there is a 50–50 chance that the competing franchise system will develop an outlet.   Thus the investor must first decide whether to make the initial $10,000 down payment.   After the decision of the competing system is known the investor must then decide whether or not to proceed with constructing the franchise outlet.   If there is competition and the market is large, the net gain during the relevant period is estimated as being $15,000; if the market is moderate there will be a net loss of $10,000.   If there is no competition and the market is large, the net gain will be $30,000; if the market is moderate there will be a net gain of $10,000.   The investor estimates that there is about a 40 percent chance that the market will be large.   Using decision tree analysis, determine whether or not the initial deposit of $10,000 should be made.

Ans.   Make the deposit (EV = $9000)

UTILITY FUNCTIONS AND EXPECTED UTILITY

14.33. For Problems 14.6 to 14.8, the extreme points of the possible monetary consequences are $-10,000 and $20,000.   Describe how you would go about developing a utility function for the individual who is involved in this investment decision.

14.34. Based on your answer to Problem 14.33, suppose the set of utility values reported in Table 14.28 has been developed.   Construct the appropriate utility curve and use it to determine whether the investor can be described as a risk averter, a risk seeker or neutral in respect to risk.   Illustrate the meaning of your conclusion in the context of this decision problem.

Ans.   The decision maker is a risk seeker.

Table 14.28   Utility Values Equivalent to Monetary Values for the Investment Decision Problem

Monetary value, $	−10,000	−2,500	2,000	10,000	14,000	18,000	20,000
Utility value	0	0.1	0.2	0.4	0.6	0.8	1.0

14.35. Determine the best act for the investment decision described in Problems 14.6 to 14.8, based on the expected utility criterion and using the utility function developed in Problem 14.34.

Ans. A_5: Invest in stock options ($EU \cong 0.230$)

Chapter 15

Bayesian Decision Analysis: The Use of Sample Information

15.1 THE EXPECTED VALUE OF PERFECT INFORMATION (*EVPI*)

Given that the several possible events, or states, are uncertain and are associated with a probability distribution, the availability of *perfect information* indicates that the decision maker knows which event will occur in respect to each individual decision opportunity. The *expected value of perfect information* (*EVPI*) is the difference between the (long-run) expected value given such information minus the expected value associated with the best act under conditions of uncertainty. Although perfect information as such is seldom available, the *EVPI* serves as an indication of the maximum value that any sample can have to the decision maker. In determining the *EVPI*, note that under conditions of uncertainty a "best act" is identified as the consistent strategy for each and every decision opportunity. On the other hand, the availability of perfect information leads to a mixed strategy in which the decision act is perfectly matched to the event, or state, for each decision opportunity. The formula for determining the expected value of perfect information is

$$EVPI = EV \text{ (with perfect information)} - EV \text{ (under conditions of uncertainty)} \quad (15.1)$$

EXAMPLE 1. Refer to Table 14.7 (page 241), where the best act under conditions of uncertainty is A_3: Order 15 units, with an expected value of $3250. If perfect information were available, act A_1 would be chosen 10 percent of the time, act A_2 30 percent of the time, and so forth corresponding to the relative frequencies of the associated demand levels. See Table 15.1. As indicated, the expected value with perfect information is $4050. Therefore, $EVPI = 4050 - 3250 = \$800$. This is the maximum amount that any sample information could be worth on the average, because it is the maximum amount by which the expected value could be increased with all uncertainty removed.

Table 15.1 Determination of the Expected Value with Perfect
Information for the Decision Situation in Table 14.7

Market demand	Probability	Best act	Conditional value of best act	Expected value
E_1: 5	0.10	A_1	$1500	$150
E_2: 10	0.30	A_2	3000	900
E_3: 15	0.40	A_3	4500	1800
E_4: 20	0.20	A_4	6000	1200
				$4050

Consider now the relationship between opportunity loss and the value of perfect information. By definition, *EOL* of the best act is the average amount of regret associated with the optimum act, as a long-run average. See Section 14.4. Given that the *EOL* of the best act is the average amount by which the best possible gain given a perfect (mixed) strategy is

257

missed, it follows that this should also be the value of perfect information for a given decision situation. Therefore, an alternative basis for determining the expected value of perfect information is

$$EVPI = EOL \text{ (Best act)} \tag{15.2}$$

EXAMPLE 2. In Example 7 of Chapter 14 (see page 241), we observed that the same decision act (A_3) was identified as being the best act whether the act with the highest EV or the lowest EOL were identified. Now, we can further observe that the EOL value of the best act ($800) also indicates the $EVPI$ for this situation. This value corresponds with the value obtained in Example 1, above.

In the above examples, note the difference between the expected value *with* perfect information and the expected value *of* perfect information. The expected value *with* perfect information indicates the long-run average result with all uncertainty removed, and is sometimes called the *expected payoff with perfect information* (*EPPI*). The expected value *of* perfect information (*EVPI*) is the average *incremental* value of removing uncertainty in the decision situation.

As was the case in Chapter 14, in this chapter we restrict our coverage to events that follow a discrete probability distribution. The determination of the value of perfect information and the value of sample information for events that follow the normal probability distribution is covered in Chapter 16.

15.2 BAYES' THEOREM

In its simplest algebraic form, Bayes' theorem is concerned with determining the conditional probability of event A given that event B has occurred. The general form of Bayes' theorem is

$$P(A \mid B) = \frac{P(A \text{ and } B)}{P(B)} \tag{15.3}$$

Formula (*15.3*) is simply a particular application of the general formula for conditional probability presented in Section 5.5. However, the special importance of Bayes' theorem is that it is applied in the context of sequential events, and further, that the computational version of the formula provides the basis for determining the conditional probability of an event having occurred in the *first* sequential position given that a particular event has been observed in the *second* sequential position. The computational form of Bayes' theorem is

$$P(A \mid B) = \frac{P(A)P(B \mid A)}{P(A)P(B \mid A) + P(A')P(B \mid A')} \tag{15.4}$$

EXAMPLE 3. Suppose there are two urns, U_1 and U_2. Urn 1 has eight red balls and two green balls, while urn 2 has four red balls and six green balls. If an urn is selected randomly, and a ball is then selected randomly from that urn, the sequential process and probabilities can be represented by the tree diagram in Fig. 15-1. The tree diagram indicates that the probability of choosing either urn is 0.50, and then the conditional probabilities of a red (R) or a green (G) ball being drawn are indicated according to the urn involved. Now, suppose we observe a green ball in step 2 *without* knowing which urn was selected in step 1. What is the probability that urn 1 was selected in step 1? Symbolically, what is $P(U_1 \mid G)$? Substituting U_1 and G for A and B, respectively, in the computational form of Bayes' theorem:

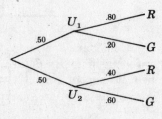

Fig. 15-1

$$P(U_1 \mid G) = \frac{P(U_1)P(G \mid U_1)}{P(U_1)P(G \mid U_1) + P(U_2)P(G \mid U_2)}$$

$$= \frac{(0.50)(0.20)}{(0.50)(0.20) + (0.50)(0.60)} = \frac{0.10}{0.40} = 0.25$$

In Example 3, note that Bayes' theorem presents the basis for obtaining what might be called a "backward conditional" probability value, since we can determine the probability that a particular urn was selected in step 1 given the observation of a sampled item from that urn in step 2. In Bayesian decision analysis this theorem provides the conceptual basis for revising the prior probabilities associated with the several events, or states, thus leading to the formulation of a posterior probability distribution (posterior to the sample information). See Section 15.3.

15.3   PRIOR AND POSTERIOR PROBABILITY DISTRIBUTIONS

This section presents the application of Bayes' theorem for the purpose of revising the several probabilities associated with the entire set of possible events, or states, in a decision situation. In this context, the *prior probability distribution* is the probability distribution which is applicable before the collection of any sample information. In Bayesian decision analysis such a probability distribution is often subjective in that it is based on judgments, although it could also be based on historical information. The *posterior probability distribution* is the probability distribution after sample information has been observed and has been used to revise the prior probability distribution by application of Bayes' theorem.

As illustrated in Section 15.2, in order to apply Bayes' theorem the prior probability of the uncertain event and the conditional probability of the sample result must be known. Typically, the conditional probabilities are determined by the use of some standard probability distribution according to the nature of the sampling situation.

EXAMPLE 4.   When a manufacturing process is in control, the proportion defective is only 0.01; when it is out of control the proportion defective is 0.10. Historically, the process has been found to be out of control 5 percent of the time, and this is the basis for the probability values indicated in Table 15.2. A sample of $n = 10$ items is inspected and one item is found to be defective. In order to use Bayes' formula to revise the prior probability values, the binomial probability distribution (see Section 6.3) serves as the basis for determining the conditional probability of the sample result given each fraction defective in turn. For instance, the probability that one item will be defective, given a sample $n = 10$ and the fraction defective 0.01, is 0.0914 by reference to Appendix 1. Note that in the present context the value of "p" in the binomial table is the fraction defective, and *not* the prior probability value associated with that fraction defective. The tree diagram for this sampling situation (Fig. 15-2) includes all of the conditional probabilities as well as the prior probabilities.

Table 15.2   Prior Probability Values Associated
             with Two Possible Levels of
             Fraction Defective in a
             Manufacturing Process

Fraction defective	Prior probability
0.01	0.95
0.10	0.05

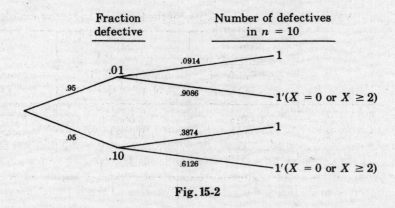

Fig. 15-2

Using formula (*15.4*), we determine the posterior probability that the true fraction defective is 0.01, given that one item was found to be defective in a sample of $n = 10$, as follows:

$$P(A \mid B) = \frac{P(A)P(B \mid A)}{P(A)P(B \mid A) + P(A')P(B \mid A')}$$

$$P(p = 0.01 \mid 1 \text{ def.}) = \frac{P(p = 0.01) \times P(1 \text{ def} \mid p = 0.01)}{P(p = 0.01) \times P(1 \text{ def} \mid p = 0.01) + P(p = 0.10) \times P(1 \text{ def} \mid p = 0.10)}$$

$$= \frac{(0.95)(0.0914)}{(0.95)(0.0914) + (0.05)(0.3874)} = \frac{0.08683}{0.10620} = 0.81761 \cong 0.82$$

We could now also apply Bayes' formula to determine the probability that the true fraction defective is 0.10 given the sample result. However, since only two levels of fraction defective are possible, this value obviously is the complement of the 0.82 determined above, or 0.18. The prior and posterior probability values for this example are summarized in Table 15.3. Note that the shift in the probability values after the sample reflects the fact that observing one defective item in a random sample of $n = 10$ is more likely with the fraction defective of 0.10 than with 0.01.

Table 15.3   Prior and Posterior Probability Distributions

Fraction defective	Prior probability	Posterior probability
0.01	0.95	0.82
0.10	0.05	0.18

Example 4 presents a direct application of the methodology in Section 15.2. When an entire set of probability values is being revised, however, a *tabular approach* for developing the posterior probability distribution is more convenient than the repeated application of Bayes' formula for determining each posterior probability value.

EXAMPLE 5. Table 15.4 illustrates the use of the tabular approach for developing the posterior probability distribution for the situation described in Example 4. For each event, the posterior probability value is determined by dividing the joint probability value in that row of column (4) by the sum of column (4). By this procedure, each entry in column (4) is equivalent to the numerator in Bayes' formula while the sum of column (4) is equivalent to the denominator. As indicated, these are the same posterior probability values as in Example 4.

Table 15.4   Revision of Probabilities for the Fraction-Defective Problem

(1) Event	(2) Prior P	(3) Conditional probability of sample result	(4) Joint probability, Col. (2) × Col. (3)	(5) Posterior P Col. (4) ÷ sum
0.01 0.10	0.95 0.05	0.0914 0.3874	0.08683 0.01937	$0.81761 \cong 0.82$ $0.18239 \cong 0.18$
Total	1.00		0.10620	1.00

15.4   BAYESIAN POSTERIOR ANALYSIS AND THE VALUE OF SAMPLE INFORMATION (AFTER SAMPLING)

The procedure by which sample information can be used to revise a prior probability distribution can now be applied to a decision problem concerned with whether or not to accept a shipment from a vendor.   The best act is first determined based on the prior distribution and then on the basis of a posterior distribution.   Finally, we determine the value of the particular sample result based on whether the identification of the best act was changed by the revision of the prior probability values.

EXAMPLE 6.   Table 15.5 shows that the fraction (proportion) defective for a shipment of 1000 items from a vendor can be at one of four levels: 0.01, 0.05, 0.10, and 0.20.   The prior probability values based on historical experience with this vendor are included in the table.   The costs associated with A_1: Accept are based on the fact that identification and removal of a defective item which becomes part of an assembled component costs \$1.00.   Thus, for a fraction defective of 0.01 there are 0.01 × 1000 = 10 defective items, which involves a cost of 10 × \$1.00 = \$10.00 for later removal.   The costs associated with A_2: Reject are based on the information that if the true fraction defective is 0.05 or less, our company is contractually obligated to accept the shipment, and thus must pay for the additional shipment expenses when the vendor returns the same shipment back to the company.   Based on the prior probability distribution, the act which has the lowest expected cost is A_1: Accept, and thus in the absence of any sample information such a shipment should be accepted routinely.   Indeed, if the best act were otherwise, it would indicate that we have "signed up" with the wrong vendor!

Table 15.5   Decision Table for the Shipment Problem Based on Use of the Prior Distribution

Fraction defective, p_i	Prior P	Conditional cost of A_1: Accept	Conditional cost of A_2: Reject	Expected cost of A_1: Accept	Expected cost of A_2: Reject
0.01 0.05 0.10 0.20	0.50 0.30 0.10 0.10	\$ 10.00 50.00 100.00 200.00	\$200.00 200.00 0 0	\$ 5.00 15.00 10.00 20.00	\$100.00 60.00 0 0
Total	1.00			\$50.00	\$160.00

Whereas the analysis in Example 6 is based on the prior probability distribution, in Example 7 we assume that sample information is available as a basis for revising the prior probability distribution.

EXAMPLE 7. For the situation described in Example 6, suppose a random sample of $n = 10$ items is selected and two of the items are found to be defective. Using the tabular procedure described in Section 15.3, the prior probability distribution is revised in Table 15.6. As expected, the posterior probability values associated with the 0.10 and 0.20 fraction defective states are larger than the respective prior probability values, because of the sample result. The conditional probabilities in Table 15.6 are based on the binomial probability distribution. As in Section 15.3, note that, when the binomial table is used, the value of "p_i" is each fraction defective in turn, and *not* the prior probability value.

Table 15.6   Revision of Probabilities for the Shipment Problem

Fraction defective, p_i	Prior P	Conditional probability of sample result, $P(X = 2 \mid n = 10, p_i)$	Joint probability	Posterior P
0.01	0.50	0.0042	0.00210	$0.0284 \cong 0.03$
0.05	0.30	0.0746	0.02238	$0.3022 \cong 0.30$
0.10	0.10	0.1937	0.01937	$0.2616 \cong 0.26$
0.20	0.10	0.3020	0.03020	$0.4078 \cong 0.41$
Total	1.00		0.07405	1.00

Bayesian posterior analysis is the process of determining a best act by revising a prior probability distribution on the basis of sample data, and then using the resulting posterior probability distribution to determine the best decision act. With the posterior probability distribution available from Example 7, in Example 8 we complete the Bayesian posterior analysis.

EXAMPLE 8. In Table 15.7, the expected cost for A_2: Reject ($66.00) is lower than the expected cost associated with A_1: Accept. Therefore, given that a sample of $n = 10$ contained two defective items, the best act from the standpoint of the Bayesian criterion of minimizing the expected cost is to reject the shipment and return it, rather than to enter the items into the manufacturing process.

Table 15.7   Decision Table for the Shipment Problem Based on Use of the Posterior Probability Distribution

Fraction defective, p_i	Posterior P	Conditional cost of A_1: Accept	Conditional cost of A_2: Reject	Expected cost of A_1: Accept	Expected cost of A_2: Reject
0.01	0.03	$ 10.00	$200.00	$ 0.30	$ 6.00
0.05	0.30	50.00	200.00	15.00	60.00
0.10	0.26	100.00	0	26.00	0
0.20	0.41	200.00	0	82.00	0
Total	1.00			$123.30	$66.00

Having illustrated the process of Bayesian posterior analysis in Examples 6 through 8, we can now consider the value associated with a sample that has already been taken. The estimated *value of sample information* (*VSI*) for a sample which has already been observed is based on the difference between the *posterior expected values* (or costs) of the best acts identified before and after sampling, or

$$VSI = \text{(Posterior expected value of best posterior act)}$$
$$- \text{(Posterior expected value of best prior act)} \qquad (15.5)$$

Thus, if the identification of the best act has not been changed as a result of the posterior analysis, then the value of the sample information is $0, even though the expected value associated with that act would generally have changed.

EXAMPLE 9.   In order to estimate the value of the sample information included in Example 8, we first note that as a result of the posterior analysis the best decision act was changed to A_2: Reject, from the best act of A_1: Accept, which was applicable without the sample.   The estimated value of the sample information which was obtained is

$$VSI = -66.00 - (-123.30) = -66.00 + 123.30 = \$57.30$$

(*Note:*   Since both of the expected values are costs in this case, they are entered as negative values above so that the *VSI* is appropriately positive.   In the long run, the sample information served to revise the prior probabilities toward a more accurate assessment.   Even though we thought that the expected cost of A_1: Accept was $50.00 based on the prior analysis, with the sample information considered we recognize that a more reliable assessment of this expected cost is $123.30.   The sample information caused us to change our decision from this act to act A_2: Reject, with the (posterior) expected cost of $66.00, thus reducing the expected cost by $57.30 from what we would have experienced had act A_1 been chosen.)

15.5   PREPOSTERIOR ANALYSIS: THE EXPECTED VALUE OF SAMPLE INFORMATION (*EVSI*) PRIOR TO SAMPLING

Preposterior analysis is the process by which the value of sample information is estimated before the sample is collected.   The basic procedure is to consider all of the possible sample outcomes, determine the estimated value in the decision process of each sample outcome, and then determine the *expected values of the sample information* (*EVSI*) by weighting each of these different values by the probability that the associated sample outcome will occur.

Example 10 illustrates the process of preposterior analysis for a sample of only $n = 1$.   Because all possible sample outcomes have to be considered, the computation of *EVSI* for samples that are not small is tedious.   However, the procedure described and illustrated below can be applied for larger samples by the use of a computer.

EXAMPLE 10.   Suppose we wish to determine the expected value of sample information associated with a sample of $n = 1$ for the decision problem described in Example 6.   Table 15.5 is the decision table for this problem, and on the basis of the prior distribution the best act is A_1: Accept the shipment, with an expected cost of $50.00 (as contrasted to A_2: Reject the shipment, with an expected cost of $160.00).   We proceed by determining the *VSI* associated with each possible sample outcome, and then combine these values to compute the *EVSI* for the sample of $n = 1$.

Step 1:   Determine the posterior distribution if zero items are defective in the sample of $n = 1$.   The revision procedure and the posterior probability distribution are presented in Table 15.8.   Note that the probability values have "shifted" somewhat in the expected direction.   Also notice that the sum of the "joint probability" column is identified as indicating the overall (unconditional) probability of the sample result being observed.   This probability value is used in the final step of determining the *EVSI*.

Step 2:   Determine the best act if zero items are defective in the sample of $n = 1$ and determine the expected values (costs) associated with the alternative acts.   As indicated in Table 15.9, the best act is A_1: Accept the shipment, which is the same act which was determined best on the basis of the prior analysis (before considering any sample information) in Example 6.

**Table 15.8 Revision of Probabilities for the Shipment Problem,
Given No Defective in a Sample of $n = 1$**

Fraction defective p_i	Prior P	Conditional probability of sample result, $P(X = 0 \mid n = 1, p_i)$	Joint probability	Posterior P
0.01	0.50	0.99	0.495	$0.5211 \cong 0.521$
0.05	0.30	0.95	0.285	$0.3000 = 0.300$
0.10	0.10	0.90	0.090	$0.0947 \cong 0.095$
0.20	0.10	0.80	0.080	$0.0842 \cong 0.084$
Total	1.00		$P(X = 0) = 0.950$	1.000

**Table 15.9 Determination of the Best Act for the Shipment Problem,
Given No Defective in a Sample of $n = 1$**

Fraction defective, p_i	Posterior P	Conditional cost of A_1: Accept	Conditional cost of A_2: Reject	Expected cost of A_1: Accept	Expected cost of A_2: Reject
0.01	0.521	$ 10.00	$200.00	$ 5.21	$104.20
0.05	0.300	50.00	200.00	15.00	60.00
0.10	0.095	100.00	0	9.50	0
0.20	0.084	200.00	0	16.80	0
				Total: $46.51	Total: $164.20

Step 3: Determine the estimated value of the information that zero items are defective in the sample of $n = 1$. Since the best act is not changed if this sample result is observed, the value of the sample is $0. Or, using formula (*15.5*):

$$VSI = \text{(Posterior expected value of best posterior act)}$$
$$- \text{(Posterior expected value of best prior act)}$$
$$= -46.51 - (-46.51) = -46.51 + 46.51 = \$0$$

Step 4: Determine the posterior distribution if one item is defective in the sample of $n = 1$. The revision procedure and the posterior probability distribution are presented in Table 15.10. Again, note that the probability values have shifted in the expected direction. Also, the sum of the "joint probability" column again indicates the overall probability of the sample result being considered, in this case that $X = 1$ given $n = 1$ and given the prior probability distribution.

**Table 15.10 Revision of Probabilities for the Shipment Problem,
Given One Defective in a Sample of $n = 1$**

Fraction defective, p_i	Prior P	Conditional probability of sample result, $P(X = 1 \mid n = 1, p_i)$	Joint probability	Posterior P
0.01	0.50	0.01	0.005	0.10
0.05	0.30	0.05	0.015	0.30
0.10	0.10	0.10	0.010	0.20
0.20	0.10	0.20	0.020	0.40
			Total $P(X = 1) = 0.050$	Total: 1.00

Step 5: Determine the best act if one item is defective in the sample of $n = 1$ and determine the expected values (costs) associated with the alternative acts. As indicated in Table 15.11, the best act is A_2: Reject the shipment, which is a change from the best act based on the prior probability distribution.

Table 15.11 Determination of the Best Act for the Shipment Problem, Given One Defective in a Sample of $n = 1$

Fraction defective, p_i	Posterior P	Conditional cost of A_1: Accept	Conditional cost of A_2: Reject	Expected cost of A_1: Accept	Expected cost of A_2: Reject
0.01	0.10	$ 10.00	$200.00	$ 1.00	$20.00
0.05	0.30	50.00	200.00	15.00	60.00
0.10	0.20	100.00	0	20.00	0
0.20	0.40	200.00	0	80.00	0
				Total: $116.00	Total: $80.00

Step 6: Determine the estimated value of the information that one item is defective in the sample of $n = 1$. Since the best act is changed if this sample result is observed, the value is determined using (*15.5*):

$$VSI = \text{(Posterior expected value of best posterior act)}$$
$$- \text{(Posterior expected value of best prior act)}$$
$$= -80.00 - (-116.00) = -80.00 + 116.00 = \$36.00$$

Step 7: Since the *VSI* associated with each possible sample outcome has now been determined, combine these values to obtain the expected value of sample information by means of the following formula:

$$EVSI = \sum (VSI_i)P(X_i) \qquad (15.6)$$

Applying (*15.6*),

$$EVSI = 0(0.950) + 36.00(0.050) = 0 + 1.80 = \$1.80$$

In the above calculation, each possible *VSI* amount is multiplied by the probability of the associated sample result occurring, and the resulting products are summed. As indicated in Steps 1 and 4 above, the probability values of the two different sample results occurring for the present problem are indicated by the sums of the "joint probability" columns in Tables 15.8 and 15.10, respectively.

15.6 EXPECTED NET GAIN FROM SAMPLING (*ENGS*) AND OPTIMUM SAMPLE SIZE

For each sample size considered, the *expected net gain from sampling* (*ENGS*) is defined as the difference between the expected value of sample information and the cost of the sample (*CS*):

$$ENGS = EVSI - CS \qquad (15.7)$$

If the *ENGS* of a sample being considered is greater than zero in value, then the sample should be taken unless some other sample has a higher *ENGS*. This matter is covered later in this section, in respect to optimum sample size.

EXAMPLE 11. For the sample size of $n = 1$ which was considered in Example 10, *EVSI* = $1.80. Suppose the cost of inspection is $1.20 per item sampled. We determine the expected net gain from taking a sample of $n = 1$ in this decision situation as follows:

$$ENGS = EVSI - CS = 1.80 - 1.20 = \$0.60$$

Therefore, it is better to take a sample of one item before deciding whether or not to accept the shipment, rather than to make the decision without the sample.

As the sample size which is being considered is increased in preposterior analysis, the *EVSI* becomes progressively larger and approaches the value of *EVPI* for the decision situation. The *optimum sample size* is the size such that the *ENGS* is maximized. Figure 15-3 illustrates the relationship among *EVPI*, *EVSI*, and *CS* as the sample size is increased. The general relationship between sample size and *ENGS* is indicated in Fig. 15-4.

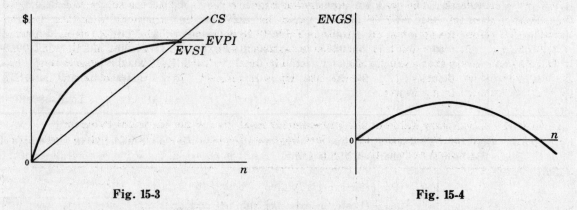

Fig. 15-3   Fig. 15-4

EXAMPLE 12. The values of *EVSI*, *CS* and *ENGS* for the shipment inspection problem discussed in Examples 10 and 11 are presented in Table 15.12, in order of sample size. The values for $n = 0$ are based on the absence of a sample while the values for $n = 1$ were determined in Examples 10 and 11. The values for $n = 2$ were determined by a procedure similar to that followed for $n = 1$, except that three possible sample results had to be considered ($X = 0$, $X = 1$, and $X = 2$). These calculations are not presented in this chapter. Since *ENGS* always "peaks" at some sample size (including possibly at $n = 0$) and then declines, we conclude from the information in Table 15.4 that the optimum sample size for this simplified problem is $n = 1$. For more realistic problems involving the consideration of larger sample sizes, the use of a computer would be required.

Table 15.12   *EVSI*, *CS* and *ENGS* for the
                     Shipment Problem According to
                     Sample Size

Sample size, n	*EVSI*	*CS*	*ENGS*
0	$0	$0	$0
1	1.80	1.20	0.60
2	2.83	2.40	0.43

In some texts in the area of Bayesian decision analysis, attention is given to determining the *overall terminal expected payoff* (*OTEP*) and *net overall terminal expected payoff* (*NOTEP*) in conjunction with preposterior analysis. For each possible sample size, the overall terminal expected payoff is the expected value of the best act before sampling plus the expected value of the sample information. This sum is reduced by the cost of sampling to determine the net overall terminal expected payoff. Thus, the overall terminal expected payoff is

$$OTEP = EV \text{ (Best prior act)} + EVSI \qquad (15.8)$$

The net overall terminal expected payoff is

$$NOTEP = OTEP - CS \qquad (15.9)$$

Finally, we should observe that if a sample is to be taken, then the best decision will depend on the observed sample result. Therefore, a complete Bayesian decision rule which involves sampling requires that the optimum sample size be identified, and further, that the best act according to various sample results be specified.

EXAMPLE 13. Table 15.13 is a summary table for the shipment inspection problem. In addition to values which were previously reported, the $OTEP$ and $NOTEP$ values are indicated for each of the three sample sizes considered. The costs are expressed as negative values so that the subtraction leading to the determination of the $NOTEP$ values could be algebraically consistent with the general formula. Therefore, the optimum sample size in Table 15.13 is the one with the largest (algebraic) value of $NOTEP$, or $n = 1$. Note that this conclusion is consistent with the result indicated in Example 12 and in Table 15.12. Given that a sample of $n = 1$ should be taken, in Table 15.13 we also observe that if the sampled item is not defective ($X = 0$), the best act is A_1: Accept. If the sampled item is defective ($X = 1$), the best act is A_2: Reject.

Table 15.13   A Summary Table of the Preposterior Analysis for the Shipment Problem and the Designation of the Best Bayesian Decision Rule (The Inspection Costs Are Expressed as Negative Numbers)

| Sample size, n | EVSI | OTEP | CS | ENGS | NOTEP | Decision rule | |
						A_1: Accept	A_2: Reject
0	$0	$−50.00*	$0	$0	$−50.00	Always	Never
1†	1.80	−48.20	1.20	0.60	−49.40	$X = 0$	$X = 1$
2	2.83	−47.17	2.40	0.43	−49.57	$X = 0$	$X \geq 1$

*This is the expected value (cost) of the best act based on the prior probability distribution and without sampling. See Table 15.7.

†The optimum sample size, based either on maximizing $ENGS$ or maximizing $NOTEP$.

Solved Problems

THE EXPECTED VALUE OF PERFECT INFORMATION

15.1. Determine the $EVPI$ for the investment decision situation in Problems 14.6 to 14.8 by determining the EOL associated with the best act based on the Bayesian criterion of expected value.

As indicated in Table 14.19, the best act from the standpoint of the expected value criterion is A_2: Corporate bonds. The opportunity-loss values for all acts are identified in Table 14.18. Thus,

$$EVPI = EOL(A_2) = 100(0.30) + 0(0.50) + 19{,}100(0.20) = \$3850$$

15.2. Determine the $EVPI$ for the shipment problem described in Example 6 by first determining the expected cost with perfect information.

Because this decision problem is concerned with costs, note that $EVPI$ in this case is determined by subtracting the expected cost with perfect information from the expected cost of the best act under conditions of uncertainty. Referring to Table 15.5, under perfect information we would accept the shipment whenever the fraction defective is either 0.01 or 0.05, and we would reject it whenever it is 0.10 or 0.20. On the basis of this decision rule, the expected cost and then *EVPI* are calculated as follows:

$$EC \text{ (with perfect information)} = 10(0.50) + 50(0.30) + 0(0.10) + 0(0.10) = \$20.00$$

$$EC \text{ (under conditions of uncertainty)} = \$50.00 \quad \text{(from Example 6)}$$

$$EVPI = EC \text{ (under conditions of uncertainty)} - EC \text{ (with perfect information)}$$

$$= 50.00 - 20.00 = \$30.00$$

15.3. In Problem 14.5 the best act in respect to how many large-screen television sets are to be ordered is determined by identifying the act with the lowest *EOL*. The best act is A_2: Order three sets, with $EOL(A_2) = \$170$. Referring to Table 14.14, demonstrate that this *EOL* is equal to the *EVPI* value which can be calculated by first determining the expected value with perfect information.

$$EV \text{ (with perfect information)} = 400(0.30) + 600(0.40) + 800(0.20) + 1000(0.10) = \$620$$

$$EV \text{ (under conditions of uncertainty)} = \$450 \quad \text{(from Problem 14.4)}$$

$$EVPI = EV \text{ (with perfect information)} - EV \text{ (under conditions of uncertainty)}$$

$$= 620 - 450 = \$170$$

BAYES' THEOREM

15.4. Box A is known to contain one penny (P) and one dime (D) while box B contains two dimes. A box is chosen randomly and then a coin is randomly selected from the box. (*a*) Construct a tree diagram to portray this situation involving sequential events. (*b*) If box A is selected in the first step, what is the probability that a dime (D) will be selected in the second step? (*c*) If a dime (D) is selected in the second step, what is the probability that it came from box A? (*d*) If a penny (P) is selected in the second step, what is the probability that it came from box A?

(*a*) See Fig. 15-5.

(*b*) $P(D \mid A) = \frac{1}{2} = 0.50$

(*c*) $P(A \mid D) = \dfrac{P(A \text{ and } D)}{P(D)} = \dfrac{P(A)P(D \mid A)}{P(A)P(D \mid A) + P(B)P(D \mid B)}$

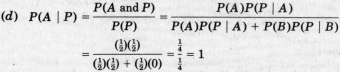

$$= \dfrac{(\frac{1}{2})(\frac{1}{2})}{(\frac{1}{2})(\frac{1}{2}) + (\frac{1}{2})(1)} = \dfrac{\frac{1}{4}}{\frac{1}{4} + \frac{1}{2}} = \dfrac{1}{3} \cong 0.33$$

Fig. 15-5

(*d*) $P(A \mid P) = \dfrac{P(A \text{ and } P)}{P(P)} = \dfrac{P(A)P(P \mid A)}{P(A)P(P \mid A) + P(B)P(P \mid B)}$

$$= \dfrac{(\frac{1}{2})(\frac{1}{2})}{(\frac{1}{2})(\frac{1}{2}) + (\frac{1}{2})(0)} = \dfrac{\frac{1}{4}}{\frac{1}{4}} = 1$$

Thus, if a penny is obtained it must have come from box A.

15.5. An analyst in a photographic concern estimates that the probability is 0.30 that a competing firm plans to begin manufacturing instant photography equipment within the next three years, and 0.70 that the firm does not. If the competing firm has such plans, a new manufacturing facility would definitely be built. If the competing firm does not have such plans, there is still a 60 percent chance that a new manufacturing facility would be built for other reasons.

(a) Using I for the decision to enter the instant photography field and M for the addition of a new manufacturing facility, portray the possible events by means of a tree diagram.

(b) Suppose we observe that the competing firm has in fact begun work on a new manufacturing facility. Given this information, what is the probability that the firm has decided to enter the instant photography field?

(a) See Fig. 15-6.

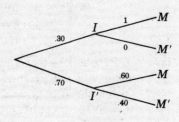

(b) $P(I \mid M) = \dfrac{P(I \text{ and } M)}{P(M)}$

$= \dfrac{P(I)P(M \mid I)}{P(I)P(M \mid I) + P(I')P(M \mid I')}$

$= \dfrac{(0.30)(1)}{(0.30)(1) + (0.70)(0.60)} = \dfrac{0.30}{0.72} \cong 0.42$

Fig. 15-6

15.6. If there is an increase in capital investment next year, the probability that structural steel will increase in price is 0.90. If there is no increase in such investment, the probability of an increase is 0.40. Overall, we estimate that there is a 60 percent chance that capital investment will increase next year.

(a) Using I and I' for capital investment increasing and not increasing and using R and R' for a rise and nonrise in structural steel prices, construct a tree diagram for this situation involving dependent events.

(b) What is the probability that structural steel prices will not increase even though there is an increase in capital investment?

(c) What is the overall (unconditional) probability of an increase in structural steel prices next year?

(d) Suppose that during the next year structural steel prices in fact increase. What is the probability that there was an increase in capital investment?

(a) See Fig. 15-7.

(b) $P(R' \mid I) = 0.10$

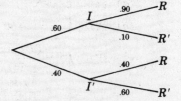

(c) $P(R) = P(I \text{ and } R) \text{ or } P(I' \text{ and } R)$

$\qquad = P(I)P(R \mid I) + P(I')P(R \mid I')$

$\qquad = (0.60)(0.90) + (0.40)(0.40) = 0.70$

(d) By Bayes' formula:

Fig. 15-7

$P(I \mid R) = \dfrac{P(I \text{ and } R)}{P(R)} = \dfrac{P(I)P(R \mid I)}{P(I)P(R \mid I) + P(I')P(R \mid I')}$

$= \dfrac{(0.60)(0.90)}{(0.60)(0.90) + (0.40)(0.40)} = \dfrac{0.54}{0.70} \cong 0.77$

PRIOR AND POSTERIOR DECISION ANALYSIS

15.7. A new product being considered by our firm will have either a low, moderate, or high level of sales. We have the choice of either marketing or not marketing the product. Table 15.14 is the decision table which indicates the probability values associated with the three possible sales levels, based on our best judgment, and the economic consequences for this decision situation.

(a) Determine the best act from the standpoint of the Bayesian criterion of maximizing expected value.

(b) Determine the maximum value that any further information can have.

Table 15.14   Decision Table for Marketing a New Product

Event	Probability	Decision act	
		A_1: Market	A_2: Don't market
E_1: Low sales	0.40	$-30,000$	$0
E_2: Moderate sales	0.40	10,000	0
E_3: High sales	0.20	50,000	0

(a) $EV(A_1) = -30,000(0.40) + 10,000(0.40) + 50,000(0.20) = \$2,000$

$EV(A_2) = \$0$

Therefore, the best act is A_1: Market the product.

(b)   Table 15.15 portrays the table of opportunity losses, or regrets, for this decision situation.   Since the $EVPI$ is equal to the EOL of the best act,

$$EVPI = EOL(A_1) = \$30,000(0.40) + 0(0.40) + 0(0.20) = \$12,000$$

Alternatively, we can determine the $EVPI$ by first determining the expected value with perfect information and then subtracting the expected value of the best act (under uncertainty) from this value:

$$EV \text{ (with perfect information)} = 0(0.40) + 10,000(0.40) + 50,000(0.20) = \$14,000$$

$$EVPI = EV \text{ (with perfect information)} - EV \text{ (under conditions of uncertainty)}$$
$$= 14,000 - 2,000 = \$12,000$$

Table 15.15   Opportunity Loss Table for Marketing a New Product

Event	Probability	Decision act	
		A_1: Market	A_2: Don't market
E_1: Low sales	0.40	$30,000	$ 0
E_2: Moderate sales	0.40	0	10,000
E_3: High sales	0.20	0	50,000

15.8.   For the decision situation in Problem 15.7, test-marketing of the product in one region results in a moderate level of sales in that region.   A review of historical sales patterns in that region indicates that for products with low sales nationally, sales in the region were moderate 30 percent of the time.   For products with a moderate level of sales nationally, sales in the region were also moderate 70 percent of the time.   For products with a high level of sales nationally, sales in the region were moderate only 10 percent of the time.

(a)   Revise the prior probabilities used in Problem 15.7, on the basis of the sample result that sales were at a moderate level in the test-market region.

(b)   Determine the best decision act on the basis of posterior decision analysis.

(a) The posterior probability distribution is determined in Table 15.16.   As would be expected, the probability that the true level of demand is moderate is increased after taking the sample results into consideration.

Table 15.16   Revision of Probabilities for Marketing a New Product Based on a Moderate Level of Sales in the Test Market

Event	Prior P	Conditional probability of sample result	Joint probability	Posterior P
E_1: Low sales	0.40	0.30	0.12	$0.2857 \cong 0.29$
E_2: Moderate sales	0.40	0.70	0.28	$0.6666 \cong 0.67$
E_3: High sales	0.20	0.10	0.02	$0.0476 \cong 0.05$
Total	1.00		0.42	1.01

(b) The best act after the sample (the Bayesian posterior act) is determined by using the posterior probabilities determined in Table 15.16 in conjunction with the conditional values presented in Table 15.14.   The expected values associated with acts A_1 (Market) and A_2 (Don't market) are

$$EV(A_1) = -30,000(0.29) + 10,000(0.67) + 50,000(0.05) = \$500$$
$$EV(A_2) = \$0$$

Therefore, as in the case of the prior analysis, the best act is A_1:   Market the product.

15.9. What is the estimated value of the sample information that was obtained in Problem 15.8? How do you reconcile this value with the observed difference in the expected value (payoff) in this risk situation after the sample as compared with before the sample?

Because the optimal act was not changed by the sample result, the sample had no value as such.   More specifically,

$$VSI = \text{(Posterior expected value of the best posterior act)}$$
$$- \text{(Posterior expected value of the best prior act)}$$
$$= 500 - 500 = \$0$$

The difference between the posterior and prior values of the optimal act is $500 - 2000 = \$-1500$.   In other words, the posterior expected payoff is $1500 less than the prior expected payoff for the same act.   However, this change took place because the sample provided more information about the uncertain states, and in this sense the sample information did not cause a change as such.   Without the sample we determined that the expected value of the best act was $2000, but after the sample we recognize that for this particular decision situation the prior expectation should be changed.   However, because we would still choose the same act as the optimal act, this knowledge does not cause us to change the eventual monetary result from that which would have occurred without the sample information.

15.10. The owner of a small manufacturing concern has the opportunity to purchase five used lathes as a group from excess equipment being disposed of by a large firm in the area.   The uncertain factor is the number of machines that will require a major overhaul before being put to productive use in his factory.   The decision to purchase them must take into account the cost of the machines to him, their value if in good condition, and the cost of overhaul. The various economic consequences for this decision are given in Table 15.17. Determine the best act for this decision situation and the expected value associated with this act.

Table 15.17   Decision Table for the Purchase of the Used Lathes

| Number of defective lathes | Probability | Decision act | |
		A_1: Purchase	A_2: Don't purchase
0	0.05	$5000	$0
1	0.10	3000	0
2	0.20	1000	0
3	0.30	−1000	0
4	0.30	−3000	0
5	0.05	−5000	0

$$EV(A_1) = 5000(0.05) + 3000(0.10) + 1000(0.20) + (-1000)(0.30) + (-3000)(0.30) + (-5000)(0.05)$$

$$= \$-700$$

$$EV(A_2) = \$0$$

Therefore, the best act is A_2: Don't purchase the machines, with an expected value of $0.

15.11. Determine the expected value of perfect information for the decision situation described in Problem 15.10.

$$EV \text{ (with perfect information)} = 5000(0.05) + 3000(0.10) + 1000(0.20) + 0(0.30) + 0(0.30)$$

$$+ 0(0.05) = \$750$$

EV (under conditions of uncertainty) = $0   (from Problem 15.10)

$EVPI = EV$ (with perfect information) − EV (under conditions of uncertainty) = $750 - 0 = \$750$

15.12. Referring to Problem 15.10, suppose that a thorough inspection of each machine is permitted, but such inspection costs $50 per machine. The owner of the manufacturing company chooses two machines at random, has them inspected and learns that neither one of these machines is in need of an overhaul. Determine the best act based on Bayesian posterior analysis.

Because the population (of five machines) is finite and relatively small in size, the probability distribution which is used to determine the conditional probabilities of the sample result must take into consideration the fact that sampling without replacement is involved in this decision situation. The required probabilities can be determined by the use of tree diagrams or by the use of the hypergeometric distribution (see Section 6.5). For the population of five machines which includes two defective machines, for example, Fig. 15-8 can be used in conjunction with the multiplication rule for dependent events to obtain the required conditional probability (see Section 5.6). In this figure, D stands for a defective machine being observed and D' stands for the observed machine being nondefective. As indicated, the probability of observing no defective item in a sample of $n = 2$ for the given population is 0.30. Conditional probabilities for other populations can be similarly determined.

The revision of the prior probability distribution based on the result that two sampled machines were both found to be nondefective is presented in Table 15.18, with the conditional probability values in the third column having been determined by either of the two procedures described above. Using the posterior probability distribution we compute the posterior expected values as follows:

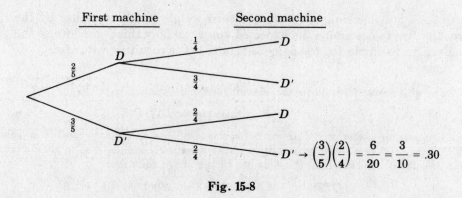

Fig. 15-8

$$EV(A_1) = 5000(0.25) + 3000(0.30) + 1000(0.30) + (-1000)(0.15) + (-3000)(0.00) + (-5000)(0.00)$$
$$= \$2300$$

$$EV(A_2) = \$0$$

Therefore, the best Bayesian posterior act is A_1: Purchase the machines, with an expected value of $2300.

Table 15.18   Revision of Probabilities for the Purchase of the Used Lathes Based on No Machines Being Defective for a Sample of $n = 2$

Number of defective lathes	Prior P	Conditional probability of sample result	Joint probability	Posterior P
0	0.05	1.00	0.05	0.25
1	0.10	0.60	0.06	0.30
2	0.20	0.30	0.06	0.30
3	0.30	0.10	0.03	0.15
4	0.30	0	0	0
5	0.05	0	0	0
Total	1.00		$P(X = 0) = 0.20$	1.00

15.13. What is the estimated net value of the sample information obtained in Problem 15.12?

$$VSI = \text{(Posterior expected value of the best posterior act)}$$
$$- \text{(Posterior expected value of the best prior act)}$$
$$= 2300 - 0 = \$2300$$
$$\text{Net } VSI = VSI - CS = 2300 - 100 = \$2200$$

Note that the net value above is *not ENGS* as discussed in Section 15.6, because this is the estimated net gain associated with a particular sample that has already been taken, not the expected value of a sample of a given size prior to sampling.

PREPOSTERIOR ANALYSIS

15.14. In Section 15.6 we indicate that the overall terminal expected payoff (*OTEP*) can be determined by adding the *EVSI* for the given sample size to the *EV* (prior). Logically, *OTEP* can also be determined by identifying the *EV* (posterior) that would be associated with each possible sample result and then weighting these values by their respective probabilities to determine the expected value. Apply this procedure to the preposterior analysis in Example 10, and demonstrate that the resulting value for *OTEP* is the same as reported in Table 15.13.

The alternative formula for the overall terminal expected payoff is

$$OTEP = \sum (\text{Posterior } EV_i) \, P(X_i) \qquad (15.10)$$

The possible posterior *EV* amounts for the sample of $n = 1$ are reported in Tables 15.9 and 15.11, while the respective probabilities of the associated sample results are reported in Tables 15.8 and 15.10. Substituting these values in the above equation,

$$OTEP = (-46.51)(0.95) + (-80.00)(0.05) = \$-48.18$$

Except for rounding error, this is the same negative value (cost) as the $\$-48.20$ reported in Table 15.13.

Supplementary Problems

THE EXPECTED VALUE OF PERFECT INFORMATION

15.15. For Problems 14.22 to 14.25, determine the expected value of perfect information by subtracting the expected values of the best act under uncertainty from the expected value of the decision opportunity under conditions of certainty. Compare your answer with the expected opportunity loss of the best act, as determined in Problem 14.25.

Ans. $EVPI = 20.20 - 18.50 = \$1.70$

15.16. For Problems 14.26 to 14.28, determine the expected value of perfect information regarding the number of spare propellers that will be required.

Ans. $EVPI = \$160$

BAYES' THEOREM

15.17. Suppose there are two urns, U_1 and U_2. U_1 contains two red balls and one green ball, while U_2 contains one red ball and two green balls.

(a) An urn is randomly selected, and then one ball is randomly selected from the urn. The ball is red. What is the probability that the urn selected was U_1?

(b) An urn is randomly selected, and then two balls are randomly selected (without replacement) from the urn. The first ball is red and the second ball is green. What is the probability that the urn selected was U_1?

Ans. (a) $P(U_1) = 2/3$,   (b) $P(U_1) = 1/2$

15.18. Refer to Problem 15.17.

(a) Suppose an urn is randomly selected, and then two balls are randomly selected (without replacement) from the urn. Both balls are red. What is the probability that the urn selected was U_1?

(b) Suppose an urn is randomly selected and then two balls are randomly selected, *but with the first selected ball being placed back in the urn before the second ball is drawn*. Both balls are red. What is the probability that the urn selected was U_1?

Ans. (a) $P(U_1) = 1$,   (b) $P(U_1) = 4/5$

15.19. Eighty percent of the vinyl material received from Vendor A is of exceptional quality while only 50 percent of the vinyl material received from Vendor B is of exceptional quality. However, the manufacturing capacity of Vendor A is limited, and for this reason only 40 percent of the vinyl material purchased by our firm comes from Vendor A. The other 60 percent comes from Vendor B. An incoming shipment of vinyl material is inspected, and it is found to be of exceptional quality. What is the probability that it came from Vendor A?

Ans. $P(A) = 0.52$

15.20. Gasoline is being produced at three refineries with daily production levels of 100,000, 200,000 and 300,000 gallons, respectively. The proportion of the output which is below the octane specifications for "name-brand" sale at the three refineries is 0.03, 0.05, and 0.04, respectively. A gasoline tank-truck is found to be carrying gasoline which is below the octane specifications, and therefore the gasoline is to be marketed outside of the name-brand distribution system. Determine the probability that the tank-truck came from each of the three refineries (*a*) without reference to the information that the shipment is below the octane specifications and (*b*) given the additional information that the shipment is below the octane specifications.

Ans.   (*a*) $P(1) = \frac{1}{6} \cong 0.17$, $P(2) = \frac{2}{6} \cong 0.33$, $P(3) = \frac{3}{6} = 0.50$; (*b*) $P(1) = 0.12$, $P(2) = 0.40$, $P(3) = 0.48$

PRIOR AND POSTERIOR DECISION ANALYSIS

15.21. A jobber has the opportunity to purchase a shipment of 10 medium-quality stereo systems manufactured abroad for $1000. However, the equipment has been in transit by ocean freighter for some time, and there is a distinct possibility of moisture damage having occurred. Based on his previous experience with the shipping company involved, the jobber estimates that there is a 20 percent chance the shipment is damaged. If the shipment is damaged, the jobber can sell the stereo sets for just $500. If no moisture damage has occurred, he can resell the entire shipment for a net profit of $300. Determine whether or not the jobber should purchase the shipment from the standpoint of the expected value criterion.

Ans.   Purchase, with $EV = \$140$.

15.22. In respect to the jobber's decision in Problem 15.21, for practical purposes "damaged" means that one-half of the stereo sets are affected, because more extensive damage would be visually obvious. The jobber pays $10 to have one randomly selected stereo set uncrated and tested, and it is found to perform adequately. Determine the best act given this sample information, and the expected value associated with this act.

Ans.   Purchase, $EV = \$212$.

15.23. What is the estimated value of the sample information which was collected in Problem 15.22?

Ans. $0, or considering the cost of the sample, $-10.

15.24. Refer to the investment decision described in Problems 14.18 to 14.21. Determine (*a*) the expected value under conditions of certainty and (*b*) the *EVPI* for this decision problem.

Ans.   (*a*) $1150, (*b*) $350

15.25. For Problems 14.18 to 14.21, by a somewhat simplified approach the investment analyst defines "upturn" to mean that (at least) 70 percent of the usual purchasers of chemical products increase their order amounts, "no change" to mean that (about) 50 percent of the purchasers increase their order amounts, and "downturn" to mean that 30 percent (or fewer) of the purchasers increase their order amounts. He contacts a random sample of 20 purchasers of chemical products and learns that 14 of them are increasing their order amounts over previous periods.

(*a*)   Revise the prior probability distribution regarding the three possible states of the chemical industry, as given in Problem 14.18, by taking this sample result into consideration.

(b) Using the posterior probability distribution, determine the best act from the standpoint of the expected value criterion and compare it with your answer in Problem 14.21.

Ans. (a) P (Upturn) $\cong 0.91$, P (No change) $\cong 0.09$, P (downturn) $\cong 0.00$;
(b) Invest in mutual fund ($EV = \$1392$).

15.26. Estimate the value of the sample information which was obtained in Problem 15.25.

Ans. $592

15.27. Using the posterior probability distribution developed in Problem 15.25, determine (a) the expected value under conditions of certainty and (b) the *EVPI* after the sample has been taken. Compare your results with those in Problem 15.24.

Ans. (a) $1437, (b) $45

15.28. Referring to Problem 14.29, suppose that the club need not commit itself to buying the blankets or beach umbrellas until 3 days before the event. Therefore, the members decide to add the weatherman's forecast as additional information. Looking at the weatherman's record, for days that are in fact cool he has correctly forecast the weather 90 percent of the time. For days that are in fact hot, he has correctly forecast the weather 70 percent of the time. For the day of the "Water Carnival" the weatherman forecasts cool weather. Revise the prior probability distribution given in Problem 14.31 based on this forecast.

Ans. P (Cool) $\cong 0.67$, P (Hot) $\cong 0.33$

15.29. Taking the weather forecast given in Problem 15.28 into consideration, determine the best decision act for the situation described in Problem 14.29.

Ans. A_1: Order blankets.

15.30. Estimate the value of the weather forecast given in Problem 15.28.

Ans. $54.60

PREPOSTERIOR ANALYSIS

15.31. In Example 10 the *EVSI* for a sample of $n = 1$ was determined to be $1.80. Using the computational procedure illustrated in Example 10, determine the *VSI* associated with a sample of $n = 2$ and with the number of defective items found being $X = 0$, $X = 1$, and $X = 2$, respectively.

Ans. $0, $23.22 and $134.14

15.32. Referring to the conditional *VSI* figures calculated in Problem 15.31, determine the *EVSI* associated with a sample of $n = 2$.

Ans. $2.83

Chapter 16

Bayesian Decision Analysis:
Application of the Normal Distribution

16.1 INTRODUCTION

This chapter deals with Bayesian decision analysis for an event (state) which is normally distributed, rather than following a discrete probability distribution. The methodology by which the mean and standard deviation for such a prior probability distribution are determined is illustrated in Section 16.2. The techniques of analysis in this case are further based on the requirement that only two decision acts are being evaluated, or compared, and that the payoff functions associated with these acts are linear payoff functions (see Section 16.3). Although these requirements may appear to be quite restrictive, a broad range of decision problems can be analyzed by these techniques.

EXAMPLE 1. A manufacturer has decided to assemble hand-held calculators for subsequent distribution by his company. The specific decision which has to be made now is whether Type 1 or Type 2 equipment is to be installed in the assembly plant. A larger capital investment is required for the Type 2 equipment, but the variable manufacturing cost is lower, which in turn leads to a higher incremental profit after the fixed (capital) cost has been covered (see Example 5). However, the Type 2 equipment would be more profitable than Type 1 equipment only at relatively higher levels of sales, which is the uncertain event in this problem. It is assumed that the decision maker's estimate of the uncertain sales level follows the normal distribution. Because the sales level estimate is the key factor in determining which type of equipment will yield the best return, it is the first area of interest in the prior analysis. In this example we have indicated that (1) our uncertainty in regard to the event follows the normal distribution; (2) two acts are being considered—purchasing Type 1 or Type 2 equipment; and (3) there is a constant incremental profit over variable cost per unit sold, which is indicative of the existence of linear payoff functions for the two acts.

16.2 DETERMINING THE PARAMETERS OF
THE NORMAL DISTRIBUTION

The prior probability distribution is descriptive of the uncertainty which is associated with the decision maker's estimate of the random event. It is not the event which follows the probability distribution, but rather, the estimate of the event. Since the estimate is based on a judgment, there is no mathematical theorem which would justify the use of the normal distribution in respect to such a judgment in any specific instance. However, for judgment situations in which an informed decision maker is aware of a number of uncertain factors which could influence the value of the eventual outcome in either one direction or the other, the use of the normal distribution has been found to be a satisfactory approximation of the uncertainty inherent in the estimate.

As described in Section 7.2, a normal distribution is defined by identifying the mean and the standard deviation of the distribution. The mean of the prior distribution can be obtained by asking the decision maker to identify the "most likely" value of the random event or by asking him for that value such that there is a 50 percent chance that the actual value will be lower and a 50 percent chance that the actual value will be higher. Note that the first approach in fact is a request for the mode of the probability distribution while the second approach asks for the median of the distribution. As indicated in Section 3.9, the mean, median, and mode are all at the same point for a normally distributed variable. The mean of the prior probability distribution is designated by M_0 in this text.

EXAMPLE 2. For the decision problem introduced in Example 1, suppose the decision maker says that the most likely level of sales nationally for the hand-held calculator is 40,000 units during the relevant period. On the basis of this judgment we designate the value of the mean of the prior distribution as $M_0 = 40,000$ units.

The prior mean is obtained by describing either the mode or median because these measures are easily described and conceptualized in a nonmathematical fashion. In the case of the standard deviation, it would be even more difficult to obtain such a prior estimate directly. Instead, the decision maker provides the boundaries for a stated probability interval, and the standard deviation of the prior distribution is determined on the basis of the observed size of the interval. As contrasted to a classical confidence interval based on sample information, an interval based on judgment is often called a *credibility interval*. The "middle 50 percent" interval is the one which is most frequently used, since this possible range of outcomes is relatively the easiest to conceptualize. Then the standard deviation is determined by observing that the middle 50 percent of the normal distribution is contained within approximately $\pm \frac{2}{3}\sigma$ units (the specific value is 0.67σ). Where the prior standard deviation is designated by S_0, the computational formula to determine the prior standard deviation by use of the middle 50 percent credibility interval is

$$\frac{2}{3}S_0 = \frac{\text{Middle 50\% interval}}{2} \qquad (16.1)$$

or

$$S_0 = \frac{3(\text{Middle 50\% interval})}{4} \qquad (16.2)$$

EXAMPLE 3. For the decision problem discussed in Examples 1 and 2, if the decision maker states that he has 50 percent confidence that the actual sales level will be somewhere between 35,000 and 45,000 units, the standard deviation of the prior probability distribution is

$$\frac{2}{3}S_0 = \frac{45,000 - 35,000}{2} = 5000 \qquad S_0 = 7500 \text{ units}$$

By the procedures illustrated in Examples 2 and 3 we have determined the values of M_0 and S_0 for total market demand. However, it is often the case that the estimate for an event such as sales is analyzed on the basis of mean results per outlet, rather than for the overall market. There are two reasons for this. First, a manager may find this easier. Second, and more importantly from the standpoint of analysis, if the prior probability distribution is to be revised on the basis of sample information, then that sample information will be obtained from randomly chosen outlets. In order to use such sample information, the prior distribution must itself be formulated on a per-outlet basis.

EXAMPLE 4. If we anticipate collecting sample information as well as managerial judgment, instead of the estimates obtained in Examples 2 and 3, we would ask for the same information on a per-outlet basis. Suppose the calculators are to be distributed through a total of 500 retail outlets in the country. If we ask the decision maker for the most likely level of sales per outlet, the answer should be $M_0 = 80$ to be consistent with his estimate of 40,000 units for the total market in Example 2.   Similarly, he should state that there is a 50 percent chance that average sales per outlet will be between 70 and 90 units to be consistent with the interval for total sales given in Example 3.   Thus, on a per-outlet basis the prior standard deviation is

$$\frac{2}{3}S_0 = \frac{90 - 70}{2} = 10 \qquad S_0 = 15$$

We have now demonstrated how the parameters of a prior probability distribution can be obtained given that the distribution is assumed to be normally distributed.   The student should be particularly alert to the fact that the prior mean and prior standard deviation are descriptive of the decision maker's estimate of the random event and his uncertainty in respect to this event.   Given that the estimate is assumed to be unbiased, it follows that M_0 is an estimate of the overall population mean μ (for example, the actual mean level of sales for all 500 retail outlets).   However, it does *not* follow that S_0 is an estimator of σ, the population standard deviation.   In this regard, it is more appropriate to think of M_0 and S_0 as being similar to $\bar{X}$ and $\sigma_{\bar{x}}$, respectively, but being based on judgment rather than on a sample.

16.3   DEFINING THE LINEAR PAYOFF FUNCTIONS AND DETERMINING THE BEST ACT

The existence of a linear payoff function indicates that the expected value (payoff) associated with an act is a linear function in respect to the uncertain level of the state.   Algebraically,

$$V(A_1) = k_1 + b_1 X \qquad\qquad (16.3)$$

$$V(A_2) = k_2 + b_2 X \qquad\qquad (16.4)$$

where V indicates the conditional value, k is the constant factor (a capital expenditure would be a negative constant), b is the incremental revenue (or cost) per unit of the random variable, and thus indicates the slope of the line, and X indicates the value of the random variable.

EXAMPLE 5.   For the decision situation described in Example 1, suppose that the capital expenditure required is $350,000 for Type 1 equipment and $450,000 for Type 2 equipment.   Because of the lower variable manufacturing cost associated with the Type 2 equipment, the incremental profit (over variable cost) is $12 per unit when this equipment is used as compared with a $10 per unit incremental profit for the Type 1 equipment.   The payoff functions are represented algebraically below, and graphically in Fig. 16-1.

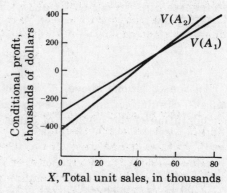

$$V(A_1) = -350,000 + 10X$$

$$V(A_2) = -450,000 + 12X$$

Fig. 16-1

The point at which the two linear payoff functions cross indicates the point of indifference in respect to choosing between the two acts, because the conditional values of the acts are equal at that point.   This is generally called the *breakeven point* in statistical decision analysis.   The specific value of the random variable at the breakeven point can be algebraically determined by setting the two equations equal to one another and solving for X_b:

$$k_1 + b_1 X_b = k_2 + b_2 X_b$$
$$b_1 X_b - b_2 X_b = k_2 - k_1$$
$$X_b(b_1 - b_2) = k_2 - k_1$$
$$X_b = \frac{k_2 - k_1}{b_1 - b_2} \qquad (16.5)$$

Having established the breakeven point, the best act can be determined graphically by observing whether the prior mean is above or below the breakeven point, and choosing the act which is optimal on that side of the breakeven point. The best act can also be identified by substituting the value of the prior mean in each payoff function and choosing the act with the highest expected value. The expected values for two decision acts which have linear payoff functions are

$$EV(A_1) = k_1 + b_1 M_0 \qquad (16.6)$$

$$EV(A_2) = k_2 + b_2 M_0 \qquad (16.7)$$

EXAMPLE 6. For the acts and payoff functions described in Example 5, the breakeven point is

$$X_b = \frac{k_2 - k_1}{b_1 - b_2} = \frac{-450{,}000 - (-350{,}000)}{10 - 12} = \frac{-100{,}000}{-2} = 50{,}000 \text{ units}$$

The prior mean was determined to be $M_0 = 40{,}000$ units in Example 2. Referring to Fig. 16-1, we can observe that this value is to the left of the breakeven point, and that act A_1 (purchase Type 1 equipment) is the best act. Alternatively, we can determine the expected value associated with each act:

$$EV(A_1) = k_1 + b_1 M_0 = -350{,}000 + 10(40{,}000) = \$50{,}000$$

$$EV(A_2) = k_2 + b_2 M_0 = -450{,}000 + 12(40{,}000) = \$30{,}000$$

Therefore, the best act is A_1 (purchase Type 1 equipment), with an associated expected value of \$50,000. Note that in determining the best act, only M_0 is required for the prior probability distribution.

The analysis presented thus far in this section has been concerned with the total market demand. As indicated in Section 16.2, however, if we anticipate the collection of sample information, an analysis on a per-outlet basis is more convenient for subsequent use of the sample results. In per-outlet analysis, the linear payoff functions are based on mean sales per outlet as the variable:

$$V(A_1) = k_1 + Nb_1\mu \qquad (16.8)$$

$$V(A_2) = k_2 + Nb_2\mu \qquad (16.9)$$

In the equations above, N is the number of outlets and μ is the average sales level per outlet. Similarly, the breakeven point in terms of mean sales per outlet must include consideration of the number of outlets involved:

$$\mu_b = \frac{k_2 - k_1}{Nb_1 - Nb_2} \qquad (16.10)$$

Finally, the expected values associated with the two acts when the linear payoff functions are based on mean sales per outlet are determined as follows:

$$EV(A_1) = k_1 + Nb_1 M_0 \qquad (16.11)$$

$$EV(A_2) = k_2 + Nb_2 M_0 \qquad (16.12)$$

EXAMPLE 7. Given that there are 500 retail outlets, then each additional unit of mean sales per outlet represents 500 additional units in total. In place of the payoff functions determined in Example 5, we have:

$$V(A_1) = k_1 + Nb_1\mu = -350,000 + (500)(10)\mu = -350,000 + 5000\mu$$

$$V(A_2) = k_2 + Nb_2\mu = -450,000 + (500)(12)\mu = -450,000 + 6000\mu$$

In place of the breakeven point for total sales reported in Example 6, on a per-outlet basis the mean breakeven point is

$$\mu_b = \frac{k_2 - k_1}{Nb_1 - Nb_2} = \frac{-450,000 - (-350,000)}{500(10) - 500(12)} = 100 \text{ units per outlet}$$

From Example 4, $M_0 = 80$ on a per-outlet basis. Therefore, the expected value associated with each act based on a per-outlet analysis is

$$EV(A_1) = k_1 + Nb_1M_0 = -350,000 + (500)(10)(80) = \$50,000$$

$$EV(A_2) = k_2 + Nb_2M_0 = -450,000 + (500)(12)(80) = \$30,000$$

These values are identical to those obtained by the total-market analysis in Example 6.

If the linear functions are concerned with costs as opposed to revenues the best act is the one with the lowest expected cost. See Problems 16.5 to 16.8.

16.4   LINEAR PIECEWISE LOSS FUNCTIONS AND THE EXPECTED VALUE OF PERFECT INFORMATION (*EVPI*)

In the context of statistical decision analysis, the term *loss function* always refers to an opportunity loss function. For the two-action problem with linear payoff functions, it follows that the loss function associated with each act will be a linear piecewise function made up of two linear pieces, or segments. This is true because on one side of the breakeven point the opportunity loss associated with a given act will be zero, while on the other side the opportunity loss increases linearly with each additional unit from the breakeven point. The process of determining linear piecewise loss functions is best presented by an example.

EXAMPLE 8. In Examples 4 through 6 the following payoff functions and breakeven point were determined:

$$V(A_1) = k_1 + b_1X = \$-350,000 + 10X$$

$$V(A_2) = k_2 + b_2X = \$-450,000 + 12X$$

$$X_b = 50,000$$

We observed in Example 6 that act A_1 is the optimum act (with no opportunity loss) when the level of sales is below the breakeven point and act A_2 is the optimum act when the sales level is above the breakeven point. For act A_1, if the actual level of sales is greater than the breakeven point, then the opportunity loss is the difference between the two incremental revenue amounts ($\$12 - \$10$) multiplied by the number of units by which the sales exceed the breakeven point. Specifically:

$$OL(A_1, X) \begin{cases} = \$2.00(X - 50,000) & \text{for } X > X_b (=50,000) \\ = 0 & \text{for } X \le X_b (=50,000) \end{cases}$$

Conversely, for act A_2 there is an increment of $\$2.00$ in the opportunity loss for each unit that the actual sales level is below the breakeven value:

$$OL(A_2, X) \begin{cases} = 0 & \text{for } X \ge X_b (=50,000) \\ = \$2.00(50,000 - X) & \text{for } X < X_b (=50,000) \end{cases}$$

The piecewise linear loss functions developed for A_1 and A_2 above are graphically portrayed in Figs. 16-2 and 16-3, respectively.

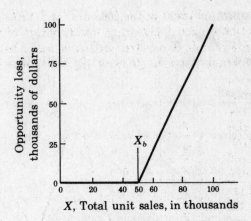

Fig. 16-2

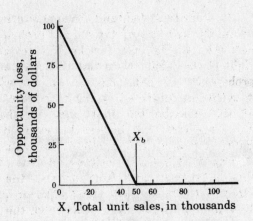

Fig. 16-3

We can observe from Example 8 that the per-unit opportunity loss for act A_1 is equal to the per-unit opportunity loss for act A_2 when each type of loss occurs. In other words, the slope of the opportunity loss function in terms of absolute value is the same for both acts for that piecewise portion that is not equal to zero. It is convenient to designate the absolute value of the slope of the loss function as b. Computationally,

$$b = |b_1 - b_2| \qquad (16.13)$$

As indicated in Section 15.1, the expected value of perfect information is the expected opportunity loss of the best act. Thus, for the two-act situation with piecewise linear loss functions, only the opportunity loss function of the best act is relevant for computing EOL. The formula to determine the expected value of perfect information for a two-action problem with piecewise linear loss functions and a normal prior probability distribution is

$$EVPI = bS_0 L(D) \qquad (16.14)$$

where $b = |b_1 - b_2|$

$S_0 =$ standard deviation of the prior probability distribution

$D = \left| \dfrac{X_b - M_0}{S_0} \right|$

$L(D) =$ the unit normal loss function for D (see Appendix 9)

EXAMPLE 9. In Example 6, the best act for the equipment purchase problem was determined to be act A_1: Purchase Type 1 equipment with an expected value of $50,000. Using information from the preceding examples, we can determine the $EVPI$ as follows:

$$EVPI = bS_0 L(D) = (2)(7500)(0.04270) = \$640.50$$

where $b = |b_1 - b_2| = |10 - 12| = 2$

$S_0 = 7500$ (from Example 3)

$D = \left| \dfrac{X_b - M_0}{S_0} \right| = \left| \dfrac{50,000 - 40,000}{7500} \right| = 1.33$

$L(D) = 0.04270$ (from Appendix 9)

The maximum amount by which the expected value in this decision situation can be increased in the long run, given the removal of uncertainty, is $640.50. Therefore, no sample information could be worth more than this amount, as a long-run average.

In order to understand the computational procedure inherent in the formula for *EVPI*, it is useful to superimpose the normal probability function on the opportunity loss function of the best act.   In Fig. 16-4, for the *EVPI* calculation in Example 9, opportunity losses occur to the right of $X_b = 50$.   Note that the greater the difference between M_0 and X_b, the lower the probability of experiencing an opportunity loss, as would be indicated by the proportion of the probability distribution that lies to the right of X_b. Therefore, the larger the value of D in the *EVPI* formula, the smaller the value of $L(D)$. Conceptually, $L(D)$ represents the product of the opportunity loss function and the probability function to the right of the breakeven point in Fig. 16-4, and can be thought of as being the *EOL* of the best act *given a loss function with a slope of 1.0 and a normal distribution with a standard deviation of 1.0*.   Therefore, the multiplication by b and by S_0 in the *EVPI* formula serves to transform the $L(D)$ value given in Appendix 9 for the unit normal loss function to the appropriate value for the given application.

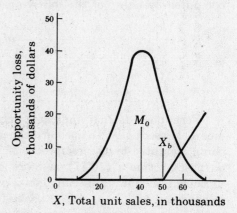

Fig. 16-4

As indicated in Sections 16.2 and 16.3, an analysis of data on a per-outlet basis is more appropriate than the total-market analysis if we anticipate subsequent collection of sample data from randomly chosen outlets.   In such a per-outlet analysis, the calculation of *EVPI* has to include consideration of the fact that the per-unit opportunity loss should represent the opportunity loss per unit change in the *mean* value per outlet.   The slope of the payoff functions of the two acts in respect to changes in the mean sales per outlet is designated by Nb_1 and Nb_2.   Therefore, the absolute value of the slope of the opportunity loss function for the per-outlet analysis is determined by

$$b = |Nb_1 - Nb_2| \qquad\qquad (16.15)$$

EXAMPLE 10.   In Example 7, the payoff functions for the two acts under consideration in terms of mean sales per outlet were identified as

$$V(A_1) = -350,000 + 5000\mu$$
$$V(A_2) = -450,000 + 6000\mu$$

The breakeven point in terms of mean sales per unit was identified as $\mu_b = 100$ units per outlet.

In Example 4 the prior mean and standard deviation on a per-outlet basis were identified as $M_0 = 80$ and $S_0 = 15$, respectively.

With the information summarized above, we determine *EVPI* for this decision problem as follows:

$$EVPI = bS_0L(D) = (1000)(15)(0.04270) = \$640.50$$

where $b = |Nb_1 - Nb_2| = |5000 - 6000| = 1000$

$S_0 = 15$

$$D = \left|\frac{\mu_b - M_0}{S_0}\right| = \left|\frac{100 - 80}{15}\right| = 1.33$$

$L(D) = 0.04270$ (from Appendix 9)

Therefore, the *EVPI* determined on the basis of mean sales per outlet corresponds with the result in Example 9 based on the total-market analysis.

16.5 BAYESIAN POSTERIOR ANALYSIS

When sample information has been collected after a prior probability distribution has been formulated, a posterior probability distribution can be determined by computing the values of the posterior mean and the posterior variance. The posterior mean is designated by M_1 and is computed by either of the following formulas:

$$M_1 = \frac{(1/S_0^2)M_0 + (1/\sigma_{\bar{x}}^2)\bar{X}}{(1/S_0^2) + (1/\sigma_{\bar{x}}^2)} \tag{16.16}$$

or

$$M_1 = \frac{M_0\sigma_{\bar{x}}^2 + \bar{X}S_0^2}{S_0^2 + \sigma_{\bar{x}}^2} \tag{16.17}$$

Formula (16.16) indicates the conceptual basis for determining the posterior mean. Essentially, the posterior mean is a weighted mean, with the prior and sample means being weighted by the reciprocal of their respective variances. However, for computational purposes formula (16.17) is more convenient. If the population standard deviation σ is unknown, then it is generally considered acceptable to use the sample standard deviation s and to substitute $s_{\bar{x}}$ for $\sigma_{\bar{x}}$ in the above formulas.

EXAMPLE 11. In Example 4 the prior mean and standard deviation for the equipment decision problem were determined to be $M_0 = 80$ and $S_0 = 15$. Suppose the calculators are manufactured on a pilot basis and distributed through nine randomly selected retail outlets. The mean sales level per outlet is found to be $\bar{X} = 110$ units with a standard deviation of $s = 18$ units. With σ unknown, we use the estimator of $\sigma_{\bar{x}}^2$: $s_{\bar{x}}^2 = \dfrac{s^2}{n} = \dfrac{324}{9} = 36$ and (16.17) to calculate the posterior mean:

$$M_1 = \frac{M_0\sigma_{\bar{x}}^2 + \bar{X}S_0^2}{S_0^2 + \sigma_{\bar{x}}^2} = \frac{(80)(36) + (110)(225)}{225 + 36} = \frac{27{,}630}{261} = 105.9 \text{ units}$$

The variance of the posterior distribution is designated S_1^2, with the square root of this value being the posterior standard deviation S_1. The conceptual basis by which the posterior variance is determined is indicated by the equation

$$\frac{1}{S_1^2} = \frac{1}{S_0^2} + \frac{1}{\sigma_{\bar{x}}^2} \tag{16.18}$$

Formula (16.18) indicates that the reciprocal of the posterior variance is equal to the reciprocal of the prior variance plus the reciprocal of the variance of the mean. Note that from the standpoint of decision analysis a larger variance indicates greater uncertainty, and that the larger the variance the smaller its reciprocal.

The computational formula derived from (16.18) is

$$S_1^2 = \frac{S_0^2\sigma_{\bar{x}}^2}{S_0^2 + \sigma_{\bar{x}}^2} \tag{16.19}$$

As was the case in determining the posterior mean, if the population standard deviation σ is unknown, the sample deviation s is generally used to compute $s_{\bar{x}}^2$ as an estimator of $\sigma_{\bar{x}}^2$.

EXAMPLE 12. Given the information in Example 11, we compute the variance and standard deviation of the posterior distribution as follows.

$$S_1^2 = \frac{S_0^2\sigma_{\bar{x}}^2}{S_0^2 + \sigma_{\bar{x}}^2} \cong \frac{S_0^2 s_{\bar{x}}^2}{S_0^2 + s_{\bar{x}}^2} = \frac{(225)(36)}{225 + 36} = \frac{8100}{261} = 31.03$$

$$S_1 = 5.57 \cong 5.6$$

After the posterior probability distribution is formulated, the best act in the decision situation is determined on the basis of this revised probability distribution and the payoff functions previously established.   As explained in Section 15.4, the sample information only has value if there is a change in the identification of the best act as the result of the prior distribution having been revised.   As in Chapter 15, the estimated value of sample information for a sample that has already been taken is

$$VSI = \text{(Posterior expected value of best posterior act)}$$
$$- \text{(Posterior expected value of best prior act)} \qquad (16.20)$$

EXAMPLE 13.   In Example 7, the payoff functions for the equipment decision problem based on mean sales per outlet were identified as:

$$V(A_1) = -350{,}000 + 5000\mu \qquad V(A_2) = -450{,}000 + 6000\mu$$

Using the posterior mean value of $M_1 = 105.9$, we determine the expected value associated with each act:

$$V(A_1) = -350{,}000 + 5000(105.9) = \$179{,}500 \qquad V(A_2) = -450{,}000 + 6000(105.9) = \$185{,}400$$

Therefore, on the basis of the Bayesian posterior analysis act A_2 is chosen, as contrasted to act A_1 being chosen on the basis of the prior analysis.   The estimated value of the sample which was obtained in this case is

$$VSI = \text{(Posterior expected value of best posterior act)}$$
$$- \text{(Posterior expected value of the best prior act)}$$
$$= 185{,}400 - 179{,}500 = \$5900$$

16.6   PREPOSTERIOR ANALYSIS AND THE EXPECTED VALUE OF SAMPLE INFORMATION (*EVSI*)

Because the prior mean is considered to be an unbiased estimator of the population mean, there is no basis for anticipating a difference between the values of the prior mean and the posterior mean before a sample is taken.   However, we can anticipate that the posterior variance will be smaller in value than the prior variance.   From Section 16.4, recall that the expected opportunity loss of the best act is dependent on the difference between the mean of the probability distribution and the breakeven point.   When the variance is reduced, the *EOL* (and thus the *EVPI*) is reduced because the difference between the mean and breakeven point is then greater in units of the standard deviation.   Conceptually, the *expected value of sample information* is the expected difference between the *EVPI* before the sample and the *EVPI* after the sample.   Thus the *EVSI* is the expected reduction in the expected opportunity loss associated with the best act as the result of taking a sample of a specified size.

The reduction in the variance between the prior and posterior probability distributions is designated S_*^2, and can be determined by either of the following formulas:

$$S_*^2 = S_0^2 - S_1^2 \qquad (16.21)$$

$$S_*^2 = \frac{S_0^4}{S_0^2 + \sigma_{\bar{x}}^2} \qquad (16.22)$$

In the computational formula (*16.22*), the value of the population standard deviation is required in order to determine the variance of the mean $\sigma_{\bar{x}}^2$.   However, this value is generally not known.   Further, a sample estimator is not available because the sample has not yet been taken.   Therefore, the value of σ has to be estimated by reference to other similar decision situations.

Once the value of S_*^2 is determined, the expected value of sample information is calculated by the formula

$$EVSI = bS_*L(D_*) \qquad (16.23)$$

where $\quad b = |b_1 - b_2|$

$$D_* = \left| \frac{\mu_b - M_0}{S_*} \right|$$

$L(D_*)$ = the unit normal loss function for D_* (see Appendix 9)

In (16.23), b is the slope of the loss function associated with the best act (see Section 16.4). D_* is similar to D in the formula for $EVPI$ presented in Section 16.4, except that S_* is in the denominator of the formula instead of S_0.

EXAMPLE 14. In Example 4 the prior mean and standard deviation for the equipment decision problem on a per-outlet basis were determined to be $M_0 = 80$ and $S_0 = 15$. For hand-held calculators manufactured by other companies we have information which indicates that the standard deviation of the sales per outlet for the time period of concern is approximately $\sigma = 20$. We can determine the expected value of the information from a market study involving nine retail outlets as follows:

$$S_*^2 = \frac{S_0^4}{S_0^2 + \sigma_{\bar{x}}^2} = \frac{(15)^4}{(15)^2 + 44.44} = \frac{50,625}{225 + 44.44} = \frac{50,625}{269.44} = 187.89$$

where $\quad \text{Est. } \sigma_{\bar{x}}^2 = \frac{\text{Est } \sigma^2}{n} = \frac{(20)^2}{9} = \frac{400}{9} = 44.44$

$$EVSI = bS_*L(D_*) = (1000)(13.71)(0.03208) = \$439.82$$

where $\quad b = |Nb_1 - Nb_2| = |5000 - 6000| = 1000 \quad$ (from Example 10)

$$D_* = \left| \frac{\mu_b - M_0}{S_*} \right| = \left| \frac{100 - 80}{13.71} \right| = 1.46$$

$$L(D_*) = 0.03208$$

Recall that in Example 13 the estimated value of sample information for a particular sample of $n = 9$ which had *already* been collected was found to be \$5900. The $EVSI$ of \$439.82 computed in Example 14 indicates that this would be the long-run average value for a sample of size $n = 9$. In many specific instances a sample will have a value of \$0, because the identification of the best act will not have been affected by the sample information.

16.7 EXPECTED NET GAIN FROM SAMPLING ($ENGS$) AND OPTIMUM SAMPLE SIZE

The expected net gain from sampling and the optimum sampling size for our equipment decision problem are determined in Example 15. See Section 15.6 for a discussion of these concepts and procedures.

EXAMPLE 15. In Example 14 we found that the $EVSI$ for a sample of $n = 9$ is \$439.82. Suppose that the cost of designing the marketing study is \$300 and the cost of obtaining the sales data from each sampled retail outlet is \$10. Given the prior probability distribution with $M_0 = 80$, $S_0 = 15$, and estimated $\sigma = 20$, we can determine the $ENGS$ associated with the alternative sample sizes of $n_1 = 9$, $n_2 = 12$, and $n_3 = 15$ as follows:

For $n = 9$: $EVSI = \$439.82$ (from Example 14)

$$ENGS = EVSI - CS = 439.82 - 390.00 = \$49.82$$

For $n = 12$:

$$S_*^2 = \frac{S_0^4}{S_0^2 + \sigma_{\bar{x}}^2} = \frac{(15)^4}{(15)^2 + 33.33} = \frac{50,625}{258.33} = 195.97$$

where   Est. $\sigma_{\bar{x}}^2 = \frac{\text{Est } \sigma^2}{n} = \frac{(20)^2}{12} = \frac{400}{12} = 33.33$

$$EVSI = bS_* L(D_*) = (1000)(14.00)(0.03431) = \$480.34$$

where $b = |b_1 - b_2| = |5000 - 6000| = 1000$

$$D_* = \left| \frac{\mu_b - M_0}{S_*} \right| = \left| \frac{100 - 80}{14.00} \right| = 1.43$$

$$ENGS = EVSI - CS = 480.34 - 420.00 = \$60.34$$

For $n = 15$:

$$S_*^2 = \frac{S_0^4}{S_0^2 + \sigma_{\bar{x}}^2} = \frac{(15)^4}{(15)^2 + 26.67} = \frac{50,625}{251.67} = 201.16$$

where $\sigma_{\bar{x}}^2 = \frac{\text{Est } \sigma^2}{n} = \frac{(20)^2}{15} = \frac{400}{15} = 26.67$

$$EVSI = bS_* L(D_*) = (1000)(14.18)(0.03587) = \$508.64$$

where $b = |b_1 - b_2| = |5000 - 6000| = 1000$

$$D_* = \left| \frac{\mu_b - M_0}{S_*} \right| = \left| \frac{100 - 80}{14.18} \right| = 1.41$$

$$EVSI = (1000)(14.18)(0.03587) = \$508.64$$

$$ENGS = 508.64 - 450 = \$58.64$$

Refer to the summarized information in Table 16.1. Of the three sample sizes considered, the optimum sample size is at $n = 12$, with the $ENGS = \$60.34$. Although all possible sample sizes were not considered, because the $ENGS$ associated with $n = 9$ and $n = 15$ are both smaller than the $ENGS$ for $n = 12$, it is obvious that by the sample size of $n = 15$ the point of the optimum sample size has been passed, and that the optimum is somewhere between $n = 9$ and $n = 15$.

Table 16.1   *EVSI, CS* and *ENGS* for the
Equipment Purchase Decision
According to Sample Size

Sample size, n	*EVSI*	*CS*	*ENGS*
0	$ 0	$ 0	$ 0
9	439.82	390.00	49.82
12	480.34	420.00	60.34
15	508.64	450.00	58.64

Finally, the *overall terminal expected payoff* (*OTEP*) and *net overall terminal expected payoff* (*NOTEP*) can be determined in conjunction with preposterior analysis. These concepts are explained in Section 15.6, where the calculations are illustrated in Example 13.

16.8   BAYESIAN DECISION ANALYSIS VS. CLASSICAL DECISION PROCEDURES

This chapter and the preceding two chapters have been concerned with Bayesian decision analysis, as contrasted to the coverage of classical decision procedures in Chapters 8 through

13. The principal techniques of classical inference are interval estimation and hypothesis testing. The principal concern of Bayesian decision analysis is the choice of a decision act. Although the classical techniques are directly concerned with estimating or testing hypotheses concerning population parameters, the results of these procedures relate to alternative courses of action, or decisions. For example, the acceptance of the null hypothesis that the average sales level for a product will be below the breakeven point would be associated with the decision not to market the product. Thus, both classical and Bayesian procedures can be concerned with the process of choosing best decision acts.

The main difference between classical and Bayesian procedures is the use of subjective (prior) information in Bayesian decision analysis and the evaluation of alternative decision acts in terms of economic consequences (or possibly utilities). The economic consequences can be formulated in terms of either conditional values (payoffs) or conditional opportunity losses (regrets). Essentially, the choice of α and β levels for the probabilities of Type I and Type II error is the basis by which the importance of the two alternative types of mistakes is assessed in hypothesis testing. The use of opportunity losses in Bayesian analysis represents a similar evaluation in a more explicit way. Whereas classical decision procedures are based entirely on the analysis of data collected through random sampling, Bayesian procedures can include the analysis of sample data (through posterior analysis), but are not dependent on the availability of such data.

From the standpoint of practical considerations, an important factor associated with the development of Bayesian decision analysis is that such analysis begins with an identification of managerial judgments, and such judgments are included in the analysis. This means that the statistical analyst is required to work closely with managerial personnel. In contrast, the exclusive orientation toward sample data in classical decision procedures does not give managers the opportunity to input their judgments into the decision analysis, and to feel that their judgments are considered to be important by the statistical decision analyst.

Solved Problems

DECISION ANALYSIS PRIOR TO ANY SAMPLING

16.1. The owner of a small manufacturing company is considering the addition of electrical generators to the line of automotive electrical equipment being manufactured. The capital investment required to manufacture the generators is $150,000, and there is a profit of $2.00 per generator sold through the established distribution system of 100 retail outlets. During the total relevant period of time, the owner estimates that the average sales of the electrical generators per retail outlet will be 700 units, and that there is a 50 percent chance that the average sales level per outlet will be between 600 and 800 units.

(a) Assuming a normal prior probability distribution, determine the mean and standard deviation of this distribution.

(b) The two possible decision acts are A_1: Manufacture the generators and A_2: Don't manufacture the generators. Formulate the linear payoff functions associated with these acts and portray them on a common graph.

(a) $M_0 = 700$ units

$$\frac{2}{3}S_0 = \frac{\text{Middle 50\% interval}}{2} = \frac{800 - 600}{2} = 100 \qquad S_0 = 150$$

(b) $V(A_1) = k_1 + Nb_1\mu = -150,000 + (100)(2)\mu = -150,000 + 200\mu$

$V(A_2) = k_2 + Nb_2\mu = 0 + (100)(0)\mu = 0$

Figure 16-5 portrays these two linear payoff functions.

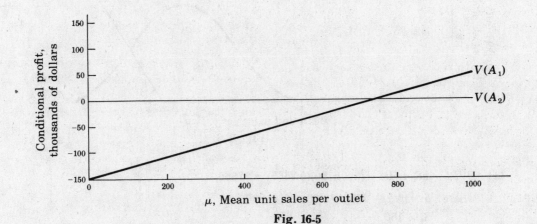

Fig. 16-5

16.2.   Determine the best act for the decision situation in Problem 16.1 by calculating the expected values associated with the two possible acts.

$EV(A_1) = k_1 + Nb_1M_0 = -150,000 + (100)(2)(700) = \$-10,000$

$EV(A_2) = k_2 + Nb_2M_0 = 0 + 100(0)700 = 0$

Therefore, the best act is A_2: Don't manufacture the generators.

16.3.   Referring to Problem 16.1,   (a) determine the breakeven value in terms of the mean unit sales per outlet, and   (b) formulate the linear piecewise loss functions for the two possible acts.   Portray the loss function of act A_2: Don't manufacture on a graph with the normal prior probability distribution superimposed on this graph.

(a) $\mu_b = \dfrac{k_2 - k_1}{Nb_1 - Nb_2} = \dfrac{0 - (-150,000)}{100(2) - 100(0)} = \dfrac{150,000}{200} = \$750$

Note that this is the mean sales volume at which the two linear payoff functions cross in Fig. 16-5.

(b) $OL(A_1, \mu) \begin{cases} = 0 & \text{for } \mu \geq \mu_b \ (=750) \\ = 200(750 - \mu) & \text{for } \mu < \mu_b \ (=750) \end{cases}$

$OL(A_2, \mu) \begin{cases} = 200(\mu - 750) & \text{for } \mu > \mu_b \ (=750) \\ = 0 & \text{for } \mu \leq \mu_b \ (=750) \end{cases}$

See Fig. 16-6.

16.4.   For Problems 16.1 to 16.3,   (a) determine the expected value of perfect information.   (b) Suppose the owner of this manufacturing firm chooses the best act as identified by the Bayesian analysis.   What is the probability that his decision will turn out to be wrong?

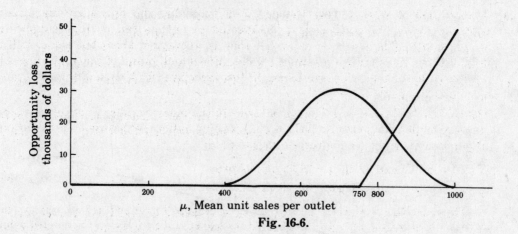

μ, Mean unit sales per outlet

Fig. 16-6.

(a) $EVPI = bS_0\,L(D) = (200)(150)(0.2555) = \$7665$

where $b = |Nb_1 - Nb_2| = |200 - 0| = 200$

$S_0 = 150$

$$D = \left|\frac{\mu_b - \mu_0}{S_0}\right| = \left|\frac{750 - 700}{150}\right| = \frac{50}{150} = 0.33$$

$L(D) = 0.2555$ (from Appendix 9)

(b) Refer to Fig. 16-6. The probability that the decision not to market the generators will turn out to be wrong is equivalent to the probability that the mean sales per outlet will exceed the breakeven of 750 units.   Converting the breakeven value into a unit-normal z value, we have:

$$z = \frac{\mu_b - M_0}{S_0} = \frac{750 - 700}{150} = 0.33$$

Therefore

$$P(\mu > 750) = P(z > 0.33) = 0.5000 - P(0 \le z \le 0.33)$$
$$= 0.5000 - 0.1293 = 0.3707 \cong 0.37$$

16.5. An office manager can purchase a photocopy machine from one of two manufacturers. The brand Y machine costs \$8000 and involves a variable cost of 5¢ per page of copy produced. Brand Z costs \$9000 but involves a variable cost of 4.5¢ per page of copy produced.

(a) Formulate the linear cost function associated with act A_1: Buy brand Y, and act A_2: Buy brand Z.

(b) The manager estimates the useful life of each machine as being 500 weeks. Reformulate the linear cost functions determined in (a) in terms of the average pages of copy produced per week.

(a) $C(A_1) = k_1 + b_1X = 8000 + 0.05X$

$C(A_2) = k_2 + b_2X = 9000 + 0.045X$

Note: These cost functions could be expressed as payoff functions by attaching negative signs to both the capital investment and the incremental costs in the above equations.   However, in comparative cost studies it is generally considered more convenient to consider the values as positive values but to label them as representing costs.

(b) $C(A_1) = k_1 + Nb_1\mu = 8000 + (500)(0.05)\mu = 8000 + 25\mu$

$C(A_2) = k_2 + Nb_2\mu = 9000 + (500)(0.045)\mu = 9000 + 22.5\mu$

16.6. (a) The volume of work during the period of time that the photocopy machine in Problem 16.5 is to be used is not expected to change (an obvious simplifying assumption!). The manager estimates that an average of about 500 copies will be produced per week on the machine. Determine which brand of machine should be purchased based on the overall expected cost associated with each of the two brands of copy equipment.

(b) Determine the breakeven volume in terms of the mean number of copies produced per week which would result in the manager being indifferent between the two brands of equipment in terms of overall expected cost.

(a) $EC(A_1) = k_1 + Nb_1M_0 = 8000 + 25(500) = \$20,500$

   $EC(A_2) = k_2 + Nb_2M_0 = 9000 + 22.5(500) = \$20,250$

Therefore, the best act is A_2: Buy brand Z, because this brand has a lower expected cost associated with it. (*Note*: If the analysis had been done in terms of expected values, the two values above would have negative signs and thus the largest value would be associated with act A_2.)

(b) $\mu_b = \dfrac{k_2 - k_1}{Nb_1 - Nb_2} = \dfrac{9000 - 8000}{500(0.05) - 500(0.045)} = \dfrac{1000}{25 - 22.5} = 400$ copies per week

16.7. Refer to Problems 16.5 and 16.6. (a) Assuming a normal prior probability distribution, the standard deviation of such a distribution can be determined based on the manager estimating any two percentile points in this distribution, and not necessarily by his identifying a middle 50 percent credibility interval. The established prior mean of 500 copies per week is of course at the 50th percentile point of the distribution. In addition, suppose the manager estimates that there is only a 10 percent chance that the average number of copies produced per week will exceed 700. Determine the standard deviation of the prior probability distribution. (b) Formulate the linear piecewise loss functions for the two acts on the basis of the mean number of copies produced per week.

(a) By reference to the standard normal distribution (Appendix 4), we observe that the value associated with the 90th percentile point is approximately $z = +1.28$. We can use a general formula for z and solve for the unknown S_0 as follows:

$$z = \frac{\mu - M_0}{S_0} \qquad S_0 = \frac{\mu - M_0}{z} = \frac{700 - 500}{1.28} = 156.25$$

(b) $OL(A_1, \mu)\begin{cases} = 2.5(400 - \mu) & \text{for } \mu > \mu_b \ (=400) \\ = 0 & \text{for } \mu \le \mu_b \ (=400) \end{cases}$

   $OL(A_2, \mu)\begin{cases} = 0 & \text{for } \mu \ge \mu_b \ (=400) \\ = 2.5(\mu - 400) & \text{for } \mu < \mu_b \ (=400) \end{cases}$

16.8. Determine the *EVPI* for the photocopy machine decision described in Problems 16.5 to 16.7.

$$EVPI = bS_0 L(D) = (2.5)(156.25)(0.1580) = \$61.71875 \cong \$61.72$$

where $b = |Nb_1 - Nb_2| = |25 - 22.5| = 2.5$

   $S_0 = 156.25$

   $D = \left|\dfrac{\mu_b - M_0}{S_0}\right| = \left|\dfrac{400 - 500}{156.25}\right| = \dfrac{100}{156.25} = 0.64$

   $L(D) = 0.1580$ (from Appendix 9)

The low value of the *EVPI* indicates that there is neither a great deal of financial risk associated with this decision-making situation, nor much expected economic gain possibility associated with sampling.

BAYESIAN POSTERIOR ANALYSIS

16.9. With reference to Problems 16.1 to 16.4, a generator similar to the one which is to be manufactured is test-marketed in 10 randomly selected outlets. The mean sales per outlet is $\bar{X} = 800$ with the sample standard deviation $s = 110$. Determine the mean and standard deviation of the posterior distribution.

$$M_1 = \frac{M_0\sigma_{\bar{x}}^2 + \bar{X}S_0^2}{S_0^2 + \sigma_{\bar{x}}^2} = \frac{(700)(1100) + (800)(22{,}500)}{22{,}500 + 1100} = \frac{18{,}770{,}000}{23{,}600} = 795.3 \text{ units}$$

where Est. $\sigma_{\bar{x}}^2 = \dfrac{s^2}{n}\left(\dfrac{N-n}{N-1}\right) = \dfrac{12{,}100}{10}\left(\dfrac{100-10}{100-1}\right) = (1210)(0.909) = 1099.999 \cong 1100$

(The finite correction factor is used in this case because $n > 0.05N$. See Section 8.2.)

$$S_1^2 = \frac{S_0^2\sigma_{\bar{x}}^2}{S_0^2 + \sigma_{\bar{x}}^2} = \frac{(22{,}500)(1100)}{22{,}500 + 1100} = \frac{24{,}750{,}000}{23{,}600} = 1048.7288$$

$$S_1 = 32.38$$

16.10. With reference to Problem 16.9,   (a) determine the best decision act (A_1: Manufacture the generators, or A_2: Don't manufacture the generators).   (b) What is the estimated value of the sample information?

(a) $EV(A_1) = k_1 + Nb_1M_1 = -150{,}000 + (100)(2)(795.3) = \$9060$

$EV(A_2) = k_2 + Nb_2M_1 = 0 + (100)(0)(795.3) = 0$

Therefore, the best act is A_1: Manufacture the generators.

(b) VSI = (Posterior expected value of best posterior act)

$\qquad\qquad$ − (Posterior expected value of best prior act)

$\qquad = 9060 - 0 = \$9060$

16.11. In Problem 16.4 the *EVPI* prior to any sample was determined to be \$7665.   (a) How is it possible for the value of sample information determined in Problem 16.10 to exceed the *EVPI*? (b) Determine the *EVPI* (posterior) for the generator manufacturing decision. That is, calculate the expected value of perfect information after the sample described in Problem 16.9 has been taken and incorporated into the analysis.

(a)   *EVPI* is the *expected* value of perfect information. Therefore, it is in fact possible that a particular sample result will have an estimated value which exceeds this long-run average value of perfect information.

(b)   *EVPI* (posterior) $= bS_1L(D_1) = (200)(32.38)(0.03667) = \$237.47$

$\qquad$ where $b = 200$

$\qquad\qquad S_1 = 32.38$

$$D_1 = \left|\frac{\mu_b - M_1}{S_1}\right| = \left|\frac{750 - 795.3}{32.38}\right| = \frac{45.3}{32.38} = 1.40$$

$\qquad L(D_1) = 0.03667$ (from Appendix 9)

16.12. The office manager in Problems 16.5 to 16.8 decides to maintain a count of the number of copies required in the department during a 5-week period before purchasing one of the brands of photocopy equipment.   He considers these 5 weeks to be a random sample of the 500-week period (again, a simplifying assumption!).   The mean number of copies for this sampled period is $\bar{X} = 450$ with the standard deviation $s = 100$.   Determine the mean and standard deviation of the posterior distribution.

$$M_1 = \frac{M_0\sigma_{\bar{x}}^2 + \bar{X}S_0^2}{S_0^2 + \sigma_{\bar{x}}^2} = \frac{(500)(2000) + (450)(156.25)^2}{(156.25)^2 + 2000} = \frac{11,986,327}{26,414.062} = 453.8$$

where   Est. $\sigma_{\bar{x}}^2 = \dfrac{s^2}{n} = \dfrac{10,000}{5} = 2000$

$$S_1^2 = \frac{S_0^2\sigma_{\bar{x}}^2}{S_0^2 + \sigma_{\bar{x}}^2} = \frac{(24,414.062)(2000)}{24,414.062 + 2000} = 1848.5655$$

$$S_1 = 42.99$$

16.13. Referring to Problem 16.12, determine   (a) the best act (A_1: Buy brand Y or A_2: Buy brand Z) on the basis of the posterior distribution, and   (b) the estimated value of this sample information.

(a) $EC(A_1) = k_1 + Nb_1M_1 = 8000 + 25(453.8) = \$19,345$

$EC(A_2) = k_2 + Nb_2M_1 = 9000 + 22.5(453.8) = \$19,210.50$

Therefore, the best act is A_2: Buy brand Z, because this brand has a lower associated expected cost.

(b)   Since the identification of the best act was not changed as the result of the sample information, the sample had no value.   Or using the general formula:

VSI = (Posterior expected value of best posterior act)

− (Posterior expected value of best prior act)

$= -19,210.50 - (-19,210.50) = \$0$

THE EXPECTED VALUE OF SAMPLE INFORMATION (*EVSI*) AND THE EXPECTED NET GAIN FROM SAMPLING (*ENGS*)

16.14. Referring to Problems 16.1 and 16.4, determine the expected value of sample information (*EVSI*) associated with a sample of $n = 10$ outlets.

Given the prior mean $M_0 = 700$, the prior standard deviation $S_0 = 150$, and the estimated standard deviation of sales per outlet $\sigma = 300$,

$$S_*^2 = \frac{S_0^4}{S^2 + \sigma_{\bar{x}}^2} = \frac{(150)^4}{(150)^2 + 8181} = \frac{506,250,000}{30,681} \cong 16,500$$

$$S_* = 128$$

where   Est. $\sigma_{\bar{x}}^2 = \dfrac{\text{Est. } \sigma^2}{n}\left(\dfrac{N-n}{N-1}\right) = \dfrac{90,000}{10}\left(\dfrac{100-10}{100-1}\right) = (9000)(0.909) \cong 8181$

(The finite correction factor is used because $n > 0.05N$.   See Section 8.2.)

$$EVSI = bS_*L(D_*) = (200)(128)(0.2339) = \$5988$$

where $b = |Nb_1 - Nb_2| = |200 - 0| = 200$

$$D_* = \left|\frac{\mu_b - M_0}{S_*}\right| = \left|\frac{750 - 700}{128}\right| = \frac{50}{128} = 0.39$$

$L(D_*) = 0.2339$ (from Appendix 9)

16.15. In Problems 16.6 and 16.7, the prior mean in terms of average copies produced per week was $M_0 = 500$ with $S_0 \cong 156$. Determine the $EVSI$ associated with a sample of $n = 5$ if Est. $\sigma = 250$.

$$S_*^2 = \frac{S_0^4}{S_0^2 + \sigma_{\bar{x}}^2} = \frac{(156)^4}{(156)^2 + 12,500} = \frac{592,240,896}{36,836} = 16,077.77$$

$$S_* = 126.80$$

where Est. $\sigma_{\bar{x}}^2 = \frac{\text{Est. } \sigma_{\bar{x}}^2}{n} = \frac{62,500}{5} = 12,500$

$$EVSI = bS_*L(D_*) = (2.5)(126.80)(0.1223) = \$38.77$$

where $b = |Nb_1 - Nb_2| = |25 - 22.5| = 2.5$

$$D_* = \left| \frac{\mu_b - M_0}{S_*} \right| = \left| \frac{400 - 500}{126.80} \right| = \frac{100}{126.80} = 0.79$$

$$L(D_*) = 0.1223$$

In Problem 16.8, the $EVPI$ was determined to be \$61.72. Thus, the expected value of a sample of just 5 weeks would serve to reduce the economic uncertainty associated with this decision situation by \$38.77, on the average.

16.16. With reference to Problem 16.15, suppose the cost of tallying the number of copies currently being produced in the department is evaluated as being \$5.00 per week. Determine the expected net gain associated with a sample of $n = 5$ weeks.

$$ENGS = EVSI - CS = 38.77 - 25.00 = \$13.77$$

Supplementary Problems

DECISION ANALYSIS PRIOR TO ANY SAMPLING

16.17. A distributor has the option of handling a new line of office furniture. Handling this line will require an additional capital expenditure of \$80,000 for new storage facilities. The incremental profit (over variable costs) associated with handling the office furniture is 10 percent of the dollar sales volume. During the period in which the capital expenditure is to be amortized, the owner of the firm estimates that the most likely dollar sales volume for the furniture will be \$900,000, and that there is a 50 percent chance the volume will be between \$750,000 and \$1,050,000.

(a) Assuming a normal prior probability distribution, determine the mean and standard deviation of this distribution.

(b) The two possible decision acts are A_1: Distribute and A_2: Don't distribute. Formulate the linear payoff functions associated with these acts and portray these payoff functions on a common graph.

Ans. (a) $M_0 = \$900,000$ and $S_0 = \$225,000$

16.18. Determine the best act for the decision situation described in Problem 16.17.

Ans. A_1 (Distribute), with $EV = \$10,000$

16.19. For Problem 16.17, (a) determine the breakeven value in terms of total dollar sales volume required. (b) Formulate the linear piecewise loss functions for the two possible acts. Portray the loss function of act A_1: Distribute, on a graph with the normal prior probability distribution superimposed on this graph.

Ans.   (*a*) X_b = $800,000

16.20.   For Problems 16.17 to 16.19,   (*a*) what is the maximum average value that any market information can be worth?   (*b*) Suppose the owner of this distributorship chooses the best act as identified by the Bayesian analysis.   What is the probability that this decision is correct?

Ans.   (*a*) $4880.25,   (*b*) $P = 0.67$

16.21.   The manufacture of a new product will require a capital investment of $100,000.   For this product, the variable cost of manufacturing will be $2.00 per unit, the selling price will be $5.00 per unit, and the marketing manager estimates that the most likely average sales level per retail outlet is 80 units.   There are 500 retail outlets.   Assuming a normal prior probability distribution, determine whether the best act is A_1: Manufacture or A_2: Don't manufacture by determining the expected values associated with these acts.

Ans. A_1: Manufacture, with EV = $20,000

16.22.   Continuing with Problem 16.21, the marketing manager states that there is a 70 percent probability that sales of the product will exceed an average of 75 units per outlet.   Determine (*a*) the standard deviation of the normal prior probability distribution and   (*b*) the expected value of perfect information.

Ans.   (*a*) $S_0 = 9.6$,   (*b*) $EVPI$ = $540

16.23.   The uncertainty inherent in the estimate of the total sales for a new product line is assumed to follow a normal distribution, with $M_0 = 7000$ units and $S_0 = 1000$ units.   The capital investment required to add the new product line is $80,000, and the markup (over variable cost) for each item sold is $10.   Indicate the best decision act for this situation (A_1: Market, or A_2: Don't market) and the associated expected value.

Ans. A_2: Don't market, with $EV = 0$

16.24.   Refer to Problem 16.23.   If the firm conducts a market study to test the product line in a sample region, what is the maximum amount that such additional information could be worth, on the average?

Ans. $833

BAYESIAN POSTERIOR ANALYSIS

16.25.   When the prior probability distribution has been determined on a total market basis, the per-outlet values of the prior mean, prior standard deviation, and the breakeven point can be determined simply by dividing each of the respective total-market values by the number of outlets involved.   For Problems 16.17 to 16.20, suppose there is a total of 800 outlets nationwide.   Determine the per-outlet values of the   (*a*) prior mean,   (*b*) prior standard deviation, and   (*c*) breakeven point.

Ans.   (*a*) $M_0 = \$1125$,   (*b*) $S_0 \cong \$281$,   (*c*) $\mu_b = \$1000$

16.26.   In relation to the transformation to per-outlet values carried out in Problem 16.25, suppose a sample of $n = 4$ outlets are randomly selected to test the marketability of the product line.   For this sample, the mean sales level for the line of office furniture is $\bar{X} = \$900$ with $s = \$300$.   Determine the   (*a*) mean and   (*b*) standard deviation of the posterior distribution of the estimated level of sales per outlet.

Ans.   (*a*) $M_1 \cong \$950$,   (*b*) $S_1 \cong \$132$

16.27. (a) On the basis of the posterior distribution determined in Problem 16.26, determine the best act (A_1: Distribute, or A_2: Don't distribute) for the decision problem described in Problems 16.17 to 16.20.

(b) What is the estimated value of the sample information obtained in Problem 16.26?

Ans.   (a) A_2: Don't distribute, (b) $4000

16.28. Referring to Problems 16.21 and 16.22, suppose the product is offered through 10 randomly selected outlets. The mean sales level of the product in these outlets is $\bar{X} = 60.0$ units with $s = 25.0$ units. Determine the (a) mean and (b) standard deviation of the posterior distribution of the estimated level of sales per outlet.

Ans.   (a) $M_1 = 68.1$,   (b) $S_1 = 6.1$

16.29. Continuing with Problem 16.28, identify (a) the best act and (b) the estimated value of the sample information which was collected.

Ans.   (a) A_1: Manufacture, (b) $0

16.30. (a) Determine the *EVPI* for Problems 16.21 and 16.22 after the sample described in Problem 16.28 has been obtained.

(b) Compare the value of the posterior *EVPI* determined in (a), above, with the *EVPI* of $540 determined prior to the sample in Problem 16.22. Explain the meaning of the change which occurred.

Ans.   (a) Posterior *EVPI* $\cong$ $2694

THE EXPECTED VALUE OF SAMPLE INFORMATION (*EVSI*) AND THE EXPECTED NET GAIN FROM SAMPLING (*ENGS*)

16.31. In Problems 16.21 and 16.22, the prior probability distribution on a per-outlet basis was determined to be $M_0 = 80.0$ and $S_0 = 9.6$. There is a total of 500 retail outlets. If the product is manufactured, it is estimated that the standard deviation of the sales level within each outlet will be about $\sigma = 30$. Determine the *EVSI* associated with a sample of $n = 10$ outlets.

Ans.   *EVSI* = $96.34

16.32. Explain the reason for the difference between the *EVSI* of $96.34 for a sample of $n = 10$ computed in Problem 16.31, and the estimated value of $0 for the sample of $n = 10$ determined in Problems 16.28 and 16.29.

16.33. In respect to the sample being contemplated in Problem 16.31, suppose the cost associated with having each outlet participate in such a study is $15. Determine the *ENGS* for a sample of $n = 10$.

Ans.   *ENGS* = $-53.66

Chapter 17

Linear Regression and Correlation Analysis

17.1 OBJECTIVES AND ASSUMPTIONS OF REGRESSION ANALYSIS

The primary objective of regression analysis is to predict the value of one variable (the *dependent variable*) given that the value of an associated variable (the *independent variable*) is known. The *regression equation* is the algebraic formula by which the predicted value of the dependent variable is determined (see Section 17.3).

The term *simple regression analysis* indicates that the dependent variable is predicted on the basis of one independent variable, whereas *multiple regression analysis* (covered in Chapter 18) is concerned with predicting the dependent variable on the basis of two or more independent variables.

The general assumptions underlying the regression analysis model presented in this chapter are that (1) the dependent variable is a random variable, (2) the independent and dependent variables are linearly associated, and (3) the variances of the conditional distributions of the dependent variable, given different values of the independent variable, are equal (*homoscedasticity*). Assumption (1) indicates that although the values of the independent variable may be designated, the values of the dependent variable must be obtained through the process of sampling.

If internal estimation is used in conjunction with regression analysis, an additional assumption is that the conditional distributions of the dependent variable, given different values of the independent variable, are all normal distributions for the population of values.

EXAMPLE 1. An analyst wishes to predict delivery time as the dependent variable based on distance as the independent variable for industrial parts shipped by truck. Suppose he chooses 10 recent shipments from the company's records such that the highway distances involved are about equally dispersed between 100 miles distance and 1000 miles distance, and he records the delivery time for each shipment. Since the highway distance is to be used as the independent variable, his selection of trips of specific distances is acceptable. On the other hand, the dependent variable of delivery time is a random variable in this study, which conforms to the assumption underlying regression analysis. Whether or not the two variables have a linear relationship would generally be determined by constructing a scatter diagram (see Section 17.2). This diagram is also used to observe whether the scatter (variance) is about equal along the regression line.

17.2 THE SCATTER DIAGRAM

A *scatter diagram* is a graph in which each plotted point represents an observed pair of values for the independent and dependent variables. The value of the independent variable, X, is plotted in respect to the horizontal axis and the value of the dependent variable, Y, is plotted in respect to the vertical axis. (See Problem 17.1.)

The form of the relationship represented by the scatter diagram can be *curvilinear* rather than linear. While regression analysis for curvilinear relationships is beyond the scope of this outline, there is a limited discussion of curvilinear trend analysis in Section 19.2. For relationships that are not linear a frequent approach is to determine a method of transforming values so that the relationship of the transformed values is linear. Then linear regression analysis can be applied to the transformed values, and estimated values of the dependent variable can be transformed back to the original measurement scale.

EXAMPLE 2. An example of a curvilinear relationship would be the relationship between years since incorporation for a company and sales level, given that each year the sales level has increased by the same percentage over the preceding year. The resulting curve with an increasing slope would be indicative of a so-called exponential relationship.

If the scatter diagram indicates a relationship that is generally linear, then a best-fitting straight line is fitted to the data. The precise location of this line is determined by the method of least squares (see Section 17.3). As illustrated in Example 3, a regression line with a positive slope indicates a direct relationship between the variables, a negative slope indicates an inverse relationship between the variables, and a slope of zero indicates that the variables are unrelated. Further, the extent of scatter of the plotted points in respect to the regression line indicates the degree of relationship between the two variables.

EXAMPLE 3. Figure 17-1 includes several scatter diagrams and associated regression lines demonstrating several types of relationships between the variables.

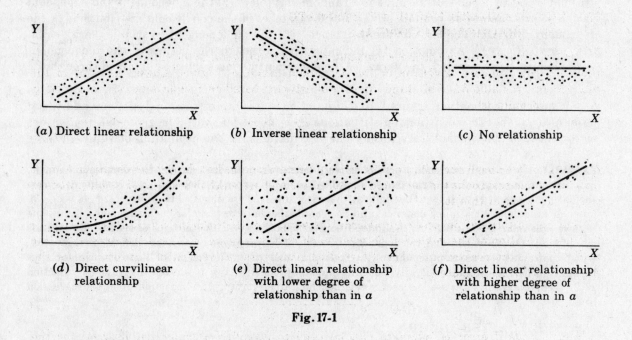

(*a*) Direct linear relationship

(*b*) Inverse linear relationship

(*c*) No relationship

(*d*) Direct curvilinear relationship

(*e*) Direct linear relationship with lower degree of relationship than in *a*

(*f*) Direct linear relationship with higher degree of relationship than in *a*

Fig. 17-1

17.3 THE METHOD OF LEAST SQUARES FOR FITTING A REGRESSION LINE

The general form of the linear regression equation for sample data is

$$\bar{Y}_x = a + bX \qquad (17.1)$$

In (17.1), $\bar{Y}_x$ is the estimated value of the dependent variable given a specific value of the independent variable, X; a is the point of intersection of the linear regression line with the Y axis (at which point $X = 0$); b is the slope of the regression line; and X is the specific value of the independent variable.

Depending on the mathematical criterion used, a number of different linear regression equations can be developed for a given scatter diagram. By the *least squares criterion* the best-fitting regression line (and equation) is that for which the sum of the squared deviations between the estimated and actual values of the dependent variable for the sample data is minimized. The computational formulas by which the values of a and b in the linear regression equation can be determined for the equation which satisfies the least-squares criterion are

$$b = \frac{\Sigma XY - n\bar{X}\bar{Y}}{\Sigma X^2 - n\bar{X}^2} \tag{17.2}$$

$$a = \bar{Y} - b\bar{X} \tag{17.3}$$

Once the regression equation is formulated, then this equation can be used to estimate the value of the dependent variable given the value of the independent variable. However, such estimation should only be done within the range of the values of the independent values originally sampled, since there is no statistical basis to assume that the regression line is appropriate outside of these limits. Also, note that the regression equation provides the basis for determining only a point estimate, and not a complete prediction interval. (See Problems 17.2 and 17.3.)

17.4 THE STANDARD ERROR OF ESTIMATE AND PREDICTION INTERVALS

The standard error of estimate conceptually is a conditional standard deviation, in that it indicates the standard deviation of the dependent variable Y given a specific value of the independent variable X. The standard error of estimate based on sample data is represented by $s_{Y.X}$; the formula is

$$s_{Y.X} = \sqrt{\frac{\Sigma (Y - \bar{Y}_x)^2}{n - 2}} \tag{17.4}$$

Note: The above formula results in $s_{Y.X}^2$ being an unbiased estimator of the unknown $\sigma_{Y.X}^2$. In some textbooks the corrected standard error of estimate is designated by $\hat{\sigma}_{Y.X}$, instead of the $s_{Y.X}$ used in this text.

For computational purposes, an alternative version of the formula which does not require the determination of the deviation between each observed value of Y and the regression line value $\bar{Y}_x$ is more convenient. The alternative computational version of the formula for the standard error of estimate is

$$s_{Y.X} = \sqrt{\frac{\Sigma Y^2 - a \Sigma Y - b \Sigma XY}{n - 2}} \tag{17.5}$$

The standard error of estimate can be used to establish a prediction interval for the dependent variable given a specific value of the independent variable. The use of $s_{X.Y}$ for this purpose is based on two assumptions about the population: (1) that the dispersion of the dependent variable is equal at all points along the regression line, and (2) that at each point the values of the dependent variable are dispersed normally in respect to the regression line. (See Problem 17.4 for an example of the computation of $s_{Y.X}$.)

Because the standard error of estimate is based on sample data, use of the t distribution is appropriate (see Section 8.5). The degrees of freedom for the t distribution are $n - 2$, because the regression equation values of a and b represent estimates of the two corresponding population parameters α and β. Thus, the basic formula for constructing a prediction interval for the dependent variable Y in simple regression analysis is

$$\bar{Y}_x \pm ts_{Y.X} \tag{17.6}$$

As explained in Section 8.5, when $n \geq 30$ then the normal probability distribution can be used as an approximation of the t distribution (some books use the rule, when $df \geq 30$). Thus, the formula for constructing a prediction interval when the sample size is relatively large is

$$\bar{Y}_x \pm zs_{Y.X} \tag{17.7}$$

Note: Two points should be particularly recognized in respect to the above formulas. First, the intervals above are called prediction intervals rather than confidence intervals because the latter term is used by statisticians when the value of a population *parameter* is being estimated. In the present context, an individual value of the dependent variable (given X) is being estimated, rather than that of a parameter. Second, use of the above formulas implies that the only uncertainty associated with predicting the value of the dependent variable is the scatter in respect to the regression line. However, since the regression line is itself based on sample data, the location of the line is also uncertain. The form of the prediction interval which takes this additional uncertainty into consideration is presented in Section 17.5. However, when the sample size n is relatively large the prediction interval defined by (17.7) is considered to be a satisfactory approximation of the complete prediction interval described in the following section. (See Problem 17.5.)

17.5 INFERENCE CONCERNING THE PARAMETERS OF THE REGRESSION LINE

We consider three separate but related topics in this section: (1) the confidence interval for the conditional mean of the dependent variable Y, given a specific value of X; (2) prediction of the individual value of Y, given X and considering the uncertainty in the location of the mean regression line value; and (3) interval estimation and hypothesis testing concerned with the slope β of the true regression line.

The point estimate for the *mean* of the dependent variable, Y, is the same as the point estimate used for predicting an individual value. It is the value $\bar{Y}_x$ obtained from the linear regression equation. The standard error of the conditional mean in simple regression analysis is represented by $s_{\bar{Y}_x}$; the basic formula is

$$s_{\bar{Y}_x} = \frac{s_{Y.X}}{\sqrt{n}} + s_{Y.X} \sqrt{\frac{(X - \bar{X})^2}{\sum X^2 - [(\sum X)^2/n]}} \tag{17.8}$$

The first term in (17.8) is analogous to the usual formula for the standard error of the mean (see Section 8.2). The second term is unique to a situation which involves regression analysis, and indicates that the standard error of the conditional mean of Y increases as the given value of X departs from $\bar{X}$. For computational convenience, an alternative formula for determining the standard error of the conditional mean is generally used:

$$s_{\bar{Y}_x} = s_{Y.X} \sqrt{\frac{1}{n} + \frac{(X - \bar{X})^2}{\sum X^2 - [(\sum X)^2/n]}} \tag{17.9}$$

Given the point estimate and the standard error of the conditional mean, the confidence interval for the conditional mean is

$$\bar{Y}_x \pm ts_{\bar{Y}_x} \tag{17.10}$$

See Problem 17.6 for the application of (17.9) and (17.10).

As was the case when predicting an individual value of the dependent variable in Section 17.4, if $n \geq 30$ then the standard-normal z value can be used in place of t in the above equation. Further, the second term in the basic formula for the standard error has a relatively small value in this case and can be dropped, leading to the following simplified expression as an approximation formula for the confidence interval for the conditional mean:

$$\bar{Y}_x \pm z \frac{s_{Y.X}}{\sqrt{n}} \qquad (17.11)$$

When the sample is small, then the uncertain location of the mean regression line value $\bar{Y}_x$ should be taken into consideration when constructing prediction or confidence intervals. To differentiate the resulting standard error from the standard error of estimate described in Section 17.4, it is designated $s_{Y\text{next}}$, in which "next" simply means the next individual value of the dependent variable Y. In some texts this standard error is called the *standard error of forecast*. The complete standard error associated with estimating an individual value of Y in regression analysis is

$$s_{Y\text{next}} = \sqrt{s_{Y.X}^2 + s_{\bar{Y}_x}^2} \qquad (17.12)$$

The computational version of the formula for the standard error of forecast is

$$s_{Y\text{next}} = s_{Y.X} \sqrt{1 + \frac{1}{n} + \frac{(X - \bar{X})^2}{\sum X^2 - [(\sum X)^2/n]}} \qquad (17.13)$$

The prediction interval for the individual value of the dependent variable given a specific value of the independent variable X is

$$\bar{Y}_x \pm ts_{Y\text{next}} \qquad (17.14)$$

The construction of a prediction interval by using the standard error of forecast is illustrated in Problem 17.7.

The final area of attention in this section is interval estimation and hypothesis testing concerned with the true slope β of the regression line. The standard error of b based on the sample data is

$$s_b = \frac{s_{Y.X}}{\sqrt{\sum X^2 - n\bar{X}^2}} \qquad (17.15)$$

The parameter β can be estimated by constructing the following confidence interval, in which the degrees of freedom associated with t are $n - 2$:

$$b \pm ts_b \qquad (17.16)$$

See Problem 17.8.

A hypothesized value of β is tested by computing the t statistic associated with the observed sample value of b, as follows:

$$t = \frac{b - \beta_0}{s_b} \qquad (17.17)$$

The most frequent null hypothesis tested is that $\beta = 0$, because such a value would indicate the absence of a relationship between the independent and dependent variables. This type of relationship is illustrated in Fig. 17-1(c). (See also Problem 17.9.)

17.6 OBJECTIVES AND ASSUMPTIONS OF CORRELATION ANALYSIS

In contrast to regression analysis, correlation analysis measures the degree of relationship between the variables. As was true in our coverage of regression analysis, in this chapter we restrict our coverage to *simple correlation analysis*, which is concerned with measuring the relationship between only one independent variable and the dependent variable. In Chapter 18, we describe multiple correlation analysis.

The population assumptions underlying simple correlation analysis are that (1) the relationship between the two variables is linear, (2) both of the variables are random variables, (3) for each variable the conditional variances given different values of the other variable are equal (homoscedasticity) and (4) for each variable the conditional distributions given different values of the other variable are all normal distributions. The last assumption is that of a *bivariate normal distribution*. Note that these assumptions are similar to the assumptions underlying interval estimation in regression analysis, except that in correlation analysis the assumptions apply to both variables whereas in regression analysis the independent variable can be fixed at various specific values and need not be a random variable.

17.7 THE COEFFICIENT OF DETERMINATION

Consider that if an individual value of the dependent variable Y were estimated without knowledge of the value of any other variable, then the uncertainty associated with this estimate, and the basis for constructing the prediction interval, would be the variance σ_Y^2. Given a value of X, however, the uncertainty associated with the estimate is represented by $\sigma_{Y.X}^2$ (or $s_{Y.X}^2$ for sample data), as described in Section 17.4. If there is a relationship between the two variables, then $\sigma_{Y.X}^2$ will be smaller than σ_Y^2. For a perfect relationship, in which all values of the dependent variable are equal to the regression line value for the given value of X, $\sigma_{Y.X}^2 = 0$. Therefore, in the absence of a perfect relationship the value of $\sigma_{Y.X}^2$ indicates the uncertainty remaining *after* consideration of the value of the dependent variable. Or, we can say that the ratio of $\sigma_{Y.X}^2$ to σ_Y^2 indicates the proportion of variance (uncertainty) in the dependent variable which remains unexplained after a specific value of the dependent variable has been given:

$$\frac{\sigma_{Y.X}^2}{\sigma_Y^2} = \frac{\text{Unexplained variance remaining in } Y}{\text{Total variance in } Y} \qquad (17.18)$$

In (17.18) $\sigma_{Y.X}^2$ is determined by the procedure described in Section 17.4 (except that population data are assumed) and σ_Y^2 is calculated by the general formulas presented in Sections 4.6 and 4.8.

Given the proportion of unexplained variance, a useful measure of relationship is the *coefficient of determination*—the complement of the above ratio indicating the proportion of variance in the dependent variable which is statistically *explained* by the regression equation (i.e. by knowledge of the associated independent variable X). For population data the coefficient of determination is represented by the Greek ρ^2 ("rho squared") and is determined by

$$\rho^2 = 1 - \frac{\sigma_{Y.X}^2}{\sigma_Y^2} \qquad (17.19)$$

For sample data, the estimated value of the coefficient of determination can be obtained by the corresponding formula:

$$r^2 = 1 - \frac{s_{Y.X}^2}{s_Y^2} \qquad (17.20)$$

Note: Formula (17.20) is based on the assumption that $s_{Y.X}^2$ and s_Y^2 are both unbiased estimators of $\sigma_{Y.X}^2$ and σ_Y^2, respectively (see Section 4.6). The standard formulas in this book include the necessary correction factors. If the two variance estimators have not already been corrected for biasedness, the second term in the above formula should be multiplied by the fraction $(n - 1)/(n - 2)$.

For computational purposes, the following formula for the sample coefficient of determination is convenient:

$$r^2 = \frac{a \sum Y + b \sum XY - n\bar{Y}^2}{\sum Y^2 - n\bar{Y}^2} \qquad (17.21)$$

Application of (17.21) is illustrated in Problem 17.10. Although this is a frequently used formula for computing the coefficient of determination for sample data, it does not incorporate any correction for biasedness and includes a slight positive bias. See Section 17.8 for the correction factor which can be used.

17.8 THE COEFFICIENT OF CORRELATION

Although the coefficient of determination r^2 is relatively easy to interpret, it does not lend itself to statistical testing. However, the square root of the coefficient of determination, which is called the *coefficient of correlation* (r) does lend itself to statistical testing, because it is included in a test statistic which is distributed as the t distribution when the population correlation ρ equals 0. Further, the arithmetic sign associated with the correlation coefficient, which is always the same as the sign associated with β in the regression equation, indicates the direction of the relationship between X and Y (positive = direct; negative = inverse). For these reasons, the coefficient of correlation rather than the coefficient of determination is more often reported as the measure of relationship. Thus, the coefficient of correlation for population data, with the arithmetic sign being the same as that for β in the regression equation, is

$$\rho = \sqrt{\rho^2} \qquad (17.22)$$

The coefficient of correlation for sample data is

$$r = \sqrt{r^2} \qquad (17.23)$$

Overall, then, the sign of the correlation coefficient indicates the direction of the relationship between the X and Y variables while the absolute value of the coefficient indicates the extent of relationship. The squared value of the correlation coefficient is the coefficient of determination and indicates the proportion of the variance in Y explained by knowledge of X (and vice versa).

EXAMPLE 4. Figure 17-2 illustrates the general appearance of the scatter diagrams associated with several correlation values.

As an alternative to (17.21), the following formula does not require prior determination of the regression values of a and b. This formula would be used when the purpose of the analysis is to determine the extent and type of relationship between two variables, but without an accompanying interest in estimating Y given X. When this formula is used, the sign of the correlation coefficient is determined automatically, without the necessity of observing or calculating the slope of the regression line. The alternative formula is

$$r = \frac{n \sum XY - \sum X \sum Y}{\sqrt{n \sum X^2 - (\sum X)^2} \sqrt{n \sum Y^2 - (\sum Y)^2}} \qquad (17.24)$$

Application of (17.24) is illustrated in Problem 17.11(b).

The sample coefficient of correlation r is somewhat biased as an estimator of ρ, with an absolute value which is too large. This factor is not mentioned in many textbooks because the

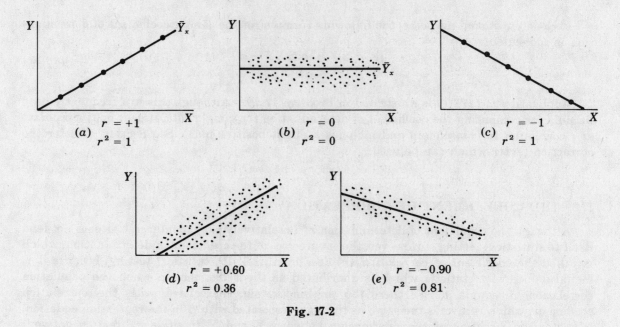

Fig. 17-2

amount of bias is slight, except for very small samples. An unbiased estimator for the coefficient of determination for the population can be obtained as follows:

$$\hat{\rho}^2 = 1 - (1 - r^2)\left(\frac{n - 1}{n - 2}\right) \tag{17.25}$$

17.9 SIGNIFICANCE OF THE CORRELATION COEFFICIENT

Typically, the null hypothesis of interest is that the population correlation $\rho = 0$, for if this hypothesis is rejected at a specified α-level we would conclude that there is an actual relationship between the variables. Given that the assumptions in Section 17.6 are satisfied, the following sampling statistic involving r is distributed as the t distribution with $df = n - 2$ when $\rho = 0$:

$$t = \frac{r}{\sqrt{\dfrac{1 - r^2}{n - 2}}} \tag{17.26}$$

Testing the null hypothesis that $\rho = 0$ is equivalent to testing the null hypothesis that $\beta = 0$ in the regression equation. (See Problem 17.12.)

17.10 PITFALLS AND LIMITATIONS ASSOCIATED WITH
REGRESSION AND CORRELATION ANALYSIS

(1) In regression analysis a value of Y cannot be legitimately estimated if the value of X is outside of the range of values which served as the basis for the regression equation.

(2) If the estimate of Y involves the prediction of a result which has not yet occurred, the historical data which served as the basis of the regression equation may not be relevant for future events.

(3) The use of a prediction or a confidence interval is based on the assumption that the conditional distributions of Y are normal and have equal variances.

(4) A significant correlation coefficient does not necessarily indicate causation, but rather may indicate a common linkage to other events.

(5) A "significant" correlation is not necessarily an important correlation. Given a large sample, a correlation of, say, $r = +0.10$ can be significantly different from 0 at $\alpha = 0.05$. Yet the coefficient of determination of $r^2 = 0.01$ for this example indicates that only 1 percent of the variance in Y is statistically explained by knowing X.

(6) The interpretation of the coefficients of correlation and determination is based on the assumption of a bivariate normal distribution for the population and, for each variable, equal conditional variances.

(7) For both regression and correlation analysis, a linear model is assumed. For a relationship which is curvilinear, a transformation to achieve linearity may be available. Another possibility is to restrict the analysis to the range of values within which the relationship is essentially linear.

Solved Problems

LINEAR REGRESSION ANALYSIS

17.1. Suppose an analyst takes a random sample of 10 recent truck shipments made by a company and records the distance in miles and delivery time to the nearest half-day. Construct the scatter diagram for the data in Table 17.1 and consider whether linear regression analysis appears appropriate.

Table 17.1 Sample Observations of Trucking Distance and Delivery Time for 10 Randomly Selected Shipments

Sampled shipment	1	2	3	4	5	6	7	8	9	10
Distance X, miles	825	215	1070	550	480	920	1350	325	670	1215
Delivery time Y, days	3.5	1.0	4.0	2.0	1.0	3.0	4.5	1.5	3.0	5.0

The scatter diagram for these data is portrayed in Fig. 17-3. The first reported pair of values in the table is represented by the dot entered above 825 on the X axis and aligned with 3.5 in respect to

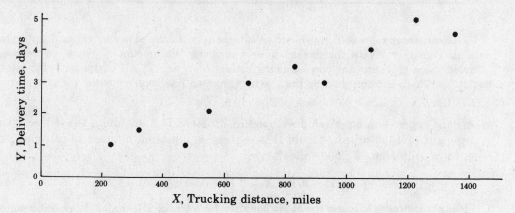

Fig. 17-3

the Y axis. The other nine points in the scatter diagram were similarly entered. From the diagram, it appears that the plotted points generally follow a linear relationship. Thus, linear regression analysis appears appropriate.

17.2. Determine the least-squares regression equation for the data in Problem 17.1, and enter the regression line on the scatter diagram for these data.

Referring to Table 17.2,

$$b = \frac{\Sigma XY - n\bar{X}\bar{Y}}{\Sigma X^2 - n\bar{X}^2} = \frac{(26,370) - (10)(762)(2.85)}{7,104,300 - (10)(762)^2} = \frac{4653}{1,297,860} = 0.0035851 \cong 0.0036$$

$$a = \bar{Y} - b\bar{X} = 2.85 - (0.0036)(762) = 0.1068 \cong 0.11$$

Therefore,

$$\bar{Y}_x = a + bX = 0.11 + 0.0036X$$

Table 17.2 Calculations Associated with Determining the Linear Regression Equation for Estimating Delivery Time on the Basis of Trucking Distance

Sampled shipment	Distance X, miles	Delivery time Y, days	XY	X^2	Y^2
1	825	3.5	2887.5	680,625	12.25
2	215	1.0	215.0	46,225	1.00
3	1070	4.0	4280.0	1,144,900	16.00
4	550	2.0	1100.0	302,500	4.00
5	480	1.0	480.0	230,400	1.00
6	920	3.0	2760.0	846,400	9.00
7	1350	4.5	6075.0	1,822,500	20.25
8	325	1.5	487.5	105,625	2.25
9	670	3.0	2010.0	448,900	9.00
10	1215	5.0	6075.0	1,476,225	25.00
Totals	7620	28.5	26,370.0	7,104,300	99.75
Mean	$\bar{X} = \dfrac{\Sigma X}{n} = \dfrac{7620}{10}$ $= 762$	$\bar{Y} = \dfrac{\Sigma Y}{n} = \dfrac{28.5}{10}$ $= 2.85$			

This estimated regression line based on sample data is entered in the scatter diagram for these data in Fig. 17-4. Note the dashed lines indicating the amount of deviation between each sampled value of Y and the corresponding estimated value, $\bar{Y}_x$. It is the sum of these squared deviations which is minimized by the linear regression line determined by the above procedure.

17.3. Using the regression equation developed in Problem 17.2, estimate the delivery time for a shipment of 1000 miles. Could this regression equation be used to estimate delivery time for a shipment of 2500 miles?

$$\bar{Y}_x = 0.11 + 0.0036X = 0.11 + 0.0036(1000) = 3.71 \text{ days}$$

It is not appropriate to use the above equation for a trip of 2500 miles because the sample data for this estimated linear regression equation included trips up to 1350 miles distance only.

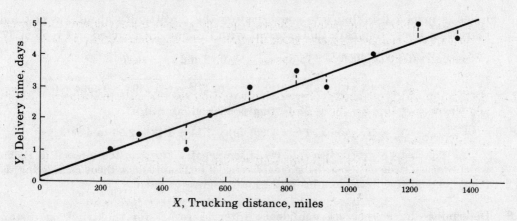

Fig. 17-4

17.4. Compute the standard error of estimate for the delivery time analysis problem, referring to values determined in the solution to Problem 17.2.

$$s_{Y.X} = \sqrt{\frac{\Sigma Y^2 - a\,\Sigma Y - b\,\Sigma XY}{n - 2}} = \sqrt{\frac{99.75 - (0.11)(28.5) - (0.0036)(26{,}370)}{10 - 2}}$$

$$= \sqrt{\frac{1.683}{8}} = \sqrt{0.2104} = 0.4587 \cong 0.46$$

17.5. From the solutions to Problems 17.3 and 17.4, construct an estimated 95 percent prediction interval for the delivery time for a shipment involving 1000 miles, without considering the uncertainty associated with the position of the regression line itself.

Since $\bar{Y}_x$ (for $X = 1000$) = 3.71 days (from Problem 17.3), and $s_{Y.X} = 0.46$ (from Problem 17.4), the 95 percent prediction interval (where $df = 10 - 2 = 8$) is

$$\bar{Y}_x \pm t\,s_{Y.X} = 3.71 \pm (2.306)(0.46) = 3.71 \pm 1.06 = 2.65 \text{ to } 4.77 \text{ days}$$

Thus, given a truck shipment involving a distance of 1000 miles, we estimate that the delivery time will be between 2.65 and 4.77 days, with a probability of 0.95.

17.6. Using the values determined in the preceding problems, construct the 95 percent confidence interval for the *mean* delivery time for a trucking distance of 1000 miles.

Given $\bar{Y}_x$ (for $X = 1000$) = 3.71 days, $s_{Y.X} = 0.46$, and the values in Table 17.2,

$$s_{\bar{Y}_x} = s_{Y.X}\sqrt{\frac{1}{n} + \frac{(X - \bar{X})^2}{\Sigma X^2 - (\Sigma X)^2/n}} = 0.46\sqrt{\frac{1}{10} + \frac{(1000 - 762)^2}{7{,}104{,}300 - (7620)^2/10}} = 0.1748 \cong 0.17$$

The 95 percent confidence interval for the conditional mean (where $df = 10 - 2 = 8$) is

$$\bar{Y}_x \pm t\,s_{\bar{Y}_x} = 3.71 \pm (2.306)(0.17) = 3.71 \pm 0.39 = 3.32 \text{ to } 4.10 \text{ days}$$

Thus, for truck shipments of 1000 miles, we estimate that the mean delivery time is between 3.32 and 4.10 days, with 95 percent confidence in this estimation interval.

17.7. Using the values determined in the preceding problems, determine the 95 percent prediction interval for the delivery time of a shipment given that a distance of 1000 miles is involved, taking into consideration the uncertainty about the position of the regression line. Compare this interval with the one constructed in Problem 17.5.

Since $\bar{Y}_x$ (for $X = 1000$) = 3.71 days, $s_{Y.X} = 0.46$ and $s_{\bar{Y}_x} = 0.17$,

$$s_{Y\,\text{next}} = \sqrt{s_{Y.X}^2 + s_{\bar{Y}_x}^2} = \sqrt{(0.46)^2 + (0.17)^2} = \sqrt{0.2405} = 0.4904 \cong 0.49$$

Where $df = 10 - 2 = 8$, the 95 percent prediction interval is

$$\bar{Y}_x \pm t s_{Y\,\text{next}} = 3.71 \pm 2.306(0.49) = 3.71 \pm 1.13 = 2.58 \text{ to } 4.84 \text{ days}$$

As expected, this prediction interval is somewhat wider than the interval in Problem 17.5, which was constructed using the standard error of estimate and without considering the uncertainty associated with the location of the mean regression value.

17.8. Determine the 95 percent confidence interval for β for the trucking distance and delivery time data discussed in the preceding problems.

Given $s_{Y.X} = 0.46$ and the values in Table 17.2,

$$s_b = \frac{s_{Y.X}}{\sqrt{\Sigma X^2 - n\bar{X}^2}} = \frac{0.46}{\sqrt{7,104,300 - 10(762)^2}} = \frac{0.46}{1,139.24} = 0.0004$$

Since $b = 0.0036$ (from Problem 17.2) and $df = n - 2 = 10 - 2 = 8$, the 95 percent confidence interval for β is

$$b \pm t s_b = 0.0036 \pm (2.306)(0.0004) = 0.0036 \pm 0.0009 = 0.0027 \text{ to } 0.0045$$

17.9. Referring to Problem 17.8, test the null hypothesis H_0: $\beta = 0$ for the trucking distance and delivery time data at the 5 percent level of significance.

$$H_0: \quad \beta = 0 \qquad H_1: \quad \beta \neq 0$$

$$\text{Critical } t(df = 8, \, \alpha = 0.05) = \pm 2.306$$

$$t = \frac{b - \beta_0}{s_b} = \frac{0.0036 - 0}{0.0004} = 9.00$$

Therefore, we reject the null hypothesis, and conclude that there is a significant relationship between trucking distance and delivery time.

CORRELATION ANALYSIS

17.10. For the trucking distance and delivery time data, the sampling procedure described in Problem 17.1 indicates that both variables are in fact random variables. If we further assume a bivariate normal distribution for the population and, for each variable, equal conditional variances, then correlation analysis can be applied to the sample data. Using values calculated in Problem 17.2, calculate the coefficient of determination for the sample data (ignore the slight biasedness associated with this coefficient).

$$r^2 = \frac{a \Sigma Y + b \Sigma XY - n\bar{Y}^2}{\Sigma Y^2 - n\bar{Y}^2}$$

$$= \frac{(0.11)(28.5) + (0.0036)(26,370) - (10)(2.85)^2}{99.75 - (10)(2.85)^2}$$

$$= \frac{16.842}{18.525} = 0.9091 \cong 0.91$$

Thus, as a point estimate we can conclude that about 91 percent of the variance in delivery time is statistically explained by the trucking distance involved. Further, given the trucking distance we can also observe that about 9 percent of the variance remains unexplained.

17.11. For the trucking distance and delivery time data, (a) calculate the coefficient of correlation by reference to the coefficient of determination in Problem 17.10, and (b) determine the coefficient of correlation by using the alternative computational formula for r.

(a) $r = \sqrt{r^2} = \sqrt{0.9091} = +0.9535 \cong +0.95$

The positive value for the correlation value is based on the observation that the slope b of the regression line is positive, as determined in Problem 17.2.

(b) $r = \dfrac{n \, \Sigma XY - \Sigma X \Sigma Y}{\sqrt{n \, \Sigma X^2 - (\Sigma X)^2} \sqrt{n \, \Sigma Y^2 - (\Sigma Y)^2}} = \dfrac{(10)(26{,}370) - (7620)(28.5)}{\sqrt{(10)(7{,}104{,}300) - (7620)^2} \, \sqrt{(10)(99.75) - (28.5)^2}}$

$= \dfrac{46{,}530}{(3602.5824)(13.6107)} = \dfrac{46{,}530}{49{,}033.668} = +0.9489 \cong +0.95$

Except for a slight difference due to rounding, the two values are the same.

17.12. Determine whether the correlation value computed in Problem 17.11(b) is significantly different from zero at the 5 percent level of significance.

$$H_0: \quad \rho = 0 \qquad H_1: \quad \rho \neq 0$$

$$\text{Critical } t(df = 8, \, \alpha = 0.05) = \pm 2.306$$

$$t = \dfrac{r}{\sqrt{\dfrac{1 - r^2}{n - 2}}} = \dfrac{0.9489}{\sqrt{\dfrac{1 - 0.9004}{10 - 2}}} = \dfrac{0.9489}{0.1116} = +8.50$$

Therefore the null hypothesis that there is no relationship between the two variables is rejected, and we conclude that there is a significant relationship between trucking distance and delivery time. Note that this conclusion coincides with the test of the null hypothesis that $\beta = 0$ in Problem 17.9. The difference in the calculated values of t in these two tests is associated with the bias in the value of r for small samples, as explained in Section 17.8.

17.13. For a sample of $n = 10$ previous loan recipients at a finance company, the correlation coefficient between household income and amount of outstanding short-term debt is found to be $r = +0.50$.

(a) Test the hypothesis that there is no correlation between these two variables for the entire population of previous loan recipients, using the 5 percent level of significance.

(b) Interpret the meaning of the correlation coefficient which was computed.

(a) $H_0: \quad \rho = 0 \qquad H_1: \quad \rho \neq 0$

$$\text{Critical } t(df = 10 - 2 = 8, \, \alpha = 0.05) = \pm 2.306$$

$$t = \dfrac{r}{\sqrt{\dfrac{1 - r^2}{n - 2}}} = \dfrac{0.50}{\sqrt{\dfrac{1 - (0.50)^2}{8}}} = \dfrac{0.50}{0.306} = +1.634$$

Therefore, the null hypothesis cannot be rejected, and we continue to accept the assumption that there is no relationship between the two variables. The observed sample relationship can be ascribed to chance at the 5 percent level of significance.

(b) Based on the correlation coefficient of $r = +0.50$, we might be tempted to conclude that because $r^2 = 0.25$, approximately 25 percent of the variance in short-term debt is explained statistically by the amount of household income. *However*, because the null hypothesis in part (a) above was not rejected, a more appropriate interpretation is that none of the variance in Y is associated with changes in X. By this approach, it is appropriate to consider the interpretation of r^2 only if the null hypothesis that there is no relationship has been rejected.

Supplementary Problems

LINEAR REGRESSION ANALYSIS

17.14. Table 17.3 presents sample data relating the number of hours spent by individual students outside of class on a course in statistics during a 3-week period, and their scores on an examination given at the end of that period. Plot these data on a scatter diagram.

Table 17.3 Hours Spent on a Statistics Course and Examination Grades for a Sample of $n = 8$ Students

Sampled student	1	2	3	4	5	6	7	8
Hours of study X	20	16	34	23	27	32	18	22
Examination grade Y	64	61	84	70	88	92	72	77

17.15. From Table 17.3, (a) determine the regression equation for predicting the examination grade given the number of hours spent on the course, and enter the regression line on the scatter diagram constructed in Problem 17.14. (b) Use the regression equation to estimate the examination grade of a student who devoted 30 hr of study to the course material.

Ans.   (a) $\bar{Y}_x = 40 + 1.5X$, (b) $\bar{Y}_x = 85$

17.16. Continuing with Problem 17.15,

(a)   construct the 90 percent prediction interval for the examination score given that a student devoted 30 hr to the course preparation, using only the standard error of estimate as the measure of uncertainty.

(b) Construct the 90 percent confidence interval for estimating the mean exam grade for students who devote 30 hr to course preparation.

Ans.   (a) 73.07 to 96.93, (b) 79.03 to 90.97

17.17. Refer to Problems 17.15 and 17.16. Construct the 90 percent prediction interval for the examination grade given that a student devoted 30 hr to the course preparation, considering the uncertainty regarding the location of the mean regression line value.

Ans.   71.63 to 98.37

17.18. For the sample information presented in Problem 17.14, (a) test the null hypothesis that the slope of the regression line is zero, using the 1 percent level of significance, and interpret the result of your test.   (b) Repeat the test for the null hypothesis that the true regression coefficient is equal to or less than zero, using the 1 percent level of significance.

Ans.   (a) Reject H_0 and conclude that there is a significant relationship. (b) Reject H_0 and conclude that there is a significant positive relationship.

17.19. Table 17.4 presents data relating the number of weeks of experience in a job involving the wiring of miniature electronic components and the number of components which were rejected during the past week for 12 randomly selected workers.   Plot these sample data on a scatter diagram.

Table 17.4   Weeks of Experience and Number of Components Rejected During a Sampled Week for 12 Assembly Workers

Sampled worker	1	2	3	4	5	6	7	8	9	10	11	12
Weeks of experience X	7	9	6	14	8	12	10	4	2	11	1	8
Number of rejects Y	26	20	28	16	23	18	24	26	38	22	32	25

17.20. From Table 17.4,   (a) determine the regression equation for predicting the number of components rejected given the number of weeks experience, and enter the regression line on the scatter diagram.   Comment on the nature of the relationship as indicated by the regression equation.   (b) Estimate the number of components rejected for an employee with 3 weeks experience in the operation.

Ans.   (a) $\bar{Y}_x = 35.57 - 1.40X$,   (b) $\bar{Y}_x = 31.37$

17.21. Continuing with Problem 17.20,

(a)   construct the 95 percent prediction interval for the number of components rejected for an employee with 3 weeks experience in the job, using only the standard error of estimate as the measure of uncertainty.

(b)   Construct the 95 percent confidence interval for estimating the mean number of rejects for employees with 3 weeks experience in the operation.

Ans.   (a) 25.67 to 37.07,   (b) 28.74 to 34.00

17.22. Refer to Problems 17.20 and 17.21.   Construct the 95 percent prediction interval for the number of components rejected for an employee with 3 weeks experience in the job by including consideration of the uncertainty regarding the location of the mean regression line value.

Ans.   25.09 to 37.65

17.23. For the sample information in Problems 17.19 to 17.20, construct the 95 percent confidence interval for estimating the value of the population regression coefficient β, and interpret the value of this coefficient.

Ans. -1.85 to -0.95

CORRELATION ANALYSIS

17.24. Compute the coefficient of determination and the coefficient of correlation for the data in Table 17.3 and analyzed in Problems 17.14 to 17.18, taking advantage of the fact that the values of a

and b for the regression equation were calculated in Problem 17.15. Interpret the computed coefficients.

Ans. $r^2 = 0.7449 \cong 0.74, \quad r = +0.863 \cong 0.86$

17.25. For the sample correlation value determined in Problem 17.24, test the null hypothesis that (a) $\rho = 0$, and (b) $\rho \leq 0$, using the 1 percent level of significance in respect to each test. Interpret your results.

Ans.   (a) Reject H_0 and conclude that there is a significant relationship. (b) Reject H_0 and conclude that there is a significant positive relationship.

17.26. For the sample data reported in Table 17.4 and analyzed in Problems 17.19 to 17.23, determine the value of the correlation coefficient by the formula which is not based on the use of the estimated regression line values of a and b. Interpret the meaning of this value by computing the coefficient of determination.

Ans. $r = -0.908 \cong -0.91, \quad r^2 = 0.8245 \cong 0.82$

Chapter 18

Multiple Regression and
Correlation Analysis

18.1 OBJECTIVES AND ASSUMPTIONS OF LINEAR
MULTIPLE REGRESSION ANALYSIS

Linear multiple regression analysis is an extension of simple regression analysis, as described in Chapter 17, to the applications involving two or more independent variables as the basis for estimating the value of the dependent variable. In the case of two independent variables, denoted by X_1 and X_2, the multiple regression equation is

$$Y_c = a + b_1 X_1 + b_2 X_2 \qquad (18.1)$$

In the above formula, Y_c, which stands for "computed Y", is analogous to the $\bar{Y}_x$ in simple two-variable analysis, without an accompanying attempt to identify the several independent variables in the subscript. (*Note*: In some textbooks and computer programs the dependent variable is designated X_1, with the several independent variables then identified sequentially beginning with X_2.)

The multiple regression equation identifies the best fitting line based on the method of least squares, as described in Chapter 17. In the case of multiple regression analysis, the best fitting line is a line through n-dimensional space (3-dimensional in the case of two independent variables). The calculations required for determining the values of the constants in a multiple regression equation and the associated standard error values are quite complex and generally involve matrix algebra. However, computer programs are widely available for carrying out such calculations, and the solved problems at the end of this chapter are referenced to the use of such a program. Specialized textbooks in regression and correlation analysis include complete descriptions of the mathematical analyses involved.

The assumptions of linear multiple regression analysis are similar to those of the simple case involving only one independent variable. For point estimation, the principal assumptions are that (1) the dependent variable is a random variable whereas the independent variables need not be random variables, (2) the relationship between the several independent variables and the one dependent variable is linear, and (3) the variances of the conditional distributions of the dependent variable, given various combinations of values of the independent variables, are all equal (homoscedasticity). For internal estimation, an additional assumption is that the conditional distributions for the dependent variable follow the normal probability distribution.

18.2 CONCEPTS IN MULTIPLE REGRESSION ANALYSIS

Constant (in the regression equation): Although the a and the several b_i values are all estimates of constants in the regression equation, in computer program output the term "constant" refers to the value of the a intercept. In multiple regression analysis, this is the estimated value of the dependent variable Y given that all of the independent variables are equal to zero.

Partial regression coefficient (or *net regression coefficient*):   Each of the b_i regression coefficients is in fact a partial regression coefficient.   A partial regression coefficient is the conditional coefficient given that one or more other independent variables (and their coefficients) are also included in the regression equation.   Conceptually, a partial regression coefficient represents the slope of the regression line between the independent variable of interest and the dependent variable given that the other independent variables are held constant.   The symbol $b_{Y1.2}$ (or $b_{12.3}$ when the dependent variable is designated by X_1) is the partial regression coefficient for the first independent variable given that a second independent variable is also included in the regression equation.   For simplicity, when the entire regression equation is presented this coefficient usually is designated by b_1.

Standard partial regression coefficient: This coefficient is often designated by β.   However, unlike the designation in simple regression analysis, the β does not identify the population parameter in this case.   Rather, it is the transformed value of a b coefficient based on the values of the independent and dependent variables being expressed in standard deviation units (i.e., in terms of z values).   Whereas b coefficients express slope in terms of the particular measurement units used for each independent variable, for comparative purposes the β coefficients are useful because they indicate the slope in terms of a common measurement system.

Standard error of estimate: This measure is analogous to that described in Section 17.4, except that the values of the several independent variables serve as the basis of the conditional standard deviation.   If two independent variables are involved, the standard error of estimate is designated by $s_{Y.12}$ (or by $s_{1.23}$ when the dependent variable is designated by X_1).

Prediction intervals in multiple regression analysis: The prediction interval for the individual (next) value of the dependent variable Y given observed values of the independent variables is determined in the same way as for simple regression analysis in Section 17.4, except that the regression equation and standard error of estimate are concerned with multiple regression.   Furthermore, the uncertainty about the true (population) values of the b coefficients and the a coefficient is not generally considered.   With the z distribution being used in place of the t distribution when the sample is at least $n \geq 30$ (some books say when $df \geq 30$), the prediction interval for an individual value of the dependent variable for the case of two independent variables is

$$Y_c \pm t s_{Y.12} \tag{18.2}$$

or

$$Y_c \pm z s_{Y.12} \tag{18.3}$$

Confidence intervals in multiple regression analysis: Typically, the only interval of interest is the estimation of the mean value of the dependent variable.   For the case of two independent variables this mean is designated $\mu_{Y.12}$ (or $\mu_{1.23}$ when the dependent variable is designated by X_1).   In a manner analogous to the prediction interval in (*18.2*) and (*18.3*), such estimation intervals typically are not concerned with the uncertainty about the position of the true regression line.   With the z distribution being used in place of the t distribution when $n \geq 30$, the estimation interval for the conditional mean of the dependent variable for the case of two independent variables is

$$Y_c \pm t \frac{s_{Y.12}}{\sqrt{n}} \tag{18.4}$$

or

$$Y_c \pm z \frac{s_{Y.12}}{\sqrt{n}} \tag{18.5}$$

Stepwise regression analysis: In such a procedure one independent variable is added to the analysis at each step of analysis, with the constant and the partial regression coefficients as well as the standard error of estimate being recalculated at each step. Typically, the first independent variable included is the one with the highest degree of association with the dependent variable. However, the computer program may allow the user to designate the sequence by which variables are added to the analysis. A stepwise regression analysis serves as the basis for the solved problems at the end of this chapter.

18.3 ANALYSIS OF VARIANCE IN LINEAR REGRESSION ANALYSIS

Both the analysis of variance and linear regression analysis utilize linear algebraic models. Consider, for example, the similarity between the equations representing the models for one-way and two-way analysis of variance in Sections 13.2 and 13.4 and the regression equations for simple linear regression in Section 17.3 and for multiple linear regression in Section 18.1, respectively. Essentially, simple linear regression analysis is the equivalent of the one-way fixed effects model of the analysis of variance when the independent variable can be measured along a continuous scale, while multiple linear regression analysis with two independent variables is equivalent to the two-way fixed effects model of the analysis of variance. Higher order models are similarly related. Although there is an equivalency between these two procedures, a particular advantage associated with regression analysis is that it is directed toward applications in prediction and estimation, rather than being primarily limited to testing the significance of the relationship among the variables. On the other hand, the analysis of variance can be used when the independent variable is not quantitative (but represents qualitative categories) or when the relationship between the variables is not linear.

Because of this equivalence, the F test can be applied in regression analysis to determine whether an independent variable, or the addition of a particular independent variable, results in a significant reduction in the variance associated with the random (dependent) variable. In this context, the *sum of squares attributable to the regression* is the sum of the squared deviations between each predicted regression line value Y_c and the overall mean of the dependent variable $\bar{Y}$. The *residual sum of squares* is the sum of the squared deviations between each observed value of the dependent variable Y and the regression line value Y_c. On the basis of these two types of sums of squares, the significance of the regression coefficient (and of the correlation coefficient) can be determined by comparing the mean square attributable to the regression with the mean square attributable to the residual. Thus the general basis for using the analysis of variance to test for the significance of the regression coefficient is

$$F = \frac{MS \text{ (Regression)}}{MS \text{ (Residual)}} \qquad (18.6)$$

In the addition of a variable in stepwise multiple regression analysis, the use of the analysis of variance is similar conceptually to the procedure represented by (18.6), except that the sum of squares attributable to the regression is evaluated in reference to the regression line associated with the previously included independent variables, rather than in reference to the overall mean $\bar{Y}$. In this respect, the F ratio is associated with the partial regression coefficient for the variable being evaluated. Mathematical development of these ideas is included in specialized textbooks on regression analysis. The use of the F test in regression analysis is illustrated in the solved problems at the end of this chapter.

18.4 OBJECTIVES AND ASSUMPTIONS OF MULTIPLE CORRELATION ANALYSIS

Multiple correlation analysis is an extension of simple correlation analysis, as described in Chapter 17, to the situations involving two or more independent variables and their degree of association with the dependent variable. As is the case for multiple regression analysis described in Section 18.1, the dependent variable is designated by Y while the several independent variables are designated sequentially beginning with X_1. (*Note*: In some textbooks and computer programs the dependent variable is designated by X_1, in which case the independent variables are designated sequentially beginning with X_2.)

The coefficient of multiple correlation, which is designated by $R_{Y.12}$ for the case of two independent variables, is indicative of the extent of relationship between two independent variables taken as a group and the dependent variable. Because it is possible for one of the independent variables to have a positive relationship with the dependent variable while the other independent variable has a negative relationship with the dependent variable, all R values are reported without an arithmetic sign.

The *coefficient of multiple determination* is designated by $R_{Y.12}^2$ for the case of two independent variables. As for the case of the simple coefficient of determination (see Section 17.7), this coefficient indicates the proportion of variance in the dependent variable which is statistically accounted for by knowledge of the two (or more) independent variables. The sample coefficient of multiple determination for the case of two independent variables is

$$R_{Y.12}^2 = 1 - \frac{s_{Y.12}^2}{s_Y^2} = 1 - \frac{\Sigma (Y - \bar{Y}_x)^2}{\Sigma (Y - \bar{Y})^2} \tag{18.7}$$

Formula (*18.7*) is presented for conceptual purposes, rather than for computational application. Because it is the orientation in this chapter that computer programs should be used for multiple regression and correlation analysis, computational procedures are not included here.

The assumptions of multiple correlation analysis are similar to those of the simple case involving only one independent variable. These are that (1) all variables involved in the analysis are random variables, (2) the relationships are all linear, (3) the conditional variances are all equal (homoscedasticity), and (4) the conditional distributions are all normal. These requirements are quite stringent and are seldom completely satisfied in real data situations. However, multiple correlation analysis is quite robust in the sense that some of these assumptions, and particularly the assumption about all the conditional distributions being normally distributed, can be violated without serious consequences in terms of the validity of the results.

18.5 CONCEPTS IN MULTIPLE CORRELATION ANALYSIS

In addition to the coefficient of multiple correlation and the coefficient of multiple determination described in the preceding section, the following concepts or procedures are unique to multiple correlation analysis.

Coefficient of partial correlation: Indicates the correlation between one of the independent variables in the multiple correlation analysis and the dependent variable, with the other independent variable(s) held constant statistically. The partial correlation with the first of two independent variables would be designated by $r_{Y1.2}$, while the partial correlation with the second of two independent variables would be designated by $r_{Y2.1}$. (If the independent variable is designated by X_1, then these two coefficients would be designated by $r_{12.3}$ and $r_{13.2}$, respectively.) The partial correlation value is different from a simple correlation value because for the latter case other independent variables are not statistically controlled. [See Problem 18.4(c).]

Coefficient of partial determination: This is the squared value of the coefficient of partial correlation described above. Indicates the proportion of variance statistically accounted for by one particular independent variable, with the other independent variable(s) held constant statistically.

Stepwise correlation analysis: Similar to stepwise regression analysis described in Section 18.2. The computer program used may add an additional independent variable to the analysis at each step in a sequential manner or by choosing the variable with the highest partial coefficient of correlation, according to user instructions. A stepwise correlation analysis typically is done in conjunction with stepwise regression analysis, and serves as the basis for the solved problems at the end of this chapter.

18.6   PITFALLS AND LIMITATIONS ASSOCIATED WITH MULTIPLE REGRESSION AND CORRELATION ANALYSIS

Two principal areas of difficulty are those associated with colinearity and autocorrelation. These are described briefly below. Detailed discussions of these problems and what can be done about them is included in specialized textbooks in regression and correlation analysis.

Colinearity (or *multicolinearity*):   When the independent variables in a multiple regression analysis are highly correlated with one another, the partial (or net) regression coefficients are unreliable in terms of meaning. Similarly, the practical meaning of the coefficients of partial correlation may be questionable. It is possible, for example, that the partial correlation for a given independent variable will be highly negative even though the simple correlation is highly positive. In general, therefore, care should be taken in interpreting partial regression coefficients and partial correlation coefficients when there are independent variables that have a high positive or negative correlation with one another.

Autocorrelation: Refers to the absence of independence in the sampling of the dependent variable Y. Particularly applicable when the Y values are time-series values, in which case the value of the dependent variable in one time period is almost invariably related to values in adjoining time periods. In such a case, the standard error associated with each partial regression coefficient b_i is understated, as is the value of the standard error of estimate. The result is that any prediction or confidence intervals are narrower (more precise) than they should be, and null hypotheses concerning the absence of relationship are rejected too frequently.

Solved Problems

The computer output presented in the following problems is based on the use of the SPSS* program named REGRESSION, which is a stepwise multiple regression program.

18.1.   Table 18.1 presents the sample data which are to be analyzed. As indicated, there is one dependent variable, Y, and there are three independent variables, X_1, X_2, and

*Norman H. Nie, et al, *Statistical Package for the Social Sciences*, 2d ed., McGraw-Hill Book Company, New York, 1975.

X_3. Referring to Fig. 18-1, which presents the first two pages of the computer output using the program REGRESSION with these data, (a) determine the total number of variables involved in the analysis. (b) The program requires that the user assign names to each of the variables in the analysis. What are the assigned names for the variables? (c) What is the mean and the standard deviation of the dependent variable?

Table 18.1   Hypothetical Data for the Sample Multiple
Regression and Correlation Problem

Sample number	Y	X_1	X_2	X_3
1	66.0	38	47.5	23
2	43.0	41	21.3	17
3	36.0	34	36.5	21
4	23.0	35	18.0	14
5	27.0	31	29.5	11
6	14.0	34	14.2	9
7	12.0	29	21.0	4
8	7.6	32	10.0	8

(a) As indicated by the "VARIABLE LIST" (in item 2) on page 1 of the output, there are four variables involved in this analysis. Under item 3 there is also reference made to the fact that the input format provides for four variables.

(b) As indicated in items 2 and 3 on page 1, the four variables have been assigned the names Y, X_1, X_2 and X_3. Y is identified as being the dependent variable in item 6.

(c) Referring to page 2 of the output in Fig. 18-1, the mean of the dependent variable Y is 28.5750, while the standard deviation is 19.3631.

18.2. Figure 18-2 presents the third page of the program output—a correlation matrix. What is (a) the simple correlation between Y and X_2? (b) The simple correlation between X_1 and X_3? (c) The correlation of any variable with itself?

(a) $r_{Y2} = 0.85846$, (b) $r_{13} = 0.72642$, (c) 1.00000 (which are the values along the diagonal of the matrix)

18.3. Page 4 of the output of the program REGRESSION includes the first two steps of the stepwise multiple regression analysis, as indicated in Fig. 18-3. That is, the first independent variable is entered into the regression equation in step 1 and the second independent variable is entered in step 2. Refer to the output for step 1 only (top part of the page).

(a)   Which independent variable was the first one to be entered into the regression equation? Why was this the first variable to be entered?

(b)   Why is the "multiple R" in fact the simple correlation value in this case?

(c)   What is the standard error of estimate associated with predicting the value of Y given a value of X_3?

(d)   Write out the regression equation for predicting Y given X_3.

(a) X_3 is the first independent variable entered into the analysis because the simple correlation between this variable and the dependent variable Y is higher than for any other dependent variable (see Fig. 18-2).

```
@NEW*PROCESSOR.SPSS
SPSS 6.01   SEPTEMBER 29, 1975
             SPACE ALLOCATION FOR THIS RUN..
               TOTAL AMOUNT REQUESTED                            9000 WORDS

             DEFAULT TRANSPACE ALLOCATION                        1125 WORDS

                 MAX NO OF TRANSFORMATIONS PERMITTED      37
                 MAX NO OF RECODE VALUES                 150
                 MAX NO OF ARITHM.OR LOG.OPERATIONS      300
               RESULTING WORKSPACE ALLOCATION                    7875 WORDS
          1.       RUN NAME         SAMPLE PROBLEM
          2.       VARIABLE LIST    Y,X1,X2,X3
          3.       INPUT FORMAT     FIXED(F3.1,X,F2.0,X,F3.1,X,F2.0)

             ACCORDING TO YOUR INPUT FORMAT, VARIABLES ARE TO BE READ AS FOLLOWS

             VARIABLE  FORMAT  RECORD     COLUMNS

                 Y       F 3. 1    1        1-  3
                 X1      F 2. 0    1        5-  6
                 X2      F 3. 1    1        8- 10
                 X3      F 2. 0    1       12- 13
THE INPUT FORMAT PROVIDES FOR   4 VARIABLES.    4 WILL BE READ
IT PROVIDES FOR  1 RECORDS ('CARDS') PER CASE.  A MAXIMUM OF   13 'COLUMNS' ARE USED ON A RECORD.
          4.       N OF CASES       8
          5.       REGRESSION       VARIABLES=Y,X1,X2,X3
          6.                        REGRESSION=Y WITH X1,X2,X3 (3)
          7.       STATISTICS       ALL

 ***** REGRESSION PROBLEM REQUIRES    128 WORDS WORKSPACE, NOT INCLUDING RESIDUALS *****

          8.       READ INPUT DATA
```

```
SAMPLE PROBLEM                                          05 MAY 76       PAGE   2
FILE   NONAME   (CREATION DATE = 05 MAY 76)

VARIABLE          MEAN       STANDARD DEV    CASES

Y                28.5750        19.3631        8
X1               34.2500         3.8452        8
X2               24.7500        12.4130        8
X3               13.3750         6.6103        8
```

Fig. 18-1

```
SAMPLE PROBLEM                                          05 MAY 76       PAGE   3
FILE   NONAME   (CREATION DATE = 05 MAY 76)

CORRELATION COEFFICIENTS

A VALUE OF 99.00000 IS PRINTED
IF A COEFFICIENT CANNOT BE COMPUTED.


            Y          X1         X2         X3

Y        1.00000     .71884     .85846     .89430
X1        .71884    1.00000     .28164     .72642
X2        .85846     .28164    1.00000     .76805
X3        .89430     .72642     .76805    1.00000
```

Fig. 18-2

SAMPLE PROBLEM

FILE   NONAME   (CREATION DATE = 05 MAY 76)   05 MAY 76   PAGE   4

* * * * * * * * * * * * * * * * *   M U L T I P L E   R E G R E S S I O N   * * * * * * * * * * * * * * * *   VARIABLE LIST   1
                                                                                                                    REGRESSION LIST 1

DEPENDENT VARIABLE..   Y

VARIABLE(S) ENTERED ON STEP NUMBER   1..   X3

MULTIPLE R   .89430   ANALYSIS OF VARIANCE   DF   SUM OF SQUARES   MEAN SQUARE   F
R SQUARE   .79978   REGRESSION   1.   2099.03270   2099.03270   23.96693
ADJUSTED R SQUARE   .79978   RESIDUAL   6.   525.48231   87.58038
STANDARD ERROR   9.35844

-------- VARIABLES IN THE EQUATION --------   ----------- VARIABLES NOT IN THE EQUATION -----------

VARIABLE   B   BETA   STD ERROR B   F   VARIABLE   BETA IN   PARTIAL   TOLERANCE   F

X3   2.61962   .89430   .53510   23.967   X1   .14651   .22502   .47231   .267
(CONSTANT)   -6.46236   X2   .41842   .59883   .41010   2.795

* *

VARIABLE(S) ENTERED ON STEP NUMBER   2..   X2

MULTIPLE R   .93358   ANALYSIS OF VARIANCE   DF   SUM OF SQUARES   MEAN SQUARE   F
R SQUARE   .87158   REGRESSION   2.   2287.47038   1143.73519   16.96712
ADJUSTED R SQUARE   .85017   RESIDUAL   5.   337.04462   67.40892
STANDARD ERROR   8.21029

-------- VARIABLES IN THE EQUATION --------   ----------- VARIABLES NOT IN THE EQUATION -----------

VARIABLE   B   BETA   STD ERROR B   F   VARIABLE   BETA IN   PARTIAL   TOLERANCE   F

X3   1.67826   .57294   .73306   5.241   X1   .64575   .96398   .28618   52.538
X2   1.65270   .41842   .39038   2.795
(CONSTANT) -10.02597

Fig. 18-3

(b) Because there is only one independent variable involved in the analysis in this first step, what is called "multiple R" is in fact the simple correlation between Y and X_3, r_{Y3}.

(c) $s_{Y.3} = 9.35844$

(d) $Y_c = -6.46236 + 2.61962X_3$

18.4. Continue referring to step 1 of the regression analysis in Fig. 18-3.

(a) Identify the F ratio associated with testing for the significance of the regression, and indicate whether this test statistic indicates a significant relationship at the 5 percent level of significance.

(b) Note that an F test statistic is also identified as the basis for determining whether the regression coefficient 2.61962 is significantly different from 0. Compare this F statistic with the F statistic identified in (a) above, and comment on this comparison.

(c) The independent variables which have not yet been entered in the analysis are identified in the lower right portion of the step 1 output, with all values being partial values predicated on use of the given variable in conjunction with X_3. Which variable not yet in the analysis has the highest partial correlation coefficient with Y, given X_3 being held constant?

(a) The F ratio is 23.96693. At the indicated degrees of freedom of 1 and 6, the critical value of F for significance at the 5 percent level is 5.99 (Appendix 8). Therefore, the reported F clearly indicates a significant relationship at this level.

(b) The F statistic for b_{Y3} is 23.967, which is a rounded version of the value discussed in (a), above. Since there is only one independent variable in step 1, it follows that the significance associated with the regression is exactly the same as the significance associated with the single regression coefficient b_{Y3}.

(c) The partial correlation between the dependent variable and X_2, which would be represented by $r_{Y2.3}$, is 0.59883, and this is higher than the partial correlation for the only other variable, X_1. Therefore, we would expect X_2 to be the next independent variable entered into the analysis in the following step.

18.5. Refer to step 2 of the regression analysis in Fig. 18-3.

(a) What additional independent variable has been entered in the stepwise regression analysis?

(b) What is the value of the coefficient of multiple correlation R?

(c) Write out the regression equation based on the use of the two independent variables.

(d) What is the standard error of estimate associated with using the regression equation to predict the value of the dependent variable?

(a) X_2, (b) $R_{Y.23} = 0.93358$, (c) $Y_c = -10.02597 + 0.65270X_2 + 1.67826X_3$,
(d) $s_{Y.23} = 8.21029$

18.6. Continue referring to step 2 of the regression analysis in Fig. 18-3.

(a) Comparison of the standard partial regression coefficients (BETA) or comparison of the F statistics for the partial regression coefficients are two ways by which the relative importance of the several independent variables in the regression equation can be determined. Which variable is more important in step 2?

(b)   Using the degrees of freedom indicated, test for the significance of the multiple regression using the 5 percent level of significance.

(c)   Using degrees of freedom of 1 and 5 in this case, determine the significance of each partial regression coefficient in the multiple regression equation.

(a)   The value of beta of 0.57294 associated with X_3 is larger than the value of 0.41842 associated with X_2.   Similarly, the F statistic of 5.241 associated with X_3 is larger than the value of 2.795 associated with X_2.   Therefore, by either comparison we conclude that the importance of X_3 is greater than X_2 in the multiple regression.

(b)   The F ratio for testing the significance of the regression is 16.96712.   At $df = 2$ and 5, the critical F for the 5 percent level of significance is 5.79.   Therefore, the regression equation (and the coefficient of multiple correlation) represents a significant relationship at the 5 percent level.

(c)   As indicated in part (a) above, the F ratios associated with the partial regression coefficients $b_{Y3.2}$ and $b_{Y2.3}$ are 5.241 and 2.795, respectively.   The critical F for significance at the 5 percent level ($df = 1, 5$) is 6.61.   Therefore, neither regression coefficient is significant.   Interestingly, when only X_3 was in the equation (step 1) the regression coefficient b_{Y3} was significant at the 5 percent level.   With the addition of a second variable, neither partial regression coefficient is itself significant.   However, as indicated in the answer to part (b), above, note that the combined relationship of the two independent variables with Y is significant.   This result is associated with the fact that X_2 and X_3 are highly correlated, and illustrates one of the difficulties associated with colinearity, as briefly explained in Section 18.6.

18.7.   Figure 18-4 completes the computer output for this sample problem.   Page 5 of the output is step 3 of the analysis, which concerns the entry of the last available independent variable X_1, while page 6 is a summary table for the completed analysis.

(a)   What is the coefficient of multiple correlation between the dependent variable Y and the three independent variables X_1, X_2, and X_3?

(b)   Test the significance of this correlation value, using the 1 percent level of significance.

(c)   Write out the regression equation based on the use of all three independent variables.

(d)   What is the standard error of estimate associated with using the regression equation to predict the value of the dependent variable?

(a) $R_{Y.123} = 0.99545$

(b)   The F ratio associated with the regression is 145.41888.   The critical value of F ($df = 3, 4$) is 16.69.   Therefore the correlation value is significant at the 1 percent level.

(c) $Y_c = -106.72668 + 3.25179X_1 + 1.33133X_2 - 0.67457X_3$

(d) $s_{Y.123} = 2.44158$

18.8.   Continue referring to Fig. 18-4.

(a)   Using degrees of freedom of 1 and 4 in this case, determine the significance of each partial regression coefficient in the multiple regression equation, using the 5 percent level of significance.

(b)   By reference to the partial regression coefficients, for which independent variable is the partial correlation with the dependent variable negative?   Since all simple correlation values were positive (page 3 of output), how can this be?

SAMPLE PROBLEM
FILE   NONAME   (CREATION DATE = 05 MAY 76)   05 MAY 76   PAGE   5

* * * * * * * * * * * * * * * * *   M U L T I P L E   R E G R E S S I O N   * * * * * * * * * * * * * * * * *
                                                                        VARIABLE LIST   1
                                                                        REGRESSION LIST 1
DEPENDENT VARIABLE..   Y

VARIABLE(S) ENTERED ON STEP NUMBER 3..   X1

MULTIPLE R   .99545   ANALYSIS OF VARIANCE   DF   SUM OF SQUARES   MEAN SQUARE   F
R SQUARE   .99091   REGRESSION   3.   2600.66968   866.88989   145.41888
ADJUSTED R SQUARE   .98728   RESIDUAL   4.   23.84532   5.96133
STANDARD ERROR   2.44158

----------- VARIABLES IN THE EQUATION -----------   ----------- VARIABLES NOT IN THE EQUATION -----------

VARIABLE   B   BETA   STD ERROR B   F   VARIABLE   BETA IN   PARTIAL   TOLERANCE   F

X3   -.67457   -.23029   .39101   2.976
X2   1.33133   .85347   .14914   79.685
X1   3.25179   .64575   .44862   52.538
(CONSTANT) -106.72668

MAXIMUM STEP REACHED

SAMPLE PROBLEM
FILE   NONAME   (CREATION DATE = 05 MAY 76)   05 MAY 76   PAGE   6

* * * * * * * * * * * * * * * * *   M U L T I P L E   R E G R E S S I O N   * * * * * * * * * * * * * * * * *
                                                                        VARIABLE LIST   1
                                                                        REGRESSION LIST 1
DEPENDENT VARIABLE..   Y

SUMMARY TABLE

VARIABLE	MULTIPLE R	R SQUARE	RSQ CHANGE	SIMPLE R	B	BETA
X3	.89430	.79978	.79978	.89430	-.67457	-.23029
X2	.93358	.87158	.07180	.85846	1.33133	.85347
X1	.99545	.99091	.11934	.71884	3.25179	.64575
(CONSTANT)					-106.72668	

Fig. 18-4

(c) If a "reverse" stepwise regression were being done, which independent variable would be the first one considered for exclusion from the complete multiple regression equation?

(a) The critical value of F ($df = 1, 4$) is 7.71. Thus, the partial regression coefficients associated with X_1 and X_2 are both significant at the 5 percent level, but the F ratio of 2.976 associated with $b_{Y3.12}$ is not significant.

(b) The partial correlation between X_3 and Y (that is, $r_{Y3.12}$) would be negative, because $b_{Y3.12}$ has the negative value -0.67457. Yet, the simple correlation r_{Y3} is not only positive, but it is also the highest positive simple correlation in the analysis. This result occurred because X_3 has a high positive relationship with both X_1 and X_2. Therefore, when X_3 is used in conjunction with X_1 and X_2, both being statistically held constant, the remaining relationship with Y is negative (but not significant). This demonstrates the difficulties associated with colinearity, as explained in Section 18.6.

(c) If we were doing a reverse stepwise regression (and such computer programs do exist) we would consider first excluding the variable X_3 from the equation, because the F ratio associated with the partial regression coefficient is smaller than the other F ratios. Further, because this F ratio is not significant [part (a), above] X_3 would in fact be eliminated from the regression equation. Yet, in the "forward" stepwise regression X_3 was the first variable entered into the analysis. What has occurred is that although X_1 and X_2 both have a high correlation with X_3, they are not highly correlated with one another. Thus, even though X_3 has the highest simple correlation with Y, the joint use of X_1 and X_2 in the regression equation would exclude any further significant contribution from X_3. Again, this demonstrates the types of difficulties associated with colinearity, as explained in Section 18.6.

Supplementary Problems

18.9. The operations manager of a plant producing ammonium sulfate has experienced difficulty with the automatic packaging equipment due to the sticking of crystals. Such sticking may be due to moisture content, shape of the crystal, or impurities. A sample of size $n = 48$ batches of ammonium sulfate with a varying percent of moisture (X_1), length to breadth ratios of the crystals (X_2), and percent impurity (X_3) were sampled for testing, with the dependent variable being flow rate of the crystal (Y) in grams per second (g/s). Table 18.2 presents the sample data. Apply a standard computer program for stepwise regression and correlation analysis for these data. What is the simple correlation (a) between Y and X_1? (b) Between Y and X_2? (c) Between Y and X_3?

Ans. (a) -0.66020, (b) -0.38558, (c) -0.68331

18.10. Refer to the computer output for Problem 18.9 to answer each of the following questions. (a) Which is the first variable entered into the regression equation by the stepwise procedure? (b) Which is the second independent variable entered into the regression equation? (c) What is the coefficient of multiple correlation when two independent variables are used? (d) What is the standard error of estimate associated with using two independent variables in the regression equation?

Ans. (a) X_3, (b) X_2, (c) 0.73860, (d) 0.86537

18.11. Continue referring to the computer output for Problem 18.9 to answer each of the following questions. (a) What is the proportion of explained variance associated with the use of all three available independent variables? (b) Test the significance of the coefficient of multiple correlation associated with the use of three independent variables, using the 1 percent level of significance.

Ans. (a) 0.57493, (b) reject H_0, the correlation is significantly different from 0

Table 18.2   Sample Data for the Analysis of Flow Rate

Sample number	X_1	X_2	X_3	Y	Sample number	X_1	X_2	X_3	Y
1	21	2.4	0	5.00	25	17	2.2	3	4.59
2	20	2.4	0	4.81	26	17	2.4	4	5.00
3	16	2.4	0	4.46	27	17	2.4	0	3.82
4	18	2.5	0	4.81	28	15	2.4	2	3.68
5	16	3.2	0	4.46	29	17	2.2	3	5.15
6	18	3.1	1	3.85	30	21	2.2	4	2.94
7	12	3.2	1	3.21	31	23	2.2	10	3.18
8	12	2.7	0	3.25	32	22	2.0	7	2.28
9	13	2.7	0	4.55	33	21	1.9	4	5.00
10	13	2.7	0	4.85	34	24	2.1	8	2.43
11	17	2.7	0	4.00	35	37	2.3	14	0.00
12	24	2.8	0	3.62	36	21	2.4	2	4.10
13	11	2.5	0	5.15	37	28	2.4	5	3.70
14	10	2.6	0	3.76	38	29	2.4	7	3.36
15	17	2.0	0	4.90	39	23	3.6	7	3.79
16	14	2.0	0	4.13	40	32	3.3	8	3.40
17	14	2.0	1	5.10	41	26	3.5	4	1.51
18	14	1.9	0	5.05	42	28	3.5	12	0.00
19	20	2.1	2	4.27	43	21	3.0	3	1.72
20	12	1.9	1	4.90	44	22	3.0	6	2.33
21	11	2.0	2	4.55	45	34	3.0	8	2.38
22	10	2.0	7	5.32	46	29	3.5	5	3.68
23	10	2.0	2	4.39	47	17	3.5	3	4.20
24	16	2.0	2	4.85	48	11	3.2	2	5.00

Source: Professor Bert M. Steece of Arizona State University.

18.12. For the computer output in Problem 18.9, test the significance of each of the partial regression coefficients in the final regression equation, using the 1 percent level of significance.

Ans.   Only the partial regression coefficient for X_3 is significant at the 1 percent level.

18.13. Review all of the steps in the multiple regression analysis for the data in Problem 18.9. If the criterion which is used in the stepwise multiple regression is that a new independent variable will be added to the equation only if the associated reduction in the unexplained variance is significant at the 1 percent level, which independent variable(s) would be included in the regression equation?

Ans. X_2 and X_3

18.14. Using the final regression equation in the computer output for Problem 18.9, construct the 95 percent prediction interval for the flow rate of a batch of ammonium sulfate which has a 15 percent moisture content, crystals for which the length is twice the breadth, and with 2 percent of impurities.

Ans.   2.88 to 6.20 g/s

18.15. Referring to the computer output for Problem 18.9, construct the 95 percent prediction interval for the flow rate of the ammonium sulfate given no information about the independent variables. Compare this interval with the one determined in Problem 18.14.

Ans.   1.38 to 6.31 g/s

Chapter 19

Time Series Analysis

19.1 THE CLASSICAL TIME SERIES MODEL

A *time series* is made up of the observed values for a sequentially ordered set of time periods. Examples of such data are annual sales for a company for the past 10 years and the number of workers employed in a given industry during the past 20 years. A time series is graphically represented by a line graph (see Section 2.8), with the time periods represented on the horizontal axis and the values of the variable represented on the vertical axis.

EXAMPLE 1. Figure 19-1 is a line chart which portrays the factory sales of domestic passenger cars in the United States for the 25-year period from 1950 through 1974. As can be observed, two years during this period in which new peaks in factory sales (to dealers) were achieved were 1955 and 1965. Although the time series includes generally rising values, two years which represent culmination of a series of declining values are 1958 and 1970. As contrasted to the *peaks* in the line chart, these low points are called *troughs* ("trŏfs").

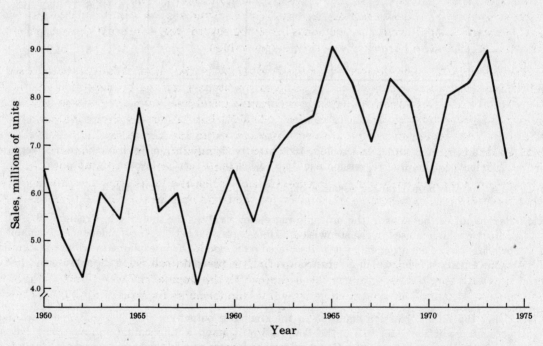

Fig. 19-1. *Source of data*: U.S. Department of Commerce, *Survey of Current Business*.

Time series analysis is the procedure by which the time-related factors that influence the values observed in the time series are identified and segregated. Once identified, they can be used to aid in the interpretation and forecasting of time series values. The classical approach to time series analysis identifies four such influences, or *components*:

(1) *Secular trend* (T):   The general long-term movement in the time series values (Y) over an extended period of time.

(2) *Cyclical fluctuations* (C):   Recurrent up and down movements in respect to secular trend which have a duration of several years.

(3) *Seasonal variations* (S):   Up and down movements in respect to secular trend which are completed within a year and recur annually.   Such variations typically are identified on the basis of monthly or quarterly data.

(4) *Irregular movements* (I):   The erratic variations from secular trend which cannot be ascribed to the cyclical or seasonal influences.

The model underlying classical time series analysis is based on the assumption that for any designated period in the time series the value of the variable is determined by the influences of the four components defined above, and furthermore, that the components have a multiplicative relationship.   Thus, where Y represents the observed time series value,

$$Y = T \times C \times S \times I \qquad (19.1)$$

The model represented by (*19.1*) is used as the basis for separating the influences of the various components influencing time series values, as described in the remaining sections of this chapter.

19.2 TREND ANALYSIS

Because trend analysis is concerned with the long-term direction of movement in the time series, such analysis is performed using annual data.   Typically, at least 15 or 20 years of data should be used, so that cyclical movements involving several years duration are not taken to be indicative of the overall trend of the time series values.

The method of least squares (see Section 17.3) is the most frequent basis used for identifying the trend component of the time series by determining the equation for the best fitting trend line.   Note that statistically speaking a trend line is not a regression line because the dependent variable Y is not a random variable, but rather, an accumulated historical value.   Further, there can only be one historical value for any given time period (not a distribution of values) and the values associated with adjoining time periods are dependent, rather than independent.   Nevertheless, the least squares method is a convenient basis for determining the trend component of a time series.   When the long-term increase or decrease appears to follow a linear trend, the equation for the trend line values, with X representing the year, is

$$Y_T = a + bX \qquad (19.2)$$

As explained in Section 17.3, the a in (*19.2*) represents the point of intersection of the trend line with the Y axis, whereas the b represents the slope of the trend line.   Where X is the year and Y is the observed time-series value, the formulas for determining the values of a and b for the linear trend equation are

$$b = \frac{\Sigma\, XY - n\overline{X}\,\overline{Y}}{\Sigma\, X^2 - n\bar{X}^2} \qquad (19.3)$$

$$a = \bar{Y} - b\bar{X} \qquad (19.4)$$

See Problem 19.1 for the determination of a linear trend equation.

In the case of nonlinear trend, two types of trend curves often used as the basis of trend analysis are the exponential trend curve and the parabolic trend curve.   A typical *exponential trend curve* is one which is indicative of a constant rate of growth during a period of years, as might apply to the sale of electronic calculators from the mid-60s to the mid-70s. See Fig. 19-2(*a*). An exponential curve is so called because the independent variable X is the exponent of b in the general equation:

$$Y_T = ab^x \qquad\qquad (19.5)$$

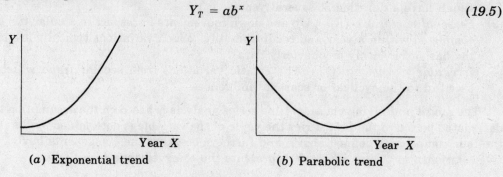

(*a*) Exponential trend   (*b*) Parabolic trend

Fig. 19-2

Taking the logarithm of both sides of (*19.5*) results in a linear logarithmic trend equation, as follows:

$$\log Y_T = \log a + X \log b \qquad\qquad (19.6)$$

The implication of the transformation into logarithms is that the linear equation for trend analysis can be applied to the logs of the values when the time series follows an exponential curve. The forecasted log values for Y_T are then transformed back to the original measurement units by taking the antilog of the values. We do not demonstrate such analysis in this outline.

A typical *parabolic trend curve* is portrayed in Fig. 19-2(*b*) and might be descriptive of such data as the number of long-distance rail passengers in the United States, which had a declining trend but then some increase following the establishment of Amtrak. The general equation for a parabolic trend curve is a second-degree polynomial of the form

$$Y_T = a + bX + cX^2 \qquad\qquad (19.7)$$

The determination of the coefficients in (*19.7*) is beyond the scope of this outline.

19.3 MEASUREMENT OF SEASONAL VARIATIONS

The influence of the seasonal component on time series values is identified by determining the seasonal index number associated with each month (or quarter) of the year. The arithmetic mean of all 12 monthly index numbers (or four quarterly index numbers) is 100. The identification of positive and negative seasonal influences is important for production and inventory planning.

EXAMPLE 2. An index number of 110 associated with a given month indicates that the time-series values for that month have averaged 10 percent higher than for other months because of some positive seasonal factor. For instance, the unit sales of men's shavers might be 10 percent higher in June as compared with other months because of Father's Day.

The procedure most frequently used to determine seasonal index numbers is the *ratio-to-moving-average method*. By this method, the ratio of each monthly value to the moving average centered at that month is first determined. Because a moving average based on monthly (or quarterly) data for an entire year would "average out" the seasonal and irregular fluctuations, but not the longer-term trend and cyclical influences, the ratio of a monthly (or quarterly) value to a moving average can be represented symbolically by

$$\frac{Y}{\text{Moving Average}} = \frac{T \times C \times S \times I}{T \times C} = S \times I \qquad (19.8)$$

The second step in the ratio-to-moving-average method is to average out the irregular component. This is typically done by listing the several ratios applicable to the same month (or quarter) for the several years, eliminating the highest and lowest values, and computing the mean of the remaining ratios. The resulting mean is called a *modified mean*, because of the elimination of the two extreme values.

The final step in the ratio-to-moving-average method is to adjust the modified mean ratios by a correction factor so that the sum of the 12 monthly ratios is 1200 (or 400 for four quarterly ratios). See Problem 19.2.

19.4   APPLYING SEASONAL ADJUSTMENTS

One frequent application of seasonal indexes is that of adjusting observed time-series data by removing the influence of the seasonal component from the data. Such adjusted data are called *seasonally adjusted data*, or *deseasonalized data*. Seasonal adjustments are particularly relevant if we wish to compare data for different months to determine if an increase (or decrease) relative to seasonal expectations has taken place.

EXAMPLE 3. An increase in lawn fertilizer sales of 10 percent from April to May of a given year represents a relative *decrease* if the seasonal index number for May is 20 percent above the index number for April. In other words, if an increase occurs but is not as large as expected based on historical data, then relative to these expectations a decline in demand has occurred.

The observed monthly (or quarterly) time-series values are adjusted for seasonal influences by dividing each value by the monthly (or quarterly) index for that month. The result is then multiplied by 100 to maintain the decimal position of the original data. The process of adjusting data for the influence of seasonal variations can be represented by

$$\frac{Y}{S} = \frac{T \times C \times S \times I}{S} = T \times C \times I \qquad (19.9)$$

Although the resulting values after the application of (*19.9*) are in the same measurement units as the original data, they do not represent actual occurrences. Rather, they are relative values and are meaningful for comparative purposes only. See Problem 19.3.

19.5   FORECASTING BASED ON TREND AND SEASONAL FACTORS

A beginning point for long-term forecasting of annual values is provided by use of the trend line (*19.2*) equation. However, a particularly important consideration in long-term forecasting is the cyclical component of the time series. There is no standard method by which the cyclical component can be forecast based on historical time-series values alone, but certain economic indicators (see Section 19.7) are useful for anticipating cyclical turning points.

For short-term forecasting, the beginning point is the projected trend value which is then adjusted for the seasonal component. Because the equation for the trend line is normally based on the analysis of annual values, the first step required is to "step down" this equation so that it is expressed in terms of months (or quarters). A trend equation is modified to obtain projected monthly values as follows:

$$Y_T = \frac{a}{12} + \left(\frac{b}{12}\right)\left(\frac{X}{12}\right) = \frac{a}{12} + \frac{b}{144}X \qquad (19.10)$$

A trend equation is modified to obtain projected quarterly values as follows:

$$Y_T = \frac{a}{4} + \left(\frac{b}{4}\right)\left(\frac{X}{4}\right) = \frac{a}{4} + \frac{b}{16}X \qquad (19.11)$$

The basis for the above modifications is not obvious if one overlooks the fact that trend values are not associated with points in time, but rather, with periods of time. Because of this consideration, all three elements in the equation for annual trend (a, b, and X) have to be stepped down.

By the transformation for monthly data in (19.10), the base point in the year which was formerly coded $X = 0$ would be at the middle of the year, or July 1. Because it is necessary that the base point be at the middle of the first month of the base year, or January 15, the intercept $a/12$ in the modified equation is then reduced by 5.5 times the modified slope. A similar adjustment is made for quarterly data. Thus, a trend equation which is modified to obtain projected monthly values and with $X = 0$ placed at January 15 of the base year is

$$Y_T = \frac{a}{12} - (5.5)\left(\frac{b}{144}\right) + \frac{b}{144}X \qquad (19.12)$$

Similarly, a trend equation which is modified to obtain projected quarterly values and with $X = 0$ placed at the middle of the first quarter of the base year is

$$Y_T = \frac{a}{4} - (1.5)\left(\frac{b}{16}\right) + \frac{b}{16}X \qquad (19.13)$$

Problem 19.4 illustrates the process of stepping down a trend equation. After monthly trend values have been determined, each value can be multiplied by the appropriate seasonal index (and divided by 100 to preserve the decimal location in the values) to establish a beginning point for short-term forecasting. See Problem 19.5.

19.6 ANALYSIS OF CYCLICAL AND IRREGULAR VARIATIONS

Annual time-series values represent the effects of only the trend and cyclical components, because the seasonal and irregular components are defined as short-run influences. Therefore, for annual data the cyclical component can be identified by dividing the observed values by the associated trend value, as follows:

$$\frac{Y}{Y_T} = \frac{T \times C}{T} = C \qquad (19.14)$$

The ratio in (19.14) is multiplied by 100 so that the mean cyclical relative will be 100.0. A cyclical relative of 100 would indicate the absence of any cyclical influence on the annual time-series value. See Problem 19.6.

In order to aid in the interpretation of cyclical relatives, a *cycle chart* which portrays the cyclical relatives according to year is often prepared. The peaks and troughs associated with the cyclical component of the time series can be made more apparent by the construction of such a chart. See Problem 19.7.

Monthly or quarterly time series values include the influence of all four components of the time series: trend, cyclical, seasonal, and irregular. By the use of the *residual method*, the effects associated with the cyclical and with the irregular components are identified by removing systematically the influences associated with the other components of the time series. The first step is to remove the effects of the trend and seasonal components by dividing the monthly values by the forecasted values based on the trend and seasonal components, as follows:

$$\frac{Y}{T \times S} = \frac{T \times C \times S \times I}{T \times S} = C \times I \qquad (19.15)$$

The ratio in (19.15) is multiplied by 100 so that thé ratio can be interpreted on a percentage basis. See Problem 19.8.

Next, a moving average of the residual values representing the cyclical and irregular components is calculated, typically for 5-month periods. Such a moving average has the short-run irregular component "averaged out," leaving the cyclical component alone. See Problem 19.9.

Finally, the short-run irregular component can be identified in the historical data by dividing the residuals containing the cyclical and irregular components by the moving average which represents only the cyclical component:

$$\frac{C \times I}{C} = I \qquad (19.16)$$

Identification of the irregular component for monthly time-series data is illustrated in Problem 19.10.

19.7 CYCLICAL FORECASTING AND BUSINESS INDICATORS

As indicated in Section 19.5, forecasting based on the trend and seasonal components of a time series is considered only a beginning point in economic forecasting. One reason is the necessity to consider the likely effect of the cyclical component during the forecast period, while the second is the importance of identifying the specific causative factors which have influenced the time series variables.

For short-term forecasting, the effect of the cyclical component is often assumed to be the same as included in recent time-series values. However for longer periods, or even for short periods during economic instability, the identification of the *cyclical turning points* for the national economy is important. Of course, the cyclical variations associated with a particular product may or may not coincide with general business cycles.

EXAMPLE 4. Historically, factory sales of passenger cars have coincided closely with the general business cycles for the national economy. On the other hand, sales of automobile repair parts tend to be counter-cyclical in respect to the general business cycle.

The National Bureau of Economic Research has identified a number of published time series that historically have been indicators of cyclical revivals and recessions in respect to the general business cycle. One group, called *leading indicators*, have usually reached cyclical turning points prior to the corresponding change in general economic activity. The leading indicators include layoff rate in manufacturing, value of new orders in durable goods industries, and the common stock price indexes. A second group, called *coinciding indicators*, are time series which have generally had turning points coinciding with the general business cycle. Coinciding indicators include the unemployment rate, industrial production index, gross national product, and dollar sales of retail stores. The third group, called *lagging indicators*, are those time series for which the peaks and troughs usually lag behind those of the general business cycle. Lagging indicators include plant and equipment expenditures, consumer installment debt, and bank interest on short-term business loans.

In addition to considering the effect of cyclical fluctuations and forecasting such fluctuations, specific causative variables that have influenced the time series values historically should also be studied. Regression and correlation analysis (see Chapters 17 and 18) are particularly applicable for such studies as the relationship between pricing strategy and sales volume. Beyond the historical analyses, the possible implications of new products and of changes in the marketing environment are also areas of required attention.

Solved Problems

TREND ANALYSIS

19.1. Table 19.1 presents data for the factory sales of domestic passenger cars from plants in the United States for the 25-year period from 1950 through 1974. Included also are the calculations needed to determine the equation for the trend line. As is typical in trend analysis, the years have been coded in the second column of this table to simplify subsequent calculations. Given this information, determine the linear trend equation for the factory sales of new passenger cars and enter the trend line on the line chart for these data.

We determine the equation for the trend line as follows:

$$\bar{X} = \frac{\Sigma X}{n} = \frac{300}{25} = 12 \qquad \bar{Y} = \frac{\Sigma Y}{n} = \frac{168.779}{25} = 6.751$$

$$b = \frac{\Sigma XY - n\bar{X}\bar{Y}}{\Sigma X^2 - n\bar{X}^2} = \frac{(2{,}194.972) - (25)(12)(6.751)}{4900 - (25)(12)^2} = 0.13052 \cong 0.131$$

$$a = \bar{Y} - b\bar{X} = 6.751 - (0.131)(12) = 5.179$$

Therefore
$$Y_T = a + bX = 5.179 + 0.131X$$

This equation can be used as a beginning point for forecasting, as described in Section 19.5. The slope of this linear equation indicates that as a long-term trend during the 25-year period there has been an average increase of about 131,000 unit sales per year. Figure 19-3 is the line chart for these time series values with the least squares trend line superimposed on the chart.

MEASUREMENT OF SEASONAL VARIATIONS

19.2. Table 19.2 presents the monthly factory sales of domestic passenger cars from U.S. plants for the period January 1970 through December 1974. Determine the seasonal indexes for such car sales by the ratio-to-moving-average method.

Table 19.2 is concerned with the first principal step in the ratio-to-moving-average method, that of computing the ratio of each monthly value to the 12-month moving average centered at that month. (*Note*: Some of the calculations in the worksheet appear to be slightly off, but actually reflect the fact that the computer analysis which was used carried more significant digits than reported in the table.)

**Table 19.1   Factory Sales of Domestic Passenger
Cars from Plants in the United States,
1950–1974, Millions of Units, and
Calculations Required for Determining
the Trend Line**

Year	Year coded, X	Factory sales, Y	XY	X^2
1950	0	6.513	0	0
1951	1	5.090	5.090	1
1952	2	4.154	8.308	4
1953	3	5.954	17.862	9
1954	4	5.352	21.408	16
1955	5	7.666	38.330	25
1956	6	5.623	33.738	36
1957	7	5.953	41.671	49
1958	8	4.132	33.056	64
1959	9	5.474	49.266	81
1960	10	6.530	65.300	100
1961	11	5.402	59.422	121
1962	12	6.754	81.048	144
1963	13	7.444	96.772	169
1964	14	7.554	105.756	196
1965	15	9.101	136.515	225
1966	16	8.337	133.392	256
1967	17	7.070	120.190	289
1968	18	8.407	151.326	324
1969	19	7.807	148.333	361
1970	20	6.187	123.740	400
1971	21	8.122	170.562	441
1972	22	8.353	183.766	484
1973	23	9.079	208.817	529
1974	24	6.721	161.304	576
Totals	300	168.779	2194.972	4900

Source: U.S. Department of Commerce, *Survey of Current Business*.

The 12-month moving totals are centered between the lines of the table because as a moving total of an even number of months the total would always fall between two months. For example, the first listed total of 6187.4 is the total unit sales (in thousands) for January through December 1970. Since 12 months are involved, the total is centered between the sixth and seventh months (between June and July 1970).

Because it is desired that the moving average be centered at each month, instead of between months, adjoining 12-month moving totals are combined to form the 2-year moving totals. Note that this type of total does not include 2 years of data as such. Rather, two overlapping 12-month periods are included. For example, the first listed total of 12,507.9 includes the January through December 1970 total of 6187.4 plus the February 1970 through January 1971 total of 6320.5.

The 12-month centered moving average is simply the 2-year centered moving total divided by 24.

Finally, the ratio to moving average in the last column of Table 19.2 is the ratio of each monthly sales value to the centered moving average for that month. This ratio is multiplied by 100 and reported as a percentage.

Table 19.2 Factory Sales of Domestic Passenger Cars from Plants in the United States, Thousands of Units: Worksheet for the Computation of Seasonal Indexes by the Ratio-to-Moving-Average Method

Year	Month	Sales	12-month moving total	2-year centered moving total	12-month centered moving average	Ratio to moving average (percent)
1970	Jan.	545.0				
	Feb.	528.4				
	Mar.	594.4				
	Apr.	627.2				
	May	684.4				
	June	758.4				
	July	464.3	6187.4	12,507.9	521.16	89.09
	Aug.	254.0	6320.5	12,831.6	534.65	47.51
	Sep.	454.2	6511.1	13,243.7	551.82	82.31
	Oct.	365.4	6732.6	13,541.6	564.23	64.76
	Nov.	341.1	6809.0	13,650.3	568.76	59.97
	Dec.	570.6	6841.3	13,685.5	570.23	100.06
1971	Jan.	678.1	6844.2	13,693.0	570.54	118.85
	Feb.	719.0	6848.8	13,901.2	579.22	124.13
	Mar.	815.9	7052.4	14,362.6	598.44	136.34
	Apr.	703.6	7310.2	15,013.6	625.57	112.47
	May	716.7	7703.4	15,802.3	658.43	108.85
	June	761.3	8098.9	16,220.4	675.85	112.64
	July	468.9	8121.5	16,230.9	676.29	69.33
	Aug.	457.6	8109.4	16,215.9	675.66	67.73
	Sep.	712.0	8106.5	16,162.3	673.43	105.73
	Oct.	758.6	8055.8	16,144.9	672.70	112.77
	Nov.	736.6	8089.1	16,259.5	677.48	108.73
	Dec.	593.2	8170.4	16,341.1	680.88	87.12
1972	Jan.	666.0	8170.7	16,266.1	677.75	98.26
	Feb.	716.1	8095.4	16,104.2	671.01	106.72
	Mar.	765.2	8008.8	16,114.4	671.43	113.97
	Apr.	736.9	8105.6	16,294.3	678.93	108.54
	May	798.0	8188.7	16,468.2	686.17	116.30
	June	761.6	8279.5	16,632.0	693.00	109.90
			8352.5			
1972 (cont.)	July	393.6	8546.3	16,898.8	704.12	55.90
	Aug.	371.0	8645.7	17,192.0	716.33	51.79
	Sep.	808.8	8763.3	17,409.0	725.37	111.50
	Oct.	841.7	8813.0	17,576.3	732.35	114.93
	Nov.	827.4	8895.1	17,708.1	737.84	112.14
	Dec.	666.2	9006.8	17,901.9	745.91	89.31
1973	Jan.	859.8	9290.7	18,297.5	762.40	112.78
	Feb.	815.5	9335.4	18,626.1	776.09	105.08
	Mar.	882.8	9192.7	18,528.1	772.00	114.35
	Apr.	786.6	9238.2	18,430.9	767.95	102.43
	May	880.1	9237.9	18,476.1	769.84	114.32
	June	873.3	9078.8	18,316.7	763.20	114.43
	July	677.5	8771.1	17,849.9	743.75	91.10
	Aug.	415.7	8457.1	17,228.2	717.84	57.91
	Sep.	666.1	8131.4	16,588.5	691.19	96.38
	Oct.	887.2	7962.2	16,093.6	670.57	132.31
	Nov.	827.1	7761.1	15,723.3	655.14	126.25
	Dec.	507.1	7506.0	15,267.1	636.13	79.72
1974	Jan.	552.1	7343.7	14,849.7	618.74	89.24
	Feb.	501.5	7343.8	14,687.5	611.98	81.95
	Mar.	557.1	7286.5	14,630.3	609.60	91.39
	Apr.	617.4	7161.9	14,448.4	602.02	102.56
	May	679.0	6834.4	13,996.3	583.18	116.44
	June	618.2	6721.3	13,555.7	564.82	109.46
	July	515.2				
	Aug.	415.8				
	Sep.	762.6				
	Oct.	608.8				
	Nov.	499.6				
	Dec.	394.0				

Source: U.S. Department of Commerce, *Survey of Current Business.*

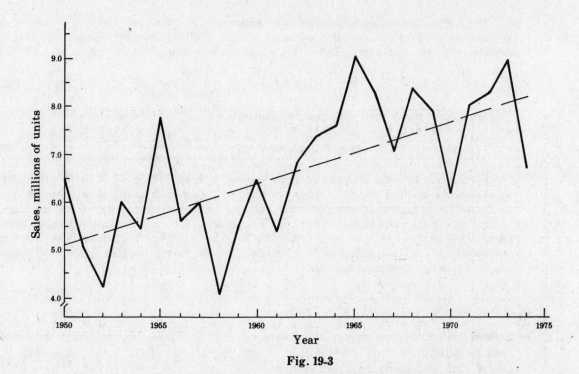

Fig. 19-3

Table 19.3 incorporates the second and third steps in determining the seasonal indexes. Again, the computer analysis which was used carried more digits than reported in this table. The modified mean for each month is the mean of the moving average percents for each month, after elimination of the highest and lowest values. For example, for January the two extreme values 89.24 and 118.86 are eliminated, with the mean of the remaining three values being 105.53.

Table 19.3 Calculation of Seasonal Indexes Using Percents of 12-Month Moving Averages

Month	1970	1971	1972	1973	1974	Modified mean, by month	Adjusted seasonal index mean × 0.9955
Jan.		118.86	98.27	112.78	89.24	105.53	105.1
Feb.		124.14	106.72	105.08	81.95	105.90	105.4
Mar.		136.34	113.97	114.36	91.39	114.16	113.7
Apr.		112.48	108.54	102.43	102.56	105.55	105.1
May		108.85	116.30	114.33	116.44	115.31	114.8
June		112.65	109.90	114.43	109.46	111.28	110.8
July	89.09	69.34	55.90	91.10		79.22	78.9
Aug.	47.51	67.73	51.80	57.91		54.86	54.6
Sep.	82.31	105.73	111.51	96.38		101.05	100.6
Oct.	64.77	112.77	114.94	132.31		113.86	113.3
Nov.	59.98	108.73	112.14	126.25		110.44	109.9
Dec.	100.07	87.13	89.32	79.72		88.22	87.8
						1205.38	1200.0

The modified means are multiplied by an adjustment factor so that the sum of the indexes is approximately 1200 for the monthly seasonal indexes (or 400 for quarterly seasonal indexes). The adjustment factor used with modified monthly means to obtain monthly indexes is

$$\text{Mo. Adj. Factor} = \frac{1200}{\text{sum of monthly means}} \tag{19.17}$$

The adjustment factor used with modified quarterly means to obtain quarterly indexes is

$$\text{Qtrly. Adj. Factor} = \frac{400}{\text{sum of quarterly means}} \tag{19.18}$$

For the data in Table 19.3, the adjustment factor is 1200/1205.38 = 0.9955; this is multiplied by each of the modified means to obtain the monthly indexes. Overall, we can observe that the month with the highest positive seasonal influence is May, with factory car sales being 14.8 percent higher than the typical month, on the average. The month with the greatest negative seasonal component is August, with factory car sales being 54.6 percent of the typical month, on the average. The latter influence is associated with the reduced factory operations for annual model changes and vacation schedules.

APPLYING SEASONAL ADJUSTMENTS

19.3. Deseasonalize the factory car sales data reported in Table 19.3 by using the monthly indexes determined in Problem 19.2. Using the results of the analysis, illustrate the use of such seasonally adjusted values.

Each seasonally adjusted value in Table 19.4 was determined by dividing the monthly value reported in Table 19.2 by the seasonal index applicable for that month and multiplying the result by 100. For instance, the adjusted value of 518.7 for January 1970 was obtained by dividing 545.0 (from Table 19.2) by 105.1 (from Table 19.3) and multiplying by 100.

As one example of the usefulness of seasonally adjusted data, note that in 1974, factory car sales dropped from 618.2 thousand units to 515.2 thousand units between June and July (Table 19.2). However, on a seasonally adjusted basis car sales in fact increased, as indicated by the respective deseasonalized values of 558.0 and 653.2 (Table 19.4). Even though an actual decrease occurred, it was not as large a decrease as would be generally expected for July, based on the seasonal index for that month.

Table 19.4 Seasonally Adjusted Data for Factory
Sales of Domestic Passenger Cars from
Plants in the United States, Thousands of
Units

Month	1970	1971	1972	1973	1974
Jan.	518.7	645.4	633.9	818.4	525.5
Feb.	501.1	681.9	679.2	773.4	475.6
Mar.	523.0	717.8	673.2	776.7	490.1
Apr.	596.8	669.5	701.2	748.5	587.5
May	596.1	624.3	695.1	766.6	591.4
June	684.6	687.2	687.5	788.3	558.0
July	588.7	594.5	499.1	859.0	653.2
Aug.	465.1	837.8	679.3	761.1	761.3
Sep.	451.5	707.7	803.9	662.1	605.1
Oct.	322.4	669.2	742.5	782.7	672.8
Nov.	310.2	669.9	752.5	752.2	454.4
Dec.	649.6	675.4	758.5	577.3	448.6

FORECASTING BASED ON TREND AND SEASONAL FACTORS

19.4. Step down the trend equation developed in Problem 19.1 so that it is expressed in months, with the base month being the first month of the base year. Use this equation to determine monthly trend values for the years 1970 through 1974 in thousands of units.

For the trend equation determined in Problem 19.1 the base year is 1950 (i.e. the year which was coded $X = 0$). The modified equation for projecting monthly trend values for which the base month is January 1950 is obtained as follows:

$$Y_T \text{ (annual)} = 5.179 + 0.131X \quad \text{(from Problem 19.1)}$$

$$Y_T \text{ (monthly)} = \left[\frac{a}{12} - (5.5)\left(\frac{b}{144}\right)\right] + \frac{b}{144}X = \left[\frac{5.179}{12} - (5.5)\frac{0.131}{144}\right] + \frac{0.131}{144}X$$

$$= (0.43158 - 0.00500) + 0.00091X = 0.42658 + 0.00091X$$

In this particular application, we further take note of the fact that the annual data used as the basis of the trend equation are in millions of units (Table 19.1), whereas the required monthly trend values are in thousands of units. Therefore, the monthly trend equation is further modified so that the projected values are in thousands of units as follows:

$$Y_T \text{ (monthly)} = 1000(0.42658 + 0.00091X) = 426.58 + 0.91X$$

Table 19.5 presents the monthly trend values for January 1970 through December 1974 based on use of the above equation. For example, January 1970 is the 240th month after the base month of January 1950, for which $X = 0$. Therefore, the monthly trend value for January 1970 is

$$Y_T \text{ (Jan. 1970)} = 426.58 + 0.91(240) = 644.98 \cong 645.0$$

Table 19.5　Monthly Trend Values for Factory Sales of Domestic Passenger Cars from Plants in the United States, Thousands of Units

Month	1970	1971	1972	1973	1974
Jan.	645.0	655.9	666.8	677.7	688.7
Feb.	645.9	656.8	667.7	678.6	689.6
Mar.	646.8	657.7	668.6	679.6	690.5
Apr.	647.7	658.6	669.6	680.5	691.4
May	648.6	659.5	670.5	681.4	692.3
June	649.5	660.4	671.4	682.3	693.2
July	650.4	661.4	672.3	683.2	694.1
Aug.	651.4	662.3	673.2	684.1	695.0
Sep.	652.3	663.2	674.1	685.0	695.9
Oct.	653.2	664.1	675.0	685.9	696.8
Nov.	654.1	665.0	675.9	686.8	697.8
Dec.	655.0	665.9	676.8	687.8	698.7

19.5. Determine forecasted monthly values for the factory car sales for the years 1970 through 1974 by applying the seasonal indexes to the monthly trend values determined in Problem 19.4. (*Note*: In the context of an actual forecasting situation such values would be determined for just several months into the future. A 5-year period is used in this problem because these values will be used to identify the cyclical and irregular components of the time series in Problems 19.8 to 19.10.)

For January 1970 the forecasted value of 677.9 in Table 19.6 was obtained by multiplying the monthly trend value of 645.0 (from Table 19.5) by the monthly index of 105.1 (from Table 19.3) and dividing by 100. The other values in Table 19.6 were obtained by the same procedure.

Table 19.6   Forecasted Monthly Values of Factory
Sales of Domestic Passenger Cars from
Plants in the United States Based on the
Trend and Seasonal Components of the
Time Series, Thousands of Units

Month	1970	1971	1972	1973	1974
Jan.	677.9	689.4	700.8	712.3	723.8
Feb.	680.8	692.3	703.8	715.2	726.8
Mar.	735.4	747.8	760.2	772.7	785.1
Apr.	680.7	692.2	703.7	715.2	726.7
May	744.6	757.1	769.7	782.2	794.8
June	719.6	731.7	743.9	756.0	768.1
July	513.2	521.8	530.4	539.0	547.6
Aug.	355.7	361.6	367.6	373.5	379.5
Sep.	656.2	667.2	678.1	689.1	700.1
Oct.	740.1	752.4	764.8	777.1	789.5
Nov.	718.9	730.8	742.8	754.8	766.9
Dec.	575.1	584.7	594.2	603.9	613.5

ANALYSIS OF CYCLICAL VARIATIONS FOR ANNUAL DATA

19.6. Determine the cyclical relatives for the data in Table 19.1.

Table 19.7 includes the factory sales of domestic passenger cars for the years 1950 through 1974 and the expected sales based on the trend equation developed in Problem 19.1. With the base year (and $X = 0$) set at 1950, the trend equation for annual data is $Y_T = 5.179 + 0.131X$.

As indicated in the last column of the table, each cyclical relative is determined by multiplying the observed time-series value by 100 and dividing by the trend value. Thus, the cyclical relative of 125.8 for 1950 was computed by solving $100(6.513)/5.179$.

19.7. Prepare a cycle chart for the annual factory sales of domestic passenger cars from 1950 through 1974, referring to the cyclical relatives in Table 19.7.

The cycle chart appears in Fig. 19-4.

ANALYSIS OF CYCLICAL AND IRREGULAR VARIATIONS FOR MONTHLY DATA

19.8. Use the residual method to identify the combined cyclical and irregular components in the monthly time-series data reported in Table 19.2.

Table 19.8 presents the monthly car sales adjusted for the trend and seasonal components, thus leaving the cyclical and irregular components as the residual. For example, the index of 80.4 for January 1970, is obtained by dividing the monthly sales, in thousands of units, of 545.0 (from Table 19.2) by the forecast based on the trend and seasonal components of 677.9 (from Table 19.6) and multiplying the ratio by 100. Thus, the resulting index of 80.4 indicates that the combined influences of the cyclical and irregular components for that month resulted in unit sales that were 19.6 percent lower than the forecasted sales based on the trend and seasonal factors.

Table 19.7   Determination of Cyclical Relatives for
Annual Factory Sales of Domestic
Passenger Cars for Plants in the United
States, 1950–1974, Millions of Units

Year	Year coded, X	Factory sales, Y	Expected sales, Y_T	Cyclical relative $100\,Y/Y_T$
1950	0	6.513	5.179	125.8
1951	1	5.090	5.310	95.9
1952	2	4.154	5.441	76.3
1953	3	5.954	5.572	106.9
1954	4	5.352	5.703	93.8
1955	5	7.666	5.834	131.4
1956	6	5.623	5.965	94.3
1957	7	5.953	6.096	97.7
1958	8	4.132	6.227	66.4
1959	9	5.474	6.358	86.1
1960	10	6.530	6.489	100.6
1961	11	5.402	6.620	81.6
1962	12	6.754	6.751	100.0
1963	13	7.444	6.882	108.2
1964	14	7.554	7.013	107.7
1965	15	9.101	7.144	127.4
1966	16	8.337	7.275	114.6
1967	17	7.070	7.406	95.5
1968	18	8.407	7.537	111.5
1969	19	7.807	7.668	101.8
1970	20	6.187	7.799	79.3
1971	21	8.122	7.930	102.4
1972	22	8.353	8.061	103.6
1973	23	9.079	8.192	110.8
1974	24	6.721	8.323	80.8

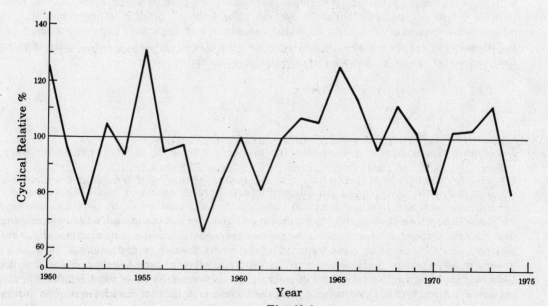

Fig. 19-4

Table 19.8   Factory Sales of Domestic Passenger Cars
from Plants in the United States,
Thousands of Units: Monthly Values
Adjusted for Trend and Seasonal
Components (Indicating the Percentage
Influence of Cyclical and Irregular Effects)

Month	1970	1971	1972	1973	1974
Jan.	80.4	98.4	95.0	120.7	76.3
Feb.	77.6	103.9	101.7	114.0	69.0
Mar.	80.8	109.1	100.7	114.2	71.0
Apr.	92.1	101.6	104.7	110.0	85.0
May	91.9	94.7	103.7	112.5	85.4
June	105.4	104.0	102.4	115.5	80.5
July	90.5	89.9	74.2	125.7	94.1
Aug.	71.4	126.5	100.9	111.3	109.6
Sep.	69.2	106.7	119.3	96.7	87.0
Oct.	49.4	100.8	110.1	114.2	96.6
Nov.	47.4	100.8	111.4	109.6	65.1
Dec.	99.2	101.5	112.1	84.0	64.2

19.9. Referring to the residuals identified in Problem 19.8, identify the cyclical component in the monthly values.   Were there any cyclical peaks or troughs during the period 1970 through 1974?

Table 19.9 presents the 5-month moving averages for the data of Table 19.8.   In reviewing these percentage indexes, we can observe that the years during which there was substantial negative influence associated with the cyclical component of the time series are 1970 and 1974.   The 1970 results coincide with a national recession, while the results for 1974 coincide with both the energy crisis and a national recession.   The year in which there was the greatest positive influence associated with the cyclical component on these monthly values was 1973, which followed recovery from the 1969–1970 recession and preceded the energy crisis.   In the inflationary environment of 1973, many car sales were also stimulated by anticipation of substantially higher prices to be charged for 1974-model automobiles.

19.10. Determine the irregular component for monthly car sales of U.S. passenger cars by reference to the residuals determined in Problems 19.8 and 19.9.

The indexes in Table 19.10 were obtained by dividing the indexes in Table 19.8, which include the influence of the cyclical and irregular components of the time series, by the respective indexes in Table 19.9, which include only the influence of the cyclical components, and multiplying by 100.   As such, these indexes indicate the percentage variation in the monthly time-series values attributable to the irregular component.   The variations (from 100) that are relatively large can generally be explained by knowledge of specific causative events.   For example, a strike at General Motors during October and November of 1970 resulted in a substantial reduction in factory car sales during these months, and settlement of this labor dispute was followed by an unusual increase in factory car sales in December of 1970.

Table 19.9 Factory Sales of Domestic Passenger Cars from Plants in the United States, Thousands of Units: 5-Month Moving Average of Monthly Values Adjusted for Trend and Seasonal Components (Indicating the Percentage Influence of Cyclical Effects)

Month	1970	1971	1972	1973	1974
Jan.		91.6	99.9	114.5	82.0
Feb.		102.4	100.7	114.2	77.1
Mar.	84.6	101.5	101.2	114.3	77.3
Apr.	89.6	102.7	102.6	113.2	78.2
May	92.1	99.9	97.1	115.6	83.2
June	90.3	103.3	97.2	115.0	90.9
July	85.7	104.4	100.1	112.3	91.3
Aug.	77.2	105.6	101.4	112.7	93.6
Sep.	65.6	104.9	103.2	111.5	90.5
Oct.	67.3	107.3	110.8	103.2	84.5
Nov.	72.7	101.0	114.7	96.2	
Dec.	79.7	100.0	113.7	90.6	

Table 19.10 Factory Sales of Domestic Passenger Cars from Plants in the United States: Percentage Variations Attributable to the Irregular Component of the Time Series

Month	1970	1971	1972	1973	1974
Jan.		107.4	95.1	105.4	93.0
Feb.		101.5	101.0	99.8	89.5
Mar.	95.5	107.5	99.5	99.9	91.8
Apr.	102.8	98.9	102.0	97.2	108.7
May	99.8	94.8	106.8	97.3	102.6
June	116.7	100.7	105.3	100.4	88.6
July	105.6	86.1	74.1	111.9	103.1
Aug.	92.5	119.8	99.5	98.8	117.1
Sep.	105.5	101.7	115.6	86.7	96.1
Oct.	73.4	93.9	99.4	110.7	114.3
Nov.	65.2	99.8	97.1	113.9	
Dec.	124.5	101.5	98.6	92.7	

Supplementary Problems

TREND ANALYSIS

19.11. Given the data in Table 19.11, determine the linear trend equation for new plant and equipment expenditures, designating 1955 as the base year for the purpose of coding the years.

Ans. $Y_T = 7.91 + 1.58X$

Table 19.11   New Plant and Equipment Expenditures for
Manufacturing Industries in the United States,
1955-1974, Billions of Dollars

Year	Plant & equipment expenditures, Y	Year	Plant & equipment expenditures, Y
1955	$11.44	1965	22.45
1956	14.97	1966	26.99
1957	15.96	1967	28.51
1958	11.44	1968	28.37
1959	12.08	1969	31.68
1960	14.48	1970	31.95
1961	13.68	1971	29.99
1962	14.68	1972	31.35
1963	15.69	1973	38.01
1964	18.58	1974	46.01

Source: U.S. Department of Commerce, *Survey of Current Business*.

19.12.   Construct a line chart for the data in Table 19.11 and enter the trend line on this chart.

MEASUREMENT OF SEASONAL VARIATIONS

19.13.   Table 19.12 presents quarterly data for new plant and equipment expenditures in the United States for the years 1970 to 1974. Determine the seasonal indexes for such expenditures by the ratio-to-moving-average method. Round all values to two places beyond the decimal.

Table 19.12   New Plant and Equipment Expenditures
for Manufacturing Industries in the United
States, 1970-1974, Billions of Dollars

Quarter	Year				
	1970	1971	1972	1973	1974
I	7.14	6.69	6.61	7.80	9.49
II	8.15	7.55	7.63	9.16	11.27
III	7.99	7.31	7.74	9.62	11.62
IV	8.66	8.44	9.38	11.43	13.63

Source: U.S. Department of Commerce, *Survey of Current Business*.

Ans.   I = 88.4,   II = 100.1,   III = 98.7,   IV = 112.8

APPLYING SEASONAL ADJUSTMENTS

19.14.   Continuing with Problem 19.13, seasonally adjust the plant and equipment expenditures.

FORECASTING BASED ON TREND AND SEASONAL FACTORS

19.15.   Step down the trend equation developed in Problem 19.11 so that it is expressed in quarters, with the base quarter being the first quarter of 1970. Use this equation to determine quarterly trend values for the years 1970 through 1974.

19.16. Determine forecasted quarterly values for plant and equipment expenditures based on the trend and seasonal components of the time series.

ANALYSIS OF CYCLICAL VARIATIONS FOR ANNUAL DATA

19.17. Determine the cyclical relatives for the annual time-series data reported in Table 19.11. Prepare a cycle chart to portray these relatives.

ANALYSIS OF CYCLICAL AND IRREGULAR VARIATIONS FOR QUARTERLY DATA

19.18. Use the residual method to identify the combined cyclical and irregular components in the quarterly time-series data reported in Table 19.12.

19.19. Referring to the residuals identified in Problem 19.18, identify the cyclical components in the quarterly time-series values by the calculation of a three-quarter moving average.

19.20. Determine the irregular component in plant and equipment expenditures between 1970 and 1974, using the results of the computations in Problems 19.18 and 19.19.

Chapter 20

Index Numbers for Business and Economic Data

20.1 INTRODUCTION

An *index number* is a percentage relative by which a measurement in a *given period* is expressed as a ratio to the measurement in a designated *base period*. The measurements can be concerned with *quantity*, *price* or *value*.

EXAMPLE 1. The Consumer Price Index (CPI) prepared by the U.S. Department of Labor is an example of a price index, whereas the Federal Reserve Board Index of Industrial Production is an example of a quantity index.

When the index number represents a comparison for an *individual* product or commodity, it is a *simple index number*. In contrast, when the index number has been constructed for a *group* of items or commodities, it is an *aggregate index number* or *composite index number*.

EXAMPLE 2. The price index of, say, 130 for butter is a simple price index indicating that the price of butter in the given period was 30 percent higher than in the base period. The same price index of 130 for the Consumer Price Index (an aggregate price index) indicates that the average price of a "market basket" of about 400 goods and services was 30 percent higher in the given period as compared with the base period.

20.2 CONSTRUCTION OF SIMPLE INDEXES

Where p_n indicates the price of a commodity in the given period and p_0 indicates the price in the base period, the general formula for the simple price index, or *price relative*, is

$$I_p = \frac{p_n}{p_0} \times 100 \qquad \text{(See Problem 20.1.)} \qquad (20.1)$$

Similarly, where q_n indicates the quantity of an item produced or sold in the given period and q_0 indicates the quantity in the base period, the general formula for the simple quantity index, or *quantity relative*, is

$$I_q = \frac{q_n}{q_0} \times 100 \quad \text{(See Problem 20.2.)} \qquad (20.2)$$

Finally, the *value* of a commodity in a designated period is equal to the price of the commodity multiplied by the quantity produced (or sold). Therefore $p_n q_n$ indicates the value of a commodity in the given period, and $p_0 q_0$ indicates the value of the commodity in the base period. The general formula for a simple value index, or *value relative*, is

$$I_v = \frac{p_n q_n}{p_0 q_0} \times 100 \qquad \text{(See Problem 20.3.)} \qquad (20.3)$$

20.3 CONSTRUCTION OF AGGREGATE PRICE INDEXES

To obtain an aggregate price index, the prices of the several items or commodities could simply be summed for the given period and for the base period, and then compared. Such an index would be an *unweighted* aggregate price index. An unweighted index generally is not very useful because the implicit weight of each item in the index depends on the units upon which the prices are based.

EXAMPLE 3. If the price of milk is reported "per gallon" as contrasted to "per quart", then the price would make a much greater contribution to an unweighted price index for a group of commodities which includes milk.

Because of the difficulty described above, aggregate price indexes generally are weighted according to the quantities q of the commodities. The question as to which period quantities should be used is the issue which serves as the basis for different aggregate price relatives. One of the more popular aggregate price indexes is *Laspeyres' index*, in which the prices are weighted by the quantities associated with the *base* year before being summed. The formula is

$$I(L) = \frac{\sum p_n q_0}{\sum p_0 q_0} \times 100 \qquad \text{(See Problem 20.4.)} \qquad (20.4)$$

Instead of using the base-year quantities as weights, the *given*-year quantities could be used. This is *Paasche's index*. The formula is

$$I(P) = \frac{\sum p_n q_n}{\sum p_0 q_n} \times 100 \qquad \text{(See Problem 20.5.)} \qquad (20.5)$$

Both the Laspeyres and Paasche methods of constructing an aggregate price index can be described as following the *weighted-aggregate-of-prices* approach. An alternative is the *weighted-average-of-price-relatives* approach, by which the simple price index for each individual commodity is weighted by a value figure pq. The values used may either be for the base year, $p_0 q_0$, or for the given year, $p_n q_n$. Typically, the base-year values are used as weights, resulting in the following formula for the weighted-average-of-price-relatives:

$$I_p = \frac{\sum (p_0 q_0)(p_n/p_0 \times 100)}{\sum p_0 q_0} \qquad \text{(See Problem 20.6.)} \qquad (20.6)$$

Algebraically, (20.6) is equivalent to Laspeyres' index, while use of given period values as weights would result in an index equivalent to Paasche's index. The reason for the popularity of the weighted-average-of-price-relatives method is that by this procedure the simple indexes for each commodity are computed first, and these simple price indexes are often desired for analytical purposes in addition to the aggregate price index itself.

20.4 LINK RELATIVES

Link relatives are indexes for which the base is always the preceding period. Therefore, for a set of link relatives for annual value of sales, each index number represents a percentage comparison with the preceding year. Such relatives are useful for highlighting year-to-year comparisons, but are not convenient as the basis for making long-run comparisons.

For the purpose of long-run comparison, if the quantities underlying the link relatives are not available these link relatives can nevertheless be converted into index numbers with a common base. For the common base year, the index, I, is set equal to 100. For each year *preceding* the base year the formula used to convert a link relative to a common-base relative is

$$I_{n-1} = \frac{I_n}{L_n} \times 100 \qquad \text{(See Problem 20.7.)} \qquad (20.7)$$

In (20.7), I_{n-1} is the index for the year preceding the year for which the index I_n is known, and L_n is the link index for the latter year.

For each year *following* the newly designated common base year, the formula used to convert a link relative to a common-base relative is

$$I_n = \frac{L_n I_{n-1}}{100} \qquad \text{(See Problem 20.8.)} \qquad (20.8)$$

20.5   SHIFTING THE BASE PERIOD

The base of an established index number series is often shifted to a more recent year so that current comparisons are more meaningful.   Assuming that the original quantities underlying the index number series are not available, the base period for an index number can be shifted by dividing each (original) index by the index of the newly designated base year and multiplying the result by 100:

$$I_{n(\text{shifted})} = \frac{I_{n(\text{old})}}{\text{old index of new base}} \times 100 \qquad \text{(See Problem 20.9.)} \qquad (20.9)$$

20.6   SPLICING TWO SERIES OF INDEX NUMBERS

An index number may often undergo change by addition of certain new products or by exclusion of certain old products, as well as by changes in the base year.   Yet, for the purpose of historical continuity it is desirable to have a unified series of index numbers available.   In order to *splice* two such separate time series to form one continuous series of index numbers, there must be one year of overlap for the two series such that both types of index numbers have been calculated for that year.   Generally, that year of overlap also is the new base, because it is the year at which new products have been added to and/or removed from the aggregate index.   The index numbers that have to be changed in the process of splicing are the indexes of the old series.   This change is achieved by dividing the new index number for the overlap year (100.0 if this is the new base) by the old index for that year and then multiplying each of the index numbers of the old index number series by this quotient.   See Problem 20.10.

20.7   THE CONSUMER PRICE INDEX (CPI)

The *Consumer Price Index* is the most widely known of the published indexes because of its use as an indicator of the cost of living.   It is published monthly by the Bureau of Labor Statistics and indicates the relative price of a market basket of about 400 items which comprise most of the continuing expenses of typical urban wage earners and clerical workers.   In terms of the standard types of aggregate price indexes discussed in this chapter, the CPI is something of a hybrid because the base year used is 1967, whereas the period used as the basis for the quantity weights is the 1960–1961 period (as of June 1976).   In 1977 a new *Consumer Price Index for All Urban Households* and an updated *Consumer Price Index for Urban Wage Earners and Clerical Workers* will be published.   Both use quantity weights based on an extensive 1972–73 survey.

Whereas the Consumer Price Index is indicative of relative prices compared to the base year, the reciprocal of the CPI indicates the value of the dollar relative to the base year:

$$\text{Value of dollar} = \frac{1}{\text{CPI}} \times 100 \qquad \text{(See Problem 20.11.)} \qquad (20.10)$$

20.8 OTHER PUBLISHED INDEXES

The *Wholesale Price Index* is published monthly by the Bureau of Labor Statistics. It is somewhat misleading in terms of its name, because wholesale or jobber prices are *not* the basis for this index. Rather, the prices studied are those involving the *first commercial transactions* for various commodities. As such, the Wholesale Price Index indicates changes in costs of raw materials to manufacturers and also is a leading indicator of subsequent changes in the Consumer Price Index.

The *Index of Industrial Production* is compiled and published monthly by the Federal Reserve Board. This index is a quantity index which indicates the total amount of goods produced in a given period relative to production in the base period. Individual indexes are also determined for specific groups and subgroups of products. Because the Index of Industrial Production indicates the current level of manufacturing, it is widely used as an indicator of general business conditions.

Solved Problems

SIMPLE INDEXES

20.1. Referring to Table 20.1, determine the simple price indexes for 1976 for the three commodities, using 1970 as the base year.

Table 20.1 Prices and Consumption of Three Commodities in a Particular Metropolitan Area, 1970 and 1976

Commodity	Unit quotation	Average price		Per capita consumption (per month)	
		1970, p_0	1976, p_n	1970, q_0	1976, q_n
Milk	quart	$0.30	$0.38	30	35
Bread	1 lb loaf	0.25	0.35	3.8	3.7
Eggs	dozen	0.60	0.90	1.5	1.0

$$\text{For milk:} \quad I_p = \frac{p_n}{p_0} \times 100 = \frac{0.38}{0.30} \times 100 = 126.7$$

$$\text{For bread:} \quad I_p = \frac{p_n}{p_0} \times 100 = \frac{0.35}{0.25} \times 100 = 140.0$$

$$\text{For eggs:} \quad I_p = \frac{p_n}{p_0} \times 100 = \frac{0.90}{0.60} \times 100 = 150.0$$

20.2. Referring to Table 20.1, determine the simple quantity indexes for the three commodities for 1976, using 1970 as the base year.

$$\text{For milk:} \quad I_q = \frac{q_n}{q_0} \times 100 = \frac{35}{30} \times 100 = 116.7$$

$$\text{For bread:} \quad I_q = \frac{q_n}{q_0} \times 100 = \frac{3.7}{3.8} \times 100 = 97.4$$

$$\text{For eggs:} \quad I_q = \frac{q_n}{q_0} \times 100 = \frac{1.0}{1.5} \times 100 = 66.7$$

20.3. Compute the simple value relatives for 1976 for the three commodities in Table 20.1, using 1970 as the base year.

$$\text{For milk:} \quad I_v = \frac{p_n q_n}{p_0 q_0} \times 100 = \frac{(0.38)(35)}{(0.30)(30)} \times 100 = 147.8$$

$$\text{For bread:} \quad I_v = \frac{p_n q_n}{p_0 q_0} \times 100 = \frac{(0.35)(3.7)}{(0.25)(3.8)} \times 100 = 136.3$$

$$\text{For eggs:} \quad I_v = \frac{p_n q_n}{p_0 q_0} \times 100 = \frac{(0.90)(1.0)}{(0.60)(1.5)} \times 100 = 100.0$$

AGGREGATE PRICE INDEXES

20.4. Compute Laspeyres' aggregate price index for 1976 for the three commodities in Table 20.1, using 1970 as the base year.

Referring to Table 20.2, the index is determined as follows:

$$I(L) = \frac{\sum p_n q_0}{\sum p_0 q_0} \times 100 = \frac{14.08}{10.85} \times 100 = 129.8$$

20.5. Compute Paasche's aggregate price index for 1976 for the three commodities in Table 20.1, using 1970 as the base year.

Using Table 20.3, we calculate the index as follows:

$$I(P) = \frac{\sum p_n q_n}{\sum p_0 q_n} \times 100 = \frac{15.50}{12.02} \times 100 = 129.0$$

20.6. Compute the price index by the weighted-average-of-price-relatives method for the three commodities in Table 20.1, using 1970 as the base year.

With reference to Table 20.4,

$$I_p = \frac{\sum (p_0 q_0)(p_n/p_0 \times 100)}{\sum p_0 q_0} = \frac{1408.00}{10.85} = 129.8$$

This answer corresponds to Laspeyres' index, calculated in Problem 20.4.

LINK RELATIVES

20.7. The dollar value of sales (in millions) for the Ford Motor Company between 1970 and 1975 is as follows: 1970, 14,980; 1971, 16,433; 1972, 20,194; 1973, 23,015; 1974, 23,621; 1975, 24,009. Determine the link relatives for these data.

The link relatives are reported in Table 20.5. For example, the link relative of 102.6 for 1974 indicates that the dollar sales for 1974 were 2.6 percent higher than dollar sales in the preceding year, 1973.

Table 20.2 Worksheet for the Calculation of
Laspeyres' Index for the Data in
Table 20.1

Commodity	$p_n q_0$	$p_0 q_0$
Milk	$11.40	$9.00
Bread	1.33	0.95
Eggs	1.35	0.90
Total	$\Sigma p_n q_0 = \$14.08$	$\Sigma p_0 q_0 = \$10.85$

Table 20.3 Worksheet for the Calculation of
Paasche's Index for the Data in Table
20.1

Commodity	$p_n q_n$	$p_0 q_n$
Milk	$13.30	$10.50
Bread	1.30	0.92
Eggs	0.90	0.60
Total	$\Sigma p_n q_n = \$15.50$	$\Sigma p_0 q_n = \$12.02$

Table 20.4 Worksheet for the Computation of the Weighted Average
of Price Relatives for the Data in Table 20.1

Commodity	Price relative, $p_n/p_0 \times 100$	Value weight, $p_0 q_0$	Weighted relative, $(p_0 q_0)(p_n/p_0 \times 100)$
Milk	126.67	$9.00	1140.00
Bread	140.00	0.95	133.00
Eggs	150.00	0.90	135.00
Total		$10.85	1408.00

Table 20.5 Ford Motor Company Sales and Link Relatives, 1970-1974

Year	1970	1971	1972	1973	1974	1975
Sales, millions of dollars	14,980	16,433	20,194	23,015	23,621	24,009
Link relative	...	109.7	122.9	114.0	102.6	101.6

Source: Ford Motor Company, *Annual Report 1974.*

20.8. Referring only to the link relatives determined in Problem 20.7, compute the value indexes for these six years using 1972 as the base year.

Table 20.6 reports the value indexes. As an example of a year preceding the base year, the value index for 1970 was determined as follows:

$$I_{n-1} = \frac{I_n}{L_n} \times 100 = \frac{I_{1971}}{L_{1971}} \times 100 = \frac{81.4}{109.7} \times 100 = 74.2$$

As an example of a year following the base year, the value index for 1974 was determined as follows:

$$I_n = \frac{L_n I_{n-1}}{100} = \frac{L_{1974} I_{1973}}{100} = \frac{(102.6)(114.0)}{100} = 117.0$$

Table 20.6   Ford Motor Company Link Relatives and Value Indexes, 1970–1974

Year	1970	1971	1972	1973	1974	1975
Link relative	...	109.7	122.9	114.0	102.6	101.6
Value index (1972 = 100)	74.2	81.4	100.0	114.0	117.0	118.9

Source: Table 20.5.

SHIFTING THE BASE PERIOD

20.9.   Shift the value indexes reported in Table 20.6 from the base year of 1972 to 1974 as the common base year for the indexes.

Table 20.7 reports the indexes computed with 1974 as the base year. As one example, the new value index for 1970 was determined as follows:

$$I_{N(shifted)} = \frac{I_{n(old)}}{\text{old index of new base year}} \times 100 = \frac{I_{1970(old)}}{\text{old index for 1974}} \times 100$$

$$= \frac{74.2}{117.0} \times 100 = 63.4$$

Table 20.7   Value Indexes Using Base Years of 1972 and 1974 for Ford Motor Company Sales

Year	1970	1971	1972	1973	1974	1975
Value index (1972 = 100)	74.2	81.4	100.0	114.0	117.0	118.9
Value index (1974 = 100)	63.4	69.6	85.5	97.4	100.0	101.6

Source: Table 20.6.

SPLICING TWO SERIES OF INDEX NUMBERS

20.10.   Table 20.8 presents two hypothetical series of price indexes: one computed for a group of commodities for the years 1965 to 1970 with the base year being 1965, and the other computed beginning in 1970 for a revised group of commodities. Thus, 1970 is the overlap year for which both indexes were determined. Splice these two series to form one continuous series of index numbers with 1970 as the base year.

The spliced series of indexes is reported in the last column of Table 20.8. The quotient which results from dividing the new index number for 1970 (100.0) by the index number for 1970 in the old series (119.2) is 0.839, and this value is used as the multiplication factor to convert each index number in the old series.

Table 20.8   Splicing Two Index Number Series

Year	Old price index (1965 = 100)	Revised price index (1970 = 100)	Spliced price index (1970 = 100)
1965	100.0		83.9
1966	103.1		86.5
1967	106.9		89.7
1968	110.0		92.3
1969	114.1		95.7
1970	119.2	100.0	100.0
1971		105.2	105.2
1972		111.3	111.3
1973		117.5	117.5
1974		124.8	124.8
1975		129.9	129.9
1976		137.7	137.7

THE CONSUMER PRICE INDEX

20.11. For the years 1967 through 1974, the Consumer Price Indexes were: 1967, 100.0; 1968, 104.2;   1969, 109.8;   1970, 116.3;   1971, 121.3;   1972, 125.3;   1973, 133.1;   1974, 147.7; 1975, 161.2.   Determine the purchasing power of the dollar for each of these years in terms of the value of the dollar in the base year—1967.

The last column of Table 20.9 reports the value of the dollar in each year.   For example, the value for 1974 was determined as follows:

$$\text{Value of dollar} = \frac{1}{\text{CPI}} \times 100 = \frac{1}{147.7} \times 100 = \$0.68$$

Thus, in 1974 the dollar was worth 68¢ in terms of 1967 dollars, on the average.

Table 20.9   Consumer Price Indexes and the Value of the U.S. Dollar, 1967-1974 (Base Year = 1967)

Year	Consumer price index	Value of dollar
1967	100.0	$1.00
1968	104.2	0.96
1969	109.8	0.91
1970	116.3	0.86
1971	121.3	0.82
1972	125.3	0.80
1973	133.1	0.75
1974	147.7	0.68
1975	161.2	0.62

Source: U.S. Department of Commerce, *Survey of Current Business.*

Supplementary Problems

SIMPLE INDEXES

20.12. Referring to Table 20.10 and using 1970 as the base year, compute the simple price relative (*a*) for butter for 1974, and (*b*) for American cheese for 1974.

Table 20.10   Factory Production and Wholesale Prices of Butter and American Cheese in the United States, 1970–1974

	1970	1971	1972	1973	1974
Butter production, millions of pounds	1136.7	1142.5	1101.9	918.6	952.1
Wholesale price, per pound	$0.704	$0.693	$0.696	$0.689	$0.674
American cheese production, millions of pounds	1425.9	1517.5	1644.3	1672.5	1832.1
Wholesale price, per pound	$0.649	$0.671	$0.714	$0.843	$0.973

Source: U.S. Department of Commerce, *Survey of Current Business*.

Ans.   (*a*) 95.7,   (*b*) 149.9

20.13. Referring to Table 20.10, compute the simple quantity relative (*a*) for butter for 1974, using 1970 as the base year, and (*b*) for American cheese for 1974, using 1970 as the base year.

Ans.   (*a*) 83.8,   (*b*) 128.5

20.14. (*a*)   Referring to the data in Table 20.10, compute the total value of the factory production of butter and of American cheese in 1970 and in 1974, respectively.

(*b*)   Using the results of part (*a*), above, compute the simple value relatives for butter and for American cheese for the given year 1974, using 1970 as the base year.

Ans.   (*b*) 80.2 and 192.6

AGGREGATE PRICE INDEXES

20.15. Refer to Table 20.11. Compute Laspeyres' price index for the price of these supplies as a group during 1975, using 1970 as the base year.

Ans. $I(L) = 150.4$

20.16. Determine the Paasche aggregate price index for the sample data reported in Table 20.11.

Ans. $I(P) = 153.0$

20.17. Determine the aggregate price index for the data of Table 20.11 by the weighted-average-of-relatives method.

Ans. $I_p = 150.3$

Table 20.11   Average Prices and Monthly Consumption of a
Selected Sample of Supplies in a Departmental
Office, 1970 and 1975

Item	Unit of quotation	Average price		Monthly consumption	
		1970	1975	1970	1975
Mimeograph paper	ream	$0.70	$1.48	4.5	8.0
Lined pads	each	0.30	0.35	10.0	16.0
Ballpoint pens	each	0.39	0.49	8.0	12.0
Pencils	doz.	0.48	0.48	1.0	1.5
Paper clips	box	0.10	0.20	2.0	3.0

LINK RELATIVES

20.18.   Convert the link relatives in Table 20.12 to quantity indexes, using 1970 as the base year.

Table 20.12   Link Relatives and Quantity Indexes for Net
Tons of Raw Steel Produced by the United
States Steel Corporation, 1970-1974

Year	1970	1971	1972	1973	1974
Link relative	. . .	86.6	112.9	114.0	96.9

Source: U.S. Steel Corporation, *1974 Annual Report*.

20.19.   (*a*)   Referring to Problem 20.18, suppose the production of raw steel for 1970 was 31.4 million tons.   Determine the net tons produced in 1974.

(*b*)   Suppose the net tons produced in 1970 was not known, but what is known is that the production of raw steel in 1973 was at 35.0 million tons.   Determine the net tons produced in 1974.

Ans.   (*a*) 33.9 million tons,   (*b*) 33.9 million tons

SHIFTING THE BASE PERIOD

20.20.   Table 20.13 lists the indexes for retail prices of dairy products and of fruits and vegetables between 1970 and 1974, with the base year being 1967.   Compute the simple price relatives for these two categories of products for 1974 using 1970 as the base, rather than 1967.

Table 20.13   Consumer Prices for Dairy Products and for Fruits and
Vegetables, 1970-1974 (1967 = 100)

	1970	1971	1972	1973	1974
Dairy products	111.8	115.3	117.1	127.9	151.9
Fruits & vegetables	113.4	119.1	125.0	142.5	165.8

Source: U.S. Department of Commerce, *Survey of Current Business*.

Ans.   Diary products: $I_p = 135.9$,   Fruits and vegetables: $I_p = 146.2$

SPLICING TWO SERIES OF CONSUMER PRICE INDEXES

20.21. Table 20.14 reports the Consumer Price Index for the years 1960 to 1969, using the base period 1957–1959, and the revised Consumer Price Index for the years 1967–1975, using the base year 1967. Splice these two series of index numbers using a common base year of 1967.

Table 20.14   Consumer Price Indexes for the Old Series
(1957–1959 = 100) and New Series (1967 = 100)

Year	Old price index (1957–59 = 100)	New price index (1967 = 100)
1960	103.1	
1961	104.2	
1962	105.4	
1963	106.7	
1964	108.1	
1965	109.9	
1966	113.1	
1967	116.3	100.0
1968	121.2	104.2
1969	127.7	109.8
1970		116.3
1971		121.3
1972		125.3
1973		133.1
1974		147.7
1975		161.2

Source: U.S. Department of Commerce, *Survey of Current Business*.

THE CONSUMER PRICE INDEX

20.22. Referring to Problem 20.21, determine the purchasing power of the dollar (*a*) in 1960 based on 1967 dollars, and (*b*) in 1970 based on 1960 dollars.

Ans. (*a*) $1.13, (*b*) $0.76

Appendix 1

Binomial Probabilities*

n	x	.01	.05	.10	.15	.20	.25 (p)	.30	.35	.40	.45	.50
1	0	.9900	.9500	.9000	.8500	.8000	.7500	.7000	.6500	.6000	.5500	.5000
	1	.0100	.0500	.1000	.1500	.2000	.2500	.3000	.3500	.4000	.4500	.5000
2	0	.9801	.9025	.8100	.7225	.6400	.5625	.4900	.4225	.3600	.3025	.2500
	1	.0198	.0950	.1800	.2550	.3200	.3750	.4200	.4550	.4800	.4950	.5000
	2	.0001	.0025	.0100	.0225	.0400	.0625	.0900	.1225	.1600	.2025	.2500
3	0	.9703	.8574	.7290	.6141	.5120	.4219	.3430	.2746	.2160	.1664	.1250
	1	.0294	.1354	.2430	.3251	.3840	.4219	.4410	.4436	.4320	.4084	.3750
	2	.0003	.0071	.0270	.0574	.0960	.1406	.1890	.2389	.2880	.3341	.3750
	3	.0000	.0001	.0010	.0034	.0080	.0156	.0270	.0429	.0640	.0911	.1250
4	0	.9606	.8145	.6561	.5220	.4096	.3164	.2401	.1785	.1296	.0915	.0625
	1	.0388	.1715	.2916	.3685	.4096	.4219	.4116	.3845	.3456	.2995	.2500
	2	.0006	.0135	.0486	.0975	.1536	.2109	.2646	.3105	.3456	.3675	.3750
	3	.0000	.0005	.0036	.0115	.0256	.0469	.0756	.1115	.1536	.2005	.2500
	4	.0000	.0000	.0001	.0005	.0016	.0039	.0081	.0150	.0256	.0410	.0625
5	0	.9510	.7738	.5905	.4437	.3277	.2373	.1681	.1160	.0778	.0503	.0312
	1	.0480	.2036	.3280	.3915	.4096	.3955	.3602	.3124	.2592	.2059	.1562
	2	.0010	.0214	.0729	.1382	.2048	.2637	.3087	.3364	.3456	.3369	.3125
	3	.0000	.0011	.0081	.0244	.0512	.0879	.1323	.1811	.2304	.2757	.3125
	4	.0000	.0000	.0005	.0022	.0064	.0146	.0284	.0488	.0768	.1128	.1562
	5	.0000	.0000	.0000	.0001	.0003	.0010	.0024	.0053	.0102	.0185	.0312
6	0	.9415	.7351	.5314	.3771	.2621	.1780	.1176	.0754	.0467	.0277	.0156
	1	.0571	.2321	.3543	.3993	.3932	.3560	.3025	.2437	.1866	.1359	.0938
	2	.0014	.0305	.0984	.1762	.2458	.2966	.3241	.3280	.3110	.2780	.2344
	3	.0000	.0021	.0146	.0415	.0819	.1318	.1852	.2355	.2765	.3032	.3125
	4	.0000	.0001	.0012	.0055	.0154	.0330	.0595	.0951	.1382	.1861	.2344
	5	.0000	.0000	.0001	.0004	.0015	.0044	.0102	.0205	.0369	.0609	.0938
	6	.0000	.0000	.0000	.0000	.0001	.0002	.0007	.0018	.0041	.0083	.0156
7	0	.9321	.6983	.4783	.3206	.2097	.1335	.0824	.0490	.0280	.0152	.0078
	1	.0659	.2573	.3720	.3960	.3670	.3115	.2471	.1848	.1306	.0872	.0547
	2	.0020	.0406	.1240	.2097	.2753	.3115	.3177	.2985	.2613	.2140	.1641
	3	.0000	.0036	.0230	.0617	.1147	.1730	.2269	.2679	.2903	.2918	.2734
	4	.0000	.0002	.0026	.0109	.0287	.0577	.0972	.1442	.1935	.2388	.2734
	5	.0000	.0000	.0002	.0012	.0043	.0115	.0250	.0466	.0774	.1172	.1641
	6	.0000	.0000	.0000	.0001	.0004	.0013	.0036	.0084	.0172	.0320	.0547
	7	.0000	.0000	.0000	.0000	.0000	.0001	.0002	.0006	.0016	.0037	.0078
8	0	.9227	.6634	.4305	.2725	.1678	.1002	.0576	.0319	.0168	.0084	.0039
	1	.0746	.2793	.3826	.3847	.3355	.2670	.1977	.1373	.0896	.0548	.0312
	2	.0026	.0515	.1488	.2376	.2936	.3115	.2965	.2587	.2090	.1569	.1094
	3	.0001	.0054	.0331	.0839	.1468	.2076	.2541	.2786	.2787	.2568	.2188
	4	.0000	.0004	.0046	.0185	.0459	.0865	.1361	.1875	.2322	.2627	.2734
	5	.0000	.0000	.0004	.0026	.0092	.0231	.0467	.0808	.1239	.1719	.2188
	6	.0000	.0000	.0000	.0002	.0011	.0038	.0100	.0217	.0413	.0703	.1094
	7	.0000	.0000	.0000	.0000	.0001	.0004	.0012	.0033	.0079	.0164	.0312
	8	.0000	.0000	.0000	.0000	.0000	.0000	.0001	.0002	.0007	.0017	.0039
9	0	.9135	.6302	.3874	.2316	.1342	.0751	.0404	.0207	.0101	.0046	.0020
	1	.0830	.2985	.3874	.3679	.3020	.2253	.1556	.1004	.0605	.0339	.0176
	2	.0034	.0629	.1722	.2597	.3020	.3003	.2668	.2162	.1612	.1110	.0703
	3	.0000	.0077	.0446	.1069	.1762	.2336	.2668	.2716	.2508	.2119	.1641
	4	.0000	.0006	.0074	.0283	.0661	.1168	.1715	.2194	.2508	.2600	.2461
	5	.0000	.0000	.0008	.0050	.0165	.0389	.0735	.1181	.1672	.2128	.2461
	6	.0000	.0000	.0001	.0006	.0028	.0087	.0210	.0424	.0743	.1160	.1641
	7	.0000	.0000	.0000	.0000	.0003	.0012	.0039	.0098	.0212	.0407	.0703
	8	.0000	.0000	.0000	.0000	.0000	.0001	.0004	.0013	.0035	.0083	.0176
	9	.0000	.0000	.0000	.0000	.0000	.0000	.0000	.0001	.0003	.0008	.0020
10	0	.9044	.5987	.3487	.1969	.1074	.0563	.0282	.0135	.0060	.0025	.0010
	1	.0914	.3151	.3874	.3474	.2684	.1877	.1211	.0725	.0403	.0207	.0098
	2	.0042	.0746	.1937	.2759	.3020	.2816	.2335	.1757	.1209	.0763	.0439
	3	.0001	.0105	.0574	.1298	.2013	.2503	.2668	.2522	.2150	.1665	.1172
	4	.0000	.0010	.0112	.0401	.0881	.1460	.2001	.2377	.2508	.2384	.2051
	5	.0000	.0001	.0015	.0085	.0264	.0584	.1029	.1536	.2007	.2340	.2461
	6	.0000	.0000	.0001	.0012	.0055	.0162	.0368	.0689	.1115	.1596	.2051
	7	.0000	.0000	.0000	.0001	.0008	.0031	.0090	.0212	.0425	.0746	.1172
	8	.0000	.0000	.0000	.0000	.0001	.0004	.0014	.0043	.0106	.0229	.0439
	9	.0000	.0000	.0000	.0000	.0000	.0000	.0001	.0005	.0016	.0042	.0098
	10	.0000	.0000	.0000	.0000	.0000	.0000	.0000	.0000	.0001	.0003	.0010
11	0	.8953	.5688	.3138	.1673	.0859	.0422	.0198	.0088	.0036	.0014	.0005
	1	.0995	.3293	.3835	.3248	.2362	.1549	.0932	.0518	.0266	.0125	.0054
	2	.0050	.0867	.2131	.2866	.2953	.2581	.1998	.1395	.0887	.0513	.0269
	3	.0002	.0137	.0710	.1517	.2215	.2581	.2568	.2254	.1774	.1259	.0806
	4	.0000	.0014	.0158	.0536	.1107	.1721	.2201	.2428	.2365	.2060	.1611
	5	.0000	.0001	.0025	.0132	.0388	.0803	.1321	.1830	.2207	.2360	.2256
	6	.0000	.0000	.0003	.0023	.0097	.0268	.0566	.0985	.1471	.1931	.2256
	7	.0000	.0000	.0000	.0003	.0017	.0064	.0173	.0379	.0701	.1128	.1611
	8	.0000	.0000	.0000	.0000	.0002	.0011	.0037	.0102	.0234	.0462	.0806
	9	.0000	.0000	.0000	.0000	.0000	.0001	.0005	.0018	.0052	.0126	.0269
	10	.0000	.0000	.0000	.0000	.0000	.0000	.0000	.0002	.0007	.0021	.0054
	11	.0000	.0000	.0000	.0000	.0000	.0000	.0000	.0000	.0000	.0002	.0005
12	0	.8864	.5404	.2824	.1422	.0687	.0317	.0138	.0057	.0022	.0008	.0002
	1	.1074	.3413	.3766	.3012	.2062	.1267	.0712	.0368	.0174	.0075	.0029
	2	.0060	.0988	.2301	.2924	.2835	.2323	.1678	.1088	.0639	.0339	.0161
	3	.0002	.0173	.0852	.1720	.2362	.2581	.2397	.1954	.1419	.0923	.0537
	4	.0000	.0021	.0213	.0683	.1329	.1936	.2311	.2367	.2128	.1700	.1208
	5	.0000	.0002	.0038	.0193	.0532	.1032	.1585	.2039	.2270	.2225	.1934
	6	.0000	.0000	.0005	.0040	.0155	.0401	.0792	.1281	.1766	.2124	.2256
	7	.0000	.0000	.0000	.0006	.0033	.0115	.0291	.0591	.1009	.1489	.1934
	8	.0000	.0000	.0000	.0001	.0005	.0024	.0078	.0199	.0420	.0762	.1208
	9	.0000	.0000	.0000	.0000	.0001	.0004	.0015	.0048	.0125	.0277	.0537
	10	.0000	.0000	.0000	.0000	.0000	.0000	.0002	.0008	.0025	.0068	.0161
	11	.0000	.0000	.0000	.0000	.0000	.0000	.0000	.0001	.0003	.0010	.0029
	12	.0000	.0000	.0000	.0000	.0000	.0000	.0000	.0000	.0000	.0001	.0002
13	0	.8775	.5133	.2542	.1209	.0550	.0238	.0097	.0037	.0013	.0004	.0001
	1	.1152	.3512	.3672	.2774	.1787	.1029	.0540	.0259	.0113	.0045	.0016
	2	.0070	.1109	.2448	.2937	.2680	.2059	.1388	.0836	.0453	.0220	.0095
	3	.0003	.0214	.0997	.1900	.2457	.2517	.2181	.1651	.1107	.0660	.0349
	4	.0000	.0028	.0277	.0838	.1535	.2097	.2337	.2222	.1845	.1350	.0873

*Example: $P(X = 3 \mid n = 5, p = 0.30) = 0.1323$

n	x	.01	.05	.10	.15	.20	.25	.30	.35	.40	.45	.50
13	5	.0000	.0003	.0055	.0266	.0691	.1258	.1803	.2154	.2214	.1989	.1571
	6	.0000	.0000	.0008	.0063	.0230	.0559	.1030	.1546	.1968	.2169	.2095
	7	.0000	.0000	.0001	.0011	.0058	.0186	.0442	.0833	.1312	.1775	.2095
	8	.0000	.0000	.0000	.0001	.0011	.0047	.0142	.0336	.0656	.1089	.1571
	9	.0000	.0000	.0000	.0000	.0001	.0009	.0034	.0101	.0243	.0495	.0873
	10	.0000	.0000	.0000	.0000	.0000	.0001	.0006	.0022	.0065	.0162	.0349
	11	.0000	.0000	.0000	.0000	.0000	.0000	.0001	.0003	.0012	.0036	.0095
	12	.0000	.0000	.0000	.0000	.0000	.0000	.0000	.0001	.0001	.0005	.0016
	13	.0000	.0000	.0000	.0000	.0000	.0000	.0000	.0000	.0000	.0000	.0001
14	0	.8687	.4877	.2288	.1028	.0440	.0178	.0068	.0024	.0008	.0002	.0001
	1	.1229	.3593	.3559	.2539	.1539	.0832	.0407	.0181	.0073	.0027	.0009
	2	.0081	.1229	.2570	.2912	.2501	.1802	.1134	.0634	.0317	.0141	.0056
	3	.0003	.0259	.1142	.2056	.2501	.2402	.1943	.1366	.0845	.0462	.0222
	4	.0000	.0037	.0349	.0998	.1720	.2202	.2290	.2022	.1549	.1040	.0611
	5	.0000	.0004	.0078	.0352	.0860	.1468	.1963	.2178	.2066	.1701	.1222
	6	.0000	.0000	.0013	.0093	.0322	.0734	.1262	.1759	.2066	.2088	.1833
	7	.0000	.0000	.0002	.0019	.0092	.0280	.0618	.1082	.1574	.1952	.2095
	8	.0000	.0000	.0000	.0003	.0020	.0082	.0232	.0510	.0918	.1398	.1833
	9	.0000	.0000	.0000	.0000	.0003	.0018	.0066	.0183	.0408	.0762	.1222
	10	.0000	.0000	.0000	.0000	.0000	.0003	.0014	.0049	.0136	.0312	.0611
	11	.0000	.0000	.0000	.0000	.0000	.0000	.0002	.0010	.0033	.0093	.0222
	12	.0000	.0000	.0000	.0000	.0000	.0000	.0000	.0001	.0005	.0019	.0056
	13	.0000	.0000	.0000	.0000	.0000	.0000	.0000	.0000	.0001	.0002	.0009
	14	.0000	.0000	.0000	.0000	.0000	.0000	.0000	.0000	.0000	.0000	.0001
15	0	.8601	.4633	.2059	.0874	.0352	.0134	.0047	.0016	.0005	.0001	.0000
	1	.1303	.3658	.3432	.2312	.1319	.0668	.0305	.0126	.0047	.0016	.0005
	2	.0092	.1348	.2669	.2856	.2309	.1559	.0916	.0476	.0219	.0090	.0032
	3	.0004	.0307	.1285	.2184	.2501	.2252	.1700	.1110	.0634	.0318	.0139
	4	.0000	.0049	.0428	.1156	.1876	.2252	.2186	.1792	.1268	.0780	.0417
	5	.0000	.0006	.0105	.0449	.1032	.1651	.2061	.2123	.1859	.1404	.0916
	6	.0000	.0000	.0019	.0132	.0430	.0917	.1472	.1906	.2066	.1914	.1527
	7	.0000	.0000	.0003	.0030	.0138	.0393	.0811	.1319	.1771	.2013	.1964
	8	.0000	.0000	.0000	.0005	.0035	.0131	.0348	.0710	.1181	.1647	.1964
	9	.0000	.0000	.0000	.0001	.0007	.0034	.0116	.0298	.0612	.1048	.1527
	10	.0000	.0000	.0000	.0000	.0001	.0007	.0030	.0096	.0245	.0515	.0916
	11	.0000	.0000	.0000	.0000	.0000	.0001	.0006	.0024	.0074	.0191	.0417
	12	.0000	.0000	.0000	.0000	.0000	.0000	.0001	.0004	.0016	.0052	.0139
	13	.0000	.0000	.0000	.0000	.0000	.0000	.0000	.0001	.0003	.0010	.0032
	14	.0000	.0000	.0000	.0000	.0000	.0000	.0000	.0000	.0000	.0001	.0005
	15	.0000	.0000	.0000	.0000	.0000	.0000	.0000	.0000	.0000	.0000	.0000
16	0	.8515	.4401	.1853	.0743	.0281	.0100	.0033	.0010	.0003	.0001	.0000
	1	.1376	.3706	.3294	.2097	.1126	.0535	.0228	.0087	.0030	.0009	.0002
	2	.0104	.1463	.2745	.2775	.2111	.1336	.0732	.0353	.0150	.0056	.0018
	3	.0005	.0359	.1423	.2285	.2463	.2079	.1465	.0888	.0468	.0215	.0085
	4	.0000	.0061	.0514	.1311	.2001	.2252	.2040	.1553	.1014	.0572	.0278
	5	.0000	.0008	.0137	.0555	.1201	.1802	.2099	.2008	.1623	.1123	.0667
	6	.0000	.0001	.0028	.0180	.0550	.1101	.1649	.1982	.1983	.1684	.1222

n	x	.01	.05	.10	.15	.20	.25	.30	.35	.40	.45	.50
16	7	.0000	.0000	.0004	.0045	.0197	.0524	.1010	.1524	.1889	.1969	.1746
	8	.0000	.0000	.0001	.0009	.0055	.0197	.0487	.0923	.1417	.1812	.1964
	9	.0000	.0000	.0000	.0001	.0012	.0058	.0185	.0442	.0840	.1318	.1746
	10	.0000	.0000	.0000	.0000	.0002	.0014	.0056	.0167	.0392	.0755	.1222
	11	.0000	.0000	.0000	.0000	.0000	.0002	.0013	.0049	.0142	.0337	.0667
	12	.0000	.0000	.0000	.0000	.0000	.0000	.0002	.0011	.0040	.0115	.0278
	13	.0000	.0000	.0000	.0000	.0000	.0000	.0000	.0002	.0008	.0029	.0085
	14	.0000	.0000	.0000	.0000	.0000	.0000	.0000	.0000	.0001	.0005	.0018
	15	.0000	.0000	.0000	.0000	.0000	.0000	.0000	.0000	.0000	.0001	.0002
	16	.0000	.0000	.0000	.0000	.0000	.0000	.0000	.0000	.0000	.0000	.0000
17	0	.8429	.4181	.1668	.0631	.0225	.0075	.0023	.0007	.0002	.0000	.0000
	1	.1447	.3741	.3150	.1893	.0957	.0426	.0169	.0060	.0019	.0005	.0001
	2	.0117	.1575	.2800	.2673	.1914	.1136	.0581	.0260	.0102	.0035	.0010
	3	.0006	.0415	.1556	.2359	.2393	.1893	.1245	.0701	.0341	.0144	.0052
	4	.0000	.0076	.0605	.1457	.2093	.2209	.1868	.1320	.0796	.0411	.0182
	5	.0000	.0010	.0175	.0668	.1361	.1914	.2081	.1849	.1379	.0875	.0472
	6	.0000	.0001	.0039	.0236	.0680	.1276	.1784	.1991	.1839	.1432	.0944
	7	.0000	.0000	.0007	.0065	.0267	.0668	.1201	.1685	.1927	.1841	.1484
	8	.0000	.0000	.0001	.0014	.0084	.0279	.0644	.1134	.1606	.1883	.1855
	9	.0000	.0000	.0000	.0003	.0021	.0093	.0276	.0611	.1070	.1540	.1855
	10	.0000	.0000	.0000	.0000	.0004	.0025	.0095	.0263	.0571	.1008	.1484
	11	.0000	.0000	.0000	.0000	.0001	.0005	.0026	.0090	.0242	.0525	.0944
	12	.0000	.0000	.0000	.0000	.0000	.0001	.0006	.0024	.0081	.0215	.0472
	13	.0000	.0000	.0000	.0000	.0000	.0000	.0001	.0005	.0021	.0068	.0182
	14	.0000	.0000	.0000	.0000	.0000	.0000	.0000	.0001	.0004	.0016	.0052
18	0	.8345	.3972	.1501	.0536	.0180	.0056	.0016	.0004	.0001	.0000	.0000
	1	.1517	.3763	.3002	.1704	.0811	.0338	.0126	.0042	.0012	.0003	.0001
	2	.0130	.1683	.2835	.2556	.1723	.0958	.0458	.0190	.0069	.0022	.0006
	3	.0007	.0473	.1680	.2406	.2297	.1704	.1046	.0547	.0246	.0095	.0031
	4	.0000	.0093	.0700	.1592	.2153	.2130	.1681	.1104	.0614	.0291	.0117
	5	.0000	.0014	.0218	.0787	.1507	.1988	.2017	.1664	.1146	.0666	.0327
	6	.0000	.0002	.0052	.0301	.0816	.1436	.1873	.1941	.1655	.1181	.0708
	7	.0000	.0000	.0010	.0091	.0350	.0820	.1376	.1792	.1892	.1657	.1214
	8	.0000	.0000	.0002	.0022	.0120	.0376	.0811	.1327	.1734	.1864	.1669
	9	.0000	.0000	.0000	.0004	.0033	.0139	.0386	.0794	.1284	.1694	.1855
	10	.0000	.0000	.0000	.0001	.0008	.0042	.0149	.0385	.0771	.1248	.1669
	11	.0000	.0000	.0000	.0000	.0001	.0010	.0046	.0151	.0374	.0742	.1214
	12	.0000	.0000	.0000	.0000	.0000	.0002	.0012	.0047	.0145	.0354	.0708
	13	.0000	.0000	.0000	.0000	.0000	.0000	.0002	.0012	.0045	.0134	.0327
	14	.0000	.0000	.0000	.0000	.0000	.0000	.0000	.0002	.0011	.0039	.0117
	15	.0000	.0000	.0000	.0000	.0000	.0000	.0000	.0000	.0002	.0009	.0031
	16	.0000	.0000	.0000	.0000	.0000	.0000	.0000	.0000	.0000	.0001	.0006
	17	.0000	.0000	.0000	.0000	.0000	.0000	.0000	.0000	.0000	.0000	.0001
	18	.0000	.0000	.0000	.0000	.0000	.0000	.0000	.0000	.0000	.0000	.0000

n	x	.01	.05	.10	.15	.20	.25	.30	.35	.40	.45	.50
25	5	.0000	.0060	.0646	.1564	.1960	.1645	.1030	.0506	.0199	.0063	.0016
	6	.0000	.0010	.0239	.0920	.1633	.1828	.1472	.0908	.0442	.0172	.0053
	7	.0000	.0001	.0072	.0441	.1108	.1654	.1712	.1327	.0800	.0381	.0143
	8	.0000	.0000	.0018	.0175	.0623	.1241	.1651	.1607	.1200	.0701	.0322
	9	.0000	.0000	.0004	.0058	.0294	.0781	.1336	.1635	.1511	.1084	.0609
	10	.0000	.0000	.0000	.0016	.0118	.0417	.0916	.1409	.1612	.1419	.0974
	11	.0000	.0000	.0000	.0004	.0040	.0189	.0536	.1034	.1465	.1583	.1328
	12	.0000	.0000	.0000	.0000	.0012	.0074	.0268	.0650	.1140	.1511	.1550
	13	.0000	.0000	.0000	.0000	.0003	.0025	.0115	.0350	.0760	.1236	.1550
	14	.0000	.0000	.0000	.0000	.0000	.0007	.0042	.0161	.0434	.0867	.1328
	15	.0000	.0000	.0000	.0000	.0000	.0002	.0013	.0064	.0212	.0520	.0974
	16	.0000	.0000	.0000	.0000	.0000	.0000	.0004	.0021	.0088	.0266	.0609
	17	.0000	.0000	.0000	.0000	.0000	.0000	.0001	.0006	.0031	.0115	.0322
	18	.0000	.0000	.0000	.0000	.0000	.0000	.0000	.0001	.0009	.0042	.0143
	19	.0000	.0000	.0000	.0000	.0000	.0000	.0000	.0000	.0002	.0013	.0053
	20	.0000	.0000	.0000	.0000	.0000	.0000	.0000	.0000	.0000	.0001	.0016
	21	.0000	.0000	.0000	.0000	.0000	.0000	.0000	.0000	.0000	.0000	.0004
	22	.0000	.0000	.0000	.0000	.0000	.0000	.0000	.0000	.0000	.0000	.0001
30	0	.7397	.2146	.0424	.0076	.0012	.0002	.0000	.0000	.0000	.0000	.0000
	1	.2242	.3389	.1413	.0404	.0093	.0018	.0003	.0000	.0000	.0000	.0000
	2	.0328	.2586	.2277	.1034	.0337	.0086	.0018	.0003	.0000	.0000	.0000
	3	.0031	.1270	.2361	.1703	.0785	.0269	.0072	.0015	.0003	.0000	.0000
	4	.0002	.0451	.1771	.2028	.1325	.0604	.0208	.0056	.0012	.0002	.0000
	5	.0000	.0124	.1023	.1861	.1723	.1047	.0464	.0157	.0041	.0008	.0001
	6	.0000	.0027	.0474	.1368	.1795	.1455	.0829	.0353	.0115	.0029	.0006
	7	.0000	.0005	.0180	.0828	.1538	.1662	.1219	.0652	.0263	.0081	.0019
	8	.0000	.0001	.0058	.0420	.1106	.1593	.1501	.1009	.0505	.0191	.0055
	9	.0000	.0000	.0016	.0181	.0676	.1298	.1573	.1328	.0823	.0382	.0133
	10	.0000	.0000	.0004	.0067	.0355	.0909	.1416	.1502	.1152	.0656	.0280
	11	.0000	.0000	.0001	.0022	.0161	.0551	.1103	.1471	.1396	.0976	.0509
	12	.0000	.0000	.0000	.0006	.0064	.0291	.0749	.1254	.1474	.1265	.0806
	13	.0000	.0000	.0000	.0001	.0022	.0134	.0444	.0935	.1360	.1433	.1115
	14	.0000	.0000	.0000	.0000	.0007	.0054	.0231	.0611	.1101	.1424	.1354
	15	.0000	.0000	.0000	.0000	.0002	.0019	.0106	.0351	.0783	.1242	.1445
	16	.0000	.0000	.0000	.0000	.0000	.0006	.0042	.0177	.0489	.0953	.1354
	17	.0000	.0000	.0000	.0000	.0000	.0002	.0015	.0079	.0269	.0642	.1115
	18	.0000	.0000	.0000	.0000	.0000	.0000	.0005	.0031	.0129	.0379	.0806
	19	.0000	.0000	.0000	.0000	.0000	.0000	.0001	.0010	.0054	.0196	.0509
	20	.0000	.0000	.0000	.0000	.0000	.0000	.0000	.0003	.0020	.0088	.0280
	21	.0000	.0000	.0000	.0000	.0000	.0000	.0000	.0001	.0006	.0034	.0133
	22	.0000	.0000	.0000	.0000	.0000	.0000	.0000	.0000	.0002	.0012	.0055
	23	.0000	.0000	.0000	.0000	.0000	.0000	.0000	.0000	.0000	.0003	.0019
	24	.0000	.0000	.0000	.0000	.0000	.0000	.0000	.0000	.0000	.0001	.0006
	25	.0000	.0000	.0000	.0000	.0000	.0000	.0000	.0000	.0000	.0000	.0001

n	x	.01	.05	.10	.15	.20	.25	.30	.35	.40	.45	.50
19	0	.8262	.3774	.1351	.0456	.0144	.0042	.0011	.0003	.0001	.0000	.0000
	1	.1586	.3774	.2852	.1529	.0685	.0268	.0093	.0029	.0008	.0002	.0000
	2	.0144	.1787	.2852	.2428	.1540	.0803	.0358	.0138	.0046	.0013	.0003
	3	.0008	.0533	.1796	.2428	.2182	.1517	.0869	.0422	.0175	.0062	.0018
	4	.0000	.0112	.0798	.1714	.2182	.2023	.1491	.0909	.0467	.0203	.0074
	5	.0000	.0018	.0266	.0907	.1636	.2023	.1916	.1468	.0933	.0497	.0222
	6	.0000	.0002	.0069	.0374	.0955	.1574	.1916	.1844	.1451	.0949	.0518
	7	.0000	.0000	.0014	.0122	.0443	.0974	.1525	.1844	.1797	.1443	.0961
	8	.0000	.0000	.0002	.0032	.0166	.0487	.0981	.1489	.1797	.1771	.1442
	9	.0000	.0000	.0000	.0007	.0051	.0198	.0514	.0980	.1464	.1771	.1762
	10	.0000	.0000	.0000	.0001	.0013	.0066	.0220	.0528	.0976	.1449	.1762
	11	.0000	.0000	.0000	.0000	.0003	.0018	.0077	.0233	.0532	.0970	.1442
	12	.0000	.0000	.0000	.0000	.0000	.0004	.0022	.0083	.0237	.0529	.0961
	13	.0000	.0000	.0000	.0000	.0000	.0001	.0005	.0024	.0085	.0233	.0518
	14	.0000	.0000	.0000	.0000	.0000	.0000	.0001	.0006	.0024	.0082	.0222
	15	.0000	.0000	.0000	.0000	.0000	.0000	.0000	.0001	.0005	.0022	.0074
	16	.0000	.0000	.0000	.0000	.0000	.0000	.0000	.0000	.0001	.0005	.0018
	17	.0000	.0000	.0000	.0000	.0000	.0000	.0000	.0000	.0000	.0001	.0003
	18	.0000	.0000	.0000	.0000	.0000	.0000	.0000	.0000	.0000	.0000	.0000
	19	.0000	.0000	.0000	.0000	.0000	.0000	.0000	.0000	.0000	.0000	.0000
20	0	.8179	.3585	.1216	.0388	.0115	.0032	.0008	.0002	.0000	.0000	.0000
	1	.1652	.3774	.2702	.1368	.0576	.0211	.0068	.0020	.0005	.0001	.0000
	2	.0159	.1887	.2852	.2293	.1369	.0669	.0278	.0100	.0031	.0008	.0002
	3	.0010	.0596	.1901	.2428	.2054	.1339	.0716	.0323	.0123	.0040	.0011
	4	.0000	.0133	.0898	.1821	.2182	.1897	.1304	.0738	.0350	.0139	.0046
	5	.0000	.0022	.0319	.1028	.1746	.2023	.1789	.1272	.0746	.0365	.0148
	6	.0000	.0003	.0089	.0454	.1091	.1686	.1916	.1712	.1244	.0746	.0370
	7	.0000	.0000	.0020	.0160	.0545	.1124	.1643	.1844	.1659	.1221	.0739
	8	.0000	.0000	.0004	.0046	.0222	.0609	.1144	.1614	.1797	.1623	.1201
	9	.0000	.0000	.0001	.0011	.0074	.0271	.0654	.1158	.1597	.1771	.1602
	10	.0000	.0000	.0000	.0002	.0020	.0099	.0308	.0686	.1171	.1593	.1762
	11	.0000	.0000	.0000	.0000	.0005	.0030	.0120	.0336	.0710	.1185	.1602
	12	.0000	.0000	.0000	.0000	.0001	.0008	.0039	.0136	.0355	.0727	.1201
	13	.0000	.0000	.0000	.0000	.0000	.0002	.0010	.0045	.0146	.0366	.0739
	14	.0000	.0000	.0000	.0000	.0000	.0000	.0002	.0012	.0049	.0150	.0370
	15	.0000	.0000	.0000	.0000	.0000	.0000	.0000	.0003	.0013	.0049	.0148
	16	.0000	.0000	.0000	.0000	.0000	.0000	.0000	.0000	.0003	.0013	.0046
	17	.0000	.0000	.0000	.0000	.0000	.0000	.0000	.0000	.0000	.0002	.0011
	18	.0000	.0000	.0000	.0000	.0000	.0000	.0000	.0000	.0000	.0000	.0002
	19	.0000	.0000	.0000	.0000	.0000	.0000	.0000	.0000	.0000	.0000	.0000
	20	.0000	.0000	.0000	.0000	.0000	.0000	.0000	.0000	.0000	.0000	.0000
25	0	.7778	.2774	.0718	.0172	.0038	.0008	.0001	.0000	.0000	.0000	.0000
	1	.1964	.3650	.1994	.0759	.0236	.0063	.0014	.0003	.0000	.0000	.0000
	2	.0238	.2305	.2659	.1607	.0708	.0251	.0074	.0018	.0004	.0001	.0000
	3	.0018	.0930	.2265	.2174	.1358	.0641	.0243	.0076	.0019	.0004	.0001
	4	.0001	.0269	.1384	.2110	.1867	.1175	.0572	.0224	.0071	.0018	.0004

Appendix 2

Values of $e^{-\lambda}$

λ	$e^{-\lambda}$	λ	$e^{-\lambda}$
0.0	1.00000	2.5	.08208
0.1	.90484	2.6	.07427
0.2	.81873	2.7	.06721
0.3	.74082	2.8	.06081
0.4	.67032	2.9	.05502
0.5	.60653	3.0	.04979
0.6	.54881	3.2	.04076
0.7	.49659	3.4	.03337
0.8	.44933	3.6	.02732
0.9	.40657	3.8	.02237
1.0	.36788	4.0	.01832
1.1	.33287	4.2	.01500
1.2	.30119	4.4	.01228
1.3	.27253	4.6	.01005
1.4	.24660	4.8	.00823
1.5	.22313	5.0	.00674
1.6	.20190	5.5	.00409
1.7	.18268	6.0	.00248
1.8	.16530	6.5	.00150
1.9	.14957	7.0	.00091
2.0	.13534	7.5	.00055
2.1	.12246	8.0	.00034
2.2	.00180	8.5	.00020
2.3	.10026	9.0	.00012
2.4	.09072	10.0	.00005

Appendix 3

Poisson Probabilities*

X	λ 0.1	0.2	0.3	0.4	0.5	0.6	0.7	0.8	0.9	1.0
0	.9048	.8187	.7408	.6703	.6065	.5488	.4966	.4493	.4066	.3679
1	.0905	.1637	.2222	.2681	.3033	.3293	.3476	.3595	.3659	.3679
2	.0045	.0164	.0333	.0536	.0758	.0988	.1217	.1438	.1647	.1839
3	.0002	.0011	.0033	.0072	.0126	.0198	.0284	.0383	.0494	.0613
4	.0000	.0001	.0002	.0007	.0016	.0030	.0050	.0077	.0111	.0153
5	.0000	.0000	.0000	.0001	.0002	.0004	.0007	.0012	.0020	.0031
6	.0000	.0000	.0000	.0000	.0000	.0000	.0001	.0002	.0003	.0005
7	.0000	.0000	.0000	.0000	.0000	.0000	.0000	.0000	.0000	.0001

X	λ 1.1	1.2	1.3	1.4	1.5	1.6	1.7	1.8	1.9	2.0
0	.3329	.3012	.2725	.2466	.2231	.2019	.1827	.1653	.1496	.1353
1	.3662	.3614	.3543	.3452	.3347	.3230	.3106	.2975	.2842	.2707
2	.2014	.2169	.2303	.2417	.2510	.2584	.2640	.2678	.2700	.2707
3	.0738	.0867	.0998	.1128	.1255	.1378	.1496	.1607	.1710	.1804
4	.0203	.0260	.0324	.0395	.0471	.0551	.0636	.0723	.0812	.0902
5	.0045	.0062	.0084	.0111	.0141	.0176	.0216	.0260	.0309	.0361
6	.0008	.0012	.0018	.0026	.0035	.0047	.0061	.0078	.0098	.0120
7	.0001	.0002	.0003	.0005	.0008	.0011	.0015	.0020	.0027	.0034
8	.0000	.0000	.0001	.0001	.0001	.0002	.0003	.0005	.0006	.0009
9	.0000	.0000	.0000	.0000	.0000	.0000	.0001	.0001	.0001	.0002

X	λ 2.1	2.2	2.3	2.4	2.5	2.6	2.7	2.8	2.9	3.0
0	.1225	.1108	.1003	.0907	.0821	.0743	.0672	.0608	.0550	.0498
1	.2572	.2438	.2306	.2177	.2052	.1931	.1815	.1703	.1396	.1494
2	.2700	.2681	.2652	.2613	.2565	.2510	.2450	.2384	.2314	.2240
3	.1890	.1966	.2033	.2090	.2138	.2176	.2205	.2225	.2237	.2240
4	.0992	.1082	.1169	.1254	.1336	.1414	.1488	.1557	.1622	.1680
5	.0417	.0476	.0538	.0602	.0668	.0735	.0804	.0872	.0940	.1008
6	.0146	.0174	.0206	.0241	.0278	.0319	.0362	.0407	.0455	.0504
7	.0044	.0055	.0068	.0083	.0099	.0118	.0139	.0163	.0188	.0216
8	.0011	.0015	.0019	.0025	.0031	.0038	.0047	.0057	.0068	.0081
9	.0003	.0004	.0005	.0007	.0009	.0011	.0014	.0018	.0022	.0027
10	.0001	.0001	.0001	.0002	.0002	.0003	.0004	.0005	.0006	.0008
11	.0000	.0000	.0000	.0000	.0000	.0001	.0001	.0001	.0002	.0002
12	.0000	.0000	.0000	.0000	.0000	.0000	.0000	.0000	.0000	.0001

X	λ 3.1	3.2	3.3	3.4	3.5	3.6	3.7	3.8	3.9	4.0
0	.0450	.0408	.0369	.0334	.0302	.0273	.0247	.0224	.0202	.0183
1	.1397	.1304	.1217	.1135	.1057	.0984	.0915	.0850	.0789	.0733
2	.2165	.2087	.2008	.1929	.1850	.1771	.1692	.1615	.1539	.1465
3	.2237	.2226	.2209	.2186	.2158	.2125	.2087	.2046	.2001	.1954
4	.1734	.1781	.1823	.1858	.1888	.1912	.1931	.1944	.1951	.1954
5	.1075	.1140	.1203	.1264	.1322	.1377	.1429	.1477	.1522	.1563
6	.0555	.0608	.0662	.0716	.0771	.0826	.0881	.0936	.0989	.1042
7	.0246	.0278	.0312	.0348	.0385	.0425	.0466	.0508	.0551	.0595
8	.0095	.0111	.0129	.0148	.0169	.0191	.0215	.0241	.0269	.0298
9	.0033	.0040	.0047	.0056	.0066	.0076	.0089	.0102	.0116	.0132

*Example: $P(X = 5 \mid \lambda = 2.5) = 0.0668$

X	λ 3.1	3.2	3.3	3.4	3.5	3.6	3.7	3.8	3.9	4.0
10	.0010	.0013	.0016	.0019	.0023	.0028	.0033	.0039	.0045	.0053
11	.0003	.0004	.0005	.0006	.0007	.0009	.0011	.0013	.0016	.0019
12	.0001	.0001	.0001	.0002	.0002	.0003	.0003	.0004	.0005	.0006
13	.0000	.0000	.0000	.0000	.0001	.0001	.0001	.0001	.0002	.0002
14	.0000	.0000	.0000	.0000	.0000	.0000	.0000	.0000	.0000	.0001

X	λ 4.1	4.2	4.3	4.4	4.5	4.6	4.7	4.8	4.9	5.0
0	.0166	.0150	.0136	.0123	.0111	.0101	.0091	.0082	.0074	.0067
1	.0679	.0630	.0583	.0540	.0500	.0462	.0427	.0395	.0365	.0337
2	.1393	.1323	.1254	.1188	.1125	.1063	.1005	.0948	.0894	.0842
3	.1904	.1852	.1798	.1743	.1687	.1631	.1574	.1517	.1460	.1404
4	.1951	.1944	.1933	.1917	.1898	.1875	.1849	.1820	.1789	.1755
5	.1600	.1633	.1662	.1687	.1708	.1725	.1738	.1747	.1753	.1755
6	.1093	.1143	.1191	.1237	.1281	.1323	.1362	.1398	.1432	.1462
7	.0640	.0686	.0732	.0778	.0824	.0869	.0914	.0959	.1002	.1044
8	.0328	.0360	.0393	.0428	.0463	.0500	.0537	.0575	.0614	.0653
9	.0150	.0168	.0188	.0209	.0232	.0255	.0280	.0307	.0334	.0363
10	.0061	.0071	.0081	.0092	.0104	.0118	.0132	.0147	.0164	.0181
11	.0023	.0027	.0032	.0037	.0043	.0049	.0056	.0064	.0073	.0082
12	.0008	.0009	.0011	.0014	.0016	.0019	.0022	.0026	.0030	.0034
13	.0002	.0003	.0004	.0005	.0006	.0007	.0008	.0009	.0011	.0013
14	.0001	.0001	.0001	.0001	.0002	.0002	.0003	.0003	.0004	.0005
15	.0000	.0000	.0000	.0000	.0001	.0001	.0001	.0001	.0001	.0002

X	λ 5.1	5.2	5.3	5.4	5.5	5.6	5.7	5.8	5.9	6.0
0	.0061	.0055	.0050	.0045	.0041	.0037	.0033	.0030	.0027	.0025
1	.0311	.0287	.0265	.0244	.0225	.0207	.0191	.0176	.0162	.0149
2	.0793	.0746	.0701	.0659	.0618	.0580	.0544	.0509	.0477	.0446
3	.1348	.1293	.1239	.1185	.1133	.1082	.1033	.0985	.0938	.0892
4	.1719	.1681	.1641	.1600	.1558	.1515	.1472	.1428	.1383	.1339
5	.1753	.1748	.1740	.1728	.1714	.1697	.1678	.1656	.1632	.1606
6	.1490	.1515	.1537	.1555	.1571	.1584	.1594	.1601	.1605	.1606
7	.1086	.1125	.1163	.1200	.1234	.1267	.1298	.1326	.1353	.1377
8	.0692	.0731	.0771	.0810	.0849	.0887	.0925	.0962	.0998	.1033
9	.0392	.0423	.0454	.0486	.0519	.0552	.0586	.0620	.0654	.0688
10	.0200	.0220	.0241	.0262	.0285	.0309	.0334	.0359	.0386	.0413
11	.0093	.0104	.0116	.0129	.0143	.0157	.0173	.0190	.0207	.0225
12	.0039	.0045	.0051	.0058	.0065	.0073	.0082	.0092	.0102	.0113
13	.0015	.0018	.0021	.0024	.0028	.0032	.0036	.0041	.0046	.0052
14	.0006	.0007	.0008	.0009	.0011	.0013	.0015	.0017	.0019	.0022
15	.0002	.0002	.0003	.0003	.0004	.0005	.0006	.0007	.0008	.0009
16	.0001	.0001	.0001	.0001	.0001	.0002	.0002	.0002	.0003	.0003
17	.0000	.0000	.0000	.0000	.0000	.0001	.0001	.0001	.0001	.0001

X	λ 6.1	6.2	6.3	6.4	6.5	6.6	6.7	6.8	6.9	7.0
0	.0022	.0020	.0018	.0017	.0015	.0014	.0012	.0011	.0010	.0009
1	.0137	.0126	.0116	.0106	.0098	.0090	.0082	.0076	.0070	.0064
2	.0417	.0390	.0364	.0340	.0318	.0296	.0276	.0258	.0240	.0223

X	λ 6.1	6.2	6.3	6.4	6.5	6.6	6.7	6.8	6.9	7.0
3	.0848	.0806	.0765	.0726	.0688	.0652	.0617	.0584	.0552	.0521
4	.1294	.1249	.1205	.1162	.1118	.1076	.1034	.0992	.0952	.0912
5	.1579	.1549	.1519	.1487	.1454	.1420	.1385	.1349	.1314	.1277
6	.1605	.1601	.1595	.1586	.1575	.1562	.1546	.1529	.1511	.1490
7	.1399	.1418	.1435	.1450	.1462	.1472	.1480	.1486	.1489	.1490
8	.1066	.1099	.1130	.1160	.1188	.1215	.1240	.1263	.1284	.1304
9	.0723	.0757	.0791	.0825	.0858	.0891	.0923	.0954	.0985	.1014
10	.0441	.0469	.0498	.0528	.0558	.0558	.0618	.0649	.0679	.0710
11	.0245	.0265	.0285	.0307	.0330	.0353	.0377	.0401	.0426	.0452
12	.0124	.0137	.0150	.0164	.0179	.0194	.0210	.0227	.0245	.0264
13	.0058	.0065	.0073	.0081	.0089	.0098	.0108	.0119	.0130	.0142
14	.0025	.0029	.0033	.0037	.0041	.0046	.0052	.0058	.0064	.0071
15	.0010	.0012	.0014	.0016	.0018	.0020	.0023	.0026	.0029	.0033
16	.0004	.0005	.0005	.0006	.0007	.0008	.0010	.0011	.0013	.0014
17	.0001	.0002	.0002	.0002	.0003	.0003	.0004	.0004	.0005	.0006
18	.0000	.0001	.0001	.0001	.0001	.0001	.0001	.0002	.0002	.0002
19	.0000	.0000	.0000	.0000	.0000	.0000	.0000	.0001	.0001	.0001

X	λ 7.1	7.2	7.3	7.4	7.5	7.6	7.7	7.8	7.9	8.0
0	.0008	.0007	.0007	.0006	.0006	.0005	.0005	.0004	.0004	.0003
1	.0059	.0054	.0049	.0045	.0041	.0038	.0035	.0032	.0029	.0027
2	.0208	.0194	.0180	.0167	.0156	.0145	.0134	.0125	.0116	.0107
3	.0492	.0464	.0438	.0413	.0389	.0366	.0345	.0324	.0305	.0286
4	.0874	.0836	.0799	.0764	.0729	.0696	.0663	.0632	.0602	.0573
5	.1241	.1204	.1167	.1130	.1094	.1057	.1021	.0986	.0951	.0916
6	.1468	.1445	.1420	.1394	.1367	.1339	.1311	.1282	.1252	.1221
7	.1489	.1486	.1481	.1474	.1465	.1454	.1442	.1428	.1413	.1396
8	.1321	.1337	.1351	.1363	.1373	.1382	.1388	.1392	.1395	.1396
9	.1042	.1070	.1096	.1121	.1144	.1167	.1187	.1207	.1224	.1241
10	.0740	.0770	.0800	.0829	.0858	.0887	.0914	.0941	.0967	.0993
11	.0478	.0504	.0531	.0558	.0585	.0613	.0640	.0667	.0695	.0722
12	.0283	.0303	.0323	.0344	.0366	.0388	.0411	.0434	.0457	.0481
13	.0154	.0168	.0181	.0196	.0211	.0227	.0243	.0260	.0278	.0296
14	.0078	.0086	.0095	.0104	.0113	.0123	.0134	.0145	.0157	.0169
15	.0037	.0041	.0046	.0051	.0057	.0062	.0069	.0075	.0083	.0090
16	.0016	.0019	.0021	.0024	.0026	.0030	.0033	.0037	.0041	.0045
17	.0007	.0008	.0009	.0010	.0012	.0013	.0015	.0017	.0019	.0021
18	.0003	.0003	.0004	.0004	.0005	.0006	.0006	.0007	.0008	.0009
19	.0001	.0001	.0001	.0002	.0002	.0002	.0003	.0003	.0003	.0004
20	.0000	.0000	.0001	.0001	.0001	.0001	.0001	.0001	.0001	.0002
21	.0000	.0000	.0000	.0000	.0000	.0000	.0000	.0000	.0001	.0001

X	λ 8.1	8.2	8.3	8.4	8.5	8.6	8.7	8.8	8.9	9.0
0	.0003	.0003	.0002	.0002	.0002	.0002	.0002	.0002	.0001	.0001
1	.0025	.0023	.0021	.0019	.0017	.0016	.0014	.0013	.0012	.0011
2	.0100	.0092	.0086	.0079	.0074	.0068	.0063	.0058	.0054	.0050
3	.0269	.0252	.0237	.0222	.0208	.0195	.0183	.0171	.0160	.0150
4	.0544	.0517	.0491	.0466	.0443	.0420	.0398	.0377	.0357	.0337

X	8.1	8.2	8.3	8.4	λ 8.5	8.6	8.7	8.8	8.9	9.0
5	.0882	.0849	.0816	.0784	.0752	.0722	.0692	.0663	.0635	.0607
6	.1191	.1160	.1128	.1097	.1066	.1034	.1003	.0972	.0941	.0911
7	.1378	.1358	.1338	.1317	.1294	.1271	.1247	.1222	.1197	.1171
8	.1395	.1392	.1388	.1382	.1375	.1366	.1356	.1344	.1332	.1318
9	.1256	.1269	.1280	.1290	.1299	.1306	.1311	.1315	.1317	.1318
10	.1017	.1040	.1063	.1084	.1104	.1123	.1140	.1157	.1172	.1186
11	.0749	.0776	.0802	.0828	.0853	.0878	.0902	.0925	.0948	.0970
12	.0505	.0530	.0555	.0579	.0604	.0629	.0654	.0679	.0703	.0728
13	.0315	.0334	.0354	.0374	.0395	.0416	.0438	.0459	.0481	.0504
14	.0182	.0196	.0210	.0225	.0240	.0256	.0272	.0289	.0306	.0324
15	.0098	.0107	.0116	.0126	.0136	.0147	.0158	.0169	.0182	.0194
16	.0050	.0055	.0060	.0066	.0072	.0079	.0086	.0093	.0101	.0109
17	.0024	.0026	.0029	.0033	.0036	.0040	.0044	.0048	.0053	.0058
18	.0011	.0012	.0014	.0015	.0017	.0019	.0021	.0024	.0026	.0029
19	.0005	.0005	.0006	.0007	.0008	.0009	.0010	.0011	.0012	.0014
20	.0002	.0002	.0002	.0003	.0003	.0004	.0004	.0005	.0005	.0006
21	.0001	.0001	.0001	.0001	.0001	.0002	.0002	.0002	.0002	.0003
22	.0000	.0000	.0000	.0000	.0001	.0001	.0001	.0001	.0001	.0001

X	9.1	9.2	9.3	9.4	λ 9.5	9.6	9.7	9.8	9.9	10.0
0	.0001	.0001	.0001	.0001	.0001	.0001	.0001	.0001	.0001	.0000
1	.0010	.0009	.0009	.0008	.0007	.0007	.0006	.0005	.0005	.0005
2	.0046	.0043	.0040	.0037	.0034	.0031	.0029	.0027	.0025	.0023
3	.0140	.0131	.0123	.0115	.0107	.0100	.0093	.0087	.0081	.0076
4	.0319	.0302	.0285	.0269	.0254	.0240	.0226	.0213	.0201	.0189
5	.0581	.0555	.0530	.0506	.0483	.0460	.0439	.0418	.0398	.0378
6	.0881	.0851	.0822	.0793	.0764	.0736	.0709	.0682	.0656	.0631
7	.1145	.1118	.1091	.1064	.1037	.1010	.0982	.0955	.0928	.0901
8	.1302	.1286	.1269	.1251	.1232	.1212	.1191	.1170	.1148	.1126
9	.1317	.1315	.1311	.1306	.1300	.1293	.1284	.1274	.1263	.1251
10	.1198	.1210	.1219	.1228	.1235	.1241	.1245	.1249	.1250	.1251
11	.0991	.1012	.1031	.1049	.1067	.1083	.1098	.1112	.1125	.1137
12	.0752	.0776	.0779	.0822	.0844	.0866	.0888	.0908	.0928	.0948
13	.0526	.0549	.0572	.0594	.0617	.0640	.0662	.0685	.0707	.0729
14	.0342	.0361	.0380	.0399	.0419	.0439	.0459	.0479	.0500	.0521
15	.0208	.0221	.0235	.0250	.0265	.0281	.0297	.0313	.0330	.0347
16	.0118	.0127	.0137	.0147	.0157	.0168	.0180	.0192	.0204	.0217
17	.0063	.0069	.0075	.0081	.0088	.0095	.0103	.0111	.0119	.0128
18	.0032	.0035	.0039	.0042	.0046	.0051	.0055	.0060	.0065	.0071
19	.0015	.0017	.0019	.0021	.0023	.0026	.0028	.0031	.0034	.0037
20	.0007	.0008	.0009	.0010	.0011	.0012	.0014	.0015	.0017	.0019
21	.0003	.0003	.0004	.0004	.0005	.0006	.0006	.0007	.0008	.0009
22	.0001	.0001	.0002	.0002	.0002	.0002	.0003	.0003	.0004	.0004
23	.0000	.0001	.0001	.0001	.0001	.0001	.0001	.0001	.0002	.0002
24	.0000	.0000	.0000	.0000	.0000	.0000	.0000	.0001	.0001	.0001

Appendix 4

**Proportions of Area
for the
Standard Normal Distribution**

Areas reported below:*

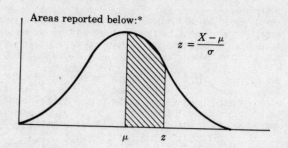

$$z = \frac{X - \mu}{\sigma}$$

z	.00	.01	.02	.03	.04	.05	.06	.07	.08	.09
0.0	.0000	.0040	.0080	.0120	.0160	.0199	.0239	.0279	.0319	.0359
0.1	.0398	.0438	.0478	.0517	.0557	.0596	.0636	.0675	.0714	.0753
0.2	.0793	.0832	.0871	.0910	.0948	.0987	.1026	.1064	.1103	.1141
0.3	.1179	.1217	.1255	.1293	.1331	.1368	.1406	.1443	.1480	.1517
0.4	.1554	.1591	.1628	.1664	.1700	.1736	.1772	.1808	.1844	.1879
0.5	.1915	.1950	.1985	.2019	.2054	.2088	.2123	.2157	.2190	.2224
0.6	.2257	.2291	.2324	.2357	.2389	.2422	.2454	.2486	.2518	.2549
0.7	.2580	2.612	.2642	.2673	.2704	.2734	.2764	.2794	.2823	.2852
0.8	.2881	.2910	.2939	.2967	.2995	.3023	.3051	.3078	.3106	.3133
0.9	.3159	.3186	.3212	.3238	.3264	.3289	.3315	.3340	.3365	.3389
1.0	.3413	.3438	.3461	.3485	.3508	.3531	.3554	.3577	.3599	.3621
1.1	.3643	.3665	.3686	.3708	.3729	.3749	.3770	.3790	.3810	.3830
1.2	.3849	.3869	.3888	.3907	.3925	.3944	.3962	.3980	.3997	.4014
1.3	.4032	.4049	.4066	.4082	.4099	.4115	.4131	.4147	.4162	.4177
1.4	.4192	.4207	.4222	.4236	.4251	.4265	.4279	.4292	.4306	.4319
1.5	.4332	.4345	.4357	.4370	.4382	.4394	.4406	.4418	.4429	.4441
1.6	.4452	.4463	.4474	.4484	.4495	.4505	.4515	.4525	.4535	.4545
1.7	.4554	.4564	.4573	.4582	.4591	.4599	.4608	.4616	.4625	.4633
1.8	.4641	.4649	.4656	.4664	.4671	.4678	.4686	.4693	.4699	.4706
1.9	.4713	.4719	.4726	.4732	.4738	.4744	.4750	.4756	.4761	.4767
2.0	.4772	.4778	.4783	.4788	.4793	.4798	.4803	.4808	.4812	.4817
2.1	.4821	.4826	.4830	.4834	.4838	.4842	.4846	.4850	.4854	.4857
2.2	.4861	.4864	.4868	.4871	.4875	.4878	.4881	.4884	.4887	.4890
2.3	.4893	.4896	.4898	.4901	.4904	.4906	.4909	.4911	.4913	.4916
2.4	.4918	.4920	.4922	.4925	.4927	.4929	.4931	.4932	.4934	.4936
2.5	.4938	.4940	.4941	.4943	.4945	.4946	.4948	.4949	.4951	.4952
2.6	.4953	.4955	.4956	.4957	.4959	.4960	.4961	.4962	.4963	.4964
2.7	.4965	.4966	.4967	.4968	.4969	.4970	.4971	.4972	.4973	.4974
2.8	.4974	.4975	.4976	.4977	.4977	.4978	.4979	.4979	.4980	.4981
2.9	.4981	.4982	.4983	.4983	.4984	.4984	.4985	.4985	.4986	.4986
3.0	.4987									
3.5	.4997									
4.0	.4999									

*Example: For $z = 1.96$, shaded area is 0.4750 out of the total area of 1.0000.

Appendix 5

Table of Random Numbers

10097	85017	84532	13618	23157	86952	02438	76520	91499	38631	79430	62421	97959	67422	69992	68479
37542	16719	82789	69041	05545	44109	05403	64894	80336	49172	16332	44670	35089	17691	89246	26940
08422	65842	27672	82186	14871	22115	86529	19645	44104	89232	57327	34679	62235	79655	81336	85157
99019	76875	20684	39187	38976	94324	43204	09376	12550	02844	15026	32439	58537	48274	81330	11100
12807	93640	39160	41453	97312	41548	93137	80157	63606	40387	65406	37920	08709	60623	2237	16505
66065	99478	70086	71265	11742	18226	29004	34072	61196	80240	44177	51171	08723	39323	05798	26457
31060	65119	26486	47353	43361	99436	42753	45571	15474	44910	99321	72173	56239	04595	10836	95270
85269	70322	21592	48233	93806	32584	21828	02051	94557	33663	86347	00926	44915	34823	51770	67897
63573	58133	41278	11697	49540	61777	67954	05325	42481	86430	19102	37420	41976	76559	24358	97344
73796	44655	81255	31133	36768	60452	38537	03529	23523	31379	68588	81675	15694	43438	36879	73208
98520	02295	13487	98662	07092	44673	61303	14905	04493	98086	32533	17767	14523	52494	24826	75246
11805	85035	54881	35587	43310	48897	48493	39808	00549	33185	04805	05431	94598	97654	16232	64051
83452	01197	86935	28021	61570	23350	65710	06288	35963	80951	68953	99634	81949	15307	00406	26898
88685	97907	19078	40646	31352	48625	44369	86507	59808	79752	02529	40200	73742	08391	49140	45427
99594	63268	96905	28797	57048	46359	74294	87517	46058	18633	99970	67348	49329	95236	32537	01390
65481	52841	59684	67411	09243	56092	84369	17468	32179	74029	74717	17674	90446	00597	45240	87379
80124	53722	71399	10916	07959	21225	13018	17727	69234	54178	10805	35635	45266	61406	41941	20117
74350	11434	51908	62171	93732	26958	02400	77402	19565	11664	77602	99817	28573	41430	96382	01758
69916	62375	99292	21177	72721	66995	07289	66252	45155	48324	32135	26803	16213	14938	71961	19476
09893	28337	20923	87929	61020	62841	31374	14225	94864	69074	45753	20505	78317	31994	98145	36168

Appendix 6

**Proportions of Area
for the *t* Distributions**

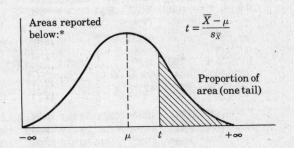

Areas reported below:*

$$t = \frac{\overline{X} - \mu}{s_{\overline{X}}}$$

Proportion of area (one tail)

−∞   μ   t   +∞

df	0.10	0.05	0.025	0.01	0.005		df	0.10	0.05	0.025	0.01	0.005
1	3.078	6.314	12.706	31.821	63.657		18	1.330	1.734	2.101	2.552	2.878
2	1.886	2.920	4.303	6.965	9.925		19	1.328	1.729	2.093	2.539	2.861
3	1.638	2.353	3.182	4.541	5.841		20	1.325	1.725	2.086	2.528	2.845
4	1.533	2.132	2.776	3.747	4.604		21	1.323	1.721	2.080	2.518	2.831
5	1.476	2.015	2.571	3.365	4.032		22	1.321	1.717	2.074	2.508	2.819
6	1.440	1.943	2.447	3.143	3.707		23	1.319	1.714	2.069	2.500	2.807
7	1.415	1.895	2.365	2.998	3.499		24	1.318	1.711	2.064	2.492	2.797
8	1.397	1.860	2.306	2.896	3.355		25	1.316	1.708	2.060	2.485	2.787
9	1.383	1.833	2.262	2.821	3.250		26	1.315	1.706	2.056	2.479	2.779
10	1.372	1.812	2.228	2.764	3.169		27	1.314	1.703	2.052	2.473	2.771
11	1.363	1.796	2.201	2.718	3.106		28	1.313	1.701	2.048	2.467	2.763
12	1.356	1.782	2.179	2.681	3.055		29	1.311	1.699	2.045	2.462	2.756
13	1.350	1.771	2.160	2.650	3.012		30	1.310	1.697	2.042	2.457	2.750
14	1.345	1.761	2.145	2.624	2.977		40	1.303	1.684	2.021	2.423	2.704
15	1.341	1.753	2.131	2.602	2.947		60	1.296	1.671	2.000	2.390	2.660
16	1.337	1.746	2.120	2.583	2.921		120	1.289	1.658	1.980	2.358	2.617
17	1.333	1.740	2.110	2.567	2.898		∞	1.282	1.645	1.960	2.326	2.576

*Example: For the shaded area to represent 0.05 of the total area of 1.0, value of *t* with 10 degrees of freedom is 1.812.

Source: From Table III of Fisher and Yates, *Statistical Tables for Biological, Agricultural and Medical Research*, 6th ed., 1974, published by Longman Group Ltd., London (previously published by Oliver & Boyd, Edinburgh), by permission of the authors and publishers.

Appendix 7

Proportions of Area for the χ² Distributions

Areas reported below:*

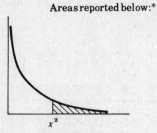

For $df = 1, 2$

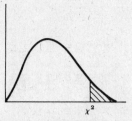

For $df \geq 3$

df	0.995	0.990	0.975	0.950	0.900	0.500	0.100	0.050	0.025	0.010	0.005
1	0.00004	0.00016	0.00098	0.00393	0.0158	0.455	2.71	3.84	5.02	6.63	7.88
2	0.0100	0.0201	0.0506	0.103	0.211	1.386	4.61	5.99	7.38	9.21	10.60
3	0.072	0.115	0.216	0.352	0.584	2.366	6.25	7.81	9.35	11.34	12.84
4	0.207	0.297	0.484	0.711	1.064	3.357	7.78	9.49	11.14	13.28	14.86
5	0.412	0.554	0.831	1.145	1.61	4.251	9.24	11.07	12.83	15.09	16.75
6	0.676	0.872	1.24	1.64	2.20	5.35	10.64	12.59	14.45	16.81	18.55
7	0.989	1.24	1.69	2.17	2.83	6.35	12.02	14.07	16.01	18.48	20.28
8	1.34	1.65	2.18	2.73	3.49	7.34	13.36	15.51	17.53	20.09	21.96
9	1.73	2.09	2.70	3.33	4.17	8.34	14.68	16.92	19.02	21.67	23.59
10	2.16	2.56	3.25	3.94	4.87	9.34	15.99	18.31	20.48	23.21	25.19
11	2.60	3.05	3.82	4.57	5.58	10.34	17.28	19.68	21.92	24.73	26.76
12	3.07	3.57	4.40	5.23	6.30	11.34	18.55	21.03	23.34	26.22	28.30
13	3.57	4.11	5.01	5.89	7.04	12.34	19.81	22.36	24.74	27.69	29.82
14	4.07	4.66	5.63	6.57	7.79	13.34	21.06	23.68	26.12	29.14	31.32
15	4.60	5.23	6.26	7.26	8.55	14.34	22.31	25.00	27.49	30.58	32.80
16	5.14	5.81	6.91	7.96	9.31	15.34	23.54	26.30	28.85	32.00	34.27
17	5.70	6.41	7.56	8.67	10.09	16.34	24.77	27.59	30.19	33.41	35.72
18	6.26	7.01	8.23	9.39	10.86	17.34	25.99	28.87	31.53	34.81	37.16
19	6.84	7.63	8.91	10.12	11.65	18.34	27.20	30.14	32.85	36.19	38.58
20	7.43	8.26	9.59	10.85	12.44	19.34	28.41	31.41	34.17	37.57	40.00
21	8.03	8.90	10.28	11.59	13.24	20.34	29.62	32.67	35.48	38.93	41.40
22	8.64	9.54	10.98	12.34	14.04	21.34	30.81	33.92	36.78	40.29	42.80
23	9.26	10.20	11.69	13.09	14.85	22.34	32.01	35.17	38.08	41.64	44.18
24	9.89	10.86	12.40	13.85	15.66	23.34	33.20	36.42	39.36	42.98	45.56
25	10.52	11.52	13.12	14.61	16.47	24.34	34.38	37.65	40.65	44.31	46.93
26	11.16	12.20	13.84	15.38	17.29	25.34	35.56	38.89	41.92	45.64	48.29
27	11.81	12.83	14.57	16.15	18.11	26.34	36.74	40.11	43.19	46.96	49.64
28	12.46	13.56	15.31	16.93	18.94	27.34	37.92	41.34	44.46	48.28	50.99
29	13.12	14.26	16.05	17.71	19.77	28.34	39.09	42.56	45.72	49.59	52.34
30	13.79	14.95	16.79	18.49	20.60	29.34	40.26	43.77	46.98	50.89	53.67
40	20.71	22.16	24.43	26.51	29.05	39.34	51.81	55.76	59.34	63.69	66.77
50	27.99	29.71	32.36	34.76	37.69	49.33	63.17	67.50	71.42	76.15	79.49
60	35.53	37.43	40.48	43.19	46.46	59.33	74.40	79.08	83.30	88.38	91.95
70	43.28	45.44	48.76	51.74	55.33	69.33	85.53	90.53	95.02	100.4	104.2
80	51.17	53.54	51.17	60.39	64.28	79.33	98.58	101.9	106.6	112.3	116.3
90	59.20	61.75	65.65	69.13	73.29	89.33	107.6	113.1	118.1	124.1	128.3
100	67.33	70.06	74.22	77.93	82.36	99.33	118.5	124.3	129.6	135.8	140.2

Proportion of area

*Example: For the shaded area to represent 0.05 of the total area of 1.0 under the density function, the value of χ^2 is 18.31 when $df = 10$.

Source: From Table IV of Fisher and Yates, *Statistical Tables for Biological, Agricultural and Medical Research*, 6th ed., 1974, published by Longman Group Ltd., London (previously published by Oliver & Boyd, Edinburgh), by permission of the authors and publishers.

Appendix 8

Values of F Exceeded with Probabilities of 5 and 1 Percent

df (denominator) rows × *df* (numerator) columns. Each cell lists the 5 percent value (top) over the 1 percent value (bottom).

df	1	2	3	4	5	6	7	8	9	10	11	12	14	16	20	24	30	40	50	75	100	200	500	∞
1	161 / 4,052	200 / 4,999	216 / 5,403	225 / 5,625	230 / 5,764	234 / 5,859	237 / 5,928	239 / 5,981	241 / 6,022	242 / 6,056	243 / 6,082	244 / 6,106	245 / 6,142	246 / 6,169	248 / 6,208	249 / 6,234	250 / 6,261	251 / 6,286	252 / 6,302	253 / 6,323	253 / 6,334	254 / 6,352	254 / 6,361	254 / 6,366
2	18.51 / 98.49	19.00 / 99.00	19.16 / 99.17	19.25 / 99.25	19.30 / 99.30	19.33 / 99.33	19.36 / 99.36	19.37 / 99.37	19.38 / 99.39	19.39 / 99.40	19.40 / 99.41	19.41 / 99.42	19.42 / 99.43	19.43 / 99.44	19.44 / 99.45	19.45 / 99.46	19.46 / 99.47	19.47 / 99.48	19.47 / 99.48	19.48 / 99.49	19.49 / 99.49	19.49 / 99.49	19.50 / 99.50	19.50 / 99.50
3	10.13 / 34.12	9.55 / 30.82	9.28 / 29.46	9.12 / 28.71	9.01 / 28.24	8.94 / 27.91	8.88 / 27.67	8.84 / 27.49	8.81 / 27.34	8.78 / 27.23	8.76 / 27.13	8.74 / 27.05	8.71 / 26.92	8.69 / 26.83	8.66 / 26.69	8.64 / 26.60	8.62 / 26.50	8.60 / 26.41	8.58 / 26.35	8.57 / 26.27	8.56 / 26.23	8.54 / 26.18	8.54 / 26.14	8.53 / 26.12
4	7.71 / 21.20	6.94 / 18.00	6.59 / 16.69	6.39 / 15.98	6.26 / 15.52	6.16 / 15.21	6.09 / 14.98	6.04 / 14.80	6.00 / 14.66	5.96 / 14.54	5.93 / 14.45	5.91 / 14.37	5.87 / 14.24	5.84 / 14.15	5.80 / 14.02	5.77 / 13.93	5.74 / 13.83	5.71 / 13.74	5.70 / 13.69	5.68 / 13.61	5.66 / 13.57	5.65 / 13.52	5.64 / 13.48	5.63 / 13.46
5	6.61 / 16.26	5.79 / 13.27	5.41 / 12.06	5.19 / 11.39	5.05 / 10.97	4.95 / 10.67	4.88 / 10.45	4.82 / 10.29	4.78 / 10.15	4.74 / 10.05	4.70 / 9.96	4.68 / 9.89	4.64 / 9.77	4.60 / 9.68	4.56 / 9.55	4.53 / 9.47	4.50 / 9.38	4.46 / 9.29	4.44 / 9.24	4.42 / 9.17	4.40 / 9.13	4.38 / 9.07	4.37 / 9.04	4.36 / 9.02
6	5.99 / 13.74	5.14 / 10.92	4.76 / 9.78	4.53 / 9.15	4.39 / 8.75	4.28 / 8.47	4.21 / 8.26	4.15 / 8.10	4.10 / 7.98	4.06 / 7.87	4.03 / 7.79	4.00 / 7.72	3.96 / 7.60	3.92 / 7.52	3.87 / 7.39	3.84 / 7.31	3.81 / 7.23	3.77 / 7.14	3.75 / 7.09	3.72 / 7.02	3.71 / 6.99	3.69 / 6.94	3.68 / 6.90	3.67 / 6.88
7	5.59 / 12.25	4.74 / 9.55	4.34 / 8.45	4.12 / 7.85	3.97 / 7.46	3.87 / 7.19	3.79 / 7.00	3.73 / 6.84	3.68 / 6.71	3.63 / 6.62	3.60 / 6.54	3.57 / 6.47	3.52 / 6.35	3.49 / 6.27	3.44 / 6.15	3.41 / 6.07	3.38 / 5.98	3.34 / 5.90	3.32 / 5.85	3.29 / 5.78	3.28 / 5.75	3.25 / 5.70	3.24 / 5.67	3.23 / 5.65
8	5.32 / 11.26	4.46 / 8.65	4.07 / 7.59	3.84 / 7.01	3.69 / 6.63	3.58 / 6.37	3.50 / 6.19	3.44 / 6.03	3.39 / 5.91	3.34 / 5.82	3.31 / 5.74	3.28 / 5.67	3.23 / 5.56	3.20 / 5.48	3.15 / 5.36	3.12 / 5.28	3.08 / 5.20	3.05 / 5.11	3.03 / 5.06	3.00 / 5.00	2.98 / 4.96	2.96 / 4.91	2.94 / 4.88	2.93 / 4.86
9	5.12 / 10.56	4.26 / 8.02	3.86 / 6.99	3.63 / 6.42	3.48 / 6.06	3.37 / 5.80	3.29 / 5.62	3.23 / 5.47	3.18 / 5.35	3.13 / 5.26	3.10 / 5.18	3.07 / 5.11	3.02 / 5.00	2.98 / 4.92	2.93 / 4.80	2.90 / 4.73	2.86 / 4.64	2.82 / 4.56	2.80 / 4.51	2.77 / 4.45	2.76 / 4.41	2.73 / 4.36	2.72 / 4.33	2.71 / 4.31
10	4.96 / 10.04	4.10 / 7.56	3.71 / 6.55	3.48 / 5.99	3.33 / 5.64	3.22 / 5.39	3.14 / 5.21	3.07 / 5.06	3.02 / 4.95	2.97 / 4.85	2.94 / 4.78	2.91 / 4.71	2.86 / 4.60	2.82 / 4.52	2.77 / 4.41	2.74 / 4.33	2.70 / 4.25	2.67 / 4.17	2.64 / 4.12	2.61 / 4.05	2.59 / 4.01	2.56 / 3.96	2.55 / 3.93	2.54 / 3.91
11	4.84 / 9.65	3.98 / 7.20	3.59 / 6.22	3.36 / 5.67	3.20 / 5.32	3.09 / 5.07	3.01 / 4.88	2.95 / 4.74	2.90 / 4.63	2.86 / 4.54	2.82 / 4.46	2.79 / 4.40	2.74 / 4.29	2.70 / 4.21	2.65 / 4.10	2.61 / 4.02	2.57 / 3.94	2.53 / 3.86	2.50 / 3.80	2.47 / 3.74	2.45 / 3.70	2.42 / 3.66	2.41 / 3.62	2.40 / 3.60
12	4.75 / 9.33	3.88 / 6.93	3.49 / 5.95	3.26 / 5.41	3.11 / 5.06	3.00 / 4.82	2.92 / 4.65	2.85 / 4.50	2.80 / 4.39	2.76 / 4.30	2.72 / 4.22	2.69 / 4.16	2.64 / 4.05	2.60 / 3.98	2.54 / 3.86	2.50 / 3.78	2.46 / 3.70	2.42 / 3.61	2.40 / 3.56	2.36 / 3.49	2.35 / 3.46	2.32 / 3.41	2.31 / 3.38	2.30 / 3.36
13	4.67 / 9.07	3.80 / 6.70	3.41 / 5.74	3.18 / 5.20	3.02 / 4.86	2.92 / 4.62	2.84 / 4.44	2.77 / 4.30	2.72 / 4.19	2.67 / 4.10	2.63 / 4.02	2.60 / 3.96	2.55 / 3.85	2.51 / 3.78	2.46 / 3.67	2.42 / 3.59	2.38 / 3.51	2.34 / 3.42	2.32 / 3.37	2.28 / 3.30	2.26 / 3.27	2.24 / 3.21	2.22 / 3.18	2.21 / 3.16
14	4.60 / 8.86	3.74 / 6.51	3.34 / 5.56	3.11 / 5.03	2.96 / 4.69	2.85 / 4.46	2.77 / 4.28	2.70 / 4.14	2.65 / 4.03	2.60 / 3.94	2.56 / 3.86	2.53 / 3.80	2.48 / 3.70	2.44 / 3.62	2.39 / 3.51	2.35 / 3.43	2.31 / 3.34	2.27 / 3.26	2.24 / 3.21	2.21 / 3.14	2.19 / 3.11	2.16 / 3.06	2.14 / 3.02	2.13 / 3.00
15	4.54 / 8.68	3.68 / 6.36	3.29 / 5.42	3.06 / 4.89	2.90 / 4.56	2.79 / 4.32	2.70 / 4.14	2.64 / 4.00	2.59 / 3.89	2.55 / 3.80	2.51 / 3.73	2.48 / 3.67	2.43 / 3.56	2.39 / 3.48	2.33 / 3.36	2.29 / 3.29	2.25 / 3.20	2.21 / 3.12	2.18 / 3.07	2.15 / 3.00	2.12 / 2.97	2.10 / 2.92	2.08 / 2.89	2.07 / 2.87
16	4.49 / 8.53	3.63 / 6.23	3.24 / 5.29	3.01 / 4.77	2.85 / 4.44	2.74 / 4.20	2.66 / 4.03	2.59 / 3.89	2.54 / 3.78	2.49 / 3.69	2.45 / 3.61	2.42 / 3.55	2.37 / 3.45	2.33 / 3.37	2.28 / 3.25	2.24 / 3.18	2.20 / 3.10	2.16 / 3.01	2.13 / 2.96	2.09 / 2.89	2.07 / 2.86	2.04 / 2.80	2.02 / 2.77	2.01 / 2.75
17	4.45 / 8.40	3.59 / 6.11	3.20 / 5.18	2.96 / 4.67	2.81 / 4.34	2.70 / 4.10	2.62 / 3.93	2.55 / 3.79	2.50 / 3.68	2.45 / 3.59	2.41 / 3.52	2.38 / 3.45	2.33 / 3.35	2.29 / 3.27	2.23 / 3.16	2.19 / 3.08	2.15 / 3.00	2.11 / 2.92	2.08 / 2.86	2.04 / 2.79	2.02 / 2.76	1.99 / 2.70	1.97 / 2.67	1.96 / 2.65
18	4.41 / 8.28	3.55 / 6.01	3.16 / 5.09	2.93 / 4.58	2.77 / 4.25	2.66 / 4.01	2.58 / 3.85	2.51 / 3.71	2.46 / 3.60	2.41 / 3.51	2.37 / 3.44	2.34 / 3.37	2.29 / 3.27	2.25 / 3.19	2.19 / 3.07	2.15 / 3.00	2.11 / 2.91	2.07 / 2.83	2.04 / 2.78	2.00 / 2.71	1.98 / 2.68	1.95 / 2.62	1.93 / 2.59	1.92 / 2.57

366

df																								
19	4.38/8.18	3.52/5.93	3.13/5.01	2.90/4.50	2.74/4.17	2.63/3.94	2.55/3.77	2.48/3.63	2.43/3.52	2.38/3.43	2.34/3.36	2.31/3.30	2.26/3.19	2.21/3.12	2.15/3.00	2.11/2.92	2.07/2.84	2.02/2.76	2.00/2.70	1.96/2.63	1.94/2.60	1.91/2.54	1.90/2.51	1.88/2.49
20	4.35/8.10	3.49/5.85	3.10/4.94	2.87/4.43	2.71/4.10	2.60/3.87	2.52/3.71	2.45/3.56	2.40/3.45	2.35/3.37	2.31/3.30	2.28/3.23	2.23/3.13	2.18/3.05	2.12/2.94	2.08/2.86	2.04/2.77	1.99/2.69	1.96/2.63	1.92/2.56	1.90/2.53	1.87/2.47	1.85/2.44	1.84/2.42
21	4.32/8.02	3.47/5.78	3.07/4.87	2.84/4.37	2.68/4.04	2.57/3.81	2.49/3.65	2.42/3.51	2.37/3.40	2.32/3.31	2.28/3.24	2.25/3.17	2.20/3.07	2.15/2.99	2.09/2.88	2.05/2.80	2.00/2.72	1.96/2.63	1.93/2.58	1.89/2.51	1.87/2.47	1.84/2.42	1.82/2.38	1.81/2.36
22	4.30/7.94	3.44/5.72	3.05/4.82	2.82/4.31	2.66/3.99	2.55/3.76	2.47/3.59	2.40/3.45	2.35/3.35	2.30/3.26	2.26/3.18	2.23/3.12	2.18/3.02	2.13/2.94	2.07/2.83	2.03/2.75	1.98/2.67	1.93/2.58	1.91/2.53	1.87/2.46	1.84/2.42	1.81/2.37	1.80/2.33	1.78/2.31
23	4.28/7.88	3.42/5.66	3.03/4.76	2.80/4.26	2.64/3.94	2.53/3.71	2.45/3.54	2.38/3.41	2.32/3.30	2.28/3.21	2.24/3.14	2.20/3.07	2.14/2.97	2.10/2.89	2.04/2.78	2.00/2.70	1.96/2.62	1.91/2.53	1.88/2.48	1.84/2.41	1.82/2.37	1.79/2.32	1.77/2.28	1.76/2.26
24	4.26/7.82	3.40/5.61	3.01/4.72	2.78/4.22	2.62/3.90	2.51/3.67	2.43/3.50	2.36/3.36	2.30/3.25	2.26/3.17	2.22/3.09	2.18/3.03	2.13/2.93	2.09/2.85	2.02/2.74	1.98/2.66	1.94/2.58	1.89/2.49	1.86/2.44	1.82/2.36	1.80/2.33	1.76/2.27	1.74/2.23	1.73/2.21
25	4.24/7.77	3.38/5.57	2.99/4.68	2.76/4.18	2.60/3.86	2.49/3.63	2.41/3.46	2.34/3.32	2.28/3.21	2.24/3.13	2.20/3.05	2.16/2.99	2.11/2.89	2.06/2.81	2.00/2.70	1.96/2.62	1.92/2.54	1.87/2.45	1.84/2.40	1.80/2.32	1.77/2.29	1.74/2.23	1.72/2.19	1.71/2.17
26	4.22/7.72	3.37/5.53	2.98/4.64	2.74/4.14	2.59/3.82	2.47/3.59	2.39/3.42	2.32/3.29	2.27/3.17	2.22/3.09	2.18/3.02	2.15/2.96	2.10/2.86	2.05/2.77	1.99/2.66	1.95/2.58	1.90/2.50	1.85/2.41	1.82/2.36	1.78/2.28	1.76/2.25	1.72/2.19	1.70/2.15	1.69/2.13
27	4.21/7.68	3.35/5.49	2.96/4.60	2.73/4.11	2.57/3.79	2.46/3.56	2.37/3.39	2.30/3.26	2.25/3.14	2.20/3.06	2.16/2.98	2.13/2.93	2.08/2.83	2.03/2.74	1.97/2.63	1.93/2.55	1.88/2.47	1.84/2.38	1.80/2.33	1.76/2.25	1.74/2.21	1.71/2.16	1.68/2.12	1.67/2.10
28	4.20/7.64	3.34/5.45	2.95/4.57	2.71/4.07	2.56/3.76	2.44/3.53	2.36/3.36	2.29/3.23	2.24/3.11	2.19/3.03	2.15/2.95	2.12/2.90	2.06/2.80	2.02/2.71	1.96/2.60	1.91/2.52	1.87/2.44	1.81/2.35	1.78/2.30	1.75/2.22	1.72/2.18	1.69/2.13	1.67/2.09	1.65/2.06
29	4.18/7.60	3.33/5.42	2.93/4.54	2.70/4.04	2.54/3.73	2.43/3.50	2.35/3.33	2.28/3.20	2.22/3.08	2.18/3.00	2.14/2.92	2.10/2.87	2.05/2.77	2.00/2.68	1.94/2.57	1.90/2.49	1.85/2.41	1.80/2.32	1.77/2.27	1.73/2.19	1.71/2.15	1.68/2.10	1.65/2.06	1.64/2.03
30	4.17/7.56	3.32/5.39	2.92/4.51	2.69/4.02	2.53/3.70	2.42/3.47	2.34/3.30	2.27/3.17	2.21/3.06	2.16/2.98	2.12/2.90	2.09/2.84	2.04/2.74	1.99/2.66	1.93/2.55	1.89/2.47	1.84/2.38	1.79/2.29	1.76/2.24	1.72/2.16	1.70/2.13	1.66/2.07	1.64/2.03	1.62/2.01
32	4.15/7.50	3.30/5.34	2.90/4.46	2.67/3.97	2.51/3.66	2.40/3.42	2.32/3.25	2.25/3.12	2.19/3.01	2.14/2.94	2.10/2.86	2.07/2.80	2.02/2.70	1.97/2.62	1.91/2.51	1.86/2.42	1.82/2.34	1.76/2.25	1.74/2.20	1.69/2.12	1.67/2.08	1.64/2.02	1.61/1.98	1.59/1.96
34	4.13/7.44	3.28/5.29	2.88/4.42	2.65/3.93	2.49/3.61	2.38/3.38	2.30/3.21	2.23/3.08	2.17/2.97	2.12/2.89	2.08/2.82	2.05/2.76	2.00/2.66	1.95/2.58	1.89/2.47	1.84/2.38	1.80/2.30	1.74/2.21	1.71/2.15	1.67/2.08	1.64/2.04	1.61/1.98	1.59/1.94	1.57/1.91
36	4.11/7.39	3.26/5.25	2.86/4.38	2.63/3.89	2.48/3.58	2.36/3.35	2.28/3.18	2.21/3.04	2.15/2.94	2.10/2.86	2.06/2.78	2.03/2.72	1.98/2.62	1.93/2.54	1.87/2.43	1.82/2.35	1.78/2.26	1.72/2.17	1.69/2.12	1.65/2.04	1.62/2.00	1.59/1.94	1.56/1.90	1.55/1.87
38	4.10/7.35	3.25/5.21	2.85/4.34	2.62/3.86	2.46/3.54	2.35/3.32	2.26/3.15	2.19/3.02	2.14/2.91	2.09/2.82	2.05/2.75	2.02/2.69	1.96/2.59	1.92/2.51	1.85/2.40	1.80/2.32	1.76/2.22	1.71/2.14	1.67/2.08	1.63/2.00	1.60/1.97	1.57/1.90	1.54/1.86	1.53/1.84
40	4.07/7.31	3.23/5.18	2.84/4.31	2.61/3.83	2.45/3.51	2.34/3.29	2.25/3.12	2.18/2.99	2.12/2.88	2.07/2.80	2.04/2.73	2.00/2.66	1.95/2.56	1.90/2.49	1.84/2.37	1.79/2.29	1.74/2.20	1.69/2.11	1.66/2.05	1.61/1.97	1.59/1.94	1.55/1.88	1.53/1.84	1.51/1.81

(continued)

df (numerator)

df (denom)	1	2	3	4	5	6	7	8	9	10	11	12	14	16	20	24	30	40	50	75	100	200	500	∞
42	4.07 / 7.27	3.22 / 5.15	2.83 / 4.29	2.59 / 3.80	2.44 / 3.49	2.32 / 3.26	2.24 / 3.10	2.17 / 2.96	2.11 / 2.86	2.06 / 2.77	2.02 / 2.70	1.99 / 2.64	1.94 / 2.54	1.89 / 2.46	1.82 / 2.35	1.78 / 2.26	1.73 / 2.17	1.68 / 2.08	1.64 / 2.02	1.60 / 1.94	1.57 / 1.91	1.54 / 1.85	1.51 / 1.80	1.49 / 1.78
44	4.06 / 7.24	3.21 / 5.12	2.82 / 4.26	2.58 / 3.78	2.43 / 3.46	2.31 / 3.24	2.23 / 3.07	2.16 / 2.94	2.10 / 2.84	2.05 / 2.75	2.01 / 2.68	1.98 / 2.62	1.92 / 2.52	1.88 / 2.44	1.81 / 2.32	1.76 / 2.24	1.72 / 2.15	1.66 / 2.06	1.63 / 2.00	1.58 / 1.92	1.56 / 1.88	1.52 / 1.82	1.50 / 1.78	1.48 / 1.75
46	4.05 / 7.21	3.20 / 5.10	2.81 / 4.24	2.57 / 3.76	2.42 / 3.44	2.30 / 3.22	2.22 / 3.05	2.14 / 2.92	2.09 / 2.82	2.04 / 2.73	2.00 / 2.66	1.97 / 2.60	1.91 / 2.50	1.87 / 2.42	1.80 / 2.30	1.75 / 2.22	1.71 / 2.13	1.65 / 2.04	1.62 / 1.98	1.57 / 1.90	1.54 / 1.86	1.51 / 1.80	1.48 / 1.76	1.46 / 1.72
48	4.04 / 7.19	3.19 / 5.08	2.80 / 4.22	2.56 / 3.74	2.41 / 3.42	2.30 / 3.20	2.21 / 3.04	2.14 / 2.90	2.08 / 2.80	2.03 / 2.71	1.99 / 2.64	1.96 / 2.58	1.90 / 2.48	1.86 / 2.40	1.79 / 2.28	1.74 / 2.20	1.70 / 2.11	1.64 / 2.02	1.61 / 1.96	1.56 / 1.88	1.53 / 1.84	1.50 / 1.78	1.47 / 1.73	1.45 / 1.70
50	4.03 / 7.17	3.18 / 5.06	2.79 / 4.20	2.56 / 3.72	2.40 / 3.41	2.29 / 3.18	2.20 / 3.02	2.13 / 2.88	2.07 / 2.78	2.02 / 2.70	1.98 / 2.62	1.95 / 2.56	1.90 / 2.46	1.85 / 2.39	1.78 / 2.26	1.74 / 2.18	1.69 / 2.10	1.63 / 2.00	1.60 / 1.94	1.55 / 1.86	1.52 / 1.82	1.48 / 1.76	1.46 / 1.71	1.44 / 1.68
55	4.02 / 7.12	3.17 / 5.01	2.78 / 4.16	2.54 / 3.68	2.38 / 3.37	2.27 / 3.15	2.18 / 2.98	2.11 / 2.85	2.05 / 2.75	2.00 / 2.66	1.97 / 2.59	1.93 / 2.53	1.88 / 2.43	1.83 / 2.35	1.76 / 2.23	1.72 / 2.15	1.67 / 2.06	1.61 / 1.96	1.58 / 1.90	1.52 / 1.82	1.50 / 1.78	1.46 / 1.71	1.43 / 1.66	1.41 / 1.64
60	4.00 / 7.08	3.15 / 4.98	2.76 / 4.13	2.52 / 3.65	2.37 / 3.34	2.25 / 3.12	2.17 / 2.95	2.10 / 2.82	2.04 / 2.72	1.99 / 2.63	1.95 / 2.56	1.92 / 2.50	1.86 / 2.40	1.81 / 2.32	1.75 / 2.20	1.70 / 2.12	1.65 / 2.03	1.59 / 1.93	1.56 / 1.87	1.50 / 1.79	1.48 / 1.74	1.44 / 1.68	1.41 / 1.63	1.39 / 1.60
65	3.99 / 7.04	3.14 / 4.95	2.75 / 4.10	2.51 / 3.62	2.36 / 3.31	2.24 / 3.09	2.15 / 2.93	2.08 / 2.79	2.02 / 2.70	1.98 / 2.61	1.94 / 2.54	1.90 / 2.47	1.85 / 2.37	1.80 / 2.30	1.73 / 2.18	1.68 / 2.09	1.63 / 2.00	1.57 / 1.90	1.54 / 1.84	1.49 / 1.76	1.46 / 1.71	1.42 / 1.64	1.39 / 1.60	1.37 / 1.56
70	3.98 / 7.01	3.13 / 4.92	2.74 / 4.08	2.50 / 3.60	2.35 / 3.29	2.23 / 3.07	2.14 / 2.91	2.07 / 2.77	2.01 / 2.67	1.97 / 2.59	1.93 / 2.51	1.89 / 2.45	1.84 / 2.35	1.79 / 2.28	1.72 / 2.15	1.67 / 2.07	1.62 / 1.98	1.56 / 1.88	1.53 / 1.82	1.47 / 1.74	1.45 / 1.69	1.40 / 1.62	1.37 / 1.56	1.35 / 1.53
80	3.96 / 6.96	3.11 / 4.88	2.72 / 4.04	2.48 / 3.56	2.33 / 3.25	2.21 / 3.04	2.12 / 2.87	2.05 / 2.74	1.99 / 2.64	1.95 / 2.55	1.91 / 2.48	1.88 / 2.41	1.82 / 2.32	1.77 / 2.24	1.70 / 2.11	1.65 / 2.03	1.60 / 1.94	1.54 / 1.84	1.51 / 1.78	1.45 / 1.70	1.42 / 1.65	1.38 / 1.57	1.35 / 1.52	1.32 / 1.49
100	3.94 / 6.90	3.09 / 4.82	2.70 / 3.98	2.46 / 3.51	2.30 / 3.20	2.19 / 2.99	2.10 / 2.82	2.03 / 2.69	1.97 / 2.59	1.92 / 2.51	1.88 / 2.43	1.85 / 2.36	1.79 / 2.26	1.75 / 2.19	1.68 / 2.06	1.63 / 1.98	1.57 / 1.89	1.51 / 1.79	1.48 / 1.73	1.42 / 1.64	1.39 / 1.59	1.34 / 1.51	1.30 / 1.46	1.28 / 1.43
125	3.92 / 6.84	3.07 / 4.78	2.68 / 3.94	2.44 / 3.47	2.29 / 3.17	2.17 / 2.95	2.08 / 2.79	2.01 / 2.65	1.95 / 2.56	1.90 / 2.47	1.86 / 2.40	1.83 / 2.33	1.77 / 2.23	1.72 / 2.15	1.65 / 2.03	1.60 / 1.94	1.55 / 1.85	1.49 / 1.75	1.45 / 1.68	1.39 / 1.59	1.36 / 1.54	1.31 / 1.46	1.27 / 1.40	1.25 / 1.37
150	3.91 / 6.81	3.06 / 4.75	2.67 / 3.91	2.43 / 3.44	2.27 / 3.14	2.16 / 2.92	2.07 / 2.76	2.00 / 2.62	1.94 / 2.53	1.89 / 2.44	1.85 / 2.37	1.82 / 2.30	1.76 / 2.20	1.71 / 2.12	1.64 / 2.00	1.59 / 1.91	1.54 / 1.83	1.47 / 1.72	1.44 / 1.66	1.37 / 1.56	1.34 / 1.51	1.29 / 1.43	1.25 / 1.37	1.22 / 1.33
200	3.89 / 6.76	3.04 / 4.71	2.65 / 3.88	2.41 / 3.41	2.26 / 3.11	2.14 / 2.90	2.05 / 2.73	1.98 / 2.60	1.92 / 2.50	1.87 / 2.41	1.83 / 2.34	1.80 / 2.28	1.74 / 2.17	1.69 / 2.09	1.62 / 1.97	1.57 / 1.88	1.52 / 1.79	1.45 / 1.69	1.42 / 1.62	1.35 / 1.53	1.32 / 1.48	1.26 / 1.39	1.22 / 1.33	1.19 / 1.28
400	3.86 / 6.70	3.02 / 4.66	2.62 / 3.83	2.39 / 3.36	2.23 / 3.06	2.12 / 2.85	2.03 / 2.69	1.96 / 2.55	1.90 / 2.46	1.85 / 2.37	1.81 / 2.29	1.78 / 2.23	1.72 / 2.12	1.67 / 2.04	1.60 / 1.92	1.54 / 1.84	1.49 / 1.74	1.42 / 1.64	1.38 / 1.57	1.32 / 1.47	1.28 / 1.42	1.22 / 1.32	1.16 / 1.24	1.13 / 1.19
1000	3.85 / 6.66	3.00 / 4.62	2.61 / 3.80	2.38 / 3.34	2.22 / 3.04	2.10 / 2.82	2.02 / 2.66	1.95 / 2.53	1.89 / 2.43	1.84 / 2.34	1.80 / 2.26	1.76 / 2.20	1.70 / 2.09	1.65 / 2.01	1.58 / 1.89	1.53 / 1.81	1.47 / 1.71	1.41 / 1.61	1.36 / 1.54	1.30 / 1.44	1.26 / 1.38	1.19 / 1.28	1.13 / 1.19	1.08 / 1.11
∞	3.84 / 6.64	2.99 / 4.60	2.60 / 3.78	2.37 / 3.32	2.21 / 3.02	2.09 / 2.80	2.01 / 2.64	1.94 / 2.51	1.88 / 2.41	1.83 / 2.32	1.79 / 2.24	1.75 / 2.18	1.69 / 2.07	1.64 / 1.99	1.57 / 1.87	1.52 / 1.79	1.46 / 1.69	1.40 / 1.59	1.35 / 1.52	1.28 / 1.41	1.24 / 1.36	1.17 / 1.25	1.11 / 1.15	1.00 / 1.00

df (denominator)

Source: Reprinted by permission from *Statistical Methods*, 6th ed., by George W. Snedecor and William G. Cochran, © 1967, by the Iowa State University Press, Ames, Iowa.

Appendix 9

Unit Normal Loss Function

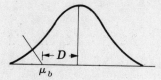

D	.00	.01	.02	.03	.04	.05	.06	.07	.08	.09
.0	.3989	.3940	.3890	.3841	.3793	.3744	.3697	.3649	.3602	.3556
.1	.3509	.3464	.3418	.3373	.3328	.3284	.3240	.3197	.3154	.3111
.2	.3069	.3027	.2986	.2944	.2904	.2863	.2824	.2784	.2745	.2706
.3	.2668	.2630	.2592	.2555	.2518	.2481	.2445	.2409	.2374	.2339
.4	.2304	.2270	.2236	.2203	.2169	.2137	.2104	.2072	.2040	.2009
.5	.1978	.1947	.1917	.1887	.1857	.1828	.1799	.1771	.1742	.1714
.6	.1687	.1659	.1633	.1606	.1580	.1554	.1528	.1503	.1478	.1453
.7	.1429	.1405	.1381	.1358	.1334	.1312	.1289	.1267	.1245	.1223
.8	.1202	.1181	.1160	.1140	.1120	.1100	.1080	.1061	.1042	.1023
.9	.1004	.09860	.09680	.09503	.09328	.09156	.08986	.08819	.08654	.08491
1.0	.08332	.08174	.08019	.07866	.07716	.07568	.07422	.07279	.07138	.06999
1.1	.06862	.06727	.06595	.06465	.06336	.06210	.06086	.05964	.05844	.05726
1.2	.05610	.05496	.05384	.05274	.05165	.05059	.04954	.04851	.04750	.04650
1.3	.04553	.04457	.04363	.04270	.04179	.04090	.04002	.03916	.03831	.03748
1.4	.03667	.03587	.03508	.03431	.03356	.03281	.03208	.03137	.03067	.02998
1.5	.02931	.02865	.02800	.02736	.02674	.02612	.02552	.02494	.02436	.02380
1.6	.02324	.02270	.02217	.02165	.02114	.02064	.02015	.01967	.01920	.01874
1.7	.01829	.01785	.01742	.01699	.01658	.01617	.01578	.01539	.01501	.01464
1.8	.01428	.01392	.01357	.01323	.01290	.01257	.01226	.01195	.01164	.01134
1.9	.01105	.01077	.01049	.01022	$.0^{2}9957$ *	$.0^{2}9698$	$.0^{2}9445$	$.0^{2}9198$	$.0^{2}8957$	$.0^{2}8721$
2.0	$.0^{2}8491$	$.0^{2}8266$	$.0^{2}8046$	$.0^{2}7832$	$.0^{2}7623$	$.0^{2}7418$	$.0^{2}7219$	$.0^{2}7024$	$.0^{2}6835$	$.0^{2}6649$
2.1	$.0^{2}6468$	$.0^{2}6292$	$.0^{2}6120$	$.0^{2}5952$	$.0^{2}5788$	$.0^{2}5628$	$.0^{2}5472$	$.0^{2}5320$	$.0^{2}5172$	$.0^{2}5028$
2.2	$.0^{2}4887$	$.0^{2}4750$	$.0^{2}4616$	$.0^{2}4486$	$.0^{2}4358$	$.0^{2}4235$	$.0^{2}4114$	$.0^{2}3996$	$.0^{2}3882$	$.0^{2}3770$
2.3	$.0^{2}3662$	$.0^{2}3556$	$.0^{2}3453$	$.0^{2}3352$	$.0^{2}3255$	$.0^{2}3159$	$.0^{2}3067$	$.0^{2}2977$	$.0^{2}2889$	$.0^{2}2804$
2.4	$.0^{2}2720$	$.0^{2}2640$	$.0^{2}2561$	$.0^{2}2484$	$.0^{2}2410$	$.0^{2}2337$	$.0^{2}2267$	$.0^{2}2199$	$.0^{2}2132$	$.0^{2}2067$
2.5	$.0^{2}2004$	$.0^{2}1943$	$.0^{2}1883$	$.0^{2}1826$	$.0^{2}1769$	$.0^{2}1715$	$.0^{2}1662$	$.0^{2}1610$	$.0^{2}1560$	$.0^{2}1511$
2.6	$.0^{2}1464$	$.0^{2}1418$	$.0^{2}1373$	$.0^{2}1330$	$.0^{2}1288$	$.0^{2}1247$	$.0^{2}1207$	$.0^{2}1169$	$.0^{2}1132$	$.0^{2}1095$
2.7	$.0^{2}1060$	$.0^{2}1026$	$.0^{3}9928$	$.0^{3}9607$	$.0^{3}9295$	$.0^{3}8992$	$.0^{3}8699$	$.0^{3}8414$	$.0^{3}8138$	$.0^{3}7870$
2.8	$.0^{3}7611$	$.0^{3}7359$	$.0^{3}7115$	$.0^{3}6879$	$.0^{3}6650$	$.0^{3}6428$	$.0^{3}6213$	$.0^{3}6004$	$.0^{3}5802$	$.0^{3}5606$
2.9	$.0^{3}5417$	$.0^{3}5233$	$.0^{3}5055$	$.0^{3}4883$	$.0^{3}4716$	$.0^{3}4555$	$.0^{3}4398$	$.0^{3}4247$	$.0^{3}4101$	$.0^{3}3959$
3.0	$.0^{3}3822$	$.0^{3}3689$	$.0^{3}3560$	$.0^{3}3436$	$.0^{3}3316$	$.0^{3}3199$	$.0^{3}3087$	$.0^{3}2978$	$.0^{3}2873$	$.0^{3}2771$
3.1	$.0^{3}2673$	$.0^{3}2577$	$.0^{3}2485$	$.0^{3}2396$	$.0^{3}2311$	$.0^{3}2227$	$.0^{3}2147$	$.0^{3}2070$	$.0^{3}1995$	$.0^{3}1922$
3.2	$.0^{3}1852$	$.0^{3}1785$	$.0^{3}1720$	$.0^{3}1657$	$.0^{3}1596$	$.0^{3}1537$	$.0^{3}1480$	$.0^{3}1426$	$.0^{3}1373$	$.0^{3}1322$
3.3	$.0^{3}1273$	$.0^{3}1225$	$.0^{3}1179$	$.0^{3}1135$	$.0^{3}1093$	$.0^{3}1051$	$.0^{3}1012$	$.0^{4}9734$	$.0^{4}9365$	$.0^{4}9009$
3.4	$.0^{4}8666$	$.0^{4}8335$	$.0^{4}8016$	$.0^{4}7709$	$.0^{4}7413$	$.0^{4}7127$	$.0^{4}6852$	$.0^{4}6587$	$.0^{4}6331$	$.0^{4}6085$
3.5	$.0^{4}5848$	$.0^{4}5620$	$.0^{4}5400$	$.0^{4}5188$	$.0^{4}4984$	$.0^{4}4788$	$.0^{4}4599$	$.0^{4}4417$	$.0^{4}4242$	$.0^{4}4073$
3.6	$.0^{4}3911$	$.0^{4}3755$	$.0^{4}3605$	$.0^{4}3460$	$.0^{4}3321$	$.0^{4}3188$	$.0^{4}3059$	$.0^{4}2935$	$.0^{4}2816$	$.0^{4}2702$
3.7	$.0^{4}2592$	$.0^{4}2486$	$.0^{4}2385$	$.0^{4}2287$	$.0^{4}2193$	$.0^{4}2103$	$.0^{4}2016$	$.0^{4}1933$	$.0^{4}1853$	$.0^{4}1776$
3.8	$.0^{4}1702$	$.0^{4}1632$	$.0^{4}1563$	$.0^{4}1498$	$.0^{4}1435$	$.0^{4}1375$	$.0^{4}1317$	$.0^{4}1262$	$.0^{4}1208$	$.0^{4}1157$
3.9	$.0^{4}1108$	$.0^{4}1061$	$.0^{4}1016$	$.0^{5}9723$	$.0^{5}9307$	$.0^{5}8908$	$.0^{5}8525$	$.0^{5}8158$	$.0^{5}7806$	$.0^{5}7469$
4.0	$.0^{5}7145$	$.0^{5}6835$	$.0^{5}6538$	$.0^{5}6253$	$.0^{5}5980$	$.0^{5}5718$	$.0^{5}5468$	$.0^{5}5227$	$.0^{5}4997$	$.0^{5}4777$
4.1	$.0^{5}4566$	$.0^{5}4364$	$.0^{5}4170$	$.0^{5}3985$	$.0^{5}3807$	$.0^{5}3637$	$.0^{5}3475$	$.0^{5}3319$	$.0^{5}3170$	$.0^{5}3027$
4.2	$.0^{5}2891$	$.0^{5}2760$	$.0^{5}2635$	$.0^{5}2516$	$.0^{5}2402$	$.0^{5}2292$	$.0^{5}2188$	$.0^{5}2088$	$.0^{5}1992$	$.0^{5}1901$
4.3	$.0^{5}1814$	$.0^{5}1730$	$.0^{5}1650$	$.0^{5}1574$	$.0^{5}1501$	$.0^{5}1431$	$.0^{5}1365$	$.0^{5}1301$	$.0^{5}1241$	$.0^{5}1183$
4.4	$.0^{5}1127$	$.0^{5}1074$	$.0^{5}1024$	$.0^{6}9756$	$.0^{6}9296$	$.0^{6}8857$	$.0^{6}8437$	$.0^{6}8037$	$.0^{6}7655$	$.0^{6}7290$
4.5	$.0^{6}6942$	$.0^{6}6610$	$.0^{6}6294$	$.0^{6}5992$	$.0^{6}5704$	$.0^{6}5429$	$.0^{6}5167$	$.0^{6}4917$	$.0^{6}4679$	$.0^{6}4452$
4.6	$.0^{6}4236$	$.0^{6}4029$	$.0^{6}3833$	$.0^{6}3645$	$.0^{6}3467$	$.0^{6}3297$	$.0^{6}3135$	$.0^{6}2981$	$.0^{6}2834$	$.0^{6}2694$
4.7	$.0^{6}2560$	$.0^{6}2433$	$.0^{6}2313$	$.0^{6}2197$	$.0^{6}2088$	$.0^{6}1984$	$.0^{6}1884$	$.0^{6}1790$	$.0^{6}1700$	$.0^{6}1615$
4.8	$.0^{6}1533$	$.0^{6}1456$	$.0^{6}1382$	$.0^{6}1312$	$.0^{6}1246$	$.0^{6}1182$	$.0^{6}1122$	$.0^{6}1065$	$.0^{6}1011$	$.0^{7}9588$
4.9	$.0^{7}9096$	$.0^{7}8629$	$.0^{7}8185$	$.0^{7}7763$	$.0^{7}7362$	$.0^{7}6982$	$.0^{7}6620$	$.0^{7}6276$	$.0^{7}5950$	$.0^{7}5640$

*The small numbers which appear as superscripts indicate the number of zeros immediately following the decimal point. For example, $.0^{2}9957$ is the value .009957.

Source: Reproduced by permission of the copyright holders, The President and Fellows of Harvard College, from the Unit Normal Loss Integral table which appears as Table IV in *Introduction to Statistics for Business Decisions* by Robert Schlaifer, published by McGraw-Hill Book Company, New York, 1961.

INDEX

Addition
    rule of for mutually exclusive events, 67, 76-77
    rule of for nonexclusive events, 67-68, 76-77
Aggregate index number, 344, 348
Aggregate price indexes, 345, 348
Alternative hypothesis, 155
Analysis of variance, 218-233
    factorial designs in, 222-223
    fixed-effects model in, 222
    incomplete block designs in, 223
    Latin Square design in, 223
    in linear regression analysis, 315, 321-324
    one-way, 218-220, 223-227
    random effects model in, 222
    randomized block design in, 220-221, 228-231
    relationship to the t test, 226-227, 229-231
    testing for interaction in, 221-222, 231-233
    two-way, 220-222, 228-233
"And under" types of frequency distributions, 12,
    21-22, 37, 40, 60
Arithmetic average, 28
Arithmetic mean, 28-30, 33-38
Autocorrelation, 317
Average deviation, 45-47, 52-59
    for grouped data, 46-47, 56-59

Bar chart, 12-13, 22-23
Base period, shifting of, 346-350
Bayes' theorem, 258-259, 268-269
Bayesian criterion, 241
Bayesian decision analysis, 1-2, 4
Bayesian posterior analysis, 261-263, 270-273,
    284-285, 292-293
Bernoulli process, 91
Bimodal distribution, 31, 35
Binomial probability distribution, 91-93, 98-102
    expressed by proportions, 92-93, 99
    normal approximation of, 112-113, 118
    Poisson approximation of, 96, 105
    table of, 355-357
    testing a hypothesized proportion, 179-180,
    188-189
Breakeven point, 279-280, 289, 291
Business indicators, 331-332
Business statistics, definition of, 1

Central limit theorem, 127, 135

Chance events, in decision tree analysis, 242, 250
Chebyshev's inequality, and confidence intervals
    for the mean, 130-131, 138
    testing the mean, 162-163, 171
Chebyshev's theorem, 130
Chi-square distributions, and the chi-square
    test, 195
    confidence intervals for the standard deviation,
    146-147, 151-152
    confidence intervals for the variance, 146-147,
    151-152
    table of, 365
Class boundaries, 8-9, 14-15, 17, 21-22
Class interval, 8-9, 14-17
Class limits, 8-9, 14-15, 17
Class midpoint, 8-9, 14-15, 17
Classical statistics, 1-2, 4
Coefficient
    of correlation, 303-304, 309-310
    of determination, 302-303, 308-309
    of multiple correlation, 316, 318-322
    of multiple determination, 316
    of partial correlation, 316-317, 321, 322-324
    of partial determination, 317
    of variation, 51, 60-61
Coinciding indicators, 331-332
Colinearity, 317, 322-324
Combinations, 73-74, 83-85
Component bar chart, 12-13, 23
Composite index number, 344
Conditional probability, 68-69, 77-78
Confidence intervals
    for the difference between two means, 142-143,
    147-149
    for the difference between two proportions,
    145-146, 150
    for the mean, 128-129, 134-138
    in multiple regression analysis, 314
    for the proportion, 144-145, 149-150
    for the standard deviation, 146-147, 151-152
    for the variance, 146-147, 151-152
Consumer Price Index (CPI), 346, 351
Contingency tables, 71-72, 82
Contingency table tests, 198-200, 210-212
Continuity correction factor (see Correction for
    continuity)

371

Continuous random variables, 89, 109
Continuous variable, 2, 4
Correction for continuity
  in the goodness of fit test, 197-198, 202-204
  for normal approximation of binomial
     probabilities, 113, 118
  for normal approximation of Poisson
     probabilities, 114, 118-119
Correlation analysis, 301-305, 308-310
  assumptions of, 302
  pitfalls and limitations of, 304-305
CPI, 346, 351
Credibility interval, 278
Critical value, of test statistic, 156
CS, 265-267, 286-287, 294
Cumulative frequency distribution, 11-12, 16,
  18-19
Cycle chart, 330, 338-339
Cyclical fluctuations, 327
Cyclical forecasting, 331-332
Cyclical variations, analysis of, 330, 338-341

Deciles, 32-33, 38-40
Decision points, in decision tree analysis, 242, 250
Decision table, 236-237, 244-250
Decision tree analysis, 242, 250-251
Degree of confidence, 128
Degrees of freedom (df), 130
  for contingency table tests, 199
  and F distributions, 183-184, 191-192
  in goodness of fit tests, 196
Dependent events, 68-69
Dependent samples, 177
Dependent variable, 297
Descriptive statistics, 1, 3
Deseasonalized data, 329, 336
Discrete random variables, 89-91, 96-98
Discrete variables, 2, 4
Disjoint events, 67
Dispersion, measures of, 44

$e^{-\lambda}$, table of, 358
ENGS, 265-267, 286-287, 294
EOL, 257-258, 267, 282-283
EPPI, 258
Estimation (see Confidence intervals)
Estimator, of population parameter, 125
EVPI, 257, 267-268, 281-283, 289-292
EVSI, 263-265, 285-286, 293-294
Exact limits, 8
Expectation of an event, as a criterion in
  decision analysis, 238, 244-245
Expected frequencies, for contingency table
  tests, 199
Expected losses, 241
Expected net gain from sampling (ENGS),
  265-267, 286-287, 294
Expected opportunity loss (EOL), 241-242,
  245-246, 257-258, 267, 282-283
Expected payoff with perfect information
  (EPPI), 258
Expected regret, 241
Expected utility (EU), 243-244, 253-254

Expected value, of discrete random variables,
  90, 96-98
Expected value (EV) criterion, 240-241, 245-250,
  280-281, 289, 291
Expected value of perfect information (EVPI),
  257, 267-268, 281-283, 289-292
Expected value of sample information (EVSI),
  263-265, 285-286, 293-294
Exponential probability distribution, 114-115,
  119
Exponential trend curve, 327-328

F distributions, in the analysis of variance,
  218-233
  table of, 366-368
  testing the difference between two variances,
    183-184, 191-192
Factorial designs, 222-223
Finite correction factor, 126-127, 132, 134-135
Fisher, R. A., 218
Fixed-effects model, 222
Folding back, in decision tree analysis, 242, 251
Forecasting, 329-332, 337-338
Frequency curve, 10-11, 15-16, 18
Frequency distribution, 8, 14-17
Frequency polygon, 10, 15, 18, 22

Goodness of fit tests, 195-198, 203-210
Grouped data, 8, 14-17

Histogram, 9, 15, 18, 20-21
Homoscedasticity, 297, 302, 313, 316
Hypergeometric distribution, 93-94, 102-104
Hypothesis testing, in the analysis of variance,
  218-233
  concerning contingency tables, 198-200,
    210-212
  concerning the differences among several
    means, 218-219, 223-225
  concerning the differences among several
    proportions, 200-203, 212-214
  concerning the difference between means of
    paired observations, 177-179, 187-188
  concerning the difference between two means,
    175-180, 184-188
  concerning the difference between two
    proportions, 182, 190
  concerning the difference between two
    standard deviations, 183-184, 191-192
  concerning the difference between two
    variances, 183-184, 191-192
  concerning goodness of fit, 195-198, 203-210
  concerning the independence of two variables,
    198-200, 210-212
  concerning the mean, 156-171
  concerning the proportion, 179-182, 188-190
  concerning the standard deviation, 183, 191
  concerning the variance, 183, 191
Hypothesized value of a parameter, 155

Incomplete block designs, 223
Independent events, 68-69
Independent variable, 297

Index of Industrial Production, 347
Index number, 344
Inferential statistics, 1, 3
Interaction, in analysis of variance, 220-222, 231-233
Intersection of two events, 67
Irregular movements, 327
Irregular variations, analysis of, 331, 340-341

Joint events, 67
Joint probability tables, 71-72, 82-83
Kurtosis, 10-11, 18-19

Lagging indicators, 332
Laspeyres' index, 345, 348
Latin Square design, 223
$L(D)$, table of, 369
Leading indicators, 331
Leptokurtic frequency curve, 10-11, 18-19
Level of significance, 155
Line graph, 13, 23
Linear payoff functions, 279-281, 288-291
Linear piecewise loss functions, 281-283, 289, 291
Linear regression equation, 298-299, 305-307
Link relatives, 345-346, 348-350
Location, measures of, 28
Loss functions, 281-283, 289, 291

Marginal probability, 72, 82
Matched pairs, 177
Maximax criterion, 239, 245-249
Maximin criterion, 238, 245-249
Maximum probability criterion, 238, 244-245
Mean, 28-30, 33-38
    for grouped data, 29, 35-37
Mean square between (MSB), 218, 223-224
Mean square error (MSE), 219, 224-225
Mean square with (MSW), 218, 223-224
Median, 30-31, 33-37
    for grouped data, 30-31, 35-37
Mesokurtic frequency curve, 10-11, 18-19
Middle 50 percent range, 45, 52, 55
Middle 80 percent range, 45, 53, 57
Middle 90 percent range, 45, 59
Minimax regret criterion, 239-240, 245-249
Mode, 31-37
    for grouped data, 31-32, 35-37
Modified mean, 329, 335
Modified ranges, 45, 52-55, 57, 59
MSB (mean square between), 218, 223-224
MSE (mean square error), 219, 224-225
MSW (mean square within), 218, 223-224
Multicolinearity, 317
Multimodal distribution, 31
Multiple correlation analysis, 316-324
    assumptions of, 316
    pitfalls and limitations of, 317
Multiple regression analysis, 313-324
    assumptions of, 313
    pitfalls and limitations of, 317
Multiplication principle for sequential outcomes, 74, 84-85

Multiplication
    rule of, for dependent events, 70-71, 78-81
    rule of, for independent events, 69-70, 78-81
Mutually exclusive events, 67

Negative skewness, 10-11, 16, 18-19
Net overall terminal expected payoff ($NOTEP$), 266-267, 287
Net regression coefficient, 314
Nonexclusive events, 67
Normal probability distribution, 110-119
    in Bayesian decision analysis, 277-294
    in hypothesis testing, 156-161, 164-168
    in interval estimation, 128-129, 134-136
    table of, 363
$NOTEP$, 266-267, 287
Null hypothesis, 155

Objective probability values, 65
OC curve, 160
Odds, 66-67, 75
Odds ratio, 66-67, 75
Ogive, 11-12, 16, 18-21
Ogive curve, 11-12, 18-19
One-sided confidence intervals
    for the difference between means, 148-149
    for the mean, 136-137
    for proportions, 151
    for the standard deviation, 151-152
    for the variance, 151-152
One-tail test, 158
One-way analysis of variance, 218-220, 223-227
Operating characteristic (OC) curve, 160
$OTEP$, 266-267, 273-274, 287
Overall terminal expected payoff ($OTEP$), 266-267, 273-274, 287

Paasche's index, 345, 348
Paired observations, 177
Parabolic trend curve, 328
Parameters, of a population, 1
Partial correlation coefficient, 316-317, 321-324
Partial regression coefficient, 314, 322-324
Payoff table, 236-237, 244-250
Pearson's coefficient of skewness, 52, 61
Percentage pie chart, 13-14, 24
Percentiles, 21, 32-33, 38-40
Permutations, 72-73, 83-84
Pie chart, 13-14, 24
Platykurtic frequency curve, 10-11, 18-19
Point estimator, 125
Poisson probability distribution, 94-96, 104-105
    normal approximation of, 113-114, 118-119
    table of, 359-362
Poisson process, 94
Population parameters, 1, 28, 125
Positive skewness, 10-11, 19
Posterior analysis, 261-263, 270-273, 284-285, 292-293
Posterior mean, 284, 292-293
Posterior probability distribution, 259-261, 270-273, 284-285, 292-293
Posterior variance, 284, 292-293

Power, in hypothesis testing, 160-161, 167-168
Power curve, 160-161
Prediction intervals, 299-300, 307
    in multiple regression analysis, 314
Preposterior analysis, 263-265, 273-274, 285-286,
    293-294
Price index, 344, 347
Price relative, 344
Prior mean, 277-278, 288, 291
Prior probabilities, 237
Prior probability distribution, 259-261, 269-272,
    277-279, 288, 291
Prior standard deviation, 278-279, 288, 291
Probability
    a priori approach to, 65
    classical approach to, 65, 74-75
    definitions of, 65-66
    personalistic approach to, 65-66
    relative frequency approach to, 65, 74-75
    subjective approach to, 65-66, 74-75
Probability distributions, 89
Probability sample, 125-126

Quantity index, 344, 347-348
Quantity relative, 344
Quartiles, 32-33, 38-40

Random effects model, 222
Random numbers, table of, 364
Random sample, 125-126
Random variable, 89
Randomized block design, 220-221, 228-231
Range, 44-45, 52-60
    for grouped data, 44-45, 55-60
Ratio-to-moving-average method, 328, 332-336
Reference contrast, 243, 251-253
Region of acceptance, of the null hypothesis,
    156-158
Regions of rejection, of the null hypothesis,
    156-158
Regression analysis, 297-301, 304-308
    assumptions of, 297
    pitfalls and limitations of, 304-305
Regression equation, 297-299, 305-307
Relative frequency distribution, 12, 20
Replication, in analysis of variance, 220-222,
    231-233
Residual method, 331, 338-341
Risk averter, 244, 253
Risk neutral, 244
Risk seeker, 244
Rounding of data, 3, 5

Sample size
    for estimating the mean, 129, 136
    for estimating the proportion, 144-145, 150
    for testing a mean, 161-162, 169
    for testing a proportion, 181-182, 190
Sample statistics, 1, 28, 125
Sampling, 1, 125-126
Sampling distribution, of the mean, 126, 132-134
Sampling without replacement, 68, 78-79, 93-94,
    102-104
Scatter diagram, 297-298, 305-307

Scientific sample, 125-126
Seasonal adjustments, 329, 336
Seasonal variations, 327
    analysis of, 328-329, 332-336
Seasonally adjusted data, 329, 336
Secular trend, 327
Significant digits, 2-5
Simple index number, 344, 347-348
Simple random sample, 126
Simple regression analysis, 297
Skewness, 10-11, 16, 18-19
    Pearson's coefficient of, 52, 61
Splicing, of index numbers, 346, 350-351
Standard deviation, 47-51, 53-60
    alternative computational formulas for,
        49-50, 53, 55-57, 59-60
    for grouped data, 48, 50, 56-60
    shortcut formulas for, 49-50, 53, 55-57, 59-60
Standard error
    of the conditional mean (in regression analysis),
        300, 307
    of the difference between two means, 142, 175-176
    of the difference between two proprtions,
        145-146, 182
    of estimate, 299-300, 307, 314, 318-322
    of forecast, 301, 307-308
    of the mean, 126, 132-134
    of the mean difference between paired
        observations, 178-179
    of the proportion, 144, 180
Standard normal distribution, 110-111
    table of, 363
Standard partial regression coefficient, 314,
    321-322
Stationary process, 91
Statistics, definition of, 1
Stepwise correlation analysis, 317-324
Stepwise regression analysis, 315, 317-324
Student's t distributions
    confidence intervals for the difference between
        means, 143, 148
    confidence intervals for the mean, 129-130,
        137-138
    table of, 364
    testing the difference between two means,
        177, 186
    testing the mean, 162, 169-170
Subjective probability values, 65-66, 74-75
Symmetrical distribution, 10-11

t distributions (see Student's t distributions)
Testing a hypothesis (see Hypothesis testing)
Test statistic, 155-156
Time series analysis, 326-343
Time series model, components of, 326-327
Tree diagrams, 70-71, 79-80
Trend, 327
Trend analysis, 327-328, 332-333, 335
Trend line, 327, 332-333, 335
Tshebyshev's inequality (see Chebyshev's
    inequality)
Two-tail test, 156-157
Two-way analysis of variance, 220-222, 228-233

Type I error, 155, 158-161, 166-168
Type II error, 155, 158-161, 166-168

Unbiased estimator, 125
Unimodal distribution, 31
Union of two events, 67
Unit normal loss function, table of, 369
Utility, 243-244, 251-254
Utility function, 244, 253

Value index, 344, 348
Value relative, 344
Value of dollar, 346, 351
Value of sample information (*VSI*), 261-263,
    271-273, 285, 292-293
Variability, measures of, 44
Variance, 47-50, 54-55, 58-59
  alternative computational formulas for,
      49-50, 55

Variance (cont.)
  analysis of, 218-233
  of discrete random variables, 90-91, 96-98
  for grouped data, 48, 50, 58-59
  homogeneity of, 218
  shortcut formulas for, 49-50, 55
Variation, coefficient of, 51, 60-61
Venn diagrams, 66, 68, 77
VSI, 261-263, 271-273, 285, 292-293

Weighted average, 29-30, 38
Weighted mean, 29-30, 38
Weighted-aggregate-of-prices approach, 345
Weighted-average-of-price-relatives approach,
    345, 348
Wholesale Price Index, 347

z distribution, table of, 363
z value, 110-111

Catalog

If you are interested in a list of SCHAUM'S
OUTLINE SERIES send your name
and address, requesting your free catalog, to:

SCHAUM'S OUTLINE SERIES, Dept. C
McGRAW-HILL BOOK COMPANY
1221 Avenue of Americas
New York, N.Y. 10020